THE ROUTLEDGE HANDBOOK OF GLOBAL PERSPECTIVES ON HOMELESSNESS, LAW & POLICY

This handbook provides a comprehensive global survey and assessment of the law and policy relating to homelessness prevention. Homelessness is regarded internationally as one of the most pressing issues facing humanity and one of the greatest social challenges of our times. This has been further amplified as a result of the Covid-19 pandemic. Across the globe, there is an enormous divergence in both experiences of and responses to homelessness from governments and state actors. This handbook examines how 28 different jurisdictions from across all six continents of the world have encountered, framed, and responded to homelessness. Written by expert scholars and leaders in their field, the book engages in a multidisciplinary and comparative analysis of homelessness as an issue of acute social concern. Understandings of homelessness are geographically, culturally, and historically situated, making analysis of each jurisdiction's approach by a national expert deeply insightful. The collection examines legal and extra-legal policy interventions targeted at reducing or preventing homelessness from across the globe. Drawing on diverse perspectives, differing cultures, and differing welfare regimes, it thus constitutes a timely evaluation of current approaches to homelessness internationally. This book will appeal to students and scholars of homelessness, sociology, social policy, anthropology, and urban sociology, as well as international and national policymakers.

Chris Bevan, Professor in Property, Housing, and Homelessness, Durham University, UK

'This is a significant reference book exploring the regulations and policies on the unresolved phenomenon of homelessness in the world by the best international experts. I would highly recommend this book.'
  Professor Sergio Nasarre-Aznar, *Professor and Founder of the UNESCO Housing Chair at the University Rovira i Virgili, Spain*

THE ROUTLEDGE HANDBOOK OF GLOBAL PERSPECTIVES ON HOMELESSNESS, LAW & POLICY

Edited by Chris Bevan

Routledge
Taylor & Francis Group
a GlassHouse Book

Designed cover image: CatLane/Getty Images/iStock collection

First published 2024
by Routledge
4 Park Square, Milton Park, Abingdon, Oxon OX14 4RN

and by Routledge
605 Third Avenue, New York, NY 10158

Routledge is an imprint of the Taylor & Francis Group, an informa business

A GlassHouse book

© 2024 selection and editorial matter, Chris Bevan; individual chapters, the contributors

The right of Chris Bevan to be identified as the author of the editorial material, and of the authors for their individual chapters, has been asserted in accordance with sections 77 and 78 of the Copyright, Designs and Patents Act 1988.

All rights reserved. No part of this book may be reprinted or reproduced or utilised in any form or by any electronic, mechanical, or other means, now known or hereafter invented, including photocopying and recording, or in any information storage or retrieval system, without permission in writing from the publishers.

Trademark notice: Product or corporate names may be trademarks or registered trademarks, and are used only for identification and explanation without intent to infringe.

British Library Cataloguing-in-Publication Data
A catalogue record for this book is available from the British Library

ISBN: 978-1-032-22700-9 (hbk)
ISBN: 978-1-032-22701-6 (pbk)
ISBN: 978-1-003-27405-6 (ebk)

DOI: 10.4324/9781003274056

Typeset in Sabon
by Apex CoVantage, LLC

CONTENTS

Acknowledgements — ix
List of Figures and Tables — x
List of Contributors — xii
Foreword — xxi

    Introduction: Learning Lessons Across Borders — 1
    Chris Bevan

PART I
Europe — 11

1. 25 Years of Devolution and a (Dis)United Kingdom Homelessness Policy — 13
   Chris Bevan, Regina Serpa, and Paddy Gray

2. Homelessness in Ireland: Law, Policy, and Practices — 38
   Mark Jordan and Padraic Kenna

3. Categorization, Selection, Displacement, and Invisibilization: Housing and Accommodation for the Homeless in France — 56
   Pascale Dietrich-Ragon and Marie Loison

4. (Still) Much Untapped Potential in Homelessness Services: Challenges and Good Practice in Germany from a Social Work Perspective — 72
   Susanne Gerull

5　Homelessness in Italy: Old Private Stories and New Public
　　Opportunities　　　　　　　　　　　　　　　　　　　　　　　96
　　Teresa Consoli and Antonella Meo

6　Homelessness and Hidden Homelessness in Spain: Tackling a
　　Somewhat Unknown Yet Increasing Phenomenon　　　　　　109
　　Núria Lambea Llop

7　Homelessness Law and Policy in Greece: Challenges and Opportunities　126
　　Nikos Kourachanis and Mando Zisopoulou

8　Norway: A Housing-Led Homeless Policy within a Weak Legal
　　Framework　　　　　　　　　　　　　　　　　　　　　　　142
　　Evelyn Dyb and Hilde Hatleskog Zeiner

9　Ending Homelessness or Managing the Homeless? – Homelessness,
　　Housing Policy, and Practice in Sweden　　　　　　　　　　159
　　Marcus Knutagård and Matti Wirehag

10　Governing Homelessness in the Netherlands: Incremental Change
　　Towards Providing Housing First　　　　　　　　　　　　　175
　　Nienke F. Boesveldt

11　The Illiberal State and Homelessness: The Case of Poland　　188
　　Adam Ploszka

12　Homelessness in Switzerland: Federalist Pathways Between
　　Ignoring, Passing on Responsibility for, and Proactive Prevention of
　　Homelessness　　　　　　　　　　　　　　　　　　　　　205
　　Matthias Drilling, Magdalena Küng, and Jörg Dittmann

PART II
North America　　　　　　　　　　　　　　　　　　　　　　223

13　Homelessness in Canada: A Wicked Problem That Requires
　　Genuine Political Commitment to Fix　　　　　　　　　　　225
　　John R. Graham, Yale D. Belanger, and Christine A. Walsh

14　The Policy of State as a Social Determinant of Health: Canada's
　　Indigenous Homelessness Policy　　　　　　　　　　　　　238
　　Yale D. Belanger

15 Homelessness in the United States of America: Dreams of a Shining City, Realities of Homelessness 257
Maria Foscarinis and Eric S. Tars

16 Innovative Policy Responses to Housing Need in the United States: Case Studies on Safe Parking, Tiny Homes, and Direct Cash Transfers 275
Daniel Brisson, Katherine Hoops Calhoun, and Jennifer Wilson

PART III
South America 299

17 'Nothing About Us Without Us': How Homeless People Protagonism Has Shaped the Law and Public Policy on Homelessness in Brazil 301
Kelseny Medeiros Pinho, Luiz Tokuzi Kohara, and Erminia Maricato

18 Public Policies for the Homeless in Chile: A Shifting Picture 320
Ignacio Eissmann and Felipe Estay

PART IV
Africa 335

19 Homelessness in Nigeria: Issues and the Way Forward 337
Andrew Ebekozien, Clinton Ohis Aigbavboa, Wellington Didibhuku Thwala, Mohamad Shaharudin Samsurijan, and Rex Asibuodu Ugulu

20 Preventing and Ending Homelessness in South Africa: Fusing Research, Policy, and Practices – Lessons from the City of Tshwane 351
Stéphan de Beer

21 The Housing Crisis and Homelessness in Zimbabwe: Examining the Exclusionary Nature of Urban Legislation and Planning Practice in Harare 369
George Masimba

PART V
Asia   385

22 Homelessness and Residential Policy in Japan   387
   Yoshihiro Okamoto

23 'Positive Non-Policy': Homeless Services and Transitional
   Rehousing Initiatives in Hong Kong and Malaysia   405
   Geerhardt Kornatowski and Constance Ching

24 Homelessness in India: A State Legislative and Civil Society
   Perspective   430
   Kalpana Goel, Mohd Tarique, Meenu Anand, and Elvis Munyoka

25 Centrality of the Home and Homelessness in Singapore   448
   Poh Leng Teo

PART VI
Oceania   463

26 From Vagrancy to Public Nuisance in 200 Years: Is It Still
   a Crime to Be Homeless in Australia?   465
   Tamara Walsh

27 Homelessness Prevention in Australian Residential Tenancies
   and Social Housing Law: The Case for Reform   481
   Chris Martin and Hal Pawson

28 A Snapshot of a Fragmented Landscape: Homelessness Law
   and Policy in Aotearoa New Zealand   500
   *Brodie Fraser, Clare Aspinall, Elinor Chisholm, Jenny Ombler,
   Sarah Bierre, Lucy Telfar-Barnard, Ellie Johnson, and Philippa
   Howden-Chapman*

Index   517

ACKNOWLEDGEMENTS

I would like to express my deepest gratitude to each and every author for their contribution to this collection. I thank you all for your insights, energy, and commitment to the project. Special mention must also go the excellent team at Routledge for assisting with the production of the book.

This handbook is dedicated to all those living with and experiencing homelessness across the globe, and to the housing, homelessness, and social policy researchers and activists engaged internationally in the collective struggle to improve the lives of homeless communities everywhere.

Chris Bevan

FIGURES AND TABLES

Figures

4.1	The development of homeless care and policy in Germany since 1945.	77
4.2	Results of the first official statistics of accommodated homeless persons.	84
4.3	Help system for cases in urgent need of housing in Germany.	88
8.1	Homelessness in Norway; number of homeless persons per 1,000 inhabitants.	147
16.1	Reported circumstances for sheltering in vehicle.	287
16.2	BCV resident and comparison group working or in school.	291
16.3	BCV resident and comparison group average frequency of emotional states.	292
16.4	Denver Basic Income Project theory of change.	295
17.1	Sufferers from the Street Community marching on their thirteenth mission (1981), holding posters with the slogan 'We are a people who want to live'.	305
18.1	Evolution of public policy on homelessness in Chile.	328
22.1	Basic homelessness self-reliance support scheme structure.	392
22.2	Expanded homelessness prevention.	399
23.1	The co-living capsule hostel project and the social housing project.	417
27.1	Homelessness service users (persons) in 2021–2022: factors cited as contributing to service user decisions to seek assistance – own analysis.	483

Tables

6.1	Causes of homelessness in Spain (2012–2022)	113
10.1	ETHOS Light typology	177
16.1	Reported reason for leaving safe lot	287
18.1	Official definitions of homelessness in Chile	325
19.1	Summary of Nigerian housing policies, programmes, and performance of public housing, 1928 to 2018	343
22.1	Reasons for living on the street	393
22.2	Employee status immediately before living on the street	395
22.3	Immediate previous occupation	395
22.4	Immediate previous residence	395

Figures and Tables

22.5	Age distribution of homeless people	397
22.6	Gender of homeless people	397
22.7	Employment status of the homeless	398
23.1	Number of registered street sleepers in Hong Kong (1980–2021)	406

CONTRIBUTORS

Rex Asibuodu Ugulu is a senior member of the Department of Quantity Surveying and the current head of department, Federal University of Technology, Owerri, Nigeria. He has authored and co-authored more than 60 accredited journal articles, conference papers, and book chapters.

Clare Aspinall is a PhD student, University of Otago, Aotearoa New Zealand. A qualitative researcher with interests in housing and homelessness, systems, equity, and effective governance, policy, and practice to prevent and address homelessness, her PhD research looks at the transferability of Housing First in Aotearoa New Zealand. She has a background in nursing and community housing governance.

Yale D. Belanger is a professor of political science, University of Lethbridge, Canada, and a member of the Royal Society of Canada, College of New Scholars, Artists, and Scientists (2017–2024).

Chris Bevan is a professor in property, housing and homelessness law at Durham Law School, Durham University, UK. His research sits at the intersection of land, housing, and social welfare law, and he has published widely on homelessness law and policy. He is also a barrister and fellow of the Royal Society of Arts.

Sarah Bierre is a senior research fellow, University of Otago, Aotearoa New Zealand. Sarah Bierre uses qualitative methodologies to look at how housing policy, politics, and law create and alleviate inequalities in access to affordable, secure, and decent housing. Her most recent work looks at the politics and narratives of rental housing standards, the consequences and experiences of eviction, and the function of the Tenancy Tribunal.

Nienke F. Boesveldt is a principal researcher on homelessness and mental health at the Sociology Department of the University of Amsterdam, the Netherlands. She has published numerous academic reports and receives broad recognition for organizing regularly, and for different target groups, workshops, lectures, and seminars, and for building a bridge between scientific knowledge and policy practice.

Daniel Brisson is a professor and the director of the Center for Housing and Homelessness Research (CHHR) at the Graduate School of Social Work, University of Denver, United States. His scholarship focuses on poverty, high-poverty neighbourhoods, affordable housing, and homelessness.

Katherine Hoops Calhoun is an assistant professor at the Ohio State University College of Social Work, United States. Her work in homelessness and poverty research is informed by her social work experience in schools, inpatient mental health, and policy advocacy.

Constance Ching is an international public health advocate and homelessness researcher. From 2003 to 2010, Constance worked in supportive housing programmes for homeless individuals at Urban Pathways and Harlem United in New York City, USA. During her time supervising a service-learning project at the City University of Hong Kong (2010–2014), she helped organize the first community homeless street count in Hong Kong through collaborations with NGOs. Since moving to Malaysia in 2014, she has been actively involved in public health advocacy and pursuing homelessness research. She obtained her master of social work from Silberman School of Social Work at Hunter College, City University of New York.

Elinor Chisholm is a senior research fellow at the University of Otago, Aotearoa New Zealand. Elinor is a qualitative and historical researcher interested in how housing and urban form contribute to well-being. Her current research projects look at the effect of housing interventions on health, the use of community rooms in multiunit housing, and public housing tenants' neighbourhood experiences.

Teresa Consoli is an associate professor of sociology of law at the University of Catania, Italy, and has been the director of the University Center on Social and Public Policy, the coordinator of the European Research Network on Southern European Societies, and a member of the Scientific Committee of the Italian Federation of Organizations for Homeless People. On homelessness, she monitored the implementation of Housing First in Italy (*European Journal of Homelessness*, 1/2016), with Antonella Meo edited the book *Homelessness in Italy* (2020), and contributed, also with Caterina Cortese, to the *Handbook on Homelessness* (2023).

Stéphan de Beer is an urbanist-theologian passionate about cities that are radically inclusive, both socially and spatially. Previously, he led a community-based organization in the inner city of Tshwane, focusing on vulnerable people and places and creating responsive social and housing infrastructure. Currently, he is a professor of practical theology and director of the Centre for Faith and Community at the University of Pretoria. With doctoral qualifications in theology and urban planning, he seeks to traverse disciplines and boundaries in undoing the apartheid city. He convenes the Urban Studio and the Unit for Street Homelessness, connecting scholarship, neighbourhoods, and the streets.

Contributors

Wellington Didibhuku Thwala is a professor at the Department of Civil Engineering, College of Science, and a director of the School of Engineering, University of South Africa (UNISA), South Africa. He has authored and co-authored more than 600 accredited journal articles, conference papers, and book chapters.

Pascale Dietrich-Ragon is a researcher in the National Institute for Demographic Studies (INED), France. Her work focuses on housing inequalities, residential precariousness, and the living conditions of working classes. She has published numerous books and articles, including 'On the Sidelines of French Society Homelessness among Migrants and their Descendants' (*Population*, 2017, no. 72) and 'Leaving the Child Welfare Services: From Institutional Housing to the Initial Steps on the Housing Market' (*Population*, 2020, no. 75).

Jörg Dittmann is a professor at the University of Applied Sciences Northwestern, Switzerland. His research is focused on poverty issues, including homelessness and social planning. He was the head of the first counting on homelessness in Switzerland.

Matthias Drilling is the head of the Institute for Social Planning, Organisational Change, and Urban Planning at the University of Applied Sciences Northwestern, Switzerland. His research focuses on the phenomenon of absolute poverty in urban contexts. He is a board member and advisor to several governmental and non-governmental institutions in Europe and acts as a research partner in EU projects.

Evelyn Dyb is a sociologist and senior researcher at OsloMet – Oslo Metropolitan University, Norway. She has researched and published widely on social housing policy and particularly on homelessness and is frequently consulted as a national expert on homelessness nationally as well as internationally.

Andrew Ebekozien is a senior research associate at the Department of Construction Management and Quantity Surveying, University of Johannesburg, South Africa, and a staff at the Department of Quantity Surveying, Auchi Polytechnic, Nigeria. He has authored and co-authored more than 150 accredited journal articles, conference papers, and book chapters.

Ignacio Eissmann is a sociologist and holds a PhD in social work (Boston College and Alberto Hurtado University). He is the co-founder of NGO Moviliza and co-founder of the Center for Research and Advocacy to Overcome Homelessness in Latin America, CISCAL. Ignacio is also the director of research and advocacy of the Jesuit Migrant Service in Chile.

Felipe Estay holds a masters in sociology (University of Bristol) and in social policy and planning (London School of Economics and Political Science). He is a PhD student of sociology in the Catholic University of Chile. He is the director of ONG Moviliza and the Center for Research and Advocacy to Overcome Homelessness in Latin America, CISCAL.

Maria Foscarinis is the founder and former executive director of the National Homelessness Law Center, United States (formerly known as the National Law Center on Homelessness and Poverty), and a lecturer in law at Columbia Law School. She has authored and co-authored dozens of book chapters and articles on homelessness and is currently working on a new book project.

Brodie Fraser is a research fellow, University of Otago, Aotearoa New Zealand. A mixed-methods researcher interested in housing inequities, social theory, public policy, and political science, they work primarily on takatāpui/LGBTIQ+ communities' qualitative experiences of homelessness and housing. They are also involved in projects on Housing First, homelessness amongst women, and children's and young people's experiences of the housing support system.

Susanne Gerull is a professor for theory and practice of social work with a focus on poverty, unemployment, homelessness, and low-threshold social work at the Alice Salomon University of Applied Sciences in Berlin, Germany. She regularly publishes articles and books on her research interests, for example, on homelessness and social work in *The Routledge Handbook of Homelessness* (Bretherton and Pleace (eds.), 2023).

Kalpana Goel is an academic in the discipline of social work at the University of South Australia. She has both practice and teaching experience in the field of social work, community development, and mental health. She has widely published inter alia on ageing population, aged care workforce, and migration. She has published an edited book, *Community work: Theories, Practices and Challenges* (2014). She is currently collaborating on a project investigating positive parenting and adolescent mental health in the South Asian context.

John R. Graham is a professor of social work, University of British Columbia, Okanagan campus, Kelowna, British Columbia, Canada, and the former director of the school. He leads the Kelowna Homelessness Research Center and is a fellow of the American Academy of Social Work and Social Welfare.

Paddy Gray is a professor emeritus of housing, Ulster University, Northern Ireland, UK. Paddy has published widely on housing and continues to inform housing policy locally, nationally, and internationally. In 2010, he was appointed the first Irish president of the Chartered Institute of Housing. He has chaired and been a board member of a number of housing organizations across the UK and Ireland. In 2012, he received an honorary fellowship of RICS; in 2015, won the UK national award for Outstanding Contribution to Work Experience; in 2017, was named the top power player in housing in the UK; and in 2019, was awarded an OBE for services to housing and communities in the Queens honours. He currently serves on the Housing Commission in the Republic of Ireland.

Hilde Hatleskog Zeiner is a researcher at the Norwegian Institute for Urban and Regional Research, Oslo Metropolitan University, Norway. She holds a PhD in social and political studies, and her research interests include multi-level governance and municipal welfare policies.

Philippa Howden-Chapman is Sesquicentennial Distinguished Professor, University of Otago, Aotearoa New Zealand. Philippa Howden-Chapman is a social scientist and co-director of He Kāinga Oranga/Housing and Research Programme and the director of the New Zealand Centre for Sustainable Cities. Her research focus is the social, cultural, and environmental outcomes from the provision and governance of high-quality public housing for tenants' well-being.

Ellie Johnson is a PhD student, University of Otago, Aotearoa New Zealand. Ellie Johnson comes from a background of applied statistics and uses quantitative methodology to explore housing as a social determinant of health. Her most recent work uses statistical methods to evaluate the Healthy Homes Initiative, a large-scale, government-funded housing intervention programme in New Zealand.

Mark Jordan is a lecturer in land and housing law at Southampton Law School, UK, and a founding member of the People, Property, and Community Centre, University of Southampton. His most recent article, 'Contesting Housing Inequality: Housing Rights and Social Movements', was published in the *Modern Law Review* (2023).

Padraic Kenna is a professor at the University of Galway, Ireland, where he lectures in land and housing law. He has published widely on housing and housing rights. His most recent contribution is *The European and International Contribution to the Right to Housing: Standards, Litigation and Advocacy* (2023).

Marcus Knutagård is an associate professor at the School of Social Work, Lund University, Sweden. His research interests include housing policy, homelessness, and the importance of place for how social work is organized – its moral geography. He is the principal investigator in several research projects on homelessness, including *RECO: Resilient Communities by Sustainable Welfare Transformation*. Another project is *Scanian homes: Reception, settlement or rejection – homelessness policies and strategies for refugee settlement*.

Luiz Tokuzi Kohara is an activist on homelessness and its related causes, beginning his work at the Organization of Fraternal Aid (1975–1987). Since 1988, he has been a member of Gaspar Garcia Center for Human Rights, São Paulo, Brazil. He holds a masters in engineering, PhD in architecture and urbanism, and has a postdoc in urban sociology and housing.

Geerhardt Kornatowski is an associate professor of human geography and urban studies at the Kyushu University Graduate School of Social and Cultural Studies, Japan. He has published books and articles on East Asian care geographies for the homeless and migrant workers, including *Diversity of Inclusivity* (2023) with Toshio Mizuuchi.

Nikos Kourachanis is an assistant professor in social policy and housing at Panteion University of Athens, Greece. His research interests are focused on social citizenship and social integration policies for vulnerable groups, such as homeless, migrants, and refugees. He has published numerous books and articles, including *Citizenship and Social Policy* (2020).

Magdalena Küng is a lead coordinator in the public administration office against domestic violence of the canton Solothurn, Switzerland. She studied sociology and law at the University of Basel, focusing on the organization of power, states, and constitutions. From 2020 to 2021, she worked as a research assistant at the FHNW, where she contributed to various research projects on homelessness. Since 2022, she has been responsible for coordinating the implementation of the Istanbul Convention in the Swiss canton of Solothurn.

Núria Lambea Llop is an international doctor in laws, postdoctoral researcher, and deputy director of the UNESCO Housing Chair and co-director of the postgraduate course on housing policies at the University Rovira i Virgili, Spain. She has been a member of several national and international research projects and published one book (*La gestión de la vivienda social en clave europea*, 2022) and various articles and book chapters on affordable and social housing, housing management, housing tenures, and tourist dwellings.

Marie Loison is an associate professor in Sorbonne Paris Nord University and the Printemps Laboratory, France. Her work focuses on the link between social representations and behaviour towards homeless people. Her current research focuses on the trajectories of homeless women and the institutional support provided from a gender perspective. She published ' "Le sans-domicilisme" – Reflections on the categories of homelessness' (*Revue française des affaires sociales*, 2023, no. 1) and 'Women homelessness. When women's shelters challenge social emergency services' (*Travail, genre et société*, 2022, no. 47).

Chris Martin is a senior research fellow in the City Futures Research Centre, UNSW, Sydney, Australia. A rental housing policy and tenancy law specialist, Chris recently worked on 'Towards an Australian and Housing and Homelessness Strategy' (2023) and 'Regulation of residential tenancies and impacts on investment' (2022), two major research projects of the Australian Housing and Urban Research Institute. Chris worked previously with the Tenants' Union of NSW, the state's specialist community legal centre for tenancy law, and is a past chair of Shelter NSW.

George Masimba is the head of Programmes for Dialogue on Shelter Trust, Zimbabwe, an affiliate of Slum Dwellers International (SDI). He holds a PhD in development studies, and his research interests centre on urbanism. He has co-authored articles on participatory urban upgrading and produced technical reports on urban infrastructure systems in Harare.

Kelseny Medeiros Pinho is a postgraduate program researcher in Federal University of ABC, Brazil. She is also an affiliated public interest lawyer at the Gaspar Garcia Center for Human Rights, São Paulo, Brazil, and is a legislative assistant to Deputy Erika Hilton, Brazil's first elected transgender woman in the Brazilian National Congress.

Meenu Anand is an associate professor at the Department of Social Work, University of Delhi, India, with extensive professional experience in gender studies and mental health for more than 24 years. She specializes as a trainer and conducts various capacity-building and gender-sensitization workshops for university teachers and several other stakeholders. She has published extensively in national and international journals. Her latest book is *Gender and Mental Health: Combining Theory and Practice* (2020).

Erminia Maricato is a retired full professor from the School of Architecture and Urbanism at the University of Sao Paulo (USP), Brazil. She served as the secretary of Housing and

Urban Development for the city of Sao Paulo (1989–1992). She established the Ministry of Cities during President Lula's first term, where she served as the vice minister (2003–2005). She received the highest award from the FPAA – Pan American Federation of Associations of Architects in 2020.

Antonella Meo is an associate professor of sociology at the University of Turin, Italy. She took part in the Italian teams of two European research programmes: *Between Integration and Exclusion: A Comparative Study on Local Dynamics of Precariousness and Resistance to Exclusion in Urban Contexts* (1998–2000), coordinated by Daniel Bertaux, and *Social Exclusion of Youth in Europe: Cumulative Disadvantage, Coping Strategies, Effective Policies and Transfer* (2015–2018), coordinated by Marge Unt. She is a member of the Scientific Committee of the Italian Federation of Organizations for Homeless People. On homelessness, she contributed to a participatory action research aimed at improving the public services system for people experiencing homelessness (*European Journal of Homelessness*, 2/2022) and edited with Teresa Consoli the book *Homelessness in Italy* (2020).

Elvis Munyoka is a passionate professional development practitioner. He is currently a PhD candidate with the Justice and Unity Society at the University of South Australia. His research focuses on the transition experiences of young people from African humanitarian backgrounds from higher education to employment. His research interests include humanitarian and community development, migration, African politics and human rights, and international development. He has extensive practical experience working with non-governmental organizations (NGOs) and government agencies in Africa and Europe.

Clinton Ohis Aigbavboa is a professor at the Department of Construction Management and Quantity Surveying and a director, DSI/NRF Research Chair in Sustainable Construction Management and Leadership in the Built Environment, University of Johannesburg, South Africa. He has authored and co-authored more than 1,000 accredited journal articles, conference papers, and book chapters.

Yoshihiro Okamoto is the chairman of Academy of Housing for Life and Well-Being, Japan. He is a professor of Housing for Life and Well-Being in Chukyo University, Japan. He has published articles, including 'A Comparative Study of Homelessness in the United Kingdom and Japan' (*Journal of Social Issues*, 2007), 'Homeless People: Single Men in Japan' (*The international Encyclopaedia of Housing and Home*. Sumith, S. J. (ed.), 2012), and 'Homelessness in Japan' (*The Routledge Handbook on Homelessness*. Bretherton, J. and Pleace, N. (eds.), 2023) with Joanne Bretherton.

Jenny Ombler is a research fellow, University of Otago, Aotearoa New Zealand. Jenny is a mixed-methods researcher with a particular interest in the relationships between policy and society and how these affect outcomes for marginalized peoples. Her current work is focused on human rights and housing.

Hal Pawson is a professor of housing research and policy and an associate director at UNSW's City Futures Research Centre, Australia. He also holds an honorary professorship at Heriot-Watt University, Edinburgh, where he worked from 1995–2011, and is a non-executive director of Community Housing Canberra. Hal is the author, with Vivienne Milligan and Judith Yates, of *Housing Policy in Australia* (2021), an author of the Homeless Monitor series in Great Britain and Australia, and numerous major research projects of the Australian Housing and Urban Research Institute (AHURI).

Adam Ploszka is an assistant professor at the Centre for Human Rights, Faculty of Law and Administration, University of Warsaw, Poland. Formerly, he was associated with the European University Institute in Florence as a Max Weber fellow. Adam is the author of many scientific publications on human rights and constitutional law.

Regina Serpa is a lecturer in housing at the University of Stirling, Scotland, and a guest researcher at Leiden University, where her research focuses on international crimmigration law – the convergence of criminal and immigration law. She is the author of the book *Migrant Homelessness and the Crimmigration Control System* (2023).

Mohamad Shaharudin Samsurijan is a professor at the School of Social Sciences and the current dean, School of Social Sciences, Universiti Sains Malaysia (USM), Malaysia. He has authored and co-authored more than 100 accredited journal articles, conference papers, and book chapters.

Mohd Tarique is an Ashoka fellow and teaches at Tata Institute of Social Sciences, Mumbai, India, and leads Koshish, the institute's project on urban poverty and destitution. He has served on various government-appointed committees, including the Supreme Court Committee for Shelters for Urban Homeless, and Govt of India, Task Force on Social Protection–Chattisgarh. Awarded the prestigious Ashoka Fellowship in 2012 for innovative leadership and social entrepreneurship and listed by Forbes India as a young achiever, he practices a 'systems approach' while seeking accountable governance on social protection.

Eric S. Tars is the senior policy director at the US-based National Homelessness Law Center, leading its human rights, civil rights, and children's rights programmes and working on cutting-edge litigation, strategic policy advocacy, and outreach and training initiatives at the international, national, and local levels. He also serves as the vice-chair of the board of the US Human Rights Network.

Lucy Telfar-Barnard is a senior research fellow, University of Otago, Aotearoa New Zealand. Lucy is an environmental epidemiologist specializing in interactions between policies and regulation in housing quality and tenure and health outcomes, particularly winter and respiratory illnesses. Current or recent projects explore Aotearoa eviction demography, housing quality priorities in public housing, and implementation of WHO Housing and Health Guidelines.

Poh Leng Teo is an associate professor and head (social work) at the Singapore University of Social Sciences, Singapore. She received her PhD (social work) and masters in public policy from the National University of Singapore. Previously, she worked at the Ministry of Social and Family Development, holding various leadership positions.

Contributors

Christine A. Walsh is a professor in the Faculty of Social Work at the University of Calgary, Calgary, Canada, and publishes extensively in the field of homelessness and immigration.

Tamara Walsh is a professor of law at the University of Queensland, Australia, and the director of the UQ Pro Bono Centre. Her research focuses on social welfare law and human rights, with a particular emphasis on homelessness, corrections, and child protection.

Jennifer Wilson is the director of research at Shopworks Architecture, a US-based firm specializing in shelters and affordable housing. She holds a PhD and MSW. As a social worker, she possesses direct practice experience in homeless service provision. She is a member of the Urban Land Institute's Health Leaders Network.

Matti Wirehag is a senior lecturer at University West, Sweden. He successfully defended his thesis on the organization of housing services for people experiencing homelessness from the University of Gothenburg in late 2022. Matti has, during the last 15 years of his professional life, been engaged in the issue of homelessness, the right to housing, and undocumented migrants' right to health and social assistance through practical social work and through development and advocacy activity locally in Gothenburg, nationally, as well as internationally.

Mando Zisopoulou is a PhD candidate in housing policy at Panteion University of Athens, Greece. She is a civil servant in the Department of Social Housing Policies at the General Directorate for Social Solidarity and Fight Against Poverty in the Ministry of Labour and Social Affairs.

FOREWORD

It is a privilege to write this foreword to welcome this important volume on homelessness, law, and policy across many continents and countries at this critical time. Not only does this volume contain detailed case studies of a number of countries; it also details many specific proposals for addressing the causes and conditions of homelessness.

Most countries in the world are experiencing a situation of 'polycrises' – an intersection of multiple crises, from security, political, economic, ecological, health, and social. Homelessness is a manifestation of these polycrises but remains a problem which is actually within the power of most wealthy countries to solve. While there is a lack of reliable worldwide statistics, homelessness is a global concern in all world regions. For those countries or organizations that have made efforts to track various forms of homelessness, the figures are alarming. For example, according to latest official figures of the United States of America, over 500,000 people were considered homeless as of 1 January 2022.[1] It should be noted that over 40% of them are people of African descent, who make up only 12% of the population.[2]

In most EU countries, homelessness has significantly increased since 2010 at least by 70%.[3] The *8th Overview on housing exclusion in Europe*, published on 5 September 2023, estimates that at least 895,000 persons live in Europe either in street situation, in emergency accommodation, or in accommodation for the homeless. In many developing nations, homelessness is either not surveyed or often the issue is named differently, but homelessness as a human rights violation is similarly persistent. The most common form is housing deprivation and exclusion, visible in the form of large under-serviced, poorly built informal settlements, often without access to safe water and sanitation and electricity, and in

---

1 The US Department of Housing and Urban Development, Office of Community Planning and Development, *The 2022 Annual Homelessness Assessment Report (AHAR) to Congress* (U.S. Department of Housing and Urban Development, December 2022).
2 See Chapters 15 and 16 in this volume on the United States of America.
3 FEANTSA and Abbé Pierre Foundation, N. Horvat and S. Coupechoux (coords), *Report: 8th Overview of Housing Exclusion in Europe 2023* (September 2023) <www.feantsa.org/public/user/Resources/reports/2023/OVERVIEW/Rapport_EN.pdf> (accessed 21 November 2023).

which residents frequently live in constant fear of forced evictions.[4] However, other forms of homelessness exist as well in the Global South, whether it is pavement dwellers, people occupying dangerous, often so-called 'unauthorized' structures, or residing in IDP or refugee camps. As pointed out in the chapters in this volume on several countries in Asia, Africa, and Latin America, large informal settlements house the most marginalized communities in the Global South, who are at the highest risk of evictions and displacement.

Although the right to adequate housing has been enshrined in the International Covenant on Economic and Social Rights since the 1960s, it is denied to millions worldwide who lack access to any form of housing or even shelter, are forced to sleep rough or in structures unsuitable for a life in safety and security.

Homelessness is not only a serious concern in terms of the right to adequate housing; if we look at morbidity and mortality rates of persons in situation of homelessness and compare those with people who are adequately housed, the difference is shocking. The median age of death for persons in street situation has, in some industrialized countries, been estimated to be 49 years, over 25 years lower than for the overall population.[5] There is no doubt that homelessness violates also the right to the highest form of attainable health, to water and sanitation, to privacy, and the right to life, which is more than mere survival but includes as well the notion of a life with dignity.[6]

Failure of public authorities to prevent and address homelessness is a state failure to uphold the most essential elements of the human right to adequate housing and other fundamental human rights that everyone should enjoy without any discrimination. Unfortunately, too many countries fail to recognize or protect economic, social, and cultural rights, such as the right to adequate housing, whose denial is almost exclusively felt by the poorest and the most marginalized. Homelessness cannot be solved without recognizing and protecting the right to housing – in fact, if not in law as well.

While the pathways into homelessness are manifold, it is possible to prevent, reduce, and end it, or at least reduce it to marginal numbers. This is particularly true for countries that have access to significant financial and other resources and have functioning public administrations. We saw how it could be done during the Covid-19 pandemic. Regrettably, those measures have all ended in most places, and we are back to square one.

For those 13 European countries where there are more reliable estimates, those persons in situation of homelessness in Europe are of course still too many, but not so many that this problem could not be dealt with: those in situations of severe forms of homelessness represent only 0.174% of their total population. This, surely, is a solvable problem. For example, Finland has actually shown that reducing homelessness is possible by adopting a housing-led approach, providing affordable housing and, if necessary, additional ambulant social support. In 1987, over 17,110 persons were counted in Finland as homeless; latest official figures from 2022 indicate 3,686 persons in various forms of homeless – a reduction by 83%.[7]

---

4 See Chapter 24 on India in this volume.
5 These are findings from research undertaken in France; see C. Vuillermoz and others, 'Mortality Among Homeless People in France, 2008–10' (2016) 26(6) *The European Journal of Public Health* 1028–33 <https://pubmed.ncbi.nlm.nih.gov/27335327/> (accessed 21 November 2023).
6 See on this in particular Human Rights Committee, 'General Comment No. 36 on Art. 6: Right to Life' <www.ohchr.org/en/calls-for-input/general-comment-no-36-article-6-right-life> (accessed 21 November 2023).
7 FEANTSA and Abbé Pierre Foundation and others (n 3) 31.

Foreword

Netherlands[8] and Singapore[9] have shown success by adopting a housing-first approach and by emphasizing prevention and care dimensions occasioned by homelessness.

I am encouraged by the fact that more and more countries have adopted national action plans to prevent and end homelessness or have started to undertake official data collection.[10] Four African countries initiated the UN General Assembly resolution 76/133[11] on affordable housing to end homelessness that was adopted in 2021, and the UN Secretary-General has recently published a comprehensive report (A/78/236),[12] arguing strongly for a human rights–based approach to prevent and end homelessness. During its EU presidency in 2021, Portugal spearheaded the establishment of the European Platform on Combatting Homelessness,[13] in which all EU states agreed to work towards ensuring by 2030 that no one sleeps rough for lack of accessible, safe, and appropriate emergency accommodation, that evictions should be prevented whenever possible, and that no one is evicted without assistance for an appropriate housing solution, when needed.

A major current concern in the global debate about how to address homelessness relates to the criminalization of homelessness. It has indeed been a particular focus of an ongoing campaign to end criminalization of homelessness that I have embarked on, together with the UN special rapporteur on extreme poverty and human rights, Olivier de Schutter.[14] Regrettably, the use of criminal and administrative law to punish the poor, the homeless, persons with mental disabilities, and other persons considered to be different, unpleasant, or deviating in their behaviour from the majority has a long and outrageous tradition. Colonialism helped export vagrancy laws globally, such as the British Vagrancy Act of 1824. Many European countries introduced similar vagrancy laws, which provided the legal basis to imprison so-called 'idle and disorderly persons', 'rogues and vagabonds', or 'incorrigible rogues' and subject them to forced labour or intern them in so-called 'workhouses'.

Regrettably also, the development of international human rights law did not immediately result in the discrediting of vagrancy or other laws criminalizing persons experiencing homelessness or poverty.

The first international human rights treaty that came into force after World War II, the European Convention on Human Rights, includes, for example, in its Article 5(1)(e) on the right to liberty and security of person, a provision allowing for the lawful detention of 'persons of unsound mind, alcoholics or drug addicts or vagrants'. In 1971, the European Court on Human Rights ruled in the so-called 'vagrancy – cases'[15] that the detention of the applicants in vagrancy centres in Belgium, where they were made to work in exchange for

---

8 See Chapter 10 in this volume.
9 See Chapter 25 in this volume.
10 For example, Germany has started, since 2022, collecting data on several forms of homelessness: see Chapter 4 on Germany in this volume.
11 <https://documents-dds-ny.un.org/doc/UNDOC/GEN/N21/400/84/PDF/N2140084.pdf?OpenElement> (accessed 21 November 2023).
12 <www.undocs.org/Home/Mobile?FinalSymbol=A%2F78%2F236&Language=E&DeviceType=Desktop&LangRequested=False> (accessed 21 November 2023).
13 <https://ec.europa.eu/social/home.jsp?langId=en> (accessed 21 November 2023).
14 B. Rajagopal, O. De Schutter and B. Van Hout, 'EU Must Treat Homeless as Rights Holders, Not Criminals' *EU Observer* (16 June 2021).
15 *Case of De Wilde, Ooms and Versyp v Belgium* 2832/66 2835/66 2899/66 <https://hudoc.echr.coe.int/eng#{%22dmdocnumber%22:[%22695483%22],%22itemid%22:[%22001-57606%22]}> (accessed 21 November 2023).

payment at a low rate, was not a violation of their right to liberty and security of person or of Article 4 of the same Convention prohibiting slavery and forced labour.

In the United States of America, it was only in the early 1970s that a succession of vagrancy laws was ruled unconstitutional by the US Supreme Court, although life-sustaining activities like sleeping or cooking continue to be criminalized by local jurisdictions or state laws. Germany's Constitutional Court ruled only in 1970 that begging and vagrancy should not be criminalized. Finland's 1883 vagrancy law was only repealed in 1987. Belgium abolished its laws against vagrancy and begging in 1993. In Greece, a provision in the penal code on vagrancy was repealed in 1994, while begging was decriminalized only in 2018. In Argentina, a police edict on vagrancy and begging was declared unconstitutional in 1995. In Mexico, there are still laws and regulations in force prohibiting begging, eating, sleeping, or performing personal hygienic activities in all or certain public places, while they are allegedly not enforced anymore.[16]

There have been several attempts to repeal the Vagrancy Act in England, Wales, and Scotland that has served as a blueprint in so many countries, especially in the formerly colonized world. While Scotland managed to repeal this law in 1982, in 2022, this infamous Act was formally scrapped in England and Wales as well, although the repeal lacks an implementation date, and there are many concerns that some form of criminalization of vagrancy or associated behaviours will continue. Indeed, this archaic law is still being used to arrest many people: more than 3,800 homeless people have been arrested in England and Wales since 2018 – more than 1,000 homeless people have been arrested for sleeping rough or begging since the UK government pledged to scrap the Act.[17]

The scrapping of vagrancy acts, the amendment of penal codes, and judgements by constitutional courts unfortunately do not mean an end to the criminalization of homelessness or sanctions and punishment for performing life-sustaining activities in public through local by-laws. In fact, in countries such as in Switzerland,[18] several Cantons reintroduced or expanded laws prohibiting begging. Hungary reintroduced the criminalization of persons experiencing homelessness in 2018. In the United States of America, many cities have made efforts to circumvent judgements aimed at decriminalizing homelessness by adopting regulations that are considered to meet the requirements of US constitutional law. Many Western states and cities are engaged in a constitutional tussle before the US Supreme Court, challenging a Ninth Circuit ruling which had held criminalization of life-sustaining activities of homeless persons to be a violation of the Eighth Amendment of the Constitution's prohibition of cruel and unusual punishment. As far as Africa is concerned, the Campaign to Decriminalize Poverty and Status made a comprehensive submission to me covering 19 African countries, indicating that in most of these countries, 'vagrancy laws' dating back from colonial period are still in force.[19] In South Asia, anti-vagrancy or 'anti-beggary' statutes were adopted during the colonial period and are systematically used to hound and harass the poor who lack adequate

---

16 See submissions <www.ohchr.org/en/calls-for-input/calls-input/call-input-decriminalization-homelessness-and-extreme-poverty> (accessed 21 November 2023).
17 On which see T. Wall, 'Thousands of Homeless People Arrested Under Archaic Vagrancy Act' *The Guardian* (2 April 2023) <www.theguardian.com/society/2023/apr/02/thousands-of-homeless-people-arrested-under-archaic-vagrancy-act> (accessed 21 November 2023); *Crisis Scrap the Act: The Case for Repealing the Vagrancy Act* (1824) <www.crisis.org.uk/media/240604/cri0220_vagrancyact_report_aw_web.pdf> (accessed 21 November 2023). See Chapter 1 on the UK in this volume.
18 See Chapter 12 on Switzerland in this volume.
19 See 'Submission on the Decriminalisation of Homelessness and Extreme Poverty' submitted to the Special Rapporteur on the Right to Adequate Housing & the Special Rapporteur on Extreme Poverty and Human

housing and income.[20] All of them are fundamentally inconsistent with modern human rights norms, including the constitutional jurisprudence of their own courts.

At the United Nations, the Guiding Principles on Extreme Poverty and Human Rights (A/HRC/21/39), as well as the Guidelines for the Implementation of the Right to Adequate Housing (A/HRC/43/43), recommend that:

> States should prohibit and address discrimination on the ground of homelessness or other housing status and repeal all laws and measures that criminalize or penalize homeless people or behaviour associated with being homeless, such as sleeping or eating in public spaces.

In June 2020, the Human Rights Council called in resolution 43/14 on states to 'take all measures necessary to eliminate legislation that criminalized homelessness'. While the UN General Assembly adopted an important resolution on homelessness (A/RES/76/133), calling homelessness an affront to human dignity in 2021, and reiterated in 2023, the resolution itself has regrettably remained silent on the issue of decriminalization of homelessness.

Given the continued difficulties to decriminalize homelessness and petty offences at the local, national, and international level, the contribution of regional human rights mechanisms to overcome the use of criminal law for petty offences must be lauded. The Principles on the Decriminalization of Petty Offences in Africa, adopted in 2017 by the African Commission on Peoples and Human Rights, the Advisory Opinion of the African Court on Human and People's Rights adopted on 4 December 2002, which states that various vagrancy laws, which continue to be in force in many African countries since colonial times, prohibiting begging, staying, or sleeping in public places, are incompatible with human rights law binding on their states, the ruling by the European Court of Human Rights (ECHR) in 2021 in the case of *Lăcătuş v. Switzerland* (application no. 14065/15) are examples that could be noted here.

Despite this judgement of the European Court, criminalization of homelessness remains a serious concern in Europe and elsewhere. On 2 February 2022, for example, the Danish Supreme Court sentenced a Lithuanian citizen to 60 days' unconditional imprisonment for begging. Since 2017, changes in the Danish Penal Code have contributed to increasing criminalization of the presence of homeless people in public spaces. Strongly condemned by civil society, the inhumane policies introduced restrictions on sleeping rough and increased punishment for begging. There is, prima facie, a strongly xenophobic element to this legislation. In debates introducing the new sanctions, it was openly stated that the aim of these policies is to target non-Danish citizens living homeless on the streets of Denmark. The figures so far confirm as well this: from 94 convictions under paragraph 197 of this Code, 91 were of non-Danes.[21]

Finally, as a recent report of a fellow UN rapporteur has pointed out,[22] more clearly than any other publication so far, homelessness can be a pathway into contemporary forms of

---

Rights by the Campaign to Decriminalise Poverty and Status (30 November 2021) <www.ohchr.org/sites/default/files/2022-03/CampaigntoDecriminalizePoverty.docx> (accessed 21 November 2023).

20 See Chapter 24 on India in this volume.
21 <www.feantsaresearch.org/en/press-release/2022/02/04/feantsa-denounces-the-criminalisation-of-homeless-people-in-denmark>.
22 Homelessness as a cause and consequence of contemporary forms of slavery: report of the Special Rapporteur on Contemporary Forms of Slavery, Including Its Causes and Consequences, Tomoya Obokata, A/HRC/54/30.

slavery, labour, and sexual exploitation and that there can also be the reverse risk: that persons subjected to contemporary forms of slavery may be at increased risk of becoming homeless. Labour and sexual exploitation may leave individuals trapped in housing, without any security of tenure, where they can be quickly pushed into homelessness. The threat of homelessness is usually a core part of the system of enslavement, for example, through slave-like labour exploitation in agriculture or in domestic work. Often, those subjected to such exploitation are housed as well by those exploiting them. If the concerned individuals want to flee the exploitation, they have literally no place to go, and no access to any alternative housing that they could afford. They are trapped in continued exploitation. If they want to exit their exploitation, they end up on the street, which in turn may keep them trapped in slavery.

Therefore, much more needs to be done to ensure that, for example, domestic and migrant workers have security of tenure that is independent from their employers. Regulations must ensure that those housed by their employers as part of the working arrangement cannot be pushed into the street when their employers end their work contracts at short notice. As the world witnessed, during the Covid-19 outbreak, in many countries, employers of migrant or domestic workers, literally overnight, ended the engagement of their assistants, workers, or servants, resulting not only in sudden job loss and loss of income, but in loss of housing, sending domestic and migrant workers to the streets, often unable to return to family members or foreign countries.

The gender dimension is critical and central to this issue. The more visible street homelessness is, in most countries, 60–80% male, while homelessness more broadly is not. In particular, women, girls, children, and LGBTQ youth usually avoid, as much as possible, the street or unsafe homeless shelters. Homelessness then takes the form of couch surfing or 'doubling up' with other people, friends, or relatives, or whoever may be willing to host the distressed person. These living arrangements hardly provide any security of tenure, and hosts can kick people into the street in a matter of minutes or hours without breaking any national law. This comes with alleviated risk of exploitation, whether labour or sexual exploitation, forcing women, girls, or youth, including LGBTQ youth, into unwanted relationships or other forms exploitation. Relationships under duress may be maintained to have a roof over the head but do not provide a safe, secure place to live in dignity. This form of homelessness is hardly visible, receives much less attention, but can be as rights violating than having to survive on the streets. It may be even more difficult to escape and is more difficult to monitor and measure. Many support services that have been established to address street homelessness do not offer adequate support and housing solutions for people trapped in this form of hidden homelessness.[23]

In the presence of these and other pervasive challenges raised by homelessness, this volume contributes significantly to our understanding of the causes and consequences of homelessness comparatively while grounding the analyses in concrete plans of actions and lessons learned. The SDG goals are farther than ever from being realized, and elimination of homelessness is not even a goal or a target within the SDG framework. In the absence of such global goal setting, the world counts on country-by-country progress, as detailed in this volume, towards achieving the end of homelessness and the fuller realization of the human right to adequate housing.

Balakrishnan Rajagopal
UN Special Rapporteur on the Right to Adequate Housing

---

23 See Chapter 6 in this volume.

INTRODUCTION
Learning Lessons Across Borders

Chris Bevan

Homelessness is a *global challenge* that warrants a *global perspective*. Yet homelessness also presents a *global opportunity* – to learn lessons across borders and to innovate and inspire new thinking and novel ways of 'seeing' homelessness from a genuinely international perspective. This collection draws on the diverse, rich tapestry of experiences of homelessness and homelessness prevention across 28 different nations from each of the permanently inhabited continents and seeks to nourish and inform debates both at the state and international level as well as within global institutions on how best to respond to and tackle this most damaging global social phenomenon and human tragedy. While every nation on Earth has its own history and socio-political landscape, the fundamental need of citizens for secure and stable housing speaks in a universal language. This core human imperative for a safe place to call 'home' is shared by all populations and is one that sounds across history and transcends country lines.

The United Nations estimates that over 1.6 billion people internationally are living in inadequate housing and over 100 million people have no housing whatsoever to call their own. Homelessness impacts every country and every community. In many parts of the world, homelessness is on the increase, fuelled by and coterminous with economic, social, and health inequalities. As this collection reveals, a broad range of powerful currents touches on homelessness, not least the tentacles of the Global Financial Crisis of 2008, which still echo in many nations of the world, but so, too, the Covid-19 pandemic, which has affected us all, but with varying degrees of severity. The pandemic both revealed but also perpetrated and exacerbated existing social global inequalities. Yet this book reveals, out of this most horrific human tragedy, that hopeful and forward-looking initiatives for homelessness prevention have sprouted. Homelessness is, as is well-known, a deeply complex problem which rests at the intersection of varied and connected social concerns. As well as housing precarity, therefore, this book demonstrates the interconnectedness of issues of housing, health, wealth, employment, politics, discrimination, and community and how these social determinants and drivers sit as enduring and dominant themes for homelessness research and for those living with homelessness. The chapters of this collection deftly map the relationship between these themes as they emerge and collide in each country studied.

Nature and Novelty of the Collection

How do different nations define *homelessness* in national and regional law and policy? What distinct conceptions and understandings of homelessness are engaged? What discourses and narratives exist within states for how they represent and construct images of those experiencing homelessness? What influence does a nation's social and geo-political history have on approaches to homelessness? What are the precise challenges, policy motivations, and impulses on homelessness, and what examples of innovative preventative practice do we find in each country? These are just some of the fascinating questions that the contributors to this groundbreaking international collection explore as they shine searching spotlights on their jurisdiction's approach to homelessness law and policy. In so doing, commanding historical accounts, probing analyses, and critiques of state policies on homelessness are offered, as well as exciting and thought-provoking recommendations for future reform.

Each chapter of this collection zooms in on homelessness in a particular country and is written by national experts with varied and diverse disciplinary backgrounds and perspectives in fields of housing, homelessness, and social policy. Writing alone or in teams, they explore the nature and scale of homelessness in their country; the definition of homelessness engaged; national, regional government, and third sector responses to homelessness; policy interventions; innovative homelessness prevention measures; and issues such as hidden homelessness set against the particular context and hinterland of that country.

This collection is not intended as a direct comparative work between countries, as 28 nations across six continents cannot be readily or, it is argued, meaningfully compared strictly with one another, given the unique socio- and geo-political conditions and history of each nation. Equally, there is no promise of an exhaustive, all-embracing, or comprehensive examination of homelessness in each country – such an endeavour would be bound to fail, as an encyclopaedic account could never be captured within the pages of just one collection. Instead, contributors were invited to offer their perspectives and insights into the issues of most importance and resonance in their country, building on their own motivations, interests, and the policy pulses and rhythms of their country. Thus, while contributors broadly examine the existing legal and policy frameworks and experiences of homelessness in their country, not all themes are explored with equal emphasis in each chapter. The great advantage of avoiding an insistence on a rigid structure for all chapters or a defined set of topics for examination is that contributors have provided broader, subtler, and more absorbing analyses – whether that be, for example, on how national strategies have been developed and delivered, the role of third sector institutions, or how individual cities or regional authorities have responded to homelessness, how the political leanings of their country have shaped perception and treatment of those living with homelessness or a focus on criminalization of homelessness and the experience of Indigenous populations.

With contributors drawn from both the Global North and the Global South, from varied and diverse backgrounds, including internationally renowned researchers, activists, advocates, directors of homelessness organizations, leaders of research centres, and more, the consequence is a book that is rich and deep in insight and real-world significance. The book contributes to knowledge in the homelessness sector by seeking to generate international debate and re-evaluation of how contrasting global experiences and action on homelessness across the world might serve as a catalyst for us, as researchers and policymakers, to 'see' homelessness differently and imagine novel ways of addressing and ending homelessness. The collection offers an unrivalled, definitive global survey and account of international

Introduction

approaches and perspectives on homelessness. The volume's novelty is found in its breadth of geographical reach and its diversity of voices, but also in its ambition as contributors trace homelessness from standpoints firmly rooted in their unique national, political, and housing stories. Taken together, the collection reveals the shifting and contrasting 'faces' or 'frontiers' of homelessness across the globe.

Structure of the Book and Chapter Outlines

The collection reaches across the six major permanently populated continents of the globe and is structured into corresponding parts covering Europe, North America, South America, Africa, Asia, and Oceania. Beginning with an examination of some of the most affluent nations of the world in Europe (Part I), and then North America (Part II), contributors urge readers to consider the ways in which wealthy nations have succeeded and the ways they have failed in framing and responding to homelessness. The collection then turns to explore the political and economic challenges and successes of South America (Part III) and Africa (Part IV) before moving to Asia (Part V), where again financial crises and demographic challenges take centre stage. The volume concludes by examining the position in Oceania (Part VI), where questions of the criminalization of homelessness, the right to housing, and discrimination of Indigenous populations remain live issues.

Part I explores Europe. In Chapter 1, on homelessness in the UK, Chris Bevan, Regina Serpa, and Paddy Gray reflect on how the different nations of the United Kingdom have responded to the homelessness problem with varying degrees of success. They trace the strategies, legislation, and political action in England and what has been achieved in Wales, Scotland, and Northern Ireland over 25 years of devolution, in a bid to illuminate the similarities and divergencies across the (dis-)United Kingdom. Chris Bevan explores the Homelessness Reduction Act 2017, which is now embedding in England and offers hope of a more serious turn to a prevention focus and additionally highlights the more proactive approach in Wales, where the work of the Homelessness Action Group has been accepted by the Welsh government and is now firmly rooted in the current Programme for Government 2021–2026. Regina Serpa highlights how the Scottish government has adopted a distinctively progressive approach to homelessness policy, founded on the establishment of a right to housing, with the objective of ending homelessness, and standing in marked contrast to more explicitly punitive welfare system in England as well as noting work around the rapid rehousing and Housing First programmes. Paddy Gray sets in context homelessness policy in Northern Ireland by referencing the political troubles in the country, the Peace Process and Good Friday Agreement. He moves to examine the rolling sequence of Northern Irish homelessness strategies from 2002 and reflects on how periods of democratic deficit in the country during which the NI Assembly has not been sitting have hampered greater progress on homelessness in the country.

In Chapter 2, Mark Jordan and Padraic Kenna offer a detailed account of the legal and policy framework on homelessness in Ireland as the country faces a rapid increase in homelessness. Drawing on a recent policy review on homelessness in Ireland, the chapter muses on the importance of wide and effective definitions of homelessness, emphasizing how prevention work cannot be seen in isolation, and noting the fascinating and continuing constitutional debates in the country on the right to housing.

In Chapter 3, Pascale Dietrich-Ragon and Marie Loison reflect on worsening housing precarity in France over the past decades and, while noting a range of innovative initiatives such as night shelters for women fleeing domestic violence and Housing First programmes, reveal that the French homelessness framework remains hierarchical, segmented, and deeply grounded in selection practices. This, they argue, does not augur well for the immediate future for homelessness in France, and they call for greater coordination between actors in the field.

In Chapter 4, Susanne Gerull outlines the definition and extensive legal framework on homelessness in Germany, noting it to be one of the strongest and most protective in Europe. Going on to explore examples of best practice across Germany's federal system from cities including Berlin, Karlsruhe and Hannover, the chapter ultimately argues that there remains much untapped potential and opportunity for greater assistance for those experiencing homelessness in Germany, if only political leaders would fully commit to making homelessness a more central (as opposed to niche) political issue and seek to involve and empower homeless people themselves in policymaking.

In Chapter 5, Teresa Consoli and Antonella Meo explore how, in Italy, only comparatively recently has homelessness risen up the media and political agenda. They explain how economics and regionality play a massive role in the homelessness story in Italy and how the Covid-19 pandemic hit the country harder than it did most European nations. With the economic divide between the richer north of the country and the poorer south, the picture remains mixed with no national standard for homelessness services. The result is a highly differentiated patchwork of provision across Italy's 20 regions. Optimism springs, however, from recently introduced minimum income schemes, the ongoing roll-out of housing-led and rapid rehousing services across Italy, and innovative examples, including self-managed shelters.

In Chapter 6, Núria Lambea Llop explores how unreliable data collection at the national level is obscuring a true assessment of the scale of homelessness in Spain and, in particular, how 'hidden homelessness' is being overlooked. Despite this, there are grounds for positivity with the National Act on the Right to Housing, which, in large measure, embraces the FEANTSA ETHOS typology on homelessness, having recently made its way through the Spanish parliamentary system. Beyond this, in the Spanish regions, exciting work is underway, for example, in the Basque Country and Catalonia, to enshrine more protective homelessness regimes into law. The chapter makes the argument for greater reliability in data gathering, more effective coordination between national, regional, and local administrations, and the creation of a continuum of tenures to guarantee affordable housing to meet households' needs.

In Chapter 7, Nikos Kourachanis and Mando Zisopoulou examine the impact of both the Greek economic crisis and the Covid-19 pandemic on social and homelessness policy in Greece and how these combined events have shaped the country's response to homelessness by reference to the particularities of the Greek welfare state. Concluding that the state's interventions remain 'characterized by fragmented actions', the authors nevertheless point to significant recent developments in housing policy in the country, including the passing of Law 5006/2022, which represents the first comprehensive approach to housing policy in Greece, and programmes such as 'My Home', 'Coverage', and 'Renovate-Rent'. Even here, however, measures risk being only temporary and not meeting the full scale of the homelessness problem in Greece.

In Chapter 8, Evelyn Dyb and Hilde Hatleskog Zeiner invite the reader to consider the position in Norway, a country (along with its Scandinavian neighbours) generally regarded as world-leading in tackling social problems such as homelessness. Norway, unlike almost

Introduction

all countries in the world, has experienced a decline in the number of homeless people in the last decade, chiefly driven, as the chapter explores, by sustained political commitment to tackling homelessness, the implementation of Housing First policies, and earmarked funding provided to Norwegian municipalities. The chapter reflects on this, the country's 'social turn', the emphasis on homeownership and how citizens, including those experiencing homelessness, are assisted to participate in the housing market.

In Chapter 9, Marcus Knutagård and Matti Wirehag offer a chapter on homelessness in Sweden, the second Scandinavian chapter in the collection. They draw attention to the differences in housing system to, for example, the UK, as in Sweden there is a unitary (as opposed to dualist) housing model. They highlight that, despite the universalist approach, many of the most vulnerable groups in Sweden still fall outside this system, finding themselves in difficult homelessness situations. The chapter highlights the central role of social services, the National Board of Health and Welfare (NBHW), the importance of national surveys on homelessness, the efforts being made to tackle the problem by seeking to prevent evictions, and the new homelessness strategy 2022 and its stated ambitions to prevent homelessness, end rough sleeping, and embed Housing First nationally. Nevertheless, the chapter underscores that the lack of consistency in measures to assist those experiencing homelessness across Sweden's municipalities remains a central challenge.

In Chapter 10, Nienke F. Boesveldt turns to consider the homelessness legal and policy framework in the Netherlands, including examining how FEANTSA's ETHOS typology is increasingly being used to draw attention to the multiple dimensions of homelessness in the country. The chapter draws attention to key preventative strands of the Dutch 2023–2030 homelessness strategy, including the 'At Home for Everyone' programme, which comprises initiatives such as 'Early On', 'Rooms with Attention', and 'Under the Rooftiles', before reflecting on positive signs for the future as the country makes a renewed and evidence-led turn towards Housing First.

In Chapter 11, Adam Ploszka discusses the 'deep crisis in the rule of law and human rights' in Poland, changes to the constitutional and political system under the Law and Justice Party in power from 2015, and makes the argument that Poland is 'no longer ... a liberal democracy'. The chapter examines the impact of this political landscape on measures on homelessness in Poland, exploring whether Poland has followed the illiberal, hostile, and stigmatizing approach towards those experiencing homelessness seen in Hungary. The chapter draws on the work of the commissioner for citizens' rights (referred to as the 'ombudsman'), who has made eradication of homelessness one of his priorities in Poland, as evidence that the country is taking a different path to Hungary. The chapter tracks the change in the social perception towards those experiencing homeless, the breaking down of stereotypes, and a shift in the language used in political debates, which, in turn, allows for tentative optimism for the future of tackling homelessness in Poland.

In Chapter 12, Matthias Drilling, Magdalena Küng, and Jörg Dittmann identify and trace the status of homelessness in Swiss society and in parliamentary debates, noting that, generally, homelessness is a poorly discussed topic in Switzerland despite its increasing visibility in urban areas. The chapter draws on the authors' own research to offer insights into the state of and responses to homelessness in Switzerland. The chapter notes that, as a result of the Covid-19 pandemic, the problem of homelessness has once again become a hot topic of discussion, and changes in legislation impacting the homelessness issue are expected from the Swiss cantons in the coming years.

Part II explores North America. In Chapter 13, John R. Graham, Yale D. Belanger, and Christine A. Walsh examine the position in Canada, the important role of Canada's third and voluntary sectors in the provision of homelessness services, set against the particular historical, geographic, and demographic challenges facing the country. The chapter draws the reader's attention to existing preventative practices and the future direction of travel for homelessness policy in Canada.

In Chapter 14, again focusing on Canada, we move to consider the impact on Indigenous populations. Yale D. Belanger offers an account of the 'mounting concern' yet 'strikingly low level of attention' paid to Indigenous homelessness and, in particular, to the scale and disproportionate nature of unsheltered homelessness experienced by the Indigenous versus non-Indigenous populations in Canada. The chapter examines the 'racism [that] underscores some of the state's Indigenous policy responses', for example, through segregation and isolation of Indigenous people from the housing market. The chapter advocates for systems innovation through self-determination to end Indigenous homelessness in Canada and a break from the institutional racism responsible for perpetuating homelessness in these communities.

In Chapter 15, in the first of two chapters exploring homelessness in the United States, Maria Foscarinis and Eric S. Tars provide a deep, thoughtful, and historical account of the homelessness 'crisis' in the United States and responses to the homelessness phenomenon from campaigners and government, presented through the prism of changing political control in the White House. The chapter reveals the authors' cautious optimism about the challenges the United States faces and opportunities for the future. Emphasis is placed on the possibilities that the Covid-19 pandemic has presented and an acknowledgement of the growth in participation in policymaking of those living with homelessness and the discourse around housing as a human right in the United States.

In Chapter 16, the second chapter on the United States, Daniel Brisson, Katherine Hoops Calhoun, and Jennifer Wilson again focus on the United States but here take a different approach, examining innovative policy responses to homelessness by exploring case studies on safe parking as a short-term sheltering option, tiny home communities as an alternative to long-term sheltering, and direct cash transfers offered to unhoused adults as a complement to existing assistance programmes.

Part III explores South America. In Chapter 17, Kelseny Medeiros Pinho, Luiz Tokuzi Kohara, and Erminia Maricato discuss the state of homelessness in Brazil, set against the political context of the country. The focus of this chapter is on the importance of participatory spaces and how the voices of those experiencing homelessness are baked into local and national action. The chapter explores the establishment of the *Movimento Nacional da População de Rua – MNPR* (National Homeless Population Movement) after the Sé Square massacre and how the formation of this social movement in Brazil has had a profound effect on the legislative landscape and development of public policies, reflecting the power and potential of social and community movements in Brazil. The chapter discusses the National Policy for the Homeless Population Law (PNPSR) – the most significant policy at a national level on homelessness – and the future challenges the country confronts including overcoming a housing model centred on emergency shelter and maintaining momentum for 'homeless people protagonism' so potent in Brazil.

In Chapter 18, Ignacio Eissmann and Felipe Estay provide an assessment of the homelessness policy framework and its effectiveness in Chile. The chapter reveals that there has been a significant increase in the recognition of homelessness as a public issue in Chile

Introduction

in the past 15 years, the growing use of a public–private working model, and ultimately argues that Chile offers valuable lessons for countries across Latin America. The chapter highlights, however, the fragility of social programmes, as many NGOs and local organizations are shouldering the financial risk of social schemes aimed at those living with homelessness. Despite major steps forward, then, homelessness services remain vulnerable. The authors conclude by offering clear recommendations for reform to homelessness policy in Chile, focusing on public investment and ensuring permanent, formal state support for those experiencing homelessness.

Part IV explores Africa. In Chapter 19, Andrew Ebekozien, Clinton Ohis Aigbavboa, Wellington Didibhuku Thwala, Mohamad Shaharudin Samsurijan, and Rex Asibuodu Ugulu explore homelessness in Nigeria, drawing attention to Nigeria's striking housing deficit, the lack of a universal, accepted definition of homelessness in the country, and the problem of forced evictions and informal settlements. Setting this discussion in the context of the root causes of homelessness and a historical account of housing policies in Nigeria, the authors set out their own clear vision for the way forward and recommendations for tackling homelessness in the country.

In Chapter 20, Stéphan de Beer presents a case study of the city of Tshwane as a potential blueprint for tackling homelessness across the whole of South Africa as the echoes of the 'apartheid city' remain in the country. The chapter draws on the instructive experiences of Tshwane, including an important, recent collaboration in the city between grassroots providers, public interest law organizations, and a Pretoria University–based research centre, to explore the benefits of innovative partnerships seeking productive fusion of research, policy, and practice. The author himself has been leading this collaboration, and the chapter is informed by the work of the successful *Tshwane Homelessness Forum*, created in the 1990s, as an attempt to coordinate services offered to homeless communities. In the absence of any national policy framework on homelessness, the city of Tshwane and other municipalities are discussed as exemplars for shifting paradigms and approaches to shaping the future of homelessness policy in South Africa.

In Chapter 21, Masimba zooms in on the housing crisis in Harare as emblematic of wider homelessness struggles in Zimbabwe. Examining the effects of exclusionary urban planning practice and the legislative framework on homelessness, the chapter demonstrates how the poor are excluded from spaces within the city and makes the case for more inclusive planning and homelessness policies across Zimbabwe.

Part V explores the response to homelessness in Asia. In Chapter 22, Yoshihiro Okamoto examines the legal framework on homelessness in Japan, informed by the country's unique economic experiences, locating the narrow, street dweller–based definition of 'homelessness' embraced in Japanese policy, and by analysing central pieces of homelessness legislation, including the Homeless Independence Support Act 2002. In so doing, the chapter identifies the key challenges facing policymaking in this area in Japan and highlights how the concept of 'employment independence' sits as the foundation of the national response to homelessness.

In Chapter 23, Geerhardt Kornatowski and Constance Ching examine the legal and policy framework on homelessness in the Hong Kong Special Administrative Region (HKSAR) and in Malaysia. The chapter engages the concept of 'positive non-policy' to provide an overview of how homeless services in Hong Kong SAR and Malaysia operate. In so doing, the chapter reveals how neither Malaysia nor Hong Kong has homelessness legislation and, as such, relies heavily on the voluntary sector to support those experiencing homelessness.

As the authors demonstrate, the positive non-policy approach allows the government to intervene in the sector without being constrained by legal obligations and by outsourcing services. The chapter captures the important colonial context, the current relationship to anti-welfarism, and concludes by noting three principal areas for development in homelessness policy.

In Chapter 24, Kalpana Goel, Mohd Tarique, Meenu Anand, and Elvis Munyoka highlight and expose the deeply class-based experience of homelessness in India. The chapter illuminates the vast scale and challenges of homelessness in a country where, as yet, the government has not committed itself to providing universal support, housing security, employment opportunities, and even safe drinking water for all its citizens. The authors detail the specific Indian experience of homelessness, including its close relationship to the world of insecure work, migrant labour, and the country's draconian anti-begging laws. Beyond this, the chapter reflects on the growing number of civil society organizations across India helping those living with homelessness, assisting women fleeing domestic violence, and children. The authors discuss current government initiatives and conclude by offering recommendations on what is needed from government if it is to succeed in challenging homelessness across the country, including shelters, which would serve as a hub for social security programmes, measures to ensure all those experiencing homelessness could live in government-provided housing, as well as the necessity for measures to guarantee access to food, health, and social security entitlements.

In Chapter 25, Poh Leng Teo explores homelessness in Singapore. The chapter examines policy responses to homelessness in this important city state and sets this against the backdrop of Singapore's relatively small geographical and population size, its high rates of homeownership, but also its wider national housing policy. In so doing, the chapter identifies the relative consistency in policy principles, as well as the shift in the role and responsibility of the state vis-à-vis social service agencies, community agencies, as well as public attitudes. It argues that Singapore's approach to dealing with homelessness can be analyzed as being multi-level and multi-pronged, comprehensive and coordinated, and timely and targeted. Examples of good practice in homelessness prevention are identified, as well as the emphasis placed on self-reliance, family support, and community partnership in Singapore.

Part VI explores Oceania. In Chapter 26, the first of two chapters on Australia, Tamara Walsh focuses on the ongoing contemporary criminalization of homelessness in Australia by examining the extent to which people experiencing homelessness continue to be impacted by the criminal law long after the Vagrancy Acts have been abolished. Through move-on powers, banning notices, search-and-seizure powers, those experiencing homelessness are still portrayed as 'offensive' and a 'public nuisance' and open to sanction for reasons connected to their housing status and poverty, such as begging. The chapter challenges the logic and fairness of this approach and concludes that criminal law responses are inappropriate to address the complex reasoning underpinning homelessness and homeless offending in Australia.

In Chapter 27, the second chapter exploring homelessness in Australia, Chris Martin and Hal Pawson take a different approach by focusing on two areas of law that, the authors argue, are the natural domain for legislative action for homelessness prevention in Australia yet have thus far been entirely neglected: the law regarding residential tenancies, and the law on social housing. The case for pursuing these reforms is made out robustly, including that the law on termination and eviction of tenants should be brought into alignment with

Introduction

Article 11(1) of the International Covenant on Economic, Social, and Cultural Rights and that social housing legislation should be amended to provide expressly that adequate housing is the right of all citizens.

In the final chapter of the collection, Chapter 28, Brodie Fraser, Clare Aspinall, Elinor Chisholm, Jenny Ombler, Sarah Bierre, Lucy Telfar-Barnard, Ellie Johnson, and Philippa Howden-Chapman reflect on homelessness law and policy in Aotearoa New Zealand. The chapter discusses how housing has increasingly become a key policy issue in political election campaigns and how the definition of homelessness is built upon but extends the ETHOS typology to include, for example, those in 'concealed homeless' living situations. The chapter explores initiatives to support people experiencing, or at risk of, homelessness in Aotearoa New Zealand, including Housing First, rapid rehousing programmes, as well as the Accommodation Supplement and Income-Related Rent Subsidy and the Sustaining Tenancies programme. The Healthy Housing Initiatives (HHIs) are also examined, which play a role in supporting people to access housing, including providing warm, dry, and healthy housing to pregnant people and low-income families with children hospitalized for housing-related conditions or who are subject to certain risk factors. As the authors reveal, despite only a small population of 5 million, Aotearoa NZ has high rates of homelessness as well as fragmentation of policy and service provision, leading to a complex and confusing process for those seeking support. Attention is also paid to the over-representation of Indigenous Māori in homelessness statistics and how, as part of the Waitangi Tribunal's Kaupapa Inquiry on Housing Policy and Services, a wider definition of homelessness has been proposed to reflect the multiple meanings of homelessness from a Māori perspective.

I hope you enjoy the collection!

Chris Bevan

PART I

Europe

1
25 YEARS OF DEVOLUTION AND A (DIS)UNITED KINGDOM HOMELESSNESS POLICY

Chris Bevan, Regina Serpa, and Paddy Gray

Housing and homelessness law and policy are a devolved matter in the United Kingdom. Devolved matters are those areas of government where decision-making has been delegated by the UK Parliament to the devolved institutions across the nations of the country, including the Scottish and Welsh Parliaments and the Northern Ireland Assembly. Any examination of the approach to homelessness law and policy in the United Kingdom must, therefore, reflect the diverse perspectives, experiences, and voices of the four nations. In this spirit, the chapter begins with an examination of the approach in England and Wales before moving to explore Scotland and, finally, closes with a discussion of the position in Northern Ireland.

Homelessness Policy in England and Wales

Homelessness in England and Wales has risen to the top of the political agenda over the last 10–15 years in response to statistics revealing stubbornly high levels of homelessness and through effective public campaigns spearheaded by homelessness charities.[1] There is, however, no single precise estimate of the extent of homelessness across the whole of the UK as each of the four nations counts homelessness separately and none fully captures the more hidden forms of homelessness behind the statistics. Homeless charity Crisis does, however, conduct an annual study which records 'core homelessness', including more traditional notions of homelessness, as well as rough sleeping, living in unconventional structures (garages, sheds), sofa surfers, and those in hostels. In its latest survey, Crisis found that over 290,000 single people, couples, and families were homeless in 2021/22. The latest data from the UK government (which records statutory homelessness) reflect an upswing in rough sleeping (up 26% on 2021, 75% on 2010)[2] and the number of households in England

---

1 For example, the campaigns led by Crisis, Shelter, and others and media attention, for example by The Guardian newspaper: see https://www.theguardian.com/society/homelessness.
2 Department for Levelling Up, Housing & Communities (DLUHC), *Rough Sleeping Snapshot in England: Autumn 2022 Table 1* (DLUHC, updated February 2023).

initially assessed by local authorities as homeless or threatened with homelessness is up 4% since July–September 2022.[3] In Wales, from April 2021 to March 2022, whilst there was a decrease in the number of households assessed as homeless (down 11% on 2019/2020), there was an increase in the number deemed threatened with homelessness (up 27%).[4] Locating accurate and current data on the demographics or profile of the homeless population in England and Wales proves challenging either because data is not robustly collected or is disparately gathered and held. Counting and identifying hidden homelessness is a particular issue here. We can glean insights from Census 2021 data, however, especially as to homeless people living in hostels or temporary shelters. Data shows that two-thirds of hostel or temporary shelter occupants were male; over half were aged between 15 and 34; a disproportionate number identified as 'Black, Black British, Black Welsh, Caribbean, African,' as part of a 'mixed or multiple ethnic group' or 'other ethnic group' compared to the rest of the population; more than twice the percentage of people identified as homeless were disabled compared to the rest of the population, more than twice the percentage reported bad or very bad health; one in three reported having no educational qualifications.[5] This data captures only a small snapshot of the homeless population – a far greater proportion of those living with homelessness do not engage with hostel/shelter accommodation. Yet, despite this, the data is instructive in providing evidence of the clear interaction of homelessness with wider social concerns around health, education, financial and opportunity disadvantage as well as discrimination. Evidence continues to demonstrate that the loss of a private sector tenancy is the greatest single cause of homelessness, and that reforms to the social welfare system are the major driver of the association between a loss of tenancies and homelessness.[6]

In England and Wales, the statutory, legal definition of *homelessness* includes a person who has no accommodation available in the UK or abroad, or no legal right to occupy the accommodation, or is part of a split household and accommodation is not available for the whole household, or if it is unreasonable for that person to continue to occupy their accommodation, or they are at risk of violence from any person, or they are unable to secure entry to their accommodation, or they live in a moveable structure but have no place to put it.[7] An individual or household that is made homeless or is threatened with homelessness[8] can approach their local authority area for housing advice and, subject to meeting a range of qualifying criteria, may be offered temporary and, ultimately, settled accommodation, which could be in either the public or private sectors. In England and Wales, homelessness law and policy are governed by legislation enacted by the UK and Welsh governments and implemented by local authorities through local housing departments. The UK's unwritten constitution does not protect the right to housing. Instead, there is a statutory framework

---

3 DLUHC, *Live Tables on Homelessness, Statutory Homelessness Live Tables, Table A1* (DLUHC, updated February 2023).
4 Welsh Government, *Statistical First Release, Homelessness in Wales, 2021–22* (Welsh Government 2022).
5 Office for National Statistics (ONS), 'People experiencing homelessness, England and Wales: Census 2021' (2023).
6 B. Watts and others, *The Homelessness Monitor: England 2022* (Crisis 2022); S. Fitzpatrick and others, *The Homelessness Monitor: Wales 2021* (Crisis 2021).
7 In England, the legal definition is provided in Sections 175–177 of the Housing Act 1996 as amended by the Homelessness Reduction Act 2017. In Wales, it is provided in Section 55 of the Housing (Wales) Act 2014.
8 *Threatened with homelessness* is defined as a person that is likely to become homeless within 56 days. This is provided by Section 175(4) of the Housing Act 1996 and Section 55(4) of the Housing (Wales) Act 2014.

that lays down enforceable entitlements to varying degrees of housing support. The entitlements in England and Wales are commonly regarded as more extensive and robust than exist in many countries. Yet, as will be explored, gatekeeping of homeless services, deep conditionality as well as inadequately funded local authorities, cuts to social security support, and long trends of increasing unavailability of social housing put enormous strain on homelessness provision in the country and can make it difficult to qualify for and generally access.

A Brief History of English and Welsh Housing Policy

The history of homelessness policy in England and Wales is a lengthy and fascinating one. Sadly, space does not permit a fulsome enquiry here.[9] The origins of the 'contemporary' homelessness legislative framework for both England and Wales can be found in the groundbreaking Housing (Homeless Persons) Act 1977,[10] which made local authorities responsible for the very first time for the long-term housing of particular groups of homeless people and offered the first statutory definition of homelessness in English and Welsh law. The 1977 Act defined certain groups considered as having 'priority need' and therefore as owed a statutory duty to be rehoused by local authorities. The homelessness duties of the 1977 Act were later consolidated into the Housing Act 1996, which, in large part, maintained the essential framework of the 1977 Act, including the definition of 'priority need', which the 1996 Act clarified. Today, in England, Part VII of the Housing 1996 Act[11] (as amended by the Homelessness Act 2002, the Localism Act 2011, the Housing and Planning Act 2016, and Homelessness Reduction Act 2017)[12] remains the key source of homelessness law, and a homeless applicant will be owed the so-called 'main housing duty' provided they are: (1) eligible for assistance,[13] (2) in 'priority need',[14] (3) not intentionally[15] homeless,[16] and (4) can demonstrate a local connection to the local authority area.[17] It must be noted, however, that there is no legal right to housing, only a right to receive housing support if the statutory hoops are surmounted. 'Priority need' is defined in Section 189 of the 1996 Act as including a pregnant woman; a person with dependent children; someone vulnerable as a result of old age, mental illness, handicap, or physical disability or other special reason; and those homeless or threatened with homelessness as a result of an emergency such as flood, fire, or

---

9 For a more comprehensive account, see, amongst others, P. Malpass, 'Fifty Years of British Housing Policy: Leaving or Leading the Welfare State?' 4(2) *European Journal of Housing Policy* 209.
10 Accounts of the significance and originality of the 1977 Act are contested: N. J. Crowson, 'Revisiting the 1977 Housing (Homeless Persons) Act: Westminster, Whitehall, and the Homelessness Lobby' (2012) 24 *Twentieth Century British History* 424; I. Loveland, *Housing Homeless Persons: Administrative Law and the Administrative Process* (OUP 1995) chapter 3.
11 On which see generally D. Cowan (ed), *The Housing Act 1996–A Practical Guide* (Jordans 1996).
12 C. Bevan, 'The Homelessness Reduction Act 2017: Furthering Not Fracturing Marginalisation of Those Experiencing Homelessness' (2022) 18(1) *International Journal of Law in Context* 41; C. Bevan, 'Governing "The Homeless" in English Homelessness Legislation: Foucauldian Governmentality and the Homelessness Reduction Act 2017' (2021) 38(3) *Journal of Housing, Theory & Society* 259; C. Bevan and E. Laurie, 'The Housing and Planning Act 2016: Rewarding the Aspiration of Homeownership?' (2017) 80(4) *The Modern Law Review* 661.
13 Eligibility is a question of immigration status; see Housing Act 1996, ss 185–86.
14 Housing Act 1996, s 189.
15 Ibid. s 191.
16 Ibid. s 175.
17 Ibid. s 199.

other disaster.[18] Housing policy in Wales is a devolved matter and has been the responsibility of the Welsh government since the Welsh devolution settlement under the Government of Wales Acts 1998 and 2006. The consequence is that the Welsh government has been able to carve out its own distinct path from that adopted in England, and in key respects, this has proved more progressive and successful in tackling homelessness in Wales. Part 2 of the Housing (Wales) Act 2014 provides the legislative framework on homelessness in Wales and displaces Part VII of the Housing Act 1996 (which still operates in England and which had been applied in Wales prior to the 2014 Act). Following recommendations of a Welsh government–funded review published in 2012,[19] Part 2 of the Housing (Wales) Act 2014 came into force in April 2015 and signalled a significant overhaul of Welsh homelessness legislation, marking a clear break from the English approach. In contrast to England (at that time), the 2014 Act introduced in Wales a keener emphasis on 'preventative' intervention for households 'threatened with homelessness', as well as introducing homelessness 'relief' duties that apply irrespective of priority need. There was, additionally, a greater focus on local authorities' development of local homelessness strategies to prevent homelessness in their areas. However, in the event that these prevention and relief measures failed, the 2014 legislation (until relatively recently) mirrored the position in England in certain respects, for example, only those households who could demonstrate priority need would be entitled to receive housing from a local housing authority. Equally, applicants who acted 'unreasonably' in not cooperating with the assistance provided or refused a suitable offer of accommodation would see their support brought to an end, and the intentionality and local connection tests of the English law survived into the Welsh legislation. That said, the Welsh approach was then, and still is, far more benevolent to homeless applicants than that in England. For example, unlike in England, Welsh local authorities can decide for themselves whether or not to consider intentionality by devising categories of people to whom the intentionality test will and will not apply (e.g. care leavers).[20] Moreover, since December 2019, local authorities are now under a duty to secure accommodation for households with children, pregnant applicants, and those under 21 (or under 25 who are care leavers) if they are in priority need, irrespective of whether they made themselves intentionally homeless, that is, the intentionality test cannot be applied. For supporters of the Welsh homelessness framework, this demonstrates the more person-centred ideology at the heart of the homelessness framework in the country and sits in contrast to the more punitive, gatekeeping model in England. There has generally been very positive support for the Welsh approach,[21] largely on the basis that the 2014 Act framework has been better funded and better managed at a political level, with a genuine commitment shown to ending homelessness in Wales.[22]

To characterize England's approach to homelessness as one solely premised on sanction and punitiveness would, however, be unnuanced and unreflective of the more recent

---

18 Ibid. s 189(1).
19 P. Mackie and others, *Options for an Improved Homelessness Legislative Framework in Wales* (Welsh Government 2012).
20 Section 78 Housing (Wales) Act 2014.
21 P. Mackie, 'The Welsh Homelessness Legislation Review: Delivering Universal Access to Appropriate Assistance?' (2014) 27(1) *Contemporary Wales* 1; Shelter Cymru, *A Brand New Start: Homelessness and the Housing (Wales) Act* (Shelter Cymru 2015); S. Fitzpatrick and others, *The Homelessness Monitor: Wales 2017* (Crisis 2017); S. Fitzpatrick and others, *The Homelessness Monitor: Wales 2015* (Crisis 2015).
22 This is underpinned by strong political commitment, for example, under the Welsh government's action plan, *Ending Homelessness in Wales: A High Level Action Plan 2021–2026* (Welsh Government 2021).

and significant turn in English homelessness policy towards prevention through the Homelessness Act 2002 and, in particular, the Homelessness Reduction Act 2017 and changes wrought by the Domestic Abuse Act 2021. Under the Homelessness Act 2002, all housing authorities in England must have a homelessness strategy founded on a close review of the state of homelessness in their authority area. Strategies must be renewed at least every five years and set out the authority's plans for homelessness prevention and for provision of accommodation and support to those who are or are at risk of becoming homeless. The centrepiece and latest major intervention on homelessness by the UK government, however, is the Homelessness Reduction Act 2017. The 2017 Act began life as a private members' bill and entered into force on 3 April 2018. Described as 'the most ambitious legal reform in decades',[23] the HRA 2017 amended Part VII of the Housing Act 1996 to 'bolt on' to the existing homelessness duties under the 1996 Act new legal duties on English local authorities in providing a sliding scale of assistance to those who are homeless or at risk of homelessness and, in key respects, is similar to (though does not go as far as) the Welsh approach under the Housing (Wales) Act 2014. The main changes introduced by the 2017 Act included a strengthened duty to provide advisory services, an extension of the period during which an applicant is considered 'threatened with homelessness' from 28 to 56 days; a new duty to assess all eligible applicants' cases (not just those unintentionally homeless and in priority need) and agree a personalized housing plan; a new duty to prevent homelessness for all eligible applicants that are threatened with homelessness; and a new duty to relieve homelessness for all eligible applicants over a period of 56 days, during which time a local authority should take reasonable steps to help them find suitable accommodation (for a minimum period of six months). This duty stops short of requiring a local authority to provide accommodation for applicants not in priority need. It also introduced a new duty on certain public bodies to refer service users who they think may be homeless or threatened with homelessness to a housing authority. The HRA 17 has been in force now for six years and has incited much political and academic debate in garnering both praise as well as scepticism from those concerned that it is framed around 'crisis prevention' rather than universal or targeted prevention, and that adequate funding has not been made available to realize the legislation's true preventative potential.[24] Early indications from stakeholders indicate, however, a positive response to the legislation, with attention drawn especially to the culture change it has ushered in local authorities towards a more personalized assessment of applicants' needs.[25] Whatever one's view of the effectiveness of the HRA 17,[26] it has signalled a significant shift in focus in England away from the traditional, purely gatekeeping of services of the 1977 and 1996 legislation as originally drafted towards a more interventionist, preventative model. That said, troubling echoes of the deep conditionality and sanction-led ideology of the past remain, as the essential framework of the 1996 Act survives intact even after enactment of the HRA 17.[27]

---

23 S. Javid, 'Secretary of State for Communities & Local Government' *Inside Housing* (March 2018).
24 See, amongst others, Bevan (n 12); S. Fitzpatrick, P. Mackie and J. Wood, *Homelessness Prevention in the UK: Policy Briefing* (Online, UK Collaborative Centre for Housing Evidence 2019).
25 *The Homelessness Monitor for England* (2022) (n 6).
26 See, amongst others, the Government's Independent Evaluation of the Homelessness Reduction Act 2017: Ministry of Housing, Communities and Local Government (MHCLG) (2020), *Evaluation of the Implementation of the Homelessness Reduction Act: Final Report* (MHCLG (2020).
27 See, amongst others, the work of Bevan (n 12).

Separately, under the recently enacted Domestic Abuse Act 2021, any household in England that is homeless as a result of domestic abuse is now automatically deemed to be in 'priority need' for the purpose of the homelessness legislation and is owed temporary accommodation, and settled housing where the prevention and relief duties of the HRA 17 fail, irrespective of whether there are dependent children in the household or the household passes the vulnerability test. This has been roundly welcomed as leading to new understandings of and responses to domestic abuse.[28]

The Impact of the Covid-19 Pandemic in England and Wales

We surfaced from the Covid-19 pandemic with a tentative but nascent hope for innovation, ingenuity, and a refreshed motivation for reform to homelessness law and policy. At the very least, there is optimism that the pandemic might show us new ways of seeing and tackling the homelessness phenomenon.[29] Both the UK and Welsh governments instigated targeted measures which, for the duration of the pandemic, changed the way homeless people were treated.[30] Under the 'Everyone In' programme, money was provided by central UK government to ensure that over 37,000 people sleeping rough or at risk of rough sleeping were given accommodation. While this was said to include people previously excluded from support because of their immigration status, research has since shown that people with less than full legal status were in fact specifically excluded from homelessness assistance under this Covid protection measure.[31] This programme also saw a shift away from the use of dormitory or hostel-style accommodation because of concerns about the health impact of close quarters housing. A similar approach was adopted in Wales – with over £50m of funding[32] – which provided that anyone sleeping rough was regarded as 'vulnerable,' therefore 'in priority need', and was entitled to accommodation. The Welsh government also offered tailored financial support to those facing financial crisis during the pandemic, including Emergency Assistance Payments, and via the Wales Council Tax Reduction Scheme.

These progressive, inclusive, and speedy responses to homelessness during the pandemic demonstrated what governments really can do and spurred a new energy for and commitment to ending homelessness. Sadly, though predictable, these financial measures (along with other related but vital interventions, such as a moratorium on evictions in the private sector, the furlough scheme for workers, uplifts in state benefits such as Universal Credit and Local Housing Allowance) have now ended. There are, additionally, enormous pressures on household incomes by the ongoing 'cost of living' crisis affecting the whole UK. Nevertheless, academics and homelessness charities are closely examining the impact of Covid-19 on the provision of

---

28 See analysis in *The Homelessness Monitor for England* (2022) (n 6).
29 See, for example, Crisis report, S. Boobis and F. Albanese, *The Impact of COVID-19 on People Facing Homelessness and Service Provision Across Great Britain* (Crisis 2020).
30 On the approach taken in England, see Housing, Communities and Local Government Select Committee, *Protecting the Homeless and the Private Rented Sector: MHCLG's Response to Covid-19* (House of Commons March 2021).
31 See, Shelter report, D. Garvie and others, *Everyone In: Where Are They Now?* (Shelter 2021), R. Serpa, 'The exceptional becomes everyday: Border control, attrition and exclusion from within' (2021) 10(9) *Social Sciences* 329; Shelter, 'Immigration and Residence Restrictions' (2023) available at: https://england.shelter.org.uk/housing_advice/homelessness/immigration_and_residence_restrictions (accessed 1 September 2023).
32 Welsh government, *Guidance for Local Authorities in Supporting People Sleeping Rough – Covid-19 Outbreak* (Welsh Government 2020).

homelessness services and are pushing to ensure a positive homelessness legacy can be realized out of the tragedy of the pandemic.[33]

Green Shoots of Optimism for Reform to Homelessness Law and Policy in England and Wales

Even prior to the pandemic, tackling rough sleeping had already been identified by the UK government and in Wales as a high priority, with the publication of various strategy documents, most recently, in England, the 2022 policy paper *Ending Rough Sleeping for Good*,[34] which has been matched with £2bn of funding over three years with the 'end goal . . . for rough sleeping to be prevented wherever possible, and where it does occur it is rare, brief and non-recurrent'. Highly ambitious in scope, the strategy is said by the government to adopt a whole system approach, including investment, not just in accommodation, but in drug and alcohol treatment, improved mental health provision, and more help into work schemes. This new strategy claims to be 'pioneering' and promises to end rough sleeping by defining what 'ending rough sleeping' means, underpinned by a new data-led framework to measure it; an expanded £500m Rough Sleeping Initiative over three years, so local areas can provide the tailored support needed to end rough sleeping and deliver long-term change through multi-year funding; a new 'prevention first' approach, which (building on the Homelessness Reduction Act 2017) will involve sector partners to develop a new framework for identifying and supporting people at risk of rough sleeping; and a new £200m Single Homelessness Accommodation Programme, to deliver up to 2,400 homes and wrap-around support by March 2025. This will provide new supported housing and Housing First accommodation and new local Integrated Care Systems (ICSs) to take account of the health and social care needs of people sleeping rough in their areas. Housing First remains a key element of UK government efforts to address rough sleeping as it does across wider Europe. Regional Housing First pilots in Greater Manchester, the West Midlands, and Liverpool were launched in 2018 and began accommodating tenants in 2019. Ongoing evaluation of these pilots[35] demonstrated a lower take-up rate than anticipated across all three regions, but for those recruited, satisfaction was noted as very high; the pilots were supporting 900 individuals as of June 2022.[36] The UK government has committed to extend the Housing First Pilots into 2024 and, thereafter, to fund Housing First services into 2025 through local areas' Rough Sleeping Initiative (RSI) programmes.

Beyond Housing First, data from local authority surveys in England signals that Housing First–type activity is flourishing outside the Housing First pilot regions, with 59% reporting

---

33 See, for example, S. Fitzpatrick, B. Watts and R. Simms, *The Homelessness Monitor England 2020: COVID-19 Crisis Response Briefing* (Crisis 2020); Local Government Association, *Lessons Learnt from Councils' Response to Rough Sleeping During the COVID-19 Pandemic* (Local Government Association 19 November 2020); House of Commons Public Accounts Committee, *COVID-19: Housing People Sleeping Rough* (House of Commons 8 March 2021); The Kerslake Commission, *When We Work Together – Learning the Lessons, Interim Report* (The Kerslake Commission July 2021); St Mungo's, Centre for Homelessness Impact Report, *Homelessness and the Pandemic: Emergency Measures During Covid-19* (St Mungo's, Centre for Homelessness Impact Report 2022).
34 DLUHC, *Ending Rough Sleeping For Good* (DLUHC September 2022).
35 MHCLG, *Evaluation of the Housing First Pilots: Second Process Evaluation Report* (MHCLG July 2021).
36 MHCLG, *Housing First Pilot: National Evaluation Reports* (MHCLG, updated September 2022).

provision in their authority area and others indicating that they are in the process of commissioning or are Housing First–type services.[37] The reform agenda in Wales is more ambitious than in England and is centred on exploring direct, statutory reforms to the homelessness framework under the Housing (Wales) Act 2004, including amending or even abolishing the priority need category.[38] In 2019, the Welsh government established an independent 'Homelessness Action Group' whose remit was to 'end homelessness in Wales', with a primary emphasis on action to reduce and prevent rough sleeping. The Homelessness Action Group has recommended even more far-reaching reforms in addition to abolishing the priority need criterion, including removing the intentionality and local connection tests,[39] and the Welsh government has committed to reviewing these matters as part of its five-year Action Plan to End Homelessness in Wales.[40] This Action Plan also sets out its aspirations for expanding rapid rehousing (which aims to cut the amount of time homeless people are stuck in temporary accommodation) 'to provide the overarching response for anyone who is experiencing homelessness or at imminent risk of homelessness'. This heavy emphasis on rapid rehousing has, however, been criticized by some charities in Wales as wrong-headed and amounting to an admission that homelessness prevention work has essentially failed.[41]

Homelessness Policy in Scotland

This section considers the development of homelessness policy in Scotland. It analyzes the divergence between UK policy and the distinctive approach taken by the Scottish government, based on a radical objective of ending homelessness. This latter approach stands in marked contrast with the more punitive and sanctions-based approach to welfare policy taken by the Westminster government. The example demonstrates some challenges of multi-level governance, highlighting the tensions between a radical set of aims, the challenges of resources (under conditions of austerity), and contemporary developments (of a global pandemic and a cost-of-living crisis). This section further considers how the tensions can be resolved within a context of political leadership, effective policy implementation, action planning and political pragmatism.

Devolution and Housing Policy

Housing policy in Scotland has been the responsibility of the Scottish government since the devolution settlement in the 1998 Scotland Act, which established the Scottish Parliament.[42] However, the foundational principles of contemporary homelessness legislation can be found in the Housing (Homeless Persons) Act of 1977, as is the case elsewhere in the UK. The statutory

---

37 See *The Homelessness Monitor for England* (2022) (n 5), Appendix 2 Local Authority survey (2021); see also Housing First England, *The Picture of Housing First in England* (Housing First England 2020).
38 See P. Mackie and others, *Review of Priority Need in Wales* (Welsh Government 2020).
39 Homelessness Action Group, *The Framework of Policies, Approaches and Plans Needed to End Homelessness in Wales (What Ending Homelessness in Wales Looks Like): Report from the Homelessness Action Group for the Welsh Government* (Homelessness Action Group 2020).
40 Welsh Government, *Ending Homelessness: A High-Level Action Plan – 2021–2026 How We Will End Homelessness in Wales* (Welsh Government 2021).
41 See, for example, comments made by Ruth Power, Chief Executive of Shelter Cymru, at the Chartered Institute of Housing Cymru's Annual Conference, Swansea, 2022.
42 D. Sim (ed), *Housing and Public Policy in Post-devolution Scotland* (Chartered Institute of Housing 2004).

homeless system established by the 1977 Act is unique in that it constitutes the only housing legislation (apart from that in France) to create, in effect, enforceable rights to settled accommodation for homeless households,[43] effectively instituting a 'progressive counter-hierarchy of power'[44] through establishing legal rights to housing.[45] These individually enforceable rights to housing are the corollary of clearly defined local authority duties towards statutorily homeless households.[46] Specifically, the 1977 Act established an enforceable duty on local authorities to accommodate certain categories of homeless families with dependent children and 'vulnerable' adults.[47]

The 1977 Act established an exceptionally broad statutory definition of homelessness, and after taking into account subsequent amendments, 'homelessness' generally is taken to refer to households who have no accommodation which one can reasonably expect to live in, as well as those facing homelessness – originally defined as threatened to be homeless within 28 days.[48] However, this broad definition has created difficulties in implementation. Generally speaking, legally enforceable individual rights to housing are different from a 'universalistic' housing policy as seen in Scandinavian countries and instead sit within a 'selective' welfare system[49] characterized by means-testing, conditionality, and targeting.[50] Furthermore, strict eligibility requirements have accompanied deep entitlements assured to households who are eligible. Individual rights to settled accommodation are consequently only extended to eligible households (such as those with recourse to public funds and other qualifying categories of applicant discussed later), and those entitled to statutory assistance under the 1977 Act and subsequent homelessness legislation.

Under the legislation, entitlement was initially restricted to 'priority need' applicants (a category which largely excludes single persons – unless deemed 'vulnerable' for some other reason) and to those who have not become 'intentionally' homeless.[51] The 'local connection' test provides a final hurdle for homeless applicants, which enables one local authority to transfer their duty to another authority (following required statutory investigations) if the main housing duty to accommodate is owed elsewhere. The result of these conditions was that there were significant gaps in homelessness legislation and few options available to those falling out with the system. Specifically, the 1977 Act and subsequent legislation excludes 'ineligible' households from the statutory system, including those who have no recourse to public funds or – prior to Britain leaving the EU – European nationals who do not have a right to reside in the UK. This exclusion applies to all constituent countries in the UK.

---

43 S. Fitzpatrick, G. Bramley and S. Johnsen, 'Pathways into Multiple Exclusion Homelessness in Seven UK Cities' (2013) 50(1) *Urban Studies* 148.
44 S. Fitzpatrick and others, *The Homelessness Monitor: England 2021* (Crisis 2021).
45 B. Watts, 'Homelessness, Empowerment and Self-Reliance in Scotland and Ireland: The Impact of Legal Rights to Housing for Homeless People' (2014) 43(1) *Journal of Social Policy* 793.
46 Fitzpatrick, Bramley, and Johnsen (n 42).
47 I. Loveland, 'Changing the Meaning of "Vulnerable" Under the Homelessness Legislation?' (2017) 39(3) *Journal of Social Welfare and Family Law* 298.
48 S. Fitzpatrick and S. Davies, 'The "Ideal" Homelessness Law: Balancing "Rights-Centred" and "Professional-Centred" Social Policy' (2021) 43(2) *Journal of Social Welfare and Family Law* 175.
49 B. Bengtsson, 'Housing as a Social Right: Implications for Welfare State Theory' (2001) 24(4) *Scandinavian Political Studies* 255; D. Gugushvili and D. Hirsch, 'Means-Tested and Universal Approaches to Poverty: International Evidence and How the UK Compares' (2014) Working Paper 640, Centre for Research in Social Policy.
50 B. Watts and S. Fitzpatrick, *Welfare Conditionality* (Routledge 2018).
51 P. K. Mackie and I. Thomas, *Nations Apart? Experiences of Single Homeless People Across Britain* (Crisis 2014).

In Scotland, the legal framework for homelessness duties and powers is contained in the Housing (Scotland) Act 1987. Following devolution, the Scottish Executive established the Homelessness Task Force in 1999 to review the impact of homelessness legislation in Scotland, whose recommendations formed the basis of the Housing (Scotland) 2001 Act.[52] The 2001 Act is widely acknowledged to be the point at which homelessness policy in Scotland first significantly diverged from the rest of the UK,[53] introducing new duties on local authorities to provide temporary accommodation for non-priority homeless households, and extended the period in which one is considered to be 'threatened with homelessness' from 28 days to two months.[54]

Subsequent legislation sought to further expand the rights of homeless households by amending the restrictions imposed by the priority-need, intentionality, and local connection tests. The Homelessness Etc. (Scotland) Act 2003 abolished the priority need test, and since 31 December 2012, all eligible and unintentionally homeless households have had a right to settled housing in Scotland.[55] The 2003 Act also made the investigation of 'intentionality' a discretionary power of local authorities and suspended local connection rules. Although these amendments were not then in force, in 2018 the Scottish Government Homelessness Rough Sleeping Action Group (HRSAG) recommended to ministers that local connection rules be abolished and that the *intentionally homeless* category be limited to the narrower definition of 'deliberate manipulation'[56] rather than behaviour which could simply be interpreted as 'foolish'.[57]

Thus, the strength of the Scottish system was in instigating a near 'universal' right to settled housing for all (eligible) homeless people.[58] However, homelessness legislation in Scotland post-devolution has been criticized for not placing greater prominence on preventative measures,[59] despite being internationally recognized as progressive[60] and considered to be the closest to a 'right to housing' in Europe.[61] Elsewhere in the UK, homelessness prevention has featured more strongly, for example, in Wales, where there has been a statutory duty on local authorities to prevent homelessness since April 2015 (Housing (Wales) Act 2014, Part 2)[62] and similar duties introduced in England from April 2018 (under the Homelessness Reduction Act 2017).

---

52 H. Pawson and E. Davidson, 'Radically Divergent? Homelessness Policy and Practice in Post-Devolution Scotland' (2008) 8(1) *European Journal of Housing Policy* 39.
53 K. McKee, J. Muir, J and T. Moore, 'Housing Policy in the UK: The Importance of Spatial Nuance' (2017) 32(1) *Housing Studies* 60.
54 Fitzpatrick and Davies (n 48).
55 Mackie and Thomas (n 51).
56 Homelessness and Rough Sleeping Action Group (HRSAG), *Ending Homelessness: The Report on the Final Recommendations of the Homelessness and Rough Sleeping Action Group* (Scottish Government 2019).
57 Fitzpatrick and Davies (n 48).
58 T. Byrne and D. P. Culhane, 'The Right to Housing: An Effective Means for Addressing Homelessness' (2011) 14 *University of Pennsylvania Journal of Social Change* 379.
59 H. Pawson, E. Davidson and G. Netto, *Evaluation of Homelessness Prevention Activities in Scotland* (Scottish Executive Social Research 2007).
60 E. S. Tars and C. Egleson, 'Great Scot: The Scottish Plan to End Homelessness and Lessons for the Housing Rights Movement in the United States' (2007) 16(1) *Georgetown Journal on Poverty Law & Policy* 187.
61 I. Anderson and R. Serpa, 'The Right to Settled Accommodation for Homeless People in Scotland: A Triumph of Rational Policy Making?' (2013) 7(1) *European Journal of Homelessness* 13; R. Serpa and E. Saunders, 'Housing in Scotland' in G. Gall (ed), *Creating a Fairer Scotland* (Pluto Press 2022).
62 P. K. Mackie, 'Homelessness Prevention and the Welsh Legal Duty: Lessons for International Policies' (2015) 30(1) *Housing Studies* 40.

Housing Options, Preventative Strategies, and the Right to Housing

Policy interventions have had considerable impact in the context of Scotland. Statutory homelessness peaked in 2005/2006 and shows a downward trend since 2010/2011. In 2014/2015, Scottish local authorities logged 35,764 statutory homeless applications, of which 28,615 were assessed as homeless.[63] This downward trend can be attributed in part to the introduction of a 'Housing Options' model in 2010. In order to focus greater attention towards prevention efforts, Housing Options broadly mirrored the approach taken in England some ten years earlier. This model of homelessness prevention involved local authorities offering households a 'holistic' advice and information service, in an attempt to avoid the need for households in crisis to make a statutory homelessness application.[64] Although there is evidence that a Housing Options approach has fostered 'gatekeeping' practices which (unlawfully) erect barriers which obstruct otherwise entitled and eligible households from accessing statutory homelessness services,[65] the associated reduction of statutory homelessness across Britain (alongside an introduction of Housing Options) is argued by some as evidence of a mix of genuine prevention and gatekeeping. In England, where more assertive, proactive prevention techniques are routinely used, gatekeeping practices are less evidenced.[66] In Scotland, the approach has been described as being a 'light touch' version compared to elsewhere in the UK, since 'Housing Options interviews' frequently culminate in a statutory homelessness application.[67]

Increases in levels of homelessness and rough sleeping seen elsewhere in the UK post-2010, particularly in the south of England, have not been experienced to the same degree in Scotland.[68] Nevertheless, rising numbers of households in temporary accommodation and an increasing proportion of social lettings to homeless households[69] indicated a need to concentrate efforts to prevent homelessness, rather than reactively respond to crises. To help address the tensions between supply and demand, a 'Housing Support Duty' was introduced under the Housing (Scotland) Act 2010 to promote prevention efforts and reduce repeat episodes of rough sleeping, by placing a new duty on local authorities (from 2013 onwards) to assess and meet the housing support needs of statutorily homeless households.

At the start of 2018, the Scottish government agreed in principle with the recommendations from the Homelessness and Rough Sleeping Action Group (HRSAG) to move towards a rapid rehousing approach; the objective of this approach is to ensure that people who find themselves homeless are supported into mainstream, settled housing as soon as possible, in order to provide a greater number of homeless households with permanent housing. The policy

---

63 *The Homelessness Monitor: England* (n 44).
64 Pawson, Davidson and Netto (n 59).
65 S. Alden, 'Discretion on the Frontline: The Street Level Bureaucrat in English Statutory Homelessness Services' (2015) 14(1) *Social Policy and Society* 63; Scottish Housing Regulator (SHR), *Housing Options in Scotland: A Thematic Review* (Scottish Housing Regulator 2014) <www.scottishhousingregulator.gov.uk/sites/default/files/publications/Housing%20Options%20Report%20-%20Web%20Version.pdf> (accessed 1 September 2023).
66 Pawson, Davidson and Netto (n 59).
67 S. Fitzpatrick, P. Mackie and J. Wood, *Homelessness Prevention in the UK: Policy Briefing* (UK Collaborative Centre for Housing Evidence (CaCHE) 2019).
68 Ibid.
69 J. Perry and M. Stephens, 'How the Purpose of Social Housing Has Changed and Is Changing' [2018] *UK Housing Review* 29.

also advocates the provision of 'wrap-around' support (to provide an intensive and individualized support service for those with complex needs), ensuring that services work effectively together to eliminate (or severely reduce) time spent in temporary accommodation.[70]

To this end, the Scottish government developed a framework for Rapid Rehousing Transition Plans, set to be adopted by all 32 local authorities in Scotland by 2023. These plans were intended to explain how all local authorities could move from their current homelessness systems towards one with rapid rehousing at the centre ('by default'). Drawing on the Welsh example, the 'Duty to Prevent' also featured in recommendations to HRSAG to complement a rapid rehousing approach in Scotland, though not yet introduced.[71] The Scottish government has been instrumental in drawing up proposals to end homelessness in Scotland. The publication of the *Ending Homelessness Together Action Plan* (the first of its kind in Britain) in 2018 highlighted the trajectory of change, under First Minister Nicola Sturgeon. In 2023, a Housing Bill was introduced which intended to produce new duties on public bodies and landlords to reduce the risk of homelessness as well as to promote more effective joint strategic planning. At the time of writing, there is no formal update on progress of the Bill. Despite these objectives, research shows that the rapid rehousing action plans have been severely under-resourced.[72] Relatedly, in February 2024, the Scottish Parliament's Local Government, Housing and Planning Committee launched an inquiry into the intensifying housing crisis in Scotland. The inquiry will explore progress (and lack thereof) on the Government's 'Housing to 2040' Strategy that aims to ensure everyone has access to safe, sustainable and affordable housing.

The Impact of the Pandemic

Research has shown how low-income groups have been disproportionately affected by the Covid-19 pandemic.[73] Within Scotland, the right to housing has been extended by measures introduced as a response to the pandemic, including a moratorium on evictions (which ended in March 2022), and the government's approach has focused on accommodating people sleeping rough and decanting night shelter accommodation using hotel or other single-room accommodation, credited as reducing rough sleeping to unprecedentedly low levels.[74] Safeguards for tenants in Scotland have also facilitated in making possession proceedings more difficult for landlords (often to the frustration of private sector landlords).[75] The effectiveness of such measures may be seen in the fact that the main reasons for homelessness applications in Scotland is relationship breakdown and violence/threat of violence (which includes domestic violence as well as other forms of abuse/threat), whereas in England the main cause is eviction or the ending of a tenancy. The pressure to provide effective

---

70 Homelessness and Rough Sleeping Action Group (HRSAG), *Ending Homelessness: The Report on the Final Recommendations of the Homelessness and Rough Sleeping Action Group* (Scottish Government 2018).
71 Ibid.
72 B. Watts and others, *The Homelessness Monitor Scotland, 2021* (Crisis 2021).
73 R. Patrick and others, *Covid Realities: Documenting Life In a Low Income During the Pandemic* (Child Poverty Action Group/Nuffield Foundation 2022).
74 Watts and others (n 72).
75 A. Evans and others, *Rent Better: Wave 2 Landlord and Letting Agent Qualitative Research Report* (Indigo House 2022).

homeless support has been exacerbated by a cost-of-living crisis, including reductions in real disposable income, caused by rapidly rising fuel and food costs. This crisis is disproportionately affecting low-income households.[76]

Tensions between Westminster and Holyrood

Scotland continues to be afflicted by significant social deprivation, with over a million people (including a quarter of a million children) described as trapped in poverty.[77] However, research studies have consistently highlighted the regressive impact of UK welfare reforms (including the impact of Universal Credit) and the significance of increased conditionality and reduced entitlement to welfare services.[78] The introduction of the Welfare Reform Act 2012, including cuts to benefits and the introduction of a new unified benefit (Universal Credit), has had significant negative impact on the most vulnerable communities and has exacerbated problems in providing effective homelessness support throughout the UK.[79]

From the perspective of the Scottish government, the ability to address homelessness and the intention to introduce a preventative approach[80] have been strictly circumscribed, as welfare and other policies (such as migration) have been a reserved matter for the UK government. Research on the geography of poverty in Scotland has demonstrated the severe impact of social deprivation,[81] and these social pressures have been exacerbated by welfare reform initiatives. It was therefore clear the Scottish government had few levers available to intervene in matters which straddled the division between reserved and devolved powers, and this has limited the ability to tackle the problem of homelessness. This is not to say that policy solutions cannot be determined elsewhere, for example, through responses by non-profit agencies, local government, or within housing practice,[82] as seen in the City of Edinburgh Council rapid rehousing pilot (which received national funding via HARSAG).

The Scottish government has adopted a distinctively progressive approach to homelessness policy, based on the establishment of a right to housing, and with the explicit objective of ending homelessness, a policy which has generated international interest.[83] The approach (based on a preventative strategy) has stood in marked contrast to homelessness policy in

---

76 H. Karjalainen and P. Levell, *Inflation Hits 9% with Poorest Households Facing Even Higher Rate* (Institute for Fiscal Studies 18 May 2022).
77 C. Birt and others, *Poverty in Scotland* (Joseph Rowntree Foundation 2021).
78 Watts and Fitzpatrick (n 50).
79 A. Power and others, *The Impact of Welfare Reform on Social Landlords and Tenants* (Joseph Rowntree Foundation 2014) <www.jrf.org.uk/report/impact-welfare-reform-social-landlords-and-tenants> (accessed 1 September 2023); P. Hickman, B. Pattison and J. Preece, *The Impact of Welfare Reforms on Housing Associations* (Collaborative Centre for Housing Evidence (CaCHE) 2018); C. Beatty and S. Fothergill, 'Welfare Reform in the United Kingdom 2010–16: Expectations, Outcomes, and Local Impacts' (2018) 52 *Social Policy & Administration* 950; C. Beatty and others, *Benefit Sanctions and Homelessness: A Scoping Report* (Crisis/Sheffield Hallam University, Centre for Regional, Economic and Social Research 2015).
80 Fitzpatrick, Mackie and Wood (n 67).
81 G. Bramley, S. Lancaster and D. Gordon, 'Benefit Take-Up and the Geography of Poverty in Scotland' (2010) 34(6) *Regional Studies* 507.
82 Communities Scotland, *Preventing Homelessness: The Role of Housing Management: Precis No. 5* (Communities Scotland 2021).
83 I. Anderson, 'Delivering the Right to Housing: Why Scotland Still Needs an Ending Homelessness Action Plan' (2019) 13(2) *European Journal of Homelessness* 131.

England, where a punitive welfare system is explicit, with little interest shown by central government to tackling the problem of homelessness. The tensions between the progressive aims of the Scottish government and the regressive restrictions of the Westminster, UK government have highlighted problems of devolved governance and the restrictions on autonomy imposed by Westminster. Implementation of policy is therefore frustrated by ideological conflict with a conservative national government, a lack of resources for action planning, and the demands of political pragmatism (where competing objectives, such as spending restrictions, are prioritized).

In the UK, selective legally enforceable rights to housing are advanced by a statutory system conveying a set of entitlements to homeless households. Scotland has established rights for homeless households, which have been expanded in successive Scottish legislation post-devolution, such as the abolition of the priority-need test and the proposed shift towards 'rapid rehousing by default'. However, research has highlighted the limitations of Scottish policy, including the need for greater attention to preventative measures, increased funding for homelessness support services, and increased attention to monitoring, implementation, and establishment of action plans.[84]

The adoption of a rapid rehousing approach, based on a 'Housing First' policy, represents an attempt to introduce a rights-based approach, but policy objectives are not implemented in a vacuum, and the objectives of housing and homeless policies have been frustrated by competing and conflicting (national) policy agendas, as well as wider economic constraints. This is particularly true for households who find themselves caught between systems, whether due to their legal status restricting their eligibility for social assistance or their employment status limiting their ability to pay for housing. With regards to accessing publicly subsidized housing and homelessness assistance, the situation becomes more complicated due to the multiple (and often conflicting) layers of governance and tensions between UK and devolved governments as well as local authorities.

Homelessness Policy in Northern Ireland

Within the UK, Northern Ireland (NI) has often been referred to as a place apart. Some commentators have argued that this is understandable, given the persistence of violence from 1968 to 1998 (widely referred to as the 'troubles') and the fact that NI politics have been determined by the co-existence of two communities with differing identities and aspirations.[85] The troubles left a brutal legacy of continued segregation by religion mainly in public sector housing, and much of this still exits today.[86] Many writers refer to a divided community, civil disturbance, and the establishment of special administrative machinery suited to the exigency of such circumstances,[87] which have played a significant role in

---

84 Ibid.
85 P. Bell, 'Direct Rule in Northern Ireland' in R. Rose (ed), *Ministers & Ministries: A Functional Analysis* (Clarendon Press 1987); S. Ogle, 'The Literature of Housing in Northern Ireland: A Critical Review of the Period Since 1970' (1989) Policy Research Institute, The Queens University of Belfast and the University of Ulster; P. Gray, 'Housing in Northern Ireland' (1994) 42(3) *Administration (Dublin)* 269; F. Boal, 'Integration & Division: Sharing and Segregation in Belfast' (1996) 11(2) *Planning Practice and Research* 151.
86 D. Capener, 'Belfast's Housing Policy Still Reflects Religious and Economic Division' *The Guardian* (3 October 2017).
87 D. Singleton, 'Housing: Towards Two Nations' (2017) *Fortnight (Belfast)*; Ogle (n 85).

determining the structure of the housing system in Northern Ireland today, which has not changed significantly since the Northern Ireland Housing Executive (NIHE) was first set up in 1971.[88] The organization still exists 52 years later, with many of its roles and responsibilities similar to when it first came into being. Some areas, however, have been added since its inception, including supporting people, housing benefit and homelessness, functions that are the responsibility of local authorities in other jurisdictions in the UK.

The History of Homelessness Policy in Northern Ireland

Direct Rule of Northern Ireland from Westminster[89] from 1971 to the Good Friday Agreement in 1998 meant that NI had housing legislation that was similar to legislation in Great Britain,[90] albeit two or three years later. Examples are the 1974 Housing Act that introduced the policy of rehabilitation rather than clearance, of which housing action areas became a key tool. This became legislation in NI as the (Northern Ireland) Order 1976. The 1980 Housing Act that introduced the 'right to buy'[91] and enhanced tenants' rights was introduced as the Housing (Northern Ireland) Order 1983, and the Social Security and Housing Benefits Act 1982 was introduced a year later as the Housing Benefits (Northern Ireland) Order 1983. But it was the legislation on homelessness that took much longer. The legislation was introduced in Britain under the Housing (Homeless Persons) Act 1977, discussed earlier in the chapter, and this Act and subsequent homelessness legislation had not applied to NI. It took another 12 years for the introduction of the new homeless legislation under the Housing (NI) Order 1988. Despite the many criticisms of the GB Act over that period,[92] the NI legislation failed to go much beyond what had been introduced across the Irish Sea.[93]

Prior to the 1988 legislation in NI, the NI Housing Executive had devised a scheme to allocate properties in a fair and equitable manner. This was important as the Cameron Commission had reported, prior to the formation of the NIHE, discrimination in housing allocations as a substantial problem.[94] As a result, a new scheme for the allocation of social housing was set up on 1 January 1974. It was originally named 'the housing allocation scheme' but was renamed 'the housing selection scheme', a points-based scheme with applicants assessed against a range of factors, including overcrowding, sharing, disrepair, lack of

---

88 The executive is a strategic housing authority for Northern Ireland and one of the largest publicly owned social landlords in Europe. Its mission statement is: 'Working in Partnership to Ensure That Everyone Has Access to a Good Affordable Home in a Safe and Healthy Community' <www.nihe.gov.uk/about-us/our-mission-vision/our-mission-values> (accessed 1 September 2023).
89 'Direct Rule' of Northern Ireland meant the administration of the country by the government of the United Kingdom sitting in Westminster, London.
90 Great Britain (GB) is the name given to the territory of England, Scotland, and Wales; Great Britain and Northern Ireland together represent the United Kingdom (UK).
91 Under this policy of the Thatcher conservative government, council house tenants were offered the opportunity to buy their council homes at large discounted prices: see A. Murie, *The Right to Buy: Selling Off Public and Social Housing* (Policy Press 2016).
92 Accounts of the significance and originality of the 1977 Act are contested: Crowson (n 10); Loveland (n 10).
93 For more on devolution of housing policy to Northern Ireland, see: C. Paris, P. Gray and J. Muir, 'Devolving Housing Policy and Practice in Northern Ireland 1998–2002' (2003) 18(2) *Housing Studies* 159; J. Muir, 'The Dynamics of Policy-Making under UK Devolution: Social Housing in Northern Ireland' (2013) 28(7) *Housing Studies* 1081.
94 See Cameron Commission Report, *Disturbances in Northern Ireland: Report of the Commission Appointed by the Governor of Northern Ireland* (Her Majesty's Stationery Office, Cmd. 532, 1969).

amenities, under-occupation, and family support. The first major review of the new scheme took place shortly afterwards, in 1975–1976, and resulted in a revised points system from October 1977, which gave higher priority to applicants expressing a local preference. It also introduced banding into the system with two principal groups of applicants: group A for non-pointed priority cases, and group B for pointed cases.

In group A, there were four priority groups, listed in what follows. Applicants who were placed in these groups were not allocated points but were given preference on the list above other applicants. Within each of these groups, priority was determined by date order:

- A1, primarily made up of homeless applicants.
- A2, for those with urgent health or welfare needs.
- A3, those living in redevelopment areas or unfit properties.
- A4, incoming workers.

Between 1977 and 1985, some 25 fine-tuning amendments were made to the scheme, but the overall structure of the pointing system remained intact until 1988.

Homelessness moved up the housing agenda, and at the beginning of 1987, a Housing Selection Scheme Review Committee was set up by the Board of the NIHE to consider whether changes should be made to its allocation scheme in terms of its operation to date and its tenant transfer policy in the light of the impending legislation. In October 1987, the Committee produced an interim report which included proposals for amendments to the scheme. After extensive public consultation, the Selection Scheme was revised, and ten amendments were introduced, including the awarding of emergency status to those applicants accepted as homeless and in priority need. Also included in the amendments was the awarding of a greater priority to applicants in shared and overcrowded accommodation and the abolition of medical and social points. The scheme remained in place until 9 July 1998, when the NIHE launched, for consultation, a revised Housing Selection Scheme. This scheme aimed to relax the residential qualifications for applicants and to remove A1 status for homeless applicants to acknowledge different levels of need. Prior to this, applicants receiving A1 status were automatically placed above those who had housing points on the general waiting list.[95]

From 1 April 1989, the Housing Executive assumed responsibility for certain homeless persons. Prior to the introduction of the 1988 Order, no public body in Northern Ireland had a statutory duty to provide emergency or temporary accommodation to those in need of it. The four Health and Social Services Boards[96] did have a discretionary power to provide such accommodation under the Health and Personal Social Services (NI) Order 1972, but before the 1988 Order, the Housing Executive had a duty to allocate dwellings to homeless persons only if they were available. If no such accommodation was, or became, available, then there was no further duty even to provide temporary accommodation.[97] The

---

95 P. Gray and G. Long, 'Homelessness Policy in Northern Ireland: Is Devolution Making a Difference?' in S. Fitzpatrick, D. Quilgars and N. Pleace (eds), *Homelessness in the UK: Problems and Solutions* (Chartered Institute of Housing 2009).
96 In Northern Ireland, health and personal social services were integrated into one structure in 1973, which was unique within the UK. Services were provided by four health and social services boards.
97 P. Gray and L. Campbell, 'Managing social housing in Northern Ireland' in C. Paris (ed), *Housing in Northern Ireland – and comparisons with the Republic of Ireland* (Chartered Institute of Housing 2021).

Housing (Northern Ireland) Order 1988 imposes a legal duty on the Housing Executive to assist people experiencing homelessness. The level of assistance provided to homeless applicants was to be determined by a number of legislative 'tests' or 'hurdles'. To qualify for Full Duty Applicant status (and therefore statutory entitlement to housing), a homeless applicant must be homeless or threatened with homelessness, in priority need, eligible for assistance, and not intentionally homeless.[98]

The new legislation required the Housing Executive to carry out investigations for those homeless or threatened with homelessness, to secure temporary accommodation where necessary, and to secure permanent accommodation for those who were unintentionally homeless and in 'priority need'. In addition to the four categories listed in Britain, the NI Order included persons without dependent children at risk from physical violence and young persons aged 16 to 21 years who were at risk of financial or sexual exploitation.

As a result of the 1988 Order, those applicants accepted as homeless were placed in the A1 category. However, over the next ten years, the proportion of those in the A groups increased from 14% to 32%, and the number of applicants contained within the A1 grouping rose from 619 to 2,777.[99] This, along with the changing nature of the waiting list, had caused concern locally as there was growing evidence of an increasing number of single persons appearing on the list, and more and more households were being housed through the priority groups only, where there was no differentiation of need or circumstances, and allocations were being made on a date order basis.[100]

It was not until January 1995 that the Board of the NIHE set up a Working Group to review the selection scheme, and this was driven by a number of legislative changes, recommendations from government and other working groups and reviews, the changes in the waiting list and applicant profile, and Policy Appraisal and Fair Treatment (PAFT) analysis. In 1996, the Department of the Environment Northern Ireland, who at that time had the responsibility for housing, published its Housing Policy Review 'Building on Success: The Way Ahead'.[101] One of the main proposals arising from the review was the creation of a common waiting list and a housing selection scheme for all social housing. Some housing associations had already been doing this, but others had their own specialist schemes.

In March 1997, a Common Housing Register was established, and this was quickly followed by a common waiting list for the allocation of all general needs housing. In November 2000, a new housing selection scheme was implemented, which was entirely points-based but did have a distinctive separate administrative category for 'complex needs' or applications requiring more specialized accommodation with support services. More objective assessment criteria were designed that were to be not only cognizant to individuals' needs but also measuring the competing needs of applicants and their different characteristics in a more sensitive way. Points were to be awarded under four assessment categories: intimidation, insecurity of tenure, housing conditions, and health and social well-being. *Urgent need* was to be renamed *housing stress* and defined on the basis of

---

98 The Housing (Northern Ireland) Order 1988, articles 3–6.
99 Ibid.
100 P. Gray and others, *Research to Inform Fundamental Review of Social Housing Allocations Policy. Final Report: Conclusions and Recommendations* (2013) <https://pure.ulster.ac.uk/en/publications/research-to-inform-a-fundamental-review-of-social-housing-allocat-8 (accessed 1 September 2023).
101 Department of the Environment Northern Ireland, *Building on Success: The Way Ahead* (1996).

whether an applicant had 30 or more points. The new scheme was also to give a substantial number of points (200) to those who were victims of sectarian, racial, or terrorist intimidation, which would give them absolute priority to facilitate immediate rehousing. Existing tenants who wished to transfer were also subject to a points-based assessment.[102]

At the same time, the 'Peace Process'[103] had been gaining momentum, with ceasefires being announced and political parties working together to come to an agreement for the future governance of the province. Subsequent referenda in the two jurisdictions of Ireland were followed by the Northern Ireland Act 1998, also known as the Good Friday Agreement, which established the new Northern Ireland Assembly and a cross-community power-sharing executive (referred to locally as 'The Executive'). It provided a framework for political settlement centred on power sharing between unionists and nationalists. It was signed by the British and Irish governments as well as the four main political parties. The devolved governance arrangements in Northern Ireland are rather different from those in Scotland and Wales. The Northern Ireland Executive and Assembly are distinctive political-administrative arrangements, comprising a mandatory coalition with no formal separation between 'government' and 'opposition'. Party political structures, which represent divisions along ethno-religious lines, are unique to Northern Ireland.

NIHE Homelessness Strategies

It was not until 2002 that the NIHE published its first homelessness strategy,[104] which was to be implemented in partnership with the statutory and voluntary sectors. In the same year, the Committee for Social Development in the Assembly published a report of an inquiry into homelessness in Northern Ireland in June 2002. That report called for homelessness to be 'accorded the highest possible priority' and made a number of important and detailed recommendations.[105]

In 2004, a report by the House of Commons Committee of Public Accounts called 'Housing the Homeless' was highly critical of NIHE for failing to produce a strategy until 14 years after it had assumed responsibility for homelessness services and considered that it had been 'complacent'.[106] The report was also highly critical of the Department for Social Development for not providing 'sufficient oversight or guidance to NIHE in order to ensure that a strategy was produced sooner.'[107]

The Housing (NI) Order 2003, which was introduced in April 2004, incorporated a number of amendments in relation to homelessness. The definition of *homelessness* was extended to include those with no accommodation 'available for his occupation in the UK or elsewhere', reflecting a change in approach to homelessness definitions elsewhere in

---

102 Gray and others (n 100).
103 By 1997, after nearly 30 years of conflict which led to over 3,500 deaths, the Provisional IRA and Loyalist paramilitaries had called ceasefires, and the majority of the main political parties were at the negotiating table.
104 Northern Ireland Housing Executive (NIHE), *The Homelessness Strategy* (NIHE 2002).
105 Northern Ireland Assembly Committee for Social Development (2001/2002) *Second Report on the Inquiry into Housing in Northern Ireland (Homelessness)* (The Stationary Office 2002).
106 House of Commons: Committee of Public Accounts, *Housing the Homeless*, HC 559, 20 May 2004.
107 House of Commons NI Affairs Committee Social Housing Provision in Northern Ireland Sixth Report of Session 2003–04.

the UK. However, despite extending the definition of *homelessness*, the legislation added an eligibility test and introduced a second intentionality test.[108] The new law allowed for a person to be deemed intentionally homeless if the NIHE is satisfied that the purpose of the arrangement is to enable the applicant to become entitled to assistance as a homeless person, and there is no other good reason why s/he is homeless or threatened with homelessness. As previously stated, the new law was seen as an opportunity missed to introduce more fundamental reforms to the legislative framework, as in Scotland, with its progressive Homelessness Etc. (Scotland) Act 2003. Compared with this legislation, the legal and policy framework in Northern Ireland had more in common with legislation in the 1970s, whereby eligibility tests were enhanced, rather than removed, as in Scotland. In many ways, 2003 marked a period whereby Northern Ireland's homelessness legislation was removed from the progressive direction being taken elsewhere in the UK.[109]

On 9 July 2007, the Minister for Social Development launched 'Including the Homeless': a strategy to promote the social inclusion of homeless people, and those at risk of becoming homeless in Northern Ireland'.[110] According to Department for Social Development (DSD) officials, this was to encourage more collaborative partnership working and joined-up integrated service provision between government departments and agencies, to identify and tackle factors that can contribute to social exclusion and to undertake positive initiatives to improve and enhance the lives and circumstances of the most deprived and marginalized people in the community. The objectives were, according to the officials,

> to prevent or reduce homelessness wherever possible; to ensure that accessible, effective, and safe provision is made for people who are homeless; and to ensure that progression to independent living is supported and encouraged wherever possible. The strategy provided a unique opportunity to address the full spectrum of issues, not only in relation to housing but from the equally important perspectives of health and social well-being and sustainability in communities, and it provided an opportunity to identify actions to address problems and barriers to good practice that existed at that time. It enabled all the key players to work together to prevent homelessness and to ensure that homeless people could gain access to the services to which they are entitled.[111]

The Housing (Amendment) Act (Northern Ireland) 2010 increased the responsibilities of the Housing Executive in relation to homelessness and anti-social behaviour. The Housing Executive was given new duties to publish a homelessness strategy every five years and a long-overdue requirement to provide free housing advice and assistance.[112]

Although the NIHE had published its first strategy in 2002, under this new legislative requirement, it published the 2012–2017 strategy that identified as its vision ensuring

---

108 The Housing (Northern Ireland) Order 2003 Chapter IV AMENDMENTS OF THE ORDER OF 1988, Articles 135–137.
109 Gray and Long (n 95).
110 Department for Social Development, *A Strategy to Promote the Social Inclusion of Homeless People, and Those at Risk of Becoming Homeless in Northern Ireland* (Department for Social Development 2007).
111 Committee for Social Development, Hansard 8 October 2009.
112 J. Muir, 'Policy Difference and Policy Ownership Under UK Devolution: Social Housing Policy in Northern Ireland' (2012) <https://pure.qub.ac.uk/en/publications/policy-difference-and-policy-ownership-under-uk-devolution-social> (accessed 1 September 2023).

that 'long-term homelessness and rough sleeping is eliminated across Northern Ireland by 2020'.[113] It aimed to do so via four strategic objectives: placing homelessness prevention at the forefront of service delivery, reducing the duration of homelessness (time spent in temporary accommodation), removing the need to sleep rough, and improving services to vulnerable homeless households.[114] Whilst it was ambitious in its approach and welcomed by many across the housing sector, it received criticism in an evaluation published in 2016 which found that 'as at November 2016, 32 of the 38 Actions were assessed as being complete, a further three were in progress (i.e. significant changes had occurred) and three were not yet complete'. Despite this, the report found that

> gaps remained in service provision and progress in delivering the Strategy had not always been rapid, including the development of preventative services. Better service coordination and interagency planning were not yet fully in place and the social blight of rough sleeping, while rare, was yet to be eradicated.[115]

Key informants interviewed for the independent *Homelessness Monitor* identified two key issues that curtailed its effective implementation: first, substantial internal changes and staff turnover in the Northern Ireland Housing Executive following a wide-ranging review of its functions,[116] and second, a failure to achieve effective inter-departmental buy-in and coordination, despite this being a core priority of the strategy.[117]

In November 2017, the NI Audit Office published a report, 'Homelessness in Northern Ireland', where it found that homelessness had risen by 32% in the last five years and was disproportionately higher compared to other parts of the UK.[118] According to the report, the government strategy in place to deal with the problem had limited success. It also highlighted that there were no regular official counts of people sleeping rough. It made nine recommendations, including the fact that NIHE needed to be more innovative in its collection, analysis, and interpretation of homelessness data, including how many households had been prevented from becoming homeless by the work of the NIHE and its partners. It also called for an annual report presenting a summary of expenditure and benchmarked cost data that can demonstrate that accommodation-based services are providing value for money. Its final three recommendations encouraged the development of a cross-departmental, outcomes-focussed approach, with particular emphasis on the role of health issues and support needs in addressing homelessness. It called for stepped-up action and coordination

---

113 Northern Ireland Housing Executive, *Ending Homelessness Together: Homelessness Strategy for Northern Ireland 2017–2022* (Northern Ireland Housing Executive 2017).
114 B. Watts and S. Fitzpatrick, 'Ending Homelessness Together in Northern Ireland: A Unique Challenge' (2017) 11(2) *European Journal of Homelessness* 117.
115 F. Boyle and N. Pleace, *The Homelessness Strategy for Northern Ireland 2012–2017: An Evaluation 2017* (Northern Ireland Housing Executive 2018).
116 Department for Social Development, *Facing the Future: Housing Strategy for Northern Ireland. Consultation on Northern Ireland Housing Strategy 2012–2017* (Department for Social Development 2012).
117 S. Fitzpatrick and others, *The Homelessness Monitor: Northern Ireland 2016* (Crisis, Joseph Rowntree Foundation 2016).
118 Northern Ireland Audit Office, *Homelessness in Northern Ireland*, CDS (Northern Ireland Audit Office 2017).

to meet the Northern Ireland Housing Executive's targets for reducing homelessness, given rises in statutory homelessness over the period of the 2012–2017 strategy.[119]

In 2017, the NIHE published its Homeless Strategy 2017–2022, 'Ending Homelessness Together',[120] following a period of consultation from 8 December 2016 to 8 February 2017. It had five core themes: to prioritize homelessness prevention, to secure sustainable accommodation and appropriate support solutions for homeless households, to further understand and address the complexities of chronic homelessness across Northern Ireland, to ensure the right mechanisms are in place to oversee and deliver this strategy, and to measure and monitor existing and emerging need to inform the ongoing development of appropriate services. The strategy was widely welcomed by the sector. In the same year, 'An Inter-Departmental Action Plan 2017–18'[121] by the Ministers for Social Development, Health and Social Care, and Justice was published with the intention of complementing the NIHE Strategy, by focusing on non-accommodation aspects of homelessness-related interventions. It set out five priority areas: health and well-being, including mental health and substance misuse; education and awareness raising, in children, young people, schools, and providers; support for those leaving places of care, including a range of institutions; support for families, including those experiencing domestic violence; and employability, financial capability, and access to benefits. A total of 14 actions within these priority areas were identified, and the year 3 action plan was published on 6 May 2022. Fitzpatrick et al. argue that the action plan, triggered by rough sleeper deaths in Belfast, and the Northern Ireland Audit Office report have both been credited with strengthening the new Homelessness Strategy's focus on prevention and housing-led solutions.[122]

In 2020, *The Homelessness Monitor* suggested that homelessness and welfare policy development in Northern Ireland had been severely hampered since January 2017 following the collapse of the Northern Ireland Assembly.[123] At the same time, the potentially serious economic, political, and social implications for Northern Ireland of a disorderly Brexit cast a long shadow over all areas of public policy. In 2018/2019, some 18,200 households were logged as homelessness presentations in Northern Ireland, of which more than two-thirds – 12,500 – were judged as 'Full Duty Applicant' cases.[124] The total number of homelessness presentations has been virtually static over the past few years, but Full Duty Applicant cases have been steadily rising, increasing by 26% since 2009/2010.[125] It highlighted the strikingly high proportion of social housing allocations accounted for by statutory homeless cases in Northern Ireland. In 2017/2018, lettings to homeless households accounted for no less than 88% of all Housing Executive lettings to new tenants, as compared with 39% of all social lets to new tenants in Scotland, and only 21% of all local

---

119 L. McMordie and B. Watts, 'The Northern Ireland Audit Office Report on Homelessness: A Missed Opportunity' (2018) 12(2) *European Journal of Homelessness* 89.
120 NIHE, *Homeless Strategy for Northern Ireland 2017–2022: Ending Homelessness Together* (Online, Northern Ireland Housing Executive 2017).
121 DfCNI, *Inter-Departmental Homelessness Action Plan: Priorities and Actions for 2017–2018* (Online, Department for Communities 2017).
122 Fitzpatrick and others (n 117).
123 S. Fitzpatrick and others, *The Homelessness Monitor: Northern Ireland 2020* (Crisis, Joseph Rowntree Foundation 2020).
124 Ibid. XIV.
125 Ibid.

authority lets to new tenants in England.[126] It went on to highlight that the overall scale of annual temporary accommodation placements had oscillated within a fairly narrow band over recent years in Northern Ireland. Nevertheless, the figure for 2017/2018 was the highest of the decade, at just over 3,000.[127]

In 2020 the NIHE published its first 'Chronic Homeless Action Plan 2019–22'[128] as a result of its commitment set out in its Homelessness Strategy 2017–2022. It defined *chronic homelessness* as 'a group of individuals with very pronounced and complex support needs who find it difficult to exit from homelessness'. It sets out how the organization plans to address gaps in services that have the most impact, or have the potential to positively impact, on the lives of those people who are experiencing, or most at risk of experiencing, chronic homelessness.

On 23 March 2022, in the midst of the coronavirus pandemic, the NIHE published its 'Ending Homelessness Together – Homelessness strategy 2022–27.'[129] It set out three strategic objectives: to prioritize homelessness prevention; provide settled, appropriate accommodation and support; and support customers to transition from homelessness into settled accommodation. It included a commitment to getting those who have experienced homelessness more involved in-service design and delivery. A year 1 action plan was published alongside the strategy, setting out 44 actions, including the expansion of Housing First provision, which was developed in previous strategies. It also includes commissioning research on local efforts to address chronic homelessness, implementing a homelessness data action plan, and ensuring effective commissioning structures are in place to prioritize funding. Around the same time, the NIHE published its Strategic Action Plan for Temporary Accommodation strategy 2022–2027[130] following a strategic review in January 2019.[131]

Looking Ahead

Power sharing in Northern Ireland resumed in early February 2024 as the Northern Ireland Assembly reconvened after a period of 2 years not sitting from February 2022. There had previously been five suspensions of the Assembly: 11 February to 30 May 2000; 10 August 2001 (24-hour suspension); 22 September 2001 (24-hour suspension); 14 October 2002 to 7 May 2007; and 9 January 2017 to 11 January 2020. Despite this, government officials, the NIHE, housing associations, public representatives, and voluntary agencies, amongst others, have worked closely together to establish a framework to end homelessness through a number of initiatives and strategies. Indeed, it has been argued that Northern Ireland is unusual in a UK context in having had a rolling sequence of national homelessness

---

126 Ibid. XII.
127 Ibid.
128 NIHE, *Chronic Homelessness Action Plan* (Online, Northern Ireland Housing Executive 2019).
129 NIHE, *Ending Homelessness Together: Homelessness Strategy 2022–2027* (Online, Northern Ireland Housing Executive 2022).
130 NIHE, *Homeless to Home: Strategic Action Plan for Temporary Accommodation 2022–27* (Online, Northern Ireland Housing Executive 2022).
131 According to *Inside Housing* (14 March 2022), in March 2022, there were 3,596 households living in temporary accommodation in NI compared with 2,065 in January 2019, the number of children in this accommodation increasing by 55% to 3763 over the same period.

strategies in place since 2002.¹³² However, levels of statutory homelessness in Northern Ireland increased rapidly in the early 2000s and have remained at historically high levels of between 18,000 and 20,000 presentations to the NIHE since 2005/2006. According to the NI Housing Bulletin published by the Department for Communities, October to December 2022, there were 44,519 applicants on the housing waiting list, which covers all of Northern Ireland.¹³³ According to homeless charity the Simon Community, the 'issue . . . has been building in Northern Ireland for 25 years, in 20 years the homelessness problem has . . . risen by 70%',¹³⁴ the same period since the Assembly was established after the Good Friday Agreement in 1998. In April 2021, an all-party Group on Homelessness (APG) was established, consisting of 11 members of the legislative assembly (MLAs): three from the Democratic Unionist Party, two from Sinn Féin, two from the Ulster Unionist Party, two from the Social Democratic and Labour Party, one from the Alliance Party, and one from the Green Party. At that time, over 42,000 households were on the housing waiting list. To date, five meetings of the group have taken place.

As outlined, Northern Ireland is distinct in the UK context for its sequence of national homelessness strategies operating since 2002. Yet the number of homeless applicants is still rising despite the many efforts and interventions by public representatives, statutory bodies, housing associations, and voluntary groups. Whilst progress has been made, it could be argued that policies have been hampered by long periods of democratic deficits, where the Assembly has collapsed, making it more difficult to build on the successes achieved. With the Assembly now back up and running, there may be cautious optimism for further progress on the homelessness issue. According to the *News letter* on 9 March 2023, the Department for Communities released statistics on homelessness that morning showing that almost 4,000 households were living in temporary accommodation in January 2023 compared with nearly 2,100 in 2019, an increase of 91%, including over 4,200 children (2,800 aged 9 and under), an increase of 74% since 2019.¹³⁵ Whilst these figures are staggering, efforts are continuing to increase the supply of housing across Northern Ireland. A Housing Supply Strategy 2022–2037 was published by the Department for Communities, setting out ambitious plans to build 100,000 houses over the life of the strategy, including 33,000 social homes.¹³⁶ In the past year, housing associations have exceeded their targets for building new homes. On 30 March 2023, the Department for Communities published a new affordable housing policy by creating an additional supply of 'intermediate rent' homes.¹³⁷

There is now a greater recognition that the NIHE must be supported in its statutory role (a role unique within the UK, where local authorities have this responsibility in the other three jurisdictions). There is an acknowledgement that homelessness needs to be tackled on a cross-departmental basis, and as part of this, the All Party Group on Homelessness

---

132 Watts and Fitzpatrick (n 114).
133 Northern Ireland Statistics and Research Agency (NISRA) Northern Ireland Housing Bulletin October–December 2022.
134 Simon Community Chief Executive, Jim Dennison report by Belfast Live, 26 December 2022.
135 J. Savage, 'Number of NI Children Living in Temporary Accommodation Continues to Rise Due to Cost-of-Living Crisis' *News Letter* (9 March 2023).
136 Department for Communities, *Housing Supply Strategy 2022–2037* (Department for Communities December 2021).
137 Department for Communities, *Intermediate Rent Policy* (Department for Communities March 2023).

is still meeting and taking evidence, helping to look at broader issues, such as prevention and support services. Indeed, speaking to *Agenda NI* in 2021, the then minister Deirdre Hargey 'indicated a recognition that homelessness was not a challenge that could be tackled in isolation and would require a whole system approach'.[138] It is difficult to know how effective these new approaches will be, but it is encouraging that there is a greater understanding across different government departments as to their roles in tackling the crisis together. The aim of the NIHE Homeless Strategy 2022–2027 is '[w]herever possible homelessness should be prevented, if homelessness cannot be prevented it should be rare, brief and non-recurring'.[139]

Conclusion: A Dis-United Kingdom Homelessness Policy

As devolution has evolved, there has been increasingly greater divergence in housing policy (as this chapter has demonstrated), which calls into question any notion of a 'UK experience' of homelessness.[140] Despite the turn to a more preventative approach in England under the Homelessness Reduction Act 2017 and recent promises of a new 'world-leading' approach to ending rough sleeping, sadly, it is hard to argue against the conclusion that the pattern of homelessness law and policy in England is one largely premised, historically and even in the contemporary law, on gatekeeping of scarce resources, sanction, and exclusion. Despite the bold political gestures there is surely cynicism and some mistrust in the sector who have heard such promises many times before. Regrettably, the policy on the ground is yet to match the rhetoric. The position in Wales is quite different, where devolution has meant that the country has been able to pursue a more progressive and distinct path at odds with that in England. In contrast to England, there is greater cause for optimism for reform in Wales. With all the Homelessness Action Group's recommendations accepted in principle by the Welsh government and now firmly rooted in the current Programme for Government 2021–2026,[141] and in the High-Level Action Plan, it is highly likely that these recommendations will reflect the shape of future reform to the homelessness framework in the country. Against this backdrop, clouds gather, with a 'cost-of-living crisis' hitting especially hard those on lower incomes and the homeless, and therefore, how much will ultimately be delivered in both England and Wales in terms of ambitious reform is yet to be determined. That said, if the pandemic has demonstrated anything, it is that when political will is harnessed, positive outcomes for the homeless are possible.

In Scotland, the political will to eradicate homelessness has been clearly articulated in primary legislation since at least 1987, when the Housing (Scotland) Act consolidated the Housing (Homeless Persons) Act 1977 to introduce new statutory duties on local authorities to provide accommodation for homeless households. Since 1999, when housing policy was devolved to the Scottish Parliament, successive Scottish governments have diverged from elsewhere in the UK by adopting an explicitly progressive, rights-based approach, based firmly on the principle of prevention. In applying a *Housing First* model, the current

---

138 D. Whelan, 'Homelessness Crisis' *Agenda NI* (June 2021).
139 NIHE, *Ending Homelessness Together* (2022) (n 129) 7.
140 McKee, Muir and Moore (n 53) 60.
141 Welsh Government, *Programme for Government* (Welsh Government 2021).

government has endorsed the idea of 'rapid housing' by default. For groups who find themselves homeless, local authorities are encouraged to provide support that can provide mainstream, settled housing as soon as possible. Local authorities are obliged to have 'Rapid Rehousing Transition Plans' to ensure an effective partnership between service providers to ensure that stays in temporary accommodation are short and supportive. The *Ending Homelessness Together Action Plan* has been adopted to ensure that preventing homelessness has a strong political priority, which can provide what *Crisis* has described as 'some of the most progressive homelessness rights in the world'. Whilst there is some uncertainty about the direction of policy of the Scottish government following the resignation of Nicola Sturgeon from leadership of the SNP in February 2023, the new first minister (Humza Yousaf) has committed himself to the continuation of a progressive homelessness strategy, demonstrated by the appointment of a dedicated housing minister (Paul McLennan). However, there still remain tensions between devolved governments and the UK government in Westminster, with England increasingly becoming the outlier in policy terms. As with other parts of the UK, homelessness policy is characterized by the frustrations of devolved governance and lack of autonomy, particularly in relation to funding. In addition, policies are frequently undermined by social security policies (as reserved matters) which are founded on conditionality and sanctions.

Northern Ireland, too, has had a unique journey regarding its housing policy and practice in particular over the past 50 years since the formation of the NIHE. Unlike other jurisdictions, many functions were removed from local authorities following the outbreak of the troubles, leaving them with limited capacity. Some of these have still not been returned, including the administration of the Supporting People programme and the administration of housing benefit, both of which remain with the NIHE, as well as the statutory responsibility for homelessness. Whilst attempts have been made to revitalize the NIHE (at the time of writing, this is still ongoing), the collapse of a functioning assembly in Northern Ireland (thankfully recently reconvened in February 2024) has not helped progress on this. The one thing, however, that policymakers and practitioners have learned to their credit over the past 50 years in Northern Ireland is resilience despite setbacks. Organizations like the NIHE, the 20 housing associations, the voluntary sector, and government departments have learned to 'get on with it' despite the difficulties they have faced. This resolve is unlikely to dissipate anytime soon. Indeed, there is a clear determination to work together in partnership to prevent homelessness and to reduce reliance on temporary accommodation.

Set in the context of 25 years of devolution, this chapter has exposed the key battle lines and foci across the four nations of the UK, which, in turn, begs broader and crucial questions as to the efficacy and appropriateness of current policy frameworks, the potentiality for new opportunities, and for novel ways of seeing and doing homelessness policy differently. In short, each nation of the UK has its own particular historical, social, and legal context into which assessments of national homelessness policy must be placed. The need for awareness of and sensitivity towards each nation's unique homelessness story emerges as a key theme from this chapter but also sounds loudly across all chapters of the wider collection. In the UK context, then, whilst the core drivers of homelessness are echoed across the four nations of the country, the approaches, successes, and failures of homelessness policy in each exude a unique character and hue, again underscoring the divergences between nations. In unearthing these differences, this chapter has therefore rendered visible what we can term 'a dis-United Kingdom' homelessness policy.

2
HOMELESSNESS IN IRELAND
Law, Policy, and Practices

Mark Jordan and Padraic Kenna

Introduction

In the last decade, according to State statistics, Ireland has 'gone through one of the most rapid increases in homelessness recorded anywhere, except in cases of natural disaster or war'.[1] This chapter provides an overview of homelessness in the Republic of Ireland that sheds light on the contemporary homelessness crisis and the State's response to it. The chapter critically examines central aspects of homelessness law and policy and presents a perspective on what the future of homelessness law and policy in Ireland could look like. In order to set homelessness in the broader Irish housing context, the chapter begins by outlining the history of homelessness in Ireland. The chapter outlines how homelessness is treated within Irish housing policy, both historically and in the present day. The distinctive 'strategy'-based approach to homelessness policy in Ireland is discussed and critically appraised. The argument is developed that the 'strategy'-based approach is beset by several long-standing limitations, most notably the narrow definition of *homelessness*, which equates homelessness with rough sleeping and numbers in emergency accommodation and therefore fails to capture or address hidden homelessness. The chapter then sets out various legal measures on homelessness prevention, including the legal definition of homelessness in Irish law and the housing obligations on local authorities under the homelessness and Traveller frameworks. The absence of rights for those experiencing homelessness is a recurring theme in Irish homelessness law, and the lack of enforceable rights goes some way towards explaining the remarkably low number of successful legal challenges to local authorities' administration of their housing functions. Following this, the discussion turns to a range of homelessness prevention practices, including distinctive rent subsidy mechanisms, homelessness agencies, data collection, tenancy support schemes, and Housing First initiatives. Although some of these initiatives have met with some successes, it is argued that they have

---

1 I. Baptista and others, *From Rebuilding Ireland to Housing for All: International and Irish Lessons for Tackling Homelessness* (COPE Galway, Focus Ireland, JCFJ, Mercy Law, Simon Communities of Ireland, and SVP February 2022) 8.

failed to stem the rapid increase in homelessness. The chapter concludes by looking to the future of homelessness law and policy, and it outlines some of the limitations of the current definition of homelessness and considers how expanding the role of legal, and constitutional, housing rights could shape law and policy in the future.

1. Housing and Homelessness in Ireland

1.1. History of Homelessness Law in Ireland

In 1983, the Simon Community introduced a Housing (Homeless Persons) Bill, modelled on the iconic English legislation of 1977, as well as a Vagrancy Law Repeal Bill. Neither was passed, but the campaign for reform prompted the Housing Act 1988, which created a definition of *homelessness*, decriminalized homelessness,[2] and made a set of obligations on local authorities towards homeless people. The legislation was the result of many years of campaigning 'to end the exclusion of homeless people from the national housing system' and ensure 'they had the same rights as other citizens'.[3] This created the first legal definition of *homelessness* since the Poor Law, which is discussed later in Section 2.

Housing authorities were obliged to carry out regular assessments of existing and prospective housing requirements. In making this assessment of housing requirements, the authority 'shall have regard' to the extent to which there are persons who are homeless or living in temporary or movable accommodation.[4] In addition, the Act included homeless people as one of the categories of people included in the local authority assessment of needs.[5] Crucially, the Act provided for State payments to agencies and providers to offer housing to homeless people, including hostels and emergency shelter.[6] As a result, the provision of accommodation for homeless people was undertaken by voluntary and charitable bodies, most of which were approved bodies (housing associations) under Section 6 of the Housing Act 1992. This legislation forms the basis of State provision for homeless people today, although it has been amended and supplemented by institutional measures, such as the establishment of the Homeless Agency, a number of strategies and action plans, and statutory obligations on local authorities to create Homelessness Action Plans (see Section 1.3).

1.2. Travellers and Homelessness

The homelessness and nomadic movement of Irish Travellers has long been recorded, yet all housing legislation and Government housing reports until the late 1980s failed to refer to Traveller accommodation needs. The *Report of the Commission on Itinerancy* (1963)

---

2 The Housing Act 1988 repealed the provisions of the Vagrancy Act 1847, which criminalized 'wandering abroad'.
3 B. Harvey, 'The Use of Legislation to Address a Social Problem. The Example of the Housing Act 1988' (1995) 4(1) *Administration* 76.
4 Section 8(2)(b). This has now been repealed and replaced with s 20 of the Housing (Miscellaneous Provisions) Act 2009, which refers to assessments of persons for eligibility for social housing support.
5 Section 9 of the Act of 1988 is replaced by S 20 of the Housing (Miscellaneous Provisions) Act 2009.
6 Housing Act 1988, s. 10.

showed that there were 1,150 Traveller families living on the roadside,[7] while there were still 591 in 2019.[8] A report by the IHREC shows that Traveller children comprised 12% of homeless children in emergency accommodation, although Travellers account for only 1% of the population in 2020.[9]

There is a special regime governing the accommodation needs of Travellers which is set out in the Housing (Traveller Accommodation) Act 1998. This Act provided for national and local Traveller Accommodation Consultative Committees[10] and placed a duty on local authorities to prepare and adopt a Traveller Accommodation Program (TAP) (see Section 2 later).[11]

1.3. Homelessness Policy

Although the provision of homeless services is mainly undertaken by voluntary and charity sector, the State, acting through the Department of Housing at national level and local authorities at local level, retains a central role in funding services and devising homelessness policy in Ireland. Eoin O'Sullivan argues that

> the current policy is best described as *reacting to homelessness* via a series of ad hoc interventions that are designed to minimise and mitigate the impact of housing instability and resultant homelessness on families and individuals, rather than the drivers of homelessness.[12]

Homelessness Strategies

Over the past three decades, the State has shaped the development of homelessness policy by devising and adopting national homelessness strategies and action plans. An extensive volume of homelessness policy has been generated in the process.[13] Indeed, a recent survey of national homelessness policy has found that since 2000, there have been well over a dozen national strategies and reports.[14] Instead of attempting to detail all the different strategies and reports here, the approach here is to draw attention to some notable features and particularly important strategy documents.

In general, the various homelessness strategies set out aspirational objectives and place considerable emphasis on the development of homelessness policy and practice through informal consultation arrangements between local authorities, health officials, and

---

7 The Stationery Office, *Report of the Commission on Itinerancy* (The Stationery Office 1963).
8 See <www.gov.ie/en/publication/6f4e1-2019-estimate-all-categories-of-traveller-accomodation/> (accessed 1 September 2023).
9 IHREC, *Submission to the Joint Committee on Key Issues Affecting the Traveller Community Irish Human Rights and Equality Commission* (February 2021) <www.ihrec.ie/app/uploads/2021/03/Submission-to-the-Joint-Committee-on-Key-Issues-affecting-the-Traveller-Community-FINAL.pdf> (accessed 1 September 2023).
10 Housing (Traveller Accommodation) Act 1998, ss 19–22.
11 Housing (Traveller Accommodation) Act 1998, s 7.
12 E. O'Sullivan, *Reimagining Homelessness for Policy and Practice* (Policy Press, U of Chicago P 2020) 75.
13 Baptista and others (n 1) 21–22.
14 Ibid.

voluntary bodies. This approach to the development of homelessness policy and practice has led to the development of some innovative and internationally distinctive practices, such as PASS (Pathway Accommodation and Support System). This is a national integrated bed and case management system that records the number of adult individuals with accompanying child dependents experiencing homelessness and residing in designated emergency and temporary accommodation. However, these strategies tend to calcify a narrow definition of homelessness that equates it with rough sleeping and living in emergency accommodation, which, consequently, fails to capture the extent of hidden homelessness in Ireland. Furthermore, despite the lofty aspirational targets in many homelessness strategies, they tend not to contain 'performance frameworks which are open to objective accountability', and many of the objectives around ending homelessness have not been met.[15] Furthermore, the absence of any real commitment to enhanced legal rights for those experiencing homelessness is a recurring feature of the strategy-based approach.[16]

Governance/Oversight Bodies

Over the past 30 years, the State has established a number of governance/oversight bodies to develop and/or coordinate homeless-related services, policies, and practices. Perhaps the single biggest institutional development in Irish homelessness policy was the establishment of the Dublin Regional Homeless Executive (DRHE – formerly known as the Homeless Agency).[17] In 2020, the DRHE spent €158.7m on homelessness services.[18] The DRHE established the Pathway Accommodation and Support System (PASS), an online server that provides important information regarding access to (emergency) accommodation. This system provides 'of-the-moment' data in terms of bed occupancy and availability. The DRHE also publishes homelessness figures and research reports on homelessness.[19]

Action Plans to Address Homelessness

Local authorities are subject to a legal requirement to prepare action plans to address homelessness.[20] This plan must be prepared in consultation with a homelessness consul-

---

15 P. Kenna, *Housing Law, Rights and Policy* (Clarus Press 2011) 265.
16 Ibid.
17 <www.homelessdublin.ie/content/files/Homelessness-Action Plan-2019-2021.pdf> (accessed 1 September 2023).
18 See 'Dublin Region Local Authority Homelessness Financial Report End of Year 2020' <www.gov.ie/en/publication/b0631-homelessness-financial-report-end-of-year-2020-dublin/#> (accessed 1 September 2023).
19 H. Morrin, *A Profile of Families Experiencing Homelessness in the Dublin Region: 2016–2018 Families* (DRHE 2019) <https://www.homelessdublin.ie/content/files/A-profile-of-families-experiencing-homelessness-in-the-Dublin-Region-2016-2018-families.pdf> (accessed 1 September 2023); H. Morrin, *Family Progression Through Homeless Services: 2016–2018* (DRHE 2019) <https://www.homelessdublin.ie/content/files/Family-Progression-through-Homeless-Services-2016-2018.pdf> (accessed 1 September 2023); DRHE, *Reported Reasons for Family Homelessness in the Dublin Region: January to June 2018* (DRHE 2019) <https://www.homelessdublin.ie/content/files/Reported-reasons-for-family-homelessness-in-the-Dublin-Region-January-to-June-2018.pdf> (accessed 1 September 2023); DRHE, *Quality Standards for Homeless Services: National Quality Standards Framework (NQSF)* (DRHE 2017) <https://www.homelessdublin.ie/content/files/Quality-Standards-for-Homeless-Services.pdf> (accessed 1 September 2023).
20 Kenna (n 15) 273.

tative forum. The members of this forum must be appointed by housing authorities in a statutorily prescribed form. In appointing members, the authority is required to appoint an employee(s) of the housing authority, the Health Service Executive (HSE), as well as persons nominated by specified bodies or the Minister – although there is no specified role of consumers of homeless services.[21]

The homelessness action plan must specify detailed measures proposed to be undertaken to address homelessness by the housing authority, the HSE, and voluntary bodies whose services include the prevention of homelessness, the reduction of homelessness, the provision of services (including accommodation), the provision of assistance (including financial), and the promotion of effective coordination of activities.[22] The homelessness action plan must be in writing and take account of a range of matters, including local housing need, the cost of any proposed measures, and the financial resources available to states. The plan must also take into account policies and objectives of the Government or Minister. As Kenna notes, these considerations place significant restrictions on the scope of any plan given that state bodies are not in a position to set out resources available to them over the three or more years of plans.[23]

At the national level, the Cross Departmental Team on Homelessness (CDT) was established in 1998, with representation from across Government departments and state agencies. In 2007, the National Homelessness Consultative Committee (NHCC) was established to provide for representation from a wide range of stakeholders in the ongoing development of Government homelessness policy. Since 2009, both groups have been meeting on joint basis. A High-Level Homelessness Task Force was established in July 2020 to provide a forum for engagement with key organizations working together to address homelessness. It also provides input on the implementation of the commitments on homelessness in the Programme for Government. The membership of the task force consists of the chief executives of DRHE, Crosscare, DePaul, Focus Ireland, the Peter McVerry Trust, Dublin Simon Community, and Threshold. In December 2021, the task force amalgamated with the National Homeless Action Committee. The aim of this Committee is to 'ensure the continued coherence and coordination of homeless related services, policies and action'.[24]

Current Government Homelessness Policy

Housing for All – A New Housing Plan for Ireland, published in 2021 by the Department of Housing, Local Government, and Heritage, sets out the most recent statement of Irish homelessness policy. This sets out the Government commitment to

> a housing-led approach as the primary response to all forms of homelessness. It includes the prevention of loss of existing housing. It also includes the provision of adequate support to people in their homes according to their needs and the provision of high levels of additional social housing.[25]

---

21 Housing (Miscellaneous Provisions) Act 2009, s 37(1). See Kenna (n 15) 276.
22 Housing (Miscellaneous Provisions) Act 2009, s 37(2).
23 Kenna (n 15) 274.
24 Baptista and others (n 1).
25 Government of Ireland, 'Housing First National Implementation Plan 2018–2021' <https://assets.gov.ie/41658/0a0d8517d31848e78ad2b54829958b9f.pdf> (accessed 1 September 2023).

While the Plan outlines a commitment to increase housing supply, it makes particular reference to increasing the building of one-bedroom units. It also contains commitments to enhance homelessness prevention practices through the expansion of health supports and street outreach services and grow the role of housing-led and Housing First approaches. It also contains a recognition for the need for further not-for-profit emergency accommodation in order to reduce the use of private hotels and B&Bs for emergency accommodation. Finally, the document re-states the Irish Government's commitment to 'work towards' eradicating homelessness in line with the objectives of the Lisbon Declaration to eradicate homelessness by 2030.[26]

A recent critical appraisal of *Housing for All* found that it contains some of the same failings that have plagued Irish homelessness policy for the past three decades. At the heart of the strategy is a narrow definition of *homelessness* that, in effect, equates homelessness with rough sleeping and people living in emergency accommodation. This narrow definition fails to capture the extent of hidden homelessness in Ireland, and as a result, 'the structural, individual and policy factors' that are generating homelessness are not being highlighted in enumeration systems.[27] The resulting lack of meaningful statistics inhibits the development of a more comprehensive, effective strategic response to homelessness. Furthermore, this narrow definition centres the policy response on people who are in what are defined as 'homeless places', that is, in emergency accommodation or on the street. As a result, 'women, young people and other populations experiencing hidden homelessness, which ultimately means no legal or physical security and may often mean limited privacy or control over living space, are undercounted in Ireland'.[28] The adoption of the ETHOS categorization, which includes 'houseless' and those living within inadequate and insecure housing, would change the situation.[29]

1.4. Contemporary Homelessness Situation in Ireland

The extent of the contemporary homelessness crisis is reflected in the extraordinary increase in numbers of people in emergency homeless accommodation. Since 2014, the number of adults in such accommodation has almost tripled from 2,500 to 7,100 in April 2022, while the number of children in such accommodation has quadrupled from under 800 to nearly 3,000 in the same period.

Homelessness and Precarious Housing

The numbers in emergency accommodation do not capture the extent of the homelessness crisis. When one considers the numbers living in precarious housing, that is, housing which is unaffordable, insecure, over-crowded, unsuitable, or unfit, a much fuller picture emerges. Statistics on those living in precarious housing are collected by local authorities as part of

---

26 Lisbon Declaration on the European Platform on Combatting Homelessness, Conference: Combatting Homelessness – A Priority for Our Social Europe (2021) <https://ec.europa.eu/social/BlobServlet?docId=24120&langId=en> (accessed 1 September 2023).
27 Baptista and others (n 1) 42.
28 Ibid. 56.
29 Source <www.feantsa.org/en/toolkit/2005/04/01/ethos-typology-on-homelessness-and-housing-exclusion; www.feantsa.org/download/ethos2484215748748239888.pdf> (accessed 1 September 2023).

their statutory housing need assessments.³⁰ Local authority assessments of housing need record that 'over the period 2016–2021, there were just over 59,000 households assessed as qualified for housing support as of June 2021, a decrease of over 32,000 households on the 2016 figure',³¹ although this drop does not reflect 'a decrease in objective need for social housing, but a policy decision to treat those households in receipt of a HAP payment as having their social housing needs'.³²

Drivers of Homelessness in Ireland

While there are numerous drivers of the homelessness crisis, Eoin O'Sullivan points out that 'the primary determinant of the residential instability experienced by those presenting to homelessness services' in Ireland is 'the housing affordability and accessibility crisis'.³³ The housing affordability crisis 'manifests itself in spiralling rents in the private rented sector that price out welfare-dependent households, despite the increase in the rent allowances, and provides a rationale for landlords to terminate tenancies in order to command higher market rents'.³⁴ At the same time, the accessibility crisis 'is demonstrated in the demand for secure social housing massively outstripping the supply'.³⁵ These twin crises can be traced to 'longer term trends in the commodification of housing' which have intensified residential instability in Ireland and across the Global North.³⁶

Traveller Housing and Homelessness

There is an acute shortage of Traveller-specific accommodation in Ireland, and many of the existing sites are in an inadequate condition.³⁷ A report released in May 2021 by the ombudsman for children condemned the poor housing conditions that 38 families, including 66 children living on a local authority halting site, were facing.³⁸ The ombudsman found that the local authority had failed to address inadequate housing conditions, including faced rodent infestations, severe overcrowding, lack of sanitation facilities, illegal dumping, unsafe electrical work, lack of adequate heating, and no safe play areas for children.³⁹ Furthermore, Irish Travellers face considerable discrimination when trying to buy or rent homes in Ireland.⁴⁰ The structural barriers faced by Irish Travellers are reflected in how approximately 7.5% of all adults and children in

---

30 Housing (Miscellaneous Provisions) Act 2009, s 20.
31 Baptista and others (n 1) 33.
32 Ibid.
33 O'Sullivan (n 12) 74.
34 Ibid.
35 Ibid.
36 Ibid.
37 *ERRC v Ireland* Complaint No. 100/2013 Decision on the Merits 2015 <www.coe.int/en/web/european-social-charter/processed-complaints/-/asset_publisher/5GEFkJmH2bYG/content/no-100-2013-european-roma-rights-centre-errc-v-ireland?inheritRedirect=false> (accessed 1 September 2023).
38 Office of the Ombudsman for Children, 'No End in Site: An Investigation into the Conditions of Children on a Local Authority Halting Site' (2021) 4 <www.rte.ie/documents/news/2021/05/no-end-in-site-final.pdf> (accessed 1 September 2023).
39 Ibid.
40 Ibid. 62.

emergency accommodation in 2016 were Irish Travellers, even though Irish Travellers comprise just 0.7% of the general population.[41]

2. Legal Measures on Homelessness Prevention in Ireland

There is an extensive legal framework around addressing homelessness in Ireland.[42] Where an applicant presents as homeless to a housing authority, the application will be addressed as part of the wider social housing support regime. An application must progress through a number of sequential steps before the applicant household will be allocated a social housing support. As a first step, the applicant household must establish that they are eligible[43] and demonstrate need for social housing support.[44] As part of this assessment, the authority will consider the housing needs of the applicant household.[45] Where an applicant presents as homeless, they must demonstrate that they meet the statutory definition of homelessness, as outlined in what follows. When the housing authority has determined that the applicant is homeless and qualifies for support, their application will progress to the allocation stage. Once eligible, applicants will be added to the housing waiting list. This scheme is administrated by local authority according to a broad notion of housing need.[46] Where an application reaches the top of the list, they will be offered a social housing support. This can take various forms, including temporary accommodation, a tenancy from a local authority, or an approved housing body. In practice, local authorities may provide emergency or temporary accommodation to the household, but the main form of social housing support for many homeless households will be financial support from the local authority in the form of Housing Assistance Payment that is paid directly to private landlords.

2.1. Definition of Homelessness

In order for a person to be regarded as being homeless, they must be considered by the housing authority to have no accommodation available to them and be unable to provide such accommodation from their own resources.[47] This legal definition of *homelessness* provides the housing authority with considerable discretion in making this crucial determination.[48] In practice, this means that the opinion of the housing or local authority officer dealing with the application is decisive, and this has given rise to different approaches.[49] Local

---

41 O'Sullivan (n 12) 67–68; Office of the Ombudsman for Children (n 38) 62.
42 See D. Browne, *Law of Local Government* (2nd edn, Round Hall 2020) chapter 14; Kenna (n 15) chapter 11.
43 Those who have a legal right to remain in the state on a long-term basis will be eligible. See Department of Environment, Community and Local Government, *Housing Circular 41* (Department of Environment 2012).
44 Household income will be assessed by local authorities, and there are three maximum income thresholds that apply to different authorities. See Department of Housing: Local Government and Heritage (DHLGH), *Social Housing Support: Household Means Policy* (DHLGH 2021).
45 Housing (Miscellaneous Provisions) Act 2009, s 20(1).
46 See Kenna (n 15) chapter 4.
47 Housing Act 1988, s 2.
48 *Tee v Wicklow County Council* [2017] IEHC 194.
49 Kenna (n 15) 804; TSA/Simon Communities/CPA, *Settlement First – Assessment of the Effectiveness of the Housing Act 1988 and the Integrated Strategy 2000 in Meeting the Housing Needs of People Who Are Homeless* (TSA/Simon Communities/CPA 2005) 5.

authorities have employed criteria such as homeless 'through no fault of their own', indigenous to the area, intentionally homeless, having no local connection, refusal of an offer of accommodation,[50] to restrict entitlement under the Act.[51] This is despite the fact that these criteria are not mentioned in the legislation. As a result, there is no commonly agreed definition of what constitutes homelessness across statutory and voluntary agencies.[52]

There is a real tension between the open textured definition of homelessness and the legal obligation on local authorities to promote equality, prevent discrimination, and protect the human rights of service users and everyone affected by their policies and plans.[53] The centrality of an individual housing officer's opinion creates a real risk of discrimination against particular groups and individuals. This is because the definition effectively allows 'agencies to widen or narrow the definition of homelessness dependent on their perspective and/or the individual that presents'.[54] These tensions are arguably exacerbated by the absence of any specified appeals procedure in respect of the local authorities' determinations.[55] Despite these criticisms, there have been few judicial review cases of local authority determinations. The reasons for this are discussed later. There have been proposals to introduce a definitive interpretation of homelessness to ensure greater consistency in the national understanding of what constitutes homelessness, but these have not been implemented.[56]

2.2. Rights, Duties, and Powers

Housing authorities are subject to a number of legal obligations to take certain actions in relation to those who are determined to be homeless. These obligations have changed over time as practices and policies have evolved, and the current regime is outlined in the Housing (Miscellaneous Provisions) Act 2009. A consistent feature of legislation in this area is how it has not placed an obligation on public authorities to provide accommodation to an applicant who is determined to be homeless. As Barrett J. pointed out in *EBS Ltd. v Kenehan*,[57] there is no constitutional or statutory right to housing in Irish law. The learned judge considered Article 8 of the European Convention on Human Rights, Article 16 of the European Social Charter (Revised), Article 11(1) of the International Covenant on Economic, Social, and Cultural Rights, and other constitutions within the European Union.[58] He then pointed out that 'the prospect that a qualified, un-enumerated right to housing may yet be found to be extant within and under our living and versatile Constitution must be a possibility'.[59]

Under the foundational Housing Act 1988, authorities were obliged to carry out regular assessments of existing and prospective housing requirements.[60] In doing so, authorities

---

50 *Doherty v South Dublin County Council (No. 2)* [2007] IEHC 4; [2007] 2 I.R. 696.
51 Ibid.; see *C v Galway County Council* [2017] IEHC 784 [17].
52 Kenna (n 15) 207.
53 Irish Human Rights and Equality Act 2014, s 42.
54 TSA/Simon Communities/CPA (n 49) 5.
55 Kenna (n 15) 207. The decision in *Meadows v Minister for Justice, Equality and Law Reform* [2010] 2 IR 701 may require local authorities to explain the reasons for their decision where that decision affects constitutional or fundamental rights.
56 TSA/Simon Communities/CPA (n 49) 11.
57 [2017] IEHC 604 para 13.
58 Ibid.
59 Ibid. para 14.
60 Housing Act 1988, s 8.

were required to have regard to the extent to which there are persons who are homeless or living in temporary or moveable accommodation. This obligation was repealed and replaced by the Housing (Miscellaneous Provisions) Act 2009.[61] This Act codified the informal consultation arrangements set out in the various strategies as well as giving a legislative basis to homelessness action plans and their implementation.[62]

Finally, it is important to note that the Minister may give general policy directions in writing to a housing authority in relation to the performance of any of its functions under the Housing Acts. The housing authority must comply any such directions and have regard to any Ministerial guidelines when performing its housing functions.[63]

Powers of Housing Authorities

Housing authorities have long been provided with broad powers to fulfil their legal duties and take actions to address homelessness.[64] Under the Housing Act 1988 (as amended), authorities are empowered to make arrangements for the provision of accommodation to those who were determined to be homeless. While authorities have the power to provide housing directly to applicants, in reality, the primary action taken by authorities is to make payments to cover the costs of homelessness provision. It is a consequence of this approach that the provision of accommodation for homeless people has mainly been undertaken by voluntary and cooperative bodies, and latterly in hotels. Thus, where a request for accommodation is made to a housing authority by, or on behalf of, a homeless person, the authority may pay for temporary lodgings or accommodation for a specified period, and the authority may require the homeless person to pay charges.[65] The provision of such accommodation does not preclude the household from being included in any assessment of housing need leading to longer-term housing.[66]

2.3. Housing Obligations and the Traveller Community

The Independent Expert Review Traveller Accommodation (2019) addressed the key areas relating to Traveller accommodation and sought to identify the barriers to the full implementation of the Housing (Traveller Accommodation) Act 1998.[67] The Expert Group identified major problems and set out some 32 recommendations in relation to four key themes: delivery reflecting need, planning, capacity and resources, governance. Some of the issues which were highlighted include the current methods of assessing Travellers' accommodation needs, supporting Travellers living in the private rented sector, allocation of social housing to Travellers, the inadequate connection between the Housing (Traveller Accommodation) Act 1998 and the planning legislation. Consultations also

---

61 Housing (Miscellaneous Provisions) Act 2009, s 20.
62 Kenna (n 15) 273.
63 Housing (Miscellaneous Provisions) Act 2009, ss 3–4.
64 Housing Act 1988, s 13.
65 Ibid. s 10(2).
66 Ibid. s 10(9).
67 D. Joyce, C. Norton and M. Norris, *Independent Expert Review Traveller Accommodation* (The Housing Agency 2019) <www.paveepoint.ie/wp-content/uploads/2019/07/Expert-Review-Group-Traveller-Accommodation.pdf> (accessed 1 September 2023).

revealed to the Expert Group other legislation that impinges on the provision of Traveller accommodation, and the Group called for that to be reviewed, in particular, the Trespass legislation, the specific legislation for the removal of temporary dwellings as introduced in Section 10 of the Housing (Miscellaneous Provisions) Act 1992 and Section 69 of the Roads Act 1993.

2.4. Legal Challenges

There have been relatively few cases of judicial review of local authority actions under the general homelessness framework. Kenna explains that the lack of case law reflects the 'absence of homeless advocacy agencies in Ireland taking test cases to establish and clarify rights'.[68] Of course, the central role of voluntary and charitable bodies in the delivery of homeless services, and their associated dependence on state funding, may explain the limited appetite for adversarial strategic litigation approaches, but other factors also play a role.

The lack of cases may reflect the narrow and minimalist nature of the statutory obligations placed on housing authorities. Unlike the express obligation on local authorities in the UK to provide housing once a household qualifies for support, the extent of the obligation on authorities in Ireland is to carry our reviews or to prepare plans to address homelessness. The Courts have been reluctant to interpret this as a mandatory obligation to provide accommodation.[69] In the handful of cases where the Courts have directed authorities to take specific actions, they have been careful to stress the exceptional facts of the case and make clear that the decision is not of wider authority.[70]

At the same time, the powers provided to local authorities to make a determination that a person is homeless and also to address homelessness are drafted in broad terms, and they confer considerable discretion on authorities to administer their housing functions as they see fit. Arguably, the boundaries of rationality and reasonableness that may be set through judicial review challenges offer minimalist control on the exercise of such powers.[71] This is particularly apparent in the Supreme Court decision in *Fagan v Dublin City Council*.[72] In determining whether a household has a reasonable requirement to live together, the Supreme Court made clear that a housing authority may consider the relationship, the separation, the custody agreement, and so forth, but the decision must be based solely on the requirements of those persons.[73] While the Court set aside the decision at the eligibility stage on the basis that the authority had taken into account an irrelevant consideration, the Court made clear that the decision did not curtail the broad discretion of the authority at the subsequent allocation stage – where the authority could prioritize those households deemed to have the greatest need.

The deference of the Supreme Court to the housing management decision of the local authority at the allocation stage is consistent with the approach taken by lower courts to

---

68 Kenna (n 15) 804.
69 *Mulhare v Cork County Council* [2017] IEHC 288.
70 *O'Donnell v South Dublin County Council* [2015] IESC 28 at 68.
71 C. O'Connell, 'The Focus of Ireland: Homelessness in the Courts Fagan v Dublin City Council [2019] IESC 96' (2020) 19(1) *Hibernian Law Journal* 119.
72 *Fagan v Dublin City Council* [2019] IESC 96.
73 Ibid. at [33].

legal challenges to determinations that a person is not homeless.[74] In *Tee v Wicklow County Council*, the Court affirmed the housing authorities' determination that an applicant was not homeless because she had the option of living with her mother in Malaysia but had chosen to come to Ireland to further her daughter's education.[75] The Court made clear that it is the opinion of the housing authority which is key and that the Court's view as to what may or may not render a person homeless is entirely irrelevant.

This deference reflects a reluctance to intervene into what is regarded by the Court as a policy decision – an interpretation perhaps aided by the drafting of the legal framework, which, as noted earlier, confers broad powers and minimalist duties on authorities.[76] It also arguably reflects the dominance of conservative interpretations of the separation of powers doctrine.[77] The Court has repeatedly expressed a reluctance to review decisions that concern the allocation of scarce public housing. However, this interpretation of the social housing support regime is somewhat outdated. Traditional 'bricks and mortar' public housing is certainly in short supply, but as O'Connell points out, there is no similar budgetary cap on Housing Assistance Payment subsidy – which has become the central vehicle for addressing homelessness in Ireland.[78]

The position adopted by the Courts has contributed to the relatively low number of legal challenges to housing management decisions. Aside from dissuading potential challenges, the Court's reasoning makes it less likely that legal aid will be available for potential challenges. This is because legal aid is only available where an applicant satisfies both an eligibility and a merits test. The marked deference of the judiciary to housing management decisions made by housing authorities means it is less likely that applicants will pass the merits stage.[79] While it is a matter of debate what weight to accord to the various factors that have limited the number of judicial review cases, the result is that housing authority management decisions are subject to minimal constraints, and this has given rise to variable, discretionary interpretations of the law.[80] Lewis argues that, in practice, 'public expectations, government policy and the weight of international convention have combined to put an obligation on housing authorities to act and provide assistance for homeless persons'.[81] But this is not the same as a legal right to housing under Irish law, and appeals to Irish constitutional rights to underpin the application of this legislation have led to calls for a referendum on a right to housing (see following).

Traveller Accommodation

The legal provisions governing Traveller accommodation have been the subject of a number of legal challenges.[82] As with the general framework, the courts have been reluctant

---

74 *C v Galway County Council* [2017] IEHC 784 [17].
75 *Tee v Wicklow County Council* [2017] IEHC 194.
76 *Ward v Dublin South County Council* [1996] 3 IR 195.
77 See *T. D. v Minister for Education* [2001] 4 IR 259.
78 O'Connell (n 71).
79 *Tee v Wicklow County Council* [2017] IEHC 623. See O'Connell (n 71) 113.
80 Kenna (n 15) 208.
81 E. Lewis, *Social Housing Policy in Ireland – New Directions* (IPA 2019) 112–13.
82 See Browne (n 42).

to interpret these provisions as imposing a duty on authorities to provide caravan sites.[83] However, litigation has established that inactivity on the part of authorities will be a breach of duty.[84] Equally, the courts have made clear that a housing authority has a duty to perform its functions in a 'rational and reasonable manner'.[85] The use of residency or 'indigenous' requirements for Travellers to qualify for local authority permanent halting site accommodation was considered in *McDonagh v Clare County Council*.[86] The court determined that three-year residency requirement was lawful but outlined that it must not be applied so rigidly that it becomes an effective bar to any considerations of an application for assistance of a deserving non-indigenous application.[87] Summarizing the mixed results of judicial challenges to the legal regime governing Traveller housing, Padraic Kenna notes the 'long struggle in the courts for adequate accommodation for Travellers' has met with limited success.[88]

One significant development is *Clare CC v Bernard and Helen McDonagh and IHREC*,[89] where the Supreme Court held that Traveller caravans and mobile homes could be treated as 'dwellings' for the purposes of constitutional inviolability protection of Article 40.5 of the Irish constitution,[90] in addition to any ECHR rights to respect for home. This decision integrated the jurisprudence of the Article 8 ECHR in *Winterstein*[91] and *Yordanova*[92] by providing for a proportionality assessment in such situations where the Travellers were being evicted from local authority land, where that local authority had not provided adequate housing for those Travellers under the relevant legislation.

3. Homelessness Preventative Practices in Ireland

In the last decade, there has been very considerable expenditure on services for people experiencing homelessness, and a number of innovative homelessness preventative practices have been introduced. These include the Housing Assistance Payment scheme, Family Hubs, Housing First initiatives, and Tenancy Support Schemes. Although these measures have achieved some relative successes, on the whole, these measures have failed to adequately respond to the scale of the crisis in Ireland, and the number of households in emergency accommodation increased by over 150% between 2014 and 2019.[93]

3.1. Housing Assistance Payment

Since the 1980s, there has been a persistent decline in local authority social housing output. This is part of a long-term trend, as successive Irish Governments have sought to transition

---

83 *O'Reilly and Others v Limerick Corporation* [1989] ILRM 182.
84 *Ward v Dublin South County Council* [1996] 3 IR 195 at 203.
85 *County Meath VEC v Joyce* [1994] 2 ILRM 210.
86 *McDonagh v Clare County Council* [2002] 2 IR 634.
87 Ibid.
88 Kenna (n 15) 817.
89 [2022] IESC 2.
90 This states that 'The dwelling of every citizen is inviolable and shall not be forcibly entered save in accordance with law'.
91 *Winterstein and Others v France*, Application No. 27013/07, Judgment 17 October 2013.
92 *Yordanova v. Bulgaria* [2013] ECHR 1768.
93 O'Sullivan (n 12) 95.

social housing policy away from a brick-and-mortar approach to a rent subsidy–based approach.[94] Central to this change has been the introduction of demand-side subsidies by local authorities, namely, Rent Supplement (RS), the Rental Accommodation Scheme (RAS), and the Housing Assistance Payment (HAP). Under current Government policy, both RS and RAS will be fully replaced by HAP in the coming years, and therefore, this section will focus on HAP.[95]

The main feature of HAP is that households source their own accommodation in the private rented sector at a market rent. Although the tenancy is between the tenant and the private landlord, the local authority pays the market rent to the landlord directly, while the tenant pays a differential rent to the local authority, which is based on household income. In general, the rent must be within the allowed HAP rent limits, which vary according to household size and the relevant area. Local authorities have discretion to increase these area HAP limits by 35% on a case-by-case basis and up to 50% in the Dublin region, where there is a risk of homelessness.[96] A major problem is the lack of availability of rented homes within the HAP rent limits, and regular surveys by the Simon Community demonstrate this problem, with very few dwellings available to rent nationally in December 2022 within the HAP rent limits.[97] A 2019 Focus Ireland survey found that 61% of families trying to exit homelessness had applied to over 20 vacancies through HAP, illustrating the difficulties in accessing suitable HAP housing.[98]

Under the Housing Act (Miscellaneous Provisions) 2009, HAP is designated as a long-term social housing support; the recipients of HAP are deemed to have their housing needs met and are removed from the housing waiting list. One of the problems with the HAP model is that it is dependent on the commitment of private landlords, who enjoy wide powers to end a tenancy. Furthermore, the HAP model is dependent on market rent system at the centre of the private rental market. In recent years, Ireland has had some of the most expensive rents in Europe.[99] Spiralling rents have frequently outstripped uprating on HAP rent limits, leaving tenants to cover the shortfall or face eviction.

3.2. Family Hubs

Family Hubs are first-response facilities for families who find themselves homeless and have no alternatives other than private hotels. The Hubs claim to provide play spaces, cooking and laundry facilities, and recreational spaces. The Hubs were originally established as a

---

94 Ibid. 77–79.
95 Ibid. 78.
96 P. Kilkenny, *Trends Analysis: Housing Assistance Payment (2014–2019)* (Department of Public Expenditure and Reform 2019).
97 Simon Communities of Ireland, *Locked Out of the Market* (Simon Communities of Ireland 2022) <www.simon.ie/wp-content/uploads/2023/01/Locked-Out-of-the-Market-December-2022-1.pdf> (accessed 1 September 2023).
98 A. E. Long and others, 'Family Homelessness in Dublin: Causes, Housing Histories, and Finding a Home' (2019) Focus Ireland, Research Briefing No. 1 <www.focusireland.ie/wp-content/uploads/2021/09/Research-Briefing-No-1-Interactive.pdf (accessed 1 September 2023).
99 Ibid. 78.

provisional attempt to reduce the 'hotelization' of family life by moving families out of hotels, B&Bs, and emergency accommodation.[100]

A report in 2017 questioned the quality of life lived in Hubs and their usefulness as *temporary* emergency accommodation.[101] A recent statement by the Committee on Housing, Planning, Community, and Local Government has revealed that Family Hubs 'restrict the capacity'[102] to lead normal and fulfilling lives and have devasting and lasting effects on family life and the well-being of both adults and children.[103] The risk of Family Hubs is the danger that they will become a lasting feature of emergency accommodation options.[104]

Another issue with Hubs is whether they are becoming a quick remedy in the circuitous housing allocation process, with many families forced to exceed the proposed three-month sojourn in these facilities. This occurs due to little or no support from housing services, rental support services, and local government. Hearne and Murphy have outlined issues faced by families in Hubs who are all competing for homes in the private rental sector.[105] Furthermore, procuring adequate HAP funding is yet another barrier for those in Hubs. To avail of HAP, families must source their own accommodation in the private rented sector and then make a HAP tenancy agreement with the landlord. However, wherein the tenancy agreement is not renewed, the local authority will continue to offer HAP funding, but the onus is on the tenant to find new accommodation – which is almost impossible today.[106] In 2019, the number of households receiving HAP had risen to 57,630[107] in comparison to 16,000 HAP recipients in 2016.[108] This reliance on HAP begs the question of suitability long-term; is HAP appropriate as the primary means of securing a home, given a history of the rented sector's inability to provide security of tenure to long-term renters in Ireland?

3.3. Housing First Initiatives[109]

In Ireland, the Dublin Housing First Demonstration Project, which ran for three years from 2011 to 2014, was a collaboration between State and voluntary agencies comprising the Dublin Region Homeless Executive (on behalf of the four Dublin local authorities), Health Service Executive (HSE), Focus Ireland, Peter McVerry Trust, Dublin Simon Community, and Stepping Stone. The project targeted 30 long-term rough sleepers. An independent evaluation (Greenwood, 2015) of the project found that Housing First clients achieved

---

100 J. Power, 'Family Hubs Are "Normalising" Homelessness-Human Rights Commission Says Three Month Limit Needed' *The Irish Times* (12 July 2017).
101 R. Hearne and M. Murphy, *Investing in the Right to a Home: Housing, HAPs and Hubs* (U of Maynooth P 2017) 6.
102 Ibid.
103 Ibid. 6.
104 Ibid. 32–33.
105 Ibid. 2.
106 <www.hap.ie/tenants/landlordandtenancy/> (accessed 1 September 2023).
107 Social Housing in Ireland 2019 – Analysis of Housing Assistance Payment (HAP) Scheme (Press Statement Social Housing in Ireland – Analysis of HAP 2019 – CSO – Central Statistics Office 2020) <www.cso.ie/en/csolatestnews/pressreleases/2020pressreleases/pressstatementsocialhousinginireland-analysisofhap2019/> (accessed 1 September 2023).
108 Hearne and Murphy (n 101) 12.
109 Government of Ireland (n 25) 50–51.

considerably greater levels of housing stability than a comparison group of service 17 users in pre-existing homeless services. Around 80–85% of tenancies were sustained among a more vulnerable group with higher support needs, compared with 50% tenancy sustainment outcomes for those accessing 'staircase' or 'continuum of care' models.[110] Following the success of the Dublin Housing First initiative, the Government launched the *National Housing First Implementation Plan 2018–2020*. This plan is directed at rough sleepers and those in emergency accommodation on a long-term basis with high support needs. It proposed to create 663 tenancies over the three-year period of the plan. The small scale of this scheme means it 'will not disrupt the flow of households into homelessness during the period of the plan' and will only 'moderate, rather than reduce', the numbers in emergency accommodation for more than six months.[111]

3.4. Tenancy Support Schemes

Threshold, a charitable agency, developed the Interim Tenancy Sustainment Protocol (ITSP) in 2014, which assists those at immediate risk of becoming homeless. Operating through the ITSP, Threshold has the means to facilitate access to increased rent supplement payments for families who have become at risk of homelessness due to a sizeable rent increase.[112] The ITSP remains with clients for the duration of the entire ITSP protocol process, providing support services for families. Between 2014 and 2019, the ITSP supported 6,339 households, including 9,707 adults and 10,622 children.[113] Though many tenants have transferred to HAP subsidiary payments, ITSP rental funding exceeds the HAP cap and its 20% discretionary payments.[114]

4. Conclusions: The Future of Homelessness law and Policy in Ireland

4.1. Defining Homelessness

In Irish housing policy, *homelessness* has tended to be equated with rough sleeping and numbers in emergency accommodation and has differentiated between homelessness and housing need. This narrow definition fails to capture the extent of hidden homelessness in Ireland and arguably obscures the scale of the homelessness crisis as well as the factors driving the crisis. It is arguable that the open textured legal definition of *homelessness* as set out in the Housing Act 1988 facilitates the adoption of a narrow conception of homelessness that is central to housing policy. As noted earlier, in practice, the definition also makes the individual housing officer's opinion central to the determination of whether a person is or is not regarded as homeless. Given the risk of discrimination and the tensions between performing this duty and the equality and human rights obligations on local authorities, it

---

110 *Peter McVerry Trust Annual Report* (2020) 11 <https://pmvtrust.ie/wp-content/uploads/2021/05/Peter-McVerryTrust-Annual-Report-2020-Online.pdf> (accessed 1 September 2023).
111 O'Sullivan (n 12) 85–86.
112 'Threshold Pre-Budget Submission to the Department of Employment Affairs and Social Protection' (2021) 5 <www.ageaction.ie/sites/default/files/_age_action_final_deasp_budget_2021.pdf (accessed 1 September 2023).
113 Ibid. 5.
114 Ibid.

is striking that there have been few successful judicial review cases of local authority determinations in this area, although, given the growing debate in Ireland about expanding the role of housing rights in Irish housing law and policy, this may well change in the future.

A recent report on tackling homelessness in Ireland[115] made some valuable recommendations on addressing homelessness in Ireland. Its first observation was that the definition of *homelessness* matters quite a lot.

> Homelessness does not exist in fixed forms and is characterised by flows from one 'population' of people to others. . . . [H]omelessness does not equate to the people living in emergency accommodation, both because households can transition in and out of emergency accommodation, but also because this population intersects with people experiencing hidden homelessness (notably, women). The most effective homelessness strategies in Europe use a wide definition of homelessness. A wider definition encompasses both specific populations that a country wishes to reduce i.e. people experiencing recurrent and sustained homelessness associated with multiple and complex needs, people in emergency/temporary accommodation and people living rough, and the other forms of homelessness that *intersect* with and are also among the *sources* of people sleeping rough or living in emergency/temporary accommodation.[116]

The report also pointed out that prevention cannot be effective in isolation – preventative services need to be able to triage effectively and to be able to offer integrated packages of support where needed. In practice, a preventative service should be able to refer someone with multiple and complex needs, at high risk of homelessness, directly to Housing First or a similar service as a preventative measure, not in the sense of stopping homelessness from recurring, but instead stopping it from happening in the first instance.[117] Homeless services and Housing First and the other responses to the personal and household crisis that is homelessness take place after the event such as eviction has occurred. The housing system should be organized to ensure an adequate supply of suitable and affordable housing, that is, social housing tends to offer better standards, more affordability, and better security of tenure. The report also highlighted the importance of the gender dynamics of homelessness. Women do not have the same trajectories through homelessness as men, domestic abuse is much more likely to be a cause of women's homelessness, and women also appear more likely to rely on friends, family, and acquaintances, experiencing hidden homelessness at higher rates. This also applies to family homelessness, which is disproportionately experienced by lone women parents both domestically and internationally, where both a tendency to rely on informal options and an association with domestic abuse are again present.[118]

---

115 Baptista and others (n 1).
116 Ibid. 92.
117 Ibid. 93.
118 R. Grotti and others, *Discrimination and Inequality in Housing in Ireland* (IHREC 2018) <www.ihrec.ie/app/uploads/2022/08/Discrimination-and-Inequality-in-Housing-in-Ireland.pdf> (accessed 1 September 2023).

4.2. Constitutional Issues and Homelessness

There is a healthy debate in Ireland on homelessness as a violation of human and housing rights. Ireland has ratified the International Covenant on Economic, Social, and Cultural Rights (ICESCR) (1966) in 1989, which obliges Ireland to respect, protect, and fulfil these rights. Ireland also ratified the European Social Charter (ESC) of the Council of Europe in 1964 and the Revised Charter in 1996, but not Article 31 on the right to housing. The reason given was that the provisions of the Constitution precluded this ratification.[119]

This resonates with the current moves on a referendum placing a specific right to housing in the Constitution.[120] As it stands at the moment, the only constitutional provisions which can be engaged are those based on a case in 1965 on 'unenumerated rights' to bodily integrity under Article 40.3.2.[121] This provides that '[t]he State guarantees in its laws to respect, and, as far as practicable, by its laws to defend and vindicate the personal rights of the citizen'. The Article has been invoked in many cases where homeless people were seeking to compel a local authority to carry out its obligations under housing legislation. Significant cases, such as *O'Reilly v Limerick Corporation*,[122] *O'Brien v Wicklow UDC*,[123] and *O'Donnell v South Dublin County Council*,[124] have all been decided on the principles of judicial deference and citing 'separation of powers' doctrines to preclude curial direction on housing allocations, prioritization, or even spending decisions. Many housing and homeless organizations are now pushing for a more substantive constitutional provision for housing, drawing on international housing rights.[125]

In conclusion, it is important to remember that addressing homelessness through legislation and court cases has limited effects. Even modern policy responses such as Housing First require dedicated, sufficient, and consistent resources. Prevention of homelessness requires actions at many levels and often requires significant 'upstream' intervention in people's housing pathways and in housing systems. In terms of ending homelessness, a recent international comparison summed up the challenges:

> One of the challenges presented by homelessness is that it is simultaneously extremely complex and very simple. It is simple to solve because all it needs is access to affordable housing and a recognition that people who are homeless are fellow human beings who need to be given choices, dignity and support that they need. It is complex because these do not turn out to be easy things for us to do.[126]

---

119 See European Committee of Social Rights (ESCR) *Fourth Report on Non-Accepted Provisions of the European Social Charter – Ireland* (ESCR 2021) 6.
120 The current Government has established a Housing Commission. See <www.gov.ie/en/campaigns/2ae5e-the-housing-commission/> (accessed 1 September 2023).
121 G. Whyte, *Social Inclusion and the Legal System: Public Interest Law in Ireland* (2nd edn, IPA 2015).
122 *O'Reilly v Limerick Corporation* [1989] ILRM 181 at 194.
123 *O'Brien v Wicklow UDC*, ex tempore (10 June 1994) High Court.
124 [2015] IESC 28.
125 See <www.homeforgood.ie/who-we-are/> (accessed 1 September 2023).
126 M. Allen and others, *Ending Homelessness? The Contrasting Experiences of Denmark, Finland and Ireland* (Policy Press 2020) 176.

3

CATEGORIZATION, SELECTION, DISPLACEMENT, AND INVISIBILIZATION

Housing and Accommodation for the Homeless in France

Pascale Dietrich-Ragon and Marie Loison

Introduction

Housing problems in large French cities have escalated since the 1990s. The homeless population increased by 50% between 2001 and 2012,[1] reflecting the growing difficulties of this vulnerable part of the population in finding housing. When people no longer have access to housing (because they have been evicted, can no longer pay their rent, etc.), they can call the 115 telephone number[2] to report their difficulties and receive temporary accommodation. However, institutional care is complicated by the saturation of these services. Thus, more and more people depend on institutional housing, at a centre or a hotel, and, in extreme cases, become roofless, the latter state being defined as sleeping in places not designed for dwelling, such as the street or makeshift shelters. Yet access to decent housing is recognized as a social right in France and enshrined in the 10th and 11th paragraphs of the Preamble to the Constitution of 27 October 1946. This status was reasserted in the Quilliot Act of 22 June 1982 ('the right to housing is a fundamental right'), the Mermaz Act of 6 July 1989, the Besson Act of 31 May 1990, and the 1998 law on the fight against exclusion. Consistent with these developments, the 'DALO' Act on the enforceable right to housing, enacted on 5 March 2007, made the French state the guarantor of the right to housing for all individuals unable to access housing through their own means. However, the contrast between this legal progress and its actual application is striking, and the situation has deteriorated further in the last few years. Population categories previously protected from homelessness, notably people with jobs, are

---

1 F. Yaouancq and others, 'L'hébergement des sans-domicile en 2012. Des modes d'hébergement différents selon les situations familiales' (2013) 1455 *Insee Première*.
2 The 115 is an emergency telephone number (like the SAMU or the fire department) that helps homeless people. It is managed by associations and financed by the state. Its objective is to inform people about their rights and to direct them to assistance services, including available accommodation.

now beset by difficulties, while new representations of rooflessness are emerging in the media. News reports frequently contain images of slums populated by migrants and drug users, the frequent eviction of whom are not accompanied by long-term solutions. The trend in housing inequalities was accentuated by the Covid-19 crisis and the widespread lockdown,[3] which increased visibility of housing exclusion. In France today, four million individuals are poorly housed, that is, without housing or living in extremely difficult housing conditions.[4] Why has housing exclusion worsened to this extent in France? Who is affected? And what types of public policy are being introduced to address the issue, and with what sort of success?

We begin this chapter by reviewing the population in France impacted by housing exclusion, before going on to assess the laws and mechanisms implemented to address the problem. Lastly, we look at the issues posed by the current system, which is based on 'sorting' the homeless and underpinned by a segmented approach in which different assistance sectors are firmly separated. Despite innovative initiatives and the desire to promote Housing First, the worsening of precariousness, the piling up of services, the lack of coordination between the actors involved, and the saturation of accommodation facilities do not augur well for an improvement to homelessness provision in France.

The Many Faces of Homelessness in France

The widely used French term 'SDF' (short for *'sans domicile fixe'*, which translates literally as 'without a fixed home') comprises a broad array of individuals and trajectories. Homeless people today no longer correspond to the traditional image of the 'vagrant' as a single jobless White man living on the margins of society.[5] The population of homeless people is expanding to include new categories of individuals with housing problems, notably young people, women, and migrants.

Definitions and Overview of Housing Exclusion in France

The French use the term 'SDF' to refer to people begging on the street and/or with a deteriorated physical appearance (dirty, smelly, tattered clothes, etc.), reflecting their social and economic vulnerability. But these individuals are not always roofless, while some people lacking this physical stigma are. The word 'homeless' is more adapted to referring to people without housing. But the homeless form a heterogenous and shifting population. Their problems range across a continuum of situations relating to housing, including living on the street, in unsanitary squats, in shelters, hotels, cabins, and cars. Not all these people sleep outside; they occupy other venues not designed for dwelling or are admitted to accommodation centres for varying periods of time. Neither is being homeless an immutable experience. The housing situations of these people vary over time, and institutional assistance sometimes requires them to alternate housing solutions, for example, spending a night with

---

3 A. Lambert and J. Cayouette-Remblière (eds), *L'explosion des inégalités: Classes, genre et générations face à la crise sanitaire, Monde en cours* (Éditions de l'Aube 2021).
4 Fondation Abbé Pierre, 'L'état du mal-logement en France. Rapport annuel n°27' (2022) <https://www.fondation-abbe-pierre.fr/actualites/27e-rapport-sur-letat-du-mal-logement-en-france-2022>.
5 P. Gaboriau, *Clochard* (Julliard 1993).

a friend, followed by two nights in emergency accommodation and one night at a hotel, and so on.

There is no consensus in France on how to define and refer to these individuals, including among researchers. Our analysis in this chapter is based on the definition of the French National Institute of Statistics and Economic Studies (INSEE), whereby a person is considered as being homeless where they use an accommodation service or sleep in a place not designed as a dwelling (for example, a public space, basement, or car park). Only in the latter case is a person qualified as roofless.[6] Consequently, in French, a roofless person (*sans-abri*) is homeless (*sans domicile*), but a homeless person is not necessarily roofless. The word used for all the people lacking a roof is 'rooflessness' (*sans-abrisme*), and the word used for people without housing is 'homelessness' (*sans-domicilisme*)[7] (and thus including situations of rooflessness).[8]

According to the most recent national survey by INSEE in early 2012,[9] conducted in mainland France, 103,000 people had used a '*service d'hébergement*' (shelters, homeless hostel, temporary accommodation, transitional supported accommodation, migrant workers accommodation . . .) or meal distribution service at least once in the week that the survey was administered. Among homeless people, 10% were roofless, 35% stayed in accommodation for the homeless, 16% in hotel rooms, and 29% in housing provided by organizations or public bodies.[10] These figures will be updated via a 'homelessness' survey planned by INSEE for 2025.

According to Fondation Abbé Pierre, based on the collection of data and compilation of research led in France on inadequate housing, 1,068,000 people did not have personal housing in 2021.[11] Of the total, the number of homeless people was estimated at 300,000, living either in an accommodation centre, an initial accommodation centre for asylum seekers, a hotel, a makeshift shelter, or on the street. Drawing on several sources, Fondation Abbé Pierre also estimates that 25,000 people live in a hotel paid from their own resources, 643,000 are hosted by family or friends,[12] 208,000 live in a mobile dwelling in poor conditions,[13] and

---

6 In contrast to the European typology Ethos, according to which roofless people may have recourse to emergency accommodation.
7 M. Loison, 'Le sans-domicilisme. Réflexion sur les catégories de l'exclusion du logement' (2023) 1 *Revue française des affaires sociales* 29.
8 We make this clarification because in France, some researchers use the term *sans-abrisme* to refer to all homeless people, whereas we wish to use the term *sans-abrisme* to describe the situation of roofless people and the term *sans-domicilisme* to describe the situation of all homeless people, including the roofless.
9 The 'Homeless' survey of people having used accommodation and free meal services was conducted in 2012 by INSEE and INED. The survey covered people aged 18 or over living in towns of over 20,000 inhabitants and having at least once, during the survey period, used an accommodation or free meal service or having used an overnight shelter, including venues set up on an exceptional basis for extremely cold weather.
10 F. Yaouancq and M. Duée, 'Les sans-domicile en 2012: Une grande diversité de situations' *France, portrait social* (Institut national d'études démographiques, 2014).
11 INSEE 2013 National Housing Survey; INSEE and INED use the term 'people without personal housing' ('*personnes sans logement personnel*') for roofless people, homeless people, or people living in caravans, homes (young worker homes, social residences, etc.), care institutions, prisons, hotels (if the person pays for the room themselves), squats, or hosted by others.
12 INSEE 2013 National Housing Survey.
13 FNASAT, *Ancrages et besoins des habitants permanents de résidence mobile: Analyse nationale des politiques départementales* (Fédération nationale des associations solidaires d'action avec les Tsiganes et les

100,000 live in makeshift dwellings.[14] Most of the indicators show a deterioration in the situation in the last few years. The number of homeless people has doubled since 2012 and tripled since 2001, while that of people who are forced to live with family or friends increased by 19% between 2002 and 2013.

The living spaces of homeless people are extremely varied, and the profiles of the people concerned have changed considerably in recent years.

The Resurgence of the 'Homeless Question'

It has long been established that the homeless population comes from the lower social classes and is faced with extreme social and economic vulnerability, often combined with life course disruptions such as relationship breakdowns and unemployment.[15] But recently, new categories of individuals have joined the homeless population, which now includes more young people, more women, and more economically active individuals, often combined with a non-French background.[16]

We have identified four key aspects for understanding housing exclusion in France and the extension of the phenomenon to new populations. The first is growing housing inequality and the rising cost of living, especially in Paris. According to the *Observatoire des Loyers de l'Agglomération Parisienne*, a rent watchdog for the Paris area, average private sector rents rose by 55% in large cities between 2000 and 2013. This trend has had the greatest impact on the most vulnerable individuals. The wealthiest households[17] devote 10% of their budget to having one room per person, while the most modest households[18] devote 33% of their budget to the same.[19] Living conditions in France have polarized socially since the 2000s,[20] with extreme inequalities in terms of location, space, and the debt service ratio, roofless individuals forming the outer edge of the spectrum of housing inequalities.

The high cost of housing destabilizes individuals who, in other contexts, could house themselves. In French cities, part of the homeless population is excluded from housing even though the individuals in question work and are often in positions essential to the functioning of society, such as building, caretaking, security, cleaning, and personal care. The new image of the 'accommodated vulnerable worker'[21] is 'invalidated' by high property

---

gens du voyage 2017) <www.fnasat.asso.fr/FNASAT-Analysenationale-Ancrageetbesoinsenhabitat2017.pdf> (accessed 1 September 2023).

14 2017 population census. In France, the census is the responsibility of the state: INSEE organizes and controls it, and the municipalities prepare and carry out the collection.

15 C. Brousse, J. Firdion and M. Marpsat, *Les sans-domicile* (La Découverte 2008).

16 P. Dietrich-Ragon, 'Aux portes de la société française: Les personnes privées de logement issues de l'immigration' (2017) 72(1) *Population* 7.

17 Households composed as a majority by people with higher-level occupations, that is, a person with a higher-level occupation living with another person with a higher-level occupation, or a person with a higher-level occupation living with a person with an intermediary occupation.

18 Couples of economically active individuals or economically active individuals without a partner.

19 F. Bugeja-Bloch, A. Lambert and A. Noûs, 'Les conditions de logement en France: Une approche multidimensionnelle des inégalités de logement selon les classes sociales' (2021) 141(4) *Revue des politiques sociales et familiales* 91.

20 J. Driant and M. Lelièvre, *Mal-logement, mal-logés: Rapport 2017–2018 de l'ONPES* (ONPES 2018).

21 P. Dietrich-Ragon and D. Remillon, 'Users of Homelessness Support Services in France in 2001 and 2012: Contrasting Housing and Employment Trajectories' (2022) 77(2) *Population* 77, 291.

market prices and discrimination on the part of private landlords selecting tenants based on financial resources, job stability, family support, and the colour of their skin.[22] Social housing could offer a solution, but the shortage is especially chronic in large French cities, Paris in particular, and waiting lists continue to grow. Social housing demand has increased by 20% since 2013, more than the growth rate of the French population (+2.8% over the same period) and the number of households (+4% between 2013 and 2018) (as reported by L'Union Sociale pour L'Habitat (USH) in 2021). On 31 December 2020, according to USH, social housing requests in France totalled 2.2 million. Without other alternatives, people turn to 'slumlords' (less selective but renting uncomfortable, unsanitary, and cramped housing units) and accommodation centres and makeshift dwellings.

The second aspect characterizing the trend in housing exclusion in France is migration. Fleeing their country for economic, political (conflict), climate, or family (violence) reasons, migrants arriving in the host country often find refuge in camps and squats[23] or unsanitary housing.[24] After the Second World War, slums in France were home to migrant populations unable to find housing elsewhere. Through considerable investment in housing, this situation was curbed starting in the 1970s. But in the last ten years, migrant camps have increased in many French cities. The number of foreigners in the homeless population rose from 38% to 53% between 2001 and 2012 and is nine times higher than in the population of mainland France.[25] Accommodation assistance for migrants is saturated, and migrants are forced to fall back on assistance structures for the roofless or marginal solutions such as makeshift dwellings. Their housing trajectories differ sharply from those of homeless people born in France. Residential downgrading is frequent among the latter (many of them having previously rented a home), as are addiction, health, and delinquency problems, but the housing exclusion of migrants more often results from administrative difficulties encountered when arriving in France (undocumented status) and problems speaking and reading French that hinder their professional integration and access to rights and housing.[26]

The third factor is the growing proportion of women, alone or with children, in the homeless population. Their number increased by 45% from 17,153 in 2001 to 24,932 in 2012, while the share of men increased by 26% in the same period (from 29,775 to 37,670). Since the mid-2010s, organizations have been concerned by the increase in the number of women, some of them with children,[27] living on the street. The National Federation of Social Assistance and Integration Organizations, FNARS,[28] decries 'a serious shortage of solutions for accommodating, rehousing and protecting these particularly vulnerable people'.[29] According

---

22 F. Bonnet and others, 'À la recherche du locataire "idéal": Du droit aux pratiques en région parisienne' (2011) 9(1) *Regards croisés sur l'économie* 216.
23 F. Bouillon, *Les mondes du squat. Anthropologie d'un habitat précaire* (PUF Partage du savoir 2009) 244.
24 P. Dietrich-Ragon, *Le logement intolérable: Habitants et pouvoirs publics face à l'insalubrité* (1st edn, Presses Universitaires de France 2011).
25 Yaouancq and others (n 1).
26 Dietrich-Ragon (n 16).
27 Numerous organizations and public policies, as well as researchers, talk about 'families' on the street when most of the time they are referring to single-parent families composed of a mother and her children. This serves to obscure the issue of homeless women.
28 Now called *Fédération des acteurs de la solidarité* (FAS).
29 <www.leparisien.fr/laparisienne/actualites/precarite-les-jeunes-femmes-seules-plus-nombreuses-a-se-retrouver-a-la-rue-02-05-2016-5760861.php> (accessed 1 September 2023).

to the *Une nuit donnée* ('on a given night') survey[30] administered in 2017 and 2018, socially isolated individuals account for the majority of people admitted to winter shelters (64%) and men form the majority (52%), but the proportion of women has increased since 2015 (from 35% in 2015 to 37% in 2016, 39% in 2017, and 48% in 2018).[31]

Focus 1: The Number of Homeless Women on the Rise

The presence of women among the homeless population was relatively hidden and under-explored until recently and little considered compared with that of homeless men. Homeless women have even been referred to as an 'invisible' population, as in the film *Les Invisibles* by Louis-Julien Petit released in 2019. This invisibility can be seen first and foremost in research work on homelessness, which, for many years in France, was largely focused on men.[32] Furthermore, while numerous women have experienced situations of vulnerability, proportionally speaking, fewer women than men have experienced homelessness. Women accounted for 52% of the French population on 1 January 2012,[33] while homeless women accounted for 38% of homeless people according to a survey carried out in 2012. Few were strictly roofless – just 1% of homeless women interviewed compared with 14% of homeless men. While the share of women among roofless people appears to have increased in the last few years (12% according to the *Nuits de la Solidarité* initiative to quantify the number of homeless people in Paris), they remain proportionally less visible than men in the public realm. The process of 'disaffiliation'[34] appears to lead them less often than men to the most extreme examples of stigma and exclusion. More exposed to gender-related violence, women are slightly better protected than men because society sees them as more vulnerable, which safeguards them in part from the most severe forms of exclusion.[35]

The fourth characteristic of the trend in the homeless population is age. Homeless individuals aged 18–25 are subject to a combination of family, financial, and educational difficulties and often come under institutional care at a very young age. When they become adults, a few temporary solutions exist,[36] provided by institutions such as *Garantie Jeunes*,

---

30 Organized by DRIHL and FAS Île-de-France, the survey was administered on the night of 22–23 February 2018, the objective being to 'better understand the profile of people calling on winter assistance solutions, particularly those calling on accommodation solutions in winter only' DRIHL, 'Les personnes accueillies dans le dispositif hivernal en Île-de-France. Résultats de l'enquête 2018 "une nuit donnée" dans les structures de renfort hivernal' *Lettre des études* (2019) 1 <www.drihl.ile-de-france.developpement-durable.gouv.fr/les-personnes-accueillies-dans-le-dispositif-a813.html> (accessed 1 September 2023).
31 DRIHL, *Les personnes accueillies dans le dispositif hivernal en Île-de-France: Résultats de l'enquête 2018 'une nuit donnée' dans les structures de renfort hivernal* (DRIHL 2019).
32 M. Loison, 'Des femmes sans domicile invisibles ? Repenser le sans-domicilisme au prisme du genre (2023) Mémoire pour l'habilitation à diriger les recherches, Conservatoire National des Arts et Métiers 2023.
33 INSEE, population estimates, France excl. Mayotte.
34 R. Castel, *Les métamorphoses de la question sociale: Chronique du salariat* (Fayard 1995); R. Castel, 'Les pièges de l'exclusion' (1995) 34 *Lien social et politiques* 13.
35 M. Loison-Leruste and G. Perrier, 'Les trajectoires des femmes sans domicile à travers le prisme du genre: Entre vulnérabilité et protection' (2019) 43(1) *Déviance et Société* 77.
36 A. Dequiré and E. Jovelin, 'Les jeunes sans domicile fixe face aux dispositifs d'accompagnement' (2012) 169(1) *Informations sociales* 126.

which works to provide young people with a monetary allowance and social support for a few months.[37] But these solutions fail to offset the exclusion of young people from social aid, as active solidarity income (RSA) is not awarded until the age of 25. This exposes young individuals with no family support to housing exclusion, particularly those exiting the child welfare system. In 2012, 23% of the people having used assistance services for the homeless in Paris said they had been in care as a child, compared with just 2% to 3% of the general population.[38]

At the other end of the life course, the elderly are also affected by homelessness. Homeless people aged over 50 are subject to increased isolation, a greater proportion of them having lost contact with their family and friends and being unemployed, retired, or in situations of disability as compared to younger people.[39] For this population, the use of accommodation or free meal services, which embody the institutional, social response at the local level, seeks to ensure that elderly homeless retain a connection with society.

The explanatory puzzle and sense-making of housing-related exclusion in France, as in many other countries, thus lies in understanding the inter-relationship between issues of housing, work, migration and social policies, and social and family relations. So what kind of public policies are being implemented to address these situations, by whom, and to what effect?

Public Policies on Homelessness: A Hierarchical, Segmented, and Competitive System

Given the increase in the number of homeless people, accommodation for the homeless accounts for a growing share of the social housing sector in France. A total of 140,400 accommodation places is offered in France to adults and families in difficulty, up 39% since end of 2012. The increase is even sharper for initial accommodation centres for asylum seekers, up 63%.[40] In 2017, 260,000 people were accommodated in emergency housing at an accommodation centre, some 17,000 more than in early 2009.[41] In addition, in response to the new faces of exclusion described earlier in this chapter, public authorities have sought to reform systems and support work to adapt to the diverse range of administrative circumstances, socio-demographic characteristics, and difficulties encountered by homeless people.[42] Today, the assistance sector, largely represented by non-governmental organiza-

---

[37] J. Couronné, M. Loison-Leruste and F. Sarfati, *La Garantie jeunes en action – Usages du dispositif et parcours de jeunes – Rapports publics – La Documentation française* (Centre d'études de l'emploi 2016).

[38] M. Marpsat and I. Frechon, 'Placement dans l'enfance et précarité de la situation de logement' (2016) 488–89 *Economie et Statistique* 37.

[39] M. Loison-Leruste, M. Arnaud and B. Roullin, 'Les personnes de 50 ans ou plus utilisant des services d'hébergement et de distribution de repas pour sans-domicile': Rapport pour l'Observatoire National de la Pauvreté et de l'Exclusion Sociale (Equipe de recherche sur les inégalités sociales, Centre Maurice Halbwachs, 2015); M. Marpsat, 'Les plus de 50 ans utilisateurs des lieux de distribution de repas chauds ou des centres d'hébergement pour sans-domicile' (2002) 25(102) *Gérontologie et société* 167.

[40] E. Pliquet, 'Hébergement des personnes en difficulté sociale: 140 000 places fin 2016, en forte évolution par rapport à 2012' (2019) 1102 *Études et résultats (Drees)*.

[41] P. Cabannes and M. Emorine, 'Hébergement d'urgence permanent: Au cours des années 2010, davantage de familles et des séjours rallongés – Résultats des enquêtes auprès des établissements et services pour adultes et familles en difficulté sociale (ES-DS) 2008, 2012 et 2016' (2021) 1184 *Études et résultats (Drees)*.

[42] V. Schlegel, 'Héberger ou accompagner les personnes sans domicile ? Une prise en charge segmentée et une professionnalisation en trompe-l'oeil' (2022) 179 *Connaissance de l'emploi*.

tions (NGOs), provides inconsistent and highly variable living conditions to recipients of accommodation owing to its hierarchical and segmented nature.

A Growing Sector Driven by Organizations and the State

The history of assistance for vagabonds and beggars has always oscillated between 'the mercy and the gallows'.[43] Until the 19th century, despite the aid provided to the 'good' poor by philanthropists and humanists, this population was significantly repressed and controlled. Hospitality and aid developed with the gradual introduction of an assistance system composed of state-run institutions and philanthropic institutions. NGOs, which worked for a large part of the 20th century to build a 'defence of the poor' in France,[44] developed gradually. While assistance for homeless people in France continues to fall within the competency of the state, the latter now delegates many of its responsibilities to NGOs, most of them charities and not-for-profits, which play a part in devising and implementing public policies.

The financing methods and origins of the sector have changed considerably. While tax incentives fostering philanthropy have led to privatization of much of the support offered to the homeless, the decentralization process afoot since 1982[45] has reduced the contribution of the state with local authorities (French departments and regions) having become the main funders of NGOs. But these organizations often lack the necessary resources depending on the specific region or territory. Public subsidies have fallen steadily since the end of the 1980s, while calls for projects and orders from public institutions, based on competition between NGOs, have steadily increased, transforming the relationship between NGOs and public authorities and serving to commodify NGOs. The development of this contractual financing has favoured large organizations who have greater human resources available to them respond to calls for tender.[46] Some of these entities have become veritable 'corporate organizations'[47] posting 'dizzying economic growth'.[48]

The activities of organizations have developed considerably and become institutionalized, forming what Julien Damon refers to as a 'bureaucratic-assistance complex operating primarily as part of a philosophical, technical, and financial register of solidarity and delivering assistance services'.[49] The extensively hierarchical and segmented nature of this system impacts the assistance available to homeless individuals.

---

43 B. Geremek, 'La Potence ou la pitié: L'Europe et les pauvres du Moyen Âge à nos jours' in J. Arnold-Moricet (tr), *Bibliothèque des Histoires* (Gallimard 1987).
44 F. Viguier, *La cause des pauvres en France*, *Domaine histoire* (SciencesPo les Presses 2020).
45 The 'Defferre' Act of 2 March 1982 on the rights and freedoms of municipalities, departments, and regions transforms the regions into full-function territorial authorities by shifting the supervision of the state onto the regions via ex post verification by an administrative judge.
46 S. Cottin-Marx, *Sociologie du Monde associatif* (La Découverte 2019).
47 M. Hély, *Les métamorphoses du monde associatif*, *Le Lien social* (Presses Universitaires de France 2009).
48 Charity organizations such as Emmaüs France today encompass 288 groups and employ over 5,500 people. French organizations and institutions managing numerous assistance systems and having posted exponential growth include *Aurore*, the Salvation Army, *les Restos du Cœur*, *le Secours Catholique*, *le Groupe SOS*, and *le Samu Social*.
49 J. Damon, *La question SDF. Critique d'une action publique*, *Le lien social* (Presses universitaires de France 2002) 177.

Hierarchy, Segmentation, and Repressive Policies

The conditions provided by assistance, accommodation, and integration systems vary considerably across the country. Initially, roofless people are referred to the 'veille sociale' services[50] (115 emergency shelter telephone number, *maraudes*[51]) and then onwards towards unconditional low-threshold aid on the lowest step of the accommodation staircase. Overnight shelters, day centres, emergency accommodation centres in collective units, or nightly hotel stays offer limited advantages in terms of the duration of accommodation (no more than a few nights), social support, and comfort (collective rooms and/or bathrooms, hard to appropriate the spaces, restrictive or impossible to remain at the centre in the day, etc.).

Slightly further up the ladder are longer 'stabilization' stays at accommodation and stabilization centres or social reintegration centres and at certain hotels. Topping the ladder, prior to social housing and private homes, are social residences (created in 1994), boarding houses (*pensions de famille*, created in 1997 and transformed into 'transition houses' (*maisons relais*) in 2002), and housing included in rental intermediation systems. The functioning of this system can be compared to that of a 'staircase of transition' to be climbed,[52] access to housing necessarily being preceded by an experience of emergency accommodation and stabilization and integration stays.

At each level of the staircase are systems intended for 'specific' categories of people with needs considered as 'special'. Accommodation centres and temporary shelter structures specialize in accommodation for isolated women, drug users, families, young people, and people with dogs, adapting the assistance provided to the type of population (on-site physicians, addictologists, psychiatrists, social workers). Subdivisions and other specialized systems have also been gradually created, including centres for lone pregnant women and the national system of accommodation for asylum seekers and refugees, composed of various structures that offer emergency accommodation to people with administrative statuses that prevent them from accessing mainstream accommodation. The divisions between the categories of, for example, homeless people, migrants,[53] and people of Roma origin,[54] generate segmentation in the fields of social intervention and public policies even though many of these populations experience the same economic and social difficulties.

---

50 'Veille sociale' services are responsible for directing homeless people or people in distress; they make an initial assessment of their medical, psychological, and social situation and direct them to structures or services adapted to their needs.

51 'Maraudes' are mobile teams of social workers and/or volunteers and/or medical or psychiatric professionals (nurses, psychologists) who travel throughout a given area and meet homeless people to delete and/or provide them with blankets, food, and other assistance. They form part of the social watch and emergency reception system.

52 I. Sahlin, 'The Staircase of Transition: Survival Through Failure' (2005) 18(2) *Innovation, European Journal of Social Research* 115.

53 E. Duvivier, 'Quand ils sont devenus visibles . . . Essai de mise en perspective des logiques de construction de la catégorie de "mineur étranger isolé"' (2009) 21(2) *Pensée plurielle* 65.

54 L. Bourgois, 'Urgence sociale et catégorisation des publics: Les "roms migrants" sont-ils des "sans-abri" comme les autres?' (2019) 71(1) *Rhizome* 42; M. Lièvre, 'Roms roumanisés, Ciurari, Ursari: Ethnicité et appartenances sociales. Ethnographie des migrants roms roumains à Montpellier' (2016) 32(1) *Revue européenne des migrations internationales* 35.

In parallel to the policies on providing people with shelter, the public authorities in France often initiate repressive action against categories of roofless people refusing assistance. This population is driven out of their homes and asked to accept offers of accommodation even if they are unsatisfactory. This situation has been observed in camps located along the Paris ring road,[55] in makeshift shelters in the *Bois de Vincennes* in Paris,[56] slums, and encampments. The repeated demolition of shanty towns and makeshift shelters reflects the determination to keep poverty under wraps and leads to the development of illegal, lasting, and visible dwellings. According to Fondation Abbé Pierre, the number of evictions from informal living spaces has increased sharply recently, with some 1,330 evictions recorded in mainland France between 1 November 2020 and 31 October 2021.

In addition to evictions, the repression of 'SDFs' persists even though vagrancy and begging have not been regarded as crimes since 1993. Assistance measures continue to co-exist with repressive measures to secure public spaces and invisibilize the existence of homeless people. This is reflected in the disappearance of public toilets in some municipalities, the use of anti-homeless repellents such as Malodor,[57] and decrees against begging and temporary campsites to evict people who could undermine the image of tourist cities in the summer.[58] Municipalities have also altered street furniture and fixtures, for example, implementing benches designed to dissuade people from adopting recumbent or reclining positions. We are thus seeing the implementation of a policy that punishes people who are already in extremely vulnerable situations.

Assistance for the homeless remains largely based on selection and a repressive approach. What are the impacts of this system on the populations concerned?

The Harmful Effects of the Assistance System

The hierarchical and segmented organization of the assistance system leads to the sorting and filtering of homeless people. Having demonstrated that the experience of the latter is characterized by worsening living conditions and the impossibility of forming roots, here we focus on two examples, overnight shelters and the 'Housing First' policy, that highlight the inflexibilities of the current system and the difficulties involved in changing it.

Selection

The current shortage of accommodation places and social housing has led to the classification of homeless people consistent with the rungs of the accommodation staircase. The classification criteria for homeless people are not the same for emergency accommodation and supported accommodation.

---

55 A. Vallet, 'Dans le petit bois en bandeau d'une autoroute parisienne' in F. Bouillon and others (eds), *Vulnérabilités résidentielles, Bibliothèque des territoires* (Éditions de l'Aube 2019) 33.
56 G. Lion, 'En quête de chez-soi: Le bois de Vincennes, un espace habitable?' (2014) 697(3) *Annales de géographie* 956.
57 In August 2007, the Argenteuil town hall triggered a major controversy. After introducing several orders to forbid begging in the town centre, by referring to an 'abnormal olfactory discomfort' caused by the presence of homeless people, the mayor purchased repellent devices to keep homeless people away from a shopping centre.
58 M. Loison-Leruste, *Habiter à côté des SDF, Habitat et sociétés* (L'Harmattan 2014).

In the emergency sector, accommodation is supposed to be unconditional, but 'vulnerability' ranks as the number one criterion for admission to a shelter. The preferred categories of public authorities are women with children, people with illnesses, and people with disabilities.[59] In the long-term support sector, priority is given to the most socially integrated individuals (or those presumed to be the easiest to reintegrate). Homeless people who work, have stable resources, were born in France, are legally documented in the country, and have local roots and a traditional lifestyle (in a couple, with children) are quicker to integrate into institutions offering long-term accommodation, which also offer a certain degree of comfort, and social support from the most qualified social workers. The people with the most advantageous characteristics in these respects experience upward mobility,[60] from the street to a shelter, and from emergency centres to supported accommodation centres. Those with the least advantageous characteristics are directed towards more short-term accommodation and housing solutions and the most perfunctory social support, generating a strong 'Matthew effect'.[61]

Regarding access to social housing, which represents the most significant way out of homelessness, applicants with the characteristics of a 'good tenant' (employed, French nationality, etc.) experience shorter waiting times. In contrast, large families, people on minimum social benefits, and people born outside France experience longer waiting times. Some people are unable to find a way out of supported accommodation because the criteria for 'climbing the staircase' are increasingly demanding in terms, for example, of independence and income, which rules the most vulnerable out of the equation. Sometimes, the 'logic of emergency,'[62] based on health risk, competes with this organization of priorities, as people in situations endangering their health or physical integrity may be rehoused on a priority basis. For the most vulnerable, obtaining assistance within a limited time period requires them to demonstrate the dramatic nature of their situation.[63]

Ultimately, housing shortage leads to the creation of categories of eligible individuals and places the poorly housed and the homeless in competition against each other. The increase in priority systems and labels designed to speed up access to housing is generating considerable inequalities as the attendant waiting lists do not offer the same opportunities or the same waiting times for accessing social housing.[64] Far from guaranteeing housing to the entire population, the enforceable right to housing has served to increase emergency assistance systems and led to a reshuffling of priorities.[65] This is reflected in painful waiting times marked by a deterioration in living conditions and numerous evictions.

---

59 V. Schlegel, 'Pauvres, déviants, malades. Travail d'inférence et catégorisations professionnelles dans la régulation de l'accès à l'hébergement des personnes sans-domicile' (2017) 30(1) *Terrains & travaux* 185.
60 Brousse, Firdion and Marpsat (n 16).
61 In reference to Matthew 13:12, whereby 'For whoever has, to him more will be given, and he will have abundance; but whoever does not have, even what he has will be taken away from him.'
62 P. Dietrich-Ragon, 'Les mal-logés parisiens face à la logique de l'urgence' (2010) 63 *Lien social et Politiques* 105.
63 The DALO law defines the legal framework for priorities, but local institutional actors and landlords then have some leeway to prioritize requests and select the priorities among the priorities.
64 P. Chauvin, 'L'administration de l'attente: Politiques et trajectoires de relogement des familles sans domicile à Paris' (Sociology PhD thesis, Nanterre, Université de Nanterre 2020).
65 P. Weill, 'Qui a le droit . . . au logement opposable?' (2013) 24(2) *Savoir/Agir* 27.

Categorization, Selection, Displacement, and Invisibilization

Long Waiting Periods, Recurrent Displacement, and Non-Take-Up

Dependence on institutions and living in accommodation structures have a substantial impact on the way people organize their private lives. In addition to issues of comfort and hygiene, accommodated individuals feel controlled by social workers and hemmed in by rules.[66] In general, they are unable to invite guest to where they live, and the hours of the centres require them to go home before a certain hour. Access to institutional accommodation is sometimes predicated on an individual separating from a pet or people close to them (for example, a partner, where couples are not admitted). Social workers can impose social or psychiatric monitoring, oversee the education of children, and ask dependent individuals to justify spending and prove that they are looking for a job. This comprehensive control can have a negative effect on some individuals and generate an attitude of withdrawal.

Another vital point is the temporary nature of accommodation, hence the 'recurrent displacement'[67] experienced by individuals. Even in long-term accommodation, homeless people are constantly reminded of the temporary nature of their situation and encouraged to seek other solutions. This pressure to leave is particularly strong among young adults accommodated by institutions, who are repeatedly reminded by social workers that they cannot stay forever.[68] Similarly, women can stay in overnight shelters for a few nights only,[69] and people in hotels are moved so that they do not take root in the institutional accommodation system. Exhortations to move, 'harness resources', and take an active approach[70] conceal an effort to avoid the shelterization[71] of social urgency, whereby institutions actively work to discourage people from getting overly dependent on accommodation solutions. The 'forced circulation' of vulnerable people leads to evictions with powerful impacts on homeless people's entire social life.[72] Unsurprisingly, the homeless are haunted by an awareness of the temporary nature of their situation, and so a strong divide develops between short-term accommodation and accommodation where they can establish themselves over the long term.

These shifts from one system to another, and the corresponding lack of stability, make people feel that they are being continually pushed around by institutions. For the most vulnerable homeless, the lack of continuity between assistance structures transforms the staircase of accommodation into the Penrose stairs, on which they could climb forever but never get any higher. The assistance system fails to establish bridges between the institutions frequented successively by individuals (child welfare, psychiatric hospital, accommodation

---

66 P. Bruneteaux, 'Les politiques de l'urgence à l'épreuve d'une ethnobiographie d'un SDF' (2007) 57(1) *Revue française de science politique* 47.
67 P. Watt, ' "This Pain of Moving, Moving, Moving": Evictions, Displacement and Logics of Expulsion in London' (2018) 68(1) *L'Année sociologique* 67.
68 P. Dietrich-Ragon, 'Quitter l'Aide sociale à l'enfance: De l'hébergement institutionnel aux premiers pas sur le marché immobilier' (2020) 75(4) *Population* 527.
69 R. Braud and M. Loison-Leruste, 'Le sans-abrisme au féminin. Quand les haltes pour femmes interrogent les dispositifs d'urgence sociale' (2022) 47 *Travail, genre et société* 131.
70 J. Barbier, 'Peut-on parler d' activation de la protection sociale en Europe ?' (2002) 43(2) *Revue française de sociologie* 307.
71 Shelterization is the process of adaptation by the homeless with long experiences of emergency accommodation structures and who end up getting used to these structures, which form the basis for their daily habits. J. Grunberg and P. F. Eagle, 'Shelterization: How the Homeless Adapt to Shelter Living' (1990) 41(5) *Hospital & Community Psychiatry* 521–525.
72 M. Desmond, *Avis d'expulsion: Enquête sur l'exploitation de la pauvreté urbaine* (P. Dardel tr, Lux 2019).

centres, etc.), leading to clipped trajectories with returns to the street and to the bottom of the staircase at the end of various stays.

Seen in this light, the preference of homeless people for alternative solutions, which appear to be more precarious, can be explained on the basis of a quest for independence and stability. Though lacking in comfort, squats and other makeshift dwellings may be chosen over hotels or hostels as they offer more autonomy, enabling inhabitants to organize their daily lives, cook, invite people over, and not be required to justify their actions.[73] For the homeless, overnight shelters and collective dorm room accommodation are at the bottom of the list in terms of expectations, behind hotels, integration accommodation, unsanitary housing, and squats, while HLM low-income housing (*habitations à loyer modéré*) is seen as the ultimate goal of their precarious housing trajectory.

Furthermore, given the lack of social housing, the increase in the number of selection criteria, and the lengthening of waiting times, homeless people are required to demonstrate patience and endurance and have (or acquire) knowledge of administrative matters.[74] They are obliged to put together a housing application file, update it regularly, and not forget to renew it every year, failing which it may be cancelled. They are also required to make appeals and request documents and assistance from various bodies and entities (including the enforceable right to housing commission, landlords, town halls, and employers). Applicants willing to play this tiring game are those with the greatest success. Others, worn out by administrative requirements and coming to see them as pointless, may lose confidence in institutions and renounce institutional assistance. As well as radically rejecting institutions, many of these individuals feel a strong sense of injustice. They may become resentful towards those who they see as being illegitimately favoured for access to social housing, pointing their fingers at recently arrived migrants and people illegally occupying dwellings, who have seemingly taken their place in the queue.

The assistance system produces considerable inequalities and is not particularly effective at removing people from accommodation structures. The organization of the system has been strongly criticized and recently been subject to structural reforms, though the latter have failed to make any significant change.

A Hard-to-Change System: Overnight Shelters for Women and the 'Housing First' Policy

The accommodation system for the homeless was criticized widely in the early 2000s, and changes were announced, on paper at least. Emergency accommodation structures were condemned for their lack of hygiene and safety and for the corresponding return to the street. Following the *Enfants de Don Quichotte* movement (see Focus 2, which follows), reforms were implemented to put an end to the continual return to the street of homeless people in emergency accommodation centres and to humanize admission conditions. The protests led to the adoption of the 'DALO' Act, introducing the enforceable right to

---

73 F. Bouillon and P. Dietrich-Ragon, 'Derrière les façades: Ethnographies de squats parisiens' (2012) 42(3) *Ethnologie française* 429; G. Lion, 'En quête de chez-soi: Le bois de Vincennes, un espace habitable?' 697(2) *Annales de géographie* 956.
74 Y. Siblot, 'Les rapports quotidiens des classes populaires aux administrations. Analyse d'un sens pratique du service public' (2005) 58(2) *Sociétés contemporaines* 85.

housing. Measures aimed at ensuring the continuity of assistance[75] and proposing 'Housing First' also sought to break with the staircase approach. But today the system remains hierarchical, and at the same time, the urgency of the situation has grown. While accommodation places have increased considerably in recent years, it is proving extremely difficult to restructure the system to the benefit of integration accommodation centres and adapted housing formats. In a notable development, accommodation places in the form of overnight stays at hotels are rising sharply.[76]

Focus 2: The DALO Act Introducing the Enforceable Right to Housing in France

In 2006, the Enfants de Don Quichotte organization (EDDQ) was created to challenge the living conditions of the homeless, some of whom were forced to sleep on the street and die of hypothermia. In December 2006, the organization erected 200 red tents on the banks of the Canal Saint-Martin in the 10th arrondissement of Paris and called on Parisians to support its work in solidarity with the homeless. On 25 December 2006, EDDQ drafted the 'Canal Saint-Martin Charter for Universal Access to Housing', which notably included the idea of making the right to housing enforceable across France. The media pressure exerted by EDDQ members throughout the country pushed the government to adopt a bill introducing the enforceable right to housing ('DALO') and comprising a raft of measures in favour of social cohesion.

Since 1 December 2008, the enforceable right to housing has been open to six priority categories of applicants: homeless people, people having been evicted and with no housing prospects, people accommodated on a temporary basis, people living in housing considered as unsanitary or unworthy, people with at least one dependent child with housing considered as substandard, and people with disabilities (or with a dependent person with a disability) with housing considered as substandard. On 1 January 2012, the right was extended to all other individuals qualifying for social housing having failed to receive a timely response to their housing application. All these categories of individuals may, via the mediation committee, lodge an appeal with the administrative court. In the event of a favourable ruling by the committee that is not followed by a resolution in a reasonable time frame, the court may order the state to house the applicant, subject to financial penalties.

---

75 Article 4 of the DALO ACT sets out the principle of the continuity of assistance as follows: 'Any person admitted to an emergency accommodation structure must receive personalized support from that structure and remain there where he or she so wishes, until he or she is directed to another solution, to a stable accommodation structure or to care or housing adapted to the individual's situation'.

76 According to a Senate-commissioned report published on 26 June 2019, the number of places in social reintegration centres increased by 14% between 2010 and 2018, while the number of places in university hospitals (CHU) and hotels rose by 182% and 249%, respectively, over the same period (source: DGCS, AHI survey). G. Arnell and J. Morisset, *Rapport d'information fait au nom de la commission des affaires sociales sur le financement public des opérateurs de l'hébergement d'urgence* (Sénat 2019).

Aware of the problems posed by a system that is struggling to reintegrate some individuals, the public authorities are exploring new systems. But the example of overnight shelters for women shows how difficult it is proving to be to effect real change. In 2018 in Paris, the first *Nuit de la Solidarité*, a campaign to count the number of roofless people on the streets of the French capital, revealed a 'new' public problem: roofless women, accounting for 12% of the total. The public authorities put the issue high on their agenda and financed the opening of new emergency systems for these women. Three overnight shelters for isolated women were opened in Paris between December 2018 and January 2019. Providing short-term and unconditional shelter accompanied by minimal social support, these structures target women considered from an institutional viewpoint as isolated, roofless, highly marginalized, with a long history of living on the street, and who no longer take up assistance services. But professionals in the field were quick to observe how ill-adapted the system was, as it admitted a different type of population to that originally intended, namely, homeless women having applied for housing and having suffered from violence (notably gender-related), especially during their migratory trajectory. In addition to this error in targeting, stemming from a lack of understanding of homeless women,[77] the response of the public authorities once again consisted in adding emergency structures lower down the staircase of accommodation, serving to simply reinforce the problems of the existing system.

A second example of the difficulty of French public policy to address homelessness can be seen in the country's 'Housing First' policy. First implemented in the United States then exported to Canada and Europe, this policy involves providing housing directly and condition-free to highly marginalized, roofless people, along with social and health support. Progress has been seen in this respect, but for now, this policy fails to address the scale of the demand. While the 'Housing First' strategy marks a disruption in approach to social housing and accommodation policy, as it calls into question the staircase model described earlier, the scope of the strategy is limited, available only in a part of France, and it addresses only a segment of the population affected by homelessness, that is, roofless people with a long history of living on the street and psychiatric problems and/or addictions.

The success of the 'Housing First' policy is also undermined by the unambitious social housing construction policy, excess demand, and the saturation of the existing housing stock. And for now, the policy has not eliminated any rungs on the accommodation staircase. As such, it could well become a 'support first' policy.[78]

Broadly speaking, reform policies are tending to reproduce the staircase approach by adding new steps to the staircase or by not fundamentally calling into question the system itself.

---

77 Yet numerous English-language studies have stressed the importance of gender-related violence causing the loss of housing: J. Calterone Williams, 'Domestic Violence and Poverty: The Narratives of Homeless Women' (1998) 19(2) *Frontiers: A Journal of Women Studies* 143.; R. Casey, R. Goudie and K. Reeve, 'Resistance and Identity: Homeless Women's Use of Public Spaces' (2007) 1(2) *People, Place and Policy Online* (September 2007) 90; and need for greater recourse to informal support: B. Edgar and J. Doherty, *Women and Homelessness in Europe. Pathways, Services and Expériences* (The Policy Press 2001).
78 R. Ballain, 'Quoi de neuf chercheurs en Auvergne-Rhône-Alpes? Logement d'abord: Deux ans plus tard, où en est-on?' *Les Actes* (June 2020).

Conclusion

Today, an entire swathe of the population in France is unable to obtain housing and falls outside the margins of French society even though many of the individuals in question have a job and modest but regular income. Some people are assisted via structures helping them to apply for low-income housing, but the most vulnerable, and those that give up on the assistance system, are relegated to outlying urban areas and wastelands or accommodation bereft of privacy, in which it is impossible to settle. Attempts at reform have done little to change the system; on the contrary, the issue is becoming more urgent, with an increase in the use of hotel accommodation and continued evictions. Repressive policies also serve to further weaken and conceal populations labelled as 'undesirable'.

Several avenues are being explored to improve this intolerable situation. For example, to find alternatives to hotel accommodation, establishments are being purchased and converted into social-purpose residences managed by organizations or social landlords. New accommodation structures are easing the rules for people with long histories of vagrancy and for whom accommodation in collective structures is ill adapted (allowing them, for example, to go out when they want, drink alcohol, and have a dog), while organizations are also promoting the 'Housing First' policy. But these initiatives have proved insufficient and tend to reproduce existing approaches and problems.

To resolve housing exclusion, an ambitious policy of promoting low-rent social housing is vital. Emphasis also needs to be placed on preventing evictions and regulating property markets.[79] Regarding assistance for the homeless, bridges need to be built between institutions to keep people from 'falling through the net' when leaving establishments. More radical political changes are also required. Some sector policies, such as migration policy, generate housing exclusion by placing people in undocumented situations. Increasingly unstable employment is largely responsible for housing insecurity, and a policy for young people should be reasserted, particularly for those exiting the child welfare system, to provide them with priority access to social housing. Resolving the issue of homelessness thus hinges as much on political housing reform as it does on initiatives in the social and employment sectors and on migration policy.

While some initiatives are heading in the right direction, it is hard to forget what Friedrich Engels had to say on unsanitary living conditions in the 19th century, namely, that if we do not fight against social inequalities, the problem, far from disappearing, simply shifts elsewhere.[80] Consequently, the root of the problem must be addressed by combating the social and wealth inequalities which have developed in France in recent years.

---

79 In France, rent caps have been introduced in several cities, including Paris.
80 F. Engels, *La question du logement (1887)* (Osez la république sociale 2012).

4

(STILL) MUCH UNTAPPED POTENTIAL IN HOMELESSNESS SERVICES

Challenges and Good Practice in Germany from a Social Work Perspective

Susanne Gerull

1. Introduction

In recent decades, the issue of homelessness has mostly been a niche topic in Germany. Not only civil society but also many political leaders associated the term exclusively with people living on the streets, although this number only makes up a part of those affected. This is and was all the more astonishing because the causes, consequences, and framework conditions of homelessness in Germany have been relatively well researched, and a differentiated system of assistance had been developed over the decades. Calls from practitioners, advocacy groups, and academia for a national strategy to overcome homelessness based on uniform national statistics on the extent of the problem have long been ignored. At the same time, Germany has robust legal provisions that allow for both preventive measures to prevent housing loss and an enforceable right to accommodation as well as support in case of social difficulties. Anyone who is homeless can report to the social authorities and apply for accommodation. For emergencies, there are low-threshold night shelters available, at least in the cities, where people can be accommodated for a few nights without any red tape. Counselling services are available, and in certain cases, people even have a legal right to them. But it is only in recent years that the target group of homeless people and people at risk of homelessness have come more into focus, as suddenly broader strata of the population were and are affected by the current lack of affordable housing.

In this chapter, the thesis is put forward and examined in more detail that there is (still) a great deal of untapped potential for homeless assistance in Germany. First, the necessary definitions are explored (Section 2), the historical background is presented (Section 3), and the current legal basis is explained (Section 4). Subsequently, the extent of homelessness in Germany is presented based on the first nationwide statistics and a supplementary report (Section 5), followed by the current status of national and local strategies to prevent housing loss and overcome acute homelessness (Section 6). After a detailed presentation of good practice from (also) a social work perspective (Section 7), the thesis in the title of the chapter is taken up and examined (Section 8). Opportunities, problems, and future challenges are discussed.

2. Definitions

The terms used for homeless people in Germany over the last century could fill a separate article. Terms such as 'homeless', 'roofless', 'non-settled', so-called 'Trebegänger' (juvenile prowlers), and many others were mainly created in the help system. They were, or are, often not self-explanatory but sometimes stigmatizing.[1]

Internationally, too, it is repeatedly stated:

> 'Homelessness is notoriously difficult to define'[2] and '[a]ny definition or typology of homelessness is, by its very nature, a social, political and cultural construct or categorization, reflecting particular assumptions held by particular actors at a particular point in time.'[3]

First, the current and relevant three terms and their definitions are presented in what follows in the form in which they are used with respect to Germany in this article: 'homeless', 'roofless', and 'cases in urgent need of housing'.

2.1. Homeless[4]

Until 2019, there was no official or legal definition of the term 'homeless' in Germany. Predominantly, the definition of the Bundesarbeitsgemeinschaft Wohnungslosenhilfe e. V.[5] (hereinafter, *BAG W*) was applied:

> Homeless is anyone who does not have housing (or homeownership) at one's disposal secured by a rental contract. Accordingly, the persons currently affected by homelessness are,
>
> - in the regulatory sector
>   - who, as a result of regulatory measures, are placed in housing without a rental contract, i.e., only with usage contracts, or are accommodated in emergency shelters
> - in the social welfare sector
>   - who are accommodated without a rental contract, whereby the costs are taken over according to the Social Code Book (SGB) XII and/or SGB II
>   - who stay in accommodations for the homeless, institutions, night shelters, asylums, and women's shelters, because no apartment is available
>   - who live as self-payers in cheap boarding houses
>   - who are temporarily staying with relatives, friends and acquaintances
>   - who are without any accommodation, living rough.

---

1 cf A. Wolf, 'Wohnungslosigkeit' in Hans-Uwe Otto and Hans Thiersch and Rainer Treptow and Holger Ziegler (eds), *Handbuch Soziale Arbeit* (Ernst Reinhardt Verlag 2018) 1855.
2 C. Hansen Löfstrand and D. Quilgars, 'Cultural Images and Definitions of Homeless Women: Implications for Policy and Practice at the European Level' in Paula Mayock and Joanne Bretherton (eds), *Women's Homelessness in Europe* (Palgrave Macmillan 2016) 46.
3 Ibid. 47.
4 In German: Wohnungslos.
5 National Federation for the Homeless in Germany.

- in the immigration sector
  - Repatriates who are not yet able to find rental housing and are accommodated in repatriate shelters

Recognized asylum seekers in emergency accommodation are included in the definition of cases in urgent need of housing but are not included in the homeless figures in the narrow sense of the term.[6]

With the entry into force of the Homeless Persons Reporting Act (WoBerichtsG) on 1 April 2020, there is, for the first time, a legal definition of the term 'homelessness', which essentially specifies the definition of the BAG W without listing the individual subgroups that fall under it:

§ 3 Definition; scope of survey
(1) Homelessness exists when

1. the use of a dwelling by a person or a majority of persons of the same household is not secured by a rental agreement or lease or by a right in rem[7]; or
2. a dwelling is not available to a person or a majority of persons of the same household for other reasons.

2.2. Roofless[8]

In Germany, a subgroup of the people mentioned in the WoBerichtsG is often referred to as 'roofless'. This usually refers to people living rough (hereinafter, rough sleepers). However, the term is not clearly defined in Germany and sometimes also includes people in night shelters or people who live in communal accommodation for homeless people – and thus *not* on the street. In addition to this confusion of terminology, it is repeatedly pointed out that the German term 'obdachlos' (roofless) is often used in a stigmatizing way. On the other hand, there has been a definition of 'rooflessness' for decades, which can be derived from the jurisprudence of the so-called police and public order laws of the 16 federal states ('Länder'). These laws regulate the state's obligation to provide shelter in cases of so-called 'involuntary rooflessness'. In a judgement from 1996, it says additionally, in the second leading sentence:

Involuntary homelessness usually occurs when the person concerned does not have a shelter that offers protection from the inclemency of the weather, leaves room for the most necessary necessities of life, meets the requirements of a decent shelter and

---

6 BAG Wohnungslosenhilfe e. V., 'Wohnungsnotfalldefinition der BAG Wohnungslosenhilfe e. V.' [2010] wohnungslos 67 (own translation). Note: Not every term can be translated directly from German in English. This applies also to further translations in this chapter.
7 This means an 'absolute' right in the sense of a sovereign right of disposal. Therefore, for example, someone with only a contract of use with a social welfare organization is, according to the definition of the law, homeless.
8 In German: Obdachlos.

does not want to live without such a shelter in the future based on a voluntary, self-determined decision of will.[9]

It thus seems sensible for several reasons to use the term 'obdachlos' ('roofless') in Germany only in the context of the state's housing obligation. However, according to the WoBerichtsG and the still-existing definition of the BAG W, rough sleepers are considered a subgroup of homeless people as a whole.

2.3. Case in Urgent Need of Housing[10]

The broader concept of 'Wohnungsnotfall ('case in urgent need of housing') was developed in 1987 by the Association of German Cities (Deutscher Städtetag) and includes two categories in addition to acutely homeless people (as defined in preceding subsections):

A person is a case in urgent need of housing if he or she is

- homeless or
- is threatened with homelessness or
- is living in unacceptable housing conditions[11]

Since then, this definition has been differentiated several times and ultimately led to the establishment of the term 'Wohnungsnotfallhilfe' ('help for cases in urgent need of housing') for the expanded assistance system. This term is intended to show the heterogeneity of the target group, but it is not defined by law. This chapter focuses on the first two groups of cases in urgent need of housing, namely, acutely homeless people (cf. 5.1 and 5.2) and people at risk of homelessness (cf. 5.3), since only for these subgroups is there a regulated responsibility within the framework in the field of social affairs (social welfare offices/ministries for social affairs). For most people in 'unacceptable housing conditions', on the other hand, depending on the reason for unacceptability, the health offices (e.g. in the case of mouldy housing), housing offices (e.g. in the case of overcrowded housing), or other authorities are primarily responsible.

Fundamentally, it can be stated that many of the housing situations described in the European Typology of Homelessness and Housing Exclusion (ETHOS)[12] can also be found in the aforementioned German definitions, but there is no exact correspondence between the respective terms and definitions.

Having explored these definitions, we will first look back at the historical background of homelessness in Germany, which is characterized by continuities of exclusion.

---

9 [1996] 1 S 470/96 (VGHBW).

10 In German: Wohnungsnotfall. The translation 'case in urgent need of housing' is internationally established.

11 F. Koch, 'Sicherung der Wohnungsversorgung in Wohnungsnotfällen und Verbesserung der Lebensbedingungen in sozialen Brennpunkten – Empfehlungen und Hinweise' [2010] *DST-Beiträge zur Sozialpolitik* 14 (own translation).

12 See <www.feantsa.org/download/ethos2484215748748239888.pdf(28.09.2022)> (accessed 1 September 2023).

3. Historical Background: Continuities of Exclusion

In Germany, assistance for acutely homeless people has historically developed from the so-called 'Nichtsesshaftenhilfe' (assistance for non-settled persons) as part of the assistance for those at risk. This background is important to understand the current structure and model of homeless assistance in Germany.

Thus, despite the modern and innovative system of assistance today (in the 2020s), continuities of exclusion of homeless people over centuries can be identified. Overcoming them requires a rigorous examination of the stages on the path from a restrictive, reprimanding, and, during National Socialism, devastating strategy in dealing with homeless people to participatory and resource-oriented services for overcoming involuntary homelessness (see Figure 4.1). This section is limited to the development of homelessness services since the mid-19th century.

Groups of the itinerant poor existed centuries ago. With the beginning of the Industrial Revolution in the German states from 1840 onwards, housing became a commodity and homelessness, thus, a relevant and visible problem.[13] At the same time, Caritas associations were founded as the basis of Catholic care for the poor. So-called sisters of mercy, women from mostly middle-class backgrounds, became involved in caring for the poor.[14] The goal here was primarily to 'influence the migrating poverty population educationally and morally'.[15] A long tradition of so-called workers' colonies developed (the first was established in 1882 on the initiative of Friedrich von Bodelschwingh), which until the 1950s were the 'welfare response [in the Federal Republic of Germany, SG] to unemployment and homelessness', with a 'strictly regulated daily work routine' for the people housed there.[16] According to § 361 of the German Criminal Code (StGB) of 1871, so-called 'vagrancy' could be punished with imprisonment for up to six weeks and subsequent incarceration in poorhouses or workhouses. In addition, at the end of the 19th century, the idea emerged that the cause of homelessness, and especially rooflessness, was a personality disorder.

To this day, this idea of a so-called 'non-settled personality' has experienced a renaissance again and again, especially in psychiatric studies.[17] The term 'non-settled' in the sense of persons migrating into communities from outside was cemented under National Socialism by the 1938 work 'Der nichtsesshafte Mensch' (*The Non-Settled Person*), authored by, among others, Nazi Standartenführer Alarich Seidler.[18] The separation of 'settled' and 'non-settled' homeless people remained 'an issue of a permanent, tenacious and recalcitrant character'[19] in Germany and led to a 'systematic orientation of help that continues to have an effect today'.[20]

---

13 See (n 1) 1856.
14 cf R. Lutz and T. Simon, *Lehrbuch der Wohnungslosenhilfe: Eine Einführung in Praxis, Positionen und Perspektiven* (Juventa 2007) 23.
15 See Wolf (n 1) 1856 (own translation).
16 R. van Spankeren and K. Stockhecke, 'Die Nichtsesshaftenhilfe auf dem Weg zum Sozialstaat (1950–1970)' [2004] *Wohnungslos* 91 (own translation).
17 See Wolf (n 1) 1857.
18 cf V. Busch-Geertsema, J. Evers and E. Ruhstrat, 'Mehr als ein Begriff... Von Wanderarmen zu Nichtsesshaften und Obdachlosen über alleinstehende Wohnungslose zu Wohnungsnotfällen' [2004] *Wohnungslos* 45.
19 H. Kiebel, 'Vierzig Jahre Bundessozialhilfegesetz. Hilfe für Nichtsesshafte, Hilfe für Gefährdete' [2001] *Wohnungslos* 51–52 (own translation).
20 F. Roscher, 'Die neue Rechtsverordnung zu § 72 BSHG – eine kritische Analyse' [2001] *Wohnungslos* 45 (own translation).

(Still) Much Untapped Potential in Homelessness Services

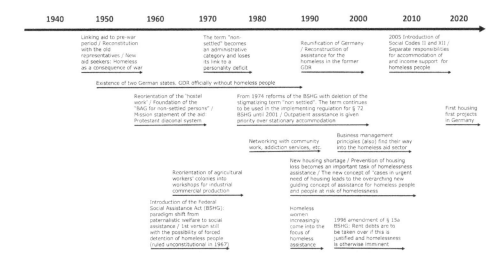

Figure 4.1 The development of homeless care and policy in Germany since 1945.
Source: Author's own presentation.

During the National Socialist era from 1933 onwards, so-called 'asocials' were also transported to concentration and extermination camps on the basis of § 361 of the Criminal Code. According to estimates, there were more than 10,000 homeless people among them.[21] This legal norm remained in force in the Federal Republic of Germany after World War II until a criminal law reform in 1974. From 1962 to 1967, homeless people could even be imprisoned indefinitely under the so-called assistance for those at risk in the Federal Social Assistance Act (§ 73 paragraph 2, sentences 1, and 2 BSHG from 1961). It was not until 1967 that the Federal Constitutional Court overturned this regulation with reference to Article 2 (2) of the Basic Law of the Federal Republic of Germany, that is, the right to freedom of the person.[22] In the German Democratic Republic, until reunification in 1990, the homeless could also be criminalized as 'asocials' and imprisoned under § 249 of the GDR Criminal Code from 1974, in repeated cases for up to five years. Other measures included residence restrictions and forced adoptions, which were regulated, among other things, in the 'Ordinance on the Tasks of Municipalities and Companies in the Education of Criminally Endangered Citizens of December 19, 1974'. Officially, however, homelessness did not exist in the GDR, which was founded in 1949.

In the Federal Republic of Germany, assistance for the homeless initially continued seamlessly from the pre-war period, with the addition of new people seeking help as a result of the war.[23] Starting in 1950, work was done on reforming welfare law, culminating in the Federal Social Assistance Act of 1961. This was decisively shaped by the guiding principle of a ruling

---

21 cf W. Ayaß, *'Asoziale' im Nationalsozialismus: Eine Einführung in Praxis, Positionen und Perspektiven* (Klett-Cotta 1995).
22 [1967] 2 BvR 335/62 (BVerfG).
23 See Wolf (n 1) 96.

by the Federal Administrative Court of 24 June 1954: 'Insofar as the law imposes obligations on the welfare agency for the benefit of the needy, the needy have corresponding rights.'[24] The reform of the Federal Social Assistance Act in 1974 introduced a legal right to 'help to overcome special social difficulties', that is, assistance *must* be granted if the requirements are met (for current forms of assistance, see Brief Overview: The Current Support System for Homeless People and People at Risk of Homelessness in Germany). However, stigmatizing descriptions of people with this legal entitlement under § 72 BSHG were still found in legal commentaries until the late 1990s.[25] At the same time, the first sociological explanatory approaches that identified and recognized homelessness as a poverty problem emerged in the 1980s to 1990s.[26] Social work thus increasingly became a central support factor for homeless people but still has to perform the balancing act of providing primarily *individual* assistance due to *structural* causes of housing need and homelessness.[27] Community-oriented approaches and specialized offers, such as addiction services, etc., have emerged. Preventive help became a new part of the help system so that homelessness should be prevented more strongly instead of having to accommodate acutely homeless people or provide them with new living space. At the same time, so-called 'Fachstellen' (specialist offices for housing assurance under municipal responsibility) developed, which were supposed to bundle resources and competences in the social authorities for the prevention and overcoming of homelessness.[28]

With the reunification of Germany in 1990, the reconstruction of assistance for homeless persons in the former GDR began, because the former institutions for 'non-settled persons' no longer existed there. Thus, assistance for the homeless in the new federal states had to be built up 'practically from scratch'.[29] The 2000s are then characterized throughout Germany by the restructuring of the welfare state on the basis of business structures and principles, which also changed homeless assistance.[30]

Even today, homeless people in Germany are still marginalized and stigmatized, for example, as 'work-shy'. Especially visibly homeless people like rough sleepers are excluded and expelled from public spaces; they have hardly any chance in the free housing market. They are also exposed to violent crimes as severe as manslaughter and even murder. It is therefore possible and necessary to speak of a continuity of exclusion of the homeless in Germany.[31]

4. Current Legal Basis

4.1. Unemployment Benefit II and Social Assistance

Since 2005, basic security benefits are paid in the form of unemployment benefit II (Social Code Book II) or social assistance (Social Code Book XII). This merger of the former social assistance, financed from taxation by the social welfare offices, and unemployment

---

24 [1954] V C 78.54 (BVerwG).
25 See Ayaß (n 21).
26 See Wolf (n 1) 1858.
27 Ibid. 1859f.
28 cf T. Specht-Kittler, 'Die neunziger Jahre – Konsolidierung und Krise' (2004) *Wohnungslos* 109, 112.
29 Ibid. 110 (own translation).
30 Ibid. 115.
31 cf S. Gerull, 'Obdachlosenfeindlichkeit. Von gesellschaftlicher Stigmatisierung bis zu Hasskriminalität' in H. Amesberger and others (eds), *Kontinuitäten der Stigmatisierung von 'Asozialität'* (Springer VS 2021).

assistance, paid as an insurance benefit by the labour offices, was also significant for homeless people and homeless assistance. Since 2005, people who are capable of work and in need of assistance have been receiving basic security benefits through the newly created job centres, while the 'remaining social assistance' was transferred to the Social Code Book XII. This included both 'basic security in old age and in the event of reduced earning capacity' and the assistance for people with special social difficulties already briefly presented in Section 3 (see in more detail in Help for People with Particular Social Difficulties). One consequence of the restructuring was that suddenly two authorities were responsible for housing homeless people: the Social Welfare Office, which checks the accommodation claim and selects suitable accommodation, and, in the case of employable homeless people, the Job Centre, which is responsible for social benefits, including the costs of accommodation.

In addition, the professionals working in the field of homeless care had to

> take on the additional task of interface management between the two Social Code Books. From both Social Code Books, they have to access the socially integrative or more labour market-oriented measures that are appropriate for their clients in each case.[32]

For 2023, the current government in Germany is planning a fundamental reform of the basic security system for those capable of working and in need of assistance under the name 'Bürgergeld' (citizen's income), which is supposed to lead to improvements for those entitled to benefits, such as the restriction of the possibility of sanctions by the job centres and more opportunities to earn extra money.

4.2. Help for People with Particular Social Difficulties

The help for people with particular social difficulties was integrated into SGB XII in 2005 and remained unchanged in terms of content, so § 72 BSHG (Federal Social Assistance Act) became §§ 67 ff. SGB XII (Social Code Book XII) with the same wording. In the meantime, the content of the regulations has remained the same for almost 50 years, 'rather an exception for the "fast-moving" social law [in Germany, SG]'.[33] According to § 18 (1) SGB XII, assistance begins 'as soon as the social welfare agency or the agencies commissioned by it become aware that the requirements for the benefit are met'. In practice, however, a sometimes quite complex application procedure presents a common barrier before assistance is granted.

A new legal ordinance on § 72 of the BSHG had already come into force in 2001, which remained in force and is still valid today. It does not contain a typology of groups of persons as before but describes living conditions and difficulties which, when combined and intertwined, lead to an legal entitlement to support services. The ordinance contains a large number of undefined legal terms 'in order to do justice to its [homelessness,

---

32 In WIS Forschung und Beratung GmbH, *Welche Auswirkungen hat Hartz IV auf die Wohnungsnotfallhilfe in NRW?* (Ruhr-Universität Bonn 2006) 10 (own translation).
33 F. Roscher, 'Die Paragraphen 67 ff. Sozialgesetzbuch XII – mehr als ein Rechtsanspruch im Wohnungsnotfall!' [2022] *Wohnungslos* 38 (own translation).

SG] very diverse manifestations'.³⁴ What remains, although erased from the law itself, is the concept of homelessness 'as a form of life characterised by "wandering" combined with "unsecured economic basis" '.³⁵ The 'traditionally separated assistance approach'³⁶ continues to exist: independent welfare organizations offer ambulatory assistance, while the municipality must fulfil its legal obligation to provide accommodation. Assistance according to §§ 67 SGB XII is offered both on an ambulatory (outpatient) and stationary (inpatient) basis, but due to the responsibility of the federal states, both the offer and structures of assistance are largely non-uniform.³⁷

Since the introduction of help for people with particular social difficulties, their independence as an assistance service compared to the so-called integration assistance ('special services for self-determined living for people with disabilities', located in SGB IX since 2020) has been questioned or controversially discussed. In this context, the lawyer Falk Roscher repeatedly states unequivocally that these are 'independent needs and assistance "worlds" '³⁸: the target group of assistance according to §§ 67 ff. SGB XII needs support in overcoming their difficulties due to their special living conditions, but the reason for assistance is not function-related impairments, as in the case of integration assistance.³⁹

4.3. The State's Obligation to Accommodate Homeless People

The 'right to housing' under Article 31 ESC (European Social Charter 1996) does not yet apply in Germany, as the revised version of the ESC of 1996 has not been ratified by Germany. However, in the definition of the term 'roofless' in Section 2, reference was already made to the state's obligation to provide accommodation in cases of so-called 'involuntary rooflessness'. This is anchored in the legal foundations of police and public order laws. Even though the 16 federal states are responsible, according to a legal opinion for the BAG W,⁴⁰ a uniform standard has emerged in case law and literature to regulate the legal relationships in the police and regulatory law when rough sleepers are admitted to emergency shelters.

According to this, 'involuntary rooflessness' represents a danger to public safety and order, which results in the obligation to avert this emergency.⁴¹ There is thus a legal entitlement to the allocation of emergency accommodation, irrespective of a claim to social benefits or a stable residence status. This legal interpretation is regularly confirmed by

---

34 A. Brühl, 'Die neue Rechtsverordnung im Licht der Gesetzes- und Ermächtigungsgrundlage (72 BSHG)' [2001] *Wohnungslos* 84 (own translation).
35 See Kiebel (n 19) (own translation).
36 See Brühl (n 34) 46 (own translation).
37 cf V. Busch-Geertsema, J. Henke and A. Steffen, *Entstehung, Verlauf und Struktur von Wohnungslosigkeit und Strategien zu ihrer Vermeidung und Behebung* (BMAS 2019) 66.
38 F. Roscher, 'Eingliederungshilfe nach neuem Recht – ein Problem für die Wohnungslosenhilfe?' in S. Gillich, R. Keicher and S. Kirsch (eds), *Alternativen zur Entrechtung und Ausgrenzung* (Lambertus 2019) 34 (own translation).
39 Ibid.
40 K. Ruder, *Grundsätze der polizei- und ordnungsrechtlichen Unterbringung von (unfreiwillig) obdachlosen Menschen unter besonderer Berücksichtigung obdachloser Unionsbürger* (BAG W-Verlag 2015).
41 Ibid. 8.

German courts, most recently by the Administrative Court of Würzburg, for example. In its judgment, the court also ruled that

> even if the homeless person is unable to be accommodated in a communal facility due to his or her inappropriate, socially harmful behaviour, this does not change the basic obligation of the security authorities to avert danger.[42]

The discretion of the authorities is thus 'reduced to zero'.[43] In practice, this is not always implemented in accordance with the law (see Good Practice: Accommodation of Acutely Homeless Persons). However, the public order law is subordinate to the law of social assistance, so a rough sleeper is 'in principle expected to pursue any social assistance claims before resorting to assistance under police law'.[44] Minimum standards must be observed for accommodation, whereby lower standards are to be applied here than for a flat. It must be humane, but only 'the so-called civilisational minimum must be guaranteed'.[45] A right to live on the street, on the other hand, only exists if no emergency accommodation is offered.[46]

4.4. Homelessness Prevention

Since the end of the 1980s, the task of not only combating homelessness but also, if possible, preventing its occurrence has become more and more the focus of homelessness assistance in the old federal states of Germany. At the same time, the broader concept of 'cases in urgent need of housing' (see Case in Urgent Need of Housing section above) has been developed, which, in addition to acutely homeless people and those in unacceptable housing conditions, also focused on the group of people threatened by homelessness. As in other European countries, evictions due to rent debts and family break-ups are the main triggers for the emergence of homelessness in Germany.[47]

In contrast to other behaviours in violation of the rental agreement as grounds for termination (e.g. unauthorized subletting, disturbance of domestic peace), Germany has very clearly formulated legal provisions for rent debts: similar to many other European countries, termination without notice can be declared after rent debts amounting to two months' rent (or more than one month's rent within two consecutive months).[48] The legal basis for this is the German Civil Code (BGB).[49] However, payment of the rent arrears within two months of service of the eviction action (so-called protection period) renders the termination

---

42 [2022] W 5 E 22.54 (VGWUERZ) (own translation).
43 See Ruder (n 41) 56f (own translation).
44 Ibid. 55 (own translation).
45 Ibid. 45 (own translation).
46 cf W. Hecker, 'Die rechtliche Regelung des Aufenthalts im öffentlichen Raum – Bedeutung für sozial ausgegrenzte Menschen' [2016] *Wohnungslos* 38–39.
47 cf P. Kenna, L. Benjaminsen, V. Busch-Geertsema and S. Nasarre-Aznar, *Pilot Project – Promoting Protection of the Right to Housing – Homelessness Prevention in the Context of Evictions* (Publications Office of the European Union 2016) 90.
48 cf S. Gerull, 'Evictions Due to Rent Arrears: A Comparative Analysis of Evictions in 14 Countries' (2014) *European Journal of Homelessness* 137, 142f.
49 § 543 (2) no. 3 BGB.

without notice invalid in Germany – even against the will of the landlord.[50] However, this does not apply 'if the termination was preceded no more than two years ago by a termination that has become invalid pursuant to sentence 1'.[51]

The Social Code Books II and XII also stipulate that the municipalities must be informed by the courts of the impending loss of housing if rent debts are the reason (or one of the reasons) for termination without notice.[52] In addition, 'they are to be taken over if this is justified and necessary and otherwise homelessness threatens to occur'.[53] Within this framework, those seeking help 'generally have a legal right to assistance, unless special circumstances exist that speak in favour of deviating from the rule'.[54] Theoretically, this gives the job centres (within the framework of unemployment benefit II according to SGB II) or social welfare offices (within the framework of social assistance according to SGB XII) a strong hand to take tertiary preventive action and prevent the impending loss of housing by taking over the rent debts. However, the authorities often only write to those affected when they receive corresponding notices from the court; proactive help, for example, through home visits, is rare. Also, applications for debt assumption are often rejected unlawfully, and those seeking help rarely go to court. If they do, for example, with the support of non-statutory welfare organizations, they have a good chance of winning the case. In 2021, the Social Court of Landshut stated: 'If the factual requirements of § 22 (8) SGB II are met, the defendant has no leeway in exercising his discretion.'[55] The general reference by the authorities to the possibility of renting substitute housing to avoid homelessness is also frequently contradicted by the courts, because 'a flat that meets the adequacy criteria must be specifically rentable for the person in need of assistance'.[56]

5. Extent of Homelessness in Germany

For decades, practitioners and researchers in Germany had called on the federal government to develop nationwide statistics on homelessness and other cases in urgent need of housing. Time and again, respective governments have refused to implement such a nationwide standardized gathering of statistics on the extent of homelessness in Germany. In 2011, they were reprimanded for this by the UN Committee on Economic, Social, and Cultural Rights (CESCR). The then federal government was requested by the Committee to submit data on the extent of homelessness with its next state report.[57] However, this did not happen. Several times, motions by parliamentary groups in the German Bundestag were rejected by respective government. A motion by the Bündnis 90/Die Grünen parliamentary group to implement such statistics was commented on by the federal government in 2015 as follows:

> Due to the responsibility of the Länder and municipalities for the care and accommodation of the homeless and roofless and for the promotion of social housing, it

---

50 § 569 (3) no. 2 sentence 1 BGB.
51 § 569 (3) no. 2 sentence 2 BGB.
52 Identical provision in § 22 (9) SGB II and § 36 (2) SGB XII (own translation).
53 Identical provision in § 22 (8), sentence 2 SGB II and § 36 (1), sentence 2 SGB XII (own translation).
54 O. Fichtner and G. Wenzel, *Kommentar zur Grundsicherung. SGB XII Sozialhilfe* (Verlag Franz Vahlen 2005) 215 (own translation).
55 [2021] S 5 AS 541/20 ER (SGLANDS), paragraph 25 and editorial principle (own translation).
56 [2021] L 16 AS 7/21 B ER (BAYLSG), paragraph 43 (own translation).
57 cf S. Krämer, 'Kinderrechte in der Wohnungsnotfallhilfe' [2016] *Wohnungslos* 65.

would, in the opinion of the Federal Government, be more appropriate to carry out surveys and analyses of homelessness and rooflessness at municipal and Land level, whereby uniform standards would be useful to ensure comparability. However, the definition of these standards is not the responsibility of the federal government, but of the competent regional authorities.[58]

Only three years earlier, the reasoning was different. At that time, a motion by the parliamentary groups of the SPD, Bündnis 90/Die Grünen, and the parliamentary group DIE LINKE to introduce it was rejected 'because the general supply situation with housing has constantly improved in recent years'.[59] As early as 1998, concrete proposals were published in a feasibility study on how at least institutionally housed homeless people could be recorded nationwide in a uniform and 'comparatively unproblematic'[60] way. According to the findings at that time, subgroups of people threatened with homelessness could also have been included in official statistics.[61] The study had been commissioned by the Federal Statistical Office on behalf of the Federal Ministry of Regional Planning, Building, and Urban Affairs (BRBS). However, it took another 22 years until the WoBerichtsG (cf. 2.1) was promulgated in 2020. In the 'Draft Law on the Introduction of Reporting on Homelessness and Statistics on Homeless Persons Accommodated', the federal government now argued that

> reliable information on the extent of homelessness and on the persons affected is required for the entire federal territory for reporting and for decisions based on social policy. The Länder therefore welcome the introduction of official nationwide statistics on homelessness in a resolution of the Conference of Ministers and Senators for Labour and Social Affairs of the Länder (ASMK) of December 2017.[62]

The Federal Council's proposal to carry out the statistical exercise on homeless persons housed as decentralized statistics was rejected by the federal government because '[b]y centralised statistics, the results can be made available much earlier'.[63] Parts of the law came into force on 1 April 2020, others were already in force from 1 January 2020. The target group and the results of the first nationwide survey are presented in what follows.

5.1. Target Group and Results of the First Official Statistics of Accommodated Homeless Persons in 2022

With a reference date of 31 January 2022, data on accommodated homeless people in Germany was collected on a legal basis for the first time. Other subgroups, such as rough sleepers, were not included. In addition, only persons who were accommodated *due to*

---

58 Deutscher Bundestag, Drs. 18/5654 of 28 July 2015, 2 (own translation).
59 Deutscher Bundestag, Drs. 17/10414 of 31 July 2012, 2 (own translation).
60 Christian König, *Machbarkeitsstudie zur statistischen Erfassung von Wohnungslosigkeit* (Statistisches Bundesamt 1998) 149 (own translation).
61 Ibid. 151.
62 Deutscher Bundestag, Drs. 19/15651 of 3 December 2019, 1 (own translation).
63 See (n 59) attachment 3, 1 (own translation).

Accommodated homeless persons: Germany, reference date, nationality, gender, age groups

Statistics on accommodated homeless persons
Germany
Accommodated homeless persons (number)

reference date, nationality, gender		age groups						
		under 18 years	18 to under 25 years	25 to under 40 years	40 to under 60 years	60 years and more	unknown	total
31.01.2022								
german	male	3060	2790	8990	15455	8285	405	38985
	female	2790	1620	3260	5290	2695	175	15830
	unknown	25	45	55	55	30	5	220
	total	5875	4460	12300	20800	11010	590	55035
foreigners	male	21045	8910	20395	17120	3280	555	71305
	female	19175	5195	13335	9815	1850	300	49670
	unknown	1105	200	365	325	75	65	2135
	total	41325	14300	34095	27265	5205	920	123110
total	male	24105	11700	29385	32575	11560	960	110290
	female	21965	6815	16590	15110	4545	480	65505
	unknown	1130	245	420	380	105	70	2355
	totat	47200	18760	46395	48065	16215	1510	178145

Figure 4.2 Results of the first official statistics of accommodated homeless persons.
Source: Statistisches Bundesamt (Destatis) 2022 (author's own translation).

homelessness are part of the statistics. Residents of, for example, homes for people with disabilities or women's shelters are also not a target group for the statistics.

A total of 178,145 accommodated homeless people was recorded as of the reporting date 31 January 2022. Figure 4.2 shows more detailed data.

Almost 56% of the persons recorded were accommodated by the municipalities/municipal associations, a good 14% by non-statutory welfare organizations. A good 27% of all recorded cases were short-term offers, for example, night shelter accommodation.

Until the first publication of the officially collected data, the BAG W regularly provided estimates on the extent of homelessness, most recently for the years 2019 and 2020. Due to other survey bases, the corresponding data are not comparable with the results of the first official statistics.

5.2. Complementary Reporting

The problems already raised in the 1998 feasibility study, such as how to record persons without accommodation,[64] were taken into account in 2020 in the Act by mandating supplementary reporting. Thus, the WoBerichtsG provides for reporting on homeless persons every two years

who

1. live temporarily in conventional housing, without that being their usual residence, or
2. who are roofless/sleeping rough.

(§ 8 [3] WoBerichtsG)

---

64 See König (n 61).

The results of the supplementary reporting on behalf of the Ministry of Employment and Social Affairs were submitted in September 2022. The survey was conducted in the week following 31 January 2022 and included unsheltered and hidden homelessness. A sample of homeless people with contact with institutions of homeless assistance or related assistance systems was surveyed, and the results were extrapolated to the population of all homeless people using inference criteria. In total, according to the report, the extrapolated number of homeless people in Germany from both groups is around 86,700. Around 37,400 homeless people were without accommodation or living in makeshift accommodation, and 49,300 were living in concealed homelessness. In addition, there are an estimated 6,600 children who were living homeless together with their parents(s), on the street or in concealed homelessness.[65]

If the homeless people recorded on the reference date (statistics of sheltered homeless people) or in the week after (extrapolated unsheltered and hidden homeless people) are added together in both surveys, the total number of acutely homeless people in Germany at the end of January/beginning of February 2022 is around 265,000. However, even this total figure does not include several subgroups of homeless people, such as people with special social difficulties in 'assisted single living' (see Figure 4.3) with only a contract of use, women in women's shelters, etc. In a new feasibility study,[66] the expansion of official reporting on other forms of homelessness was examined in parallel (§ 4 WoBerichtsG); corresponding recommendations are currently being discussed (as of September 2022) but could be implemented in 2024 at the earliest.

6. National and Local Strategies to Prevent Housing Loss and Overcome Acute Homelessness

More and more countries are developing national and/or local strategies to prevent housing loss and overcome acute homelessness. The basis is usually valid data on the extent of 'cases in urgent need of housing'. Objectives are formulated in concrete terms so that the success of the assistance measures implemented within this framework can be verified. A positive example in Europe is Finland, whose governments have been legally anchoring programmes to reduce homelessness since the mid-1980s and have thus arrived at less than 5,000 in 2020,[67] after approximately 20,000 acutely homeless people in the mid-1980s.[68]

In Germany, there is currently no national strategy in the context of 'cases in urgent need of housing'. For years, such a strategy was rejected with the same arguments as the nationwide uniform collection of data on the extent of the problem. For example, the

---

65 cf Gesellschaft für innovative Sozialplanung und Sozialforschung e. V. and Kantar Public, *Empirische Untersuchung zum Gegenstand nach § 8 Absatz 2 und 3 Wohnungslosenberichterstattungsgesetz*, Research Report 605 (BMAS 2022) 13.

66 Gesellschaft für innovative Sozialplanung und Sozialforschung e. V., *Machbarkeitsstudie für eine regelmäßige Berichterstattung gemäß § 8 Absatz 4 Wohnungslosenberichterstattungsgesetz*, Research Report 606 (BMAS 2022).

67 cf ARA, *The Housing Finance and Development Centre of Finland, Report 2021: Homelessness in Finland 2020* (ARA 2021) 3.

68 cf H. Tainio and P. Fredriksson, 'The Finnish Homelessness Strategy: From a "Stair-Case" Model to a "Housing First" Approach to Tackling Long-Term Homelessness' (2009) *European Journal of Homelessness* 181–82.

federal government answered a parliamentary question by the Bündnis 90/Die Grünen parliamentary group in 2015: 'The federal government is not planning a federal programme against homelessness. Such a programme would be the responsibility of the Länder and municipalities.'[69] In November 2020, the European Parliament passed a resolution on tackling homelessness rates in the EU, calling on its members to develop national strategies:

> [The European Parliament] [c]alls on the Member States to tackle the issue of homelessness urgently by adopting long-term, community-based, housing-led, integrated national homelessness strategies, as encouraged by the EU's social investment package.[70]

In the course of implementing the first nationwide reporting on homelessness, the demand for a national strategy against homelessness was also taken up by politicians. In the coalition agreement 2021–2025 between the Sozialdemokratische Partei Deutschland, Bündnis90/Die Grünen, and the Freie Demokratische Partei (FDP), the goal was announced 'to overcome homelessness and homelessness by 2030 and . . . to establish a national action plan for this purpose'.[71] Further details on this are not agreed in the coalition agreement, but a participatory draft is currently (early 2024) being clarified by the stakeholder groups involved and will then be put to a parliamentary vote. However, following the government's decision, the responsibility for the issue of homelessness has changed within the federal government. Thus, only social welfare issues remain the responsibility of the previously responsible Ministry of Labour and Social Affairs. The Federal Minister for Housing, Urban Development, and Construction has taken over the other responsibilities and also tweeted on 3 February 2022 that her ministry would coordinate the process of implementing a national action plan.[72]

Germany's largest state, North Rhine-Westphalia (NRW), on the other hand, launched its first programme to prevent homelessness as early as 1996 and has since supported innovative project approaches in regular action programmes and promoted a whole series of research projects. A coordination group with representatives from municipalities, regional associations, the housing industry, non-statutory welfare organizations, ministries, professional associations, etc. has been providing support for the action programmes since 2009.[73] Data on the extent of homelessness has been collected there since the 1960s. In the city state and federal state of Berlin, the former social senator, together with her state secretary, launched a so-called master plan to overcome homelessness and rooflessness by 2030, which is to be followed up by her successor in office and the current government coalition as a basis for future work.[74]

---

69 Deutscher Bundestag, Drs. 18/4261 of 9 March 2015, 9 (own translation).
70 European Parliament, 'P9_TA(2020)0314, resolution of 24 November 2020 on tackling homelessness rates in the EU (2020/2802(RSP))' 5.
71 Koalitionsvertrag 2021–2025. Zwischen der Sozialdemokratischen Partei Deutschlands (SPD), Bündnis 90/Die Grünen und den Freien Demokraten (FDP): Mehr Fortschritt wagen. Bündnis für Freiheit, Gerechtigkeit und Nachhaltigkeit (2022).
72 See <https://twitter.com/klara_geywitz/status/1499038558140649476(06.09.2022)> (accessed 1 September 2023).
73 cf MAGS: Ministerium für Arbeit, Gesundheit und Soziales des Landes NRW, *Aktionsprogramm "Hilfen in Wohnungsnotfällen": Maßnahmen zur Prävention und Bekämpfung von Wohnungslosigkeit* (MAGS 2018) 9.
74 E. Breitenbach and A. Fischer, 'Berliner Masterplan zur Überwindung von Wohnungs- und Obdachlosigkeit bis zum Jahr 2030' (2021) <https://www.tagesspiegel.de/berlin/so-konnte-berlin-obdachlosigkeit-bis-2030-beenden-4221163.html>.

7. Homelessness Good Practice in Germany

This section describes assistance approaches and projects in the sense of homelessness good practice in Germany. What they all have in common is that social work support is part of the concepts and measures, as their target groups are often affected by multi-problem situations, such as poverty, social difficulties, and/or psychological stress in addition to homelessness as a central problem. First, a compact overview of assistance for 'cases in urgent need of housing' in Germany is given. This is followed by two selected practical examples each on the prevention of housing losses, in the context of accommodating acutely homeless people, and on the provision of homeless people with their own housing and aftercare. First of all, selected problems and challenges in the respective fields of action are outlined.

7.1. Brief Overview: The Current Support System for Homeless People and People at Risk of Homelessness in Germany

The following Figure 4.3 shows a compact overview of the most important pillars of the support system for 'cases in urgent need of housing' in Germany. Due to the federal responsibilities and the special features that have developed over decades, not all offers can be listed in detail, and the focus here is on the already-established services. Housing First, for example, is only listed under 'other services', as there is currently no uniform legal basis and form of financing for the many projects that are springing up. The overview is divided into legal bases, financing, service providers, and service variants of the respective subsystems.

The fundamental shape of the aid system shown in Figure 4.3 has existed in this form for decades, with only incremental changes or minor modifications. Nevertheless, new target groups have emerged in the support system in recent years, which lead to new challenges and require innovative ideas and approaches. These include, for example, vulnerable non-German EU citizens or homeless LGBTQI* people. In addition, homeless families are increasingly appearing in the help system again, after the homelessness of children was considered to have been overcome in the 1990s. On the other hand, self-advocacy groups of homeless and formerly homeless people have been emerging as new players in the field, demanding participation and co-determination. There is still a lot of need for action here, and a rethink is necessary on the part of the professional actors, including social workers, who sometimes still display paternalistic and caring attitudes towards their users.[75] The following practical examples show that the help system is currently producing new approaches and that politics and administration are also developing new strategies to overcome homelessness.

7.2. Good Practice: Prevention of Housing Losses

As already made clear in Section 4, Germany has long had legal regulations in the field of tenancy and social law, which are actually an excellent basis for preventing the loss of housing, at least in the case of rent debts. Nevertheless, housing preservation often fails because of the job centres or social welfare offices, which are responsible for approving the corresponding applications. In this context, 'good practice' means interventions and, above all, practical concepts that guarantee implementation of the legal requirements or offer other

---

[75] cf S. Gerull, *Spaghetti oder Reis? Partizipation in der Wohnungslosenhilfe* (Schibri-Verlag 2018).

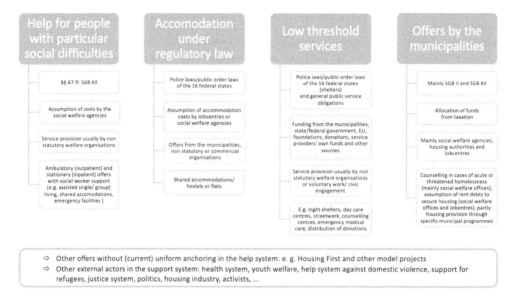

Figure 4.3 Help system for cases in urgent need of housing in Germany.
Source: Author's own presentation.

solutions. Innovative approaches benefit from the fact that preventive assistance in the event of imminent loss of housing 'is possible at different stages, both in extrajudicial and judicial proceedings and ultimately also during the enforcement process'.[76] The prerequisite for this is that the responsible authorities become aware of the impending loss of housing – through the district courts when an eviction action is filed (see Homelessness Prevention), through the affected tenants themselves or also non-statutory welfare organizations that have become aware of the problem situation and contact the authorities on behalf of the tenants. According to various empirical studies, the sooner the tenants are contacted, the greater the chances of them being able to keep their apartments.[77]

At the end of the 1980s, the Association of German Cities (Deutscher Städtetag, see Case in Urgent Need of Housing) developed the concept of the 'Fachstelle Wohnungssicherung' (specialized offices for housing security) in municipal responsibility which brought control of prevention of housing loss into one administrative unit (as opposed to several units as existed previously). Despite positive experience, this concept has not caught on throughout Germany. Nevertheless, the city of Karlsruhe is one of the major German cities whose department for housing security of the social and youth welfare office was transformed into such a 'Fachstelle Wohnungssicherung' in 2007.

76 MAGS: Ministerium für Arbeit, Gesundheit und Soziales des Landes NRW, *Wohnungsnotfallhilfen vorausschauend planen und präventiv handeln. Eine Praxishilfe für Kommunen und freie Träger der Wohlfahrtspflege* (MAGS 2019) 56 (own translation).
77 See Roscher (n 38) 89.

The City of Karlsruhe: 'Fachstelle Wohnungssicherung'[78]

Team 2 of a total of four teams of the Karlsruhe 'Fachstelle Wohnungssicherung' is responsible for the task 'prevention'. In addition to preventing the loss of housing, especially due to rent debts, the team is also responsible for acquiring housing. According to the team's own statement, it tries to 'exhaust all legal possibilities to prevent people from losing their homes due to a notice of termination or an eviction action and to prevent housing losses due to missing rent payments'.[79] When a threatened loss of housing becomes known, the General Social Service tries to establish contact, also through outreach assistance, and to arrange assistance for rent arrears settlement and rent protection. This is done until the eviction date announced by the bailiff. In 2019 and 2020, 41% of the eviction dates already set were prevented in this way. By assigning their own income in the amount of the monthly rent to the prevention team and forwarding this income to the landlord, new rent arrears can also be prevented in the long term.

As early as 2003, a dissertation demonstrated the success of outreach assistance in the form of home visits when social welfare offices are informed of eviction complaints.[80] While the employees of social welfare offices mostly were reluctant to engage in outreach work until 2004, such intervention became almost unthinkable after the merger of social welfare and unemployment assistance and the resulting responsibility of the job centres (see Unemployment Benefit II and Social Assistance). Exceptions, as outlined earlier for the city of Karlsruhe, unfortunately only confirm this rule. The transfer of prevention to an independent agency is also rather rare. In isolated cases, however, the landlords themselves become active, as the following example shows.

Bielefeld: When It Is Urgent – Outreach Prevention by 'Mobile Mieterhilfe Bielefeld'[81]

The Mobile Mieterhilfe ('Mobile Tenant Assistance') of the non-statutory welfare organization 'Bodelschwinghsche Stiftungen Bethel' is commissioned by a Bielefeld housing company to make three outreach contacts with the company's tenants who are threatened with losing their homes. These take place at different times of the day, even after 6:00 p.m. If no one is found during the first contact attempt, a second appointment is announced by dropping a letter in the mailbox or leaving a notice on the apartment door. If no contact can be made by the third (again unannounced) appointment, a business card is left with a handwritten note. The success rate of preventing apartment loss is 89% (as of 2019).

---

78 cf R. Heibrock, *Gesamtkonzept Wohnungslosenhilfe 97 – Zwölfter Sachsstandsbericht 2021* (Stadt Karlsruhe 2021) 13f.
79 Ibid. 11 (own translation).
80 S. Gerull, *Behördliche Maßnahmen bei drohendem Wohnungsverlust durch Mietschulden* (KBW Fachbuchverlag 2003) 168ff.
81 MAGS: Ministerium für Arbeit, Gesundheit und Soziales des Landes NRW (n 76) 14 (own translation).

7.3. Good Practice: Accommodation of Acutely Homeless Persons

As the overview in Figure 4.3 shows, there are different options for accommodating acutely homeless people in Germany. In the following example, 'good practice' is presented on the basis of emergency overnight stays that are open all day and an outreach project for the placement of non-German EU citizens, among others, in the regular legal aid system.

In Germany, night shelters must be provided by the competent authorities due to the enforceable right to accommodation in case of 'involuntary homelessness', as emergency care must be provided immediately (see The State's Obligation to Accommodate Homeless People). Uniform standards for these shelters do not exist; only the federal state of North Rhine-Westphalia has issued recommendations in this regard in 2022.[82] Most of the night shelters in Germany are only open at night. This poses many problems for those affected, even if there are counselling and accommodation services open during the day, for example, warming rooms/day care centres for homeless people. They have to carry their belongings around with them or deposit them in a safe place. If they have no income, they have to organize every day anew how to get food, drink, and fresh clothes, where they can take a shower or use a toilet. During the coronavirus pandemic, the authorities tried to enforce lockdowns with the slogan 'stay at home'. In Berlin, therefore, three so-called 24/7 facilities for rough sleepers were created in 2020.

Berlin: 24/7 Facilities for Rough Sleepers[83]

Contrary to the responsibilities of the 12 Berlin districts for the provision and financing of night shelters, in 2020, the Senate Department for Integration, Labour, and Social Affairs (SenIAS) implemented three unconditional shelters, open 24/7, at short notice and without red tape. In a very short time, a total of 400 new places for rough sleepers was created. According to an evaluation of the offer,

> the facilities offered above all the possibility of leaving everyday problems behind: no worries about where to sleep the next night, about food or sanitary facilities. Leaving these worries behind made it possible for the residents to actively strive for a change in their lives and to make use of the social counselling [offered there, SG].[84]

The offer has not yet become permanent, so the three facilities were closed again after a few months. However, their success led to the fact that 24/7 facilities and their funding continue to be discussed in practice and politics and have even made it into the current coalition agreement of the Berlin government as an offer to be examined. Two further facilities were funded by EU REACT until November 2022.

---

82 cf MAGS: Ministerium für Arbeit, Gesundheit und Soziales des Landes NRW, *Empfehlungen des Ministeriums für Arbeit, Gesundheit und Soziales des Landes Nordrhein-Westfalen zur Ausgestaltung der ordnungsrechtlichen Unterbringung von obdachlosen Menschen* (MAGS 2022).
83 cf A. Lupprich, 'Bedingungslose Unterbringung: In der Obdachlosenpolitik eröffnete die Corona-Krise neue Möglichkeiten' (2020) 170 *WZB-Mitteilungen* 30.
84 Ibid. 31 (own translation).

Accommodation under regulatory law takes place not only in night shelters but also mainly in residential homes run by non-statutory or commercial organizations, which are called temporary but can often last for years or even decades. As is known from counselling practice and now confirmed by an analysis of the German Institute for Human Rights 2022, these shelters do not always comply with human rights. Single people, but also families with children, who are accommodated there often live in cramped conditions, without privacy and peace, and under sometimes catastrophic sanitary and hygienic conditions. In addition, there are conflicts and even violent attacks among the residents.[85]

However, homeless non-German EU citizens who exercise their right to freedom of movement are often denied even this possibility when their application for social benefits is rejected. A Berlin project has therefore been offering outreach counselling in the mother tongue for this group of people for years.

Berlin: Outreach Counselling of the 'Frostschutzengel 2.0'[86]

The project 'Frostschutzengel' (roughly translated as 'frost protection angels') was established in 2012 from donations. It offers outreach social counselling in low-threshold facilities of the Berlin homeless aid. The special feature of the counselling is that it is also offered in English and several Eastern European languages by native speakers. This enables them to reach migrants from non-German EU countries, among others, who are often denied access to regular assistance by the responsible social welfare offices. Through individual counselling and support, but also networking with other support services, existing access barriers can be dismantled, and people can be referred to appropriate support services. In some cases, with their help, it is possible to enforce – in court, if necessary – that those seeking help are accommodated by the social welfare offices in transitional shelters or hostels, instead of continuing to move from night shelter to night shelter. According to their own statement, the guiding principle of their work is a human rights–based approach that grants basic rights to all people, regardless of their nationality or residence status.

Most recently, the project was financed with funds from the Fund for European Aid to the Most Deprived (FEAD), as well as the executing non-statutory welfare organization GEBEWO pro's own funds. In 2018, it was awarded the FEANTSA Ending Homelessness Award 2018.[87]

---

85 cf C. Engelmann, *Notunterkünfte für Wohnungslose menschenrechtskonform gestalten. Leitlinien für Mindeststandards in der ordnungsrechtlichen Unterbringung* (Deutsches Institut für Menschenrechte 2022) 14.
86 cf M. Eigmann, B. Friedrich and S. Gerull, 'EU-Migrant_innen in der niedrigschwelligen Wohnungslosenhilfe' in Stefan Gillich, Rolf Keicher and Sebastian Kirsch (eds), *Ohne Wohnung in Deutschland* (Lambertus 2017) 287, 292ff.
87 See <https://frostschutzengel.de/en/> (accessed 1 September 2023).

7.4. Good Practice: Housing Provision and Aftercare

The German housing market has been tight and strained for a long time, and people who are on low incomes or otherwise socially disadvantaged in particular barely have a chance to find adequate and affordable housing. A study on the development of housing conditions and social housing provision in Germany shows an undersupply of 18% of all tenant households in 2018 – despite declining numbers of tenant households overall on the one hand and income growth on the other.[88] Homeless people usually have to put themselves at the back of the queue in the competition for housing. Even if they are on social benefits and have proof that their housing costs are covered, they are dependent on municipal programmes and targeted projects to provide housing for homeless people due to the often stigmatizing attributions on the part of potential landlords.

Appropriate Municipal Instruments include:[89]

- Guarantee declarations to cover possible rent defaults and damage to the apartment
- The use of existing occupancy rights
- Influencing the allocation practice in the municipal housing stock
- Contractual agreements between municipalities, independent providers, and housing companies

Furthermore, additional housing for homeless people can be developed through social projects. Following the model of the Social Rental Agencies (SRA) in Belgium, so-called 'Soziale Wohnraumhilfen' (Social Housing Agencies) have been increasingly created in Germany in recent years, which acquire normal housing and – in contrast to the broader target group in Belgium – explicitly provide or rent it to homeless people. As a result of a comparative study, it is stated:

> Although the quantitative success in housing provision remains limited in view of the many times higher numbers of homeless people, the findings nevertheless indicate that these organisations are very successful in (re)integrating people with particular social difficulties into housing and in securing housing.[90]

An example of this in terms of good practice is the Soziale Wohnraumhilfe gGmbH from Hannover.

---

88 cf A. Holm and others, 'Die Verfestigung sozialer Wohnversorgungsprobleme. Entwicklung der Wohnverhältnisse und der sozialen Wohnversorgung von 2006 bis 2018' (2021) 217 in Working Paper Forschungsförderung 47.
89 See Heibrock (n 79) 107ff.
90 A. Steffen, 'Dauerhafte Wohnraumversorgung wohnungsloser Menschen – Eine Ersterhebung eines neuen Organisationstypus' (2018) 2 *Zeitschrift für Sozialreform* 187 (own translation).

> ### Hannover: Soziale Wohnraumhilfe gGmbH[91]
>
> The non-profit organization Soziale Wohnraumhilfe (SWH) from Hannover initiates the construction of new flats within the framework of social housing. These are usually built on former church properties. Through corresponding occupancy rights, the flats are rented out with regular tenancy agreements by SWH as the landlord to 'cases in urgent need of housing' (see Case in Urgent Need of Housing). In addition, individual flats are also acquired and rented. For this purpose, a cooperation agreement was concluded with three private housing companies in 2016:[92] The homeless assistance facilities in Hannover report interested persons for flats to SWH, which forwards these reports to the housing companies after checking them. They check individually whether suitable flats can be offered in the near future. Through cooperation with the Diakonisches Werk[93] Hannover, tenants receive social work support if needed. A handyman is also part of the assistance offered. In 2022, SWH managed around 260 publicly subsidized flats in the city and the Hannover region.

In 2013, the results of a comparative study on 'Housing First' funded by the European Commission were published.[94] One of the aims was to examine the potential and limitations of the Housing First approach in Europe. Despite the positive results from the evaluated projects from five cities in the European Union, it took several years before the first Housing First projects were implemented in Germany as well. Two of them started simultaneously in Berlin in 2018 and were evaluated by the author with an identical research design. In addition to a gender-mixed project, the first Housing First project in Europe for women only[95] was launched in Berlin.

> ### Berlin: Housing First für Frauen Berlin[96]
>
> The Berlin Senate Department for Integration, Work, and Social Affairs financed 'Housing First für Frauen Berlin' (Housing First for Women Berlin) of the Sozialdienst katholischer Frauen e. V. (Social Services of Catholic Women e. V.) from October 2018 to September 2021 as a model project within the framework of Housing First. The goal of acquiring 30 flats for homeless women in multi-problem situations during the model phase was even exceeded despite the tight situation in the Berlin housing market: 38 women were provided with their own housing and

---

91 See Lupprich (n 84) 42.
92 See <www.swh-hannover.de/app/download/18861908/Vereinbarung+WW+Text.pdf> (accessed 1 September 2023).
93 Social welfare organization of Germany's Protestant churches.
94 cf V. Busch-Geertsema, *Housing First Europe: Final Report* (2021) 14 <https://housingfirsteurope.eu/research/housing-first-europe-final-report/>.
95 Regarding the term *women*, the project's executing agency explains in the concept that it 'basically refers to all women: heterosexual women, lesbians, transwomen, bisexual women and intersex people who live in the female gender role'. Sozialdienst katholischer Frauen e. V., 'Konzeption Housing First für wohnungslose Frauen' updated status from 20 June 2018, 5.
96 cf S. Gerull, *Evaluation des Modellprojekts 'Housing First für Frauen Berlin'* (ASH Berlin 2021).

> received an unconditional offer of support. Although only women who had previously lived on the street or in similarly precarious housing situations were included in the project, a housing stability of 100% was achieved at the end of the three-year evaluation. None of the women had lost their flat. The interviews with the users as well as the quantitative surveys show that some of the women had specifically applied for this Housing First project because they felt understood and taken care of there as women. In the final questionnaire, the support received was rated as very good by almost 86% of the respondents and as good by the rest.[97]

The project continued to be funded after the model phase. The coalition agreement of the new Berlin government provides also for the expansion of the programme (this concerns both evaluated Housing First projects). In the Berlin master plan of the former social senator (see National and Local Strategies to Prevent Housing Loss and Overcome Acute Homelessness), the goal was even formulated to 'make Housing First the standard approach in homeless assistance'.[98]

8. Outlook: Opportunities, Problems, and Future Challenges

For decades, Germany's federal system has meant that neither the collection of uniform nationwide data on the extent of homelessness nor a national strategy to overcome it was seen as a social and housing policy task. At the same time, individual states such as North Rhine-Westphalia have promoted their own innovative projects, which in many cases have inspired other states to develop and implement similar programmes. Nevertheless, it must be emphasized that even by European comparison, the federal legislation in the field of homelessness prevention and support for homeless people is exemplary. This potential is not (yet) always sufficiently exploited, but the current decisions of political leaders give hope that homelessness will leave its niche existence in the long run and will be considered a problem relevant to society as a whole. Finally, the state must also guarantee the dignity of homeless people in view of the German Basic Law if 'successful action in the sense of a successful . . . life . . . is (no longer) possible for them'.[99] This includes taking responsibility for the continuities of exclusion and stigmatization of homeless people. This also challenges the professionals in the field of homeless care. Their mission is to counteract both exclusion mechanisms: 'The economic exclusion through different models of rent protection and the socio-cultural exclusion by being available as a permanent contact in case of conflict.'[100]

There is an urgent need for greater involvement of affected people in the decisions about the design of assistance offers. Social workers must also make greater use of their political mandate, which is available to them by virtue of their profession. Besides the mandates given by their clients (help) and by society (control), the so-called third mandate comes from the profession itself and is based on scientific knowledge and the professional code of

---

97 cf Heibrock (n 78).
98 See MAGS (n 76) 11.
99 See (n 4) 39.
100 S. Lotties and W. Rosenke, 'Beschaffung von und Zugang zu eigenem Wohnraum als Kernelement Ambulanter Wohnhilfen – Grundprinzipien, Praxiserhebungen und Empfehlungen' [2022] *Wohnungslos* 41, 46 (own translation).

ethics.[101] The examples of good practice in this chapter have shown that innovations in Germany are only possible because of political decisions. Structural problems (such as housing shortages) can only be solved through structural measures (access to housing, including for marginalized groups). The pathologization of homeless people, on the other hand, must be resolutely opposed.

A 'return' to the invisibility of homeless people is no longer possible due to current developments in Germany, since, for example, the collection of nationwide data on the extent of the problem has been enshrined in law as a milestone. This must now be extended to other subgroups of homeless people as far as possible, especially the regular recording of rough sleepers. In addition, it is necessary to react flexibly to new target groups or groups that have reappeared in the assistance system, such as non-German EU citizens, LGBTIQ*, families, etc. All actors must be involved in this process: from politics to administration, welfare, practice, science, and finally, homeless people themselves.

---

101 cf S. Staub-Bernasconi, 'Human Rights and Their Relevance for Social Work as Theory and Practice' in L. M. Healy and R. J. Link (eds), *Handbook of International Social Work: Human Rights, Development, and the Global Profession* (OUP 2012) 34.

5
HOMELESSNESS IN ITALY
Old Private Stories and New Public Opportunities

Teresa Consoli and Antonella Meo

Introduction

Homeless people in Italy can easily get food and, in almost all the big Italian cities, will be able to access a night shelter. Service provision is usually based on common emergency accommodation provided by public and/or private organizations and therefore focused on basic, essential, and material needs. In big cities, additional services are available, including outreach support, help centres, legal assistance, human rights protection, and health and psychological support. In recent years, Housing First services have been actively promoted in many regions of Italy and are increasingly getting more political and social support.

Unfortunately, this is not the case evenly all over the national territory, as local services for the homeless are provided by regional and local authorities and are highly differentiated according to available resources and the social policies of local administration. In Italy, there still are no basic levels of assistance nationally granted, but the latest national plans against poverty, combined with the EU Next Generation Plan and the National Resilience Plan, are moving towards the introduction of greater local social services for homeless people. This chapter considers the state of homelessness in Italy and is organized as follows: after exploring the definition and the main features of homelessness in Italy, it describes the most relevant aspects of the legal and political framework set in the specific Italian national context. The chapter then moves to examine examples of homelessness preventative practice in Italy. The final section is devoted to offering reflections on the future of homelessness law and policy in Italy.

The Definition of Homelessness in Italy

The first research on homelessness in Italy dates back about 30 years.[1] However, it is only in more recent times that the phenomenon has caught the media's attention because of the

---

1 L. Berzano, 'Il vagabondaggio nella metropoli' in P. Guidicini (ed), *Gli studi sulla povertà in Italia* (Franco Angeli 1991); M. Pellegrino and V. Verzieri (eds), *Né tetto né legge: L'emarginazione grave, le nuove povertà,*

increasing number of people living on the streets in Italy. In 2014, according to the latest available research by the Italian National Institute of Statistics (ISTAT), there were more than 50,000 homeless people.[2] It was the international economic crisis that began in 2007 and hit Italy in 2008, its continuation and intensification, that again reignited issues that seemed to have lost relevance in Italy, drawing attention to the phenomena of poverty, impoverishment, and inequality in the country.[3] Specifically, homelessness has become the subject of renewed attention in the past decade, both because it is on the rise in all large- and medium-sized Italian cities but also because it has recently increasingly become the subject of political interest.

ISTAT carried out the first survey on the homeless population in 2011[4] as part of a research project about the conditions of people living in extreme poverty, thanks to an agreement between ISTAT, the Italian Ministry of Labour and Social Policy, the Italian Federation of Organizations working with Fio.PSD,[5] and the Italian Caritas organization.[6] The survey sought to estimate the hitherto unknown scale of homelessness as well as demographic and social characteristics of this population.

In 2014, a second survey was conducted by ISTAT, again in collaboration with the Ministry of Labour and Social Policies, Fio.PSD, and Caritas Italiana.[7] It was estimated that 50,724 homeless people, in the months of November and December 2014, used at least one soup kitchen or night shelter in the 158 Italian municipalities where the survey was carried out. This estimate was based on a sample survey and was subject to error due to observing only a section, rather than the whole, of the population: the count of homeless people was based on data collected by the services available in the territories. This data corresponds to 2.43 per thousand of the population regularly registered, a value higher than it was three years earlier, when it was 2.31 per thousand (47,648 persons). In comparison with 2011, the main features of homeless people were identified as follows: they were mostly men (85.7%), foreigners (58.2%), and under 54 years of age (75.8%) – although, following the decline in foreigners under 34 years of age, the average age showed a slight increase (from 42.1 to 44.0) – and, most had a low level of educational attainment (only one-third held at least a secondary school diploma). The percentage of people who had been living on the street for more than two years almost doubled and specifically increased between the two surveys from 27.4% to 41.1%, and those who had been living on the street for more than four years increased from 16% to 21.4%.

ISTAT surveys have returned a complex and varied picture of homelessness, despite the fact that in the public debate in Italy, the dominant image of homelessness remains that of a lonely, alcoholic man experiencing chronic forms of street life and in strong

---

i senzafissa dimora (Edizioni Gruppo Abele 1991), A. Tosi, *Abitanti. Le nuove strategie dell'azione abitativa* (Il Mulino 1994).

2 ISTAT, *The Homeless: Year 2014* (ISTAT 2015).
3 A. Meo and T. Consoli (eds), *Homelessness in Italia. Biografie, territori, politiche* (FrancoAngeli 2020).
4 ISTAT, *The Homeless: Year 2011* (ISTAT 2012).
5 fio.PSD is a non-governmental umbrella organization within the homelessness sector in Italy. It is a full member of FEANTSA. Since 1980, fio.PSD has been promoting analysis, studies, and advocacy action for improving services and protection of the most vulnerable people. Currently, 130 organizations are members. For details, visit <www.fiopsd.org/en>.
6 Caritas Italy is a pastoral organization of the Italian Bishop's Conference founded in 1971. It connects 218 diocesan Caritas committed in their daily activities to support the most vulnerable people.
7 ISTAT (n 2).

psycho-physical distress. No further national survey on the homeless population has subsequently updated this picture, but annual Caritas reports, based on interviews with people using the services, have focused on extreme poverty and homelessness, offering more insights on the phenomenon of homelessness. In 2019, the Caritas report[8] on extreme poverty also focused on homelessness and revealed a high percentage of foreigners (67% of the total) entering local centres, mainly men and the young (18–34), declaring housing distress.

During the initial phase of the Covid-19 pandemic, according to another Italian Caritas report,[9] there was a sharp increase in people asking for support,[10] from 195,541 users (2019) to 445,585 people (April to June 2020), and the incidence of newcomers was strong (+105%). The proportion of Caritas service users aged 18–34 increased from 20% to 23% between 2019 and 2020. The Caritas report 2021[11] found that 22,527 homeless people were offered services in the 2,663 local centres where the survey took place. Homeless people accounted for 16.3% of the total number of people 'listened to', mostly male (69.4%), foreigners (64.3%), with an average age of 44 years old, and were served mostly in Caritas counselling services in northern Italy. In Italy, as ISTAT documented,[12] in the year of the pandemic, absolute poverty increased, reaching the highest level since 2005. Almost half of all poor households were found to rent a house. Non-national individuals in absolute poverty measured over 1.5 million, with an incidence of 29.3%, against 7.5% for national citizens. In 2021 absolute poverty remained stable, but in 2022 it worsened largely due to a sharp acceleration in inflation. In addition, more widespread absolute poverty was confirmed among renter households.

As regards research on homelessness, in Italy, the concepts of poverty and social exclusion have traditionally represented the two main theoretical pillars within which homelessness was framed in the 1990s and has subsequently developed.[13] If the major difficulties in interpreting homelessness highlighted by the international debate are related to the complexity of the relationship between its two constituent dimensions, housing distress and social distress, in the Italian example, the dominant interpretation among researchers and social workers placed emphasis, from the outset, on the housing problem in the strict sense as deeply intertwined with social problems of marginality and poverty.[14] Since the first studies, the homelessness phenomenon has been analyzed in Italy as a problem of extreme poverty and severe marginalization.[15] The economic crisis of 2008 and the increasing rel-

---

8 CARITAS Italiana, *Rapporto annuale: Dati 2019* (CARITAS Italiana 2019).
9 CARITAS Italiana, *Gli anticorpi della solidarietà: Rapporto 2020 su povertà ed esclusione sociale in Italia* (CARITAS Italiana 2020).
10 Caritas counselling services are 'advice and support places': they offer material and relational supports generated through food distribution, information, economic support (occasionally), housing provision (occasionally), intermediation with other territorial services.
11 CARITAS Italiana, *Oltre l'ostacolo: Rapporto 2021 su povertà ed esclusione sociale in Italia* (CARITAS Italiana 2021).
12 ISTAT, *Poverty in Italy: Year 2020* (ISTAT 2020) <www.istat.it> (accessed 1 July 2021).
13 A. Meo, 'Vivere in strada: Carriere di povertà e pratiche di sopravvivenza. Uno sguardo sociologico sui senza dimora' in R. Gnocchi (ed), *Homelessness e dialogo interdisciplinare* (Carocci 2009).
14 Tosi (n 1).
15 N. Negri, 'Reti di rischio e percorsi di povertà' in G. A. Micheli and A. Tulumello (eds), *Percorsi e transizioni* (Franco Angeli 1990); M. Bergamaschi, *Ambiente urbano e circuito della sopravvivenza* (Franco Angeli 1999); L. Gui, *L'utente che non c'è* (Franco Angeli 1995).

evance of housing exclusion have prompted researchers to assign greater importance to the multiple factors that are interwoven and together cause homelessness.[16] Several issues and characteristics of homelessness have drawn the particular attention of researchers as well as social workers, including homeless people who do not belong to any group of severe marginalization, do not present themselves in a state of extreme degradation, nor seem to manifest forms of chronicity and dependence on the welfare circuit. Individuals who live 'on the margins' of society, whose existence, however, does not appear to be completely disengaged from either the labour market or the social fabric.[17]

In 2019, 5% of the Italian population lived in conditions of severe housing deprivation (against an EU-25 average of 4%), a percentage that rose to 7% for the poorest and 12.3% for the poorest minors. Pre-Covid estimates reported 50,000 eviction judgments, an increase of 57% in ten years (from 2006 to 2016), of which the share of those concerning backlog payments increased from 75% to 89%.[18]

The health and economic crises related to the pandemic have aggravated the situation. The Covid-19 pandemic, in fact, hit the Italian economy harder than it did other European countries, bearing down on an already economically and socially fragile country with low economic growth and high unemployment. Housing distress is taking on the characteristic of a genuine emergency in Italy, exacerbated by the pandemic, and there is an increase in homelessness, as more people have turned to shelters.

The Legal and Policy Framework on Homelessness in Italy

The general legal and policy framework according to which homelessness has been treated in Italy and the services that homeless people can receive echo the basic structure and the latest changes to the Italian welfare system. The Italian welfare regime possesses specific characteristics that have been deeply analyzed by scholars across different disciplines,[19] characteristics that can be briefly described as demonstrating:

- High polarization between categories of eligible beneficiaries and categories excluded from welfare services, commonly termed *insiders* vs *outsiders*.
- Strong differentiation of welfare service provision among the 20 Italian regions.
- An absence of provision of homogeneous low-threshold services offered at the local level for people in extreme poverty and need.

---

16 Housing-related issues were already prominent as the main drivers for increasing levels of homelessness identified in the large majority of EU countries. See: I. Baptista and E. Marlier, *Fighting Homelessness and Housing Exclusion in Europe: A Study of National Policies* (European Social Policy Network, European Commission 2019); Housing Europe Observatory, *The State of Housing in Europe 2021* (Housing Europe Observatory 2021).
17 A. Meo, 'Homelessness: Perché e come occuparsene' in T. Consoli and A. Meo (eds), *Homelessness in Italia: Biografie, territori, politiche* (FrancoAngeli 2020).
18 ISTAT, *Rapporto sul Benessere equo e sostenibile: 2019* (ISTAT 2020).
19 M. Ferrera, *Il welfare state in Italia: Sviluppo e crisi in prospettiva comparata* (Il Mulino 1984); M. Ferrera, *Le politiche Sociali: L'Italia in prospettiva comparata* (Il Mulino 2012); M. Ferrera, V. Fargion and M. Jessoula, 'Alle radici del welfare all'italiana: origini e futuro di un modello sociale squilibrato' in *Collana storica della Banca d'Italia* (Marsilio 2012); N. Negri and C. Saraceno, *Le politiche contro la povertà in Italia* (Il Mulino 1996); C. Gori (ed), *Il welfare sociale in Italia* (Carocci 2014); L. Bifulco, *Il welfare locale* (Carocci 2015).

These characteristics have multiplier effects when it comes to homeless people, as housing policies have never been considered a pillar of the welfare system in Italy but, on the contrary, residualized in the general structure of the public definition of well-being.[20] As a matter of fact, after a post-war reconstructive phase during the 1950s (INA-casa) and some national plans in the 1970s (GESCAL), the main aim of public housing policy in Italy has been to support individual and family property.[21]

As a direct consequence of this Italian approach to welfare, and given the 'territorial' access to welfare rights, during the 1980s and 1990s, homeless people were excluded from many services and could only get access to shelters, dormitories, or other kinds of usually low-threshold services and even then only if locally available. The role of municipalities and the competences of people working in local services were strategic in those years but were progressively lost because of the continuous cuts to public welfare services.

Since 2000, a national law reforming social policies and local welfare services[22] has promoted the provision and planning of resources and strongly supports the implementation of a minimum basic standard of social services at a national level (LEAS). Article 28 of Law 328 specifically makes reference to interventions for people in extreme poverty and homelessness and increased the amount of money the national Fund of Social Policies (FNPS) allocated to empower local services dedicated to this population. Law 328 also recognized as main actors of this new planning process bigger administrative units, territorial 'Ambits', built through the association of neighbouring municipalities with a need-oriented and accountable territorial organization of services.

This wave of systematic change was stopped by a limited two-year provision of the FNPS and constitutional reform (Titolo V), which reinforced the role of regions and supported the requests for decentralization and regional autonomy which are still active today after 20 years.[23]

According to the situation briefly described and to the multi-level governance profiled by the Law 328, still today the planning and endowment of social services in Italy remain the responsibility of regional and local municipalities organized in Ambits, while the national government defines and implements national minimum standards (LEAS).

The absence of any provision for adequate long-term investment of the FNPS aimed at supporting structural welfare reform led to a progressive decrease and almost a closure of the National Fund in 2012–2013. As a result, local services were gradually cut, and the economic crisis of 2008 shaped an evident nationwide deterioration in the condition of people living in poverty. Nonetheless, innovative, interesting, and mainly voluntaristic interventions were, at this time, animating the territories and regions of Italy, providing in some cases the only available services to people in extreme poverty and need.

---

20 L. Padovani, 'Italy' in P. Balchin (ed), *Housing policy in Europe* (Routledge 1996); M. Olagnero, 'Politiche abitative: contesti e coorti di accesso all'alloggio di edilizia pubblica' in N. Negri (ed), *Percorsi e ostacoli: Lo spazio della vulnerabilità sociale* (Trauben 2002); S. Mugnano, *Non Solo Housing* (Franco Angeli 2017).
21 M. Filandri, *Proprietari a tutti i costi* (Carocci 2015); A. Tosi, *Le Case dei Poveri* (Mimesis 2016).
22 L 328/2000, for the first time in Italy, defines a national integrated system of interventions and social services.
23 G. Viesti, *Verso la secessione dei ricchi? Autonomie regionali e unità nazionali* (Laterza 2019). In 2018, three regions – Lombardia, Veneto, and Emilia-Romagna – on the results of a public consultation, requested more autonomy from the central administration, but other regions followed this, and at present there is law reform on 'differentiated autonomy' being proposed by the government.

Following a bottom-up approach, competences widely acquired by social workers, psychologists, and educators, and also the analysis on the progressively more articulated content of homelessness, have been represented in Italy by the Fio.PSD, experimenting with new approaches and services shared at the European and international level. The European Consensus Conference on Homelessness in 2010[24] focused the attention of national policies, and in line with the EU 2020 European Strategy, which involved fio.PSD, Ministry of Labour and Social Policies, regions, metropolitan cities, and other entities, a debate was launched in Italy together with actions necessary to fight homelessness. As a result, in 2015, following also the National ISTAT survey on homelessness of 2014, Italy approved and published the first official document setting parameters and implementing social services for homeless people, including guidelines for tackling severe adult marginality in Italy, the first attempt to overcome the traditional emergency approach, recommending adoption of an 'integrated and strategic approach', citing housing-led and Housing First programmes.[25] These guidelines were the first official national planning document in the sector, a benchmark and standard for different levels of government to implement interventions and social services dedicated to extreme poverty and homelessness. The work of programming and implementation of actions, the allocation of structural funding for homeless people, and the integrated use of national resources and European funds have helped stimulate the debate on homelessness in recent years, including encouraging researchers to take a closer look at changes in policy paradigms, the role of policies and services, also opening a space for greater dialogue and comparison with wider European experiences and literature.

Unfortunately, neither the national Law 328 nor the national guidelines effectively grant a national standard for services on homelessness, and there is a high differentiation across Italy's 20 regions as regards the provision of welfare services. These differences have markedly increased in the last years, especially between the regions of the north and the south of the country. Economic and social differences between northern and southern Italy have always been relevant in the history of the construction of the Italian nation state but have been exacerbated in the last years because of a clear political will to enhance a federalist approach to fiscal and social welfare and to not compensate appropriately for existing inequalities.[26] What emerges, then, is a high degree of fragmentation and heterogeneity of services reflecting an emergency approach to homelessness. As a result, where available, there are locally managed night shelters; some are integrated with flexible services, but the main direct or indirect service provider is not the public sector or the state but rather the third sector and volunteers in place of absent municipalities, therefore reinforcing the emergency approach.[27]

---

24 The report 'Homelessness and Homeless Policies in Europe: Lessons from Research' was prepared by V. Busch-Geertsema and others and published by FEANTSA in 2010 <www.feantsa.org/download/fea_020-10_en_final8900978964616628637.pdf> (accessed 1 September 2023).

25 The document guidelines for tackling severe adult marginality in Italy accessible online <www.lavoro.gov.it/temi-e-priorita/poverta-ed-esclusione-sociale/focus-on/Poverta-estreme/Documents/Linee-di-indirizzo-per-il-contrasto-alla-grave-emarginazione-adulta.pdf> (accessed 1 September 2023).

26 C. Saraceno, D. Benassi and E. Morlicchio, *Poverty in Italy: Features and Drivers in a European Perspective* (Policy Press 2020); G. Viesti, *Centri e periferie. Europa, Italia, Mezzogiorno dal XX al XXI secolo* (Laterza 2021); C. Giorgi, *Welfare, Attualità e Prospettive* (Carocci 2022).

27 From a report on homelessness services in Europe produced by the European Observatory on Homelessnes (EOH), Italy has been placed in the category of '[l]ow and medium intensity non-housing focused support and only some intensive, housing – focused support': *Homelessness Services in Europe: EOH Comparative Studies on Homelessness* (EOH 2018).

In this context, specific policies against homelessness have been directly promoted and experimented with by the fio.PSD, for example, 'Network Housing First Italia', which supports pilot initiatives implementing a Housing First approach in Italy. Without national or public support, more than 50 members implemented 35 projects in ten different regions, rolling out this new approach to homelessness as pilot projects firstly in 2014–2016 and again in 2017–2019.[28] This experience reflects a fascinating attempt at a national, bottom-up social homelessness policy, providing monitoring and evaluation processes. As a result, Housing First has been progressively recognized as an innovative response to homelessness, and it has been included in the national guidelines and financed through competitive projects via European funds, Fund for European Aid to the Most Deprived (FEAD), and Italy's National Operational Programme for Inclusion (PON).

The experimental phase of Housing First in Italy contributed to knowledge exchange on homelessness, nourishing the public debate and legitimizing policies focused on alternatives to older services for tackling the phenomenon of homelessness. Fifty million euros have been invested in financing innovative services for homelessness, such as Housing First and housing-led projects, through public notice 4/2016[29] and further increased by L.33/2017. In the same years, Italy approved Law Decree 147/2017 and finally introduced a national measure against poverty firstly named Reddito di Inserimento (REI), which, after one year, was changed by the new government into Citizenship Income (RdC). Article 21 of this decree defines a '[n]etwork for protection and social inclusion' as the national actor responsible for the planning of different funds for poverty and the coordination of social services. The network is delivered at regional levels and seeks to bring together local and national services in the fight against poverty. In the wake of the pandemic, the network produced two relevant plans: the National Plan for Interventions and Social Services 2021–2023 and the National Poverty Plan 2021–2023. The first is the planning instrument for the national fund on social policy, while the second is focused on services targeted at tackling poverty. Both documents inform and define the basic level of national service (LEAS) on extreme poverty, and more particularly, the national poverty fund finances Housing First, registered residence, shelter services, and social and emergency services, assigning 20 million euros for each of the three planned years for extreme poverty and homelessness, according to Article 7 c.9 of Decree 147.

At the same time, the Recovery and Resilience National Plan[30] is further financing temporary housing and shelters based on the idea that the highest concentration of extreme

---

28 For the first years, there are many publications reporting the methods and results – Cortese (ed) 2016; Consoli and others (2017); Molinari e Zenarolla (2018) – and for the last two years, the fio.PSD report <www.fiopsd.org/wp-content/uploads/2020/12/Report-finale-Monitoraggio-fio.PSD-Housing-First-2019.pdf (accessed 1 September 2023).

29 Minister of Labour and Social Policies, Public notice 4/2016 assign 25M Euro on the national plan devoted to 'Inclusion' and specifically oriented towards people in extreme poverty and homelessness.

30 The pandemic, and the ensuing economic crisis, prompted the EU to formulate a coordinated response at both the conjunctural level, with the suspension of the Stability Pact and substantial economic support packages adopted by individual member states, and at the structural level, in particular with the launch in July 2020 of the Next Generation EU (NGEU) programme. Italy is the first beneficiary, in absolute value, of the two main instruments of the NGEU: the Facility for Recovery and Resilience (RRF) and the Recovery Assistance Package for the Cohesion and Territories of Europe (REACT-EU). The RRF alone guarantees resources of €191.5 billion, to be deployed over the period of 2021–2026, of which 68.9 billion are non-repayable grants. Italy also intends to use fully its financing capacity through RRF loans, which, for our country, is estimated at 122.6 billion.

poverty is in urban and metropolitan areas, and this requires greater service provision and the need to strengthen the territorial units, renamed as 'Social Territorial Ambits'. In relation to Housing First, by 2026, 177.5 million euros will have been provided to implement bespoke projects aimed at increasing individual autonomy and empowerment of homeless people, while 275.5 million euros have been devoted to shelters to provide centres offering low-threshold services to people in need. More recently, the European programme REACT EU has provided 280 million euros for measures aimed at enhancing social inclusion through the implementation of First Social Service, which should be integrated within the network of local services already operative or financed by the Recovery and Resilience National Plan (RRNP) Funds.

By way of a tentative conclusion, we can see that the legal and policy framework on homelessness and extreme poverty in Italy is rapidly changing. Funds and projects financed nationally and through the European Funds and by RRNP are oriented towards housing-led services, but in order to be effective, all these interventions have to be integrated within a broader, effective national housing policy which has been completely abandoned in recent years, with the result that Italy has the lowest rate of public housing of all European countries.[31] In any event, after a long period of non-provision of services and cutting of local provision, there is now an attempt to build a new infrastructure of local public social services as well as some interesting examples of Housing First and housing-led initiatives in some small and big cities which can be considered as the first safety net for people in extreme poverty in Italy. Unfortunately, however, Citizenship income has recently been abolished by the new right-wing government. From the beginning of 2024, in fact, it will be replaced by two different measures: the 'inclusion allowance' and 'training and employment support,' the latter aimed at the so-called able-bodied and presumably employable poor.

Examples of Homelessness Preventative Practice in Italy

Italy has, in recent year, closed the gap with the rest of Europe by introducing the aforementioned nationwide minimum income scheme.[32] After an earlier experimental pilot measure introduced in 2012, several minimum income measures followed including Citizenship Income, which was operative from April 2019 to December 2023 when it was abolished. Although the name 'Citizenship Income' suggested a universal, unconditional basic income, the Citizenship Income was actually a selective, means-tested measure targeted at poor households and was conditional on participation in job-search activities. This was an important step forward in Italy's strategy to combat poverty and social exclusion, despite the fact that the eligibility criteria were very stringent. Eligibility criteria included a household income under €9,360 per year, savings under €6,000, no second property costing more than €30,000, and also ten years of residence in Italy, and the last two years continuously spent in Italy. These were constraints that penalized many foreigners and homeless people, although, under pressure from fio.PSD, the government provided that civil registration was a subjective right for all Italian and foreign citizens, EU and non-EU, legally residing in the territory. However, the measure had a homelessness prevention function in preventing

---

31 See <www.housingeurope.eu>.
32 M. Raitano, M. Natili and M. Jessoula, *Two Decades on, Italy Finally Introduces a National Minimum Income Scheme* (European Social Policy Network Flash Report June 2018).

people from losing their housing, by providing an additional €280 to top up the monthly benefit for households who rent their accommodation, whereas a €150 top-up was paid to beneficiaries who held a mortgage (independent of household size). Citizenship Income was abolished at the end of 2023 and, from 1st January 2024, has been replaced with two new subsidies: first, the 'inclusion allowance' for those who care for minors, the elderly or disabled family members; and secondly, 'training and employment support' for unemployed people who are ineligible for 'inclusion allowance' and are actively seeking work.

While, as mentioned, the national landscape is characterized by extreme territorial differentiation of services to support the homeless and by an overall orientation that is still focused on emergency provision and centred on so-called primary needs, with service provision mainly focused on shelters,[33] the National Plan of Interventions and Social Services 2021–2023, in line with RRNP, proposes overcoming the emergency approach, calling for the adoption of an integrated strategic model, the strengthening of services, widespread reception, integrated caretaking, and the development of housing inclusion pathways with an approach that is also preventative. The territorial units aforementioned, such as Social Territorial Ambits, are urged to plan activity to strengthen the network of services in order to be able to intercept and intervene to help individuals and families in difficulty before they lose their homes and/or become chronically homeless. However, only a very limited provision of preventative services is, at the moment, available in Italy.

As international comparative research has noted, homelessness prevention has recently become a prominent element in the national strategies of many EU countries (e.g. Denmark, Finland, Ireland, Luxembourg, and the Netherlands).[34] These strategies mostly focus on secondary forms of prevention, namely, prevention activity designed to support people who are at high risk of becoming homeless in the near future or who have recently become homeless. They include actions such as emergency rentals, security deposits, help with moving costs, mortgage and utility assistance, tenant–landlord mediation efforts, and vocational education and training interventions.[35] International data show that prevention is most effective when it is part of an integrated homelessness strategy.[36] Prevention must be combined with rapid housing services that can end homelessness quickly when a family or individual has become homeless without warning or has sought help too late for prevention to work. Housing-led and Housing First services can be used in a preventative logic, especially for people with high support and assistance needs. Integration with health, mental health, housing, drug and alcohol addiction, and other services is important. For prevention to be successful, there must also be a sufficient supply of adequate housing, with affordable rents and legal protection for tenants' rights.

As noted earlier, in Italy, housing-led and Housing First services are the least common form of homelessness services, although they are increasingly appearing to some extent in

---

33 T. Consoli and A. Meo (eds), *Homelessness in Italia: Biografie, territori, politiche* (FrancoAngeli 2020).
34 Baptista and Marlier (n 16); see Chapters 2 and 10 of this collection on Ireland and the Netherlands respectively. The growing emphasis on preventative measures on homelessness globally is a pervasive theme running through all chapters of this book.
35 T. Byrne and others, 'Rapid Rehousing for Persons Experiencing Homelessness: A Systematic Review of the Evidence' (2021) 38(4) *Housing Studies* 1.
36 D. P. Culhane, S. Metraux and T. Byrne, 'A Prevention-Centered Approach to Homelessness Assistance: A Paradigm Shift?' (2011) 21(2) *Housing Policy Debate* 295; N. Pleace, *Preventing Homelessness: A Review of the International Evidence* (Research Report, Simon Communities of Ireland 2019).

many large Italian cities. However, the rationale guiding such services is still predominantly reparative rather than preventative in the country, but in the future, it may move towards a preventative ideology. The RRNP, in particular, provides for a series of interventions aimed at tackling serious adult marginality and homelessness, by proposing the implementation of temporary housing and access to low-threshold multifunctional centres.

Following the introduction of dedicated funds for extreme poverty and severe marginalization introduced in recent years, funds that the RRNP has now increased, even smaller cities have begun to change their approach in response to homelessness. Cities under 250,000 inhabitants (Biella, Grosseto, Brescia, Padua, Livorno, Siena, etc.) have chosen not to open dormitories or make people wait for access to public housing but have decided to start small-scale Housing First/housing-led services.[37] This is something new on the Italian scene. In contrast, major cities, such as Bologna, Turin, and Genoa, characterized by a more diverse range of services (including Housing First), have invested additional resources in developing an integrated strategic intervention model.

Here, the case of the city of Turin is particularly interesting. The city has a long tradition of initiatives and services for the homeless and an active role is taken by the municipal administration,[38] but in recent decades, the city's homelessness service provision, inspired by the staircase approach, has seen many limitations and critical issues, including growing numbers of people who, for years, have used low-threshold services without any real prospect of leaving the welfare circuit, with a shift from a person-centred to a place-centred approach that reduces the right of homeless people to self-determination. The city has employed government funds to strengthen the local policy system, by initiating a co-planning process for the development of activities and projects dedicated to the inclusion of homeless citizens in conditions of severe marginality.[39] In Turin, through joint and continuous planning between social services, health services, third sector entities, associations, social cooperatives, and foundations, avenues for reform and for the development of a Turin homelessness system of services have been identified. These include an increase in opportunities to exercise the right to housing for homeless citizens, those staying in dormitories, or on the street, by offering wider and more diversified housing resources inspired by the principle of rapid rehousing, as well as secondary prevention and social inclusion interventions to address the chronic status and deterioration of living conditions within the welfare services, with particular attention on the preservation and exercise of skills and abilities. In addition, there are experimental projects of tertiary prevention aimed at supporting citizens who have gained access to housing but who, if not adequately supported, risk 'falling back' into the previous condition of marginality and thereby losing their homes.

---

37 Osservatorio fio.PSD, *I servizi come agenti di cambiamento nel contrasto alla homelessness: Report di Monitoraggio qualitativo fio.PSD sui servizi finanziati con risorse Avviso 4/2016 e Fondo Povertà* (Caterina Cortese and Roberta Pascucci eds, Osservatorio fio.PSD March 2021).

38 The Turin municipality was one of the first to join the Italian Housing First Network and to take part in the first experimental programme with its own pilot project. See: D. Leonardi, 'Divenire homeless: Quale ruolo assumono i servizi di accoglienza nella definizione delle identità?' in T. Consoli and A. Meo (eds), *Homelessness in Italia: Biografie, territori, politiche* (FrancoAngeli 2020).

39 See: C. Campagnaro and others, 'Re-Orienting the Turin Reception System to Address Homelessness. Findings from an Italian Participatory Action-Research Study' (2022) 16(2) *European Journal of Homelessness* 97.

New projects of rapid rehousing are also being planned and implemented in other contexts in Italy.[40] Alongside prevention, as the first line of defence against homelessness, as international research has shown, rapid rehousing services are important and are designed to minimize the duration of homelessness, as there will be situations in which homelessness occurs suddenly or in which people only seek assistance after becoming homeless.

The Covid-19 crisis has, additionally, prompted the government and the regions to launch emergency initiatives aimed at coping, temporarily, with the economic difficulties faced by poor tenants seeking to avoid the risk of eviction. The 'Cure Italy Decree' suspended the execution of eviction orders for both residential and non-residential buildings from March 2020 to June 2021. The same decree increased the funds and extended the interventions of the national 'Solidarity Fund', which allows those holding a mortgage contract for the purchase of their first home to benefit from suspension of instalment payments in the event of 'temporary' economic difficulties. Law No. 77, enacted on 17 July 2020, substantially increased, for the year 2020, the resources of the National Fund for Supporting Access to Rented Housing (Laws No. 431/1998, 124/2013 and 80/2014), that is, the fund that allows local authorities to grant subsidies to low-income families to decrease the incidence of the cost of rent on family income. The Budget Law for 2021 (Article 234 of Law No. 178 of 30 December 2020) further increased the resources of the fund for the entire year of 2021. This intervention significantly strengthened an existing measure to support tenants in economic distress due to the pandemic and, thus, helped reduce the risk of evictions.[41] However, despite these emergency measures, structural weaknesses in housing policies persist, and public intervention remains uneven, fragmented, and unable to provide adequate responses to the multiple housing needs in Italy.[42] Several interconnected structural factors contribute to the problem of widespread housing distress, which were already present before the pandemic. These include rising housing costs in the rental housing market, deregulation of the rental housing market, low or declining public investment in the supply of social housing, the imbalance between the supply of and demand for affordable housing, and the impact of the tourism industry in large cities on the supply of affordable rental housing.[43]

The Future of Homelessness Law and Policy in Italy

Since the turn of the millennium, housing need has once again become a pressing social issue. Housing vulnerability is taking on entirely new dimensions. In fact, the economic crisis, major humanitarian emergencies, the coronavirus pandemic, and an aging population have put Italy's already-compromised housing system under even greater stress. The

---

40 Osservatorio fio.PSD, *I servizi come agenti di cambiamento nel contrasto alla homelessness. Report di Monitoraggio qualitativo fio.PSD sui servizi finanziati con risorse Avviso 4/2016 e Fondo Povertà*, C. Cortese and R. Pascucci (eds) (03/2021).
41 M. Natili, M. Jessoula, M. Raitano, E. Pavolini, *Politiche per la casa e per i senza dimora in Italia. Sfide e prospettive in prospettiva comparata* (SOCIAL COHESION PAPER 1/2021).
42 T. Poggio and D. Boreiko, 'Social Housing in Italy: Old Problems, Older Vices, and Some New Virtues?' (2017) 4(1) *Critical Housing Analysis* 112.
43 Social spending on housing in Italy does not reach 0.1% of GDP, compared with 0.4% for the EU-27, 0.5% in Germany, and 0.7% in France (Eurostat 2019). A significant portion of public spending on housing policies is allocated through tax breaks (exemptions and deductions), which, however, have grown mainly for middle and upper incomes. Matteo Jessoula and Emmanuele Pavolini (eds), *La mano invisibile dello stato sociale: Il welfare fiscale in Italia* (il Mulino 2022).

pandemic has, however, shown that it is possible to find alternative solutions to night-only shelters, by including the active participation of service users (the successful case of self-managed shelters in Savona is emblematic). It has also highlighted the strong limitations of a traditional and emergency system that requires sustainable and long-term reprogramming with the introduction of new cultural models of intervention, innovations, approaches, and dimensions of social work that are targeted at the prevention of severe deprivation and housing poverty. The issue of social inclusion rights, access to housing, and a fair system of protection must become the main focus.

The RRNP is an opportunity for change in the way the homeless are assisted. Italy's efforts to transform responses to homelessness into policies of prevention highlight the importance of international commitment to a programme for innovation.

The national government, as seen from the first months of the pandemic, managed to adopt anti-crisis measures (reprogramming and simplified procedures for the use of structural funds, especially for the distribution of material on FEAD resources). At the same time, in some regions (i.e. Piedmont, Friuli Venezia Giulia, Veneto, Puglia), some projects or good practices have spread in the homelessness service sector, such as extraordinary investment in shelters open 24/7 (city of Turin), socio-health protocols for the prevention of contagion (Milan, Genoa), and extraordinary night shelters for highly vulnerable groups (Palermo, Livorno).

Equally, the Housing First approach and housing-led (HF/HL) policies have now become a more serious part of the national debate on homelessness. Thanks to the FioPSD in Italy and to FEANTSA and the Housing First Europe Hub,[44] this approach has spread from Canada and the USA and is now gaining attention finally all over Europe.[45] But still at present, many municipalities and different territories experience difficulties in implementing the model and the approach because of economic constraints, or due to the unavailability of social (public) housing, as well as a lack of cooperation from private landowners. But there are also administrative issues related to the role of local municipalities, including the problem of adding homeless people to the already long queue for public housing. Nonetheless, Housing First/housing-led are now part of the services financed through the RRNP, and they will be implemented in 600 social Ambits across Italy. Together with these projects, the RRNP is also financing a temporary housing service, in other words, providing temporary housing for families, individuals, and small groups that can be hosted for a maximum of 24 months. All these projects will be monitored by FioPSD and the Ministry of Labour and Social Policies. It will be crucial to learn if, and in what ways and what directions, these measures might lead to broader structural changes in the provision and development of local policies.

Along these lines, and together with other European actors, such as the European Housing First Hub, there is growing pressure in Italy to commit to 'end homelessness', as some countries have declared.[46] The debate is focused on the need to adopt a systems perspective, a change in approach which has been recently proposed by the fio.PSD at the national level through a Consensus Conference (hosted in Rome in 2022). The call is for working towards

---

44 See <https://housingfirsteurope.eu> (accessed 1 September 2023).
45 S. Tsemberis, 'Housing First: The Pathways Model to End Homelessness for People with Mental Illness And Addiction Manual' (2011) 5(2) *European Journal of Homelessness* 235; D. Padgett, B. Henwood and S. Tsemberis (eds), *Housing First* (FrancoAngeli 2018).
46 M. Allen and others, *Ending Homelessness? The Contrasting Experiences of Denmark, Finland and Ireland* (Policy Press 2020).

the goal of ending homelessness using the principle of Housing First, not imposing strict procedures but supporting a transition, a change in culture and thinking, 'a structural and operational shift in the governance of homelessness form a system that manages homelessness to one that aims to eliminate it'.[47] The challenge is to move from an understanding of individual need to facing the risk of becoming homeless and offering flexible Housing First services in a bid to achieve the overall goal of ending homeless.[48] The change proposed is challenging but extremely interesting, especially insofar as it seeks to offer better conditions and life chances for homeless people, to offer them a 'home', dignity, and respect. The possibility of all these changes is strongly connected to the skills and the competences of national and local administrations in Italy to sustain the motivation for and implementation of change, not following the perspective of public order, as well as rethinking the *public* dimension of homelessness.[49] At present, homelessness is still perceived as a private issue, or as a problem of decorum,[50] in many quarters in Italy and is, therefore, treated repressively by many local administrators. In order to bring about a real change in the public policies on homelessness in Italy, the first steps must be connected with the empowerment and monitoring of national and local integrated planning and with the provision of regular and reliance data about homelessness in the country, opening a public debate on policy and the role of the state towards extreme poverty and the risks of becoming homeless.

---

47 Fio.PSD, Italian Consensus Conference (1 June 2022) <www.fiopsd.org/wp-content/uploads/2022/09/Manifesto_ENG_CC_2022-scaled.jpg> (accessed 1 September 2023).

48 S. Jones, F. Albanese and M. Revelli, *Achieving a New System Perspective to Ending Homelessness Through Housing First: A Policy and Practice Guide* (Housing First Europe Hub 2020) <https://housingfirsteurope.eu/publication/publication-achieving-a-new-systems-perspective-to-ending-homelessness-through-housing-first-a-policy-and-practice-guide/ (accessed 1 September 2023).

49 T. Consli, 'Ripensare la dimensione pubblica della Homelessness' in T. Consoli and A. Meo (eds), *Homelessness in Italia Biografie, territori, politiche* (FrancoAngeli 2020) 231–50; M. J. Stern, 'The Emergence of Homelessness as a Public Problem' (1984) 58(2) *Social Science Review* 291; E. O'Sullivan, *Reimagining Homelessness: A Blueprint for Policy and Practice* (Bristol UP 2020).

50 T. Pitch, *Contro il decoro, L'uso politico della pubblica decenza* (Laterza 2013).

6
HOMELESSNESS AND HIDDEN HOMELESSNESS IN SPAIN

Tackling a Somewhat Unknown Yet Increasing Phenomenon

Núria Lambea Llop

The Concept and Scope of Homelessness in Spain

An Uncertain Concept Leading to a Lack of Reliable Data on the Phenomenon of Homelessness

As happens at a European level,[1] there is neither a common definition nor a standard methodology for dealing with and quantifying the homelessness issue in Spain.[2] The dictionary of the Royal Spanish Academy does not yet include the word 'homeless' (*sinhogar*) or 'homelessness' (*sinhogarismo*).[3]

Official data on homelessness at a national level is provided by the Spanish National Institute of Statistics (*Instituto Nacional de Estadística*, INE) through the 'Survey on homeless people'. However, this data is collected and published at irregular intervals (2005, 2012, and 2022)[4] and with certain methodological biases.[5] The survey covers roofless and houseless situations, as well as illegal occupation and supported accommodation for the homeless

---

1 As methodologies and sources vary from country to country, there are no comparable data on homelessness at a European level. However, FEANTSA and Fondation Abbé Pierre estimate that 700,000 homeless people are sleeping rough or living in emergency or temporary accommodation across the EU today, which means there has been an increase of 70% in the space of ten years. C. Serme-Morin and O. Lamas (coords), *Fifth Overview of Housing Exclusion in Europe 2020* (Fondation Abbé Pierre and FEANTSA 2020) 11.
2 Therefore, we will introduce and analyze the concept and data of each existing instrument and regulation.
3 Although there have been some proposals: the UNESCO Housing Chair of the Rovira i Virgili University proposal in 2018 (also suggesting a new meaning of the word 'home' -*hogar*-) which did not succeed, and the Hogar Sí Foundation proposal (in 2021 and currently in 2022 as well) <https://hogarsi.org/sinhogarismo-rae/> (accessed 1 September 2023). RAE states the existence of a proposal to include the neologism 'sinhogarismo' to its dictionary <www.rae.es/observatorio-de-palabras/sinhogarismo> (accessed 1 September 2023).
4 Fernández-Evangelista argues that despite this survey being the main source of statistical information to monitor the homelessness issue (complemented with the night counts), its high economic cost prevents carrying it out regularly: G. Fernández-Evangelista, 'El acceso a la vivienda social de las personas sin hogar' (DPhil thesis, Universitat Autònoma de Barcelona 2015) 269.
5 A. Sales-Campos, 'How Many Homeless People Live in Spain? Incomplete Sources and Impossible Predictions' (2015) 9(2) *European Journal of Homelessness* 215.

(from the FEANTSA ETHOS typology),[6] but only regarding people who are in contact with the services provided by public bodies or NGOs. The last survey is from 2022,[7] and results showed that 28,552 homeless people were assisted in shelters and food services during that year (an increase of 24.5% over 2012), the significant majority being men (76.7%), but with a steady increase in women (17.3% in 2005, up to 23.3% in 2022).[8] INE also has a survey on support centres for homeless people, the last taking place in 2020.[9]

A definition of and data on homelessness were provided in the Comprehensive National Homelessness Strategy 2015–2020. This instrument recognized the ETHOS typology of homelessness but expressly mentioned that the Strategy only focused on providing concrete solutions to homeless people within the categories of roofless and houseless (considering the needs of the rest of the population deemed to be at social risk when establishing preventive action lines).[10] As regards data, it estimated a total number of homeless people in the range of 25,000 to 30,000,[11] noting that it could increase to 36,300. These numbers were calculated based on the INE data from 2012, the night counts from cities, and the number of people known to be living in cars, caves, staircases, hallways, and so on.[12] The Strategy also highlighted an overall increase in the number of young people, people over 45, and (young) women among the homeless population. The recently approved National Strategy to Combat Homelessness in Spain 2023–2030 (30 June 2023) also considers the dimension of homelessness established by the ETHOS typology, while continuing to focus on roofless and houseless categories. The Strategy, which highlights an increase of the phenomenon (based on the INE survey on homeless people 2022 data), is structured around two general goals: to eradicate roofless people by 2030 and to prevent people living rough.

At a local level, many Spanish cities undertake counts (and censuses) regularly to give an approximate number of people sleeping rough; the current outcome gives an estimated 5,385 roofless people in Spain, even though it refers only to municipalities and regions that have undertaken these overnight counts, conducted during different timelines (between 2009 and 2021). In general terms, the highest numbers (in absolute terms) are concentrated in large cities, such as Barcelona, with 1,636,732 inhabitants (1,231 roofless people in 2022), and Madrid, with 3,305,408 inhabitants (650 roofless people in 2018).[13] As these initiatives are taken at a local level and methodologies differ, there is a proposal (created in

---

6 FEANTSA has developed a comprehensive European Typology of Homelessness and Housing Exclusion (ETHOS), which identifies four main categories of living situation (rooflessness, houselessness, insecure housing, and inadequate housing) that are subdivided into 13 operational categories. The ETHOS Typology is widely accepted in the scientific field and used for data collection purposes, for policy purposes, and also for developing, monitoring, and evaluating policies.
7 INE, *Encuesta sobre las personas sin hogar* (INE 2022).
8 The particular case of women and (hidden) homelessness can be seen in P. Cabrera, M. José Rubio, and J. Blasco, *¿Quién duerme en la calle?: Una investigación social y ciudadana sobre las personas sin techo* (Fundació Caixa Catalunya 2008) 31 and in Fernández-Evangelista (n 4) 307.
9 INE, *Encuesta de centros y servicios de atención a las personas sin hogar* (INE 2020).
10 'National Comprehensive Strategy on Homelessness 2015–2020' 10ff. <https://www.mdsocialesa2030.gob.es/derechos-sociales/servicios-sociales/Personas-sin-hogar/docs/StrategyHomeless20152020English.pdf>.
11 These same numbers appear already in a rough calculation undertaken in a scientific report of 2008: Cabrera, José Rubio and Blasco (n 8) 25.
12 National Comprehensive Strategy on Homelessness (n 10) 19.
13 Numbers collected by the Arrels Foundation <www.arrelsfundacio.org/persones-sense-llar/problematica/espanya/> (accessed September 2023).

the context of the aforementioned National Strategy 2015–2020) for a common methodology for the analysis of the circumstances giving rise to residential exclusion in Spain, particularly focusing on night-time counts.[14] It aims to foster these counts among the Spanish regions and cities and to develop a common methodology to harmonize and compare data.

In terms of legislation, it is only with the 12/2023 National Act on the Right to Housing that the concept of homelessness has been regulated legally at a national level in Spain. However, there have been grounds for dispute,[15] springing from the fact that this concept was not contemplated in the draft bill and, thus, was hastily added to the final version of the bill that was presented before the Parliament. While the first version established an imprecise definition that excluded most of the circumstances within the insecure and inadequate categories of the ETHOS typology,[16] the wording finally selected in the Act (Article 3.l) includes a broader (albeit somewhat chaotic) definition, more aligned with the ETHOS typology. On the other hand, some autonomous regions regulate the concept of homeless people within the framework of their housing legislation, such as the Basque Country and Catalonia,[17] to include them as a vulnerable group that needs access to accommodation or housing. Both define *homelessness* as a housing problem and provide a broad and inclusive definition of this concept, in line with the ETHOS typology. All in all, while some (and increasingly) Spanish instruments acknowledge the full range of homelessness and residential exclusion typologies (but not all), the existing data is scarce, outdated, and fragmented and fails to reveal the full extent of the homelessness problem in Spain.

The Process of Urbanization and the Phenomenon of Hidden Homelessness

The aforementioned numbers (mainly related to roofless and some cases of houseless people) are only the tip of the iceberg of a much larger problem, as there is a whole range of hidden homelessness that is more difficult to identify. Many of these hidden homelessness situations are the result of the unstoppable global process of urban growth (urbanization)[18] accompanied by a context of unemployment (worsened by the coronavirus crisis 2020/2021 and inflation crisis 2021/2023) and job insecurity, as well as a lack of affordable and social housing in urban areas and a deficient territorial cohesion policy. All this impacts negatively on people who need to live in cities in Spain, mainly due to the greater abundance of employment opportunities or the presence of support networks, but lack sufficient economic resources to access housing (mortgage or rent) without becoming overindebted. A 2020 report on shared housing in Barcelona[19] highlights some of these hidden homelessness situations. Regarding insecure housing, it discusses cases of people having to share housing or

---

14 Ministerio de Derechos Sociales y Agenda 2030, 'Propuesta de una metodología común para el análisis de las situaciones de exclusión residencial en España: Los recuentos nocturnos de personas sin hogar' (2021) <https://www.mdsocialesa2030.gob.es/derechos-sociales/servicios-sociales/Personas-sin-hogar/docs/Recuentos_nocturnos.pdf>.
15 S. Nasarre-Aznar, 'El Proyecto de Ley de Vivienda 2022' (2022) *FEDEA, Colección Apuntes No. 2022/11* 13.
16 This was also highlighted by the General Council of the Judiciary. General consideration no. 76 of its Report on the Right to Housing National Bill (27 January 2022).
17 18/2007 Catalan Act on the right to housing (art. 3.m) and 3/2015 Basque Country Housing Act (art. 3.m).
18 S. Nasarre-Aznar (coord.), *Concrete Actions for Social and Affordable Housing in the EU* (The Foundation for European Progressive Studies 2021) 133.
19 G. Caballé-Fabra and others, *L'habitatge compartit a Barcelona i la seva adequació als estàndards internacionals* (Ajuntament de Barcelona 2020).

even rooms (with family, friends, or strangers) due to economic difficulties, unemployment, and/or job insecurity, or to other circumstances, such as a family breakdown, even though sometimes they are hidden behind 'collaborative' formulas, such as co-living or co-housing; room rentals, which are not covered under the Urban Leases Act, meaning, tenants are not protected; subtenancies without the consent of the landlord; squatters; people at risk of being evicted;[20] or those suffering from domestic violence. Concerning cases of inadequate housing, the report references people living in overcrowded conditions, such as the dwellings commonly known as 'hot beds' for immigrants or 'beehive apartments',[21] living in shacks or in tiny and deprived apartments that have inadequate living conditions (e.g. housing lacking accessibility or basic amenities or damp housing), or housing in shipping containers, provided that they do not meet habitability requirements.[22]

Indicators that impact and trigger hidden homelessness are the Spanish rates of housing cost overburden (9.9%, but 11.4% in urban areas), housing overcrowding (6.4%, but 7.1% in urban areas), and severe housing deprivation (3.4%, but 4.4% in urban areas).[23] INE data also states that 19.7% of the Spanish population lives in dwellings with particular housing deficiencies.[24] Meanwhile, the FOESSA Foundation estimates (undertaking questionnaires and fieldwork) that more than 4.5 million people are living in inadequate housing and more than 2 million are in insecure housing in Spain.[25]

Homelessness, a Complex Phenomenon on the Rise

According to INE (2022),[26] starting from scratch after arriving from another country (28.8%), losing a job (26.8%), and housing eviction (16.1%) are the main causes of homelessness in Spain. The data have slightly changed from the INE 2012 study, as seen in Table 6.1. It should be noted that the first cause of homelessness in the 2022 data was not contemplated as an option in the 2012 questionnaire.[27]

---

20 It remains to be seen what will happen with all those vulnerable households (even squatters) granted a moratorium on evictions due to the coronavirus situation (ending 31 December 2023), considering the lack of a functional, diversified supply of affordable and social housing in Spain.

21 Beehive housing is not legal but is an existing practice in large cities such as Madrid or Barcelona, with companies offering 2.6 or 3 square metre apartments for 200 euros per month, not as a tourist experience, but as a permanent housing solution. 'Un nuevo proyecto de 'pisos colmena' reaviva el conflicto del Ayuntamiento de Barcelona con estas viviendas' *El Periódico* (3 May 2022) <www.elperiodico.com/es/barcelona/20220503/proyecto-pisos-colmena-conflicto-ayuntamiento-barcelona-13601665> (accessed June 2023).

22 A pilot project estimates that there are 9,274 homeless people in the city of Barcelona, according to the ETHOS Typology, Generalitat de Catalunya, *Marc d'acció per a l'abordatge del senselarisme a Catalunya 2022–2025* 131. Thus, far from the numbers obtained by the night counts (e.g., 1,231 in 2022).

23 Data from Eurostat 2021 (2020 for the latter). The 27 EU average is worse than Spanish rates in overcrowding (17.1%) and severe housing deprivation (4.3%) <https://ec.europa.eu/eurostat/statistics-explained/index.php?title=Living_conditions_in_Europe_-_housing> (accessed 1 September 2023).

24 Data <www.ine.es/dyngs/ODS/es/indicador.htm?id=4909> (accessed 1 September 2023).

25 G. Fernández-Maíllo (ed), *VIII Informe sobre exclusión y desarrollo social en España 2019* (Fundación FOESSA 2019) 252. *Insecure housing* understood as precarious tenure, risk of eviction due to economic problems, and domestic violence, and *inadequate housing* being substandard housing, dwellings with serious construction deficiencies, severe overcrowding issues, living in degraded environments, and lack of basic supplies.

26 INE, *Survey on Homeless People* (INE 2022).

27 Addiction problems (12.6%) and leaving a juvenile facility (2.7%) are also new options in the INE 2022 questionnaire. Questionnaire <www.ine.es/daco/daco42/epsh/cuesti_epshper22.pdf> (accessed 1 September 2023).

Table 6.1 Causes of homelessness in Spain (2012–2022)[28]

2012		2022	
Grounds	%	*Grounds*	%
Losing a job	45	Starting from scratch after arriving from another country	28.8
Could no longer pay for housing	26	Losing a job	26.8
Relationship breakdown	20.9	Housing eviction	16.1
Changing location	13	Could no longer pay for housing	14.7
Housing eviction	12.1	Relationship breakdown	14.1
Household violence situation	9.7	Addiction problems	12.6
Having been deprived of liberty	7.5	Hospitalization	11.1
Hospitalization	6.8	Changing location	9.6
Termination of the tenancy contract	5.8	Household violence situation	9.6
Building in ruins, demolished, or burnt down	3.7	Termination of the tenancy contract	8
		Having been deprived of liberty	7.2
		Leaving a juvenile facility	2.7
		Building in ruins	2.5
		Other grounds	15.2

Source: Author's own analysis.

All in all, we can conclude that the main grounds for becoming a homeless person in Spain are related to structural problems: (1) immigration (the foreign population is over-represented among the homeless people: 49.9%); (2) unemployment or precarious/unstable jobs[29] (71.2% of unemployment among homeless people, and half of these are not looking for a job due to health or work permit issues);[30] (4) housing; and (5) relationship breakdown (nearly 2 million between 2005 and 2021[31]).[32] Housing-related grounds prevail,

---

28 The sum of percentages is greater than 100 because people could choose several grounds.
29 A 2019 FOESSA report highlights that poor job quality and problems accessing and retaining housing are among the main causes of social exclusion in the country, and that young people are more severely affected by these problems. Fernández-Maíllo (n 25) 217.
30 Spain is a country with 6.2% of structural unemployment and 31% of youth unemployment. Data from INE 2021, *Tasa de paro de larga duración por edad y periodo* and INE 2022, *Encuesta de población activa, EPA, Tercer trimestre 2022*, respectively. Also, Gestha (the trade union of technicians of the Spanish Finance Ministry) estimated in 24.52% the average black economy rate between 1991 and 2015 in Spain. Information <www.gestha.es/index.php?seccion=actualidad&num=735> (accessed 1 September 2023).
31 1,853,997. Data from INE 2021, *Nulidades, separaciones y divorcios*.
32 'Under Spanish civil law, nullity, separation and divorce usually entail the loss of possession of the family home to one of the spouses . . . also the case for *de facto* or legal partnerships.' S. Nasarre-Aznar and R. Maria Garcia-Teruel, 'Evictions and Homelessness in Spain 2010–2017' in P. Kenna and others (eds), *Loss of Homes and Evictions Across Europe: A Comparative Legal and Policy Examination* (Edward Elgar

accounting for 38.8% altogether (housing eviction, lacking economic resources to pay for housing, and termination of the tenancy contract). In fact, most homeless people consider that having housing (82%) or a job (78%) would help them overcome their homelessness.[33]

The transition from eviction to homelessness is closely linked to the availability of personal support (e.g. family and friends), social support (e.g. homeless shelters and services), financial support and resources, as well as the rapid provision of rehousing options.[34] Overall, homelessness is a complex and multifaceted issue, and eviction is often just one part of a chain of events that perpetuate it.

Despite the lack of consensus in terms of defining and measuring homelessness, the general perception is that the phenomenon has increased in the last decade, not only in Spain, but also in nearly all EU member states.[35] More precisely, homelessness in its different forms (squatting, hidden, roofless, etc.) is regularly highlighted as one of the main challenges concerning housing within EU countries.[36] Covid-19 has also led to an increase in the most severe examples of homelessness,[37] and in Barcelona, for example, 22% of the people living rough became roofless during the pandemic, according to Arrels Foundation.[38]

The Existing Legal and Policy Framework on Homelessness in Spain

Homelessness, considering only roofless and some houseless situations, has historically been considered an issue confined to the social services arena, addressed at a local level and following a 'staircase' model (rather than a housing-led model).[39] The main services offered are shelter or temporary accommodation, food, hygiene, specialized social assistance, information and guidance, and public subsidies.[40]

2018) 316. These authors also state that divorce is considered an important cause of default in the payment of housing, as 'the spouse that leaves the family home usually has to pay the mortgage on it, plus compensation/alimony to the other spouse, plus child support maintenance and other compensations'.

33 All data from 2022, INE (n 26).
34 P. Kenna and others (eds), *Pilot Project – Promoting Protection of the Right to Housing – Homelessness Prevention in the Context of Evictions* (European Commission 2016).
35 I. Baptista and E. Marlier, *Fighting Homelessness and Housing Exclusion in Europe: A Study of National Policies* (European Commission 2019) 49; C. Serme-Morin and S. Coupechoux (coords), *Sixth Overview of Housing Exclusion in Europe 2021* (Fondation Abbé Pierre and FEANTSA 2021) 10ff.
36 Nasarre-Aznar (n 18) 133.
37 FACIAM (coord), *Exclusión social y COVID-19: El impacto de la pandemia en la salud, el bienestar y las condiciones de vida de las personas sin hogar* (FACIAM 2021) IV.
38 Arrels Fundació, *Viure al carrer en temps de pandèmia: Enquesta a les persones que viuen al ras* (Arrels Fundació 2021) 26. In the same vein, a 2020 study on the use of emergency shelters during Covid-19 in this city reveals how 40% of people assisted were not roofless or houseless but were residing in inadequate or insecure housing before the pandemic, while 32% became roofless due to this health and economic crisis: A. Sales-Campos, 'Características de la población sin hogar atendida en Barcelona durante la emergencia sanitaria de la Covid-19' (Actas VIII Congreso REPS, Servicio Editorial de la Universidad del País Vasco, Bilbao 2022) 471.
39 Fernández-Evangelista (n 4) 257, 287.
40 Municipal registration must be facilitated to homeless people (even roofless), so as they can have access to the mentioned services and facilities. *Resolución de 29 de abril de 2020, de la Subsecretaría, por la que se publica la Resolución de 17 de febrero de 2020, de la Presidencia del Instituto Nacional de Estadística y de la Dirección General de Cooperación Autonómica y Local, por la que se dictan instrucciones técnicas a los Ayuntamientos sobre la gestión del Padrón municipal* (BOE 2 May 2020, No. 122).

If we consider the broad concept of homelessness (ETHOS typology), Spain has passed a significant number of regulations focused on the most vulnerable groups[41] (both at national and regional levels) as a result of, first, the 2007 Global Financial Crash (GFC) and, later, the coronavirus and Ukraine war crises. Some of the measures adopted include the suspension of evictions for non-payment of mortgage or rent (or even due to squatting), extraordinary extensions of tenancy contracts, forced social rents, housing expropriations to provide social tenancies, rental (emergency) subsidies, public loans or other public subsidies, rent and rent increase caps in private rental contracts, electricity discount vouchers, debt restructuring or negotiation, urgent measures for the protection of mortgage debtors, increasing – by all means, both positive incentives and coercive measures[42] – the social rental housing stock, and so on.[43] Most of these are reactive short-term measures, some of them amended many times (to embrace more vulnerable groups) and some declared unconstitutional, bringing legal uncertainty to the housing legal system. And very few provide reliable data on the suitability of the measures regulated, nor do they incorporate cost–benefit calculations or mechanisms for their ex-post evaluation.[44] The result is incoherent multi-level legislation that creates legal uncertainty and does not provide necessary, broader structural measures to tackle the housing issue.[45] It is yet to be seen what will occur when the continuous renewal of the suspension of evictions comes to an end on 31 December 2024.[46]

Homelessness is, however, a complex and multidimensional phenomenon that has a cross-impact on many fields – housing, economics, health, labour, social assistance, education, foreign policy/migration, consumer protection, among others. But in Spain, it lacks specific and special legislation. The multi-level administration system in Spain implies that competences related to these areas are handled at different levels (state, regional, and local). The state has exclusive responsibility for establishing basic conditions for the preservation of equality in terms of rights and duties, labour legislation, civil law legislation, and planning the basis of economic activity, while the autonomous regions have powers related to land planning, urbanism and housing, social assistance, and health and hygiene. Meanwhile, municipalities assess social needs and provide immediate attention to people at risk of (or who are already suffering from) social exclusion.[47] In that sense, homelessness is

---

41 In some of these regulations, social services are given the role of determining whether a person is at risk of residential exclusion or of being in another type of vulnerable situation. See, for example, Royal Decree Laws 11/2020 and 37/2020 or State Housing Plans 2018–2021 and 2022–2025, or Catalan Acts 24/2015 and 4/2016, among others.
42 Some of them (and whether they were declared unconstitutional) are in S. Nasarre-Aznar, *Los anos de la crisis de la vivienda. De las hipotecas subprime a la vivienda colaborativa* (Tirant lo Blanch 2020) 469.
43 See, for example, Royal Decree-Laws 6/2012 and 27/2012, Acts 1/2013 and 25/2015 at national level and Acts 14/2015, 24/2015, 4/2016, 11/2020, 1/2022 and Decree-Law 17/2019 at Catalan level, among others. Also, Royal Decree-Laws 8/2020, 11/2020 and 37/2020 adopting measures as a response to the Covid-19 crisis and Royal Decree-Laws 6/2022 and 11/2022 introduced as a result of the Ukrainian war.
44 R. Maria Garcia-Teruel and S. Nasarre-Aznar, 'Quince años sin solución para la vivienda: La innovación legal y la ciencia de datos en política de vivienda' (2022) 789 *Revista Crítica de Derecho Inmobiliario* 183.
45 Nasarre-Aznar (n 18) 44.
46 Extended by Royal Decree-Law 8/2023, 27 December. BOE 28 December 2023, No. 310.
47 See the division of competences in Articles 148 and 149 of the Spanish Constitution and Articles 25 Act 7/1985, 2 April, regulating the Bases of the Local Regimes (BOE 3 April 1985, No. 80).

not tackled using a coordinated approach involving different administrative levels[48] (and different departments at the same level) which hinders efforts to engage a comprehensive approach to this complex issue, creating loopholes and disruption.[49]

The *Comprehensive National Homelessness Strategy 2015–2020* was the first national instrument to provide an integrated policy framework of action to tackle homelessness, in line with EU requirements. However, it was poorly implemented due to a confused alignment of objectives and measures (because of unclear concepts and lack of real data on the phenomenon), lack of leadership and coordination between multi-level governments, and lack of a specific budget and a failure to give political priority to the matter. These are the conclusions of an evaluation of this strategy (2020),[50] which also put forward recommendations for the design of a new national strategy, finally approved in 2023.[51] Despite these shortcomings, the instrument was viewed as a key reference and resource by some regional and local governments aiming to develop their own strategic plans, for example, Comunidad de Madrid (2016–2021), Basque Country (2018–2021), and Galicia (2019–2023)[52] at a regional level, and Madrid (2015–2020), Barcelona (2016–2020), Las Palmas de Gran Canaria (2017–2021), or Zaragoza (2018) at a local level. Another national instrument that could have an impact on homelessness policies is the *National Strategy to Prevent and Tackle Poverty and Social Exclusion 2019–2023*,[53] as it expressly classifies *homeless people* as a priority group for housing policies (in fact, its forerunner instrument was the institutional framework for homelessness policies, prior to the adoption of the *Homelessness Strategy of 2015*).

A number of regional laws on social services discuss homeless or roofless people as rights-holders,[54] entitled to shelter or temporary accommodation, while other regional laws refer to wider terms, such as *social exclusion* or *social urgency*.[55] In the housing field, the 12/2023 National Act on the Right to Housing[56] offers a broad but imprecise and quite

---

48 V. Marbán-Gallego and G. Rodríguez-Cabrero, 'Las políticas sociales de lucha contra el sinhogarismo en la Unión Europea y España: Alcance, efectividad y principales limitaciones y prioridades' (2020) 72 *Gizarte zerbitzuetarako aldizkaria: Revista de servicios sociales* 5, 13.
49 Nasarre-Aznar (n 18) 44.
50 Instituto para la Evaluación de Políticas Públicas, *Evaluación intermedia de la Estrategia Nacional Integral para Personas Sin Hogar (2015–2020): Informe final* (Ministerio de Política Territorial y Función pública 2020) 118ff.
51 National Strategy to Combat Homelessness in Spain 2023–2030 (30 June 2023).
52 Catalonia started the elaboration of a *Comprehensive Strategic Plan* (Agreement GOV/161/2016, 20 December. DOGC 22 December 2016, No. 7272) that was never finished and in 2022 has passed a *Framework for Action to tackle homelessness in Catalonia 2022–2025* (Agreement GOV/59/2022, 29 March. DOGC 31 March 2022, No. 8638).
53 *Estrategia Nacional de Prevención y Lucha contra la Pobreza y la Exclusión Social 2019–2023*.
54 'Homeless people' in Act 16/2019, 2 May, on Social Services of the Canary Islands and 'roofless people' in Extremadura and Navarra Social Services Acts (Act 14/2015, 9 April and Act 15/2006, 14 December). Asturias and Castilla y León Social Services Acts (Act 1/2003, 24 February and Act 16/2010, 20 December) refer to them as 'bystanders' (*transeúntes*) and Balearic Islands and Catalonia Social Services Acts (Act 4/2009, 11 June and Act 12/2007, 11 October) refer to 'social need due to lack of housing'.
55 For example, Aragón (5/2009, 30 June), Castilla-la Mancha (14/2010, 16 December), La Rioja (7/2009, 22 December), the Basque Country (12/2008, 5 December) or Comunidad Valenciana (3/2019, 18 February) Social Services Acts.
56 Although the Bill received more than 800 amendments (Enmiendas e índice de enmiendas al articulado. 121/000089 Proyecto de Ley por el derecho a la vivienda, BOCG 27 May 2022, No. 89/3) and a critical analysis from the General Council of the Judiciary (see the Report on the Right to Housing National Bill, 27 January 2022), the Act was finally passed in May 2023.

disordered definition of homelessness (Article 3.l), expressly mentioned only once again in Article 14, when describing cases of exceptional vulnerability, and it only regulates broad policy issues.[57] At a regional level, some autonomous regions expressly include homeless people in their Housing Acts, such as the Basque Country or Catalonia,[58] defining the issue as an issue of residential exclusion and framing the homeless as beneficiaries of certain housing or accommodation programmes.[59]

It is worth mentioning the Catalan legislative proposal on transitional and emergency measures to tackle and eradicate homelessness (2022),[60] aimed at categories 1, 2, and 3 of the ETHOS typology (arguing that these are the most separable categories, in need of specific legislation, and which can be treated homogeneously, fully, and coherently in a legal text). Its ultimate purpose is to eradicate these categories of housing deprivation. And to do so, it provides measures intended to afford real and effective assistance to this group, recognizes rights and the need to provide services to guarantee them a dignified life, and delivers a decent residential space. Thus, as well as creating a registry of entities for homeless people and creating inter-departmental, inter-administrative, and participatory bodies, it also regulates rights for homeless people pertaining to one of those first three categories, standing out, among them, the right to a decent residential space as a subjective right that is enforceable before the courts (Article 12). Also, the 15/2022 national comprehensive Act on equal treatment and non-discrimination[61] explicitly categorizes homeless people as a group that should not be excluded from healthcare services (Article 15) or from any social service (Article 16), taking into consideration their particular needs when designing housing and urban planning policies (Article 20). It does not, however, provide any definition of *homeless people*.

Housing plans are the main mechanism for establishing housing policies, and in the aftermath of the coronavirus crisis, the *National Housing Plan 2018–2022* was amended[62] to introduce a new programme specifically focused on providing immediate housing solutions to victims of gender-based violence, people evicted from their primary residence, homeless people, and other particularly vulnerable people.[63] This programme endures with the current *National Housing Plan 2022–2025*[64] (Articles 35 to 42), the funding of which is provided as a priority (together with rent subsidies for tenants in a situation of supervening vulnerability). Before that, the *National Housing Plan 2009–2012*[65] contemplated homeless people as a group entitled to access protected accommodation for particularly vulnerable groups, but this programme was not regulated in the subsequent *Plan 2013–2016*.

---

57 See an in-depth study of the Right to Housing National Bill in Nasarre-Aznar (no. 15), where the author also highlights the risk of the future Act being declared partially unconstitutional.
58 Housing Act 3/2015 and Right to Housing Act 18/2007, respectively.
59 'Alojamientos dotacionales' (Article 3.j) and 'viviendas de inserción' (Article 70) in Catalonia and 'alojamientos dotacionales' in the Basque Country (Article 23).
60 Arrels Fundació, 'Entidades sociales y mundo académico trasladamos al Parlament de Cataluña una propuesta de ley para hacer frente al sinhogarismo' *Arrels Fundació* (25 January 2022) <www.arrelsfundacio.org/es/propuesta-ley-sinhogarismo/> (accessed September 2023).
61 Act 15/2022, 12 July, integral para la igualdad de trato y la no discriminación. BOE 13 July 2022, No. 167.
62 Royal Decree 106/2018, 9 March. BOE 10 March 2018, No. 61. Amended by Orden TMA/336/2020, 9 April. BOE 11 April 2020, No. 101.
63 Considering the ETHOS Typology, all these situations would already be regarded as homelessness.
64 Royal Decree 42/2022, 18 January. BOE 19 January 2022, No. 16.
65 Royal Decree 2066/2008, 12 December. BOE 24 January 2008, No. 309.

Therefore, the homelessness issue has begun to be addressed by public policies in Spain, and the concept has even been introduced legally, but it is nevertheless poorly defined. The existence of multi-level government and different fields and competences related to homelessness in Spain hinders the effectiveness of the measures adopted and means that the level of commitment and the steps taken in this field vary significantly between regions and municipalities. Moreover, housing regulations that focus on this vulnerable group are generally oblivious to the complexity of the problem and, above all, to the realities of roofless and houseless people.[66]

Analyzing Existing Measures to Prevent and Tackle Homelessness in Spain

Structural Measures

A European project on evictions and homelessness (ordered by the European Commission, 2016)[67] highlighted the importance of not only focusing on reactive measures (once eviction has taken place) when tackling evictions and homelessness but also fostering structural and treatment measures to achieve a comprehensive intervention against this phenomenon. Primary (structural), secondary (treatment), and tertiary (reactive) prevention measures[68] combined can work effectively. Moreover, structural measures may be more costly in the short term but end up being less costly in the medium and long term (expenditure on resources and overnight stay services, expenditure on health services) – not to mention the cost to the physical and mental health of the person suffering from this situation. In that sense, even though the main Spanish measures employed to tackle homelessness are categorized as either treatment or reactive actions, targeting only the most severe forms of homelessness, we can highlight some key structural measures:

1. Regarding the diversification of tenures, which prevents overindebtedness and evictions, two sets of measures should be highlighted:

    a. The introduction of two new types of housing tenure into the Catalan Civil Law:[69] shared ownership and temporal ownership.[70] These intermediate tenures contribute to the creation of a *continuum* of housing tenures (both in the private and social sector), facilitating access to homeownership in an affordable and sustainable way[71] and creating a true alternative to full homeownership and the rental market. Temporal ownership is also used by the Catalan government to sell dwellings to third-sector institutions and

---

66 Marbán-Gallego and Rodríguez-Cabrero (n 48) 14.
67 Focused on studying the (back then) 28 EU countries considered successful in preventing evictions and homelessness. Kenna and others (n 34).
68 These three conceptual classifications were originally proposed in V. Busch-Geertsema and S. Fitzpatrick, 'Effective Homelessness Prevention? Explaining Reductions in Homelessness in Germany and England' (2008) 2 *European Journal of Homelessness* 69.
69 Through Act 19/2015, 29 July. BOE 8 September 2015, No. 215.
70 See H. Simón-Moreno, N. Lambea-Llop and R. Maria Garcia-Teruel, 'Shared Ownership and Temporal Ownership in Catalan Law' (2017) 9(1) *International Journal of Law in the Built Environment* 63.
71 'In Spain, the huge wave of evictions that took place after the 2008 financial crisis combined with the lack of a functional, diversified supply of affordable housing were what caused the increase in the homeless population.' Serme-Morin and Coupechoux (n 35) 15.

to municipalities.⁷² At a state level, a cooperative model is being explored and developed to provide affordable housing,⁷³ and there are some co-housing projects in operation in Spain already; however, it is a model with some obstacles, and replicability is not easy.⁷⁴

b. Different positive incentives to increase the social rental housing stock. Here we find regional and local programmes that aim to draw vacant private dwellings into the social rental sector⁷⁵ (some of them similar to rental housing agencies), obtaining better results when combined with rehabilitation subsidies. We also find rights of pre-emption and first refusal,⁷⁶ as well as the creation of non-profit entities along the lines of the Dutch or English housing association model (e.g., the Habitat3 Foundation), even though a legal framework for social housing management providers does not yet exist.⁷⁷ A REIT-like company,⁷⁸ Primero H, has also been created to acquire and provide affordable/social housing, especially to homeless people,⁷⁹ a group often excluded from entitlement to scarce social housing stock.

2. Condominium legislation regulates the right of the disabled and elderly (over 70) to require the removal of structural barriers from the condominium, even if an agreement has not been reached among the homeowners.⁸⁰ However, regulation itself is not sufficient (the percentage of total universal accessibility remains very low)⁸¹ and requires increases in population awareness and financial support.

3. Legal recognition of the subjective right to housing in the Basque Country, in its 3/2015 Housing Act (Article 6.2).⁸² This is a breakthrough in Spain,⁸³ as the right to housing is not a

---

72 Shared and temporal ownership are chosen as one of the 50 best solutions to prevent and tackle homelessness and housing exclusion in C. Clark-Foulquier (coord), *50-Out-of-the-Box Housing Solutions to Homelessness and Housing Exclusion* (The Housing Solutions Platform 2019) 112.

73 M. Pareja-Eastway and T. Sánchez-Martínez, 'More Social Housing? A Critical Analysis of Social Housing Provision in Spain' (2017) 4(1) *Critical Housing Analysis* 124, 128.

74 S. Nasarre-Aznar and H. Simón-Moreno, 'Spain' in C. U. Schmid (ed), *Ways Out of the European Housing Crisis* (Edward Elgar 2022) 25.

75 For example, The Catalan Housing intermediation network – see Nasarre Aznar (n 18) 29; or the Basque Bizigune Programme – Clark-Foulquier (coord) (n 79) 40. See more measures in N. Lambea-Llop, *La gestión de la vivienda social en clave europea* (Tirant lo Blanch 2022) 285ff.

76 For example, Compulsory pre-emption rights in favour of the Catalan government to acquire dwellings coming from mortgage enforcements or *datio in solutum* (usually from banks). Art. 2 Decree-Law 1/2015, 24 March. BOE 1 June 2015, No. 130. Other examples in Andalucia (art. 73 Act 1/2010, 8 March. BOE 30 March 2010, No. 77) or Extremadura (art. 125 Act 11/2019, 11 April. BOE 15 May 2019, No. 116).

77 See a proposal in Lambea-Llop (n 75) 509ff.

78 SOCIMIs are listed real estate investment companies created in 2009 (Act 11/2009, 26 October. BOE 27 October 2009) to boost the rental market in Spain. They are similar to real estate investment trusts (REITs) and are allowed to trade on an official stock market and pay no corporation tax.

79 It is still early to evaluate the success of this instrument. In March 2022, they had acquired five dwellings in Madrid. 'Primero H SOCIMI adquiere las primeras cinco viviendas en el municipio de Madrid generando arrendamientos asequibles' *Hogar Sí* (3 March 2022) <https://hogarsi.org/primero-h-socimi-primeras-viviendas-arrendamientos-asequibles/> (accessed 1 September 2023).

80 Art. 10.b Spanish Condominium Act 49/1960, 21 July (BOE 23 July 1960, No. 176) and art. 553–25.5 Catalan Civil Code (Act 5/2006, 10 May, BOE 22 June 2006, No. 148).

81 A 2018 study on housing accessibility showed how only 0.6% of the people surveyed lived in a condominium that was universally accessible: S. Nasarre-Aznar and H. Simón-Moreno, *Accesibilidad de las viviendas en España* (Mútua de Propietarios 2018).

82 18 June. BOE 13 June 2015, No. 166.

83 See the impact, beneficiaries, results, and obstacles encountered regarding this measure in Nasarre-Aznar (n 18) 32.

subjective right in the Spanish Constitution but a programmatic principle. Nevertheless, this recognition does not guarantee direct allocation of rental housing in practice (due to a lack of stock) but rather a benefit of 250 euros/month (exclusively targeted on the payment of rent).[84]

Treatment Measures

Secondary prevention measures are those focused on people deemed as high risk of becoming homeless, and they can be put into effect at different stages of an eviction process: prior to the default, after the default but prior to the filing of a judicial claim, after the claim has been made, and once the court has made its ruling. Spain has implemented several measures, such as housing (emergency) benefits, discounts on electricity bills (and even a prohibition on cutting off the utilities of vulnerable consumers), housing advice and counselling, mediation services, legal aid to defend against judicial claims seeking evictions, and datio in solutum or moratoriums on evictions.

As a result of the consequences of the 2007 GFC and the coronavirus crisis, a plethora of new and multi-level (national and regional) pieces of legislation and policies has been introduced to prevent, tackle, and respond to evictions, as mentioned earlier. Most of these were of a transitory nature (intended to counteract the immediate effects of the crisis), despite some of them being extended for several years.[85] The measures implemented under these regulations have also led to a work overload for social services departments responsible for assessing the vulnerability of households.

Contrary to those transitory and intrusive measures, we can highlight some measures that have proved positive and effective:

- Institutional mediation services assisting with negotiations between financial bodies or institutional landlords and debtors/tenants to avoid evictions.[86] They exist in several regions and municipalities, such as the Catalan service *Ofideute* (created in 2010), a free information/advice service for households at risk of losing their home because of difficulties in meeting mortgage loan payments, monthly rent (if the landlord is a financial institution), or personal loans. There is also a 'Good Banking Practices Code' at the national level (regulated by Royal Decree Law 6/2012 and Act 1/2013) that includes loan rescheduling, postponement of payments, reduction of interest rates, and finally, a datio in solutum. Despite being voluntary, it is accepted by many lending institutions (83 in 2022).[87]
- Interaction between courts and social services and possible suspension of eviction procedures. In addition to specific protocols designed to enhance this interaction that already

---

84 6,137 people were granted this right until 2020, but only 1,172 were directly allocated. Departamento de Planificación Territorial, Vivienda y Transportes. Gobierno Vasco. *Plan director de Vivienda 2021–23. Diagnóstico normative-programático* 12.
85 Moratoriums on evictions of especially vulnerable households, regulated by Royal Decree-Law 6/2012 and Act 1/2013 and amended 3 times, now in effect until May 2024 (by virtue of Royal Decree-Law 6/2020, 10 March).
86 Highlighted as best practice in Spain for social and affordable housing solutions in Nasarre-Aznar (n 18) 38.
87 Resolution 18 July 2022 of the *Secretaría de Estado de Economía y Apoyo a la Empresa*. BOE 1 August 2022, No. 183.

existed previously (e.g. in Catalonia or Aragón), an amendment of the Civil Procedure Law in 2019 (by Royal Decree-Law 7/2019, March 1)[88] regulated the court's obligation to inform social services of ongoing eviction procedures for rent arrears or the termination of tenancy agreements, and a subsequent amendment in 2023 (by Act 12/2023) extends the notification to the regional and local administrations responsible for housing and social assistance and also urges them to adopt measures such as a proposal for social housing, financial support, subsidies, etc. when tenants are considered socially or economically vulnerable; the procedure might also be suspended for two to four months (applicable to natural or legal persons), to find a solution (Article 441.5, amended by Act 12/2023, in relation to Article 250.1.1° Civil Procedure Law).

Finally, the preventative role played by notaries public and land registrars (prior to default) as well as the support received from the family circle (after the default and/or eviction) have prevented many evictions leading to homelessness.[89] The Spanish legal system also regulates the obligations that relatives have in relation to the maintenance of other relatives (Articles 143 and 144 Spanish Civil Code and Article 237 Catalan Civil Code), an important measure, given half of the homeless population according to the 2022 INE Survey have children.

What Covid-19 Measures in Spain Taught Us

Covid-19 led to an increase in the more severe types of homelessness, the stoppage of different support resources, an increase in the number of different problems to face, and a decline in the strength of social networks and support services (accompanied by an increase in isolation).[90] It has also revealed, once again, the special vulnerability of homeless people, for whom it was impossible to comply with measures taken by government to tackle the health crisis (lockdowns, improved hygiene, social distancing).

Nevertheless, it also showed that it is possible to rapidly implement accommodation policies on a massive scale for this vulnerable group.[91] Also, the creation of centres or facilities specifically aimed to sheltering homeless (mainly roofless) people, or using hotels, tourist accommodation, or public buildings, gave an opportunity to provide 24/7 care, support, and attention from different kinds of services; collect comprehensive statistical data as well as information about the different profiles and needs of this vulnerable group; and design medium- and long-term work plans.[92] The pandemic also brought about an awareness of the need for spaces that allow for social distancing. However, whether these policies

---

88 BOE 53-2019, No. 55.
89 Nasarre-Aznar (n 42) 332.
90 FACIAM (n 37).
91 By means of creating temporary and emergency accommodation places and using hotels, tourist accommodation, public buildings and so on. Serme-Morin and Coupechoux (n 35) 17.
92 However, concentrating people with such different profiles and special problems (e.g., mental health or addiction issues) in these temporary facilities also generated tensions and harmful community dynamics. J. Uribe-Vilarrodona, 'Personas en situación de calle, políticas públicas y pandemia' (2022) 10 *Ciudadanías. Revista de Políticas Sociales Urbanas* 1, 5, 24.

will remain in place, will be fostered, and improved after the pandemic remains to be seen, as a large number of these temporary facilities have already been closed.[93]

Reactive Measures

The importance of working on structural and treatment measures has been highlighted, yet the implementation of reactive (tertiary prevention) measures is key to mitigating the potential harm caused when an eviction has already taken place and, ultimately, preventing an evicted household from becoming or remaining long-term homeless. In that sense, a body of good practices exists in Spain that should be emphasized.

The first one is the minimum income protection after mortgage or rent default, as it assures that vulnerable households retain a decent minimum income that cannot be seized by creditors, ensuring a minimum standard of living and facilitating rent payments for rehousing.[94] Debt relief and debt cancellation is an integral part of this process too.[95]

A second set of good practices is related to rapid rehousing mechanisms. Apart from the existence of night shelters, homeless hostels, temporary accommodation, or reception centres,[96] there are good practices geared towards providing access to permanent housing. One example is the Catalan Economic and Social Emergencies Assessment Board,[97] which provides a special and quick allocation procedure for assigning social rental housing to the most vulnerable groups (including homeless people). However, the lack of social housing means long waiting lists exist and new programmes are being created to allow public authorities to rent private dwellings (now also being used to avoid imminent evictions of vulnerable households).[98] The second one is the introduction, since 2014, of Housing First programmes[99] in Spain, even though the exact number of dwellings connected to this programme is unknown – an average of 439 in 2020 according to INE (an increase of 30.1% since 2018),[100] and between 600 and 1,000 according to the 2021 report by the non-profit organization Hogar Sí.[101] Despite these programmes having higher initial costs than other shelter solutions for homeless people, they generate savings in the costs related to external services and resources. They also show a high housing retention rate and positive outcomes in aspects such as personal hygiene, health, safety, and social support.[102]

---

93 Sales-Campos (n 38) 472, 479; Uribe-Vilarrodona (n 92) 17, 24.
94 Kenna and others (n 34) 155.
95 See Act 25/2015, 28 July. BOE 29 July 2015, No. 180.
96 INE, *Encuesta de centros y servicios de atención a las personas sin hogar* (INE 2020).
97 Arts. 73–75 Decree 75/2014, 27 May. DOGC 29 May 2014, No. 6633.
98 For example, 'Reallotgem.cat' or '60/40' Programmes.
99 According to the Fondation Abbé Pierre and FEANTSA, systems based on access to permanent housing and Housing First 'have proven successful throughout the pandemic by enabling self-isolation and requiring a lot less planning to prevent the spread of the virus'. Serme-Morin and Coupechoux (n 35) 21.
100 INE, *Encuesta de centros y servicios de atención a las personas sin hogar* (INE 2020).
101 Hogar sí, *Conocer para actuar: Políticas públicas de sinhogarismo en Europa* (Hogar Sí. Fundación Rais 2021) 20.
102 S. Panadero-Herrero, J. Martín-Fernández and L. Henar-Lomeña, *Assessment of the Housing First Methodology in Spain. Solutions to Homelessness: Executive Report* (Provivienda and Hogar Sí 2021). Another report evaluating the effectiveness of the specific Program 'Primer la Llar' in Barcelona stated that additional complementary medium-term measures are needed to maintain these positive results for the health or personal development of the beneficiary of the programme, and that some changes cannot be measured

The existence of Networks for Homeless People (e.g. in Barcelona[103] or Tarragona[104]) allows for collaborative work at the public, third sector, and academic levels, to tackle the complexity of the homelessness phenomenon. Networks focus on different objectives: creating and sharing data/material, knowledge, and experiences; coordinating organizations to provide comprehensive support to complex homeless situations; defining the resources/services and policies needed; and raising awareness among citizens and institutions. Finally, other important measures include the development and implementation of regional and local homelessness strategic plans and night counts.

Looking to the Future: Challenges to and Recommendations for Tackling Homelessness in Spain

Homelessness is on the Spanish public agenda. National and regional legislation has started to expressly address it, while comprehensive strategies now appear at different levels to tackle this phenomenon. However, a clear legal concept has not yet been defined, and data are limited and fragmented, obscuring the full extent of the issue. In terms of regulation, homelessness has a cross-impact affecting many fields and all levels of government in a multi-level administration. Political priority, a specific budget, and coordination between all levels of government are needed to successfully implement effective homelessness strategies.

All these issues are common in many EU countries.[105] Homelessness is a problem on the rise at the EU level, increasing in complexity due to the concatenation of three crises in the last 15 years, but Spain is not at the bottom of the list.[106] Family plays an essential role in prevention,[107] as do the best practices outlined in this chapter. Still, Spain has experienced, in the last decade, the introduction (and subsequent amendment) of a plethora of multi-level legislation, at times incoherent or contradictory, creating legal uncertainty. Several

---

in the short term. Ivàlua, *Avaluació del programa 'Primer la Llar' per a persones sense llar: Avaluació de l'efectivitat. Informe definitiu* (Ajuntament de Barcelona 2018).
103 <www.sensellarisme.cat/es/> (accessed 1 September 2023).
104 <https://observatorisocial.tarragona.cat/col·laboracio-en-espais-de-participacio-2/impulsem-espais-de-participacio/xarxa-datencio-integral-de-persones-sense-llar/> (accessed 1 September 2023).
105 Marbán-Gallego and Rodríguez-Cabrero (n 48) 12.
106 The rising trend over the last few years is lower than in some central and north European countries. C. Serme-Morin (coord), *Second Overview of Housing Exclusion in Europe 2017* (Foundation Abbé Pierre and FEANTSA 2017) 10; C. Serme-Morin and S. Coupechoux (coords), *Third Overview of Housing Exclusion in Europe 2018* (Foundation Abbé Pierre and FEANTSA 2017) 10. However, as these are non-comparable data sets, we can provide more specific indicators. One is night counts, where numbers in Paris or Brussels are three and five times higher than in Barcelona, for example (which is a high difference even if counts included the metropolitan area). Serme-Morin and Coupechoux (n 35) 26. Other indicators are housing cost overburden rates: by degree of urbanization (10.1% in ES, 20.3% in DK, 11.8% in BE or 11.4% in DE), or by age (+65: 4.9% ES, DK 18%, 11.4% BE, DE 10.3%; 25–29 years old: 9.8% ES, 22% DK, 18.2% NL). The overburden rate among social housing tenants is 11% in BE and 9.1% in FR and FI (8.2% in ES). Sergio Nasarre-Aznar, 'Los retos de la vivienda en España en clave europea' (Disenso 2023) 12; Eurostat <https://ec.europa.eu/eurostat/databrowser/explore/all/popul?lang=en&subtheme=livcon.ilc.ilc_lv.ilc_lvho.ilc_lvho_hc&display=list&sort=category&extractionId=ILC_LVHO07A> (accessed 1 September 2023).
107 Help from older relatives was possible because most of them were outright homeowners. Nasarre-Aznar (n 42) 333.

transitory and reactive measures have been introduced, instead of fostering those that are structural and preventative.

Beyond wider structural problems related to homelessness (such as unemployment, job insecurity and low wages, relationship breakdown, or immigration legislation) and the need to overcome the 'staircase' model, treatment and reactive measures in the housing field must be combined with structural measures to combat homelessness. With this in mind, the following key recommendations for tackling homelessness for the future of Spain can be made:

1. There is a need for harmonization of concepts (homelessness typologies) and methodologies to collect data on the homelessness phenomenon and, subsequently, provide reliable data on the matter. In that sense, research is key, and so is creating or fostering existing housing (or homelessness) observatories and institutes to tackle the lack of data and advanced research on this field, helping develop proper housing policies by providing reliable and in-depth data or undertaking accurate consultations and research.[108] Also increasing literacy in this field, by transferring and communicating trustworthy housing research to all interested groups.
2. Providing reliable data to the social housing sector and creating a legal framework for social housing providers to allow them to grow, consolidate, and increase the social rental housing sector.[109] Housing association–like institutions may help increase this stock and also provide services complementary to housing, such as social support, training, occupational integration, or a working plan, necessary when coping with such complex situations.
3. The importance of recognizing the complexity of the homelessness issue in regulations and policies in Spain and tackling it by adopting a comprehensive approach. Policies must take a long-term view if they are to be sustainable and coherent. Measures taken should address the real needs of the homeless based on reliable data and should provide cost–benefit calculations, monitoring, and ex-post evaluation.
4. There is a need for fostering better coordination among administrations (national, regional, and local) and between departments (housing, social services, health, labour). Public administration must be proactive, identifying (hidden) homelessness situations and implementing appropriate measures. So it is important to design protocols at both regional and local levels to prevent, tackle, and react to evictions and homelessness situations. Creating or consolidating existing networks for homeless people facilitates joint work between institutions and organizations at local or regional level to offer comprehensive support and coordinate services and resources, also providing fulsome data and raising awareness of the issue.
5. Finally, a continuum of tenures should be created to guarantee affordable housing, adaptive to each household's distinct and particular needs, by extending the regulation of shared and temporal ownership to a national legal system and amending the Urban Leases Act. Housing tenancies' regulation should balance both landlords' and tenants' interests,[110] and this Act should also include room rental regulation[111] and special regula-

---

108 Some examples in Nasarre-Aznar (n 18) 40.
109 See a legal framework proposal in Lambea-Llop (n 75) 509ff.
110 E. Molina-Roig, *Una nueva regulación para los arrendamientos de vivienda en un contexto europeo* (Tirant lo blanch 2018) 681ff.
111 H. Simón-Moreno, 'Capítol 22. El lloguer d'habitacions' in S. Nasarre-Aznar, H. Simón-Moreno and E. Molina-Roig (dirs), *Un nou dret d'arrendaments urbans per a afavorir l'accés a l'habitatge* (Atelier 2018) 293.

tion for social housing tenancies to provide the flexibility that social housing providers require for different social households' needs (so they do not evade this Act and the security offered to tenants).[112] A legislative amendment is also needed to provide legal security to both parties in co-living and cooperative housing models.[113] Schemes such as rehabilitation for rent should, additionally, be adopted to create housing solutions for less economically affluent households.[114]

All in all, identifying and quantifying the homelessness phenomenon is the key first step to addressing it in Spain and, at the same time, doing so from a holistic viewpoint which engages meaningfully with the different levels of preventative measures that such a complex issue demands.

---

112 N. Lambea-Llop presents a proposal for the regulation of social rents in Lambea-Llop (n 75) 561.
113 H. Simón-Moreno, 'Las cooperativas de viviendas en régimen de cesión de uso: ¿Una alternativa real a la vivienda en propiedad y en alquiler en España?' (2020) 134 *REVESCO. Revista de Estudios Cooperativos* 1.
114 R. Maria Garcia-Teruel, *La sustitución de la renta por la rehabilitación o reforma de la vivienda en los arrendamientos urbanos* (Tirant lo blanch 2019).

7
HOMELESSNESS LAW AND POLICY IN GREECE
Challenges and Opportunities

Nikos Kourachanis and Mando Zisopoulou

Introduction

This chapter describes the effects of multiple crises – economic, refugee management, Covid-19 pandemic – that Greece had to face in the last decade impacting the phenomenon of homelessness as well as the methods and measures that the Greek state has adopted in an attempt to deal with these issues. In so doing, this chapter explores the existing legal and policy framework pertaining to homelessness in Greece, examines the new regulatory framework for alleviating the housing problem in Greece, specifically Law 5006/2022, and finally, reflects on the future of homelessness law and policy in Greece. The chapter begins with a discussion of the homelessness context in Greece prior to the economic crisis of 2009.

Homelessness in Greece Before the Economic Crisis

Social policy measures for the protection of homeless people in Greece, in the period before the economic crisis of 2009, were based on structured planning or specific targeting of vulnerable people. Until the 1990s, high rates of homeownership in Greece and the crucial supportive role of the Greek family in social protection effectively hid and obscured the scale and severity of extreme social problems such as homelessness in the country with life-threatening consequences.[1] At the same time, the arrival of particular population groups (such as economic immigrants, asylum seekers, and refugees) in Greek territory with neither suitable, private accommodation nor any family protection or support – and, as such, finding themselves exposed to many social risk and vulnerabilities – led to the emergence of the contemporary homeless phenomenon in Greece and forced the Greek state to take certain social policy measures. During the 1990s, only three social structures for temporary accommodation of the homeless operated in Athens, providing

---

1 V. Arapoglou, 'The Governance of Homelessness in Greece: Discourse and Power in the Study of Philanthropic Networks' (2004) 24(1) *Critical Social Policy* 102.

only 155 beds. However, in this period, further measures to deal with homelessness were taken, including the creation of the Homeless Center of the Municipality of Athens; civil society initiatives, such as the organization *Friends of the Homeless*; the magazine *Dromoloya*; and NGO *Arsis*. Finally, there has, for many decades, if not hundreds of years and, perhaps, even since records began, been intervention from church bodies supporting vulnerable groups and the homeless.[2]

At this point, it is worth mentioning the government's proposal from June 2004, in the context of the Athens Olympic Games, to transport drug users and homeless citizens to special temporary accommodation facilities.[3] The true intention was to clear the streets, to conceal the evident and visible problem of homelessness. This measure was strongly criticized by the Greek public, who regarded the practice as 'cleansing' the city of extreme marginalization in advance of the Olympic Games rather than as a genuine social interventionist policy.[4]

Historically, the choice and preference of the Greek state in pursuing homelessness measures has been to adopt short-term planning on a case-by-case social action basis. This has resulted in a residual, fragmented, and managerial social policy framework for the homeless. According to this approach, the focus has been on the action of voluntary agencies and the church, while state social policy was only activated in emergency situations. Even in cases where state social policy was activated and the state intervened, this intervention was centred on and shaped by the short-term contours of political priorities in Greece and not on wider social policy theories or academic research, evidence, or developments.[5]

Simultaneously, incoming economic migrants into Greece during the 1990s were turned into an object of exploitation, living in conditions of impoverishment and precarity. The influences of the Europeanization plan aimed at the entry of Greece into the Economic Monetary Union (EMU) as well as the costs of the 2004 Olympic Games in Athens together had an ambivalent effect on the social policies aimed at tackling the lack of housing in the country. Despite this, since the mid-1990s and, in particular, in the early 2000s, the population groups targeted for social support and protection, including the homeless, have been expanded. Unfortunately, given the absence of any broader, comprehensive social plan, and with little political will, no meaningful or substantial reforms were forthcoming in the field of housing and homelessness.

Housing services and provision in Greece, as in many other Southern European countries, represent a particularly weak pillar of the welfare state,[6] which has resulted in either a residual development or even a complete lack of development of social housing policies in these countries. The problem of housing insecurity intensified in Southern European countries during the 1990s and in combination with the implementation of mild neoliberal reforms, such as the tendency towards shrinking or reducing of the social protection system built in the 1980s by the Greek Social Democrat government, led to a new and highly

---

2 N. Kourachanis, *Homelessness Policies. The Greek Residual Approach* (Papazisi 2017) (in Greek).
3 Ibid.
4 A. Sapounakis, 'National Updates of Policies and Statistics on Access to Housing and Homelessness in Greece' (2004) Unpublished report for the European Observatory on Homelessness, FEANTSA.
5 N. Kourachanis, 'Confronting Homelessness in Greece During the Economic Crisis' (2015) 10(2) *Social Cohesion and Development* 113.
6 J. Allen and others, *Housing and Welfare in Southern Europe* (Blackwell Publishing 2004); T. Maloutas, 'The Broadening and Mystified Margins of Urban Deprivation' (2012) 6(2) *European Journal of Homelessness* 13.

visible form of poverty, namely, homelessness.[7] The residual nature of state intervention in the housing sector and limited responses to the homelessness problem shifted responsibility for social support for the homeless away from the state towards charitable and religious institutions.[8] Over the past decade, the sovereign debt crisis in Greece and the extensive cuts to the Greek social protection system that followed led to a double pressure on the 'housing problem', as households lost a significant part of their incomes, and at the same time, any support from social benefits was increasingly weakened, due to austerity policies imposed by the Troika, pushing many more Greek citizens into poverty and, ultimately, homelessness.[9]

Today in Greece, the social protection system is characterized by consolidation of limited and residual social management and support along with emergency intervention. It is not informed by a coherent grid or wider supportive network of housing services. The services that do exist are more in line with the 'staircase model' of housing services. Despite this, in recent years, measures have begun to be taken and developed that are part of the Housing First approach to homelessness now seen in countries across the world, without, however, forming part of a wider, integrated framework for dealing with the homelessness problem in Greece. This typology of residual housing services focusing on emergency provision and increased levels of social control is intertwined with extensive cuts to public spending introduced by governments in Greece over the last decade, informed by a distinctly neoliberal approach to management of social problems, such as the tendency towards the reduction of social spending and the re-commodification of social policy.[10]

The Economic Crisis and the Need for a National Homelessness Policy

The period of Greek austerity policies, which began following the 2009/2010 fiscal crisis, highlighted the multiple problems inherent in the breakdown of social cohesion, the violent impoverishment of the population, and the inability to combat social exclusion in Greek society.[11] The outbreak of the crisis rapidly hit the Greek labour market, resulting in a sharp increase in unemployment. This period was marked by what might be regarded as a form of social collapse that could not be managed, at least in the first phase of this period, which is generally seen as covering the years 2010–2014. During this time, dramatic effects of austerity and associated policies could be observed in Greece, particularly in employment and in the private sector. By way of illustration, research identified a severe deterioration in all social indicators during this decade, as evidenced from data exploring the risk of poverty and social exclusion,[12] which increased from 27.7% in 2010 to 35.7% in 2016. Moreover,

---

7 V. Arapoglou and K. Gounis, *Contested Landscapes of Poverty and Homelessness in Southern Europe: Reflections from Athens* (Palgrave Macmillan 2017).
8 Arapoglou (n 1).
9 Kourachanis (n 2).
10 N. Kourachanis, 'Homelessness Policies in the Liberal and the Southern European Welfare Regimes: Ireland, Portugal, and Greece' (2020) 30(2) *Housing Policy Debate* 121.
11 Maloutas (n 6); D. Papadopoulou, *Sociology of Exclusion in the Age of Globalization* (Topos 2012) (in Greek).
12 *At risk of poverty or social exclusion*, abbreviated as AROPE, corresponds to the sum of persons who are either at risk of poverty or severely materially and socially deprived or living in a household with a very low work intensity. For further analysis, please see <https://ec.europa.eu/eurostat/statistics-explained/index.php?title=Glossary:At_risk_of_poverty_or_social_exclusion_(AROPE)> (accessed 1 September 2023).

unemployment rates rose from 7.8% in 2008 to 24.9% in 2015, and long-term unemployment rates from 3.9% in 2008 to 18.2% in 2015. Material deprivation rates increased from 21.8% in 2008 to 40.7% in 2016, while the housing burden of poor households went from 18.1% in 2010 to 40.9% in 2016.[13] In this unfavourable socio-economic climate, social policy was reorganized with an almost exclusive focus on managing only the most extreme forms of poverty and social exclusion, which were exacerbated by the austerity policies imposed by the Greek state.[14]

At the level of social welfare structures, a first horizontal form of intervention during the economic crisis was implemented in the context of fiscal adjustment programmes. Its purpose was the development of emergency intervention measures to mitigate the extreme social consequences of the implementation of the memorandum commitments.[15] Characteristic here is the creation of the 'National Network of Direct Social Intervention', which put into operation the 'Social Structures for Direct Response to Poverty', co-financed by the European Social Fund and implemented by municipalities and NGOs. Services such as social grocers, clinics, pharmacies, time banks, dormitories, and homeless day centres were instituted to relieve vulnerable groups from the adverse effects of austerity. At the end of 2014, the implementation of measures under the Food Aid Fund for the Needy (TEBA) was approved.[16]

The crisis highlighted yet further the pathologies of the Greek economy and legitimized calls for reform and even dismantlement of the problematic social protection system. Thus, the inefficient and fragmented Greek welfare state transformed, in just a few years, its philosophy towards a residual mode of management of the most serious social problems and phenomena, for example, poverty and social exclusion, and shifted responsibility for remaining socio-economic strata to a capitalistic mode of social policy based upon citizens' employment status.[17] Among the first victims of the radical restructuring of the Greek economy was social policy. The rapid increase in unemployment; the shrinking of wages, in both public and private sectors; the restructuring of collective agreements; the flexibility of labour relations; and the increase in insecure work are just some of the developments that contributed significantly to the impoverishment of Greek society.[18] The result was an increase in the number of homeless people and people facing housing insecurity. An important indication of this housing insecurity was the upswing in non-performing mortgage loans as a percentage of GDP from 10% in 2010 to 45% in 2020.[19] Another key factor was

---

13 Eurostat, 'Income and Living Conditions Data' (2022) <https://ec.europa.eu/eurostat/documents/203647/16195750/EU-SILC+DOI+2022%2C+release+1%2C+version+3.pdf/7809416e-c92d-a745-46ba-3db9182f3398?t=1689074323657#:~:text=Short%20description%3A%20The%202022%20release,is%20available%20for%20eligible%20researcher> (accessed 1 September 2023).
14 Arapoglou and Gounis (n 7); D. Papadopoulou and N. Kourachanis, *Homeless and Social Exclusion in Crisis Greece* (Topos 2017) (in Greek).
15 This refers to the 'Memorandum of Understanding' which set out the commitments of the Greek state to the European Commission, ECB, and IMF in return for financial aid during the crisis.
16 N. Kourachanis, 'Homelessness Policies in Crisis Greece: The Case of Housing and Reintegration Programme' (2017) 11(1) *European Journal of Homelessness* 59.
17 A. Kapsalis, V. Koumarianos and N. Kourachanis (eds), *Social Policy, Authoritarian Neoliberalism and Covid-19* (Topos 2021) (in Greek).
18 I. Kouzis, 'Crisis and Memorandums Deregulate the Employment' (2016) 6 *Journal of the Hellenic Social Policy Association [Koinoniki Politiki]* 7 (in Greek).
19 Eurostat, 'Income and Living Conditions Data' (2022) <https://ec.europa.eu/eurostat/web/income-and-living-conditions/data/database>

the surge in rents, especially in large urban centres – a typical example being the 29.8% increase in rents in central areas of the municipality of Athens from 2016 to 2018.[20]

In particular, during the first years of the sudden collapse in social structures and drop in living standards, there was an intensification of street homelessness and people in housing support or living occasionally with relatives or friends. The term 'neo-homelessness' [νεοάστεγοι] emerged in public discourse in Greece during this time to describe those who lost their homes as a result of economic and social hardship caused by the crisis, to differentiate them from those who the public already and routinely considered 'homeless', that is, vulnerable groups, such as drug addicts, the mentally ill, or immigrants.[21]

Despite the lack of reliable, official data and measurements of the phenomenon of homelessness in this period, the fact of its increase is considered a fact based on indications derived from the preceding analysis. In spite of the rapid increase in the number of homeless people – leading to a tragic familiarization of the Greek people with the phenomenon and bringing home the undeniable need to deal with it – there was no corresponding institutional and regulatory framework to recognize and protect this vulnerable social group. The right to housing has been constitutionally guaranteed in Greece since 1975. However, the basis for the formulation of a national homelessness policy was laid only in 2012 with Article 29 (para. 1 and 2) of Law 4052/2012 (Official Gazette 41 section A), when homeless people as a population were first institutionally recognized as a vulnerable group in need of special protection. Prior to this, there was a lack of any organized action plan for the prevention, rehabilitation, or rehousing of the homeless, and the measures that were implemented were sporadic and fragmentary. This, along with the absence of official data and a data collection system for recording the numbers of homeless people, must now be seen as significant inhibiting factors preventing more effective resolution of the phenomenon of homelessness in Greece.

In 2012, the Directorate of Social Perception and Solidarity of the Ministry of Labour, Social Security, and Welfare,[22] recognizing the growing problem of homelessness resulting from the economic crisis, addressed a call to relevant government ministries, public bodies, as well as civil society partners with the aim of legislating for the homeless to be recognized as a vulnerable group, as beneficiaries of social protection, and for the preparation of an action plan to tackle the problem of homelessness in Greece, in combination with the search for a realistic and sustainable funding base for the implementation of the action plan. In the same year, the homeless were legally recognized under Law 4052/2012 of the Ministry of Labour, as amended by Law 4254/2014. Specifically, according to Article 29 (para. 1 and 2) of Law 4052/2012 (Official Gazette 41 section A):

> The homeless are recognized as a vulnerable social group to which social protection is provided. Homeless persons are all persons legally residing in the country, who lack access or have precarious access to adequate accommodation, privately owned, rented or rent-free, that meets the technical requirements and has basic amenities for water and electricity. The homeless include especially those who live on the streets,

---

20 Ibid.
21 Papadopoulou and Kourachanis (n 14).
22 For further details about the responsibilities of this body, see <www.moh.gov.gr/articles/ministry/organogramma/yphresies/47-dieythynsh-koinwnikhs-antilhpshs-kai-allhleggyhs> (accessed 1 September 2023).

in hostels and those who are hosted, out of need, temporarily in institutions or other closed structures, as well as those who live in inappropriate accommodation.

Subsequently, targeted interventions were designed and implemented in order to create a safety net for the most vulnerable groups of the population, such as the pilot scheme of the 'Social Solidarity Income';[23] the Fund for European Aid to the Most Deprived (FEAD),[24] for the distribution of food and types of basic material assistance to economically vulnerable households with accompanying measures for their social reintegration; the 'National Network of Direct Social Intervention', with targeted actions for the homeless population, specifically the homeless night shelters and homeless day reception centres; as well as the 'Housing and Reintegration' Programme,[25] which concerned the provision of independent housing to homeless people, with parallel support services to address their wider social and health problems as well as access to subsidized work. During the period of the Greek economic crisis, the contribution of third-sector organizations, such as NGOs, was especially notable, with measures to support the homeless mainly in dealing with the most extreme and publicly visible examples of homelessness, such as living on the street and providing services aimed at meeting basic human needs, such as soup kitchen initiatives.

Despite these moves and legal recognition of the homeless in 2012, it was only in 2018 that the 'National Strategy for Homelessness' was announced. This Strategy, in which FEANTSA's expanded ETHOS typology (2006) of homeless people was adopted, was based on the following five strategic axes: (1) prevention of homelessness; (2) immediate intervention; (3) improvement of housing conditions for those population groups living in inadequate conditions; (4) work integration; and (5) coordination, monitoring, and evaluation. Under each of these dimensions, specific measures were presented, both existing and those planned for the future.

Importantly, during both the financial and refugee crises of 2015–2016, there were conflicting opinions about the extent and severity of homelessness in Greece, most opinions being unsound, however, due to the lack of any official definition of *homeless people* and the absence of commonly accepted established procedures for accurate data collection and enumeration.[26]

Although legal and institutional recognition of homeless people as a vulnerable social group was established in 2012, measures aimed at precisely capturing the scale of homelessness in Greece were delayed. The institutionalization of the National Mechanism of Coordination, Monitoring, and Evaluation of the Social Integration and Social Cohesion Policies, pursuant to Law 4445/2016, established the basis for development of a special mechanism for recording and monitoring the number of homeless people. In 2018, a pilot project for counting homeless people was carried out in seven large municipalities of the country: Athens, Piraeus, Thessaloniki, Heraklion, Ioannina, N. Ionia, and Trikala. The pilot referred to those who lived either on the street or in homeless structures (homeless

---

23 Joint Ministerial Decision 39892/GD1.2/2014 – Official Gazette 3018/B/7 November 2014. Its nationwide application was institutionalized by Law 4445/2016.
24 Law 4314/2014.
25 The programme was implemented within the framework of the Housing, Feeding, and Social Care Actions for the Homeless, Article 29 of Law 4052/12.
26 V. Arapoglou, C. Dimoulas and C. Richardson, 'Counting the Homeless in Greece' (2021) 14 *Social Policy* 115.

night shelters and open day centres for the homeless) and supported apartments. The programme was implemented by the Ministry of Social Solidarity, which assigned research responsibility for the project to Panteion University. The aim of this pilot recording scheme was twofold: first, to test the selected tools and procedures for counting homelessness in Greece and, secondly, to engage local communities and NGOs in the creation and operation of a permanent mechanism employing mutually agreed institutional procedures for the regular enumeration of the homeless population.[27]

After an initial survey, the point-in-time technique was adopted as the most appropriate method for counting homelessness, and the research was supported by a number of tools, such as a digital platform, structured questionnaires to conduct surveys on the street and in shelters, survey guides, and evaluation questionnaires. According to the results of the survey in the aforementioned municipalities, the number of people living in homeless conditions amounted to 1,645 people, of which 691 lived on the street and 954 in hospitality structures (homeless night shelters, open day centres for the homeless, and supported apartments).[28]

The findings of the pilot count demonstrated that, despite efforts to combat homelessness within the framework of emergency services that had been instituted since 2012, six years later, a large proportion of the housing needs of the homeless remained unmet, especially in large urban centres. The value of the findings' analysis and the conclusions from this project remain undisputed to this day. However, despite the fact that this pilot project was a rigorous and scientifically underpinned tool for counting the homeless population, it was not sufficiently utilized. Although this project was an opportunity for public administration to introduce an institutional mechanism for gathering information and monitoring the problem of homelessness in Greece and an institutional forum for cooperation, knowledge sharing and learning between central and local authorities and NGOs, its implementation was not continued after 2019 due to a change of government. A key consequence of this has been that the data on the number of homeless people gathered in 2018 has become a vital snapshot of and insight into the growing problem of homelessness in Greece but a static snapshot rather than a starting point for continuous monitoring of the phenomenon of homelessness and the impact of social policies on it.

The Impact of the Covid-19 Pandemic on Homelessness and Ideological Transformation in Social Policy in the Western World and in Greece

The emergence of the pandemic in Greece represented a new form of crisis in a landscape of existing and former crises impacting the country, starting with the economic crisis and continuing with the refugee crisis.[29] This whole tumultuous decade in Greece was managed chiefly through governmental tools of individual responsibility, repression, and political shock, with intense deregulation in various fields of social policy in favour of the market.[30]

---

27 Ibid.
28 N. Kourachanis, *Final Issue of Methodology, Method of Organization, Procedures and Tools for Recording the Homeless* (P1.1 IDIKA 2018) (in Greek).
29 N. Kourachanis, 'Asylum Seekers, Hotspot Approach and Anti-Social Policy Responses in Greece (2015–2017)' (2018) 19(4) *Journal of International Migration and Integration* 1153.
30 C. Dimoulas and G. Kouzis, 'Introduction' in C. Dimoulas and G. Kouzis (eds), *Crisis and Social Policy: Deadlocks and Solutions* (Topos 2018) (in Greek).

The Covid-19 pandemic spread on a global scale at the beginning of 2020, changing global priorities in the social policy realm. The handling of the pandemic has been marked by a new phase in the attempt to accelerate the restructuring of social protection systems,[31] introducing stronger elements of authoritarianism, personal responsibility, and neoliberalism. This trend pre-dated Covid-19 with varying intensity in distinct countries but, in many cases, was accelerated by the pandemic.

The crisis of the post-war welfare state and the predominance of neoliberalism in the Western world brought about structural rearrangement in the philosophy of social policy, mainly the abandonment of the agenda for social cohesion and the limitation of social interventions within a logic of managing extreme poverty.[32] The welfare mix of this philosophy included an increased reliance and emphasis on civil society and private social policy actors as substitutes for state involvement and accompanied by state shrinkage. The legitimization of these changes was grounded in the shift from collective to individual responsibility for the social situation of citizens.[33]

This created a framework of repressive and low-quality social benefits, which sought to cover only the most basic needs of the extreme poor – a framework in which there is no state monopoly. On the contrary, civil society and the private sector of the economy were involved in undertaking social initiatives, by developing voluntary and socially responsible activities.[34] Extreme poverty was managed by promoting emergency services.[35] Emergency housing services, social assistance, and material assistance to meet the most essential needs for survival have been established in several welfare states in the Western world (from the 1980s onwards) in order to manage the growing number of extreme poor and newly homeless resulting from extensive cuts to welfare states.[36] Indicative measures that reflect this trend are the granting of a minimum guaranteed income, often shifting all the burden of responsibility to the individual for his or her so-called 'integration', as in the case of France.[37]

The Great Recession of 2008 brought about pronounced developments in the same direction of the neoliberalization of social policy in Greece, leading to greater convergence with the trends prevailing in the wider Western world.[38] The acceleration of the privatization processes of social benefits was largely facilitated by the legitimization of the rearrangements in

---

31 J. Nunes, 'The COVID-19 Pandemic: Securitization, Neoliberal Crisis, and Global Vulnerabilization' (2020) 36(5) *Saúde Pública* e00063120.
32 C. Papatheodorou, 'Economic Crisis, Poverty and Deprivation in Greece: The Impact of Neoliberal Remedies' in S. Mavroudeas (ed), *Greek Capitalism in Crisis: Marxist Analyses* (Routledge 2014).
33 B. J. Brown and S. Baker, *Responsible Citizens: Individuals, Health and Policy Under Neoliberalism* (Anthem Press 2012).
34 N. Kourachanis, *Citizenship and Social Policy. From Postwar Development to Permanent Crisis* (Palgrave Macmillan 2020).
35 K. Hopper and J. Baumohl, 'Held in Abeyance: Rethinking Homelessness and Advocacy' (1994) 37(4) *The American Behavioral Scientist* 522; B. R. O'Shaughnessy and others, 'Home as a Base for a Well-Lived Life: Comparing the Capabilities of Homeless Service Users in Housing First and the Staircase of Transition in Europe' (2021) 38(3) *Housing, Theory and Society* 343.
36 R. Levitas, 'The Concept of Social Exclusion and the New Durkheimian Hegemony' 16(46) *Critical Social Policy* (1996) 5.
37 D. Papadopoulou, *Sociology of Exclusion in the Age of Globalization* (Topos 2012) (in Greek).
38 Nunes (n 29); N. Kourachanis, 'The Evolution of Social Security System in Greece' in M. Zakowska and D. Domalewska (eds), *Balkans – Social Security. Experience, Challenges, Perspectives* (Brill Publications 2021).

the welfare mix, further enhancing the role of NGOs and businesses.[39] The focus of social interventions was the systematization of emergency services in order to prevent images of impoverishment or even death among constantly expanding impoverished groups, as seen clearly in Greece.[40]

With the emergence of the pandemic and, above all, with the way it has been managed globally by neoliberal governments, it seems, in certain aspects, to promote an even greater contraction of social protection[41] combined with aspects of neoliberalization, individual responsibility, and authoritarianism at the heart the adopted reforms. The international emphasis on individual responsibility and the prevalence of a logic of self-protection prevail as dominant prescriptions for managing the pandemic. After all, as Lowenheim[42] has noted, neoliberal politics in recent decades seem to be limited to the logic of individual responsibility of citizens as the central driver of social responsibility. Thus, self-protection measures, such as the logic of self-protection and enforced lockdowns and staying at home, instead of policies to support public health, education, and transport systems,[43] were adopted as the main practices to curb the health crisis in many countries across the Western world. However, this management model leaves exposed those populations who are unable to access affordable housing, care for themselves, or adhere to public health measures and, therefore, unable to provide adequate self-protection for themselves.[44] Thus, many neoliberal governments explicitly stated during the pandemic that they were not willing to protect those citizens who could not protect themselves, for example, if they were homeless or otherwise impacted by housing insecurity,[45] did not have sufficient income or resources, and did not have access to basic public goods such as public health.

In relation to Greece more specifically, several of the preceding aspects were keenly observable in the response of the Greek authorities to the pandemic. The Greek model of managing the pandemic during the first period (March to May 2020) was considered one of the most successful within the EU, although a policy strongly imbued with the logic of self-protection and individual responsibility was implemented. However, it remained a management model that ultimately lacked any form of social care and support for those experiencing extreme poverty. In fact, in some cases, the lack of social intervention was combined with political practices of authoritarianism and, further, neoliberalization, such as forcing people to stay at home and fining homeless citizens for living on the street despite curfews.[46]

---

39 E. Stockhammer, 'The Euro Crisis, European Neoliberalism and the Need for a European Welfare State' (2012) 50 *Soundings* 121.
40 Papadopoulou and Kourachanis (n 14).
41 M. Petmesidou, 'The Pandemic and the Future of the Welfare State' in H. Kondylis and A. Benos (eds), *COVID-19 Pandemic and Contemporary Threats to Public Health* (Topos 2021) (in Greek).
42 O. Lowenheim, 'The Responsibility to Responsibilize: Foreign Offices and the Issuing of Travel Warnings' (2007) 1(3) *International Political Sociology* 203.
43 R. Horton, 'Offline: Covid-19 and the NHS – a "National Scandal"' (2020) 395(10229) *The Lancet* 1022.
44 D. Rogers and E. Power, 'Housing Policy and the COVID-19 Pandemic: The Importance of Housing Research During This Health Emergency' (2020) 20(2) *International Journal of Housing Policy* 177.
45 D. Silva and M. J. Smith, 'Social Distancing, Social Justice, and Risk During the COVID-19 Pandemic' (2020) 111(4) *Canadian Journal of Public Health* 459.
46 A. Kapsalis, V. Koumarianos and N. Kourachanis (eds), *Social Policy, Authoritarian Neoliberalism and Covid-19* (Topos 2021) (in Greek).

The Current Legal and Policy Framework Pertaining to Homelessness in Greece

During the last decade in Greece, as in most EU states, the problem of homelessness has been addressed either by horizontal public social welfare policies to combat poverty and social exclusion (Guaranteed Minimum Income (GMI); Fund for European Aid to the Most Deprived (FEAD) programmes) or by direct housing policies (Housing Allowance; 'Housing and Work for the Homeless' programmes). The effectiveness of Greek policies to prevent and address homelessness depends, on the one hand, on their specialized targeting of people with an objectively high risk of exclusion from housing (people who experience repeated and prolonged homelessness with additional problems of mental health and drug use or alcohol) and, on the other hand, to people who are unable to secure decent housing conditions in free market conditions. In this context, the interconnection and complementarity of the already-implemented national financial support social programmes for households experiencing conditions of extreme poverty or with low incomes (and are burdened with the cost of renting a main residence) aim to provide an expanded service network. The beneficiaries of GMI and FEAD programmes, with specific institutional interventions, include individuals or families who live on the street or are accommodated in homeless shelters, especially people in Athens.

Some of these financial support social programmes in the context of addressing the housing problem and homelessness in Greece are part of the staircase service approach for homeless people, and some are part of the Housing First approach.[47] The staircase service approach includes the GMI programme, 'Housing Allowance' (as a preventive measure), and the provision of shelters offering services to the homeless.

The already-mentioned GMI represents the most fundamental welfare change during the last ten years of the austerity policies in Greece and warrants further discussion.[48] GMI is a form of intervention that belongs to the so-called 'third generation' welfare mechanisms, which have been developing since the 1980s and combine benefit support with active employment policies.[49] In particular, it combines financial support for population groups facing problems of extreme poverty with the preparation and monitoring of individual action plans aimed at the return to employment and the social reintegration of their beneficiaries.

Although the issue of the GMI has been the subject of debate for more than two decades, its roll-out in Greece garnered strong reactions from many parts of the political spectrum. For years it has been the subject of rhetorical or partisan interest from political parties and interest groups. Evidence of this can be seen in the repeated proposals for its adoption at different times and originating from different right-wing and left-wing political parties.[50]

---

47 N. Kourachanis, 'Housing as a Base for Welfare in Greece: The Staircase of Transition and Housing First Schemes' (2022) 22(2) *International Journal of Housing Policy* 1.
48 C. Dimoulas, 'The Implementation of the Social Solidarity Income in Greece' (2017) 7 *Journal of the Hellenic Social Policy Association* 7 (in Greek); T. Sakellaropoulos, V. Lalioti and N. Kourachanis, 'The Social Impact of the "Social Solidarity Income" in Greece: A Qualitative Interpretation' (2019) 13(2) *Social Cohesion & Development* 5.
49 Y. Kazepov and S. Sabatinelli, 'Minimum Income and Social Integration: Institutional Arrangements in Europe' (2006) Working Paper, ILO.
50 V. Lalioti, 'The Curious Case of the Guaranteed Minimum Income: Highlighting Greek "Exceptionalism" in a Southern European Context' (2016) 26(1) *Journal of European Social Policy* 80.

Ultimately, the GMI was established as part of the Medium-term Framework Fiscal Strategy 2013–2016 (Law 4093/2012), which provided for its pilot implementation from 2014 in two regions of the country. Finally, its implementation was extended to a total of 13 municipalities, instead of the two that had been initially indicated, with unclear and non-transparent selection criteria.[51] GMI's nationwide implementation took place in February 2017. The programme is based on three pillars: income support, the interface with social integration services, and the interface with activation services aimed at introducing or reintroducing beneficiaries into the labour market and social reintegration. Moreover, it refers to three different target groups living in conditions of extreme poverty: single-person households, multi-person households, and the homeless.[52]

The GMI is particularly concerned with homeless people living in transitional homeless shelters and in shelters for women who are the victims of violence and aims to strengthen the ability of the users of these shelters to gradually progress to independent living. Homeless users of this accommodation, as beneficiaries of the programme, receive not only the financial support but also all other support services flowing from the coordination with social integration services and services aimed at getting the beneficiaries into the labour market and education.[53]

In 2015, the introduction of the Humanitarian Crisis Response Programme also provided for the rent subsidy measure. Law 4320/2015 enacted, among other measures, the rent allowance, which provided for the granting of a rent allowance to Greek families and individuals living in conditions of extreme poverty and without the possibility of housing in a privately owned property in the place of their permanent residence. This programme was perhaps the most relevant measure related to the problem of homelessness in Greece. It is undoubtedly a preventive measure of social policy which, over time, shows characteristics of residualization.[54]

The initial implementation of the programme did not appear to be sufficient either in terms of the level of benefits or in terms of the number of beneficiaries it reached. Subsequently, under Law 4472/2017, the programme was renamed Housing Allowance and expanded, becoming a more substantial and supportive intervention for the prevention and/or treatment of housing insecurity for low- or middle-income households living in rented accommodation. This welfare programme assists households with the cost of renting their main residence. The Housing Allowance currently provides 70 to 210 euros per month, depending on the composition of the beneficiary unit, has a total annual budget of 300 million euros from state budget resources, and in 2021, the average number of beneficiary households in Greece amounted to 260,000 (this figure comprising only those able to satisfy several eligibility criteria).[55]

In the field of homelessness more specifically, starting in 2013, targeted interventions were designed and started to be implemented in order to create a safety net for the most vulnerable groups of the population, such as the 'National Network of Direct Social Intervention'. This was part of a national effort to form a network of 'Social Structures for Direct

---

51 Dimoulas (n 48).
52 V. Lalioti, N. Kourachanis and C. Skamnakis, 'Through the Eyes of Beneficiaries: The Greek "Social Solidarity Income" (SSI) Experience' (2019) 3 *Journal Autonomie Locali e Servizi Sociali* 1.
53 Sakellaropoulos, Lalioti and Kourachanis (n 48).
54 Kourachanis (n 16).
55 Ministerial Decision D13/ 10747/256/6 March 2019 – Official Gazette 4500/B/29 September 2021.

Responses to Poverty' [Κοινωνικές Δομές Άμεσης Αντιμετώπισης της Φτώχειας], in which 51 municipalities, 46 NGOs, five local government organizations, eight public sector bodies, and 18 private sector bodies participated.

As part of this work, there were targeted measures for the homeless population, specifically the homeless night shelters and open day centres. Other actions included opening social grocers, social aids, and social pharmacies in many municipalities of the country. Homeless night shelters provide accommodation but operate only at night and cover the urgent housing needs of those living on the street. The beneficiaries of this service are homeless people who are legally resident in the country, though such shelters have, in the past, only had a capacity for 55 homeless people each night, despite the fact that homelessness has increased significantly in the last decade in Greece. The open day centres for the homeless are direct accommodation structures that operate only during the day in order to address the basic needs of the homeless. They provide services of psychosocial support, primary health care, personal care and hygiene, as well as connection with services, nourishment, psychological support, legal assistance, counselling, and health, social, and professional reintegration.[56]

Moreover, in 2016, and still operating today, transitional hospitality hostels were introduced.[57] These are structures offering accommodation for a certain, limited period of time. Additionally, there are supported apartments which are independent living structures again offering housing for a certain period of time in properties that are leased or owned by the operating agency.

All these services are targeted at the successful transition of homeless people up the scale of protected forms of services from one step to the next in a gradual process, that is, to less protective forms, so that, with the appropriate support, they can eventually find themselves in stable housing in order to achieve the goal of access to independent autonomous living and social reintegration. At this point, it is worth mentioning street work, which involves specialized scientists (mainly social workers) directly approaching and helping people living on the street. Street work is one of the most important homeless support actions in Greece. In addition to immediate relief services such as first aid, nursing, medical advice, and providing basic necessities, street work additionally contributes to connecting and networking of the homeless with the services they require to meet their needs. In Greece, street working services are offered by public bodies funded by the state, but also civil society, through non-governmental organizations.[58]

In contrast to the dominant 'staircase' model of transitional housing services, minor initiatives which share some characteristics of the Housing First approach have been implemented in the last seven years in Greece in order to house homeless people.[59] Within the framework of the Housing First approach, 'Housing and Work for the Homeless' is included as a permanent programme for the immediate housing and social integration of individuals and families living in conditions of homelessness. The 'Housing and Work for the Homeless' programme was established by Law 4756/2020 and is a continuation of

---

56 Kourachanis (n 5).
57 Ministerial Decision D23/ 19061-1457/2016 – Official Gazette 1336/B/12 May 2016.
58 N. Kourachanis, 'Social Policy and Homelessness Services, Athens Social Atlas' (2019) <www.athenssocialatlas.gr/en/article/social-policy-and-homelessness-services/ (accessed 1 September 2023).
59 Kourachanis (n 47).

corresponding programmes that were implemented in 2014 and 2018 from resources of the primary surplus of the state budget.

The programme provides a rent subsidy for up to 18 months, to cover basic expenses for household goods and utilities, as well as an employment subsidy for up to 12 months. At the same time, it provides psychosocial support to beneficiaries with the aim of empowering and mobilizing them so that they can gradually assume responsibility for solving everyday problems and can re-integrate smoothly into society. In its new phase, the programme aims to reintegrate 600 households/800 beneficiaries every two years at a cost of 10 million euros and is a first but fundamental step in addressing homelessness and the accompanying problems. Beneficiaries of the programme might be (1) families and people hosted in transitional homeless hostels and dormitories, (2) families and individuals registered by the Social Services of the municipalities as homeless living on the street or in unsuitable accommodation, (3) women who are accommodated in hostels for women victims of violence and do not have access to housing, and (4) people who are accommodated in temporary hospitality hostels of social reintegration units of certified treatment programmes for dependent persons and do not have access to a residence.[60]

What does support look like on the ground? Today, if a Greek citizen is in a situation of homelessness, he can report to the Social Service of his municipality. Thereafter, a certificate of homelessness is issued, and the Social Service puts him in contact either with homeless accommodation facilities provided by the specific municipality or, in the event that the municipality does not have accommodation facilities, puts him in contact with accommodation facilities in the nearest municipality. In addition, he is provided with assistance in gathering the necessary supporting documents that will enable him to receive all the benefits to which he is entitled. In the municipalities in which the 'Housing and Work for the Homeless' programme is implemented Social Services inform and assist in its participation.

The Future of Homelessness Law and Policy in Greece

Today, the housing and homelessness problem in Greece, as a consequence of the collapse of the economy and the long-term recession that the country has been experiencing for the last ten years, is a priority sitting at the top of the government's agenda, an issue which it is called upon to address immediately and effectively. Both in Greek society and across the political spectrum, there is a general and common acceptance that there is a lack of an integrated housing policy comprising corresponding strategies, methods, and tools to tackle the social phenomenon of housing insecurity and homelessness. The existing housing policy is restricted to measures and programmes concerned exclusively with homelessness and the thresholds of housing insecurity. But even this minimum social safety net is insufficient and weak to cover wider housing needs in a period of rising housing insecurity. In addition, and crucial to appreciate, is that there is a complete absence, so far, of any state-run social housing system in Greece, with the result that housing needs are covered exclusively by the free market. This is an aggravating factor and a further block on finding solutions to the homelessness problem in the country.

In addition, the housing problem is exacerbated due to the lack of a clear and effective framework for the protection of citizens' main residence ('main residence' is the one used

---

60 Ministerial Decision D13/42815 Official Gazette 2788/B/30 June 2021.

to cover permanent housing needs and has been declared to the Greek tax authorities).[61] Particularly, given that a key feature of the housing culture in Greece is homeownership, it is easy to understand that the shift towards lending by banking institutions, especially after the 1990s, made thousands of families captive to bank loans. The multiple crises that Greek society has had to deal with has created a dystopian financial environment in terms of mortgage repayments. The consequence of this situation has been the need for state protection of the primary residence in cases of inability to repay loan obligations.

In terms of housing protection, during the period of the austerity policies in Greece, an important exception in the direction of managing extreme poverty was the 'Katseli Law'. This law protected a large number of overindebted households from the confiscation of their main residence by the banks. It helped low-income households, the unemployed, and pensioners while providing more favourable terms for repaying their debt.[62] The amendment of the 'Katseli Law' by the 'Stathakis Law' in 2018 led to a tightening of the protection framework and limitations on its scope to benefit citizens.

However, the complete withdrawal of the primary residence protection framework for overindebted borrowers came in the midst of the pandemic. At the same moment when government policy imposed staying at home as the dominant prescription for managing the Covid-19 pandemic, it simultaneously made the 'Bankruptcy Law' the new tool for managing non-performing loans. The vote in favour of Law 4738/2020, 'Debt settlement and provision of a second chance and other provisions' ('Bankruptcy Law'), took place in October 2020 amid pandemic conditions and measures to restrict the movement of citizens by the government. The 'Bankruptcy Law' is an attempt to codify all procedures aimed at preventing or dealing with insolvency. Its passing came from the requirement to incorporate Community Directive 1023/2019 into domestic legislation. The main object of the 'Bankruptcy Law' is to deal with 'non-performing loans',[63] focusing on the regulation of the existing position but also the creation of a framework, with the aim of preventing the existence of non-performing loans going forward. It is, to a large extent, a state intervention with a punitive logic for those who fail to consistently meet their loan obligations. The basic philosophy of Law 4738/2020 is the formation of uniform bankruptcy procedures as a vehicle for the release of legal and natural persons from non-performing debts. The result of this weakening of the protection framework governing the first home is that a large section of the middle and lower social classes in Greece are now exposed to the risk of housing insecurity or even homelessness.[64]

Recently, the Greek government, recognizing the housing crisis as a major problem of society, passed Law 5006/2022. The purpose of this law was to constitute the first comprehensive approach to housing policy in Greece. The key points of the law are the 'My

---

61 Article 217 of Law 4738/2020 (Official Gazette A' 207).
62 A. Sapounakis and E. Komninou, 'The Issue of Evictions in Greece' in N. Kourachanis (ed), *Housing and Society: Problems, Policies and Movements* (Dionicos 2019) (in Greek).
63 A loan is considered non-performing when the borrower is more than 90 days late in paying the agreed interest or instalments. Non-performing loans are also called bad loans ('red loans'). See <www.bankofgreece.gr>.
64 D. Papadopoulou and N. Kourachanis, 'Bankruptcy Law as an Aspect of Authoritarian Neoliberalism and Individual Responsibility in the Era of the Pandemic Covid-19' in A. Kapsalis, E. Koumarianos and N. Kourachanis (eds), *Social Policy and Authoritarian Neoliberalism in the Era of the Covid-19 Pandemic* (Topos 2021) (in Greek).

Home' programme, the institution of a social land-for-apartment exchange system and the strengthening of the utilization of private houses for social housing, through the 'Coverage' and 'Renovate–Rent' programmes.

The 'My Home' programme concerns the granting of low-interest or interest-free loans from credit institutions to young individuals or young couples, with the aim of acquiring a main residence with the participation of the Greek Public Employment Service (DYPA) in the financing of the loans. The social land exchange system for apartments is a new form of partnership between the public and private sectors, with the specific purpose of encouraging private contractors to build real estate on undeveloped plots owned by general government bodies in return (from the state to private individuals). Apartments on the land are leased to citizens with a state-controlled rent or lease price. The 'Coverage' programme refers to the utilization of properties which were allocated in the past for housing applicants for international protection in order to meet the housing needs of young people. In particular, beneficiaries of the programme are people aged 25 to 39 years old who are included in the beneficiary units of the Minimum Guaranteed Income. The 'Renovate–Rent' programme aims to activate dormant private building stock for housing by renting them out, subsidizing their renovation or repair, setting social criteria in the selection of owners.

The 'My Home' programme is of interest to a larger number of beneficiaries and has gained the attention of a significant portion of Greek society it being consistent with the Greek housing culture as it has been shaped since the 20th century with the main characteristics of owner-occupation and lending. At the same time, it is obvious that the age limit of the beneficiaries is directly linked to their future ability to repay the loan and is not based on any other social criterion. Lending as a means of acquiring a residence requires the existence of a guaranteed and continuous income that comes either from work or from financial support in the context of family ties that exist in Greek society. Therefore, one could conclude that the specific programme is a tool that preserves the pathogenic characteristics of the South European social model, such as the strengthening of owner-occupied housing, which in the future may lead to the commercialization of housing, but also to economic dependence between family members. In addition, the attraction and popularity of the programme are expected to cause a partial increase in property prices. Therefore, it can be said that the 'My Home' programme cannot be regarded as a sustainable solution to the current housing crisis and, on a strict view, is not, in any meaningful way, connected with the treatment of or solution to homelessness, as it does not refer to or offer support for vulnerable social groups.

The introduction of a social land-for-apartment exchange system and the possible future programmes leading to its implementation appears to represent a time-consuming process with questionable social benefits. A further disincentive is the high risk involved in weighing the value of the public property that will be required for a social compensation programme against the net social benefit as a result of the involvement of private sector participation. However, adopting an optimistic outlook and with a strong regulatory framework, the social land-for-apartment exchange system could be a useful tool if it is integrated into a robust system of social housing in the context of a holistic housing policy.

Undoubtedly, the activation of dormant private or public building stock, however, is extremely important. Yet the necessity of the 'Renovate–Rent' programme is called into question as there are no clear data on the dormant private building stock in Greece. Moreover, documenting the real reasons for not renting a residence is inherently difficult. This programme seems to serve communication policy goals rather than a coordinated method of housing crisis mitigation.

Perhaps the most important action established by this law is the 'Coverage' programme, as it refers exclusively to the institution of social housing, directly offering housing at low or no cost to people with very low incomes. However, it is a fairly inward-looking programme with significant limitations in its application both due to the small number of properties that will be made available and the terms of negotiation between the state and landlords. In particular, it is problematic that the terms of negotiation with the landlords are already defined in a previous programme framework of cooperation which did not have the same objectives as the 'Coverage' programme. This means that the rental prices of the properties participating in the programme, in combination with their relatively small number, cannot effectively impact the rental prices on the free market. However, this is a real step towards the institution of social housing because, through its implementation, a system of agencies and new procedures will be developed and tested in practice, which will have the potential to promote, in the future, more mature and adequate social housing programmes, with the ultimate goal of mitigating the housing crisis and effectively dealing with homelessness in Greece.

In conclusion, despite the recognition of the housing problem and the clear intention to formulate a robust housing policy, the Greek government's approach is characterized by fragmented actions. The housing problem in Greece did not arise suddenly or abruptly. The growth of housing and homelessness issues has followed a gradual evolution over, at least, the last 15 years, while its beginnings can be traced back decades. However, neither its treatment nor its prevention has been effectively addressed through a proper housing policy. Moreover, an aggravating factor has been the significant time lag between identifying the problem and taking action. Even today, the actions taken by the Greek state to deal with homelessness and housing insecurity are characterized by fragmentation, by measures delivering only short-term effectiveness, and in many cases, by inefficiency. It is clear that the establishment of individual measures of questionable effectiveness can in no way be considered a comprehensive policy formulation with vision, strategy, method, and tools aimed at tackling homelessness. Therefore, even if some of these measures, including recent efforts discussed earlier, have a positive impact on alleviating the problem, they are not a real safety net against homelessness and housing insecurity in Greece but instead offer only insufficient and temporary solutions.

8
NORWAY
A Housing-Led Homeless Policy within a Weak Legal Framework

Evelyn Dyb and Hilde Hatleskog Zeiner

Introduction

The approach to homelessness has historically, throughout the Western world, fluctuated between care, help, and punishment, as well as a good measure of moralism.[1] In Norway, a shift occurred with the introduction of national surveys in 1996. The surveys, which quantified and described the homeless population, spurred a change in homelessness policy,[2] from moralization to assistance, and from social policy to housing policy. The shift took place in the context of developments in the national housing policy, from general to selective instruments,[3] and increased attention to groups with special needs.

Homeless persons are one of the groups prioritized in the present housing policy. The municipalities are obliged to provide temporary housing to their homeless residents. The homeless person may contact the social services directly or be referred from other services, most typically health and care services, or correction facilities. Although there is no legal right to housing, the municipalities have an obligation to assist those who are unable to obtain suitable housing. A new law clarifies and strengthens this obligation, specifying that the municipalities shall provide individually tailored assistance to the disadvantaged on the housing market, but stops short of providing an individual right to housing.[4]

---

1 D. Garland, *Punishment and Modern Society: A Study in Social Theory* (Clarendon Press 1990); L. Wacquant, *Punishing the Poor: The Neoliberal Government of Social Insecurity* (Duke UP 2004); E. O'Sullivan, 'Varieties of Punitiveness in Europe. Homelessness and Urban Variety' (2012) 6(2) *European Journal of Homelessness* 69.
2 L.-M. Ulfrstad, *Bostedsløs i Norge. Kartlegging av bostedsløse i kontakt med hjelpeapparatet* (Norwegian Building Research Institute 1997).
3 J. Sørvoll, *Den boligsosiale vendingen: Norsk boligpolitikk fra midten av 1990-tallet i et historisk perspektiv* (2011) in: *NOU 2011: 15*, Appendiks 2, 171; E. Dyb, 'Reinventing Homelessness Through Enumeration in Norwegian Housing Policy: A Case Study of Governmentality' (2021) 3(5) *Housing, Theory and Society* 564.
4 Lov-2022-12-20-121: Lov om kommunenes ansvar på det boligsosiale feltet (Act on Municipalities' Responsibilities in the Social Housing Field) <https://lovdata.no/dokument/NL/lov/2022-12-20-121> (accessed 1 September 2023).

The shift from (mainly) social to housing policy has had a major impact on policy and governance. Norway adopted a housing-led policy on homelessness, signalled by use of the term 'houseless' rather than 'homeless' in public documents and research.[5] Nevertheless, housing has been designated the wobbly pillar of the welfare state.[6] In Norway, homeownership is the norm, and the legal and normative basis of the right to housing is weaker than the more solid pillars of pensions, education, and healthcare. At the local level, where much of the implementation of homeless policy occurs, responsibility lies with social and healthcare services. As a result, the tension between punishment and care persists in present-day homelessness governance.

The chapter is structured as follows: The first section provides a historical overview of the field. The second discusses 'homelessness' as a new concept in Norwegian welfare policy and presents the scale and profile of the homeless population in Norway. The legal framework for homelessness policy is addressed in the third section, while the fourth section considers measures and initiatives to prevent and counter homelessness and the overall political governance of the field. The concluding section discusses the way forward.

Background: The Vagrancy Act of 1900

The Vagrancy, Beggary, and Drunkenness Act of 1900 (the Vagrancy Act) governed how homelessness was conceptualized and tackled throughout much of the 20th century. The Act primarily targeted adult men of working age who could not document permanent employment, and defined a *vagrant* as a person who 'indulges in ineptness or drifting around in such circumstances that there is reason to assume that he is fully or partially obtaining the means of his life in the event of criminal acts or by the immoral occupational of others'.[7] The status as a vagrant was derived from the person's connection to working life, and the concept did not address homelessness as such but, rather, 'the workless proletariat, which has become the great scourge of the towns'.[8] The preparatory work of the Vagrancy Act illustrates that it sought to criminalize a specific lifestyle and people associated with that lifestyle and also affected marginalized people in the labour market, including construction workers who moved between construction sites in search of work.[9] Violations of the Act were met with imprisonment or detention in correctional facilities or penal workhouses. The authorities considered the penal workhouse to be part of the cure for alcoholism and vagrancy,[10] while the inmates perceived that they had reached the bottom of the social ladder.[11]

---

5 *Houseless* translates into *homelessness* in English-language texts, and the latter term is consistently used in this text.
6 U. Torgersen, 'Housing: The Wobbly Pillar Under the Welfare State' in B. Turner, J. Kemeny and L. Lundqvist (eds), *Between State and Market: Housing in the Post-industrial Era* (Almqvist & Wiksell 1987).
7 Elden/Store norske leksikon, lovteksten/Lovdata.
8 T. Kalberg, *Løsgjengerloven av 1900 og løsgjengerloven av i dag* (Department of Sociology and Human Geography, University of Oslo 1970) 15.
9 T. Kalberg, 'Anleggsslusk' in F. Burmann and O. Ramsøy (eds), *Fra de hjemløses verden* (Department of Sociology and Human Geography, University of Oslo1975) 28.
10 N. Christie, *Tvangsarbeid og alkoholbruk* (Universitetsforlaget 1960); A. Omsted, *Fra Mangelsgården til Sing. Iakttakelsen og erfaringer hjemme og ute* (Aschehoug 1949).
11 A. Bratholm, 'Kriminologiske kommentarer til løsgjengerloven og løsgjengeromsorgen' in *Løsgjengeromsorgen – en utfordring* (Universitetsforlaget 1969) 149.

Throughout the 1960s, the Vagrancy Act was heavily debated and criticized. The backdrop was growing institutional criticism – criticism of the prison system and the focus of social sciences on vulnerable groups in general, which spurred the development of *deviant sociology*.[12] The paragraph of the Vagrancy Act which criminalized homelessness came to symbolize an unworthy form of social and institutional control with one of society's weakest groups.[13] When it was repealed in 1970, penal workhouses were also discontinued.[14] This created the impression that the Vagrancy Act as a whole was repealed.[15] As we will see, however, some sections were retained. The section on begging was retained until 2006. By then, it was a sleeping paragraph, but the presence of migrants begging in the streets put it back on the public agenda. A compromise was struck, whereby the section was repealed but the municipalities were given authority to adapt local regulation on begging.

Repealing the Vagrancy paragraph was of great symbolic significance. However, few alternative policies or services for the homeless were introduced. In the big cities, the most important measure remained hostels with large dormitories. Social services relied on private providers who specialized in renting rooms to homeless people. Thirty years after the repeal of the Vagrancy paragraph, and after massive criticism from several stakeholders, Oslo municipality appointed a group with the mandate to map services for homeless people.[16] As a follow-up to the group's reporting on highly reprehensible conditions, the municipality established the 'hospice project' with the purpose of assessing the hospices and considering alternatives for the residents. As a result, some residents were offered an ordinary council apartment or were helped to rent a home in the private market. In parallel with this work, the first national survey of people experiencing homelessness was carried out in 1996. A new survey in 2003, which was to become a series over several decades, showed that the number of homeless people in Oslo had halved since 1996.

National Homeless Surveys

The Norwegian National Homeless Surveys provide an overview of developments in the homeless population over several decades. Registration of population characteristics on an individual level provides data to profile the population and identify subgroups of homeless individuals.[17] The method was developed and used in Sweden for the first time

---

12 E. Goffman, *Asylums: Essays on the Social Situation of Mental Patients and Other Inmates* (Doubleday 1961); E. Goffman, *Stigma: Notes on the Management of Spoiled Identities* (Prentice-Hall 1963); H. Becker, *Outsiders: Studies in the Sociology of Deviance* (The Free Press 1963); M. Foucault, *Birth of the Clinic: An Archaeology of Medical Perception* (Routledge 1963/1973); Y. Hammerlin, *Hard mot de harde, myk mot de myke. Norsk kriminalomsorg i anstalt* (Universitetsforlaget 2021).
13 P. Sundby and others, *Løsgjengerne – en skjønnhetsflekk på velferdssamfunnet?* (Universitetsforlaget 1968).
14 It should be noted, however, that to the Norwegian Roma, the repeal was of little importance. Until the late 1980s, when the Norwegian Mission for travellers was discontinued, various laws were applied to intern them in labour camps. Today, the criminalizing aspect of homelessness is more often applied to various groups of poor migrants and non-nationals.
15 T. Mathiesen, 'Et 40-års jubileum' (2010) 4(3) *Rus & Samfunn* 8.
16 The report from the group is not public; the authors have access to the report.
17 L. Benjaminsen and others, 'Measurement of Homelessness in the Nordic Countries' (2020) 14(3) *European Journal of Homelessness* 139.

in 1993.[18] In Sweden, the survey was carried out by the authorities. In Norway, the first nationwide survey was initiated by a research group, the Norwegian Building Research Institute (NBI), which had no specific political or governance purposes. Denmark has also adopted this definition and method, and the three countries mentioned have continued essentially the same definition of homelessness and survey method up to the present day, while Finland, as a fourth in the group of Nordic countries, uses a slightly different method and definition.[19]

The first survey in Norway resulted in a 'new' category of homeless persons.[20] Definitions based on socially deviant appearances and lifestyles were rejected. Instead, *homelessness* is defined in terms of position in or outside the housing market. In the survey, housing situations are defined and organized hierarchically in ten housing circumstances, from owned and rented dwellings all the way down to rough sleeping. A person is considered homeless if he/she has no privately owned or rented accommodation and (1) is reliant on occasional or temporary lodging; (2) lives temporarily with friends, acquaintances, or relatives; (3) stays in an institution and is due to be discharged within two months without access to accommodation; (4) stays in a correctional facility and is due to be released within two months without access to accommodation; or (5) sleeps rough. Those who live permanently with next of kin or in sublet accommodation are not considered homeless.

The registration of the homeless population in Norway is carried out by a wide range of health and welfare services. The most important respondents (service) are the municipal social services (the municipal department of the Norwegian Labour and Welfare Administration NAV), which by legislation are responsible for assisting homeless persons with their housing issues (discussed further later). Other respondents include municipal health and care services, state-owned hospitals and specialized healthcare institutions, prisons, NGOs, and other private agencies providing services for the homeless. The survey is cross-sectional, measuring homelessness at a particular point in time (week 48), and the number of homeless people throughout the year will be higher.

This method has its strengths and weaknesses. It is important to note that homeless people not known by the services will not be registered, and hence not included in the national homeless data. On the other hand, many of the services involved in the registration are in contact with people not using facilities for homeless people and who otherwise would be regarded as part of the 'hidden homeless' category. Although the operational definition comprises a range of living situations, there is always a risk of reproducing the institutional identities associated with homelessness representations of the traditional 'vagrant'. For instance, children who are homeless with their parents were not included until the fourth national survey in 2008.[21] Even though families with children staying in temporary accommodation were known to the local authorities before 2008, applying the term *homelessness* to these families did not sit well with the traditional image of 'the homeless person'.

Throughout the 24 years of national surveys, the definition of *homelessness* has remained unchanged, ensuring regular and timely data throughout this period. However,

---

18 E. Borgny and A. Qvarlander, 'Hjemløse i Sverige' in W. Runquist and H. Swärd (eds), *Hemlöshet. En antologi om olika perspektiv & förklaringsmodeller* (Carlssons bokförlag 2000).
19 Benjaminsen and others (n 17) 139.
20 Ulfrstad (n 2).
21 E. Dyb and K. Johannessenv, *Bostedsløse i Norge 2008 – en kartlegging* (NIBR Report 2009) 17.

the groups of people living as homeless or in marginal housing situations have changed. The EEA Agreement[22] grants citizens from EU and EEA countries free movement within the internal market, and the 2004 and 2007 EU enlargements have led to an influx of labour immigration in particular from Eastern European countries. Whereas most immigrants succeed in the labour and housing market, a small group is relegated to begging or engaging in temporary, informal work. Refugees without residence permits find themselves in a similar situation. Poor visitors and undocumented migrants are denied access to mainstream services and are served by low-threshold facilities. As a result, they are not counted in national surveys. Migration is defined as a major and growing homelessness problem in Europe,[23] for which many European countries are reluctant to take responsibility.[24]

Numbers and Profile of Homelessness in Norway

Redefining *homelessness* did not necessarily alter the common understanding of the concept.[25] The institutional identity of homelessness is shaped within the hostels, shelters, and other institutions that have given homeless people a roof above their head.[26] Moreover, the laws and regulations that govern the sector shape specific institutionalized identities and concepts. Throughout seven surveys, the most prominent characteristics of homelessness that are revealed are: male, mid-30s, single, born in Norway, with a long history of homelessness and substance abuse. The profile is quite close to that of the homeless population in Denmark, and largely similar to homelessness in Sweden.[27] This reproduction of the 'old vagrant' is explained by the well-developed security net of the Nordic welfare states, which results in a rather small homeless population dominated by persons with multiple social and health issues.

Norway differs from most European countries in that there has been a steady decline in the number of homeless people in recent decades. In 2020, 3,325 adults were homeless in Norway. The highest numbers were registered in 2012 (6,259 people) and 1996 (6,200 people). The number has almost halved in the period from the first survey to the last.

Figure 8.1 shows that the number of homeless people per 1,000 inhabitants was higher in 1996 than in 2012, although the number was about the same. The relative decline, from 1.5 per 1,000 to 1.26 per 1,000 inhabitants, is explained by population growth during this period. The last two surveys (2016 and 2020) have shown a decrease in absolute and relative numbers.

---

22 The Agreement on the European Economic Area, includes the 27 EU states, Iceland, Lichtenstein, and Norway.
23 <https://mailchi.mp/feantsa/feantsa-migration-newsletter-8> (accessed 1 September 2023).
24 K. Hermans and others, 'Migration and Homelessness: Measuring the Intersections' (2020) 14(3) *European Journal of Homelessness* 13.
25 M. Spector and J. I. Kitsuse, *Constructing Social Problems* (Cummings Publishing Company 1977).
26 M. Järvinen and N. Mik-Meyer, *At skabe en klient. Institutionelle identiteter i socialt arbejde* (Hans Reitzels Forlag 2004).
27 L. Benjaminsen, *Hjemløshed i Danmark 2019: National kortlægning* (VIVE – The Danish National Centre for Social Research 2019); The National Board of Health and Welfare (Socialstyrelsen), *Homelessness 2017 – Extent and Character* (The National Board of Health and Welfare 2017).

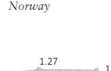
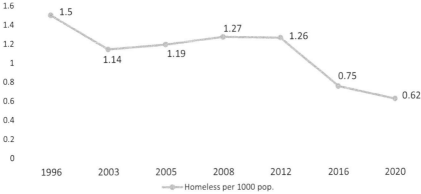

Figure 8.1 Homelessness in Norway; number of homeless people per 1,000 inhabitants.
Source: Authors' own presentation.[28]

A significant proportion of homeless people in Norway has complex problems and requires assistance from several services. In 2020, one in two had a substance abuse problem, one in three a mental illness, and one in four suffered from both substance abuse and mental illness. Although the proportion of homeless people suffering from substance abuse has declined progressively, the overall characteristics of the homeless population has remained stable throughout the surveys. For the majority, social assistance or benefits are the main income. Fewer than one in ten have a source of income, indicating some form of labour market affiliation. The proportion of foreign-born homeless is increasing. In 2020, 67% were born in Norway, compared to 86% in 2003. The proportion of women remains relatively stable and constitutes between 25 and 30% of the homeless population. By and large, homeless women do not differ from the general profile of the population. Of the small minority that is homeless with their children, few suffer from substance abuse, mental illness, or long-term homelessness.

There are essentially two explanations for the decline in the number of homeless people in Norway. One is that changing political governments have prioritized measures to tackle homelessness. In 1996, the high number of homeless people and their dispersal across the country surprised central and local authorities alike. The findings triggered more research funding, and the resulting research both confirmed known information and presented new findings revealing the poor state of services and provisions for the homeless.[29] From 2001 to today, there has been a succession of national initiatives and programmes to reduce homelessness and improve conditions for the group.[30] Over time,

---

28 See E. Dyb and H. H. Zeiner, *Bostedsløse I Norge 2020 – en kartlegging* (Report, NIBR 2021) 10.
29 L. M. Ulfrstad, *Hjelpeapparatet for bostedsløse. Om hjelpeapparatet i Oslo, Bergen, Trondheim og Stavanger* (Norwegian Building Research Institute 1999); L. J. Solheim, *Vår tids legdefolk? Bustadsløyse i mindre kommunar* (Østlandsforskning 2000).
30 The Housing Bank: *Project Homeless (2001–2004)*; The Government/The Housing Bank: *The Pathway to a Permanent home (2005–2007)*; The Housing Bank's *Housing social development program from 2009–2015* followed by The Housing Bank's *Municipal program (2016–2020)*; The Government: *Housing for Welfare (2014–2020)*; The Government: *National Strategy for Social Housing Policy (2021–2024)*.

the target group has been broadened, but countering homelessness remains central. This sustained effort has clearly paid off.[31]

The second explanation is the housing-led focus of the programmes. The only countries in Europe to have a pronounced housing-led focus on national homeless policies – Finland and Norway – are also the only countries that can document a decline in homelessness. In Norway, in keeping with the housing-led approach, responsibility for homelessness is included in national housing policy, with the Norwegian State Housing Bank as the executive directorship, thus signalling that access to housing is key. Hence, the issue is no longer whether the homeless deserve a home, but whether they should be included in the larger group of people in need of home-based services. In contrast to the Vagrancy Act, which criminalized homelessness, the current approach equates the housing needs of the homeless with that of groups traditionally considered 'worthy needy', such as the elderly or people with disabilities. Nevertheless, there is still some distance between stated national ambitions and the reality of local-level implementation.

Statutory Frameworks Governing Social Housing

The housing-led policy on homelessness is implemented in a market-driven housing system. A series of liberalizations in the housing and finance sectors in the 1980s has rendered Norway one of the most market-driven housing sectors in Western Europe.[32] Cooperative housing was transformed into a self-owning sector, and private rental estates were sectioned and converted into condominiums. Today, almost 80% of Norwegian households are homeowners. A 'well-functioning housing market' has been an important objective in Norwegian housing policy over the past two decades.[33] The rental market, which accounts for 20%, is mostly commercial with unregulated rents. Most landlords are non-professionals, renting out one or a few homes, and these can be quickly pulled off the market, for example, by landlords selling an extra dwelling during a period of spikes in house prices. Figures for the share of social rental dwellings vary depending on whether the dwellings for specific groups, which are not allocated only on socio-economic criteria (e.g., for the elderly, persons with functional deficits), are included. But the sector accounts for less than 5% of the housing stock.

The Housing Bank was established in 1946 and has since represented the most important national housing policy instrument. Over the past 30 years, and in line with liberalization of housing policy, its role has shifted from a state bank to an executive welfare directorate under the ministry responsible for housing policy.[34] Today it manages parts of legislation as well as social and economic policy instruments. Implementation takes place mainly in the municipalities. The municipalities are obliged to provide statutory services or welfare benefits. The provision of non-statutory services depends on the municipalities' resources and priorities. However, Norwegian municipalities have a high degree of autonomy regarding

---

31 E. Dyb, 'Counting Homelessness and Politics: The Case of Norway' (2017) 1(2) *European Journal of Homelessness* 15.
32 M. Stamsø, 'Housing and the Welfare State in Norway' (2009) 32 *Scandinavian Political Studies* 195.
33 Sørvoll (n 3).
34 Ministry of Local Government and Regional Development, KDD (April 2022).

priorities and service provision, and the quality and extent of both statutory and non-statutory services vary across municipalities.

The laws and regulations regulating the housing sector operate at various levels. Some address obligations on a structural level; others regulate individual rights and the authorities' obligations towards individuals. *The Planning and Building Act*[35] regulates planning and building and works on a structural level. The Act provides rules on the processing of state, regional, and municipal plans, with municipal plans being particularly salient to social housing issues. The Act does not require municipalities to incorporate housing for homeless and social housing purposes specifically, but the general provisions, in Article 3–1f, state that the planning shall 'promote the health of the population and counteract social health differences, as well as help prevent crime'. Article 17, on development agreements between the municipality, the landowner, and/or the developer, is a tool for implementing the municipality's land use plan in cooperation with private stakeholders and includes social considerations. The municipalities decide the content and priorities of their area and community plans. However, with reference to the Planning and Building Act, and with support in the *Public Health Act*,[36] national housing authorities have increasingly emphasized and called for social housing objectives and considerations to be incorporated into the overall municipal plans.[37]

The *Housing Cooperatives Act*[38] and the *Condominium Act*[39] regulate different forms of cooperative ownership and include provisions on the rights and duties of individual unitholders, finances, and accounts, and handling of joint ownership (outdoor areas, stairways, etc.). The laws safeguard the rights and duties of homeowners, but they have a section that can be used to give municipalities access to social housing, counteract unwanted concentration, and provide greater social mix. As a primary rule, the Act states that a person can own only one unit (dwelling) in a housing cooperative. But there are some exceptions. 'Legal entities' may own at least one dwelling in smaller cooperatives and condominiums and up to 10% of the dwellings in a housing cooperative and condominiums with more than five units.[40] Legal entities, which are most important for the procurement of housing for social purposes, include municipalities and 'companies, foundations or others that have entered into a cooperation agreement with the state, county or municipality to provide housing for the disadvantaged'. Some municipalities have used the section, also referred to as the 'ten-per-cent rule', to buy rental properties in housing cooperatives and condominiums or to enter into agreements with commercial actors who buy homes to rent out for social purposes.

At the individual level, the right to assistance with housing problems is provided in laws regulating social services and health services in municipalities. The two laws are

---

35 The Planning and Building Act Lov om planlegging og byggesaksbehandling (plan- og bygningsloven) – Lovdata <https://lovdata.no/dokument/NL/lov/2008-06-27-71> (accessed 1 September 2023).
36 The Public Health Act Lov om folkehelsearbeid (folkehelseloven) – Lovdata <https://lovdata.no/dokument/NL/lov/2011-06-24-29> (accessed 1 September 2023).
37 <www.veiviseren.no> (the Wizard) Comprehensive Housing Policy Planning, The Wizard <https://husbanken.no/kommune/veiviseren> (accessed 1 September 2023).
38 The Cooperative Housing Act Lov om burettslag (burettslagslova) – Lovdata <https://lovdata.no/dokument/NL/lov/2003-06-06-39?q=burettslag> (accessed 1 September 2023).
39 The Condominium Act Lov om eierseksjoner (eierseksjonsloven) – Lovdata <https://lovdata.no/dokument/NL/lov/2017-06-16-65#KAPITTEL_5> (accessed 1 September 2023).
40 Article 4–2 in The Cooperative Housing Act, Article 24 in The Condominium Act.

managed by the social sector and the health sector, respectively. *The Act Relating to Social Services in the Labour and Welfare Administration (the Social Services Act)*[41] regulates assistance to households and people experiencing financial and/or social exclusion in the housing market. Article 15, titled 'Dwellings for disadvantaged', states: 'The municipality shall contribute to acquiring housing to disadvantaged persons who are not able to attend to their interest in the housing market.' The Act establishes a duty to assist the disadvantaged, not an individual right to housing, and is not perceived by the municipalities to be a statutory obligation. Article 27, titled 'Temporary accommodation', imposes an obligation on the municipalities 'to provide temporary accommodation for those unable to manage on their own', an obligation that the county governor has established shall be provided in kind, not in cash. The municipality is also obliged to assist homeless people registered as domiciled in another municipality if the person is without other options.[42] Several paragraphs in the Social Service Act are understood to amplify the municipalities' obligation towards the homeless – for example, Article 1, titled 'Objective of the Act', states that its aim is to improve the living conditions of the disadvantaged and contribute to social and financial security, including the opportunity for an independent life and housing.

Article 3–2a of the *Act of Municipal Health and Care Services (the Health and Care Services Act)*[43] establishes that the municipality is responsible for providing nursing facilities and residential care homes. In general, the Act regulates municipal health services, including services to homeless people with substance abuse and/or other serious health problems.

The Act of Housing Allowance and Municipal Housing Subsidy (the Housing Allowance Act)[44] provides for housing allowance, which is a means-tested housing subsidy for low-income households. The upper-income limit and the rate of the allowance are regulated by governmental decree. The Act stipulates the principles for calculation of the rate. The dwelling shall meet the requirements of adequate housing, which generally means an independent dwelling with its own entrance, bathroom, and cooking equipment. The aim of the *housing subsidy* is to assist disadvantaged households to permanently settle in a suitable dwelling. The Act endows municipal case managers with significant autonomy in carrying out the assessment regarding the use of the subsidy. For example, the subsidy can be used to buy a dwelling (usually on top of a loan), to refinance a mortgage, to re-settle in an adapted dwelling, or to improve a current dwelling. The municipalities may choose to assist a few households with a large sum or allocate smaller sums to many households or subsidize the construction of a building or buy dwellings earmarked for people at disadvantage in the housing market. A secondary law regulates the allocation of the subsidy to

---

41 Act relating to social services in the labour and welfare administration Lov om sosiale tjenester i arbeids- og velferdsforvaltningen (sosialtjenesteloven) - Lovdata <https://lovdata.no/dokument/NL/lov/2009-12-18-131?q=sosialtjenesteloven> (accessed 1 September 2023).
42 A. Kjellevold, 'Retten til bolig og oppfølgingstjenester En utredning for Kommunal- og regionaldepartementet/Boligutvalget' in NOU 2011: 15 Appendiks 1, 152.
43 Act of Municipal Health and Care Services Lov om kommunale helse- og omsorgstjenester m.m. (helse- og omsorgstjenesteloven) – Lovdata <https://lovdata.no/dokument/NL/lov/2011-06-24-30?q=kommunale%20helse%20og%20omsorgstjenester> (accessed 1 September 2023).
44 Act of Housing Allowance and Municipal Housing Subsidy (the housing allowance act) av 2012 Lov om bustøtte og kommunale bustadtilskot (bustøttelova) – Lovdata <https://lovdata.no/dokument/NL/lov/2012-08-24-64?q=bostøtte> (accessed 1 September 2023).

acquire rental housing for the disadvantaged in the housing market.[45] Both municipalities and private companies that have entered into an agreement with a municipality committing the company to rent out dwellings to households chosen by the municipality can receive the subsidy.

The Regulations of Loans from the Housing Bank of 2022[46] replaced several regulations on different types of loans. The Housing Bank manages and allocates various loans designed to support the objectives of housing policy. *The start-up loan*, introduced in 2004, and regulated by secondary law (Section 5), is a subsidized loan provided by the state through the Housing Bank and managed by the municipalities. The target group is low-income households whose income is deemed sufficiently stable to pay the mortgage for the next years. In 2014, a change in the regulations strengthened the emphasis on households experiencing long-term difficulties in accessing housing, particularly families with children. There is variation between the municipalities both in the management of the loans and in the assessment of who should be the main target group. The housing subsidy is often allocated to top up the start-up loan. Section 3 of the secondary law regulates municipalities and other stakeholders with the objective of acquiring rental dwelling for people and households in disadvantaged position. The condition for assigning loans to companies and stakeholders is that they enter into an agreement with the municipality, which gives the municipality the right of disposal of the given dwelling for a minimum of 20 years.

Finally, the *Regulations on Competence Grants for Social Housing Work from the Norwegian State Housing Bank*[47] contribute to increasing competence in social housing work and policy, as well as the dissemination of knowledge about the housing market and public housing policy in general. The grant may not be used to fulfil the statutory tasks of municipalities. Individual grants should be allocated based on priorities given by the Ministry of Local Government and Regional Development. The Housing Bank may provide further guidelines for awarding and calculating grants. As was the case with the now-discontinued *Regulations of Grants for Experiments with New Housing Models from the Norwegian State Housing Bank*,[48] the regulation pertains to knowledge development and innovation in the section of the housing sector that addresses the needs of people and households with special housing needs and/or home services. In a mainly market-based sector and with autonomous municipalities, development projects with state funds are an important way of managing the implementation of housing policies. Unlike, for example, the UK, Norway has no tradition of education in social housing management.[49]

---

45 Forskrift om tilskudd til utleieboliger fra Husbanken – Lovdata <https://lovdata.no/dokument/SF/forskrift/2017-12-18-2235?q=forskrift%20tilskudd%20til%20utleieboliger> (accessed 1 September 2023).

46 Forskrift om lån fra Husbanken – Lovdata <https://lovdata.no/dokument/SF/forskrift/2019-11-18-1546?q=lån%20fra%20Husbanken> (accessed 1 September 2023).

47 See <https://lovdata.no/dokument/SFO/forskrift/2011-02-23-193?q=Forskrift%20om%20kompetansetilskudd%20til%20boligsosialt> (accessed 1 September 2023). The grant, which was discontinued in 2023, aimed to contribute to the development and testing of new housing models for people disadvantaged in the housing market and have special needs, as well as facilitate attempts to create a greater diversity of housing supply. Municipalities, companies, and other stakeholders with projects within the scope of the grant could apply for the grant.

48 See <https://lovdata.no/dokument/SF/forskrift/2021-12-20-3779?q=boligmodeller> (accessed 1 September 2023).

49 I. Anderson, E. Dyb and S. Ytrehus, *Meeting the Needs of Homeless People: Interprofessional Work in Norway and Scotland. A Pilot Study* (NIBR 2012).

Proposals to Strengthen the Individual Right to Housing

Development of the social housing field (elaborated in the next section) has highlighted the weak legal foundations of the right to housing in Norway. During the last decade, government initiatives have sought to strengthen the individual right to housing, but without imposing a duty on local governments to provide housing to homeless or other disadvantaged people and households. Discussion and assessment of the legislative amendments emphasize the dilemmas tied to the legislative frame on housing in a welfare state with autonomous municipalities and a market-driven housing system.

Amendments to the Social Services Act and the Municipal Health Services Act in 2012 aimed to strengthen the individual right to housing. A judicial review of the consequences of the amendments concluded that the wording of the proposal increases the responsibility of municipalities to help provide housing for disadvantaged people in the housing market. However, this duty is not tantamount to a right to housing for citizens in need of assistance from their municipalities.[50] Prior to the proposal, Kjellevold concluded that the proposed amendment did not significantly strengthen citizens' right to housing.[51] Nevertheless, Kjellevold concluded that several sections of the two laws combined, in concert with rights embedded in other regulations, put strong pressure on municipalities to provide housing for disadvantaged people, including the homeless. In particular, the right to an individual plan settled in the *Act of Patients and User Rights* and laws regulating health services imposes obligations on municipalities.[52] Patients and users in need of long-term and coordinated health and care services have the right to an individual plan, the purpose of which is comprehensive and coordinated services. The legislation also stipulates that municipal and national services must cooperate on the plan. A significant proportion of the homeless population will have the right to an individual plan, in particular, homeless people with both an addiction and a mental illness and experiencing long-term homelessness. Yet the 2020 homeless survey indicates that only 5% of homeless people actually have an individual plan.[53] The proportion is lower than it was in the 2016 and 2012 surveys.

The Act on Municipalities' Responsibilities in the Social Housing Field[54] *(the Social Housing Act)* was passed and came into force on 1 July 2023. It aims to increase municipalities' duties in the field. Section 1 states that the purpose of the Act 'is to help disadvantaged people in the housing market to acquire and retain a dwelling, which has satisfactory standards and size, located in a neighbourhood that is good for the persons who are going to live there'. The Act specifies and clarifies municipalities' duty to assist disadvantaged people in the housing market already specified in the Social Services Act and underlines the responsibility of all stakeholders involved in the field to cooperate and

---

50 Hjort: *Rettslig betydning av lovendringer for kommunene (Legal consequences of the legislative amendments for the municipalities)* (2012) (internal document).
51 Kjellevold (n 42) 152–60. (2011).
52 Act of Patient and User Rights <https://lovdata.no/dokument/NL/lov/1999-07-02-63?q=pasient%20og%20bruker (accessed 1 September 2023); Act of establishing and implementation of mental health care <https://lovdata.no/dokument/NL/lov/1999-07-02-62?q=psykisk%20helsevern> (accessed 1 September 2023). Act of specialist health service etc <https://lovdata.no/dokument/NL/lov/1999-07-02-61?q=spesialisthelsetjeneste> (accessed 1 September 2023).
53 Dyb and Zeiner (n 28).
54 Act on municipalities' responsibilities in the social housing field https://lovdata.no/dokument/NL/lov/2022-12-20-121 (accessed 1 September 2023).

coordinate their work. Furthermore, the Act clarifies municipalities' obligations to take social housing considerations into account in their social and land-use plans. The Act was prepared by the Ministry of Local Government and Regional Development, which emphasized that the Act did not impose new tasks on the municipalities. Before passing the bill, a preparation paper was sent out for public consultation.[55] Discussions and arguments during this preparatory work reflect the true state of social housing policy and illustrate dilemmas in social housing work and policy, particularly related to the obligation to assist in providing housing for disadvantaged people in the housing market, also referred to as 'accomplice liability'. One of the arguments for tightening the accomplice liability is that ambiguity in current legislation and practice generates, among other things, undesirable discrimination between municipalities. *Social housing work* is a relatively new term in Norway, and the content of the term may be perceived differently between municipalities. The Ministry points to significant variation and failures in the municipalities' approaches to social housing work.[56]

Whilst the Social Housing Act is intended to contribute to greater equality in the approach of the municipalities, the Ministry has underscored the importance of safeguarding municipal self-government as enshrined in the *Local Government Act*.[57] The Local Government Act stipulates that municipal self-government should be limited only to the extent that it is necessary to meet national objectives. State earmarked funds in the municipalities have played a key role in the development of social housing work. As the Ministry points out, there has been a shift in state funding from mainly earmarked funds to framework funding. Whereas framework funding reinforces municipal self-government, it is not necessarily conducive to greater equality in the provision for citizens. Finally, the Ministry points out that obtaining a dwelling is both an individual responsibility and that adequate housing is one of the four pillars of the welfare state, together with education, health services, and pensions. The argument about housing as the fourth pillar equal to the other three pillars under the welfare state was strongly emphasized in Green Paper 2011:15[58] and is maintained in later public documents.[59] As mentioned earlier, however, Torgersen, who coined the phrase 'pillars under the welfare state', used the metaphor to characterize housing as the wobbly pillar.[60]

The Ministry's preparation paper and the Act itself detail various forms of assistance municipalities are obliged to provide in securing housing for disadvantaged citizens. The Act imposes tighter procedural requirements for case processing and requires municipalities to make decisions for each individual assistance measure they implement. The law thus strengthens citizens' right to appeal to the county governor against decisions made. The

---

55 The Ministry of Local Government and Regional Development: Bill on municipal responsibility towards disadvantaged in the housing market. Consultation paper Kommunenes oppgaver og ansvar på det boligsosiale området <www.regjeringen.no/contentassets/d0ecae28c67b4600a2553fdd1ff3265b/ny-boligsosial-lov-om-kommunens-ansvar-overfor-vanskeligstilte-pa-boligmarkedet-horing.pdf (accessed 1 September 2023).
56 Norwegian Board of Health Supervision (Helsetilsynet), *Det heng dårleg saman* (Report 6/2019; cited in KDDs Consultation Paper 21).
57 Act relating to municipalities and county authorities, paragraphs 2–1 and 2–2 <https://lovdata.no/sok?q=The+local+government+act (accessed 1 September 2023).
58 NOU 2011:15, *Rom for alle* (Room for all).
59 Meld. St. 17 (2012–2013) *Byggje – bu – leve*.
60 Torgersen (n 6).

county governor has a supervising role and serves as the court of appeal in several areas of health and welfare services.

A review of the consultation responses[61] to the Act shows that the municipalities, which are the implementing stakeholder, while supporting a social housing law, also have objections and proposals for clarifications. The majority of municipalities who responded were wary of the requirement that the dwelling should have a 'satisfactory standard and size', as well as the requirement that the dwelling be located in a neighbourhood that suits the individual: Section 1. The main argument is that the proposed formulation places too great a restriction on both local self-government and local discretion. Most of the larger municipalities have submitted consultation responses, and although there is a reasonably differentiated housing stock in these municipalities, adequate housing to disadvantaged people is in short supply. The municipalities argue that municipalities must have sufficient leeway in balancing individual needs with available municipal and private housing. Some consultation responses called for more clarity on how far a municipality's duties should extend within a primarily market-based housing sector. Although the municipality assists in finding a home in the private market, the tenancy is a private legal agreement between landlord and tenant. So too is the purchase of a home a private legal transaction. Even if the municipality awards start-up loans and subsidies, the purchase of a dwelling is an important decision for the individual, who must have the right and responsibility to assess desirable quality and neighbourhood conditions within their own financial framework.[62]

Many municipalities maintain that the proposed obligation to formalize in writing decisions on every single service, advice, and guidance to a client, which is a prerequisite for realising the client's right to appeal, will create more administration and delay case processing. A local authority argues that the Ministry's stipulation that social housing services should be made statutory is flawed: 'But statutory legislation alone does not lead to increased municipal budgets. It will be the same funds that will be distributed to an increasing number of statutory purposes.'[63] There is some disagreement among the consultative bodies concerning whether the 2023 Act will consolidate social housing work and policy in one law or whether it deals only with parts of this field. The Bar Association mainly supports the law but nevertheless maintains that restricting regulation to a limited part of the social housing field would be inexpedient. Significant provisions will remain in other Acts and secondary laws.[64] This is particularly true for the Social Services Act, which covers several of the elements in the new 2023 law, but also for regulations on housing support, housing grants, and start-up loans.

---

61 All bills are sent out for consultation to a wide range of bodies, depending on who will be affected, for example, ministries, government agencies, the county governor, municipalities, labour unions, other organizations (including NGOs), and other private stakeholders. Consultative bodies and statements for the social housing law are listed here <www.regjeringen.no/no/dokumenter/horing-ny-boligsosial-lov/id2786962/?expand=horingsinstanser&lastvisited=undefined> (accessed 1 September 2023).

62 For example, Consultation Response from Bærum Municipality <www.regjeringen.no/no/dokumenter/horing-ny-boligsosial-lov/id2786962/?uid=51e16d15-42b0-4e88-adeb-24e50e4d73e8> (accessed 1 September 2023).

63 Consultation Response from Sandnes Municipality <www.regjeringen.no/no/dokumenter/horing-ny-boligsosial-lov/id2786962/?uid=512d5415-07f4-4958-94af-e9a6ece1692b> (accessed 1 September 2023).

64 See the Norwegian Bar Association (Advokatforeningen) <www.regjeringen.no/contentassets/c554ce16bdc34dcb8a97e12418d210d7/advokatforeningen.pdf?uid=Advokatforeningen> (accessed 1 September 2023).

Some consultative bodies maintain that the new law does not go far enough in legislating for the right to housing. Jussbuss, a free legal aid initiative run by law students, says the law should be clearer about who is disadvantaged and consequently entitled to assistance, and that the duty to assist should be emphasized more strongly. Based on the experience of users of their legal services regarding the low quality of some council housing stock, Jussbuss supports legislating for suitable standards and sizes of the dwelling, and for requirements regarding the quality of the neighbourhood.

Soft Measures and Funding

Norway has achieved significant results in combatting homelessness. Achievements for other disadvantaged groups are more uncertain. The definition of 'disadvantaged in the housing market' has varied, resulting in a corresponding variation in the number of affected people and households.[65] As a result, the number of disadvantaged people in the housing market is an uncertain measure of success or failure of social housing policy. Homelessness, in contrast, has been a high priority in Norway in several national programmes since 2000. A clear definition and regular surveys of homelessness are prerequisites for measuring homelessness and allows us to measure and evaluate the extent of political achievements in the area.

To compensate for weak legislation and local autonomy, state programmes to prevent and reduce homelessness all apply soft and educational instruments of governance, as well as funding, to implement policy in the municipalities. The first state initiative, *Project Homeless* (2001–2004), was an experimental project with participation from the seven largest municipalities. Its aim was to develop methods and models for working with and reducing homelessness, reflecting limited knowledge about social housing work both locally and nationally. A housing-led policy emerged during the project period, signalling that assisting homeless people to acquire a home was a priority and, moreover, that the allocation of a dwelling should not be conditional. This was a radical new approach to assisting homeless persons with multiple issues, and slogans like 'everyone can live, it depends on the assistance and follow-up services' were launched.[66]

The subsequent programme, the *Pathway to a Permanent Home (2005–2007)*, was recognized in an international peer review under the European Commission specifically for being based on a housing-led policy.[67] Unlike *Project Homeless*, however, this programme operated with performance targets and principally included all municipalities. The national government set out specific targets that municipalities should collectively achieve during the project period. For example, the number of petitions for eviction should be reduced by 50%, and the number of evictions should be reduced by 30%. Time limits were also set for stays in temporary accommodation, and accommodation facilities were required to meet certain quality criteria. Evaluation of the programme found that the municipalities prioritized working with a selection of targets based on local needs and capacities, and

---

65 L. R. Thorsen, *Vanskeligstilte på boligmarkedet. Hvordan måle og hvem er utsatt på boligmarkedet?* (Report 2017/6, Statistics Norway 2017).
66 I. L. S. Hansen and S. Ytrehus, *Alle skal bo, det er tjenestene det kommer an på* (Fafo Housing for Welfare (2014–2020) 2005).
67 B. Edgar, *National Strategy to Prevent and Tackle Homelessness: The Pathway to a Permanent Home* (European Commission, DG Employment, Social Affairs and Equal Opportunity 2006).

national authorities had limited instruments of governance to influence the overall target achievement.[68]

The last two programmes, *Housing for Welfare (2014–2020)*[69] and the present government strategy *Everyone Needs a Safe Home (2021–2024)*,[70] include several target groups, but homelessness remains a central issue. However, the time gap between 2008 and 2013, from the end of the *Pathway to a Permanent Home* to the launching of *Housing for Welfare*, was covered by the *Housing Banks's Social Housing Development Programme (2009–2014)*, succeeded by the *Housing Bank's Municipal Programme (2015–2020)*. The two programmes played a key role in the implementation of the *Housing for Welfare* strategy. In the two programmes, the competence and development aspects are clearly stated. In addition, municipalities were differentiated by the extent of social housing challenges, and the programmes were based on long-term and reciprocal agreements between municipalities and the Housing Bank. Finally, all the programmes themselves are instruments of field development and state policy implementation. Moreover, educational and learning instruments permeate all the programmes, from participation in networks to exchange experiences between municipalities and other stakeholders and guidance from the Housing Bank. Courses in social housing work have also been established in educational institutions.

A recent study has found that the sustained efforts of the Housing Bank, combined with substantial earmarked funds for development purposes in the municipalities, have been important factors behind the decline in homelessness in Norway from 2012 to 2016.[71] All national programmes were accompanied by earmarked government funding. The funding increased substantially in 2005 with the introduction of the Social Housing Competence Fund. The Competence Fund, which was expanded during the following decade and, at its peak, reached EUR 8.2 million per year (2015 and 2016), was made available to municipalities with the aim of developing local homelessness projects and measures but also for research purposes. This competence funding was included in the municipalities' ordinary budget framework from 2017. The Labour and Welfare Administration (NAV) also allocated earmarked funds to the municipalities to develop follow-up housing support for former homeless with complex needs (in the period 2004–2019).

Lack of affordable and social housing remains the major obstacle to access to both the rental market and homeownership among disadvantaged and other households with limited income. The Housing Bank and the municipalities have developed new instruments designed to provide housing for social purposes in the private market. *Assignment agreements* and *allocation agreements* between municipalities, private housing, and construction companies are aimed at increasing municipalities' access to social rental housing. The

---

68 E. Dyb, M. K. Helgesen and K. Johannessen, *På vei til egen bolig. Evaluering av nasjonal strategi for å forebygge og bekjempe bostedsløshet* (Report 15, NIBR 2008). For an English summary of the evaluation see The Pathway to a Permanent Home <www.regjeringen.no/en/dokumenter/the-pathway-to-a-permanent-home/id576721/> (accessed 1 September 2023).

69 Bolig for velferd. Nasjonal strategi for boligsosial arbeid (2014–2020) <www.regjeringen.no/no/tema/plan-bygg-og-eiendom/boligmarkedet/Housing-for-welfare-National-strategy-for-housing-and-support-services-2014-2020/id2351129/> (accessed 1 September 2023).

70 Alle trenger et trygt hjem. Nasjonal strategi for den sosiale boligpolitikken (2021–2024) (We All Need a Safe Place to Call Home: National Strategy for Social Housing Policy) (2021–2024) <www.regjeringen.no/contentassets/c2d6de6c12d5484495d4ddeb7d103ad5/we-all-need-a-safe-place-to-call-home-national-strategy-for-social-housing-policies-2021-2024.pdf (accessed 1 September 2023).

71 E. Dyb, *Færre bostedsløse – hva er forklaringen?* (Report, NIBR 2019) 9.

assignment agreement has a duration of 20 years and gives the municipality the right, but not the obligation, to assign up to 40% of the dwellings in new projects to disadvantaged households. Up to 85% of the project can be financed with loans from the Housing Bank. The *allocation agreement* has a framework of 30 years and gives the municipality the right to dispose of all dwellings in a project. The municipality is not obliged to use all, but the dwellings must nevertheless be rented out for social purposes. In addition to loans from the Housing Bank, these housing projects can be financed with grants, totalling up to 85% of the costs. The arrangement *From Tenancy to Homeownership* can be carried out in different ways, depending on the local housing market. The principle is that the resident is given a right to buy the property after a period as a tenant, and that part of the rent is included in the mortgage.

Social housing programmes have had a consistent focus on the most disadvantaged. Homeless people with drug addiction and mental illness are explicitly mentioned in all the programmes, including the latest strategies and programmes, which have a broader perspective beyond homelessness. The introduction of the concept of Housing First, which has been imported from the United States[72] and has had a huge breakthrough in Western Europe,[73] has reinforced the housing-led policy in the municipalities. Housing First is a programme to assist people with complex needs to settle and retain their housing and is just one type of project in a broader housing-led strategy.

Conclusion

Over the last decades, housing policy in Norway has shifted from a universalist model with the general housing supply at the centre to a narrower housing policy, primarily addressing the needs of particularly vulnerable groups.[74] The change is referred to as 'the social turn'.[75] Acquiring a home has always been a private responsibility, and throughout history, there has been variation as to what extent and with what tools the state has supported the general housing supply.[76] Perhaps a historical coincidence, but the trend towards a more targeted social housing policy has coincided with the development of a homelessness policy. Through homelessness programmes, which have expanded to include other groups, this homelessness policy has been important in developing the 'new' social housing policy and in transforming the Housing Bank from a mere bank to a welfare agency.[77]

This chapter has described how national authorities have developed new tools to assist the homeless and other disadvantaged people in the housing market in Norway. At the same time, the objective of homeownership for the majority has been strengthened in general housing policy. The conservative government, which was in office from 2013 to

---

72 S. Tsemberis, I. Gulcar and M. Nakae, 'Housing First, Consumer Choice and Harm Reduction for Homeless Individuals with Dual Diagnosis' (2004) 94(4) *American Journal of Public Health* 651.
73 V. Busch-Geertsema, 'Housing First Europe – Results of a European Social Experimentation Project (2014) 8(1) *European Journal of Homelessness* 13.
74 E. Reiersen and E. Thue, *De tusen hjem. Den Norske Stats Husbank 1946–96* (Ad Notem Gyldendal 1996); E. Dyb, *Bostedsløs Politikk og Praksis* (Gyldendal Akademisk 2020).
75 Sørvoll (n 3) 171.
76 B. Bengtsson, 'Bostaden som social rettighet: Den generella bostadspolitikens logikk' in A. Lindbom (ed), *Den nya bostadspolitiken* (Boréa 2021).
77 J. Sørvoll, *Husbanken og boligpolitikken 1996–2021* (Cappelen Damm Akademisk 2022); Dyb (n 3).

2021, operated under the slogan that as many people as possible should own their own home. The incumbent government (from autumn 2021), led by the Social Democratic Party, has maintained this emphasis on homeownership. The introduction to the current social housing strategy (2021–2025) states: 'It is first and foremost a private responsibility to acquire a dwelling, and most people do so on their own. Housing policy is therefore largely about stimulating well-functioning housing markets through efficient planning and construction processes.'[78]

The legislation as well as financial and other tools which are intended to help homeless people and other disadvantaged people get satisfactory housing are increasingly adapted to this ownership-focused market. It assists people and households who lack financial opportunities to buy a home and accumulate capital in real estate, hence levelling the playing field in a context where most citizens are homeowners. As this chapter has shown, the success of homelessness policy in Norway can be explained by long-standing national programme activity accompanied by earmarked funding to municipalities, and a focus on housing-led homeless policies.[79]

---

78 Alle trenger et trygt hjem. Nasjonal strategi for den sosiale boligpolitikken (2021–2024) (n 70).
79 Dyb (n 31).

9
ENDING HOMELESSNESS OR MANAGING THE HOMELESS? – HOMELESSNESS, HOUSING POLICY, AND PRACTICE IN SWEDEN

Marcus Knutagård and Matti Wirehag

Introduction

Municipalities are responsible for housing provision in Sweden, but social services (*Socialtjänsten*) tend to be the only organization within the Swedish welfare system responsible for the management of homelessness. Social services are organized at the municipal level, which means that there are 290 different social service organizations in Sweden governed by the Social Services Act and Social Welfare Committees consisting of politicians at the municipal level. The way social services manage this issue of homelessness has a significant impact on the lives of people experiencing homelessness in Sweden. The following quote, taken from the website of a Swedish municipality (Mönsterås municipality), aimed at offering guidance to people experiencing homelessness, offers a strong starting point to understand how homelessness is perceived and managed in Sweden:

> If you are living in homelessness or at risk of becoming homeless, social services can give you advice and support. You who are currently living in homelessness know how hard it is. Therefore, we want to give you the guidance you need to solve your housing situation. Many believe that social services can help you with housing, which is not entirely accurate. Primarily you need to take responsibility for your own situation and look for housing all across the country. This includes everyone, even families. If, despite all efforts you would be eligible for emergency housing provided by the social services, you need to contribute to the housing cost based on your financial situation. An individual assessment of your situation and possibilities is always conducted. If you are at risk of being evicted, you can contact the personal and family counselling services[1] for advice and support.[2]

---

1 Personal and family counselling services are a division of the broader social services department in Sweden.
2 The authors' translation of information found on Mönsterås Municipality's webpage <www.monsteras.se/omsorg-och-stod/hemloshet/> (accessed 1 September 2023).

Similar information as the one presented can be found on many Swedish municipalities' websites. The preceding information highlights one of the central issues people experiencing homelessness are facing today in Sweden when applying for help. Social services are not a housing agency and can only provide housing following homelessness in particular cases for people considered to have special difficulties, such as substance misuse, mental illness, and/or considerable debt. This means that those experiencing homelessness, for example, solely due to poverty will have a hard time accessing housing services even though they might be eligible for financial aid from social services. Since social services are the only organization responsible for managing the practical aspects of homelessness in Sweden, there is currently a significant gap between the needs of those experiencing homelessness on the one hand and the services actually available on the other. This gap is just one of several issues with which social services in Sweden are currently struggling in relation to homelessness policy and practice.

To understand the context of homelessness policy and practice in Sweden, a number of key background issues must be addressed. One of these issues is understanding the central drive and motivation of Swedish housing policy. Throughout the 21st century, a cornerstone in the Swedish's welfare model has been the universal ambition of having a unitary housing system[3] that provides adequate housing to all Swedish citizens at a reasonable cost. Municipal public housing companies, housing allowances, and municipal housing agencies have been the principal instruments deployed in pursuit of this universal policy.[4] The Swedish unitary housing system differs from that, for example, in the UK, which has built its housing policy upon a dualist housing system. In a dualist housing system, a major share of the rental housing market is unregulated, and rents are set based on a market-driven logic, while a smaller section of the market is regulated social housing, where housing is designated for low-income groups.[5] In Sweden, there has been strong political resistance against moving towards a dualist housing system.[6] Despite the universal ambition of Swedish housing policy, several of the most vulnerable groups in Sweden still fall outside of this system, finding themselves in difficult homelessness situations. Policies and practices designed to manage and tackle homelessness have therefore been developed as particular solutions within the specific conditions of the Swedish welfare state. However, the nature of these responses as well as the actors responsible for implementing homelessness policy have varied over time in Sweden. Löfstrand[7] argues that a shift of responsibility for ownership and management of homelessness started in the 1990s as the Swedish unitary housing system began to adapt to a market-driven climate.

---

3 J. Kemeny, *From Public Housing to the Social Market: Rental Policy Strategies in Comparative Perspective* (Routledge 1995).
4 T. Salonen (ed), *Nyttan med allmännyttan* (Liber 2015); M. Grander, *For the Benefit of Everyone? Explaining the Significance of Swedish Public Housing for Urban Housing Inequality Dissertation Series in Migration, Urbanisation, and Social Change* (Faculty of Culture and Society, Malmö University 2018); M. Nilsson, *Från Barnrikehus till sociala hyreskontrakt: Den selektiva bostadspolitikens ursprung och förändring 1933–1994* (Nordic Academic Press 2021).
5 J. Kemeny, 'Comparative Housing and Welfare: Theorising the Relationship (2001) 16 *Journal of Housing and the Built Environment* 53.
6 B. Bengtsson and others (eds), *Varför så olika? Nordisk bostadspolitik i jämförande historiskt ljus. Andra reviderade upplagan* (Égalité 2013).
7 C. Löfstrand, 'Hemlöshetens politik – lokal policy och praktik [The Politics of Homelessness – Local Policy and Praxis]' (Dissertation, Égalité 2005).

Municipal public housing companies adopted a more business-oriented approach, and consequently, many public housing companies increased their demands on potential tenants. At the same time, municipal housing agencies lost their legal mandate to distribute rental apartments based on the needs of applicants. Both changes created a higher threshold for people with social issues to enter the ordinary housing market in Sweden.[8] As part of this shift, homelessness transformed from being a structural housing issue of both state and municipal concern into a municipal homelessness issue mainly handled on an individual level by social services.[9]

Social services had, up to that point in time, only been responsible for handling housing for a selective group of people living with homelessness, such as those with substance misuse and mental illness without housing. So when homelessness to a larger extent became a municipal responsibility, it was delegated to social services that had hitherto only been handling a selective group of people. Since then, homelessness as a wider social issue has occupied an ambiguous place within social services. The reluctance of social services to take full responsibility for the homelessness phenomenon has led to a situation where homelessness organizationally has been subordinated to already-existing housing solutions used to help client categories with substance use and mental illness.[10] That said, precisely how each local housing service provides for homeless people in their area has developed since the 1990s and differs enormously between municipalities. Social services across Sweden's 290 municipalities are free to structure and develop their organization and approach based on local conditions, as part of municipal autonomy established in the Municipal Act (*Kommunallag*),[11] as long as they uphold their legal obligations under the Swedish Social Service Act (*Socialtjänstlag*).[12] This means that social services are responsible for providing, financing, and organizing housing services for people experiencing homelessness in their area, but they are free to organize their precise interventions based on local circumstances. Because of this, the structure, interventions, and actors involved in providing services for homeless people vary widely across Sweden.[13] Despite this broad local discretion, studies show that the delivery of local housing services for persons living in homeless shelters across Sweden is organized, at a broad level, in a similar manner, and municipalities learn and develop through networking and contacts with neighbouring municipalities.[14] Today, the types of interventions used within local housing services for people experiencing homelessness range from emergency housing to different forms of short-term housing solutions, such as rooms or apartments in collective accommodation with or without staff. It can also consist of different types of long-term housing solutions consisting of ordinary apartments subleased through social services. Social services pay for the housing, but it can differ depending on the situation and on individual assessment. It can be paid as a housing allowance to clients who then pay the rent, or it can also be paid

---

8 Löfstrand (n 7); Grander (n 4).
9 I. Sahlin, *På gränsen till bostad: avvisning, utvisning, specialkontrakt* (Arkiv 1996); Löfstrand (n 7).
10 Löfstrand (n 7); H. Swärd, *Hemlöshet: Ett komplext problem i ett föränderligt samhälle* (3rd edn, Studentlitteratur 2021).
11 The Municipal Act 2017:725.
12 SSA 2001:453.
13 Sahlin (n 9).
14 C. Hansen Löfstrand and M. Nordfeldt (eds), *Bostadslös!: Lokal politik och praktik* (Gleerups Utbildning AB 2007).

directly to service providers.[15] The types of solutions used and the extent of local housing solutions vary between municipalities, where larger and more urban municipalities seem to have a wider menu of interventions than smaller and more rural municipalities.[16]

Definition of Homelessness

In Sweden, it is *Socialstyrelsen* – the National Board of Health and Welfare (NBHW) – that is responsible for the development of a national definition of *homelessness*. This is one of the few policy issues concerning homelessness that is managed at a national level. However, municipalities are free to construct parallel definitions based on their local conditions should they wish, which presents one of several problems with accessing and interpreting available statistics on homelessness across Sweden. Today, in Sweden, around 33,250 people are, according to the official Swedish definition, living in different forms of homelessness.[17] The official, national Swedish definition of homelessness, which is the responsibility of the NBHW, is based on four homelessness situations: (1) acute homelessness, living rough, or in acute housing provided by social services; (2) being in an institution and not having any housing prior to release, or being in an institution even though they should have been released because they lack their own housing; (3) long-term housing provided by social services; and (4) in private, short-term living arrangements that are due to expire within three months and there has been contact with social services due to this situation.[18] Based on the NBHW's official statistics on homelessness, the number of homeless people was found to be 9,903 in 1993, 8,400 in 1999, 13,000 in 2005, 34,000 in 2011, and 33,250 in 2017 (the latest survey conducted in Sweden). The big gap between 2005 and 2011 is due to a clarification made by the NBHW to the around 1,400 organizations responding to the survey, in relation to which situations it regarded as being included in the survey. It is therefore likely that the surveys predating 2011 underestimated the number of homeless people in Sweden.[19] The Swedish definition connects to parts of the European Typology of Homelessness and Housing Exclusion (ETHOS[20]) developed by FEANTSA,[21] a European organization that monitors the homelessness issue at a European level. The ETHOS typology is considerably wider than the Swedish definition and includes 13 situations divided into four different groups: roofless, houseless, insecure housing, and inadequate housing. The Swedish definition includes the first two groups.[22] However, this does not include undocumented migrants or destitute EU migrants or other groups living in circumstances of hidden homelessness, out of reach for local homeless housing services.

---

15 M. Knutagård, *Skälens fångar: Hemlöshetsarbetets organisering, kategoriseringar och förklaringar* [Prisoners of Reasons: Organization, Categorizations and Explanations of Work with the Homeless] (Égalité 2009); M. Knutagård, 'Homelessness and Housing Exclusion in Sweden' (2018) 12(2) *European Journal of Homelessness* 103.
16 M. Blid, 'Ett folkhem för alla? Kommunala insatser mot hemlöshet' (Doktorsavhandling, Institutionen för socialt arbete, Mittuniversitetet 2008).
17 NBHW 2017.
18 Socialstyrelsen (NBHW) 2017.
19 Socialstyrelsen (NBHW) 2011, 9.
20 European typology of homelessness and housing exclusion.
21 European federation of organizations working with the homeless.
22 M. Knutagård, J. Heap and K. Nelson, *Thematic Report on National Strategies to Fight Homelessness and Housing Exclusion – Sweden, European Social Policy Network* (ESPN European Commission 2019).

This means that homelessness as a social problem is likely significantly underestimated in the Swedish context. It is hard to accurately estimate how many people are living in hidden homelessness with very unreliable estimates, indicating anything form 10 to 50,000 persons.[23] The exclusion of undocumented migrants and destitute EU migrants living in homelessness is one of several problematic issues in current homelessness policy and practice in Sweden. However, it is not only non-citizens living in homelessness that are falling outside the purview of current homelessness policy and practice. In recent years, social services in the larger cities have reported that more and more people without mental health and substance abuse problems have contacted them in need of housing. Traditionally, social services in Sweden do not assist people to secure housing without severe social issues. The result is that there are groups of people experiencing homelessness in Sweden that, to varying degrees, are excluded from local social services.[24]

The national surveys of homelessness, together with several studies on homelessness in Swedish municipalities, directly or indirectly describe three modes of homelessness: (1) visible homelessness, which refers to all those homeless people and that are known by social services or organizations cooperating with social services – these groups are those tracked in the NBHWs official statistics on homelessness; (2) hidden homelessness, which refers to all those living with homelessness but that are unknown to social services, for example, undocumented migrants or destitute EU migrants who are homeless (there is today no reliable data on the size of this group, but it can safely be assumed that they live in dire housing circumstances);[25] (3) structural homelessness, referring to all those living in homelessness and who, while lacking the social issues that make them eligible for housing assistance through social services, at the same time, have trouble accessing housing on their own. It is unclear how many people in Sweden experience structural homelessness. In some of the larger cities in Sweden, policies limiting access to housing assistance through social services for the structurally homeless have been developed in the last couple of years.[26] Hidden homelessness as well as structural homelessness challenge current praxis and highlight the difficulties that social services have when facing the heterogenous and ever-evolving state of homelessness as a social issue.[27] Despite the fact that certain demographics in Sweden are excluded from the official statistics, the level of homelessness (per 1,000 inhabitants) is still higher in Sweden than its Nordic neighbours despite sharing similar welfare systems.[28]

---

23 Socialstyrelsen (NBHW) 2017.
24 K. Hermans and others, 'Migration and Homelessness: Measuring the Intersections' (2020) 14(3) *European Journal of Homelessness* 13.
25 Swärd (n 10), M. Wittchag and others, 'Living Situation Among Undocumented Migrants in Sweden: The Effects of Exclusion from Fundamental Housing Rights' [2020] *International Journal of Social Welfare* 1; T. Samzelius, 'A Vicious Circle of Silent Exclusion: Family Homelessness and Poverty in Sweden from a Single-Mother Perspective' (PhD dissertation, Malmö University 2020); C. Listerborn, 'The New Housing Precariat: Experiences of Precarious Housing in Malmö, Sweden' [2021] *Housing Studies* 1.
26 I. Sahlin, 'Moving Targets: On Reducing Public Responsibilities Through Re-Categorising Homeless People and Refugees' (2020) 14(1) *European Journal of Homelessness* 27.
27 Ibid.; W. Runquist, *Hur har andrahandslägenheter i Malmö kommun fördelats till hemlösa över tid? En studie av prioriteringar och exkluderingar* (Research Reports in Social Work; Vol. 2021, No. 5) (Socialhögskolan, Lunds universitet 2021).
28 Knutagård (n 15); L. Benjaminsen and others, 'Measurement of Homelessness in the Nordic Countries' (2020) 14(3) *European Journal of Homelessness* 159.

The Right to Housing Assistance

The Swedish definition of homelessness is rarely used as a tool to assess the right to housing by social workers within social services. Instead, social services base their assessments on current case law. The responsibility for assisting homeless people with their housing needs is defined in the Social Services Act (*Socialtjänstlag*) (SSA). The law stipulates that social services have a general responsibility to provide all persons residing within the municipality with the support they need (SSA Chapter 2 §1) and assist in upholding a reasonable living situation (SSA Chapter 4§1). The Supreme Administrative Court in Sweden (SAC) (*Högsta förvaltningsdomstolen*), in one of its rulings,[29] concluded:

> In those cases where a person applying for housing is entirely without housing and the need cannot be fulfilled in any other way, it is the local social welfare committee that is responsible to provide housing. This means that the social welfare committee needs to make sure the individual in question has somewhere to stay and/or assists with the costs of housing.

However, the right to access housing in any particular from is not defined in the SAC decision; instead, a decision on the type of assistance that should be provided is taken in each individual case. Therefore, the right to housing for individuals is not clearly stated either in current law or in case law.[30] In decision 1990 ref 119 and decision 2004 ref 130, the SAC offered clarifications regarding the right to access housing. The opinion of the SAC is that individuals have the right to assistance in the form of housing through social services if the person applying for assistance is homeless and has special difficulties in finding housing for themselves.[31] Interpretation of this SAC opinion is, to a large extent, up to the politicians sitting on local social welfare committees (governed by their local politicians), social workers, as well as the 12 administrative courts that are spread across Sweden.[32] Through case rulings in administrative courts across Sweden, the phrase 'special difficulties' encountered by people experiencing homelessness has been interpreted as including types of mental health issues, substance misuse, a history of repeated evictions, and/or considerable debt.[33] In the last couple of years, there have been examples of municipalities trying to restrict access to housing assistance in a number of different ways. By way of example, stricter interpretations of the right to housing assistance have, in some municipalities, been advocated by municipal legal counsel (lawyers working for the municipalities guiding them in interpretations of different laws), such as concerning structural homelessness.[34] Another example here is a municipality in the south of Sweden that created two types of homeless categories, the voluntarily homeless (people who had been evicted or could not take care

---

29 1990 ref 119.
30 T. Holappa, *Om socialnämndens olika roller som biståndsgivare och hyresvärd (2018): En kommentar till JO:s beslut den 18 maj 2017, dnr 416–2016* (Nordisk Socialrättslig Tidskrift 2018) 17–18, 201–6.
31 Ibid.
32 Sahlin (n 26).
33 Runquist (n 27) 58.
34 P. Kjellbom, 'Socialtjänsten gör fel – hemlösa ska få hjälp' [The Social Services Does It Wrong – Homeless Persons Should Receive Help], Debate Article, Svenska Dagbladet (31 July 2019) <www.svd.se/ socialtjansten-gor-fel–hemlosa-har-ratt-till-hjalp (accessed 1 September 2023).

of their previous home) and involuntarily homeless (people who had become homeless due to unforeseen events and were actively applying for housing across the whole of Sweden). These two categories were, according to the local social welfare committee, a clarification of current case law, and the recommendation to social services was that they should use this tool when assessing the right to housing assistance in their area – only providing housing to the involuntarily homeless.[35]

It is not only the municipalities that have become stricter in their interpretations of the right to housing assistance in recent years. Judicial review of the right to housing assistance has also reflected a stricter approach in recent times. In a case in the court of appeal (*Hovrätten*) in 2018, a person who had documented mental health issues and significant debt was not considered to have special difficulties in relation to her housing situation.[36] This ruling has had some impact on how social services have interpreted the right to housing assistance despite the fact that rulings of the court of appeal have only a limited value in relation to rulings of the SAC.[37]

A further but separate legal issue in relation to the right to housing assistance through social services concerns tenancy law. Housing assistance can be provided according to SSA Chapter 4§1. The relationship between the social welfare committee and the individual is, in most of these cases, the concern of public law (*offentlig rätt*), which governs the state's responsibilities towards its citizens. Another possibility for the local social welfare committee is to enter into a lease agreement with individuals. In these cases, the lease concerns civil law, and the Land Code (*Hyreslagen*)[38] becomes applicable.[39] How the legal aspects of housing assistance are handled by social services in Swedish municipalities is unclear. In a case reviewed by the parliamentary ombudsman in 2017, a social welfare committee had terminated a contract with short notice. The parliamentary ombudsman's opinion was that the Committee had acted correctly. However, the ombudsman concluded it was important that individuals received correct information concerning the legal aspects of their housing assistance.[40]

The right to housing assistance also highlights the tension between civil and human rights in Sweden. Almost all assistance in the form of housing provided in Swedish municipalities is based on an assessment by social services. This means that access even to a single night at a shelter requires an individual assessment that itself, therefore, creates a barrier, a threshold to access even the most basic housing support. In some municipalities, for example, Gothenburg and Stockholm, there are limited 'Roof Over Your Head' guarantees that do not require an assessment by social services; however, these are often very temporary services only open when the temperature drops below a certain level (often a couple of degrees below 0 degrees Celsius). Further, the 'Roof Over Your Head' guarantee (for example, in Stockholm) can be seen as a political and perhaps rhetorical device rather than a new intervention, since this right is already established in the Social Services Act (2001:453), which provides that '[e]ach municipality is responsible

---

35 H. Brandberg, 'Politikerna vill ah riktlinjer om hemlöshet' *Sydöstran* (23 October 2019).
36 Runquist (n 27).
37 Ibid.
38 Land Code (Hyreslagen) 1970:994.
39 Holappa (n 30) 202.
40 Ibid. 204.

for social services within its boundaries and has the ultimate responsibility that individuals receive the support and assistance they need'.[41] The threshold to access housing assistance, as well as the exclusion of undocumented migrants and other non-citizens living in homelessness from housing assistance through social services, shows that Sweden does not live up to the formulations in Article 11 of the convention of economic and social rights that was ratified by Sweden in 1967, which defines all people's right to housing. Sweden has previously been criticized for its differentiation in the treatment of citizens and non-citizens concerning access to basic human rights such as healthcare. Paul Hunt, the special rapporteur on the right to healthcare, wrote after his mission to Sweden in 2007 that the right to vote may be confined to citizens but human rights are, in principle, to be enjoyed by all people.[42]

The Provision of Local Housing Services for Those in Homelessness

The housing assistance provided within local housing services for people experiencing homelessness was, for a large part of the 20th century, run by social services and the municipalities themselves.[43] In the early 1990s, the Swedish welfare system began a transformative process towards restructuring based on the ideas of a new public management governance model. The transformation started with a change in the Municipal Act (*Kommunallag*),[44] which gave municipalities and counties the possibility to transfer municipal responsibilities to corporations, NGOs, or individual businesses, while the exercise of public authority remained with the municipalities.[45] As Hartman explained:

> One way to describe this transformation is as a shifting from a welfare state to a welfare society. In both models, the goal is the same, to ensure that all citizens can access welfare services when needed and regardless of individual economic capacity.[46]

The difference between the models lies in the mode of production. In the welfare state model, the politically governed public sector is a central actor providing welfare services. In the new model, the welfare society, the production of welfare services could be provided by several different for-profit, non-profit, and municipal actors competing in a welfare service market. In this market, different public actors, such as social services, became procurers of different types of services, ordered through a tender system. The service providers bid on these tenders, and the most financially competitive bids are contracted to deliver the service.

This restructuring and shift towards public procurement transformed the organization of social services and its different departments in Sweden. The Personal and Family Counselling Service (PFS) is the section within social services that, in most municipalities,

---

41 Social Services Act, Chap. 2 Section 1.
42 P. Hunt, 'Report of the Special Rapporteur on the Right of Everyone to the Enjoyment of the Highest Attainable Standard of Physical and Mental Health: Mission to Sweden' (2007) A/HRC/4/28/Add.2.
43 Swärd (n 10).
44 The Municipal Act 2017:725.
45 L. Hartman (ed), *Konkurrensens konsekvenser: vad händer med svensk välfärd?* (SNS Förlag 2011).
46 Ibid. 9.

handles the issue of homelessness.[47] The PFS has undergone a vast privatization since the 1980s and beyond. One key illustration is the number of private care placements in residential care homes for children and young persons, which increased by 3,728% between 1982 and 2010.[48] However, the greatest transformation towards privatization seemed to take place during the 1980s and 1990s, reaching its peak in the 2000s.[49] Swärd[50] describes this change as a shift towards a welfare pluralist system, where more and different types of actors, with different ideas[51] and ideologies on how to solve social issues such as homelessness, gained influence over the services delivered to those service users. This pluralist system can make it harder to gain insight into how services were delivered, as well as understanding the ideologies and ideas upon which different actors built their services, since there are more actors involved and the openness toward social services might be lower form private and non-profit actors than from municipal actors.[52] Hartman[53] studied the consequences of privatization within the PFS in Sweden and demonstrated that the educational level among employees in residential care homes for young and children, a similar sector as the housing services for homeless people, was lower among for-profit actors than for municipal actors. They also argued that the privatization of sectors within social services was problematic, as the incentives for private actors differed as compared to those of municipal actors. Private actors might, for example, wish to keep clients in care longer than needed, rather than finding a new client, to secure continued funding. As highlighted by Hartman,[54] some services, including homelessness provision, operate as an atypical sector within the welfare state. Firstly, what makes these services different from many other privatized sectors within the welfare society is that the people receiving support from social services are often the most vulnerable groups in society, most likely with the least economic and social resources, and who have no choice but to turn to the state for help. Secondly, placements in the local housing services for homeless people are not based on individual choice, as with many other welfare sectors in Sweden, where clients themselves have a louder voice in choosing and changing services. Equally, whether a homeless person receives housing support depends on an assessment and decision from social services. There is little possibility for people experiencing homelessness themselves to be involved in this decision, and it is most often the needs of the procurer of the services, that is, social services, and not the client itself which are determinative of the extent of support provided. Therefore, the voices of the homeless go unheard, and the possibility of changing services is lower than in other welfare sectors, for instance, in eldercare.[55]

---

47 Some of the largest cities who organize housing services for people experiencing homelessness have developed a special homelessness section within the social services, dealing with housing as well as other issues that they consider relevant in relation to homelessness.
48 Hartman (n 45).
49 Ibid.
50 Swärd (n 10).
51 Hartmann (n 45).
52 E. Dyb and M. Loison, 'Impact of Service Procurement and Competition on Quality and Standards in Homeless Service Provision' (2007) 1 *European Journal of Homelessness* 119.
53 Hartman (n 45).
54 Ibid.
55 Ibid.

Actors in Local Housing Services Provided to Homeless People

How this change has affected the organization of local housing services for the homeless is still, in some ways, unclear. Previous research has demonstrated that more for-profit as well as non-profit actors have become involved in providing housing for the homeless in Sweden during the 1990s.[56] However, no overarching national studies have been conducted on the extent, experience, and efficacy of for-profit, non-profit, and municipal actors and how they are distributed across Sweden. A study comparing France and Norway has shown that the privatization of housing services for homeless people increases the risk of fragmentation of the sector, as well as increased use of short-term insecure housing solutions.[57] A recent study comparing the quality of housing services for homeless people across the EU highlighted the importance of gathering more detailed information and data on both what type of services are provided as well as the providers themselves.[58] In Sweden, more specifically, there are some studies exploring the actors involved in housing service provision for the homeless. One larger study focused on the providers themselves,[59] while several others describe the actors involved while focusing on other issues.[60] These studies collectively demonstrated that there are three types of actors involved in local housing services provided for the homeless in Sweden. There are social services who are the procurer of services; there are the 'active' actors, such as for-profit, non-profit, and municipal actors, who are selling and producing different forms of housing support; and there are 'passive' actors that only provide the accommodation used in these services but do not take an active part in the formal delivery of the services themselves.[61] Dyb and Loison[62] demonstrated that NGOs dominated the provision of housing services for homeless people in France, while in Norway, local authorities dominate the service provision of housing for homeless people. In Sweden, the mix of actors is still limited, but a forthcoming study shows that a slight majority of the actors in the homelessness housing services section are private actors, followed by municipal actors, while around 10% are non-profit actors.[63]

Löfstrand[64] examined the provision of local housing services for homeless people in the second largest city in Sweden. She identified two forms of for-profit actors entering the homelessness sector. The first type consisted of hostels and hotels that previously had been part of the tourist industry but, at some point, began providing rooms to local authorities. The second type of for-profit actor Löfstrand found 'start[s] out with homelessness as their

---

56 M. Nordfeldt, 'Hemlöshet i välfärdsstaden: en studie av relationerna mellan socialtjänst och frivilliga organisationer i Stockholm och Göteborg' (Doctoral thesis, Uppsala University 1999); Swärd (n 10).
57 Dyb and Loison (n 52).
58 N. Pleace, I. Baptista and M. Knutagård, *Housing First in Europe: An Overview of Implementation, Strategy and Fidelity* (Housing First Europe Hub 2019).
59 Nordfeldt (n 56), comparing two highly urbanized municipalities.
60 Löfstrand (n 7); Sahlin (n 9); Knutagård (n 15); Blid (n 16).
61 Nordfeldt (n 56); I. Sahlin, 'Exkludering av bostadslösa genom gränskontroll och disciplin' in F. Petterson and T. Davidsson (eds), *Social exkludering: Perspektiv, Process, problemkonstruktion* (Studentlitteratur AB 2016) 89.
62 Dyb and Loison (n 52).
63 M. Wirehag and J. Mellberg, 'Growth, Range, and Variation of Actors within Local Housing Services for Persons Living in Homelessness in Sweden, 2011–2018' (2023) 6(2) *Tidsskrift for Boligforskning* 122.
64 C. Löfstrand, 'Hemlöshet som affärsidé: Policyförändringar, diskurser och realiteter' (2009) [Homelessness as Business: Policy Changes, Discourses, and Realities] (Unpublished manuscript, Department of Sociology, University of Gothenburg).

original business idea, offering temporary special housing *and* support for the homeless clients, just like a municipality agency would do. This latter type has become increasingly common since the beginning of the current decade'.[65] Olsson and Nordfeldt,[66] in their study of four Swedish municipalities, also demonstrated that non-profit organizations played an important role in providing housing services to those groups in most acute need; at the same time, non-profit actors had started to become service providers by bidding on tenders and delivering housing solutions on behalf of social services to homeless people.

Examples of Homelessness Preventative Practice in Sweden

The main intervention for preventing homelessness in Sweden is the work around prevention of evictions. A key measure by which homelessness can be prevented here is by social services taking over the lease of a property from a tenant. There are variations between different municipalities, but often, the social contract runs for a month at a time with one week's notice. In this way, the lease is turned into a social contract and becomes a part of the so-called secondary housing market. Some municipalities have built up a good organization for preventing evictions in this way and have established a strong collaboration with both private and public housing companies. But there is more work to be done. The NBHW conducts open comparisons of the services that municipal social services and healthcare providers offer. In the comparison exercise in 2020, 62% of the municipalities stated that they had outreach work to prevent evictions. The data shows, however, that there are surprisingly not many municipalities that have systems in place for preventing families with children from being evicted. For those who do, it is common to use home visits and provide help with debts and other financial matters. Rent arrears significantly increase the risk of households becoming evicted, and so work in this area can be very effective. However, the open comparison showed that only 20% of the municipalities had planned for how they would work to prevent homelessness and how to tackle housing exclusion in their area. Even though some municipalities work closely with housing companies on joint strategies to provide housing for excluded groups, only 41% of them had written agreements on how this should be done. The lack of agreements and systems for preventative work might be one explanation for the increase in enforced evictions. In 2021, Sweden saw the highest number of evictions since 2011. In 2011, there were 9,244 applications and 2,802 enforced evictions. In 2021, there were 6,675 applications and 2,672 enforced evictions. The year before, in 2020, the number of enforced evictions was 2,209.[67] In 2022, the numbers dropped slightly, with 6,563 applications and 2,620 enforced evictions. A key explanation for the increased evictions in Sweden as compared to many countries is the Covid-19 pandemic. Many European countries banned evictions during the pandemic. Sweden did not. Moreover, we can also see that the number of children affected by enforced evictions has increased. In 2011, there were 663 children affected by enforced eviction. In 2021, 572 children were impacted. The year before, in 2020, 449 children

---

65 Ibid. 26.
66 M. Nordfeldt and L.-E. Olsson, 'Homelessness and the Tertiary Welfare System in Sweden – the Role of Welfare State and Non-Profit Sector' (2008) 2 *The European Journal of Homelessness* 157.
67 The Swedish Enforcement Authority <www.kronofogden.se/om-kronofogden/statistik/statistik-om-vrakningar> (accessed 1 September 2023).

were affected by enforced eviction.[68] In 2022, the number of children affected by enforced evictions increased slightly to 575 children. The statistics from the Swedish Enforcement Authority only include evictions from the ordinary housing market. This is an important point, since most homeless families with children are housed within the so-called secondary housing market. If households get evicted from their social contracts, this is not, therefore, included in the statistics. Equally, at the time of writing, there are no statistics on how many families with children are being evicted or moved around within the so-called secondary housing market. In the national homelessness count in Sweden in 2017, more than 24,000 children had at least one parent in a homelessness situation.[69] An increasing number of households belong to what is referred to as the structurally homeless category. The lack of housing makes it difficult, if not impossible, for these families to get an apartment on their own. Another complicating factor is that newly produced rental housing is very expensive, and the rents are far higher than the housing costs that social services accept and pay.[70] Poor families or households cannot demand these newly produced apartments, since the rental costs are too high for social services to accept when paying social benefits. This creates a very real catch-22.

One key change in the work tackling homelessness in Sweden is the introduction of Housing First programmes in 21 of the 290 municipalities.[71] Housing First was first introduced in Stockholm and in Helsingborg in 2010, and at the time of writing, more municipalities are about to start up their own Housing First programmes. Housing First was first developed by Sam Tsemberis and the Pathways to Housing in New York in the 1990s. Originally, it was based on eight core principles, of which housing as a human right was but one of them. Today, the Pathways Housing First Institute highlights five core principles: consumer choice, separation of housing and treatment, provision of services to match needs, recovery-oriented service philosophy, and social community integration.[72] In the Swedish context, homelessness services have been and, to a large extent, still are based on a 'staircase model'. In the staircase model, the clients must show that they are housing-ready before they can progress to the next step. This often includes a requirement of undergoing treatment before they can get an apartment. Different housing options within the staircase model are often connected with specific rules that do not apply if you were to rent a home on the ordinary housing market. Housing First differs in many ways from the staircase logic. In Housing First, housing is seen as a prerequisite to be able to deal with other potential problems. The support provided in Housing First is based on the individual's needs and wishes.[73] Research has shown that the Housing First programmes have very positive results in ending homelessness. The tenants remain housed, and the housing retention rates are often between 80 and

---

68 Ibid.
69 The National Board of Health and Welfare <www.socialstyrelsen.se/globalassets/sharepoint-dokument/artikelkatalog/ovrigt/2017-11-15.pdf> (accessed 1 September 2023).
70 I. Sahlin, 'Bostadsmarknad, bostadspolitik och hemlöshet' in H. Swärd (ed), *Den kantstötta välfärden* (Studentlitteratur AB 2017).
71 Pleace and others (n 58).
72 <www.pathwayshousingfirst.org> (accessed 1 September 2023).
73 D. Culhane, S. Fitzpatrick and D. Treglia, 'Contrasting traditions in homelessness research Between the UK and US' in L. Teixeira and J. Cartwright (eds), *Using Evidence to End Homelessness* (Policy Press 2020).

90%.⁷⁴ The results from the Swedish experiences with Housing First so far correspond with those from international programmes. In one of the municipalities, the city of Helsingborg, the housing retention rate has been more than 80% for a decade. These are very good and solid results. It shows that the results can be sustainable over time, not only during the pilot phase. Institutional support and a widespread understanding of what Housing First is have been shown to be important factors when implementing the programme.⁷⁵

The introduction of a new homelessness strategy⁷⁶ from the government in 2022 has increased the interest in starting up Housing First services. The strategy will run from 2022 to 2026 and consists of four goals:

1. Homelessness must be prevented.
2. No one should live on the street.
3. The Housing First method should be introduced nationally.
4. The social perspective in community planning must be strengthened.

In February 2023, municipalities could apply for funding (for the second time, the first being in September 2022) for Housing First (105 municipalities applied). The total amount of money was €6,330,605. It is expected that the same amount of money will be provided per year throughout the strategy, specifically focusing on funding projects regarding the strategy's third goal.

Unfortunately, homelessness preventative work seems to be the first thing to be taken away if the municipality is required to make cuts in its budget. It can also be more difficult to measure preventative effects, but preventative work is a key ingredient to end homelessness. Homelessness is related to housing policy, and in a majority of the Swedish municipalities, there is a shortage of rental housing that households can apply to access. Newly produced rental housing is often too expensive, and older stock with lower rents are attractive for all and in demand. Even though many municipalities work actively with preventing evictions, there is more work to be done around evictions and the impact on children of the household – especially considering that the Convention of the Rights of the Child is now implemented in law in Sweden as of January 2020. In practice, it should result in the child receiving stronger legal protection and social workers having better legal tools in their work with children. However, the distinction between socially homeless and structurally homeless has caused an increased pressure on households of diverse ethnic backgrounds, especially those households comprising single mothers with children. There is still very little evidence of any effects of the new legislation. Structurally homeless families are forced to live in very precarious housing situations for long periods of time. Children are more than ever affected by enforced evictions. Sahlin concludes that children have always been at the core of social services' responsibility, but today, '[i]t is nevertheless remarkable that, in Malmö, homeless

---

74 L. Benjaminsen and M. Knutagård, 'Homelessness Research and Policy Development: Examples from the Nordic Countries' (2016) 10(3) *European Journal of Homelessness* 45; M. Knutagård and others, 'Homelessness' (2020) 1 Research Brief 14 <https://forte.se/app/uploads/sites/2/2020/09/forskning-i-korthet-en-hemloshet.pdf> (accessed 1 September 2023).
75 Knutagård and others (n 74).
76 <www.regeringen.se/contentassets/5a5f795a1db144ec8dfe36cd60114ed7/regeringens-strategi-for-att-motverka-hemloshet-2022-2026.pdf> (accessed 1 September 2023).

women (born abroad) and their children are judged to be less "deserving" than, e.g., homeless single men (born in Sweden) with substance abuse or mental health problems'.[77]

Housing First might have the capacity to push Swedish municipalities towards more housing-led solutions. Contemporary research argues that homelessness strategies ought to be integrated between different levels of government and have a clear focus on prevention. For those experiencing homelessness, the interventions should be aimed at minimizing the duration of that homelessness by way of rapid rehousing.[78] Notably, however, and until very recently, Sweden did not have a national homelessness strategy (in particular from 2009 to 2022).[79] Before that, both Norway and Denmark were very much inspired by both the definition of *homelessness* in Sweden and also the national strategy. However, the responsibility of homelessness in Sweden was pushed further towards the municipal level. The new legislation that was introduced in 2011 that stated that public housing companies were to act for profit increased the marketization of housing policy in Sweden. After the strategy ended, most of the involved officials within the NBHW left for new assignments. The result is that our neighbouring Scandinavian countries have ongoing national homelessness strategies, and they can also point to lower numbers of homeless people per thousand inhabitants in their countries.[80] Norway has 0.7 homeless per thousand inhabitants, compared to 3.3 in Sweden.[81] Housing First is based on the principle of housing as a human right, and this principle is consistent with Swedish legislation and societal goals, but since housing is not only a basic human need but also a commodity, the homeownership ideology tends to dominate the Swedish housing market. One area for potential momentum in transforming housing policy and for launching a new homelessness strategy in Sweden is that the government has given the NBHW the role of coordinating a national network of municipalities working with Housing First, and they have also put funding directed towards implementation or development of already-existing Housing First programmes. This is the first time that the government in Sweden has put money towards a specific evidenced-based method within the homelessness field aimed at prevention. It is too early to say what impact this will have on homelessness work in Sweden, but it is a clear direction towards housing policy that is informed by research, and this is to be welcomed.

The Future of Homelessness Law and Policy in Sweden

During the spring of 2022, an official Swedish government report on how to lower the thresholds for citizens to access housing[82] was published. The report highlighted four important areas where policy needed to be improved, including housing supply, distribution, demand, and the management of housing stock. The report particularly highlighted the need to focus on the intersection between local housing services for the homeless provided by social services and general measures on the ordinary housing market. Another

---

77 Sahlin (n 26) 43.
78 <https://ec.europa.eu/social/BlobServlet?docId=26185&langId=en> (accessed 1 September 2023).
79 E. Dyb and others, 'Governing Through Definitions and Numbers: Analysis of the Nordic Homeless Registrations as Instruments of Governing Homelessness' (2021) 15(3) *European Journal of Homelessness* 161.
80 Benjaminsen and others (n 26).
81 <https://forte.se/app/uploads/sites/2/2020/09/forskning-i-korthet-en-hemloshet.pdf> (accessed 1 September 2023).
82 SOU 2022:14.

key suggestion in the report was for national regulation on how landlords select potential tenants. The demands (e.g. income requirements and what types of income are accepted – some landlords do not accept social benefit as an income) used by landlords should be transparent, be available to potential landlords and, in some cases, municipalities. Another recent development in homelessness policy in Sweden, a report was produced on how to prevent and counteract homelessness,[83] published during the autumn of 2021 by NBHW. This report identified several key issues concerning homelessness policy and practice in need of reform. One of the issues was the lack of affordable housing provided to social services by local landlords to sublease to people experiencing homelessness. Another issue was the demands made by landlords to transform the contracts that were subleased through social services onto rental contracts with tenure. The lack of a coherent measure of homelessness across Swedish municipalities was a further issue highlighted in the report. One of the key outcomes of the report was a state-funded initiative to promote and develop Housing First as a method across Swedish municipalities, as discussed earlier in this chapter. During the spring of 2022, approximately 3 million euros was made available for Swedish municipalities that wished to start new or develop current Housing First interventions. As mentioned earlier, the amount of money has increased even with the change of government, so there seems to be continued governmental support for this strategy. Much can be said about both the amount of money and how the goals can be implemented, but also measured and evaluated, but the national strategy will probably be significant in increasing the interest in introducing Housing First programmes. We do know that there are special challenges for smaller municipalities to make Housing First work, since they do not have all the resources within their municipal boundaries. They will likely have to find ways to collaborate with neighbouring municipalities. The issues of homelessness policy highlighted in recent government reports concur with research findings from the last ten years. Research studies have highlighted several different issues pertaining to homelessness policy and practice in Sweden. One of these issues relates to the access and availability of homelessness services for specific groups, such as EU migrants and undocumented migrants living in homelessness who are currently excluded from most interventions due to their legal status.[84] Another issue relating to access concerns the growing number of people with low or no incomes living in a double exclusion, where they are not eligible for housing services through social services since they lack the qualifying social problems, such as substance misuse and/or mental illness/debt that social services require, nor can they fulfil the requirements set by landlords on the ordinary housing market.[85]

As this chapter has explored, a major and further problem in Sweden is the different approaches to homelessness policy and practice seen across divergent municipalities and how housing services for the homeless are organized quite distinctly in different geographic areas. One of the key aspects highlighted in research regarding municipal differences relates to specific terms, rules, and regulations used to structure the different housing interventions

---

83 Att förebygga och förhindra hemlöshet (NBHW 2021).
84 Sahlin (n 26); M. Wirehag, 'Gatekeeping, Managing Homelessness and Administrating Housing for the Poor: The Three Functions of Local Housing Services for the Homeless in Sweden' (2021) 15(1) *European Journal of Homelessness* 83.
85 SOU: 2022:14.

used across Sweden. Research[86] has shown, for example, that how municipalities organize the transition from a subleased contract rented by social services into a contract with tenure varies widely across the country. Some municipalities have active strategies for this transition, while social services in some municipalities renew the subleased contracts for long periods of time without a structured method of transition in place. This creates situations where more and more people are living in insecure subleased contracts for long periods of time. Simultaneously, people living in housing provided by social services are considered homeless according to the Swedish definition of *homelessness*, creating a situation where the more people that social services house through social contracts, the more people will be counted as homeless within this specific homelessness categorization.

There are several possibilities for policy reform and avenues for improving the state of homelessness provision in Sweden. Swedish municipalities need coherent and strict guidelines regarding how subleased contracts are handled and how the transition into tenure is organized. One opportunity would be to set a maximum limit for how long a contract could be subleased through social services before it should be transformed into a contract with tenure. Since there is no national regulation available, social services must coordinate and structure this matter at a local level in cooperation with local landlords who have few incentives to let contracts transform into tenured leases. The European Platform on Combatting Homelessness (EPOCH) is one example on how ending homelessness has become a greater priority on a European level. This, together with the newly initiated national homelessness strategy with funding directed towards Housing First, may lead Sweden to shift to a more integrated homelessness policy, where there is an increased collaboration between the state, regions, and municipalities. Contemporary research points towards the importance of focused prevention activity as a key intervention in combatting homelessness. Another is rapid rehousing for those who experience homelessness and Housing First for those with higher support needs. The results so far show that Housing First works, but it is still a small part in a wider system of homelessness intervention. Housing First will not work without housing. Therefore, it is important to work closely with housing companies. Traditionally, the municipal housing companies have taken a large share of social responsibility. Since 2011, the legislation has been used to push them towards working more and more for profit. If neither municipal nor private housing companies step in, new actors are needed. One example of how this might operate is the City Mission in Stockholm, which is in the process of building housing for people with lower incomes.[87] Considering the growth in the number of people that are defined as structurally homeless, Sweden faces a huge challenge to build more housing that people with lower income can access without increasing sociospatial inequality and without exacerbating the division of 'us and them' in local communities between city districts and different municipalities and region.

---

86 Wirehag (n 84).
87 <www.stadsmissionen.se/vad-vi-gor/boende/hyreshus-byggs-i-farsta-strand> (accessed 1 September 2023).

10
GOVERNING HOMELESSNESS IN THE NETHERLANDS

Incremental Change Towards Providing Housing First

Nienke F. Boesveldt

Introduction

In the Netherlands, current law and policy on homelessness are geared towards deinstitutionalizing and decentralizing homeless shelters and protected housing facilities. The broader context is that of a retreating welfare state, budget cuts to social services, a growing homeless population of 32,000 people in 2021,[1] a shortage of affordable housing, and public concerns about social mixing, exclusion, and neighbourhood liveability.[2] By outlining recent changes in policy and legislation, this chapter seeks to characterize and examine what we might call 'the Dutch approach' to homelessness.

Defining Homelessness in the Netherlands

According to the Social Support Act of 2015,[3] those without a home – whether due to risks to safety because of domestic violence or their inability to maintain themselves – are entitled to shelter and support from a social worker specialized in homelessness. These services are available in the larger municipality within a region meaning people may need to travel to use these services and leave their own social support network behind. Since 2019, Statistics Netherlands has defined homeless people as those without a permanent residence. It includes people who sleep in the open air; people who sleep in covered public areas, such as stations, bicycle sheds, and shopping malls; people who sleep in their cars or make use of temporary social or emergency shelters; and people who, on a non-structural or irregular or temporary basis, rely on friends, acquaintances, or family members. The official statistics

---

1 Statistics Netherlands 2021. These figures underestimate the total number of homeless persons as they do not include key groups, including women in reception centres fleeing domestic abuse, couch surfers, minors, people above 65, and undocumented persons. Figures on the number of people at risk of becoming homeless or experiencing serious difficulties in exercising their right to housing are unavailable.
2 K. Leidelmeijer, J. Frissen and J. van Iersel, *Resilience in Housing Associations Ownership* (Aedes 2020).
3 wetten.nl – Regeling – Wet maatschappelijke ondersteuning 2015 – BWBR0035362 (overheid.nl).

have been criticized for underestimating the number of homeless people: they do not include women in reception centres fleeing domestic abuse, couch surfers, minors, people above 65, and undocumented people while the number of people at risk of becoming homeless or experiencing serious difficulties in exercising their right to housing also remains unknown.

The new 2023–2030 Dutch national action plan on homelessness, *Eerst een Thuis* (First a Home),[4] uses a broader definition of *homelessness* to prevent people from becoming homeless in the first place: 'We want to prevent people from becoming homeless. That is why we look at the groups that are at risk of homelessness.'[5] The action plan thus covers people who live in unstable housing (e.g. temporarily living with family or friends, living without a rental contract, living under the threat of domestic violence), inadequate housing (e.g. non-residential addresses, such as holiday homes), and unconventional quarters (e.g. campers, squats). The action plan also identifies individuals leaving institutions (detention centres, mental healthcare facilities, homeless shelters, protected housing, and youth services) as a group at increased risk of becoming homeless. The plan states, at present, that current monitoring is insufficient to provide targeted guidance on the basis of quantitative data. When collecting data on homelessness, therefore, moves are being made towards the use of the European Typology of Homelessness and Housing Exclusion (ETHOS) Light definition. In 2022, at the time of writing the action plan, it was only possible for most municipalities to monitor categories 2 and 3 from the ETHOS Light classification. In the plan, therefore, it has been agreed that the Ministry of Health, Welfare, and Sport will commission research into the possibilities for engaging all categories of ETHOS Light at a national level from 2023. It has also been agreed that, in 2024, municipalities will use the ETHOS Light classification in Housing and Care policies as well as in local prevention activities. From 2025 and beyond, an annual count based on the ETHOS Light classification can then be carried out.

The European Typology on Homelessness and Housing Exclusion (ETHOS) is increasingly being used to draw attention to the multiple dimensions of homelessness in the Netherlands. ETHOS seeks to provide standardized, comparable measures of homelessness in the European Union.[6] In Belgium, the census has already been carried out in various cities and regions, and the Dutch team follows the approach as applied in Belgium. The first two studies making use of the ETHOS typology were conducted in two Dutch municipalities in 2023, while other municipalities have expressed interest.[7] The fact that municipalities are responsible for homelessness policy explains the difficulty of monitoring the homeless population. These studies, therefore, are seen as a much-needed step forward, with the

---

4 Nationaal Actieplan Dakloosheid: Eerst een Thuis <https://open.overheid.nl/documenten/ronl-bb529bd58ad-c8061e5c058d2fe9671197ba6244f/pdf> (accessed 1 September 2023).
5 Ibid. 19.
6 B. Edgar, 'The ETHOS Definition and Classification of Homelessness and Housing Exclusion' (2012) 6(2) *European Journal of Homelessness* 219.
7 S. Schel, M. Kuijpers, D. Wewerinke, A. Scheepers, J. De Vries and L. Van Doorn *'Ledereen telt mee. Resultaten eerste ETHOS telling van dak- en thuisloosheid in regio Brabant Noordoost-Oost. Utrecht'* (2023) Hogeschool Utrecht; D. Wewerinke, S. Schel, M. Kuijpers, J. De Vries and L. Van Doorn *'Ledereen telt mee. Resultaten eerste ETHOS telling dak- en thuisloosheid regio Noordoost Brabant. Utrecht'* (2023) Hogeschool Utrecht; ETHOS telling dak- en thuisloosheid in regio Noordoost-Brabant, Kansfonds <www.kansfonds.nl/themas/dak-en-thuisloosheid/telling/> (accessed 1 September 2023).

Table 10.1 ETHOS Light typology

	Operational category		Living situation	Definition
1	People living rough	1	Public space/external space	Living in the streets or public spaces without a shelter that can be defined as living quarters
2	People in emergency accommodation	2	Overnight shelters	People with no place of usual residence who move frequently between various types of accommodation
3	People living in accommodation for the homeless	3 4 5 6	Homeless hostels Temporary accommodation Transitional supported accommodation Women's shelter or refuge accommodation	Where the period of stay is less than one year
4	People living in institutions	7 8	Healthcare institutions Penal institutions	Stay longer than neeed due to lack of housing No housing available prior to release
5	People living in non-conventional dwellings due to lack of housing	9 10 11	Mobile homes Non-conventional budiling Temporary structure	Where the accommodation is used due to a lack of housing and is not the person's usual place of residence.
6	Homeless people living temporarily in conventional housing with family and friends (due to lack of housing)	12	Coventional housing, but not the person's usual place of residence	Where the accommodation is used due to a lack of housing and is not the personal's usual place of residence

Source: W. Edgar, M. Harrison, P. Watson, and V. Busch-Geertsema, *Measurement of Homelessness at European Union Level* (European Commission 2007).

hope that the whole country will adopt the typology, ultimately improving conditions for all homeless people in the Netherlands.

Historical Background to Homelessness in the Netherlands

Homelessness in the Netherlands has only recently been acknowledged as a social problem.[8] In the late 1970s, the country counted roughly 10,000 heroin addicts; as in many

---

8 L. Deben and D. Greshof, 'Zwerven zonder zorg; daklozen in Nederland' in K. Schuyt (ed), *Het sociaal tekort; veertien sociale problemen* (De Balie 1998).

other countries, the heroin epidemic of the 1980s[9] dramatically increased the number of homeless people. The numbers swelled again in the 1990s with the de-institutionalization of the mental health sector, which saw the closing of psychiatric hospitals, leading many within the long-stay population to move back to the city.[10] Many former psychiatric patients thus came to live in protected housing and homeless shelters.[11]

At the turn of the millennium, the four largest cities in the Netherlands – Amsterdam, Rotterdam, The Hague, and Utrecht – all had highly visible homeless populations living in public spaces in poor conditions for extended periods of time. Initially, the main policy response targeted visible homelessness on the streets and sought to reduce the number of people sleeping rough by expanding services.[12] This led to the housing of half of the country's homeless population in shelters, many of whom stayed permanently.[13] However, this institutionalization[14] and hospitalization[15] of homeless people was seen as undermining the ability of individuals to ever again live independently. By 2003, the congestion in shelters became a policy issue.

In response to this congestion as well as problems of coordination between public services,[16] the central government and the four major cities launched an interministerial programme titled the *Plan van Aanpak Maatschappelijke Opvang* (Approach to Social Relief) in 2006. By 2014, research had found that the most vulnerable citizens benefitted most from individualized care and support covering all areas of their lives. The key factors behind the success were strong financial backing, policy urgency, and cooperation between parties.[17]

With greater policy attention for homelessness in the 2000s, the number of homeless people in the Netherlands reached a low of 17,800 in 2009.[18] The number then swelled to 27,000 in 2012 and 39,000 in 2018 before declining again to 32,000 in 2021.[19] Particularly pronounced among young people and those with migration backgrounds, homelessness in the Netherlands has been traced to the international financial crisis of 2007–2008,

---

9 M. C. A. Buster, 'Prevalence, Mortality and Morbidity Among Heroin Users and Methadone Patients' (thesis, University of Amsterdam 2023); G. Blok, *Ziek of zwak: Geschiedenis van de verslavingszorg in Nederland* (Uitgeverij Nieuwezijds 2011).
10 L. Verplanke and J. W. Duyvendak, *Onder de mensen? Over het zelfstandig wonen van psychiatrische patiënten en mensen met een verstandelijke beperking* (Amsterdam UP 2010).
11 J. Theunissen and others, *Een karig en sober leven maar niet ontevreden: Vermaatschappelijking van de chronische patiënt in de stad deel II* (Arkin, GGZ inGeest, HVO Querido 2014).
12 L. Van Doorn, *Een tijd op straat: Een volgstudie naar (ex-)daklozen in Utrecht* (NIZW 2002).
13 N. Nuy, *De odyssee van thuislozen* (SWP 1998); Interdepartementaal Beleidsonderzoek, *De opvang verstopt* (IBO Maatschappelijke opvang 2003).
14 D. P. Culhane, S. Metraux and T. Byrne, 'A Prevention-Centered Approach to Homelessness Assistance: A Paradigm Shift? (2011) 21(2) *Housing Policy Debate* 295.
15 L. Gulcur and others, 'Housing, Hospitalization, and Cost Outcomes for Homeless Individuals with Psychiatric Disabilities Participating in Continuum of Care and Housing First Programmes' (2003) 13 *Journal of Community and Applied Social Psychology* 171.
16 J. Wolf, *Uitburgering. Rede ter verkrijging hoogleraarschap Maatschappelijke Opvang* (SWP 2002).
17 M. Tuynman and M. Planije, ' "Het kán dus!" Een doorbraak in het Nederlandse dakloosheidsbeleid. Evaluatie Plan van Aanpak maatschappelijke opvang in de vier grote steden, 2006–2014' [' "So It's Possible!" A Breakthrough in Dutch Homelessness Policy: Evaluation of Plan of Approach for Social Care in the Four Major Cities, 2006–2014'] (Trimbos 2014).
18 Ibid.
19 Statistics Netherlands 2021.

increased municipal responsibilities for protected housing and youth care, and the gradual dismantling of the social housing sector.[20]

In 2020, the Council for Public Health and Society issued an advisory report[21] that prompted the government to rethink its approach to housing vulnerable households. While homelessness was previously within the purview of the Ministry of Health and Welfare, the latest policy initiatives extend responsibility to the Ministry of Internal Affairs,[22] which is also responsible for housing. This signifies the new framing of homelessness in the Netherlands: from primarily a health issue to one of housing.[23] The emphasis on providing Housing First also informs the aforementioned multi-ministerial national action plan on homelessness[24] presented as the new national solution to homelessness in 2022.

Existing Legal and Policy Framework on Homelessness in the Netherlands

This section covers both existing legislation and softer forms of guidance and intervention. It first outlines two criteria by which homeless people are rendered ineligible for services. The first is that they are deemed 'self-sufficient'; the second is that they are deemed as lacking 'ties to the locality'. This denial of services takes place in a context where larger and smaller municipalities have unequal access to national funding, while homeless individuals are often drawn to urban areas. The section also discusses the associated areas of healthcare and law enforcement that pose challenges for coordination.

Exclusion from Services

In implementing the Social Support Act, municipalities must decide whether individuals are entitled to services by their own criteria of self-sufficiency and priority needs. People who are denied services generally have fewer physical and mental health problems. They also tend to be more self-sufficient in providing for their own basic needs, with access to support from family/friends and with minimal police contact.[25]

For example, the municipality of Amsterdam has, since 2013, based its decisions to grant access to services on an individual's ties to the city and level of self-sufficiency. Only those struggling with self-reliance are assessed to be in need of the municipality's homelessness services; previously, it was everyone with a housing need.[26] A study exploring denial of

---

20 Statistics Netherlands 2019
21 Herstel begint met een huis. Dakloosheid voorkomen en verminderen, Raad voor Volksgezondheid en Samenleving <www.raadrvs.nl/documenten/publicaties/2020/04/21/herstel-begint-met-een-huis-dakloosheid-voorkomen-en-verminderen#:~:text=Op%20dinsdag%2021%20april%202020%20heeft%20de%20Raad,Den%20Haag.%20U%20kunt%20de%20uitzending%20hier%20terugkijken> (accessed 1 September 2023).
22 Ministry of Internal Affairs, 'Ontwerp Nationale Omgevingsvisie' (2021) <https://open.overheid.nl/documenten/ronl-806e6cdb-efbe-4cf7-9841-48de0d9b9e55/pdf> (accessed 1 September 2023).
23 N. F. Boesveldt and D. Loomans, 'Housing the Homeless: Shifting Sites of Managing the Poor in the Netherlands' *Urban Studies* (2023); available at: https://doi.org/10.1177/00420980231208624 (accessed 16 February 2024).
24 Nationaal Actieplan Dakloosheid (n 4).
25 N. Runtuwene and M. Buster, *Monitor – Maatschappelijke Opvang 2010–2013* (GGD/Epidemiologie, documentatie en gezondheidsbevordering 2014).
26 Ibid.

social support to homeless people in Amsterdam[27] found that 0.2% of the city's population was considered homeless, with 30–40% of that number served by one or more homelessness services that cater to people with serious mental illness. This left 60% of the registered homeless population not receiving any services. Of the 11–12% of homeless people who were sleeping outside on any given night, the majority had no access to services due to their level of self-sufficiency and/or lack of local connection.

In determining whether a person has a right to shelter, municipalities often determine whether they ties to the locality. While 'local connection' has no legal basis in the Social Support Act, this fact would come as a surprise to many municipal employees implementing the policy. This condition for admission undermines the right to access social shelters as laid down in Dutch law. As a result, homeless people often fall through the cracks.

Amsterdam policy documents from 2018 reveal that ties to the locality have been key admission criteria for social care since 2010. The city claims that 'these criteria prevent large numbers of people turning to Amsterdam for social care and the already high pressure on facilities and the housing market becoming disproportionately large'.[28] The most recent 2022 policy document references ties to the locality, the care framework, and one's social network[29] as the three factors that determine whether a person has a connection to the Amsterdam region. All three are weighted equally and serve to determine in which region the applicant is most likely to receive services.

To test the accessibility of social shelters in the Netherlands, 43 central municipalities were visited by researchers posing as homeless in 2015, 2017, and 2018. Each of the 43 central municipalities was visited five times; in total, the undercover researchers made 215 visits to reception desks. In 2015 and 2017, they were offered a place to sleep that night 51% of the time; in 2018, 57% of the time. When access to services was refused, the most frequently cited reason was a lack of local ties.[30] As no formal decision was communicated, these decisions were impossible to appeal.[31] When a homeless person was deemed both a migrant and self-sufficient, the risk of being turned down doubled.[32]

At the national level, the right to social assistance is shrouded in legal controversy. Take, for instance, the law that states that residents in the country who need support must always receive it.[33] The European Court of Justice has ruled against the Dutch interpretation of the free movement directive and access to shelters. In addition, the European

---

27 N. F. Boesveldt, 'Denying Homeless Persons Access to Municipal Support' (2019) 12(3) *International Journal of Human Rights in Healthcare* 179.
28 *City of Amsterdam, Handboek Maatschappelijke Opvang – procedures en afspraken* [Handbook Social Relief Procedures and Regulations] version 4 (2018) 28 <www.amsterdam.nl/zorgprofessionals/wmo-documenten/maatschappelijke/> (accessed September 2023).
29 *Kortdurende opvang Maatschappelijke opvang Beschermd wonen Handboek voor Professionals* [Short-Term Social Care Protected Living Handbook for Professionals] <www.amsterdam.nl/sociaaldomein/zorgprofessionals/wmo-documenten/beschermd-verblijf-en-begeleid-thuis/> (accessed 1 September 2023).
30 National Institute for Mental Health and Addiction, *Practical Test for National Accessibility to Social Care* (National Institute for Mental Health and Addiction 2018).
31 M. Gielen and others, *Landelijke toegankelijkheid maatschappelijke opvang en beschermd wonen. Onderzoek naar de knelpunten en oplossingsrichtingen* (Significant Public in opdracht van Ministerie voor Volksgezondheid, Welzijn en Sport 2019).
32 Boesveldt (n 27).
33 See wetten.nl – Regeling – Wet maatschappelijke ondersteuning 2015 – BWBR0035362 <https://wetten.overheid.nl/BWBR0035362/2023-07-01> (accessed 1 September 2023).

Committee for Social Rights has found that the Netherlands disproportionately denies emergency assistance to both regular and irregular migrants by using restrictive criteria for 'vulnerable groups' when, in fact, everyone within the state's jurisdiction has a right to emergency shelter.[34]

Municipalities in the Netherlands typically work together in regions of five to eight smaller municipalities, in which the largest municipality is responsible for the provision of emergency shelters and protected living arrangements. The larger municipalities usually also receive the regional budget for the provision of shelters and protected housing. The smaller municipalities will have budgets for lighter support, up to two hours a week. If clients require more support than this to stay in their own home, this is only possible in the larger municipalities. While the smaller municipalities may pay for the additional hours of support after all, more challenging residents are often not served and asked to claim services in the larger municipalities.

Problems of Coordination

The governance of homelessness in the Netherlands is complicated by the overlap of structural issues that lead to homelessness. In both policy and practice, the services for homelessness and mental health are entwined. Alongside the municipalities, the actors involved include housing associations, healthcare providers, health insurance companies, and the police. There are further divisions of tasks within these bodies; social support and housing, for example, come under different municipal departments, while treatment services for mental health and addiction are the competence of private insurance companies. Finally, a significant proportion of the homeless in any given year spend time in prison. Cooperation with detention services may also prevent relapses into homelessness.

The associated areas of mental health and addiction services are poorly coordinated. Since 2015, longer-term and more intensive care has been organized through the Long-Term Care Act, implemented regionally by private health insurance companies. Additionally, since 2015, the Recovery Vision in mental healthcare[35] has led to the de-institutionalisation of supported housing facilities. The idea behind this policy was that 60% of people living in protected housing could live independently, provided that appropriate supervision and support were provided in the community. A parallel development was the transformation of assertive community teams (hospitals without walls)[36] into flexible ACT (FACT)[37] teams that serve larger numbers of medium-care patients. These FACT teams, however, do operate in many places but are not operative everywhere in the country. The range of services they offer has also been scaled down, for example, in supporting clients in their daily activities.

---

34 FEANTSA Complaint No. 86/2012.
35 The Recovery Vision in the mental healthcare sector starts from the idea that recovering is not just about getting better but also means learning to deal with a mental illness and regaining more control over one's own life. Recovery here is about victory and discovery. Resuming Social Roles and Regaining One's Own Identity <www.health.nsw.gov.au/mentalhealth/psychosocial/foundations/Pages/recovery.aspx>.
36 Sam Tsemberis Interviews Len Stein about Assertive Community Treatment – YouTube (2023 <www.youtube.com/watch?v=683yoITWZxc> (accessed 1 September 2023).
37 See 'Wat Is F-ACT?' *F-ACT Nederland* <www.f-actnederland.nl/wat-is-f-act/>.

In the region of The Hague, specialized, supported housing is seen as the most promising solution for people discharged from mental health institutions. A longitudinal study of homelessness and protected housing in The Hague[38] found that after preparing the transfer to the next location, the previous residential facility no longer has anything to do with the client. The vital continuity valued by clients is lacking. The following quote from a healthcare worker in a social shelter and sheltered housing chain illustrates the necessity of suitable follow-up locations:

> These [mental health and addiction] organizations say if you've finished treatment then you must leave. Of course, finished is not the right term . . . : the emergency is over. We recently had someone come out of the sheltered clinical setting into a social shelter who then stabbed someone. While these are isolated incidents, they are happening more often. Then the emergency is suddenly acute again. The environment is not good at all for such a person; nor is just [living] in a neighbourhood without any support. Then you have FACT teams, it all works well on paper, but in practice it is not easy at all.

Here we see the lack of continuity in guidance and support following treatment in clinical settings. While night care is deemed a suitable follow-up setting, experiences from the social shelter and sheltered housing chain tell a different story. Employees of one of the smaller municipalities in our study told us that when a homeless client requires serious mental healthcare, the general practitioner and associated nurse practitioner for mental health are no longer part of the treatment trajectory, an omission that does little to help local reintegration.

The study demonstrated that homeless shelters and protected housing institutions were often cautious in releasing their clients as they were concerned about relapse and overcrowding. We saw that budgets and resources were insufficient to support warm (i.e. smooth) transfers. For example, a representative of people with mental health problems told us many care providers maintain a strict separation between counsellors who provide intramural and extramural support. Dean and Roel, both former supported housing clients whom we interviewed, were transferred to a new outpatient counsellor after they had left the hospital. Both indicated they had to get accustomed to their new supervisors. While this did not create major problems for Roel as he got along with his outpatient supervisor, this was not the case for Dean. Due to his past experiences involving multiple outpatient counsellors over a short period of time, it took Dean longer to build relationships of trust. He, therefore, decided to stop his education. He told us in our third interview that as a result of too many changes in guidance and support, he was no longer asking for help.

Mental healthcare is often criticized as operating in isolation without cooperation with other care providers. For example, opportunities have been missed because housing supervisors are not consulted. The mental health district teams are experimenting with an approach that involves more case management and engagement of parties such as social workers. Several stakeholders, however, indicated that the waiting lists for the district teams are far too long. As a result, people regularly stay longer than necessary in mental healthcare clinics; they do not leave because appropriate support and treatment cannot be offered in the community. We also heard of clients leaving without further care when inpatient

---

38 N. F. Boesveldt, 'Regio Den Haag Study' (2022) <https://nienkeboesveldt.com/index.php/onderzoeksregios-en-rapportages/regio-den-haag/ (accessed 1 September 2023).

treatment and its associated financing ends, creating risky situations for these individuals. Several municipal stakeholders are now experimenting with neighbourhood walk-in centres for mental healthcare.

Since 2004, municipalities in the Netherlands have been responsible for care following detention.[39] Different municipalities are currently working on a vision and approach for supporting people returning from prison, including improved cooperation with penitentiary institutions to have a clearer picture of released citizens. A longitudinal study in the municipality of Utrecht showed how (administrative) discontinuity in their trajectories while being imprisoned increased the risk of recurrent homelessness. Three of the four research participants who had been imprisoned during their five-year trajectory had fines replaced by (partial) custody; they were detained for between three days and six months in a penitentiary institution outside Utrecht.

Three of the four research participants who had been detained were arrested unexpectedly. Although the court's verdict was known in each case, the date of detention was unclear to them. In some cases, this was due to a pending appeal which was later found to have been rejected. In another case, the participant, due to physical complaints, was unable to perform the specified community service; in the absence of a timely alternative, he was picked up by the police. One participant told us he was unaware of the exact date of detention as he only had a postal address, not a fixed residential address.

The Example of Richard

Richard's trajectory, which went from protected living through residential detention to living in night shelters, made him increasingly vulnerable. Due to an unpaid fine, Richard also spent a month in prison. Although the verdict had been reached some time ago, he was not well informed about when he should serve his sentence, partly due to the uncertainties surrounding Covid-19. Earlier this year, he was unexpectedly picked up by the police at his protected housing facility. His one-month sentence later increased to four months to replace community service.

Three weeks before Richard was to be released, he was told that he could not keep his room at the protected housing facility. He turned down his case manager's offer for probation and social guidance, indicating he found it unnecessary and did not trust others with his data. At the time of our fourth interview, Richard was staying in a 24-hour shelter and, without an income, and was in the process of claiming benefits. He had yet to recover his belongings from the protected housing facility and was looking with the city team about where he might go. At the time of our final interview, he was in a homeless shelter, suffering psychosis. By that time, Richard had been in unstable housing for at least one year.[40]

---

39 The Department of Correctional Institutions, the Association of Dutch Municipalities, and the probation service have agreed to work with detainees from the outset of detention to reintegration. The initiative lies with the detainee <www.dji.nl/documenten/publicaties/2019/12/23/bestuurlijk-akkoord-kansen-bieden-voor-re-integratie> (accessed 1 September 2023).
40 See <www.nienkeboesveldt.com/Boesveldt-2021-Rapportage-Voorkomen-Herhaalde-Dakloosheid-Utrecht-derde-meting.pdf>.

Detention is often seen as a time when people have more peace, space, and regularity than in a homeless shelter. While much could be achieved by preparing one's return to society during detention, people with the highest recidivism rates often do not indicate any need for help, underlining the importance of being proactive. People in detention must navigate poorly coordinated systems, including the probation service, social services offered by the municipality, and healthcare administered by private health insurance companies. These bureaucracies rarely communicate and sometimes work at cross-purposes. It is currently very difficult for municipalities to know whether they have enough suitable places for people returning from detention. Municipalities rarely know how many protected housing facilities are financially supported by the national judiciary in their areas. Protected housing facilities are also unequally distributed across the country, with, for example, many more places available in The Hague than in other large municipalities such as Amsterdam and Rotterdam.[41]

Preventing Homelessness

One of the five action points that make up the 2023–2030 strategy on homelessness[42] seeks to prevent people from becoming homeless in the first place. It emphasizes social inclusion, establishing meaningful daily routines at work or school, financial support to access healthcare, and strengthening informal support and relationships.[43] The policy acknowledges that when the foundations of adequate living conditions, self-management, and informal care are missing, people will continue to fall through the cracks. Focusing on prevention also increases the chance that people will not require professional help, reflecting the broader emphasis on self-reliance in the Social Support Act.

The policy emphasizes both prevention and recovery care so that 'an effective well-covering system of early detection and types of support are available and failure and relapse are prevented'.[44] It further references the importance of providing information, client support, legal protection, and access to facilities and services, including investing in crisis intervention, neighbourhood outreach, and reducing the stigma surrounding homelessness.[45] While the proposed actions to improve access to information and combat stigma are generic solutions applicable to all professionals, the other actions target people at risk of imminent homelessness and focus on preventing homelessness. The policy proposes:

1. Countering stigmatizing images.
2. Reliable, accessible information on all areas of life.

---

41 See *Digitale landkaart DJI*, Forensische Zorg <www.geowebonline.nl> (accessed 29 March 2023) For insights on detention and reintegration from the Amsterdam Action Centre for Safety and Care, see p. 49 of the *Derde Rapportage Voorkomen Herhaalde Dakloosheid Utrecht* [third report on preventing recurrent homelessness in Utrecht].
42 Nationaal Actieplan Dakloosheid (n 4).
43 Reference is also made to the prevention alliance established in the previous policy period: 'An Alliance for Prevention and Early Detection specially set up for this purpose will, with financial support from the national government, allow (central) municipalities to analyze the process of prevention and early detection and to advise on concrete steps for improvement.'
44 Nationaal Actieplan Dakloosheid (n 4) 19.
45 Ibid.

3. Investment in good outpatient guidance, independent client support, and socio-legal advice.
4. Investing in outreach and crisis intervention.
5. Connecting the medical and social domains and care for the uninsured.
6. Release from an intramural setting should not lead to homelessness.
7. Eviction should not lead to homelessness.

Concrete proposals for action in 2023–2024 are contained in the Ministry of Internal Affairs' *Een Thuis voor Iedereen* (At Home for Everyone) programme,[46] which contains a mandatory emergency regulation under which people leaving intramural institutions receive priority for housing. The programme includes the following initiatives:

- *Vroeg Eropaf* (Early On) starts by identifying payment arrears. The municipality receives reports from, for example, health insurers, energy suppliers, and housing corporations. Early response teams will contact the resident to see if help is needed. If so, the team will check for problems in other areas of life; a plan of action must offer residents a way forward in often difficult circumstances. A Vroeg Eropaf employee will accompany the resident to debt assistance and/or relevant, connected partners when necessary. A national comparative study has addressed how this service is implemented by municipalities.[47]
- *Kamers met Aandacht* (Rooms with Attention) is a non-profit organization that seeks to reduce homelessness among young people aged 18 to 23, especially those leaving youth care services, by offering temporary housing with a family. Alongside outpatient guidance, informal support is available from housemates and neighbours. A next step needed to upscale this initiative would require more support from mortgage lenders.
- *Onder de Pannen* (Under the Rooftiles) is a national initiative to prevent long-term homelessness. Finding oneself on the street after a divorce or bankruptcy is not uncommon, given the current housing shortage. By offering people housing for one year, they get the opportunity to look for their own place in peace. Anyone who has an empty room can register as a landlord, including people living on benefits, with allowances, or in (social) rental housing. This support from the housing sector and landlords to allow subletting was unexpected, since subletting in social housing tends to be strictly prohibited in the Netherlands.
- Housing First – the theory and practice of prioritizing permanent independent housing rather than treatment and short-term shelters – is gaining popularity in Dutch public discourse. Determining eligibility and priority, however, remains a key challenge.
- Resource Group Assertive Community Treatment (R-ACT)[48] is an experimental form of collaboration between all healthcare providers in Amsterdam to support residents with complex needs in a more targeted way. The resource group model is based on the

---

46 Programma, 'Een thuis voor iedereen' <www.rijksoverheid.nl/documenten/rapporten/2022/05/11/programma-een-thuis-voor-iedereen> (accessed 1 September 2023).
47 See A. L. Scheepers, L. van den Dries, J. R. L. M. Wolf 'Informatie, interventies en praktijkvoorbeelden bij preventie van dakloosheid. Bijlage bij de uitgaven van de Preventie Alliantie' (Nijmegen: *Impuls, Radboudumc* 2022) <https://impuls-onderzoekscentrum.nl/wp-content/uploads/bijlage-info-interventies-en-voorbeelden-bij-preventie.pdf> (accessed 16 February 2024).
48 See <https://ract.nl> (accessed 1 September 2023).

principle that clients set their own treatment goals and have a strong say in what their treatment looks like. Nineteen healthcare professionals and 115 clients are currently involved in the programme in Amsterdam.[49] This method has been successful in keeping people on the waiting list from actually using protected housing or homelessness services.

The Future of Dutch Homelessness Law and Policy

New national policy documents[50] propose wider definitions of homelessness geared towards its prevention. At a time when more and more people are falling into poverty due to, for example, soaring energy bills, the broader framing of the issue is both promising and timely. One early challenge is the apparent instability of the, since January 2022, installed coalition government that proposed this more preventative policy.

According to conservative estimates, almost 40,000 people in the Netherlands are now homeless, a sharp increase over the past decade. The current system is expensive, relatively ineffective,[51] and poorly coordinated. Much of the help provided to homeless and vulnerable people entails temporary rather than sustainable solutions. In response, the Dutch government, in the spring of 2022, decided to renew its approach to homelessness based on the success of local *Housing First* programmes. Housing First is an evidence-based approach to support vulnerable people by providing stable, independent housing without conditions, alongside intensive personalized case management.[52]

It is promising that the agenda for combating homelessness is now based on scientific evidence. The findings of research on Housing First initiatives in the Netherlands have long suggested that a home is the solution to homelessness. But this newfound recognition by the government does not mean that all will be smooth sailing from now on. For example, there are currently no quality standards for Housing First initiatives or for the education of professionals. There are currently 47 Housing First initiatives in 93 municipalities – a cautious starting point for national coverage, as homeless people in the Netherlands now have an estimated 10% chance of accessing Housing First programmes, highlighting the lack of both affordable housing and unconditional access to it. While the Dutch government accepts a 'best-effort obligation' to achieve sufficient housing, there is no legal right to a home in the Netherlands. While the Netherlands has a large – albeit shrinking – stock of social housing, it remains insufficient.

The current system of prioritized housing means homeless people must compete with other vulnerable home seekers such as refugees. The homes required to accommodate those discharged from reception facilities and sheltered housing are not yet always provided in local agreements between municipalities and housing associations, besides the

---

49 See <https://ract.nl/>(accessed 16 February 2024).
50 See Nationaal Actieplan Dakloosheid (n 4).
51 N. F. Boesveldt, *Planet Homeless: Governance Arrangements in Amsterdam, Copenhagen, and Glasgow* (PhD thesis, Eleven International Publishing 2015); C. van Everdingen and others, 'A Comprehensive Assessment to Enable Recovery of the Homeless: The HOP-TR Study' (2021) 9(9) *Frontiers in Public Health* 661517.
52 S. Tsemberis and R. F. Eisenberg, 'Pathways to Housing: Supported Housing for street-Dwelling Homeless Individuals with Psychiatric Disabilities' (2000) 51 *Psychiatric Services* 487.

other competing groups, such as refugees.[53] For the new system to succeed, public housing must become a national priority, and municipalities must provide sufficient social housing stock. The key is to focus on local practices to achieve nationally formulated goals. In the Netherlands, it is the task of the Senate and the House of Representatives to assess whether legislation conflicts with the constitution. Unlike many other European countries, the Netherlands does not have a constitutional court. While ministers often state that housing is a fundamental right,[54] they do not make this explicit in policy.[55]

Although a place of one's own is a marked improvement over emergency shelters and institutions, housing-led approaches can still entail punitive, controlling, and conditional practices. For example, in a recent study, we observed the growing use of conditional rental contracts for permanent housing which require that tenant behaviour is deemed (at times arbitrarily) acceptable to other residents. Transgression of the rules can lead to eviction and ouster from the regional social rental sector. This brings the threat of sanctions back into the housing-led approach as housing becomes, once again, not a right but a conditional instrument that can be taken away.[56] In a strict Housing First system, there are no additional requirements for individuals to obtain a home; they do not need to prove that they are 'ready' for housing. Although there is broad support for the Housing First idea, the tendency to assess who could and should live independently, and thus gain access to housing, remains ubiquitous.[57] Truly unconditional access to housing would require a transformation of the sector.

A final consideration lies in the fact that many of the strategies to prevent homelessness in the Netherlands are rooted in private, bottom-up solidarity. These initiatives fit what the government has long touted as 'social innovations' in which solutions for unmet needs are jointly produced, with the state being only one stakeholder among many.[58] These private social support initiatives, however, point to a wider issue of decreasing public solidarity: they are filling the gaps left by professionals in the shrinking welfare state. This welfare state, in which deflection of action is combined with budgetary constraints, poses a risk to the future of services required to meet complex needs. All in all, this chapter, exploring incremental change towards providing Housing First, has outlined both promising policies and strong initiatives in homelessness monitoring and prevention that can be seen in the Netherlands but also has highlighted the challenging multi-level context of coordination and shifting definitions and interpretations of responsibilities in which attempts to structurally end homelessness are situated.

---

53 Every six months, the central government determines how many refugees permitted to stay in the Netherlands municipalities must give a place to live <www.rijksoverheid.nl/onderwerpen/asielbeleid/huisvesting-asielzoekers-met-verblijfsvergunning> (accessed 1 September 2023). The central government does not determine how many previously homeless people municipalities must give a place to live.
54 Letter to Parliament, 'Cabinet Presents Renewed Housing-First Approach to Homelessness' (2022) <www.rijksoverheid.nl/actueel/nieuws/2022/06/01/kabinet-presenteert-vernieuwde-aanpak-dakloosheid-wonen-eerst> (accessed 1 September 2023).
55 M. Schmit, N. F. Boesveldt, and A. Jansen, 'Housing First as a system approach: what does this require from the Netherlands? (2023) 17(2) *European Journal of Homelessness* 171 <https://www.feantsaresearch.org/public/user/Observatory/2023/EJK_17_-_2/EJH_17-2_A12_v02.pdf> (accessed 16 February 2024).
56 Boesveldt and Loomans (n 23).
57 Schmit, Boesveldt and Janssen (n 55).
58 P. Hirst, 'Renewing Democracy Trough Associations' (2002) 73 *The Political Quarterly Publishing Co. Ltd.* 409.

11

THE ILLIBERAL STATE AND HOMELESSNESS

The Case of Poland

Adam Ploszka

Introduction

Poland is in the midst of a deep crisis in the rule of law and human rights. Changes made to the constitutional and political system from 2015 onwards have led to a situation where Poland can no longer be described as a liberal democracy.[1] In the course of dismantling democratic standards, the Law and Justice Political Party, which governed in Poland from 2015 to the end of 2023, to a large extent, followed the path determined by the Hungarian populist government.[2] Among the elements that form the identity of the illiberal Hungarian state we find a hostile and discriminatory attitude towards homelessness,[3] which eventually led to the constitutional amendment legalizing the criminalization of homelessness.[4]

---

1 Cf W. Sadurski, *Poland's Constitutional Breakdown* (OUP 2019); M. Wyrzykowski, 'Experiencing the Unimaginable: The Collapse of the Rule of Law in Poland (2019) 11(2) *Hague Journal on the Rule of Law* 417; Cf. also A. Ploszka, 'It Never Rains but It Pours.: The Polish Constitutional Tribunal Declares the European Convention on Human Rights Unconstitutional' (2023) 15 *Hague Journal on the Rule of Law* 51.
2 Cf. G. Halmai, 'The Making of "Illiberal Constitutionalism" with or Without a New Constitution: The Case of Hungary and Poland' in D. Landau and H. Lerner (eds), *Comparative Constitution Making* (Edward Elgar Publishing 2019); T. Drinóczi and A. Bień-Kacała, *Illiberal Constitutionalism in Poland and Hungary: The Deterioration of Democracy, Misuse of Human Rights and Abuse of the Rule of Law* (Routledge 2021).
3 Cf: E. Tessza Udvarhelyi, '"If We Don't Push Homeless People Out, We Will End Up Being Pushed Out by Them": The Criminalization of Homelessness as State Strategy in Hungary' (2014) 43(6) *Antipode* 816; B. Misetics, 'Criminalisation of Homelessness in Hungary' in S. Jones (ed), *Mean Streets: A Report on the Criminalisation of Homelessness in Europe* (FEANTSA 2013) 101.
4 Cf. Article 6 of Seventh Amendment of the Fundamental Law of Hungary, effective as of 15 October 2018. The process that led to the adoption of this amendment started long before – in 2012. After the Budapest city council led by a FIDESZ majority enacted a local ordinance that banned homelessness from public places, the Orbán government extended the ban to the entire country. However, in November 2012, the Constitutional Court found the law unconstitutional, because it prohibited homelessness as a status, and due to this, it violated the human dignity of people who could not afford a place to live. (Decision 38/2012. (XI. 14.) AB.) In reaction to this judgement, the Fourth Amendment to the Fundamental Law in 2013 was adopted, which, among other things, reversals of a declaration of unconstitutionality by the Constitutional Court authorized both the national legislature and local governments to declare homelessness unlawful. The Fourth Amendment added the following Section 3 to Article XXII of the Fundamental Law: 'In order to

In this chapter, I pose and respond to the research question of whether the Polish government has followed the Hungarian approach in relation to homelessness. This will also make it possible for me to provide an answer to the more general question of whether or not there is a single illiberal Central European approach to homelessness.

The chapter is structured as follows. In the first part, I will provide a broader picture of the phenomenon of homelessness in Poland and its social and legal determinants. This piece is part of a broader comparative law project on law and policy and homelessness; outlining some of these issues will enable further comparative analysis. The broader perspective also allows us to establish the starting point in 2015, when Law and Justice came to power, thus creating a reference point for an assessment of the actions (or lack thereof) from 2015 onwards.

In the second part, I will provide an overview of the Polish illiberal government's approach to homelessness. To do this, I will juxtapose and analyze selected actions in the field of homelessness rights and freedoms taken by the independent Polish National Human Rights Institution, the Commissioner for Citizens' Rights (hereinafter referred to as the 'Ombudsman' and with the Polish abbreviation, RPO) in the period of Adam Bodnar's term (2015–2020). The choice of this time period is clear: Bodnar's term started almost at the same time as Law and Justice came to power; the new Ombudsman made eradication of homelessness in Poland one of his priorities,[5] justifying this by stating that homelessness could not be reconciled with the human dignity guaranteed to everyone in the Polish Constitution.[6] Thus, an analysis of the Polish government's responses to the selected actions of the RPO in this area of the rights and freedoms of the homeless makes it possible to examine and reconstruct the approach of the illiberal Polish government towards homelessness as it concerns rights and freedoms.

Background and Context on Homelessness Prevention in Poland

The phenomenon of homelessness is permanently inscribed in the image of Polish society. It is thus not surprising that the prevention of homelessness is widely discussed in the social sciences in Poland.[7]

---

protect public order, public security, public health and cultural values, an Act or a local government decree may, with respect to a specific part of public space, provide that staying in public space as a habitual dwelling shall be illegal'. Finally, the Seventh Amendment of the Fundamental Law was adopted, which concluded the process of criminalization of homelessness. Cf in more detail in G. Halmai, 'The Evolution and *Gestalt* of the Hungarian Constitution' in *Ius Publicum Euroepaeum* (OUP forthcoming).

5 Cf: R. Mędrzycki, 'Działalność Rzecznika Praw Obywatelskich w Polsce w zakresie ochrony osób w kryzysie bezdomności i zagrożonych bezdomnością w latach 2005–2015 w świetle raportów RPO' (2020) 20(1) *Zeszyty Prawnicze* 229.
6 Cf. Full transcript of the proceedings of the Sejm Committee on Justice and Human Rights (No 259) 7 July 2015 <https://orka.sejm.gov.pl/zapisy7.nsf/0/E94D2CF5C4A6CD3CC1257E82004A859D/%24File/0480207.pdf> (accessed 1 September 2023).
7 Cf. for example some English-language publications: A. Burak and A. Ferenc, 'Defining and Measuring of Homelessness: Poland' (2021) 52(1) *Problemy Polityki Społecznej. Studia i Dyskusje* 24; M. Mostowska and K. Dębska, 'An Ambiguous Hierarchy of Inequalities: The Political Intersectionality of Older Women's Homelessness in Poland' (2020) 29(4) *Journal of Gender Studies* 443; cf also some important Polish-language publications: A. Duracz-Walczak, *Bezdomni* (CRRS 1996); P. Dobrowolski and I. Mądry (eds), *Ubodzy i bezdomni* (Wydawnictwo Uniwersytetu Śląskiego 1998); A. Przymeński, *Bezdomność jako*

Analyzing this phenomenon from a historical perspective, we can see that although historical research on homelessness in current Polish lands goes back to the Middle Ages,[8] it is only relatively recently, after the First World War and Poland's return to the world map, that homelessness was legally recognized as a social problem by the resurgent Polish state.[9] After the Second World War, when the communists came to power, the existence of homelessness within the People's Republic of Poland was denied, as it could not be reconciled with the socialist system that was supposed to take care of all citizens. People experiencing homelessness were hidden from society, for example, by placing them in so-called workers' hotels. The precise word 'homeless' was, at that time, eliminated from dictionaries. The problem of homelessness reappeared again after the democratic breakthrough of 1989. The scale of homelessness was raised as a result of political transformations and the introduction of a market economy.[10]

Tackling homelessness after 1989 was never a key priority for consecutive Polish governments. Until 2000, the very notion of a 'homeless person' was not defined by law.[11] The first government strategy covering this issue was adopted in 2014[12] as a prerequisite for EU funding. The very first survey conducted by the Polish government to estimate the population of the people experiencing homelessness[13] was made only in 2009.[14] According to the latest (2019) results of a survey conducted by the Polish government, the population of homeless people in crisis in Poland was 30,330, of which 83.6% were men (25,369 people), while 16.4% were women (4,961 people).[15]

---

kwestia społeczna w Polsce współczesnej (Wydaw. Akademii Ekonomicznej 2001); M. Dębski (ed.), *Problem bezdomności w Polsce. Wybrane aspekty – diagnoza Zespołu Badawczego* (Gdańsk 2011).

8 S. Grodziski, *Ludzie luźni. Studium z historii państwa i prawa polskiego* (Nakładem Uniwersytetu Jagiellońskiego 1961).

9 See Social Welfare Act of August 16, 1923 [PL. Ustawa z dnia 16 sierpnia 1923 roku o opiece społecznej], published in Journal of Laws in 1923, No. 92, item 726. Cf: Dominika Cendrowicz, 'Zadania administracji publicznej z zakresu pomocy osobom bezdomnym w II Rzeczypospolitej' (2019) Prawo Tom 327 *Sto lat polskiej administracji publicznej* 39.

10 L. Stankiewicz, *Zrozumieć bezdomność* (Wydawnictwo UWM 2002).

11 Information on the results of the audit of the implementation of the Social Assistance Act in the field of homelessness prevention [PL. Informacja o wynikach kontroli z realizacji ustawy o pomocy społecznej w zakresie zapobiegania zjawisku bezdomności] Warszawa 1997 <http://bip.nik.gov.pl/kontrole/wyniki-kontroli-nik/kontrole,1464.html (accessed 1 September 2023). This provision was added by Article 21(1)(a) of the Act of 21 January 2000 amending certain acts related to the functioning of public administration, published in *Journal of Laws* in 2000, No. 12, item 136.

12 Resolution No. 165 of the Council of Ministers of 12 August 2014 on the adoption of the programme titled 'National Programme for Counteracting Poverty and Social Exclusion 2020: A New Dimension of Active Integration' [PL: *Uchwała nr 165 Rady Ministrów z dnia 12 sierpnia 2014 r. w sprawie przyjęcia programu pod nazwą 'Krajowy Program Przeciwdziałania Ubóstwu i Wykluczeniu Społecznemu 2020. Nowy wymiar aktywnej integracji'*] published in *Monitor Polski*, item 787.

13 In this chapter, I am using the terms 'person experiencing homelessness' and 'person in homelessness crisis' intentionally to replace the commonly appearing 'homeless person(s)' or 'the homeless'. This change was intended to emphasize the transient nature of homelessness and move away from the stereotypical and stigmatizing term 'homeless person'.

14 Ministerstwo Pracy i Polityki Społecznej Departament Pomocy i Integracji Społecznej, Bezdomność w Polsce – diagnoza na dzień 31 stycznia 2010, Warszawa 2010.

15 <www.gov.pl/web/rodzina/wyniki-ogolnopolskiego-badania-liczby-osob-bezdomnych-edycja-2019> (accessed 1 September 2023). The counting process was conducted in the following way. In winter, on the coldest night possible, people who were in institutions providing help to the homeless and non-residential

The Existing Legal Framework Pertaining to Homelessness in Poland – Constitution of Poland

Homelessness prevention and eradication have solid legal foundations in the Polish legal system. The Constitution of the Republic of Poland of 1997[16] *expressis verbis* refers to the eradication of homelessness, stating in 75.1 that:

> Public authorities shall pursue policies conducive to satisfying the housing needs of citizens, in particular combating homelessness, promoting the development of low-income housing, and supporting activities aimed at acquisition of a home by each citizen.

Article 75 was included in the catalogue of constitutional rights, which, according to Article 81 of the Constitution, may be asserted within the limits set by law. The drafters of the Constitution gave this provision the character of a 'programmatic norm'. This kind of legal norm defines, as a rule, the duties of public authorities. The question that is still being answered in the jurisprudence of the Constitutional Tribunal relates to the extent to which a subjective right of the individual can be derived from this provision.

In one of the historic first judgments relating to this provision, the Constitutional Tribunal formulated an opinion on the possibility of individuals deriving rights from Article 75 of the Constitution. The Constitutional Tribunal came to the conclusion that Article 75 of the Constitution, on economic and social rights, may be the basis for a constitutional complaint[17] in the following three special situations: (1) whenever the legislator applied means that may not lead to the implementation of a constitutional goal; (2) whenever a statute restricts a citizen in such a manner that it violates the essence of law; (3) whenever the statutory legal regulation does not take account of the minimum right delineated by its essence.[18] The Tribunal, however, has not defined, either in this or subsequent case law, what is to be understood by the 'essence of the law' or by the 'minimum law' contained in that provision. It is legitimate to conclude that the essence of the right set forth in Article 75 of the Constitution is the obligation of public authorities to provide shelter to a citizen unable to meet their own housing needs.[19]

However, in later jurisprudence of the Constitutional Tribunal, the opposite approach towards Article 75 providing a subjective right to housing was adopted. The Constitutional Tribunal expressed a definitive view rejecting this subjective right in case K 5/03, stating

---

places where such people stay were counted. Clearly, this methodology does not include all the homeless, for example, people who, for different reasons, are temporarily in transit or temporarily received assistance from a family member or other organizations that are not included in the counting process.

16 The Constitution of the Republic of Poland of 2nd April 1997, published in Journal of Laws No. 78, item 483.
17 According to art 79.1. of the Polish Constitution: 'In accordance with principles specified by statute, everyone whose constitutional freedoms or rights have been infringed, shall have the right to appeal to the Constitutional Tribunal for its judgment on the conformity to the Constitution of a statute or another normative act upon which basis a court or organ of public administration has made a final decision on his freedoms or rights or on his obligations specified in the Constitution.'
18 Judgment of the Constitutional Tribunal of 14 May 2001, Case No. SK 1/00, OTZU 2001, no. 4, item 84.
19 This line of reasoning corresponds with the interpretation of the right to housing by the UN Committee on Economic, Social and Cultural Rights in 'General Comment No 4: The Right to Adequate Housing (Art. 11 (1) of the Covenant)' Un. Doc. E/1992/23, par. 7.

that this provision had the nature of a programming norm, formulating strategic priorities of state policy. The manner in which these policies are to be implemented has not been determined, nor is the strategic priority of this provision absolute. Accordingly, Parliament has broad discretion in the implementation of the programmatic objectives contained in this provision, particularly as to the choice of time, intensity, dynamics, and manner of implementation of the programmatic objectives contained therein. Thus, the Tribunal held that programmatic provisions, which include Article 75 of the Constitution, cannot be raised as a standard of review in a framework of constitutional complaint, as they do not create a subjective right. At the same time, however, it is permissible to invoke this provision as a standard of review for abstract control.[20]

In one of the most recent judgments of the Constitutional Tribunal, the Tribunal came to the conclusion that the content of Article 75 makes it possible to determine a certain minimum scope of constitutional guarantees in all spheres indicated therein, inter alia, in the sphere of the obligations to prevent homelessness. In the opinion of the Constitutional Tribunal, the allegation of violation of this provision by the legislator may be formulated when public authorities do not undertake any action or they create apparent solutions that, in practice, do not lead to realization of the constitutional objectives set out in this provision.[21]

To conclude, although Article 75 refers directly to the prevention of homelessness, the approach of the Constitutional Tribunal to this provision has limited its practical meaning. Consequently, other constitutional guarantees, including Article 30 of the Constitution, which protect human dignity, have gained much greater significance.

The importance of human dignity was best characterized in the Constitutional Tribunal judgment in case no. K 11/00, where the Tribunal ruled on the constitutionality of the lack of legal guarantees protecting people against eviction onto the streets, which would make them homeless.[22] Interestingly, in this case, the Ombudsman, who initiated the proceedings by his motion, raised a claim of incompatibility of the questioned regulation with Article 75 of the Constitution. The Tribunal, however, came to the conclusion that Article 75 of the Constitution is not adequate to provide protection to persons evicted from housing. This inadequacy, in the opinion of the Constitutional Tribunal, results from the fact that this provision does not specify criteria for tackling homelessness or legal measures serving this purpose.

While deciding on the incompatibility of the regulations with the Constitution, the Constitutional Tribunal concluded that the constitutional lawmaker made human dignity a constitutional concept and made it a reference point for a system of values on which the Constitution evolved, and the foundation of the entire legal system in the state. As noted

---

20 Judgment of the Constitutional Tribunal of 23 September 2003, Case No. K 5/03, OTK ZU 2003, no. 7A, item. 77, para 28. Cf. also judgement of the Constitutional Tribunal of 18 January 2011, Case No. P 44/08, OTK ZU 2011, No. 1A, item. 1. As regards abstract control: in the Polish legal system, certain state bodies, including, among others, the Ombudsman, based on Article 191 of the Constitution of the Republic of Poland, have the competence to initiate proceedings before the Constitutional Tribunal by lodging with the Constitutional Tribunal a motion in any case (also without any relation to a concrete individual case, hence the name abstract control) remaining within the competences of the Constitutional Tribunal as defined in Article 188 of the Constitution of the Republic of Poland.
21 Judgment of the Constitutional Tribunal of 18 October 2017, Case No. K 27/15, OTK-A 2017, item. 74.
22 Judgment of the Constitutional Tribunal of 4 April 2001, Case No. K 11/00, OTK ZU 2001, no. 3, item 54, para. 57.

by the Tribunal, dignity must not be understood as a feature or a set of rights assigned by the state because it has a primary position in relation to the state. Hence, both the legislator and the authorities applying the law must respect the meaning of the term *dignity*, to which every human being is entitled. Furthermore, the Tribunal concluded that the prohibition on violating human dignity as defined in Article 30 is absolute and applicable to everyone. The duty to respect and protect dignity was imposed on the public authorities of the state. As a consequence, all actions of the public authorities should account for the existence of a certain autonomy zone within which a person may fully realize their social potential, and that those actions should not lead to the creation of legal or real-world situations that deprive an individual of their sense of dignity. In the context of the public authorities' duty to respect and protect dignity, the Tribunal concluded that:

> [A] premise for respecting . . . human dignity includes, among other things, the existence of a certain material minimum that provides the individual with the ability to function in the society on their own and to create opportunities for each person to fully develop their personality within their cultural- and civilizational surroundings.

This concept of 'certain material minimum' has been further developed in the jurisprudence of the Tribunal.[23]

Thus, to sum up, in the context of the constitutional framework, the Constitutional Tribunal has outlined certain requirements for the legislator in the field of tackling homelessness and in the field of state duties to support people in a homelessness crisis. In truth, these requirements are minimalistic. The issue of homelessness, as indicated by the limited number of judgments delivered by the Tribunal on the matter, does not occupy a significant position in the jurisprudence. Clearly, this lack of jurisprudence results from a relatively low interest in the field of homelessness from state institutions and citizens that are entitled to initiate proceedings before the Constitutional Tribunal.

The Existing Statutory Legal Framework on Homelessness in Poland: The Social Welfare Act

Although the Constitution of Poland provides that the obligation to tackle homelessness lies with public authorities, the legislator has attributed this task mainly to local government.[24] According to the Local Government Act, the obligation to provide social assistance (including to people in homelessness crisis) rests with the lowest local government unit – the commune (*gmina*).[25] In fact, assistance for people suffering homelessness is, to a large

---

23 A. Ploszka, 'The Right to Subsistence Minimum and Its Role in the Protection of People Living in Extreme Poverty – the Polish Experience' (2018) 24 *Comparative Law Review* 225.
24 Cf: D. Cendrowicz, *Zadania jednostek samorządu terytorialnego w zakresie pomocy osobom bezdomnym z perspektywy zasady pomocniczości* (Difin 2020); R. Mędrzycki, *Zadania administracji publicznej w zakresie przeciwdziałania bezdomności* (Wydawnictwo Naukowe 2017); I. Lipowicz, *Bezdomność – problemy prawne, innowacyjne rozwiązania* (Fundacja Didactics 2016).
25 Art. 7.1.6 Act on Commune Self-government of 8 March 1990, published in *Journal of Laws* from 2022, item 559.

extent, provided by non-governmental organizations, which are commissioned by particular communes to provide services.[26]

The definition of a 'homeless person' in Polish law is relatively simple.[27] A person can be recognized by law as a 'homeless person' under two conditions: first, a person that does not reside in a residential unit (dwelling which is suitable for habitation), and, secondly, a person not registered in any premises for permanent residence. Alternatively, the legal definition of a 'homeless person' also covers persons that do not reside in a residential unit and do have a permanent residence registration but where there is no possibility of living where that person is registered.

This definition serves as a basic tool for social assistance authorities in Poland. However, it does not cover all people suffering homelessness who are not entitled to benefit from the social welfare system. This definition does not include, for example, people who, being *de facto* homeless, use the help of other people to satisfy their housing needs (e.g. by staying with family or friends from time to time). Nor does this definition include people who are living in substandard conditions (in overcrowded apartments, of a very low standard, with no electricity or access to running water), or people threatened with homelessness (who find themselves in a situation directly leading to homelessness).

An analysis of the Social Welfare Act allows us to reconstruct the Polish model of assistance for the homeless – assistance provided, as mentioned earlier, by local communes and NGOs acting on their behalf.[28] This model can be best described by referring to the metaphor of stairs. A person experiencing homelessness may receive various types of assistance in overcoming homelessness. A significant part of this is of a low-threshold nature, such as the possibility of using a night shelter or receiving a meal and necessary clothing. However, to get more specialized assistance (i.e. to climb up the staircase), such as a 24-hour night shelter, combined with services aimed at strengthening social activity, and gaining independence in life, which in fact is necessary to reverse homelessness, the person must fulfil a number of conditions, often locally determined. Only having passed through successive steps of assistance does the prospect of housing appear. Securing housing takes time and is connected with compliance with all relevant conditions, for example, meeting particular personal goals, such as realization of an individual programme for getting out of homelessness, including, first of all, permanent abstinence from alcohol. In the case of failure at any of the previous levels, the person suffering homelessness has to start the journey again from the beginning.[29] In contrast to the 'stairs-step' approach, a model based on the Housing First

---

26 On particular challenges and good practices in the field of homelessness prevention, cf. publications issued after annual conferences organized by the Polish National Federation for Solving the Problem of Homelessness, which is an umbrella organization associating NGOs operating in Poland in the field of homelessness. In particular: J. Wilczek (ed), *Pokonać bezdomność: Dobre praktyki w zakresie pomocy osobom bezdomnym* (Ogólnopolska Federacja Rozwiązywania Problemu 2018); P. Olech, L. Węsierska-Chyc and J. Wilczek (eds), *Streetworking, mieszkania, współpraca: Dobre praktyki w pomocy osobom bezdomnym* (Ogólnopolska Federacja na rzecz Rozwiązywania Problemu Bezdomności 2019); J. Wilczek (ed), *Pokonać bezdomność 2020. Materiały konferencyjne i dobre praktyki* (Ogólnopolska Federacja na rzecz Rozwiązywania Problemu Bezdomności 2020).
27 Art. 6.8. of the Social Welfare Act of 12 March 2004, published in *Journal of Laws* from z 2021 r. item. 2268.
28 Cf. in particular Articles 48–49 of the Social Welfare Act.
29 Cf: J. Wilczek, 'Wstęp. O potrzebie zmiany systemu przeciwdziałania bezdomności' in J. Wilczek (ed), *Programy mieszkaniowe w przeciwdziałaniu bezdomności – dobre praktyki i refleksja systemowa* (Ogólnopolska Federacja na rzecz Rozwiązywania Problemu Bezdomności 2017) 7.

concept is gaining increasing attention in academic debate and social practice in Poland. Although it is being tested by many cities in Poland, it is still not clearly grounded in law in the Social Welfare Act.[30]

Challenges to Homelessness Preventative Practice and Homelessness Law and Policy in Poland: The Activities of the Ombudsman

As mentioned in the introduction, the rights of homeless people have been in the Ombudsman's sights for many years and, since 2015, have become his priority. However, the RPO, thanks to his competences defined by the Constitution, giving him the mandate to protect the rights of citizens, does not deal with homelessness policy in a general sense, instead focusing his activity on the *legal* aspects of homelessness.

The Ombudsman is obliged to inform Parliament annually about his activities and report on the degree of respect accorded to the freedoms and rights of citizens.[31] Analysis of the reports published for the years 2015 to 2020 demonstrates that the issue of homelessness was of particular interest to the RPO, although activities related to the defence of the rule of law have dominated this term of office.[32] However, it is worth mentioning – as a form of good practice – that at the beginning of the term, the Expert Committee on Homelessness Prevention was established by the Ombudsman. It was composed of various stakeholders involved in homelessness prevention in Poland. The purpose of establishing this Committee was for the Ombudsman to acquire knowledge on legal problems connected with reducing homelessness (and its prevention). In addition to this, over time, the Committee has also become a platform for dialogue with various state institutions on problems identified by the RPO.

Based on an analysis of the annual information presented by the RPO to Parliament for the years 2015–2020, we can observe that the Ombudsman, among his various competences,[33] most often used so-called 'general interventions' (PL: *wystąpienia generalne*) in which he addressed to different state authorities the existence of specific problems concerning the law and policy on homelessness. In general, this instrument is one of the most important tools in the Ombudsman's practice to solve the legal and social problems submitted in complaints made by citizens. General interventions allow the Ombudsman to present to the competent state authority recommendations on what should be changed in the law or in the operation of public institutions to improve human rights standards in Poland.

General interventions submitted by the Ombudsman in the period of 2015–2020 allow us to identify key issues in the area of homelessness perceived from a human rights perspective. Responses to them make it possible to reform the approach of government-controlled institutions to the problem of homelessness. The most important of these general

---

30 J. Wygnańska, 'Ocena wierności NM, Fundacja Najpierw Mieszkanie Polska' <https://najpierwmieszkanie.org.pl/publikacje/artykul/ocena-wiernosci-najpierw-mieszkanie/> (accessed 1 September 2023).
31 According to art 212 of the Polish Constitution.
32 A. Bodnar 'The Role of the Commissioner of Human Rights of the Republic of Poland in the Fight for Rule of Law in Poland' in A. Bodnar and J. Urbanik (eds), Περιμένοντας τους Βαρβάρους. *Law in a Time of Constitutional Crisis* (Verlag CH Beck 2021).
33 Cf. Art. 12–17 The Commissioner for Human Rights Act of 15 July 1987, published in Journal of Law from 2020, item 627.

interventions – relating to problems of a systemic nature, juxtaposed with the responses to them – will be examined later.

The Ombudsman's focus on general interventions requires some comment. First, in the information analyzed, in the field of homelessness, there was not a single example of the RPO exercising the competence of joining pending court proceedings, which the Ombudsman is entitled to do. Here, we can formulate a hypothesis that there is no noticeable activity of those experiencing homelessness and of non-governmental organizations helping them before the courts. Among possible explanations for this, one can highlight – for formal reasons – the difficulty in accessing courts in Poland. However, determination of the precise reasons requires a separate study.

Secondly, the crisis in the rule of law has had an impact on homelessness prevention and eradication. Due to the destabilization by Law and Justice of the Constitutional Tribunal,[34] the Ombudsman lost his ability to initiate abstract control of the constitutionality of legal regulations. This competence was popularly referred to as 'the Ombudsman's atomic weapon' and was usually deployed by the RPO as a result of the failure, or unsatisfactory response, of public authorities to earlier general addresses. Over the years, especially in the context of eviction from premises, it was the judgments of the Constitutional Tribunal issued in the proceedings initiated by the Ombudsman that forced the legislator to make changes to the law. However, the Ombudsman, despite receiving unsatisfactory responses to his general interventions (discussed later), did not exercise this competence during the period in question. The only judgment that was delivered during this period, which related, again, to evictions, was delivered as the result of a motion filed by the Ombudsman just before the constitutional crisis in Poland started.[35]

Thus, in the area of homelessness, the Ombudsman either did not have or could not use the judicial mechanisms for the protection of individual rights. This explains why the RPO concentrated his activity on attempts to establish a dialogue with governmental institutions.

Lack of Coordination of Public Administration Activities in the Field of Homelessness

One of the first general interventions of the Ombudsman at the beginning of his term in 2015 was referred to the Prime Minister. In his intervention, the Ombudsman proposed the appointment of a government plenipotentiary whose task would be to coordinate the activities and initiatives of various government branches in the area of homelessness prevention.[36]

The Ombudsman justified this proposal by pointing out that homelessness prevention not only ensures appropriate places to live but also requires providing the homeless with a possibility to exercise rights and freedoms, including inter alia access to public services,

---

34 Cf: W. Sadurski, 'Polish Constitutional Tribunal Under PiS: From an Activist Court, to a Paralysed Tribunal, to a Governmental Enabler' (2019) 11 *Hague Journal on the Rule of Law* 63.

35 Judgment of the Constitutional Tribunal of 18 October 2017, Case No. K 27/15, OTK-A 2017, item. 74.

36 Dated 17 November 2015, ref. IV.7217.91.201, *Information on the activities of the Human Rights Commissioner in 2015 and the state of respect for human and civil liberties and rights* [PL: *Informacja o działalności Rzecznika Praw Obywatelskich w roku 2015 r. oraz o stanie przestrzegania wolności i praw człowieka i obywatela*] 180 <https://bip.brpo.gov.pl/sites/default/files/Informacja%20roczna%202015.pdf> (accessed 1 September 2023).

especially to medical care, legal aid, or public education. It is also about providing people experiencing homelessness with the basic conditions for a dignified life, that is, adequate nutrition, basic clothing, and the opportunity to take care of personal hygiene. Finally, it is not possible to prevent homelessness without limiting the factors that cause it (such as poverty, unemployment, domestic violence, addiction to narcotics, mental disorders, excessive indebtedness, and lack of a sufficient number of places in hospitals and nursing homes), as well as therapeutic activities supporting the process of getting out of homelessness.

As all these issues fall within the competences of many branches of government administration (public administration, construction, local planning and zoning, budgeting and public finance, education, labour education, labour, justice, social security, or health), there is a need to coordinate these various branches to makes homelessness prevention effective. According to the Ombudsman, this kind of special plenipotentiary of the Prime Minister may also initiate systemic actions that go beyond the competences of particular sectors of government administration.

The Prime Minister's Office responded to that intervention by declaring that the establishment of a separate body within the structure of government administration dealing exclusively with the coordination of actions in the field of homelessness would be pointless due to the financial cost connected with it. In the government's opinion, the phenomenon of homelessness is indeed a complex and acute social problem, but it is not the only social group that requires the care of the public administration. The government perceives homelessness prevention and eradication as an element of wider social policy, which seems to be consistent with European recommendations in the field of tackling homelessness.[37]

The Ombudsman, when close to the end of his term, in December 2019, repeated his intervention.[38] In his reply, a representative of the Prime Minister's Office pointed out that the issue of homelessness was a subject of concern and interest to the competent state administration institutions. The Prime Minister's Office declared that within the Council for Public Benefit Activity (PL: *Rady Działalności Pożytku Publicznego*), which is an advisory body to one of the ministries, there is a Team for Social Participation of the Elderly (PL: *Zespół ds. Partycypacji Społecznej Osób Starszych*), whose purview includes activities for the improvement of the conditions of homeless people.[39] The government's position has therefore not changed.

Local Connection Rules That Violate the Constitutional Freedom of Choice of the Place of Residence and Sojourn

Defining precisely which public administration entities are responsible for providing support to the homeless is a challenge of at least European proportions.[40] The Act on Social Welfare

---

37 Ibid., letter dated 7 January 2016.
38 General intervention dated 18 December 2019, ref. no: IV.7217.89.2019, *Information on the activities of the Human Rights Commissioner in 2020 and the state of respect for human and civil liberties and rights* [PL: *Informacja o działalności Rzecznika Praw Obywatelskich w roku 2020 r. oraz o stanie przestrzegania wolności i praw człowieka i obywatela*] 335.
39 Ibid., letter dated 6 February 2020.
40 I. Baptista, L. Benjaminsen and N. Pleace, 'Local Connection Rules and Access to Homelessness Services in Europe' in *EOH Comparative Studies on Homelessness* (European Observatory on Homelessness, FEANTSA 2015).

provides, in Article 101(2), that in the case of a person in homelessness crisis, the municipality that is locally competent is the one where that person was last registered as a permanent resident. This way of determining the local competence authority serves as an exception to the general rule that the locally competent municipality is determined in accordance with the current place of residence of the person applying for a benefit. This legal regulation may produce a situation where people applying for support to overcome homelessness are forced by law to apply for support in a place with which they do not have any relationship at that time. This exact place may be located hundreds of kilometres away from their current 'home'.

In consecutive general interventions presented to the ministry responsible for social affairs in 2018 and 2020, the Ombudsman pointed out that this provision effectively hinders support for the homeless. The RPO pointed out that this may raise doubts in light of constitutionally guaranteed freedoms of Polish citizens to choose their place of residence and sojourn.[41] The Ombudsman proposed several solutions, starting from minor modifications to this provision to the creation of a so-called basket of guaranteed benefits offered (and therefore financed) not by local administration but by central governmental administration.

In response to these interventions, the ministry responsible for social affairs eventually acknowledged this legal obstacle to homelessness prevention. However, neither of the proposals to improve the situation of the homeless has been adopted. The ministry's action was limited to sending a legal but non-binding recommendation to the municipalities suggesting they use the exception stipulated by the Act on Social Assistance, which allows for assistance to the municipality of residence (not registration) in a situation when it is not in line with the will of the homeless person and is justified by their personal circumstances.[42] Such an action cannot, however, be considered a solution to the problem; the granting of a social welfare benefit is, in fact, conditional on the goodwill of the social worker, who determines if the exception defined by law is engaged.

Lack of Access to Medical Care for Those in Homelessness Crisis

Having to live in non-residential conditions creates both physical and mental health risks.[43] People in homelessness crisis are in particular need of access to medical care. Although the Constitution of Poland in Article 68.2 provides that '[e]qual access to health care services, financed from

---

41 Cf. Article 51.1. of the Polish Constitution (in official translation available at the following link): 'Freedom of movement as well as the choice of place of residence and sojourn within the territory of the Republic of Poland shall be ensured to everyone' <www.sejm.gov.pl/prawo/konst/angielski/konse.htm> (accessed 1 September 2023).

42 General intervention dated 11 October 2018, ref. no. III.7065.193.2018 z r., with answer dated: 20 December 2018, *Information on the activities of the Human Rights Commissioner in 2018 and the state of respect for human and civil liberties and rights* [PL: *Informacja o działalności Rzecznika Praw Obywatelskich w roku 2018 r. oraz o stanie przestrzegania wolności i praw człowieka i obywatela*] 284, as well as General intervention dated 4 June 2020, ref. no III.7065.43.2020, with answer dated 26 June 2020, *Information on the activities of the Human Rights Commissioner in 2020 and the state of respect for human and civil liberties and rights* [PL: *Informacja o działalności Rzecznika Praw Obywatelskich w roku 2020 r. oraz o stanie przestrzegania wolności i praw człowieka i obywatela*] 338 <https://bip.brpo.gov.pl/sites/default/files/Informacja_RPO_za_2020.pdf> (accessed 1 September 2023).

43 Cf. J. Romaszko and others, 'The Incidence of Pulmonary Tuberculosis Among the Homeless in North-Eastern Poland' (2013) 8(2) *Open Medicine* 283.

public funds, shall be ensured by public authorities to citizens, irrespective of their material situation', those experiencing homelessness, but more broadly people that are not earning, face problems in accessing medical care. This category of potential patients is often unable to complete the formalities needed to have the right to medical care financed from public funds.

This problem has been reported in every year of the Ombudsman's tenure. The RPO, in his general intervention in 2016, also pointed out that homeless people have problems with access to the necessary health services, medications, and medical equipment after leaving hospital, living in shelters, and other facilities for the homeless. Moreover, there are great difficulties connected with the realization of the right to long-term care by the homeless. The lengthy procedure of admission to nursing homes and social welfare homes often results in the need for long-term and expensive hospitalization.[44]

Interestingly, the government initially, in 2016, announced that it would undertake reform of the healthcare system to address this problem, which was a clear indication of its awareness of the problem. The Ministry of Health declared its plan to amend the Act on Health Care Services financed from public funds[45] to guarantee that each person using healthcare services within the scope of basic healthcare services would not incur the costs of the healthcare services provided to them, even if there were difficulties confirming their entitlement to those services.[46] Ultimately, however, no such reform was undertaken.

Therefore, in general interventions in 2017 and in 2018, the Ombudsman argued again that the health insurance system theoretically created the basis for coverage of the indicated groups of people but is dependent on going through a rigorous and complicated procedure. It is difficult to expect this from a person in homelessness crisis.

On this occasion, the Minister of Health did not agree with the RPO's concerns. In the opinion of the Minister, the challenges described by the Ombudsman did not result from the law, as the Act on Health Care Services financed from public funds does not limit access to healthcare services for people who are uninsured. The problem is, 'the aversion of the homeless to obtaining a decision from social assistance about the right to benefits'. (PL: '*Problemem jest niechęć osób bezdomnych do uzyskania decyzji z pomocy społecznej o prawie do świadczeń*'.) The procedure to be followed in specific cases may seem too formal; however, it is not aimed only at people in homelessness crisis but also at a wider group of citizens meeting income criteria referred to in the Social Welfare Act.[47]

---

44 General intervention dated 15 March 2016, ref. no. V.7010.17.2016, *Information on the activities of the Human Rights Commissioner in 2016 and the state of respect for human and civil liberties and rights* [PL: *Informacja o działalności Rzecznika Praw Obywatelskich w roku 2016 r. oraz o stanie przestrzegania wolności i praw człowieka i obywatela*] 263 <https://bip.brpo.gov.pl/sites/default/files/Informacja%20RPO%202016%20do%20druku.pdf> (accessed 1 September 2023).

45 Act on healthcare services financed from public funds of 27 August 2004, published in *Journal of Laws* from 2022, item 2561.

46 Ibid., Letter dated 3 August 2016.

47 General intervention dated 10 November 2017, ref. no. V.7010.82.2017, *Information on the activities of the Human Rights Commissioner in 2017 and the state of respect for human and civil liberties and rights* [PL: *Informacja o działalności Rzecznika Praw Obywatelskich w roku 2017 r. oraz o stanie przestrzegania wolności i praw człowieka i obywatela*] 364 <https://bip.brpo.gov.pl/sites/default/files/Informacja%20roczna%20RPO%20za%20rok%202017.pdf> (accessed 1 September 2023). General intervention dated 5 March 2018, ref. no. V.7010.17.2016, answer dated 5 April 2018, *Information on the activities of the Human Rights Commissioner in 2018 and the state of respect for human and civil liberties and rights* [PL: *Informacja o działalności Rzecznika Praw Obywatelskich w roku 2018 r. oraz o stanie*

The situation, therefore, remains systemically unresolved. As a result of this, a number of bottom-up, third-sector, and other voluntary initiatives have been taken, the best example of which is the functioning of a medical clinic in Kraków and Warsaw, run by doctors, where the homeless can get medical help and medicines for free.[48]

In another general intervention from 2019 referred to the ministry responsible for social affairs, the RPO highlighted the problem of providing homeless people with access to necessary healthcare services, medicines, and medical products after their discharge from hospital, shelters, and other facilities for the homeless. The Ombudsman pointed out that hospitals still refer people experiencing homelessness and requiring medical care either 'nowhere,' to the street, or to facilities unsuitable for accommodating people unable to take care of themselves. There are also problems with long-term care, including a protracted procedure of admission, especially for persons of undetermined identity, and those without an ID card, to care facilities, and to social welfare homes often resulting in the need for long-term and expensive hospitalization.[49]

In response, the Minister indicated that already in 2017, discussions were underway with the Ministry of Health, which supervises medical bodies, aimed at improving the functioning of the existing assistance system. During discussions, there was a strong emphasis on the need to improve cooperation between social assistance centres and hospital social services, especially as regards dependent patients leaving hospital. As a result, a letter was sent to all directors of general hospitals concerning the need to provide adequate care to needy people (in particular, the lonely or those deprived of the possibility of support in their existing environment) through placement in nursing and care facilities, especially when the person concerned requires intensive medical care.[50]

This problem, therefore, still remains unsettled. It has concrete implications for human life. In 2019, there was the death – widely reported publicly – of two homeless men discharged from hospital without shelter. This case is still under investigation by the Ombudsman.[51]

The Criminalization of Begging

One of the most fundamental problems faced by people in housing precarity in Poland is the criminalization of homelessness, or poverty more broadly. Although staying in public places or rough sleeping is not subject to penalty *per se*, certain everyday activities related

---

przestrzegania wolności i praw człowieka i obywatela] 291 <https://bip.brpo.gov.pl/sites/default/files/Informacja%20Roczna%20Rzecznika%20Praw%20Obywatelskich%20za%20rok%202018.pdf> (accessed 1 September 2023).

48 Cf websites <https://sln.org.pl/> (accessed 1 September 2023).
49 General intervention dated 8 March 2019, ref. no. III.7065.60.2019, *Information on the activities of the Human Rights Commissioner in 2019 and the state of respect for human and civil liberties and rights* [PL: *Informacja o działalności Rzecznika Praw Obywatelskich w roku 2019 r. oraz o stanie przestrzegania wolności i praw człowieka i obywatela*] 285 <https://bip.brpo.gov.pl/sites/default/files/INFORMACJA%20RPO%202019.pdf> (accessed 1 September 2023).
50 Ibid., letter dated 29 March 2019.
51 Cf: RPO press release: Citizen Rights Commissioner investigates death of two people in homelessness crisis who died in spring shortly after being discharged from Warsaw's Praga Hospital to a shelter [PL: *RPO wyjaśnia sprawę śmierci dwóch osób w kryzysie bezdomności, które zmarły wiosną wkrótce po wypisaniu ich z warszawskiego Szpitala Praskiego do schroniska*] <https://bip.brpo.gov.pl/pl/content/rpo-wyjasnia-sprawe-smierci-osob-w-kryzysie-bezdomnosci> (accessed 1 September 2023).

to life without a home are penalized, mainly by the Code of Petty Offences.[52] It is worth noting that the whole Code of Petty Offences was enacted under the previous Constitution, the Polish People's Republic of 1952, and therefore is based on a profoundly different axiology than the currently binding Constitution. The Code penalizes, inter alia, bathing in forbidden areas,[53] indecent behaviour in public spaces[54] (which could take the form of defecating in public areas, streets, passageways), and fouling and littering public places,[55] as well as begging in public places. The latter is worth paying a little more attention to, as a demand for its decriminalization has been publicly expressed.

According to Article 58 of the Code of Petty Offences, begging is committed if the perpetrator begs and (1) has a means of subsistence and (2) is able to work or (3) commits obtrusive or fraudulent begging.[56] In 2017, the Ombudsman, in his general intervention, requested decriminalization of the most basic form of begging (not obtrusive or fraudulent begging). The argument raised in his intervention was based on the disproportionality of the restriction of individual freedom by this provision.[57] As this intervention remains unanswered in 2021, after the ECtHR delivered the *Lăcătuş v Switzerland* judgment in 2021, the RPO issued another general intervention referring to this issue.[58]

In response to this intervention, the Minister of Justice did not share the Ombudsman's opinion that this form of begging (or any other) should be decriminalized. The Ministry declared that provision of Article 58 § 1 of the Code of Petty Offences indirectly created a pattern of behaviour desired by the legislator, which, at the same time, reflected a social attitude by which citizens were expected to show maturity and take responsibility for their own life, including actively securing means of subsistence for themselves in a manner that was socially acceptable.[59]

Positive Aspects in the Field of Homelessness Law and Policy

Although analysis of the annual information provided by the Ombudsman shows a rather negative, or at least, indifferent attitude of the illiberal authorities towards homeless people in Poland, it should be noted that the picture is not so clear-cut.

---

52 Code of Petty Offences of 20 May 1971, published in *Journal of Law* 2021, item. 2008.
53 See Article 55. This offence is subject to a fine of up to PLN 250 (approximately €60) or a reprimand.
54 Article 140 penalized by detention, the restriction of liberty, a fine of up to PLN 1,500 (approximately €365) or a reprimand.
55 Fouling and littering public places, in particular, roads, streets, squares, gardens, lawns, and green areas, is subject to a fine of up to PLN 500 (approximately €120) or a reprimand under Article 145 of the Code.
56 Liability for mere begging may consist of a fine of up to PLN 1,500 (approximately €365) or a reprimand. Liability for obtrusive or fraudulent begging may be the penalty of detention or restriction of liberty.
57 General intervention dated 29 November 2017, ref. no. II.501.7.2017, *Information on the activities of the Human Rights Commissioner in 2017 and the state of respect for human and civil liberties and rights* [PL: *Informacja o działalności Rzecznika Praw Obywatelskich w roku 2017 r. oraz o stanie przestrzegania wolności i praw człowieka i obywatela*] 364 <https://bip.brpo.gov.pl/sites/default/files/Informacja%20roczna%20RPO%20za%20rok%202017.pdf> (accessed 1 September 2023).
58 General intervention dated 23 January 2021, ref. no: II.501.7.2017.MM <https://bip.brpo.gov.pl/sites/default/files/Do_MS_ws_karania_zebractwa_23.01.2021.pdf> (accessed 1 September 2023).
59 Letter dated 6 April 2022 <https://bip.brpo.gov.pl/sites/default/files/2022-04/Odpowiedz_MS_06.04.2022.pdf> (accessed 1 September 2023).

In response to the Ombudsman's general intervention supported by the National Electoral Commission (PL: *Państwowa Komisja Wyborcza*), the Regulation of the Minister of Internal Affairs defining the rules of registering electors was changed. Presence on this register is a *sine qua non* condition in order to be able to vote in elections. Homeless people have struggled to be added to the electoral register due to the requirement to provide an address at which they reside. Amendments to the law introduced in 2018 have led to a situation where, in order to be added to the electoral register, it is sufficient to leave information on how to contact the voter without the need to provide an address.[60]

It should also be noted that every year the Ministry of Social Policy organizes a competition in which it allocates a sum of about 5 million PLN (about 1.1 million EUR) for activities of non-governmental organizations aimed at tackling and solving the problem of homelessness.

Concluding Observations: The Future of Homelessness Law and Policy in Poland – The Emerging Role of Cities in the Field of Homelessness

The Law and Justice Party in 2015 won the parliamentary and presidential elections in Poland with a special emphasis on social issues.[61] Therefore, one might expect that social policy would have been of particular interest to the institutions ruled by this party, and thus also the issue of homelessness. The analysis carried out in this chapter demonstrates that the eradication of homelessness was not a major issue of interest for the Law and Justice government. The legal obstacles in homelessness eradication policy highlighted by the Ombudsman, the resolution of which would, on the whole, not involve spending, have not been treated with due consideration.

At the same time, however, Law and Justice policy regarding homelessness was not so different from the policies of previous liberal governments. It must be noted that the homelessness prevention system in Poland has occasionally been evaluated by the Supreme Audit Office, an independent state audit body. In 2014 (that is, before Law and Justice came to power), the Supreme Audit Office found that assistance provided by the Polish state to the homeless was mainly of an interventionist and ad hoc nature, intensifying during autumn and winter. However, there is a lack of year-round, systemic activity supporting a way out of homelessness.[62] The evaluation undertaken in 2020 (that is, after five years of the Law and Justice government) was equally critical. The Supreme Audit Office noticed that the number of homeless people in Poland had been systematically decreasing for several years (between 2015 and 2020, it dropped by almost six thousand) but at the same time declared that it was impossible to determine to what extent this decrease was an effect of state

---

60 Cf: *Information on the activities of the Human Rights Commissioner in 2018 and the state of respect for human and civil liberties and rights* [PL: *Informacja o działalności Rzecznika Praw Obywatelskich w roku 2018 r. oraz o stanie przestrzegania wolności i praw człowieka i obywatela*] 237–38 <https://bip.brpo.gov.pl/sites/default/files/Informacja%20Roczna%20Rzecznika%20Praw%20Obywatelskich%20za%20rok%202018.pdf> (accessed 1 September 2023).
61 Cf: R. Markowski, 'Creating Authoritarian Clientelism: Poland After 2015' (2019) 11 *Hague Journal on the Rule of Law* 111.
62 Information on the results of the audit: Public Administration Activities in Support of the Homeless [PL: *Informacja o wynikach kontrolii: Działania administracji publicznej na rzecz bezdomnych*] (Warszawa 2014) <www.nik.gov.pl/plik/id,6740,vp,8559.pdf> (accessed 1 September 2023).

actions or resulted from other causes. According to the Supreme Audit Office, the homelessness prevention system, which consists of activities undertaken by the government and local government bodies as well as non-governmental organizations, was neither coherent nor effective. It did not provide the homeless with life chances and vocational stimulation which would enable them to achieve independence in life.[63]

At the same time, however, without observing an improvement in the situation of homelessness in Poland, it cannot be said that the situation of the homeless community has worsened. Therefore, there is a certain difference in the Polish government's approach to this issue from that of the Hungarian government.

In the context of Poland, one cannot ignore the phenomenon that is part of broader European trends related to the increasingly active role of cities in the arena of human rights implementation.[64] One may even risk a broader hypothesis, the confirmation or denial of which, however, requires deeper analysis, that this activity of cities, at least in Poland, increases in inverse proportion to the government's actions lowering human rights standards.

A demonstration of this broader trend is that some cities around Europe have adopted the Homeless Bill of Rights. This Bill is inspired by FEANTSA (the European Federation of National Organisations Working with the Homeless), a European non-governmental organization which, together with the Abbé Pierre Foundation, developed the model Homeless Bill of Rights. This Bill includes 11 rights, the most important of which is the right to exit homelessness. The Bill of Rights not only sets out a list of rights but also defines their scope and substance.[65]

In Poland, the idea of the Homeless Bill of Rights has gained strong support from the Ombudsman. At a press conference in 2018, the year of the local elections in Poland, the Ombudsman endorsed the idea of municipal adoption and implementation of the Bill. The RPO also developed and distributed a special leaflet addressing basic concerns about the concept and wording of the Bill.[66] The Bill was ultimately adopted by one Polish city, Gdańsk. Other municipalities, including Warsaw, the nation's capital, and Kraków, have publicly declared an intention to adopt the instrument and started work on a large scale that is to lead not only to the enactment of the Bill but also to its implementation in the local legal order.[67]

---

63 Information on the results of the audit: Actions Supporting and Activating the Homeless [PL: *Informacja o wynikach kontroli działania wspierające i aktywizujące osoby bezdomne*] (Warszawa 2020) <www.nik.gov.pl/plik/id,22486,vp,25161.pdf> (accessed 1 September 2023).
64 R. Hirschl, *City, State: Constitutionalism and the Megacity* (OUP 2020); B. Oomen, M. F. Davis and M. Grigolo (eds), *Global Urban Justice. The Rise of Human Rights Cities* (CUP 2016); M. Grigolo, *The Human Rights City, New York, San Francisco, Barcelona* (Routledge 2020).
65 The text of the Bill is available at the website of Housing Rights Watch <www.housingrightswatch.org/sites/default/files/Template%20Homeless%20Bill%20of%20Rights%20EN_0.pdf> (accessed 1 September 2023). On the Bill itself and its implementation by individual European cities, cf: A. Ploszka, 'A Homeless Bill of Rights as a New Instrument to Protect the Rights of Homeless Persons' (2020) 16(4) *European Constitutional Law Review* 601.
66 See the leaflet *Skuteczna pomoc w walce z kryzysem bezdomności, Karta Praw Osób Doświadczających Bezdomności- pytania i odpowiedzi* [Effective Assistance in Tackling the Homelessness Crisis, the Bill of Rights of Persons Experiencing Homelessness: Q&As] (Warsaw 2018).
67 See The Mayor of Warsaw's response to the Ombudsman's intervention letter concerning the adoption of the Warsaw Homeless Bill or Rights, dated 13 December 2019, available online at the Ombudsman's

The activities of selected cities in Poland are not limited to the adoption or consideration of the Bill but have a broader, more practical dimension. In addition to fulfilling the legal obligations of communes to prevent homelessness and provide support to the homeless, cities also undertake certain innovative solutions to the problem of homelessness, such as implementing programmes based on the idea of Housing First and creating assistance in the form of intervention hostels as a response to the growing problem of homelessness in the LGBT+ community.[68] These are just a few examples of the many innovative initiatives.

In conclusion, one might draw attention to a recurring retort often heard in Polish public debate, namely, the yardstick of humanity, and how this yardstick is or is not being engaged in support of the most vulnerable in Polish society. The application of this yardstick to state policy on homelessness may lead to a pessimistic assessment of the state of humanity in Poland. However, thanks to, among other things, the activities of the Ombudsman examined in this chapter, one can observe a change in the social perception of homelessness, breaking down certain stereotypes, including perhaps the fundamental and pervasive stereotype that homelessness is a personal choice. This shift in perception can be seen, for example, in changes of language in the public debate which more and more is referencing the concept of 'homelessness crisis' or 'the experience of homelessness' rather than merely 'homelessness' alone. A deeper societal understanding of homelessness and the need to eradicate it is therefore emerging and increasingly featuring in Polish public discourse. This allows, tentatively, and with cautious optimism, for a hypothesis to be formed that change in the perception of homelessness in the country may, in the future, translate into more active and effective state policy on ending homelessness in Poland.

---

website <https://bip.brpo.gov.pl/pl/content/rpo-czy-warszawa-podpisze-karte-praw-osob-doswiadczajacych-bezdomnosci> (accessed 1 September 2023). as well as The Mayor of Kraków's response, dated 16 September 2021, available online at the Ombudsman's website <https://bip.brpo.gov.pl/pl/content/miejska-karta-praw-osoby-doswiadczajacej-bezdomnosci-rpo-pisze-do-prezesa-zarzadu-zwiazku> (accessed 1 September 2023).

68 Such hostels have been created in Poznan and Warsaw. Cf: The report 'The social situation of LGBTA people in Poland. Report for 2019–2020' produced by the Campaign Against Homophobia and Lambda Warsaw Association [PL: *raport 'Sytuacja społeczna osób LGBTA w Polsce. Raport za lata 2019–2020' sporządzony przez Kampania Przeciw Homofobii oraz Stowarzyszenie Lambda Warszawa.*] <https://kph.org.pl/wp-content/uploads/2021/12/Rapot_Duzy_Digital-1.pdf> (accessed 1 September 2023).

12
HOMELESSNESS IN SWITZERLAND

Federalist Pathways Between Ignoring, Passing on Responsibility for, and Proactive Prevention of Homelessness

Matthias Drilling, Magdalena Küng, and Jörg Dittmann

Introduction

Homelessness is a poorly discussed topic in Switzerland. And yet people who sleep on the streets, who beg or look for a place to sleep at night, are increasingly part of urban society in the country. In order to raise public and political awareness of the issue through research activities, the authors of this chapter began some years ago by addressing the issue through national research, through EU networks, and in the context of social work education. In order to offer insights into the state of and responses to homelessness in Switzerland, this chapter draws on some of the authors' own studies to give as comprehensive an account as possible of the homelessness landscape in Switzerland. The chapter is structured accordingly: the first section provides an overview of homelessness in Switzerland, how it is researched and tackled. In so doing, this section reveals a lack of clarity in both the definition of homelessness and the availability of reliable data on homelessness in Switzerland – this despite there being a number of Swiss national laws pertaining to the issue. This first section also explores how, in Switzerland, responsibility for homelessness is constantly shifting between the federal government, the cantons, and the municipalities. In the second part, a historical perspective is taken, and justifications provided as to why homelessness in Switzerland has, until relatively recently, been of such little interest in Parliament and politics. Links are made, above all, to drug policy and how homelessness has hitherto mainly affected young people with substance addiction. In the third section, the current legal and policy framework on homelessness in Switzerland is examined. It does so by presenting two recent studies that could act as changemakers for policy in Switzerland: a first national census of homelessness and a national study on the approach of cantons and municipalities. Both studies provide a basis for revisiting the issue of homelessness from an evidence-based perspective and, additionally, for justifying legal reforms that provide entitlements and protections for people without a place to live. The section also discusses examples of homelessness preventative practice in Switzerland. In the final section, the chapter turns to consider the future of homelessness law and policy in the country.

Matthias Drilling, Magdalena Küng, and Jörg Dittmann

Homelessness in Switzerland

A Lack of Definition of Homelessness

Switzerland has no official definition of *homelessness* – something that is not unusual in Europe, as the report of the European Social Policy Network ESPN identifies.[1] As a result, calculating the true number of homeless people in Switzerland proves challenging, as estimations vary wildly depending on the understanding of homelessness engaged, with numbers ranging enormously from 900 to 3,000 people, to 28,000 (on a broad conception of people who have been homelessness at any point during their lifetime). At times, no attempt at all has been made to measure the scale of the issue in Switzerland on the basis that it is simply too difficult to capture.[2] The lack of clarity and definition has various consequences for Switzerland including that an internationally comparable assessment of the problem becomes almost impossible due to the incomparability of locally collected figures that do not represent or reflect the national picture. At the national level, the lack of a definition of homelessness makes it difficult to legislate and thus to secure entitlements for those affected. On the other hand, Switzerland is a Federal Republic comprised of 26 cantons or 'states', under which sit 2,131 municipalities (as of January 2024), which are the lowest level of administrative division in the country. At the cantonal and municipal level, it, therefore, becomes impossible to compare existing statistics from homelessness services and thus clarify the extent and profile of homelessness even in the same city.

Nevertheless, and despite the fact that the legal subject of the 'homeless person' does not exist in any legally defined sense in Switzerland, homeless people do have certain subjective rights, including some that are linked to the right to accommodation. The Swiss Federal Constitution (FC) guarantees all people in Switzerland, regardless of their residence status, two basic social rights that guarantee certain state benefits in the form of individual legal protections. These are the right to assistance in emergency situations (Article 12 FC) and the right to primary education (Article 19 FC). Article 12 of the Federal Constitution is directly relevant to the issue of homelessness, since, as a fundamental right, it establishes 'subjective, directly applicable and, in principle, judicially enforceable claims to certain benefits of the community'. However, the right to assistance in emergency situations only guarantees those benefits that are essential for a dignified existence and prevents those affected from falling into a so-called 'undignified beggar's existence'.[3] Thus, anyone who is objectively able to provide for themselves does not fulfil the requirements of Article 12 and cannot make a claim under it. Moreover, the emergency assistance article does not establish any concrete benefits, such as a basic income.[4] In practice, Article 12 is applied primarily in the area of asylum and in the case of foreign nationals without a right of residency in Switzerland. According to Article 80, para. 1, of the Integration and Asylum Act (AIG),[5] the cantons are responsible for its implementation.

---

1 I. Baptista and E. Marlier, *Fighting Homelessness and Housing Exclusion in Europe: A Study of National Policies* (Synthesis Report, European Social Policy Network 2019).
2 See the discussion in Section 3.1.
3 BGE 131 I 166, 172.
4 SODK (2012): Zur Nothilfe für Ausreisepflichtige Personen des Asylbereichs (Nothilfeempfehlungen) vom 29. Juni 2012 <https://ch-sodk.s3.amazonaws.com/media/files/2012.06.29_Nothilfeempfehlungen_sw_d_WEB.pdf 10> (accessed 1 September 2023).
5 Bundesgesetz über die Ausländerinnen und Ausländer und über die Integration, see <https://fedlex.data.admin.ch/filestore/fedlex.data.admin.ch/eli/cc/2007/758/20200401/de/pdf-a/fedlex-data-admin-ch-eli-cc-2007-758-20200401-de-pdf-a.pdf> (accessed 1 September 2023).

In addition to the fact that the Federal Constitution recognizes few individual social rights, there is the issue of the justiciability of these norms. Justiciability presupposes a certain degree of political consensus as to what the content of a norm should be, or what rights it grants. Müller has argued that a right to housing can never be concretized because no quantitative and qualitative criteria can be found that would allow a court to make a precise judgement. It is impossible for a court to decide which housing is appropriate and for whom.[6] In contrary logic to the assumption that constitutional norms only make sense if their enforceability is clarified, there are repeated voices advocating a right to housing in a programmatic way, that anchoring a right to decent housing in the Federal Constitution should oblige the state to become active in the area of housing provision and to develop programmes that tackle homelessness and precarious housing situations. The fact that there is no nationally recognized, justiciable right to housing in Switzerland is, then, also frequently criticized, both nationally and internationally.[7] As has been argued in this section, at the federal level, there is no law that specifically deals with the prevention of homelessness. However, that is not to say there are no legal protections or no legal references to homelessness in Swiss law. What follows is a brief overview of the legal foundations that are relevant for the protection of people who are threatened or affected by homelessness in Switzerland. This begins with a discussion of Switzerland's welfare state as it pertains to homelessness.

Switzerland as a Welfare State

There are no provisions in the Federal Constitution that would define Switzerland as a welfare state. Nevertheless, the Federal Constitution contains various elements that are reflective of a welfare state. Regardless of the absence of specific mention of the idea of the 'welfare state', however, it is clear that the idea of the welfare state must be an inherent part of a modern understanding of any democracy:

> A state that guarantees people legal equality, respects their rights of freedom, provides procedures based on the rule of law and allows its citizens to participate in important political decisions, but does not care whether the actual conditions for exercising these rights are also met, is not fully fulfilling its task. Today, Switzerland has a duty to provide its citizens with a certain degree of social security and thus to create the basis for ensuring that equality of rights and other rights do not remain mere theory.[8]

Any discussion of a state's obligations pertaining to social welfare must raise the issue of homelessness, because the consequences of threatened or a loss of secure housing have far-reaching consequences for citizens beyond just the arena of housing; various other rights protected by the constitution are engaged (e.g. rights of freedom, democratic participation, etc.). Securing livelihoods must not only be limited to averting material hardship but must

---

6 J. P. Müller, *Soziale Grundrechte in der Verfassung?* (Helbing & Lichtenhahn 1981) 21.
7 M. Drilling, E. Mühlethaler and G. Iyadural, *First Country Report on Homelessness Switzerland* (Institute for Social Planning, Organisational Change and Urban Development, ISOS 2020) 19.
8 U. Häfelin, W. Haller and H. Keller, *Schweizerisches Bundesrecht* (Schulthess Verlag 2012) 56.

also 'enable a minimum level of participation in social and societal life'.[9] Switzerland is therefore obliged to ensure that all people are provided with the actual conditions necessary to be able to exercise their rights. Among the welfare state components in the Federal Constitution are the regulations on competence in various social areas (Section 8 of the Federal Constitution, 'Housing, work, social security and health'), but also the preamble, the article on the 'aims' of the Constitution, the programmatic social goals, and the obligation of the economy to serve the common interest (Article 94, para. 2, Federal Constitution).[10] The idea of the welfare state as a guarantor of freedom and equality rights also manifests itself 'in the inclusion of norms with a social component in the most diverse areas of law'.[11] Such elements can be found in tenancy law, labour law, or assistance for victims of (domestic) violence.[12] Issues of housing and homelessness are usually categorized under the legal field of social security, which can be divided into social insurance law and social assistance law. However, because other areas of law can also have social elements, other laws that relate to housing issues must be considered in addition to the classic laws pertaining to social security – that is, social and emergency assistance. To sum up: Switzerland provides a welfare state, but not all the aspects of welfare are in the responsibility of the federal state (see following sections).

The Cantons as Responsible Bodies

Switzerland is a federalist constitution, which means that the federal state, the cantons, and the municipalities are in close collaboration and, together, constitute the welfare system. While preventing and combating unemployment is a state task, tackling homelessness is one of the tasks of the cantons and municipalities (Federal Constitution Article 115 FC). Article 115 FC is a so-called 'competence norm', which imposes a constitutional duty on the cantons to organize support for people in need in their canton area. In this respect, the federal state only assumes the competence to regulate exceptional circumstances. The state does the latter in the Federal Act on the Competence of Assistance to People in Need (ZUG). This Act determines which canton is specifically responsible and regulates the reimbursement of support costs among the cantons (Article 1, para. 1 and 2 ZUG). The ZUG defines as 'in need' anyone who cannot adequately or in a timely manner provide for his or her subsistence from his or her own resources. According to common understanding, subsistence also includes accommodation. Need is assessed according to the regulations and principles applicable at the place of support (Article 2, paras. 1 and 2 ZUG). If persons with Swiss citizenship are in need of immediate assistance outside their canton of residence, the canton of residence must provide this (Article 13, para. 1 ZUG). Furthermore, the canton of residence reimburses the costs of emergency assistance to the canton that supports those in need (Article 14, para. 1 ZUG). Finally, the canton of residence that supports the

---

9 P. Coullery, 'Der Anspruch auf existenzsichernde Leistungen und seine verfassungsrechtlichen Grundlagen. Rechtsgutachten zuhanden der Schweizerischen Konferenz für Sozialhilfe' (2018) <www.soziothek.ch/der-anspruch-auf-existenzsichernde-leistungen-und-seine-verfassungsrechtlichen-grundlagen 18 (accessed 1 September 2023).
10 U. Kieser, *Schweizerisches Sozialversicherungsrecht* (Dike 2017) 20.
11 Ibid. 1.
12 C. Häfeli, *Das Schweizerische Sozialhilferecht. Rechtsgrundlagen und Rechtssprechung* (Interact Verlag für Soziales und Kulturelles 2008) 16.

person in need in an emergency and demands reimbursement of the costs from the canton of residence must notify the canton of the case for support as soon as possible (Article 30, para. 1 ZUG). The regulations of the ZUG, therefore, allow for support for homeless people regardless of whether they claim assistance in their own canton or in another canton. The cost recovery system also establishes contact between the cantons (or, if they are the implementing authorities, the municipalities). Such contacts are considered extremely valuable in fostering joint strategic development in terms of providing meaningful assistance to the homeless.

The Institution of Social Assistance

One of the most important pillars of the Swiss welfare system is social assistance. Individual social assistance can be divided into personal and material or economic social assistance.[13] Personal social assistance essentially consists of counselling and can be granted even if there is no entitlement to material social assistance. The cantons are responsible for the organization of social assistance. Because they are responsible for social assistance, it is regulated by cantonal social assistance laws. These laws differ both in how assistance is set up and in the division of competences between the cantons and municipalities. In some cantons, social assistance is fully the responsibility of the canton, while others have extensive communal autonomy and corresponding communal social services. There is no federal law on social assistance.

Providing suitable accommodation is one of the tasks of social assistance, and housing costs are a significant part of material social assistance. Therefore, municipal social assistance is the central point of contact for people who are threatened or affected by homelessness. However, this only applies to citizens who live or have lived in the municipality previously. Anyone who becomes homeless and leaves the municipality where they previously lived ends up in limbo because no municipal service is available, and nothing more than emergency assistance is offered. However, even those who are helped are expected to live as cheaply as possible. Children are not entitled to a room of their own.[14] However, even modest living conditions place a heavy burden on a household budget. In addition to questions of housing costs, housing security and quality are also regular problems for social assistance recipients.[15] It would be wrong to assume that all people living in a precarious housing situation are entitled to social assistance because there are prerequisites, like Swiss nationality, citizenship, or a specific duration of labour market experience. In addition, it is quite commonplace that people in need are not aware of their right to social assistance. The Swiss Conference for Social Welfare (SKOS)[16] notes that since the tightening of the Foreigners and Integration Act, foreigners in need are increasingly deregistering from social

---

13 C. Hänzi, 'Leistungen der Sozialhilfe in den Kantonen' in Häfeli (n 12) 91.
14 SKOS Richtlinien: Wohnen <https://rl.skos.ch/lexoverview-home/lex-RL_A_1> (accessed 1 September 2023).
15 SKOS, 'Grundlagenpapier Wohnen. Herausforderungen und Handlungsansätze aus Sicht der Sozialhilfe' (2020) 2 <https://skos.ch/fileadmin/user_upload/skos_main/public/pdf/grundlagen_und_positionen/grundlagen_und_studien/2020_Grundlagendokument_Wohnen.pdf> (accessed 1 September 2023).
16 The Swiss Conference for Social Welfare SKOS is the national professional association for social welfare. Members of the SKOS are all cantons, many municipalities, various federal offices, and private social welfare organizations. The SKOS is committed to the design and development of fair and effective social assistance in Switzerland.

assistance because they are concerned about their residence rights. This failure to receive due benefits means that social assistance can no longer fully perform its task of promoting social integration, with the result that healthcare and individuals' housing situation are jeopardized.[17]

Housing Promotion

The Housing Promotion Act of 2003 has two objectives: firstly, it aims to create more housing for low-income households, and secondly, it aims to promote access to homeownership. The provisions of the Act are intended to benefit families, single parents, people with disabilities, elderly people in need, and people in education. The Federal Ministry of Housing has initiated various programmes based on the Housing Promotion Act. These provide a basis for increasing the number of non-profit housing units in Switzerland. For people who are affected or threatened by homelessness, this programme is probably out of reach. However, they can benefit from the Housing Promotion Act if housing is created that is reserved for people who have difficulties securing housing on their own.

Historical Pathways: Homelessness in Swiss Parliamentary Debates

In order to inform discussion of the Swiss contemporary approach to homelessness, the historical political debates around homelessness are, in this section, placed in context. For a very long time, homelessness was not discussed in the Swiss Parliament.[18] This changed in 1955, when the popular initiative[19] 'for the protection of tenants and consumers (continuation of price control)' was accepted by the population. This concluded a phase of closer political framing of housing supply and numerous target group–specific protection goals. Some 15 years later, the 'Referendum for the Right to Housing and the Extension of Family Protection' (1970)[20] was rejected. The popular initiative called for a right to housing to be enshrined in the Constitution: 'The Confederation recognises the right to housing and takes the necessary measures to safeguard it so that families and individuals can obtain housing that meets their needs and whose rent or costs do not exceed their financial capacity.'[21] Although the scale of construction increased in the 1970s, the situation of residential construction remained strained. The tensions between a capitalist-oriented housing industry, the liberal state organs, and numerous critical Marxist university institutes made

---

17 SKOS, 'Anpassungen bei der Sozialhilfe für Personen aus Drittstaaten' (2020) 1 <https://skos.ch/fileadmin/user_upload/skos_main/public/pdf/grundlagen_und_positionen/positionen/2020_Stellungnahme_Sozialhilfe-Drittstaaten.pdf> (accessed 1 September 2023).
18 For detailed information about parliamentary debates up to the 1960s, see Drilling, Mühlethaler and Iyadural (n 7).
19 In Switzerland, the *popular initiative* describes the political right to obtain a desired constitutional amendment. As the term implies, popular initiatives originate from the people, including citizens, parties, or interest groups, excluding parliament and the government itself.
20 Federal laws and other enactments of the Federal Assembly are subject to an optional referendum in accordance with Article 141 of the Federal Constitution. The vast majority of laws and enactments come into force without first being the subject of a referendum. However, if Swiss citizens gather 50,000 signatures within 100 days of the publication of a new law, a national referendum will be held. The referendum is therefore a cornerstone of direct democracy in Switzerland.
21 Drilling, Mühlethaler and Iyadural (n 7) 28.

the question of interventionist measures by the state an object of keen debate. As a result, the wholesale company *Denner* supported a referendum to set up a housing fund (Denner Initiative) 'from which mortgage loans with low, socially graded interest rates for the construction of apartments and old people's homes as well as contributions to the development of building land were to be paid'.[22] But even this petition for a referendum was rejected in favour of a counter-proposal, which only spoke of 'granting the federal government general competence to promote housing construction and the acquisition of residential property and house ownership'.[23] However, the intention to keep the development of rents as the focus of social policy led to another popular initiative in 1977.[24] Here, too, the focus was on the protection of tenants, with rent controls and making termination of tenancy agreements more complex. But this popular initiative 'for effective tenant protection' was also rejected on 25 September 1977.

A first National Council meeting took place between the two referendums, during which homelessness was addressed directly. Via an agenda item 'Narcotics Change' on 10 October 1974, parliamentarian Bratschi introduced the idea of emergency shelter and opened the debate on the link between drug consumption and homelessness that continued in Switzerland until the 1990s:

> An emergency shelter, called 'Sleep-in', also accommodates 30 young people night after night. For them, the 'sleep-in' should not be the final destination; it is, however, because there are no corresponding cantonal institutions that could take over this care task. We can only be dismayed and simply state: the drug wave has overrun us.[25]

Since the 1980s, parliamentary activity, debates, and popular initiatives have vacillated widely on a regular basis on the issues of low-cost housing, protection of tenants, and homelessness on the one hand, and drug consumption problems, homelessness, and support on the other. The success of initiatives in the area of rent protection remained limited. On 21 March 1986, the popular initiative 'For an effective tenant protection' was rejected; in 1999, the federal initiative 'Homeownership for all'; in 2003, the popular initiative 'Yes to fair rents'; and on 23 December 2012, the popular initiative 'Secure living in old age' also all failed. The issue of homelessness in these years was primarily tackled as a problem of drug consumption and no longer as an issue of housing construction, as it had been in previously. By way of cost estimates in the National Council meeting of 18 June 1992, parliamentarian Leemann highlighted the 3.1 million Swiss francs demanded for preventive measures in the field of drug addiction and advanced an argument for conformity of approach with homelessness support and with simultaneous action by the Confederation and the cantons.[26] Parliamentarian Plattner's suggestion concerning help for the homeless in the field of drug prevention was again raised on 3 October 1994. On the occasion of the popular initiatives 'Youth without Drugs' and 'For a Sensible Drug Policy' (Droleg-Initiative),

---

22 <https://anneepolitique.swiss/APS/de/APS_1972/APS1972_I_6_c_2_print.html> (accessed 1 September 2023).
23 Ibid.
24 Drilling, Mühlethaler and Iyadural (n 7) 28.
25 Ibid. 29.
26 Ibid.

parliamentarian Gysin linked the issue of homelessness even more clearly with drug policy in the National Council on 21 March 1996:

> We have a viable, integrated four-pillar model, as it is on the table at the Federal Government. We've been living this in Basel for six to seven years. We have well-developed, functioning survival support with three drug consuming rooms, emergency sleeping places, soup kitchens, day structures and other institutions.[27]

And in the late summer of the same year, Plattner renewed his idea in the Upper Chamber (17 September 1996) that drug prevention was, above all, also effective as a means of helping the homeless. In this context, two documents are relevant, which refer to the accommodation of homeless people with an addiction illness (Motion Bischof of 3 June 1992 and Motion Dormann of 6 December 1993). These two documents demonstrate the narrow definition of homelessness adopted at that time in that it was mainly related to drug consumption. The National Council argued for a further push and action on the topic of homelessness through a motion by Leutenegger Oberholzer for the 'Federal Housing Decree' of 21 March 1991 and the de Dardel motion of 9 March 1993. Leutenegger Oberholzer pleaded for 'fifteen percent of this to be used specifically for the housing supply for socially disadvantaged population groups and their specific housing needs'.[28] The parliament withdrew the application after a debate. The de Dardel motion,[29] which was submitted to the National Council on 12 December 1993, also did not proceed any further. Under the title 'People without Permanent Residence and the Right to Housing', de Dardel asked the Federal Council to include the right to housing as a political objective and to enshrine it in the Federal Constitution.

It was a further ten years, however, before the issue of homelessness would be more widely discussed in the National Council again. On 23 September 2014, parliamentarian Marra submitted an interpellation titled 'Emergency Shelters for the Homeless in Switzerland'. With its questions to the Federal Council, it catapulted the issue of homelessness to the institutional level, in particular, the issue of the division of action between the Confederation and the cantons. It saw the people concerned as being torn between these two governmental levels. Marra thus addressed the following issue:

> There are, however, great differences between the cities in terms of policy in this area. Some do not shy away from 'sending' their homeless to other cantons where emergency shelter places might be offered. In most cases, this depends on the social policy of the city or canton. Article 12 of the Federal Constitution, however, states: 'Anyone who finds himself in need and is unable to take care of himself is entitled to assistance and care and to the means which are indispensable for a decent existence.' Marra asked whether it was 'normal' for 'certain cities to fulfil their duty by taking on this task as their responsibility, while others simply sit back and rely on the existing offer?'[30]

27 Ibid.
28 Ibid. 30.
29 Ibid.
30 Ibid. 30f.

Homelessness in Switzerland

In its reply, the Federal Council rejected any responsibility. It played down the problem by writing that 'the homeless are part of the reality of Swiss cities' and admitted that it had 'no overall view of the situation in the cities' and 'therefore cannot comment on the practice of referring to other cities'.[31] The Federal Council also did not consider the lack of national data as grounds for a new survey and hoped that the 'Conference of Cantonal Social Directors (SODK) will deal with the subject'.[32] On 12 December 2014, the motion was archived as completed. Two years later, Marra passed a postulate on the same topic under the title 'emergency sleeping places'. She wanted to know from the Federal Council how the SODK or other bodies of federal social policy had dealt with this issue.[33] In its reply, the Federal Council made it clear that there was no need for action in the context of the National Dialogue on Swiss Social Policy: 'We have thematised the issue in this context, but I must also point out that no need for intervention was ultimately identified.'[34] In the years that followed and to date, homelessness has not been discussed in the Parliament. The last interpellation was in 2016, when parliamentarian Addor asked if 'asylum seekers are preferred to our homeless'.[35] The Federal Council replied that due to the lack of data, it was impossible to answer the question.

The Current Legal and Policy Framework Pertaining to Homelessness in Switzerland

As explained so far, the approach to addressing homelessness in Switzerland is strongly concentrated in the cantons and municipalities. How they tackle the issue will be explored in this section of the chapter by engaging two recent case studies: the first study, Dittmann et al. 2022,[36] measured the extent of homelessness in the eight largest cities in Switzerland. This was the first time that figures on the extent and profile of homelessness were made available in Switzerland. A second study, Drilling et al. 2022,[37] conducted a survey of all the then 2,160 municipalities in Switzerland and identified the scale of the homelessness problem and how the municipalities act to prevent and combat homelessness. Taken together, these two studies offer a vital insight into the state of homelessness in contemporary Switzerland.

Defining the Problem: Homelessness as Connected with Social Rights

The results of the survey by Dittmann et al. which was conducted in December 2020 and March 2021 focused on the eight of the largest cities in Switzerland and surveyed the users

---

31 Ibid. 31.
32 Ibid.
33 Ibid.
34 <www.parlament.ch/de/ratsbetrieb/amtliches-bulletin/amtliches-bulletin-die-verhandlungen?SubjectId=38944#votum2> (accessed 1 September 2023).
35 Drilling, Mühlethaler and Iaduraj (n 7) 31.
36 J. Dittmann and others, 'Ausmass, Profil und Erklärungen der Obdachlosigkeit in acht der grössten Städte der Schweiz' (2022) LIVES Working Paper 93 <www.centre-lives.ch/sites/default/files/2022-09/93_2022%20Forschungsbericht_OBDACH_Dittmann_Dietrich_Stroezel_Drilling%20-%20formatted%20-%20with%20authorship%20changes.pdf> (accessed 1 September 2023).
37 M. Drilling and others, *Obdachlosigkeit in der Schweiz. Verständnisse, Politiken und Strategien von Kantonen und Gemeinden* (Bundesamt für Wohnungswesen 2022) <www.bwo.admin.ch/bwo/de/home/wie-wir-wohnen/wohnen-und-armut/publikationen-bwo/obdachlosigkeit.html> (accessed 1 September 2023).

of 62 care structures. Due to the lack of a definition of homelessness, the study used the ETHOS categories of homelessness and exclusion from the housing market (developed by FEANTSA in 2017).[38] A total of 1,182 people were interviewed on the day of the census. Of these, 46% were homeless 38.5% were sleeping rough, and the remaining 61.5% were sleeping in an emergency shelter on the day of the survey. Although the total number of people experiencing homelessness extrapolated from these figures seems low compared to other European countries (depending on the extrapolation model, the estimate varies between 918 and 2,740 people sleeping outside or in an emergency shelter on an ordinary day in December 2020 in Switzerland), the study also revealed another finding: 80% of all 1,182 respondents had already experienced one of the two forms of homelessness during their lives. Homelessness in Switzerland is thus associated with a revolving door effect, although the study could not determine how long the respective states of housing insecurity and homelessness lasted and how frequently they changed. As far as experiences of homelessness over a lifetime are concerned, the authors of the study, using the EU-SILC, estimated that '28,718 people in Switzerland have been homeless (at least) once during their lives'.[39] So while 0.02% of the population in Switzerland is currently homeless (for comparison, in Germany it is said to be 0.44%),[40] 0.4% of the total population in Switzerland has experienced homelessness. The survey also indicated that the distribution of homeless people varies greatly within the participating cities. The highest number of homeless people was found in Geneva. For every 100,000 inhabitants (aged 18 and over), 210 people were homeless there, while in Lausanne, the figure was 150. The cities of Bern (58), Basel (46), and Lugano (38) followed somewhat behind these figures. After that came Zurich, Switzerland's largest city in terms of population, with 29 homeless people per 100,000 inhabitants. Lucerne and St. Gallen had the lowest numbers of homeless people in the city comparison exercise. Concerning the profile of homeless people, the survey identified a strong link between homelessness and migration policy: only 16.8% of the homeless people were Swiss nationals, and 83.2% had a foreign nationality. Of the immigrants, the majority reported being from Romania (19.5%), Nigeria (11.5%), and Algeria (9.1%). Immigrants are therefore shown to be significantly more likely to be homeless than one may anticipate from the demographic data – immigrants representing 26% of the permanent resident population of Switzerland. Of the respondents, 61.1% reported having no official residence status. They are considered 'sans-papiers'. The 2022 study by Dittmann et al. thus clearly identified that the legal and political framework relating to homelessness in Switzerland should therefore be oriented towards the right of residence.

Geography Matters

The 2022 research conducted by Drilling et al. explored how the cantons and municipalities, as bodies of the state, act to combat and prevent homelessness. In addition, the study also addressed the threat of losing housing and explored the potential preliminary stages of homelessness, that is, precarious, insecure, and inadequate housing. The survey of the

---

38 FEANTSA 2017: European Typology of Homelessness and Housing Exclusion <www.feantsa.org/download/ethos2484215748748239888.pdf> (accessed 1 September 2023).
39 Dittmann (n 24).
40 Ibid.

cantons showed that they generally recognized that the prevention and combating of homelessness was the responsibility of the state. However, the implementation in this regard varied greatly. Very few cantons had developed an overall assistance system or even a policy field towards homelessness, which meant that the extent and scale of homelessness and its precursors were only vaguely known. Many experts in the cantonal administrations consider support to be closely linked to social assistance, which is why homelessness is primarily tackled through the structures of social and emergency assistance and thus a problem of individuals (instead of a structural problem, such as the housing market). This reaches its limits when people do not meet the eligibility criteria for social assistance or do not come forward. On the other hand, the cantons have established several best practices, ranging from regional cooperation to cantonal housing provision and strengthening social planning approaches. The survey of municipalities demonstrated that homelessness and the threat of losing housing could be estimated in terms of numbers. Homelessness was found to be mainly a challenge for municipalities in large- and medium-sized agglomerations, especially for the six Swiss cities with more than 100,000 inhabitants (in line with the Dittmann et al. study discussed earlier). But as a country characterized by significant divergences between rural and urban areas, the municipalities in Switzerland are affected very differently. Therefore, the study was based on a typology of the Federal Office for Spatial Planning, which distinguishes between urban, peri-urban, and rural areas and assesses the municipalities according to their centrality (centrality, for example, in terms of a concentration of jobs, affordable and rental housing, transport hubs, shopping centres of regional importance). Here it was evident that municipalities with a high centrality function were more or less equally affected by the issue of homelessness, regardless of whether they were located in a rural, peri-urban, or urban area. Thus, the functional importance of a municipality in terms of its economic, social, or cultural centrality as well as its housing market could therefore be key pull factors of homelessness. This aligned with the answers from respondents which indicated that the higher a municipality estimated the number of people living in homelessness or threatened by losing their homes in its municipality area, the more strained they assessed the housing market in that municipality as being.

Dealing with the threat of loss of housing is also a key task in municipalities, in particular those in peri-urban and rural areas. The municipalities acknowledged their limitations in combating homelessness and threatened loss of housing: most municipalities do not have their own accommodation facilities; cooperation is rare, and support from the cantons and the federal government is not guaranteed. At the same time, the municipalities do formulate access criteria for their assistance, criteria which themselves can lead to exclusion and migration problems. The Drilling et al. study, therefore, demonstrated that a strategy to combat homelessness must also deal with spatial planning and geographical matters if it is to succeed.

Legal Framework in Most Affected Cities: Three Types of State Responsibility

Based on the results of the 2022 Drilling et al. study, the authors developed a typology that seeks to inform analysis of the homelessness situation in Switzerland by describing what is happening today on the ground. Key axes of the typology are the interplay of state and non-state actors, the distribution of responsibility, and the role of state entities. The typology describes ideal, system 'types'. While these 'types' cannot be found as such in the field, they are identified and are to be understood and deployed as idealized, summarizing systems to be used as guiding frameworks in assessing and responding to homelessness in Switzerland.

The first type identified is 'absence of a state assistance system' and is characterized by the complete structural absence of a state. Intervention by authorities in favour of people without shelter or in precarious housing situations can take place, but it has no influence on the structures of the welfare state. There is no state disposition; the state does not proactively intervene to provide accommodation to those affected. In type 1, the state only provides the minimum that the law obliges it to do and provides temporary accommodation in emergency situations. Type 1 is also characterized by the fact that there is no institutionalized, plannable procedure for how the state deals with homelessness. There are no predefined procedures. Rather, when confronted with a situation of homelessness, the authorities spontaneously activate their private contacts to support those affected. Just as there are no predetermined procedures for establishing contact between the authorities and the affected person or group of persons, there are no official points of contact in an informal assistance system. Contact with the authorities must be made by the persons concerned themselves, for example, by telephone or e-mail. Contact can also be arranged through third parties, for example, a relief organization, a church, or where a private person brings the case to the attention of the authorities. Whether the authority then approaches the person directly or is referred by a third party is irrelevant for this type. The only characteristic of communication in this assistance system is that the communication that takes place activates and involves the authorities themselves. The lack of predefined assistance results in the service being offered as strongly determined by the network of the people who take over the case. Personal contacts, experience, existing informal networks with aid organizations and churches, as well as the individual assessment of the situation are more important here than in other systems. Ad hoc solutions such as renting a holiday home or resorting to unused living spaces that the authorities know about through their private networks are not uncommon.

In the second type, 'system with state involvement', the state plays a more active role, but without establishing a corresponding field of services. The involvement takes the form of an exchange with those organizations that are operationally active in the field of homelessness assistance in the canton, triaging activities between these organizations and those affected, and offering financial support for organizations. The authorities take on the task of ensuring that the services provided by voluntary organizations and private individuals do not have to be discontinued due to financial bottlenecks. This kind of support can take various forms, depending on what the organizations in the support system need: service contracts for specific services, providing spaces for shelters, providing land for housing projects, financing projects, providing networking opportunities, providing information, materials and basic documents, support for the development or further development of wider strategies. Common to all assistance provided by the state is that in this type 2 of assistance, the concrete needs of the implementing agencies are addressed. It is characteristic here that the state only becomes active when it has knowledge of the needs of the help system. It does not act proactively. The authorities do not specify which services have to be provided but build on the existing network of services and secure it through their involvement. The state also does not motivate the further development of existing services but can respond if this is identified as an area of need. The involvement of the authorities also has a formative, consolidating effect, as in this type, non-governmental organizations have to fulfil certain requirements or report back in order to receive funding, for example. This can increase the professionalism and transparency of the system. Most of the needs of homeless people are met by voluntary actors (such as non-profit associations, NGOs, spontaneously formed groups, and private individuals). Voluntary organizations are financed by donations and sometimes also by the unpaid commitment of staff. It is also significant that the provision of housing and professional counselling is often a greater challenge for volunteers and non-profit organizations than other forms of assistance, for example, in the provision of information, meals, everyday activities, or education. Housing and appropriate care require financial resources that voluntary organizations rarely have.

Type 3, 'state-led system of services', can be considered as a development of the state involvement seen in type 2, because the authorities are much more involved. What exactly motivates this further involvement is multifaceted. It can be a demand from politics or the aid system itself, or a development in connection with an overall strategy or similar. What is important is that the canton defines for itself an area of support needed by the homeless and becomes active normatively and strategically as well as operationally. The goal does not have to be that all tasks in the field of homelessness assistance are carried out by state agencies; rather, it is a matter of overall coordination as well as the definition of services for which the state, that is, the canton or the municipalities, is financially responsible.

Type 3 also involves monitoring and evaluation tasks and active participation in the further development of assistance to the homeless. Here, the authorities can develop their own services or make use of existing networks. The authorities establish contacts with NGOs and associations and involve private individuals on an institutionalized level and build on this in order to actively participate in homeless assistance. To sum up the evidence-based 'ideal' model: The coordination of a homeless assistance system contains various elements and is led by state actors. In particular, the cantonal authorities are involved in monitoring the situation and evaluating the effectiveness of existing services. They can also develop instruments that facilitate cooperation between the organizations involved, such as regular exchange meetings. They commission expert reports, develop strategies, and provide basic papers or training elements. It is also characteristic of each governmental performance field that the canton monitors itself, reviews the effectiveness of measures, and reports to parliament and the public.

Examples of Homelessness Preventative Practice in Switzerland

Due to the federal structure of homeless assistance in Switzerland, there is a diversity of preventative practice in the country. Regarding 'comprehensive solutions', a number of examples of best practice stand out: one canton[41] maintains a 'Coordination Office for Precarious Housing Conditions', which is tasked with identifying precarious housing conditions and combating them in cooperation with other cantonal services, the owners, and tenants, as well as relevant third parties. The overriding goal is to preserve housing. In another canton, the care of persons without shelter is separated from the seven existing regional social services and brought together to be managed by a single organization or foundation. The foundation coordinates the entire cantonal homeless

---

41 Cantons have shared their experiences with the authors and provided examples of best practice anonymously and are, as a result, not specifically identified here.

assistance and is controlled and financed by the canton. In a further canton, the medical officer of the canton, the social services department, the child and adult protection authorities, the cantonal police, and the public prosecutor's office come together to work within a wider 'emergency group'. They meet regularly and function as an exchange body between the individual administrative offices and the authorities. The group also takes on tasks, including evaluation and monitoring, development of strategies, and promotion of understanding as to the roles of the various agencies and bodies of the group. In urban municipalities, moreover, investments are being made in strategies to preserve affordable housing. Here, the promotion of social and cooperative housing is a promising strategy. One canton has been actively promoting housing for over 40 years. In 2018, around 3,800 of the total 740,000 dwellings throughout the canton were already subsidized housing. Another canton proactively provides land for projects for homeless people. In another canton, there is a housing promotion strategy that specifically champions affordable housing; in addition, there is the Housing Promotion Act, which offers a legislative framework and serves as an anchor for cantonal measures at the legislative level. Currently, politicians in this canton are establishing a public law housing foundation that acquires or builds affordable housing.

The Future of Homelessness Law and Policy in Switzerland

The most important and influential change that could be made in Switzerland if the country is to make progress towards a more inclusive and better-functioning democracy in which all people are able to exercise their rights of freedom and participation would be if Switzerland was to become more deeply embedded in international conventions where homelessness is rarely seen as an isolated phenomenon at the legal level but rather as part of a broader legal framework of social welfare, poverty reduction, and the right to adequate housing.

The International Declaration of Human Rights of 1948 (Article 25)[42] and the International Covenant on Economic, Social, and Cultural Rights (ICESCR) of 1966 (Article 11)[43] recognize adequate housing as part of the right to an adequate standard of living. Other international human rights treaties address the right to adequate housing or aspects thereof, such as the protection of one's own home and privacy or protection against discrimination in access to housing.[44] In addition, a right to housing is also provided at the European level within the framework of the 'EU Social Charter' (EU Social Charter 1999) and the 'European Pillar of Social Rights'.[45] The right to adequate housing is, moreover, enshrined in the 'Agenda 2030 for Sustainable Development'.[46] Objective 11.1 on inclusive development of cities and settlements also provides for 'access to adequate, safe and affordable housing and basic services for all by 2030'.

Homelessness was described by the first Special Rapporteur on the Right to Decent Housing, Miloon Kothari (2000–2008), as 'perhaps the most visible and serious symptom

---

42 <www.ohchr.org/EN/UDHR/Pages/Language.aspx?LangID=ger> (accessed 1 September 2023).
43 <www.ohchr.org/en/professionalinterest/pages/cescr.aspx> (accessed 1 September 2023).
44 See, for example, the Antiracism Convention (Art. 5), the Women's Rights Convention (Art. 14), the Children's Rights Convention (Art. 27), the Migrant Workers Convention (Art. 43) or the Disability Rights Convention (Art. 28).
45 <www.ohchr.org/Documents/Publications/FS21_rev_1_Housing_en.pdf> (accessed 1 September 2023).
46 <www.un.org/Depts/german/gv-70/band1/ar70001.pdf> (accessed 1 September 2023).

of a lack of respect for the human right to decent housing'.[47] Homeless people experience particular difficulty in exercising this right to respect due to discrimination and stigmatization. Given the seriousness of the multiple violations of the fundamental rights of homeless people, the Special Rapporteur has even spoken of a 'global human rights crisis' in connection with the global increase in homelessness, which urgently requires a global response (OHCHR 2015).[48] In addition to quantitative and qualitative monitoring of homelessness in each country, Farha called on the states to take the following specific measures: establish right-based strategies to prevent and combat homelessness, eliminate all policies and structures that discriminate directly or indirectly against homeless people, and ensure access for homeless people to legal assistance when their rights are violated (OHCHR 2016).[49]

A human rights–based housing strategy does not see homeless people or people living in inadequate housing as recipients, beneficiaries, or 'objects' of housing, as many housing programmes and policies do, but rather as rights-holders and active citizens who are empowered to participate in decisions concerning their lives and in the defence and protection of their rights. Housing strategies should thus respond to the lived experience and promote the participation of the people concerned.[50]

A right to accommodation is also provided at European level. The EU Social Charter,[51] which was adopted by the Council of Europe in Turin in 1961 and entered into force in 1999 in a second, revised version, lays down the fundamental social, cultural, and economic rights of all European citizens, including the right to housing (Article 31):

In order to ensure the effective exercise of the right to housing, the Contracting Parties undertake to take measures designed to that end: (1) to promote access to housing of sufficient standard; (2) to prevent and reduce homelessness with a view to its gradual elimination; (3) to make housing costs affordable for people without sufficient resources.

Such a right to housing was also proposed by the European Commission in 2016 in the Twenty Principles of European Social Rights ('European Pillar of Social Rights').[52] Principle 19 on 'Housing and Assistance for the Homeless' provides for access to social housing or

---

47 M. Kothari, S. Karmali and S. Chaudhry, *The Right to Adequate Housing* (National Human Rights Commission 2006) 51.
48 <https://documents-dds-ny.un.org/doc/UNDOC/GEN/G15/294/52/pdf/G1529452.pdf?OpenElement> (accessed 1 September 2023).
49 The Office of the United Nations High Commissioner for Human Rights (OHCHR), *Adequate Housing as a Component of the Right to an Adequate Standard of Living Note by the Secretary-General* (OHCHR 2016).
50 Human Rights Council, 37th Session (26 February–23 March 2018), *Report of the Special Rapporteur on Adequate Housing as a Component of the Right to an Adequate Standard of Living, and on the Right to Non-Discrimination in This Context* 4 <www.institut-fuer-menschenrechte.de/fileadmin/Redaktion/PDF/Sonstiges/Bericht_Sonderberichterstatterin_Recht_auf_Wohnen_Recht_auf_Nichtdiskriminierung.pdf> (accessed 1 September 2023).
51 <www.coe.int/de/web/conventions/full-list/-/conventions/rms/090000168007cf92> (accessed 1 September 2023).
52 <https://ec.europa.eu/commission/priorities/deeper-and-fairer-economic-and-monetary-union/european-pillar-social-rights/european-pillar-social-rights-20-principles_en> (accessed 1 September 2023).

housing assistance for the needy, protection of vulnerable people from eviction, and provision of shelter and social inclusion services for the homeless.

Switzerland is committed to respecting universal human rights and economic, social, and cultural rights, as described in the ICESCR. It acceded to the ICESCR in 1992 but has not yet ratified the protocol.[53] The EU Social Charter has not been ratified by Switzerland either, although this has been demanded by various actors for several years, and the legal conditions for ratification have been fulfilled according to a report by the Federal Council.[54] At the same time, Switzerland participates neither in the form of statements nor through active contribution to initiatives and resolutions of the European Union on ending homelessness mentioned earlier. By signing the ICESCR, Switzerland has accepted the obligation to report regularly on the implementation of the covenant and thus also to demonstrate its commitment to advancing the right to housing. If one reads Switzerland's reports to the UN Committee, it is noticeable that the right to housing provided for in Article 11 of the ICESCR is taken up and commented on in individual passages. However, it plays only a marginal role overall and is not systematically documented and reflected upon in its implementation in Switzerland. Switzerland's reporting on the implementation of the ICESCR has repeatedly triggered heavy criticism, not only from the UN Committee, but also from actors within Swiss civil society. In its recommendations to Switzerland in 2010, the UN Committee expressed fundamental criticism of the Swiss approach. The Committee regretted that most of the provisions of the ICESCR in Switzerland are only programmatic and social objectives, not binding provisions. This means that some provisions are not strictly enforceable and cannot be appealed to national courts.[55] Although the UN Committee does not specifically address the right to housing in this context, its criticism surely extends to this. The first report from Switzerland to the UN on the implementation of the ICESCR acknowledges that the Swiss Federal Constitution does not guarantee any right to housing as such and that a corresponding referendum (popular initiative 'Right to housing and extension of family protection') was rejected in 1970. The right to accommodation is only recognized under constitutional law in individual cantons. It is precisely this lack of a national, binding, enforceable right to housing that forms part of the comprehensive criticism raised by Swiss non-governmental organizations (NGOs) of Switzerland's first report on the implementation of the ICESCR.[56]

A second debate is taking place in Switzerland regarding the non-ratification of the EU Social Charter by Switzerland. Although Switzerland signed the Social Charter in 1976, both attempts (1987 and 2004) to ratify it have so far failed. Switzerland is thus one of

---

53 <www.eda.admin.ch/eda/de/home/aussenpolitik/voelkerrecht/internationale-uebereinkommenzum schutzdermenschenrechte/internationaler-pakt-wirtschaftlich-soziale-kulturelle-rechte.html> (accessed 1 September 2023).

54 Federal Council, 'Bericht des Bundesrates über die revidierte Europäische Sozialcharta' [Report of the Federal Council on the Revised European Social Charter] (2014) <www.admin.ch/opc/de/federal-gazette/2014/5611.pdf> (accessed 1 September 2023).

55 Economic and Social Council 45th Session (2010) 2 <http://www2.ohchr.org/english/bodies/cescr/docs/co/E.C.12.CHE.CO.2-3.doc> (accessed 1 September 2023).

56 See M. Beck Kadima and others, *Internationaler Pakt über wirtschaftliche, soziale und kulturelle Rechte (Pakt I). 1. Kommentar schweizerischer Nichtregierungsorganisationen zum ‹Ersten Bericht der Schweiz zur Umsetzung des Internationalen Paktes über wirtschaftliche, soziale und kulturelle Rechte* (GSP 1998) <www.humanrights.ch/cms/upload/pdf/020612_ngo_sozialpakt.pdf> (accessed 1 September 2023).

the few member states of the Council of Europe that have not ratified the Social Charter.[57] Starting in 2007, a third attempt at ratification took place over more than ten years with the 'Pro Social Charter' campaign of the professional association Avenir Social. The first interim result presented by the Federal Council in 2014 was a report confirming that the legal situation in Switzerland meets the requirements for ratification.[58] Given that there was no prospect of ratification due to the current political make-up in Switzerland, the campaign was discontinued in autumn 2018.

Switzerland has not positioned itself in relation to the 'European Pillar of Social Rights', in relation to housing-specific demands in the European Strategy 2020, or in relation to resolutions on combating homelessness. Individual references can only be found in statements by actors such as political parties or trade unions. The Social Democrats, for example, are in favour of agreements between Switzerland and the EU based on the 'European Pillar of Social Rights'.[59] The Swiss Confederation of Trade Unions[60] is also committed to improving living and working conditions by ensuring that new EU social achievements, such as the 'Pillar of Social Rights', are adopted in Switzerland. However, Switzerland is very unlikely to make any moves in this direction at the national level because it shifts responsibility to the cantons and municipalities in accordance with the principle of federalism.

Despite these partly legally binding principles, there has been little structural change in Switzerland in recent years vis-à-vis the problem of homelessness and exclusion from the housing market. This is likely to change. In the course of the Covid-19 pandemic, the problem of homelessness became even more apparent: around 10% of the population in Switzerland was suddenly dependent on emergency aid and free food.[61] Politicians did not expect this extent, but in the reactions to it, homelessness once again became a hot topic of discussion. Supported by a new research project on 'frontline work in humanitarian disasters',[62] it looks inevitable that greater attention will be paid to the issue of homelessness in Switzerland and in particular the role of non-state actors in the future. In particular, changes in legislation impacting the homelessness issue are expected from the cantons, which in turn will have an impact on the associated municipalities and how they tackle the social phenomenon of homelessness.

---

57 See Council of Europe Data on Ratification (2017) <https://rm.coe.int/16806f399d> (accessed 1 September 2023).
58 Federal Council (n 42).
59 See <https://lienseurope.ch/aufruf/> (accessed 1 September 2023).
60 See <www.sgb.ch/fileadmin/user_upload/Dokumente/Kongress2018/Resolution/Resolution_4_de.pdf> (accessed 1 September 2023).
61 S. Roduit and others, 'Être sans-abri en temps de crise sanitaire: l'ambivalence des réponses institutionnelles' [Being Homeless in a Health Crisis: The Ambivalence of Institutional Responses] in S. Mimouni and E. Rosenstein (eds), *COVID-19: Les politiques sociales à l'épreuve de la pandémie* (Social Policies in the Face of the Pandemic) (Seismo 2022).
62 <www.nfp80.ch/en/lPhDB7VM1yUuIjet/project/frontline-work-in-humanitarian-crises-state-and-non-state-cooperation> (accessed 1 September 2023).

PART II

North America

13
HOMELESSNESS IN CANADA
A Wicked Problem That Requires Genuine Political Commitment to Fix

John R. Graham, Yale D. Belanger, and Christine A. Walsh

Introduction

Canada is a federal system with three levels of government. There is one national government, ten provinces, three territories, and the municipal or local level. As we elaborate in this chapter, this political system is highly determining of homelessness responses. If one becomes homeless, there are practical steps that can immediately occur. Local government–run emergency services (911) can be phoned toll-free if the individual is in danger. There are public spaces – shopping centres, libraries, police stations – that can be accessed until an individual determines the next steps. Nearly a third of individuals use shelters only for one night, but shelters can be difficult to locate and access. Emergency phone numbers – often 211, sometimes 311 – can be called toll-free to assist an individual to identify rent banks, housing help centres, food banks, shelters, drop-in centres, or meal programmes.[1] There are income security programmes offered by higher levels of government, housing programmes frequently provided by third or voluntary sectors, but sometimes governmental sectors, and a vast patchwork quilt of social policies that are relevant to homelessness response and upstream homelessness prevention.[2]

Homelessness is a long-standing public issue in Canada. As early as the 17th century, there was public interest in societies' 'vagrants', with focus later shifting to residents of 'tenements' and 'skid rows'. Contemporary understandings of – and quantitative interest in – homelessness appear to date back to the 1980s in both Canada and the United States, including two early indirect estimations conducted in the United States. An early Canadian development occurred in 1992, with the city of Calgary's first Point-in-Time Count – in their words, 'a survey that counts the number of people experiencing homelessness on a particular night'. They have continued to conduct counts every two years. Other cities

---

1 T. Gulliver, 'I'm Homeless: Now What?' *Homeless Hub* (2014) <www.homelesshub.ca/resource/i%E2%80%99m-homeless-now-what#:~:text=Many%20cities%20across%20Canada%20have,in%20centres%20or%20meal%20programs> (accessed 1 September 2023).
2 J. R. Graham, M. L. Shier and R. Delaney, *Canadian Social Policy: A New Introduction* (5th edn, Pearson Canada 2017).

followed suit, with counts dating back to 1999 in Edmonton, 2002 in Metro Vancouver, and 2006 in Toronto.

In 2001, Alberta formed the 7 Cities on Housing and Homelessness group to coordinate local plans and align funding, also coordinating provincial homeless counts in 2008 and 2014. While 2016 represented a transition period during which a provincially coordinated Alberta count and a new federally coordinated national count of select communities took place at different times, by 2018 Canada had its first truly nation-coordinated count of individuals experiencing homelessness across 61 participating communities. But there remains obvious variance and unknowns in the Canadian data. Indeed, the Homelessness Partnering Secretariat (HPS) has regularly used the estimate that between 150,000 and 300,000 individuals experience homelessness in Canada each year, with advocates often employing the higher number.[3]

According to the most recent estimates from the Canadian Observatory on Homelessness, homelessness costs $7 billion per year in such expenses as police, justice, healthcare, temporary shelters, and other items. An investment of $55 billion over ten years would solve chronic homelessness.[4]

Canada is a northern country occupying two-fifths of the North American continent but with sparse settlement, with the overwhelming majority of the country's 38 million people concentrated largely within 300 kilometres of the American border, and with over 82% in an urban setting. Whether urban or rural, remote or not, the cold temperatures are a threat in wintertime, and severe heat in the summer can cause death.

Our housing situation is made additionally complex by the nature of our Canadian polity. Canada is a federal political system. Under the Canadian Constitution, Sections 91 and 92, federal and provincial powers are designated. The federal government has the most robust revenue capacity through income, sales, corporate taxes and tariffs. Provinces rely on transfer of federal monies as well as income and sales taxes. Municipalities, which have historically been the government of last resort for broad areas of social welfare, can be created or disbanded by provincial writ and have no constitutional authority. They rely on transfers from higher levels of government and various other revenue sources, including property taxes, which are erratic because of economic downturns.[5]

And yet each level of government is manifestly involved in homelessness response systems and policies. The federal government has jurisdiction over such income security programmes as employment insurance; it also oversees a $70 billion national housing strategy.[6] Canada's national homelessness strategy seeks to 'reduce chronic homelessness nationally by 50% by fiscal year 2027 to 2028'.[7] But there remain challenges, as we shall elaborate. The policy emphasizes Housing First, local priorities, coordinate access systems, a federal Homeless Individuals and Families Information System (HIFIS) data collection and case management system 'that allows multiple service providers in the same community to

---

3 S. Gaetz and others, 'The State of Homelessness in Canada 2016' *Homeless Hub* <www.homelesshub.ca/SOHC2016> (accessed 1 September 2023).
4 G. Mason, 'Close to Home' *Globe and Mail* (Canada, 17 December 2020) D1, D5–D6.
5 Graham and others (n 2).
6 Canada Mortgage and Housing Corporation, 'National Housing Strategy' <www.cmhc-schl.gc.ca/en/nhs> (accessed 1 September 2023).
7 Government of Canada, 'About Reaching Home: Canada's Homelessness Strategy' <www.infrastructure.gc.ca/homelessness-sans-abri/index-eng.html> (accessed 1 September 2023).

access real-time data and to increase coordination of services. HIFIS supports daily operations, data collection and the development of a national portrait on homelessness'. Points-In-Time counts are supported and locally based approaches to Indigenous homelessness, and homelessness in the far territorial north and in rural and remote regions are expected to receive greater attention.[8]

Provinces are responsible for universal healthcare services, various income security programmes such as employment insurance and income security for the unemployed and disabled, housing strategy, as well as complex funding programmes for local homelessness responses. Various regional management and local systems coordination fall to provincial governments, as do, in most provinces, some semblance of housing policy coordination, oversite, and in some provinces, outright housing stock construction.[9] Municipalities, for their part, facilitate zoning policies and approval processes that are key to the development of affordable rental housing.[10] Local jurisdictions develop, and coordinate, homelessness prevention plans. Homelessness response systems are, however, notoriously in silos. Health, mental health, substance misuse, child welfare, income security, housing construction, and other response systems operate in relative isolation to one another. So too are local, provincial, and federal policies and response systems are often uncoordinated.

Canada is the product of European colonialism, and the long, woeful history of subjugating Indigenous peoples continues to the present day. Canada is a diverse country with an explicit policy of multiculturalism inaugurated in 1971. Indigenous peoples, people of colour, LGBTQ2, the disabled, the working class, and other vulnerable people are especially prevalent in homeless populations. Linguistic issues are likewise important. The country has two official languages – English and French; since 1974, French is the sole official language in Quebec, although there remains a substantial English-speaking minority. In and outside of Quebec, minority language concerns remain important, and homelessness services do not always make the mark; this is also true of the hundreds of other languages – whether they are Indigenous or representative of the country's cultural mosaic from other lands.

Homelessness is best understood as the intersection of private trouble and public issues. An individual experiences a private issue, such as the end to a relationship, abruptly leaving a family home, losing a job, or rapid onset of psychosis. And this intersects with public issues.[11] The latter include the 1993 end to the federal homelessness social housing financial commitment, considerable cutbacks to mental health, child welfare, substance misuse, and related programmes since the early 1990s – the cumulative effect of which are being felt with great acuity today. Added to this is the dreadful problem of housing unaffordability and unavailable affordable housing stock. International data ranks Canada as among the higher OECD countries with respect to housing unaffordability, and cities like Vancouver

---

8 Ibid.
9 Homeless Hub, 'Appendix A: Ontario's Housing and Homelessness System' *Homeless Hub* <www.homelesshub.ca/toolkit/appendix-ontario%E2%80%99s-housing-and-homelessness-system> (accessed 19 March 2023); See also Quebec, 'About Homelessness' <www.quebec.ca/en/family-and-support-for-individuals/homelessness/about> (accessed 19 March 2023 and 1 September 2023).
10 Institute on Municipal Finance & Governance, 'Finance and Governance Solutions for Stronger Cities' (2022) <https://munkschool.utoronto.ca/imfg/wp-content/uploads/2022/04/imfgwdw_no1_housing_april_5_2022_.pdf> (accessed 1 September 2023).
11 C. Wright Mills, *People, Power, and Politics* (L. Horowtiz ed, OUP 1963) 395.

and Toronto are as expensive as Boston, Sydney, Seattle, Rome, Los Angeles, and other international cities.[12] While provinces and many municipalities claim robust responses to homelessness, including claims of hitting targets of affordable housing constructs,[13] many regions of the country suffer from insufficient affordable housing. An Ontario housing report called for the doubling of home construction over the next decade and the greater densification of cities.[14] Many municipalities rejected the report, and NIMBY responses locally were pervasive. The province did not adopt most of the report's recommendations.[15]

In terms of definitions of *homelessness* in Canada, one of the better definitions is associated with the Canadian Observatory on Homelessness:

> Homelessness describes the situation of an individual, family or community without stable, safe, permanent, appropriate housing, or the immediate prospect, means and ability of acquiring it. It is the result of systemic or societal barriers, a lack of affordable and appropriate housing, the individual/household's financial, mental, cognitive, behavioural or physical challenges, and/or racism and discrimination. Most people do not choose to be homeless, and the experience is generally negative, unpleasant, unhealthy, unsafe, stressful and distressing. Homelessness describes a range of housing and shelter circumstances, with people being without any shelter at one end, and being insecurely housed at the other. That is, homelessness encompasses a range of physical living situations, organized here in a typology that includes 1) Unsheltered, or absolutely homeless and living on the streets or in places not intended for human habitation; 2) Emergency Sheltered, including those staying in overnight shelters for people who are homeless, as well as shelters for those impacted by family violence; 3) Provisionally Accommodated, referring to those whose accommodation is temporary or lacks security of tenure, and finally, 4) At Risk of Homelessness, referring to people who are not homeless, but whose current economic and/ or housing situation is precarious or does not meet public health and safety standards. It should be noted that for many people homelessness is not a static state but rather a fluid experience, where one's shelter circumstances and options may shift and change quite dramatically and with frequency.[16]

The present chapter offers an overview of the structures and background of homelessness in Canada. In the end, it argues that no jurisdiction seems to take responsibility for its resolution. And the problem does not seem to be solvable. In the end, housing needs to

---

12 I. McCugan, 'More Construction, Housing Supply Likely to Result from Political Pressure' *Globe and Mail* (16 April 2022) B9.
13 F. Bula, 'Cities Reject Blame for Housing Woes' *Globe and Mail* (24 March 2022) A6.
14 Ontario, 'Report of the Ontario Housing Affordability Task Force' (February 2022) <https://files.ontario.ca/mmah-housing-affordability-task-force-report-en-2022-02-07-v2.pdf> (accessed 1 September 2023).
15 A. Bozikovic, 'Ontario's Housing Crisis Demands Big Change, and Doug Ford Blinked' *The Globe and Mail* (30 March 2022) <www.theglobeandmail.com/canada/article-ontarios-housing-crisis-demands-big-change-and-doug-ford-blinked/> (accessed 1 September 2023).
16 S. Gaetz and others, 'Canadian Definition of Homelessness' *Homeless Hub* (6 December 2012) <www.homelesshub.ca/sites/default/files/COHhomelessdefinition.pdf> (accessed 1 September 2023). See also H. Echenberg and L. Munn-Rivard, 'Defining and Enumerating Homelessness in Canada' (*Library of Parliament*, 18 December 2020) <https://lop.parl.ca/sites/PublicWebsite/default/en_CA/ResearchPublications/202041E> (accessed 1 September 2023).

be affordable and available, support for those who need it must be adequate, and the risk factors that lead to homelessness need to be properly funded, staffed, and utilized so that cycles of chronic homelessness do not continue to contribute to what feels to many to be a wicked – or difficult to resolve – problem.

Canada's Third/Voluntary Sector

Canada's third sector, otherwise known as the not-for-profit sector, offers 'socially mixed non-market housing provided through community-based and municipal non-profit organizations'.[17] Situated within their local contexts, third sector organizations are distinct from government and corporate realms and address the housing needs of minority groups, while governments concentrate on majority needs.[18] Prior to 1993, the third sector's range was limited, as federal and provincial housing programmes provided oversight of Canada's 700,000 units of social housing stock (5% of Canada's total housing stock).[19] The third sector rose to prominence following the federal government's withdrawal from the social housing arena in the mid-1990s. Government officials accurately predicted that the third sector would offer the required affordable housing to offset those in core housing need.[20] As Dreier and Hulchanski noted, the third sector taught us that 'local and community-based organizations can create good-quality housing and that this housing can remain a permanent community asset'.[21] Three types of non-profit housing make up the third sector in this regard: municipal, private, and cooperatives.[22] The third sector was also responsible for providing community housing services, such as 'group homes, housing registries, transitional housing and shelters for women and children at risk, and emergency shelters'.[23]

Non-profit organizations remain important housing providers in Canada, providing upwards of two-thirds of the social housing stock.[24] Limited federal and provincial funding has, however, compromised the third sector's effectiveness. Poorly financed and often unable to retain experienced staff, third sector agencies work together to address housing needs by forging multi-sectoral partnerships furthering mutual goals. Despite these efforts, as a result of the loss of social housing combined with low-cost housing disappearing due to market forces and demolition, the risk of homelessness became more pronounced as individuals fled substandard housing or were forced out due to rental competition. By 1999, in the wake of its reconfigured housing policy that had become increasingly dependent

---

17 P. Dreier and J. D. Hulchanski, 'The Role of Nonprofit Housing in Canada and the United States: Some Comparisons' (1993) 4 *Housing Policy Debate* 43, 52.
18 J. J. Rice and M. J. Prince, *Changing Politics of Canadian Social Policy* (2nd edn, U of Toronto P 2013).
19 S Pomeroy, 'The Fiscal Impact of Expiring Federal Social Housing Operating Subsidies' (*Focus Consulting*, February 2014) <www.focus-consult.com/wp-content/uploads/The-fiscal-impact-of-expiring-federal-subsidies-1-2.pdf> (accessed 1 September 2023).
20 D. Rewniak, 'Third Sector Housing: An Examination of Third Sector Housing Initiatives and a Comparison of the Private and Non-Profit Rental Markets in Inner-City Winnipeg' (MCP thesis, University of Manitoba 1997).
21 Dreier and Hulchanski (n 17) 57.
22 I. Skelton, 'Cooperative and Nonprofit Housing in Winnipeg: Toward a Re-Engagement of the Provision Infrastructure' (2000) 9 *Canadian Journal of Urban Research* 177.
23 T. Carter, 'Current Practices for Procuring Affordable Housing: The Canadian Context' (1997) 8 *Housing Policy Debate* 593, 625.
24 N. Van Dyk, 'Financing Social Housing in Canada' (1995) 6 *Housing Policy Debate* 815.

on third sector organizations, the federal government was forced to admit that affordable housing was needed. More to the point, as the federal government instituted cuts to social housing, homelessness was on the rise. A number of funding programmes followed, including the three-year national homelessness prevention strategy (1999–2002, $753M), and in 2006 the two-year Homelessness Partnering Strategy ($269.6M), which was extended for five years in 2009.

As Walker noted, rather than fund additional low-cost housing construction, the federal government targeted 'the problem of homelessness'.[25] Within a decade, the Wellesley Institute proclaimed homelessness in Canada to be a 'national crisis'.[26] In recent years, estimates reveal that over 235,000 people couch surf, stay in emergency shelters, or live on the street. The housing affordability crisis dating to 2017 combined with the Covid-19 pandemic's impact on employment is just the most recent issue highlighting the need for Canada to revive social housing. Federal reliance on the third sector remains a key pillar of its $72 billion to its National Housing Strategy (NHS), which was launched in 2017. The federal government has spent more than $26.5 billion to support the creation of over 106,100 units and the repair of over 254,600 units.[27] This does not represent a return to the pre-1993-era social housing in Canada. It does, however, beckon to the third sector that their efforts and expertise are much needed. For example, the 2022 budget allocated $200 million to the existing Affordable Housing Innovation Fund, of which $100 million was assigned to support non-profits, co-ops, developers, and rent-to-own companies building new rent-to-own units.[28] Unfortunately, despite the third sector offering an established infrastructure of networked organizations boasting significant expertise and knowledge, which could, if effectively managed, ground the much-touted integrated systems response to homelessness, the problem of homelessness continues.

Indigenous Peoples

In recent decades, Indigenous homelessness has generated greater academic consideration and policy attention.[29] This much-welcomed shift nevertheless continues to obscure the fact that since the 1960s, Indigenous peoples have been disproportionately represented in the homeless population and remain at risk for homelessness. Trends differ by province and territory, but the evidence clearly illustrates that in every jurisdiction, Indigenous rates of homelessness outpace those of any other ethnocultural group in Canada. Indigenous homelessness, as a phenomenon, is difficult to quantify and evaluate because of limited data, which narrows our ability to effectively respond.[30] Few local studies exist, and no national

---

25 R. Walker, 'Social Housing and the Role of Aboriginal Organizations in Canadian Cities' (2008) 14 *IRPP Choices*.
26 Wellesley Institute, 'Precarious Housing in Canada' (2010) <www.wellesleyinstitute.com/wp-content/uploads/2010/08/Precarious_Housing_In_Canada.pdf> (accessed 1 September 2023).
27 Canada, 'Creating Nearly 17,000 Homes for Canadians Across the Country' (August 2022) <https://pm.gc.ca/en/news/news-releases/2022/08/30/creating-nearly-17000-homes-canadians-across-country> (accessed 1 September 2023).
28 Canada, 'Budget 2022' (2022) <https://budget.gc.ca/2022/report-rapport/chap1-en.html> (accessed 1 September 2023).
29 For more, see Chapter 14 of this collection on Canada and indigenous homelessness.
30 Y. D. Belanger, G. Weasel Head and O. Awosoga, 'Housing of Urban Indigenous People in Urban Centres: A Quantitative Perspective' (2012) 2 *Aboriginal Policy Studies* 4.

studies have been conducted, surveying First Nations reserve homelessness. Numerous comprehensive studies have been published elaborating on urban Indigenous homelessness specifically. Yet these findings are substandard when compared to the volume of research produced annually about homelessness more generally. We do know that Indigenous homelessness is influenced by various trends ranging from off-reserve migration as well as higher urban Indigenous birth and fertility rates. Recently, analysts have begun to grapple with the effect of intergenerational trauma[31] and how unique notions of homeland influence homelessness trends.[32]

Indigenous homelessness is a growing policy concern that is underscored by unique forces, suggesting that it is an institutionalized problem requiring meaningful policy responses.[33] Based on the last census, there are roughly 1.8 million First Nations, Metis, and Inuit people, which comprise Indigenous people in Canada.[34] Many Indigenous peoples live in First Nations communities, known also as reserves, and an estimated 58% live in cities. In the post-1867 period, after the numbered treaties (1871–1877) were signed, Indigenous peoples were relocated and isolated to First Nation reserves. Indian officials elsewhere did their best to restrict Metis and Inuit movement. During this period, Canada's civilization policy was developed, grounded by a belief in Indigenous peoples' assimilation into Canadian society.[35] Consequently, nominal funding was directed to reserve housing, which soon developed into a mix of traditional Indigenous architecture and European-style housing. Since reserves were slated to decommission once assimilation was completed, neither sewage nor drinking water infrastructure was installed.[36] As a reserve housing crisis took root in the 1950s, Indigenous peoples began to leave reserves. By the 1960s, Indigenous urbanization was in full swing. Those leaving reserves plagued with deteriorating housing and poor economic prospects confronted similar scenarios upon moving to nearby towns and cities.[37] Notably, the lack of reserve housing programmes meant that urban Indigenous émigrés were not prepared about the importance of homeownership, and few had the capital needed to buy a house. Those lucky enough to obtain rentals often did not fully comprehend their responsibilities as renters and found their tenancies short-lived affairs.[38]

---

31 P. Menzies, 'Understanding Aboriginal Intergenerational Trauma from a Social Work Perspective' (2007) 27 *Canadian Journal of Native Studies* 367.
32 G. Weasel Head, ' "All We Need Is Our Land": An Exploration of Urban Aboriginal Homelessness' (MA thesis, University of Lethbridge 2011); Y. D. Belanger and G. Lindstrom, ' "All We Need Is Our Land": Exploring Southern Alberta Urban Aboriginal Homelessness' in E. J. Peters and J. Christensen (eds), *Indigenous Homelessness: Perspectives from Canada, Australia and New Zealand* (U of Manitoba P 2016) 161.
33 Belanger, Weasel Head and Awosoga (n 30); Y. D. Belanger, 'Can an Emergency Response Translate into Practicable Policy? Post-Flood Provincial-First Nations Housing in Alberta' in M. Papillon and A. Jeneau (eds), *Canada. The State of the Federation 2013: Aboriginal Multi-Level Governance* (McGill-Queen's UP 2015) 259; Belanger and Lindstrom (n 32).
34 Statistics Canada, *Census in Brief: Housing Conditions Among First Nations People, Métis and Inuit in Canada from the 2021 Census* (Minister of Industry 2022).
35 J. Nichols, *A Reconciliation Without Recollection? An Investigation of the Foundations of Aboriginal Law in Canada* (UTP 2019).
36 S. Olsen, 'Making Poverty: A History of On-Reserve Housing Programs, 1930–1996' (DPhil dissertation, UBC 2016).
37 Belanger, Weasel Head and Awosoga (n 30).
38 Y. D. Belanger, 'A Critical Review of Canadian First Nations and Aboriginal Housing Policy, 1867-Present' in N. Nichols and C. Doberstein (eds), *Exploring Effective Systems Responses to Homelessness* (Canadian Observatory on Homelessness 2016) 442.

The stage was thus set for the trends we are currently witnessing. Though we lack substantive data, Belanger[39] estimated that of the 633,306 urban Indigenous people nationally, roughly 6.97% were homeless on any one night, compared with 0.78% of the mainstream population. Put another way, more than 1 in 15 urban Indigenous people were homeless, compared to 1 out of 128 non-Indigenous Canadians. This meant that urban Indigenous people were more than eight times as likely to be or become homeless than non-Indigenous urban folks. The author's (Belanger) informal evaluation of the 2018 Point-In-Time (PIT) Counts measuring community-based sheltered and unsheltered homeliness rates suggests that these trends remain the same. As for reserve communities, between 2006 and 2013, the government of Canada provided $2.3 billion in on-reserve housing support to First Nations, which contributed to an annual average of 1,750 new units and 3,100 renovations annually.[40] In May 2015, the Canadian Broadcast Corporation reported that the federally sponsored $300M First Nations Market Housing Fund established in 2008 had produced 99 new reserve homes to date – out of a proposed target seeking 25,000 privately owned dwellings by 2018.[41] Canada's Indigenous housing policy can be described as little more than ad hoc, attitudes that are evident in the equally laissez-faire approach to Indigenous homelessness policy that has done little to mitigate growing rates of Indigenous homelessness.

One positive outcome that we can point to is the creation of a definition of Indigenous homelessness. Intended to shed light on the complex drivers of Indigenous homelessness, the goal is to offer policymakers a lens to aid in both responding to and for preventing Indigenous homelessness. As Thistle explains, Indigenous homelessness 'is not defined as lacking a structure of habitation; rather, it is more fully described and understood through a composite lens'.[42] Further, it is 'a human condition that describes First Nations, Métis and Inuit individuals, families or communities lacking stable, permanent, appropriate housing, or the immediate prospect, means or ability to acquire such housing'.[43] Indigenous people experiencing these kinds of homelessness 'cannot culturally, spiritually, emotionally or physically reconnect with their Indigeneity or lost relationships'. Unfortunately, a lack of government intervention leaves First Nations without the necessary supports to improve reserve housing needed to offset what we hypothesize is growing homelessness. Urban Indigenous peoples likewise allege government programmes do not effectively integrate Thistle's taxonomy and as such remain inadequate to the task of facilitating the systemic changes needed to alleviate off-reserve homelessness.[44]

Though academics were headed in this direction, policymakers are now breaking away from deficit perspectives undergirded by settler colonial beliefs seeking the expulsion of

---

39 Y. Belanger (2014), 'Infographic Wednesday: Urban Aboriginal Homelessness in Canada' *Homeless Hub* (19 February 2014) <www.homelesshub.ca/blog/infographic-wednesday-urban-aboriginal-homelessness-canada> (accessed 1 September 2023).
40 Canada, 'Proceedings of the Standing Senate Committee on Aboriginal Peoples' (2013) <www.parl.gc.ca/content/sen/committee/412/APPA/01EV-51063-E.HTM> (accessed 1 September 2023).
41 D. Beeby, 'First Nations $300M Federal Housing Fund Builds JUST 99 Homes' *CBC News* (27 May 2015).
42 J Thistle, *Indigenous Definition of Homelessness in Canada* (Canada Observatory on Homelessness Press 2017) <www.homelesshub.ca/sites/default/files/attachments/COHIndigenousHomelessnessDefinition.pdf> (accessed 1 September 2022).
43 Ibid. 6.
44 Ibid.

Indigenous peoples from towns and cities. Research has also evolved to interpret Indigenous homelessness from various perspectives, which helps improve how policymakers react. Still, the response is slow, as both urban Indigenous populations and First Nations populations grow in communities lacking accessible and appropriate housing in hostile colonial space.

Examples of Homelessness Preventative Practice in Canada

Between 2009 and 2013, a $110 million five-year demonstration project in five Canadian cities (Vancouver, Winnipeg, Toronto, Montréal, and Moncton) involved a randomized controlled field trial of Housing First – the well-known principle that you house homeless individuals first and then tackle related issues of substance misuse, social well-being, or other psychosocial issues. It found Housing First to be successful.[45]

One of the country's significant NGO actors is the Canadian Alliance to End Homelessness, formed in 2012. In 2015, the CAEH, with 21 participating communities, initiated the 20,000 Homes Campaign, whose goal was 'to house 20,000 of Canada's most vulnerable homeless people by July 1, 2018'[46] – in part inspired by the successful 100,000 Homes Campaign in the United States.

As the initiative moved forward, greater emphasis was placed on community-embedded strategies, such as 'using real-time data, creating coordinated homeless systems and embracing strategies for continuous performance improvement in addition to a focus on urgently housing our most vulnerable homeless neighbours'.[47] The 2018 goal was hit in 2019, after which the revised strategy became 'Built for Zero' (BFZ), in which communities reach 'functional zero' chronic homelessness and then expand those efforts to all forms of homelessness.

Indeed, the BFZ campaign is one of the more encouraging developments in Canada. As the BFZ website puts it, BFZ processes help to get communities to hit and sustain 'functional zero on chronic homelessness', by which one means three individuals or less than 0.1% of that community's last point in time count of homeless people.[48] Key to this initiative is a byname list, in which service providers are able to track individual service users and determine what their service needs might optimally be. Much of the BFZ priorities have focused on veterans' homelessness.

Medicine Hat, Alberta (population 63,000), is one of the country's earliest jurisdictions to capitalize on a byname list, in 2010, and is now considered one of the country's earliest places to functional zero. As the BFZ initiative puts it:

> Since 2009, more than 1,323 people (358 chronically homeless) who were homeless or at-risk of becoming homeless have gotten a place to live, including 328 children through Housing First programs. An even greater number of people have been

---

45 Mental Health Commission of Canada, 'National Final Report: Cross-Site at Home/Chez Soi Project' (2014) <www.mentalhealthcommission.ca/wp-content/uploads/drupal/mhcc_at_home_report_national_cross-site_eng_2_0.pdf> (accessed 1 September 2023).
46 Built for Zero Canada, 'About Us' (2023) <https://bfzcanada.ca/about-us/> (accessed 1 September 2023).
47 Ibid.
48 Built for Zero Canada, 'Functional Zero Homelessness Question and Answer Document' (11 February 2021) 2 <https://bfzcanada.ca/wp-content/uploads/Functional-Zero-QA.pdf> (accessed 1 September 2023).

stabilized or housed through diversion and rapid resolution. At the same time, shelter use has reduced by 64% overall, including children in shelters and family violence.[49]

But a great deal more needs to be done. The federal government needs to provide provinces with adequate funding. Provinces, because of the Canadian Constitution, are responsible for education, income security, health, human services, and many other related areas that are preventative and ameliorative in respect to homelessness. Historically – and, to a great extent, this continues today – local governments have been seen as the responsible place of last resort. Prior to the comprehensive welfare state of the 1940s to 1970s, local governments were responsible for unemployment relief, and by-laws were there to permit or restrict rooming houses and other mechanisms that dealt with homelessness. Local governments are still much involved – but their powers are limited. Provinces may create or disband them at provincial writ, and their funding mechanisms are limited to property tax, user fees, and transfers from higher levels of government. Meanwhile, a patchwork system persists – involving all three levels of government, NGOs, and the private sector which builds and sometimes runs housing services. But all the systems that are involved in the solutions to homelessness – be they housing-related, health, income security, employment policies/practices – remain siloed, and in the direct homelessness-serving sector, data structures are, while improving in some places, years behind where they should be. Nor are supports adequate for the many people who require supportive housing, and housing remains unaffordable to so many.

The Future of Homelessness in Canada: Problems, Opportunities, and Challenges

The last three decades represent a unique era in Canada's homelessness programming history. After the Liberal Party defeated the Progressive Conservatives in 1993, Prime Minister Jean Chretien initiated a slate of social programming cutbacks that claimed the federal social housing programme.[50] The Liberal cuts structurally changed the policy environment, forcing officials and not-for-profit agencies working with the homeless to revise their relationship to one another while refashioning their economic and frontline intervention strategies. Retreating from social housing provision, however, created the conditions that amplified an existing social crisis. Here we see the origins of the saying that homelessness is a policy choice on the part of the federal government. The resulting downsizing crushed the social housing programme, led to the Canada Assistance Plan demanding provinces meeting national welfare standards being scrapped, and began to increase reliance on extra-government agents to help manage the homelessness crisis.[51] Finally, rather than adopting full-on a systems approach to eradicate homelessness, a process that would seek to modify homelessness's institutional causes, the federal government adopted a crisis management plan. Though the federal government's retreat from social housing policy and its reliance

---

49 BFZ Canada, 'Bright Spot: Canada's First Functional Zero Chronic Homelessness Proof Point' (24 June 2021) <https://bfzcanada.ca/bright-spot-canadas-first-functional-zero-chronic-homelessness-proof-point/> (accessed 1 November 2023).
50 Graham (n 2).
51 Rice (n 18).

on the third sector is well documented, less attention has been paid to Canada's chosen crisis management model. As the Office of the Auditor General of Canada's (OAG) report *Chronic Homelessness* suggested, the federal government's confidence in crisis management strategies led by multiple agencies remains problematic and, in fact, may be exacerbating the situation.[52]

Released in November 2022, the OAG's report excoriated Canada Mortgage and Housing Corporation's (CMHC) management of the National Housing Strategy, and its programme partners, Infrastructure Canada and Employment and Social Development Canada. Reaffirming its support for the $78.5 billion National Housing Strategy, an essential strategy seeking to reduce chronic homelessness by 50% by 2028, the OAG reported an 11% increase in chronic homelessness nationally when Infrastructure Canada spent $1.36 billion, or 40% of Reaching Home funding, whereas the CMHC spent roughly $4.5 billion and committed $9 billion of National Housing Strategy funding.[53] Of particular concern was the failure of each of the programme's leads to guarantee judicious data collection or provide timely analyses, which made it impossible for the OAG to determine whether homelessness and chronic homelessness had increased or decreased since 2019.[54] Even more troubling was the CMHC's lack of accountability, as captured by the agency's declaiming accountability for addressing chronic homelessness despite leading the National Housing Strategy.[55] The OAG responded by recommending improving accountability through enhanced programme integration, and that Infrastructure Canada should collect and analyze data in a timely manner and the CMHC should determine whether its programmes are helping vulnerable groups.

What the OAG did not discuss was our enduring reliance on crisis management and, with it, the costly policy interventions and adaptations that must take precedence over equally, if not more, expensive systems approaches to ending homelessness. The latter demands we develop unique strategies that may be measured in years, if not decades. Crisis management, however, is appealing to politicians trapped in four-year election cycles and who must quickly respond to new and ongoing pressures. Integrated models embracing a mix of crisis management and systems change remain the most advantageous approach. But as recent events have shown, crisis management remains vulnerable to extreme shocks. Take Medicine Hat as an example, a mid-sized Alberta town that achieved international acclaim in 2021 after it announced an end to chronic homelessness. By September 2022, however, the Canadian Broadcast Corporation reported the return of chronic homelessness for various reasons. Notably, Covid-19's onset in March 2020 resulted in both higher unemployment and elevated eviction rates. Emergency measures such as the Canada Emergency Response Benefit (CERB) were unable to offset these trends, especially since CERB frequently compromised an individual's ability to access social benefits. The local shelters' absorptive capacity was also overwhelmed, which left clients unhappy with overcrowding and little choice but to live outside.[56] Just as Covid-19 began to subside, inflation hit, raising the cost

---

52 Office of the Auditor General of Canada, 'Chronic Homelessness' (2022) <www.oag-bvg.gc.ca/internet/docs/parl_oag_202211_05_e.pdf> (accessed 1 September 2023).
53 Ibid. 7–8.
54 Ibid. 12–14.
55 Ibid. 8.
56 B. Labby, 'Medicine Hat Says It Ended Homelessness a Year Ago, but It Didn't Last Long' *CBC News* (3 October 2022) <www.cbc.ca/news/canada/calgary/homeless-medicine-hat-point-in-time-count-1.6600717> (accessed 1 September 2023).

of living and leading to rent hikes that excluded many from affording accommodations. As of this writing, a recession is anticipated, which comes with it a drop in the gross domestic product (GDP) and homeless population increases.[57] Responding to such exogenous shocks demands nimble responses, and crisis management enables the quick reallocation of budgeted resources. The latter are, however, not apportioned with emergency contingencies in mind, and because there is only so much money to go around, crisis management responses to economic and health shocks we have experienced dating to March 2020 deplete budgets.

An interesting policy paradox develops that is based on our need to accept homelessness as inevitable to ensure ongoing funding of support, or to fight for its resolution, which demands longitudinal and pricey strategies that may, in the short term, compromise the health and socio-economic stability of the homeless. Developing mixed models is the most practical strategy but, as noted, not the most politically appealing, for governments limited to four-year cycles are not incentivized to fund ten-year (or longer) strategies. The question we seem to be struggling with is this: Do we accept the inevitability of homelessness to ensure ongoing supports? Or do we seek to end a crisis that, in part, is a political policy choice and, in part, an adaptable phenomenon that demands creative and nimble policy responses? Though crisis management may appear to be the less-expensive approach that helps mitigate the worst impacts of homelessness on the individual, we also need to attack the institutional drivers of homelessness, despite its costs and long-term commitment, if we are to create an adaptable response strategy that can provide the supports to ensure temporary relief while challenging issues that are, in nature, systemic.

The recent national trend of homeless encampments, or tent cities, is troubling. Once believed to be the exclusive purview of large cities, in 2022, elected officials in mid-sized and smaller local governments across Canada discovered that their communities were no longer immune to this phenomenon. Encampments represent an assertion of identity that act to enhance a vulnerable community while shaming all government levels into action. As we have witnessed in Lethbridge (Alberta, 2016 population 92,730) and Kitchener (Ontario, 2017 population 242,368), to name two sites, local opposition to homeless visibility has translated into clean-sweep programmes in the name of citizen safety. In effect, the previous war on homelessness has arguably developed a new meaning, as municipal officials engage in the criminalization of homeless communities to satisfy local demands to make the homeless once again invisible. Several critical linked issues demand our attention. Municipalities that were once the front line of service delivery, or played a vital coordinating role, are undermining programme impacts by abandoning a duty of care responsibility for the homeless. Our worry is that small- and mid-sized communities refuse to acknowledge that homelessness is not just a big-city problem, but that they must start playing a more substantial role that demands local officials avoid criminalizing tent cities and their occupants. This represents a basic example of how the crisis management model is ineffective in combatting the obvious systemic issues, and how the resulting policy outcomes play out daily on the front line. Complicating the war on homelessness by going to war with the homeless is

---

57 N. Falvo, 'Calm Before the Storm: The Great Recession's Impact on Homelessness' *Homeless Hub* (2010) <www.homelesshub.ca/resource/calm-storm-great-recession's-impact-homelessness> (accessed 1 September 2023).

inevitable without promoting the efforts needed to both manage the immediate needs of a social crisis by policy choice that will never end absent longitudinal systems change.

These are equally wider issues of public policy. But they involve all of us. Poverty is manifested by cheap consumer products and services that create precarious and low-paying jobs. Canada has a genuine problem with predatory financial institutions including payday loan operations and banks that do not service adequately those unhoused or vulnerable to homelessness. The private sector – which houses so many who are vulnerable to homelessness – does a very poor job creating sufficient housing stock as well as reliable systems of tenancy over the longer term.

Canada requires governments to genuinely commit to ending homelessness. Housing needs to be affordable, available, and support for those who need it must be adequate, and risk factors that lead to homelessness must be tackled, services properly funded, staffed, and accessed, so that cycles of chronic homelessness do not continue to contribute to what feels to many to be a wicked – or difficult to resolve – problem. There needs to be a massive rethinking of governmental and societal priorities: a shift manifestly away from predatory capitalism that disadvantages the poor and ignores the very real class basis of a gamed capitalist system.

14

THE POLICY OF STATE AS A SOCIAL DETERMINANT OF HEALTH

Canada's Indigenous Homelessness Policy

Yale D. Belanger

Introduction

Indigenous homelessness is a mounting concern in Canada and vastly underreported in official government census data and correspondence. A 2022 Statistics Canada study shows that 'First Nations people living off-reserve (12%), Métis (6%), and Inuit (10%) were more likely to have experienced unsheltered homelessness than the non-Indigenous population'.[1] First Nations individuals with Registered or Treaty Indian status living on reserve were almost twice as likely to live in crowded housing compared with those who lived off reserve (35.7% versus 18.4%).[2] Though macro-trends such as these remain highly publicized, detailed Indigenous homelessness data are deficient, and the available data and analyses are dated. Take two oft-cited articles by Belanger, Weaselhead and Awosoga from 2012 and 2013 that estimated 6.97% of urban Indigenous people were homeless on any one night compared to 0.78% of the non-Indigenous population. The authors also concluded that 1 in 15 urban Indigenous people was homeless and that they are eight times more likely to be or to become homeless than non-Indigenous urban individuals.[3] These findings endure as an important starting point for government, third sector, and academic analyses, which means that Canada's Indigenous homelessness response strategies 'are being struck in the absence of reliable data'.[4]

Data is not the only concern for government officials, and academics privilege the study of urban Indigenous homelessness.[5] Urban Indigenous peoples are a grouping of individu-

---

1 S. Uppal, *A Portrait of Canadians Who Have Been Homeless* (Statistics Canada 2022).
2 Statistics Canada, *Census in Brief: Housing Conditions Among First Nations people, Métis and Inuit in Canada from the 2021 Census* (Minister of Industry 2022).
3 Y. Belanger, G. Weaselhead and O. Awosoga, 'Housing of Urban Aboriginal People in Urban Centres: A Quantitative Perspective' (2012) 1 *Aboriginal Policy Studies* 4; Y. Belanger, O. Awosoga and G. Weaselhead, 'Homelessness, Urban Aboriginal People, and the Need for a National Enumeration' (2013) 2 *Aboriginal Policy Studies* 4.
4 Ibid.
5 Belanger, Weaselhead and Awosoga (n 3); J. Anderson and D. Collins, 'Prevalence and Causes of Urban Homelessness Among Indigenous Peoples: A Three-Country Scoping Review' (2014) 29 *Housing Studies* 959.

als representing various Indigenous communities who may be living within their traditional homelands but who may not live in their landed (federally sanctioned) communities. In 2016, the federal government adopted the term 'Indigenous' to describe the constitutionally recognized First Nations, Métis, Inuit, and their kin. In 2021, 1,807,250 people self-identified as Indigenous, representing 4.9% of the total Canadian population. Of these, 1,048,405 (58.0%) identified as First Nations, 624,220 (34.5%) as Métis, and 70,540 (3.9%) as Inuit.[6] Is homelessness a significant issue in each of these communities? Does it differ in each setting? If it does, how so? Why do we privilege urban Indigenous homelessness research? Or refuse to disentangle the assorted community trends when formulating policy? Despite the prevalence of Indigenous homelessness, our grasp of the issues unfortunately remains informal and contingent on anecdotal evidence. Individually and collectively, we do not fully understand how these communities cope.

Indigenous homelessness is 'a crisis that should be considered an epidemic'[7] and one that 'cannot be decontextualized from the uneven economic and community development, institutionalization, landlessness, and cultural genocide experienced in different degrees and scales'.[8] Contemporary Indigenous homelessness is directly liked to government institutions such as the reserve system and the *Indian Act*, which federal officials mobilized to constrain individual and group rights, disregard treaties, prohibit ceremonies, promote urbanization, and cultivate residential schools.[9] Grasping Indigenous homelessness starts by asking how the state, through domestic law and policy and its ongoing reliance on the aforesaid institutions, makes Indigenous peoples vulnerable to homelessness. As this chapter argues, Canada's tactics dating to its 1867 founding remain informed by racist ideas that reproduce structural and procedural inequities that act as key determinants negatively influencing Indigenous health. Reading and Wien confirm that whereas 'the mechanisms and impact of colonization as well as historic and neo-colonialism are similar among all Aboriginal groups, particular policies such as the Indian Act have been patently deleterious to the lives and health of First Nations people'.[10] Indigenous homelessness is, as this chapter contends, a distal determinant of health, which leads us to conclude that Indigenous homelessness is a policy choice that we have the power to correct.

Definition and the Context of Indigenous Homelessness in Canada

Prior to the 1980s, homelessness was not thought of as a significant problem in Canada, and when it was acknowledged, its cause was attributed to large-scale natural disasters that left scores without shelter. Well after the century's turn, homelessness was

---

6 Statistics Canada, *Indigenous Population Continues to Grow and Is Much Younger Than the Non-Indigenous Population, Although the Pace of Growth Has Slowed* (Statistics Canada 2022) <https://www150.statcan.gc.ca/n1/en/daily-quotidien/220921/dq220921a-eng.pdf?st=iXegVayi> (accessed 1 September 2023).
7 C. Patrick, *Aboriginal Homelessness in Canada: A Literature Review* (Canadian Homelessness Research Network 2014); J. Thistle and J. Smylie, 'Pekiwewin (Coming Home): Advancing Good Relations with Indigenous People Experiencing Homelessness' (2020) 192 *Canadian Medical Association Journal* E257.
8 E. Peters and J. Christensen (eds), *Indigenous Homelessness: Perspectives from Canada, Australia and New Zealand* (UMP 2016).
9 J. Nichols, *A Reconciliation Without Recollection? An Investigation of the Foundations of Aboriginal Law in Canada* (UTP 2019).
10 C. Reading and F. Wien, *Health Inequalities and the Social Determinants of Aboriginal Peoples' Health* (National Collaborating Centre for Aboriginal Health 2009) 8.

considered an urban phenomenon influenced by individual choices to dodge gainful employment.[11] The Great Depression (1929–1939) led to increased homelessness rates in an era whose leaders started to contemplate how macro-economic forces influenced homelessness trends. Slowly, social attitudes shifted from theorizing homelessness as an individual/urban phenomenon to that of a complex social, physical, and geographic phenomenon. By the 1980s, the cause of homelessness was attributed to an intersection of an array of forces ranging from a lack of affordable and adequate housing to a dearth of social supports that barred many people from affording even poor-quality housing.[12]

During the next three decades, the definition of *homelessness* evolved into a detailed, six-page description.[13] Created by the Canadian Observatory on Homelessness, a four-part typology is employed to accommodate gender; Indigenous historical, experiential, and cultural perspectives; and numerous populations, including youth, women, families, people with mental health and addiction issues, seniors, veterans, immigrants, refuges, racialized people, and members of the LGBTQ2S communities. Homelessness is:

> the situation of an individual, family or community without stable, safe, permanent, appropriate housing, or the immediate prospect, means and ability of acquiring it. It is the result of systemic or societal barriers, a lack of affordable and appropriate housing, the individual/household's financial, mental, cognitive, behavioural or physical challenges, and/or racism and discrimination. Most people do not choose to be homeless, and the experience is generally negative, unpleasant, unhealthy, unsafe, stressful and distressing.[14]

The brief mention of Indigenous peoples does not signal issue evasion, for in 2017, the Observatory published a complementary Indigenous definition. Working alongside Indigenous elders, academics, frontline workers, and government officials, Métis-Cree scholar Jesse Thistle drew from their ideas to define Indigenous *homelessness* as 'a human condition that describes First Nations, Métis and Inuit individuals, families or communities lacking stable, permanent, appropriate housing, or the immediate prospect, means or ability to acquire such housing'. Thistle rejects characterizations such 'as lacking a structure of habitation', arguing that they hinder our ability to interpret and appreciate Indigenous homelessness 'through composite lens of indigenous worldviews' or to distinguish that 'Indigenous peoples experiencing these kinds of homelessness cannot culturally, spiritually, emotionally, or physically reconnect with their indigeneity or lost relationships.[15] They suggested 12 dimensions of Indigenous homelessness: historic displacement, contemporary geographic separation, spiritual disconnection, mental disruption and imbalances, cultural

---

11 A. Solenberger, *One Thousand Homeless Men: A Study of Original Records* (Charities Publication Committee 1911).
12 D. Hulchanski, 'Keynote Address' (Growing Home: Housing and Homelessness in Canada, Calgary, 18 February 2009) <www.tdrc.net/uploads/file/2009_hulchanski.pdf> (accessed 1 September 2023).
13 S. Gaetz and others, *Canadian Definition of Homelessness* (Canadian Observatory on Homelessness 2012).
14 Ibid.
15 J. Thistle, *Indigenous Definition of Homelessness in Canada* (Canadian Observatory on Homelessness Press 2017) 6.

disintegration and loss, overcrowding, relocation and mobility, going home, nowhere to go, escaping or evading harm, emergency crisis, and climatic refugee homelessness.[16]

Recognizing differences in experiences, an Indigenous-specific definition, the experts argue, helps strengthen response strategies through improved public policy and funding pathways to counter a still-predominant understanding of Indigenous homelessness as the product of deviant and culturally backwards peoples, which has 'left a lasting legacy of dependency for many individuals and communities'.[17]

Confederation (1867) and Indigenous Peoples: Institutionalizing the Jurisdictional Divides

Prior to discussing Canada's homelessness policy, an institutional overview is offered to contextualize why Indigenous peoples continue to demonstrate significantly higher rates of homelessness.

Indigenous leaders were not invited to contribute to, nor were they consulted about, the Confederation deal negotiated starting in 1864.[18] They were effectively bystanders who were expected to assimilate into Canada and assent to its legal and policy decrees following the enactment of the *Constitution Act* 1867. Canadian federalism divided governing powers between federal and provincial orders of government with the federal order of government (Section 91) assigned exclusive legislative authority over 'Indians, and lands reserved for the Indians' (Subsection 24). Considered to be wards of the state lacking political agency, the diversity of Indigenous peoples in Canada was collapsed into an administrative term, 'Indians', that colonial and later federal officials used to fashion policies aimed at civilizing some Indigenous peoples while (largely) ignoring others.[19] To act on the narrowest interpretation of its responsibility, Canada enacted the *Indian Act* in 1876 that permitted the federal government to, among other provisions, define who is an 'Indian' (and, therefore, which Indigenous peoples are excluded from the federal government's limited consideration of its responsibilities), create an 'Indian' Registry, confine 'Indian' people to reserves, and replace traditional governing systems with imposed, foreign political models.[20]

Decades of Indigenous and provincial challenges followed, disputing Canada's narrow reading of its responsibility as relevant to only registered status 'Indians' normally resident on a reserve. In 1939, the Supreme Court decided that the Inuit were included in the term 'Indians' in the Constitution, after which the federal government intermittently included Inuit in its policies and programmes.[21] In 2016, the Supreme Court of Canada ruled that

---

16 See G. Lindstrom and others, *Understanding the Flow of Urban Indigenous Homelessness: Examining the Movement Between Treaty 7 First Nations and Calgary's Homeless-Serving System of Care* (Calgary Homeless Foundation 2020).
17 P. Menzies, *Orphans Within Our Family: Intergenerational Trauma and Homeless Aboriginal Men* (UTP 2005) 68; A. Leach, 'The Roots of Aboriginal Homelessness in Canada' (2010) 23 *Parity* 12.
18 E. Whitcomb, *Rivals for Power: Ottawa and the Provinces: The Contentious History of the Canadian Federation* (James Lorimer & Company 2017).
19 N. Dyck, *What Is the Indian 'Problem? Tutelage and Resistance in Canadian Indian Administration* (MUP 1991).
20 P. Palmater, *Beyond Blood: Rethinking Indigenous Identity* (UBC 2011); Sébastien Grammond, *Identity Captured by Law: Membership in Canada's Indigenous Peoples and Linguistic Minorities* (MQUP 2009).
21 *Re Eskimos* [1939] S.C.R. 104.

non-status Indians and Métis are included as 'Indians' under 91(24).[22] *Daniels* clarified with certainty that the division of powers (91/92) makes *all* Indigenous peoples a federal government responsibility, though it has refused this recognition in word or deed. The status/non-status divide foretold an extended period of extreme government parsimony for fear of fostering 'Indian' dependency.[23] Noticeably, policy did not allow for Indigenous people to be off reserve (rural, town, urban) and First Nations residents – they could either choose to remain 'Indian' or become a Canadian citizen entitled to a separate set of rights and privileges.[24]

The Fathers of Confederation further drew upon the British colonial civilization agenda that historically excluded Indigenous political participation.[25] A fundamental institution of civilization was First Nations self-government.[26] Then and now, Canada delimits the powers accessible to First Nations governments and the roles the federal government is expected to satisfy through laws, policies, and self-government institutions.[27] Most First Nations (about 600) operate under the *Indian Act*, meaning, they are delegated forms of government analogous to municipalities, while those First Nations that have a self-government agreement with Canada (fewer than 50) operate outside of the *Indian Act* under their own, federally directed constitutions not unlike provinces. Urban Indigenous peoples' demands for self-government duties have been duly ignored, in large part due to the federal government's erroneous view about its limited responsibilities.

Indian Act band leaders challenge the *Indian Act*'s prominence by claiming an inherent right to self-determination, which they insist confirms their capacity to regulate their own laws, priorities, and policies and negotiate with federal and provincial governments on matters of law and public policy.[28] Notably, the *Indian Act* limited the scope of band council authority, which nurtured a milieu of financial dependence Indian Affairs officials feared would develop, which undermined band governments' ability to effectively respond to local matters inducing homelessness.[29] Dating from the 1860s until the 1970s, band council officials had no say in federally created First Nations housing policies (their input remains constrained). The federal desire to improve Indigenous housing conformed to the societal diffusion of housing, gender, and family-related ideals, which was expected to achieve full expression with Indigenous urbanization. Consequently, the housing interests of communities destined for decommission were deemed irrelevant.[30]

---

22 *Daniels v. Canada (Indian Affairs and Northern Development)* 2016 SCC 12 [2016] 1 S.C.R. 99.
23 D. Neu and R. Therrien, *Accounting for Genocide: Canada's Bureaucratic Assault on Aboriginal People* (Zed Books 2003).
24 J. Borrows, ' "Landed" ' Citizenship: Narratives of Aboriginal Political Participation' in W. Kymlicka and W. Norman (eds), *Citizenship in Diverse Societies* (OUP 2000).
25 P. Price, *Questions of Order: Confederation and the Making of Modern Canada* (UTP 2020).
26 Nichols (n 9); W. Daugherty and D. Madill, *Indian Government Under Indian Act Legislation, 1868–1951* (Department of Indian Affairs and Northern Development, Treaties and Historical Research Centre 1980).
27 B. Titley, *A Narrow Vision: Duncan Campbell Scott and the Administration of Indian Affairs in Canada* (UBC 1986).
28 See A. Manuel and Grand Chief R. Derrickson, *The Reconciliation Manifesto: Recovering the Land, Rebuilding the Economy* (James Lorimer & Company 2017).
29 M. Kelm and K. Smith, *Talking Back to the Indian Act: Critical Readings in Settler Colonial Histories* (UTP 2018).
30 A. Perry, 'From "the Hot-Bed of Vice" to the "Good and Well-Ordered Christian Home": First Nations Housing and Reform in Nineteenth-Century British Columbia' (2003) 50 *Ethnohistory* 587.

When Indigenous housing was built, it was to clarify assimilation's rewards, even if it was not extended to all community members.

A quick word: Indigenous sovereignty is not being ignored. Jurisdiction is offered as 'the apparatus through which sovereignty is rendered meaningful' and is aptly 'not a technicality of sovereignty'.[31] Jurisdiction embodies the 'authority to have authority', which the state consequently translated into its legitimate power to uphold the law.[32] Daily jurisdictional processes remain the means by which Canada did and continues to undermine Indigenous nations' sovereign territoriality and self-determination.[33] As of the 1870s, the institutional context assigning responsibility for all Indigenous peoples to the federal government was set, which remains the status quo in 2024. Federal policy therefore is the source of structural and procedural inequities that help ensure Indigenous peoples remain vulnerable to homelessness. As discussed later in the chapter, Indigenous self-determination is a most promising option to creating an expedient, provisional pathway enabling Indigenous leaders to build up jurisdictional mechanisms needed to reduce Indigenous homelessness and improve housing conditions. More on this in what follows.

Indigenous Homelessness: The Historic Reality

Indigenous homelessness was rarely acknowledged because social and political convention held that homelessness was exclusively an urban matter. Since Indigenous peoples living in First Nation, Métis, or Inuit communities were deemed rural peoples, homeless was not plausible. Indian agents charged with promoting Canada's civilization programme frequently reported overcrowding, considering it an echo of historic traditions encouraging living in close communion.[34] The overcrowding that persisted with the advent of Western-style housing was also dismissed.[35] In the spirit of self-help housing, admixture of limited federal funding, welfare contributions, and individual and band contributions allowed residents to purchase materials to construct their own homes – which underscored First Nations housing policy until the 1960s, when federally sponsored First Nations housing construction emerged.[36]

Beyond the federal government's gaze, several studies in the early 1900s linked overcrowding and deteriorating First Nations housing to the inter- and extra-community spread of disease.[37] Still, it would be 1958 before Harry Hawthorn, Cyril Belshaw, and Stuart Jamieson published the first significant socio-economic study of First Nations in British Columbia, which dedicated a chapter to First Nations housing and overcrowding. The

---

31 S. Pasternak, *Grounded Authority: The Algonquins of Barrier Lake Against the State* (UMP 2017).
32 Ibid. 3.
33 S. Dorsett and S. McVeigh, *Jurisdiction* (Routledge-Cavendish 2012); S. Pasternak, 'Jurisdiction and Settler Colonialism: Where Do Laws Meet?' (2014) 29 *Canadian Journal of Law and Society* 145.
34 See, for example, R. Brownlie, *A Fatherly Eye: Indian Agents, Government Power, and Aboriginal Resistance in Ontario, 1918–1939* (UTP 2003).
35 Perry (n 30).
36 S. Olsen, 'Making Poverty: A History of On-Reserve Housing Programs, 1930–1996' (DPhil dissertation, UBC 2016); Y. Belanger, 'A Critical Review of Canadian First Nations and Aboriginal Housing Policy, 1867-Present' in N. Nichols and C. Doberstein (eds), *Exploring Effective Systems Responses to Homelessness* (Canadian Observatory on Homelessness 2016).
37 Truth and Reconciliation Commission of Canada, *Honouring the Truth, Reconciling for the Future* (MQUP 2015).

three authors questioned the accepted social belief that First Nations overcrowding was a product of too few homes and too many people (supply and demand), after their appraisal of the 'adjustments of the Indian to the Canadian economy and society' confirmed staggering overcrowding and poor housing conditions.[38] Their assessment indicated that overcrowding was not due to an 'Indian' failure to assimilate but was the result of government neglect. If left unabated, they warned, existing conditions would produce significant negative intergenerational effects.[39]

Overcrowding implied homelessness, and as Hawthorn et al. warned, it began to push First Nation residents into nearby towns and cities, which set the stage for the growth of urban Indigenous homelessness.[40] Subsequent decades of political, academic, and grey literature and free press reporting would elaborate Indigenous homelessness's characteristics and impacts.[41] Overcrowding as a theme nevertheless endured. In 2015, as an example, the Standing Senate Committee on Aboriginal Peoples' survey of First Nations housing distinguished between *overcrowding* and *homelessness*.[42] Thistle's ensuing definition and the Observatory's general explanation, both of which classify *overcrowding* to be a fundamental concern, propose the existence of homelessness in Indigenous communities that, as is the case today, exacted a terrible social, economic, and political toll.

The Senate Committee did, however, express its unease with negative impacts associated with the lack of legal and policy clarity regarding responsibility for First Nations housing.[43] Quoting from the Royal Commission on Aboriginal Peoples (RCAP) final report in 1996, the Senate Committee identified that Canada's historic obsession with establishing responsibility for Indigenous peoples left them institutionally vulnerable to homelessness and housing risk while hindering Indigenous efforts at formulating crucial policy interventions.[44] For example, some of Canada's earliest housing legislation in the 1930s that was intended to alleviate homelessness denied Indigenous peoples access.[45] Legislation and policy were not the only sources of exclusion. The Central Mortgage and Housing Corporation (later the Canada Mortgage and Housing Corporation, est. 1946), created to ensure favourable mortgage rates for homebuyers, was also First Nations–inaccessible and inapplicable to northern and Inuit populations.[46]

Indigenous homelessness remains an abstract phenomenon. How it is defined and understood remains reliant on mainstream decision-makers, whose choices act to constrain Canada's 'ability to develop promising policy and frontline interventions to combat the

---

38 H. Hawthorn, C. S. Belshaw and S. M. Jamieson, *The Indians of British Columbia: A Study of Contemporary Social Adjustment* (UCP 1958) iv.
39 Ibid.
40 M. Wente, *Urban Aboriginal Homelessness in Canada* (Faculty of Social Work, U of Toronto P 2000).
41 Belanger (n 36).
42 The Standing Senate Committee on Aboriginal Peoples, *Interim Report of the Standing Senate Committee on Aboriginal Peoples: Housing on First Nations Reserves: Challenges and Successes* (The Standing Senate Committee on Aboriginal Peoples 2015) 18.
43 Ibid. 3.
44 Canada, 'The Royal Commission on Aboriginal Peoples' (1996) <www.bac-lac.gc.ca/eng/discover/aboriginal-heritage/royal-commission-aboriginal-peoples/Pages/introduction.aspx> (accessed 1 September 2023).
45 P. Begin and others, *Homelessness* (Library of Parliament 1999) 35.
46 J. Miron, *Housing in Postwar Canada: Demographic Change, Household Formation, and Housing Demand* (MQUP 1988); A. Rose, *Canadian Housing Policies, 1935–1980* (Butterworth and Company 1980).

situation'.⁴⁷ Contemporary Canadian officials, for example, still employ the word 'homelessness' to deliberate urban Indigenous trends while favouring the term 'overcrowding' to discuss First Nations concerns. What remains unacknowledged is the Indigenous homelessness crisis dating to the 1960s in First Nations, Métis, and Inuit communities, and which gained momentum among the urban Indigenous population in the 1980s.⁴⁸ This is discussed next.

Homelessness Policy in Canada

Dedicated national homelessness policies were uncommon in Canada until the 1990s, when pronounced national homelessness trends forced the federal government to institute a national homelessness prevention strategy. Homelessness had existed to this point, with those without homes portrayed as vagrants, beggars, and transients, as individuals unable to manage their lives. The Great Depression revealed that economic factors out of an individual's control were impactful, which meant that homelessness was no longer considered exclusively a consequence of personal (ir)responsibility.

Starting in 1935, the *Dominion Housing Act* (DHA) targeted young homebuyers of modest economic means to grow personal homeownership rates *and* generate employment opportunities through homebuilding.⁴⁹ Replacing the DHA in 1938, the *National Housing Act* encouraged new home construction and programmes to stimulate home repair and modernization and finance rental accommodations.⁵⁰ Complementing this slate of legislative changes was the Rowell-Sirois Commission (est. 1937–1941), a Royal Commission established to identify federalism's failings and suggest recommendations for change to help improve all Canadians' standard of living.⁵¹ The Commission's report set the stage for the welfare state's advent, and though it notionally discussed housing, the latter would become a lynchpin of public health, economic development, community development, individual security, and education policy. Housing's capacity to underwrite national economic planning and offset Depression-era social issues was appealing, and this launched an enduring conversation about housing's role in national development.⁵²

Post–World War II, homelessness was considered a by-product of substandard housing, poor federal and provincial policies, and macroeconomic forces.⁵³ Recognizing its need to respond, Canada signalled its institutional, legal, and ideological readiness to improve

---

47 Y. Belanger and G. Lindstrom, ' "All We Need Is Our Land": Exploring Southern Alberta Urban Aboriginal Homelessness' in E. Peters and J. Christensen (eds), *Indigenous Homelessness: Perspectives from Canada, Australia and New Zealand* (UMP 2016).
48 J. Thistle, *From The Ashes: My Story of Being Métis, Homeless, and Finding My Way* (Simon & Shuster Canada 2019).
49 S. Chisholm, *Affordable Housing in Canada's Urban Communities: A Literature Review for Canada Mortgage and Housing Corporation* (CMHC 2003); D. Hulchanski, 'The 1935 Dominion Housing Act: Setting the Stage for a Permanent Federal Presence in Canada's Housing Sector' (1986) 15 *Urban History Review* 19.
50 R. Harris and G. Arku 'Housing and Economic Development: The Evolution of an Idea Since 1945' (2006) 30(4) *Habitat International* 1007.
51 R. Wardhaugh and B. Ferguson, *The Rowell-Sirois Commission and the Remaking of Canadian Federalism* (UBC 2021).
52 See Canada, *Housing in Canada 1945–1986: An Overview and Lessons Learned* (CMHC 1987).
53 See N. Falvo, 'Three Essays on Social Assistance in Canada: A Multidisciplinary Focus on Ontario Singles' (DPhil thesis, Carleton University 2015).

national housing and living conditions with the CMHC's creation.[54] Building on these changes, war-worker housing construction began in the 1940s, after which some social housing construction occurred in the 1950s.[55] The latter strategy grew in scope to 1984, when programme cuts heralding federal government's developing reliance on private market solutions fuelled neoliberal reforms promoting greater individual responsibility. The welfare state withered, Canada ceased social housing funding and then devolved its responsibilities to the provinces.[56] Homelessness rates across Canada rose, trends that would continue well into the 2000s and beyond.

The federal government implemented several funding programmes beginning with the three-year *National Homelessness Initiative* (NHI)($753M) in 1999 (extended for five years in 2004). Intended to provide direct funding to communities to support local efforts addressing homelessness priorities, it was renamed the *Homelessness Partnering Strategy* (HPS). The HPS shifted from a generalized policy approach to endorsing Housing First, which 'provides people with immediate access to permanent housing with no housing "readiness" or compliance requirements, is recovery-oriented and centres on consumer choice, self-determination and community integration'.[57] With the *National Housing Strategy* in 2016, the federal government created a ten-year, $2.2 billion investment in homelessness strategies. In 2019, with the *National Housing Strategy Act*, the federal government enshrined the right to adequate housing in federal law. *Reaching Home: Canada's Homelessness Strategy* (est. 2019) was mandated to support the needs of the most vulnerable Canadians; improve access to safe, stable, and affordable housing; and reduce chronic homelessness by 50% by 2027–2028.[58]

Despite these achievements, the federal response remains uncoordinated if not ably funded, and no joint federal, provincial, and/or municipal programmes operate to address Indigenous homelessness and/or housing issues. Many programmes do, however, include Indigenous funding pathways. The *National Homelessness Initiative* renewed in 2004, for instance, directed $45 million to the *Urban Aboriginal Homelessness* (UAH) module that led to 382 projects.[59] The more recent *Reaching Home* strategy includes an Indigenous module privileging urban Indigenous organizations to promote 'greater flexibility and support in determining their own initiatives, local priorities and collaboration with Indigenous partners'.[60] Programs such as the CMHC's *Indigenous Shelter and Transitional Housing Initiative* provide $724.1 million to construct 38 shelters and 50 transitional homes across Canada, including urban areas and the North.[61]

---

54 G. Suttor, *Still Renovating: A History of Canadian Social Housing Policy* (MQUP 2016).
55 Ibid.
56 E. Wooley, 'Why Wasn't Homelessness a Social Problem Until the 1980s?' (2015) <www.homelesshub.ca/blog/why-wasnt-homelessness-social-problem-until-1980s> (accessed 1 September 2023).
57 Homeless Hub, 'Housing First' <www.homelesshub.ca/about-homelessness/homelessness-101/housing-first> (accessed 1 September 2023).
58 Canada, 'Budget 2022' (2022) <https://budget.gc.ca/2022/report-rapport/chap1-en.html> (accessed 1 September 2023).
59 Belanger, Awosoga and Weasel Head (n 4).
60 Canada, 'About Reaching Home: Canada's Homelessness Strategy' (2023) <www.infrastructure.gc.ca/homelessness-sans-abri/index-eng.html?wbdisable=true> (accessed 1 September 2023).
61 CMHC, *Indigenous Shelter and Transitional Housing Initiative* (CMHC 2022) <www.cmhc-schl.gc.ca/en/professionals/project-funding-and-mortgage-financing/funding-programs/all-funding-programs/shelter-and-transitional-housing-initiative-for-indigenous> (accessed 1 September 2023).

The lack of Indigenous participation at the policy tables means that programmes at times include problematic elements, such as demanding a distinction-based approach privileging the unique rights, interests, and circumstances of the First Nations, the Métis Nation, and Inuit. *Reaching Home*, for example, fails to clearly define which 'Indigenous peoples' have programme access while employing language that appears to limit access of urban Indigenous peoples, a group that comprises 61% of the national Indigenous population. Currently, the Assembly of First Nations (AFN) and the federal government are deploying $35.8 million *Reaching Home* dollars to jointly develop a First Nations distinction-based approach to homelessness.[62] The government's ongoing reliance on this policy framework, which is reliant on group differentiation, leads to a chaotic funding and programmatic environment.

To summarize, Canada creates housing policy that relies on a combination of social housing subsidies and third sector agencies for programme delivery. Indigenous homelessness responses similarly rely on the creation of large funding programmes that unfortunately assign responsibility for planning and budgeting to varied institutions lacking effective coordination. Indigenous homelessness programming thus remains dependent upon national homelessness policies that combine targeted programmes and those offering Indigenous funding streams. An evident urban Indigenous institutional presence in some cities and Friendship Centres attempt to support federal or provincial programmes.[63] Indigenous homelessness's scale dwarfs most organizations' financial ability to respond, however. After appraising two decades of national homelessness programmes, general interventions may be effective in helping Indigenous peoples with finding temporary shelter, but they are ineffective in assisting individuals' permanent exit from the streets.

Homelessness Law and Policy: Prevention and Innovation

Indigenous homelessness programming relies heavily on housing schemes. In First Nations, since 1996, the CMHC (a Crown corporation) had provided oversight and financial subsidies promoting local homeownership opportunities. In 2022, Canada committed $190 million over five years to support Métis housing and $845 million to support Inuit housing.[64] Federal First Nations (reserve) housing is a CMHC obligation that emphasizes 'future planning and community control of reserve housing decisions and to gradually relieve the reserve housing crisis'.[65] First Nations, however, create by-laws, community plans, regulations, and zoning while administering and managing the majority of their local housing stock. Federal programmes do not cover the full cost of housing, a deficiency that First Nations try to accommodate by creating funding for multi-year housing plans. Those desiring shelter are expected to secure funding from other sources for their housing needs,

---

62 Employment and Social Development Canada, *Canada's Reaching Home Strategy: National First Nations Homelessness Symposium* (Employment and Social Development Canada 2021).
63 See D. Newhouse, The Invisible Infrastructure: Urban Aboriginal Institutions and Organizations' in D. Newhouse and E. Peters (eds), *Not Strangers in These Parts: Urban Aboriginal Peoples* (Ottawa Policy Research Initiative 2003) 243.
64 Canada, *Canada and Métis Settlements General Council announce housing investments from Budget 2022 for Métis settlements of Alberta* (Crown-Indigenous Relations and Northern Affairs 2022).
65 O. Kleer Townshend, *Aboriginal Law Handbook* (Carswell 2008) 274.

including shelters charges and private sector loans'.[66] Local supports are often funded by existing national programmes (e.g. *Reaching Home*), whereas in rare cases, where local homelessness programming exists (i.e. shelters, food banks, soup kitchen), they are internally funded and coordinated.

Northern Indigenous housing is a separate domain operating in a 'highly complex field with a multiplicity of governmental, quasi-governmental, and non-governmental actors'.[67] In 2006, the federal government, under its Northern Housing Trust programme, allocated $300 million over three years towards social housing units in Canada's three northern territories. The Yukon and NWT each received $50 million. In the latter case, the territorial government provided matching funding under its *Affordable Housing Initiative*.[68] Meanwhile, Nunavut received $200 million, but across the territories, these funds did not result in a significant increase in the number of public housing units overall and were instead used to replace aging public housing units.[69] In 2009, Canada dedicated $200 million for social housing provision in the three northern territories. Though a considerable amount of funding has been committed to northern housing over the past 15 years, this strategy of doling out funding packages has not enabled the formation of a consistent and sustained housing strategy, nor is it suited to the task of adding housing stock.[70]

Several urban housing programmes in southern Canada date to the early 1970s, and some of them remain crucial homelessness mitigation strategies. Most prominent was the CMHC-delivered Urban Native Housing Program (UNHP).[71] It fulfilled two unified objectives by offering support to Indigenous non-profit organizations and co-op groups that owned and/or operated urban rental housing projects, which in turn helped satisfy a federal government promise to build or acquire 50,000 housing units to house anticipated urban Indigenous émigrés.[72] Despite its uptake by numerous Friendship Centres and tribal councils, by 2015, fewer than 20,000 UNHP units had been built nationally.[73] The UNHP nevertheless 'outperformed the mainstream non-profit and rent supplement programmes on a variety of well-being indicators' driven by 'improved access to social services' that led clients to feel 'more secure, settled and independent'.[74]

---

66 Assembly of First Nations, 'National First Nations Housing and Related Infrastructure Strategy' (2018) <https://afn.ca/all-news/bulletins/assembly-of-first-nations-bulletin-housing-priorities-national-first-nations-housing-and-related-infrastructure-strategy/#:~:text=The%20National%20First%20Nations%20Housing%20and%20Related%20Infrastructure%20Strategy%2C%> (accessed 1 November 2023).
67 G. Wilson, C. Alcantara and T. Rodon, 'Multilevel Governance in the Inuit Regions of the Territorial and Provincial North' in M. Papillon and A. Juneau (eds), *Canada: The State of the Federation 2013: Aboriginal Multilevel Governance* (MQU 2015) 53.
68 Northwest Territories, Northwest Territories Housing Corporation (2009) <www.fin.gov.nt.ca/sites/fin/files/nwthc-2009-10.pdf> (accessed 1 September 2023).
69 N. Falvo, 'Homelessness in Yellowknife: An Emerging Social Challenge' *Homeless Hub* (2011).
70 J. Christensen, *No Home in a Homeland: Indigenous Peoples and Homelessness in the Canadian North* (UBC 2017).
71 R. Walker, 'Social Housing and the Role of Aboriginal Organizations in Canadian Cities' (2008) 14 *IRPP Choices* 7.
72 S. Pomeroy, 'A New Beginning: A National Non-Reserve Aboriginal Housing Strategy' in J. P. White and others (eds), *Aboriginal Policy Research Vol. IV: Setting the Agenda for Change* (Thompson 2007).
73 Ibid. 235.
74 Walker (n 71).

At a regional level, the Lu'Ma Native Housing Society (est. 1980) in Vancouver, British Columbia, operates 500 affordable housing units for low-income Indigenous peoples while guaranteeing Indigenous employee, management, and board representation. In southern Alberta, Treaty 7 Housing Society (est. 1981) offers long-term sustainability that, for decades, helped alleviate urban Indigenous homelessness. And the Métis Urban Housing Corporation and the Métis Capital Housing Corporation Settlements manage 900 affordable housing units in 14 Alberta urban centres.[75] Despite these accomplishments, the rapidly growing community of urban Indigenous peoples face difficulty instituting provincial Indigenous and municipal funding arrangements due to a provincial aversion to extending provincial services to landed Indigenous people living outside of their communities (municipalities are similarly refusing to engage).[76] Urban Indigenous peoples are consequently 'left to create policies' matching their needs, even if they often lack the 'capacity to do so adequately'.[77]

It is encouraging to see all provinces developing Indigenous housing policies, and three provinces (British Columbia, Alberta, Nova Scotia) are clear leaders. The Tripartite First Nations Housing Memorandum of Understanding (2008), signed by the Province of British Columbia, the First Nations Leadership Council, and Canada, commits the signatories to formulating inclusive approaches to improve housing for a mix of First Nations communities, individuals, and families living on and off reserve.[78] The final agreement highlighted a need to, among other concerns, increase affordable housing stock, to improve the adequacy of and access to housing, and to contribute to the prevention and reduction of homelessness.[79] Provincial participation in Nova Scotia's Tawaak Housing Association (est. 1981), a private, non-profit housing corporation, is restricted to partially funding the organization.[80] The province of Alberta responded to devastating flooding in 2013 that left dozens of families homeless in two First Nations, by signing two memoranda of understanding with and directing more than $180 million to the Siksika ($83 million) and Stoney Nakoda ($98 million) First Nations to rebuild homes and infrastructure.[81] This, in part, inspired the New Democratic Party–led Alberta government to implement a $120 million Indigenous Housing Capital Program in 2018 that the succeeding United Conservative Party (UCP)–led government gutted in 2020.[82]

Though Indigenous homelessness programmes remain rare, Housing First, when applied, shows promise. Housing First is 'a recovery-oriented approach to ending homelessness'

---

75 Métis Housing: Métis Urban and Capital Housing <www.metishousing.ca/mtis-housing-home-page/> (accessed 1 September 2023).
76 J. Anthony Long, M. Boldt and L. Little Bear (eds), *Governments in Conflict: Provinces and Indian Nations in Canada* (UTP 1988).
77 C. Hanselmann, *Urban Aboriginal People in Western Canada. Realities and Policies* (Canada West Foundation 2001) 10.
78 British Columbia, 'Aboriginal Housing Initiatives' (2014) <www.housing.gov.bc.ca/housing/Aboriginal-Housing/> (accessed 1 September 2023).
79 Y. Belanger, 'Can an Emergency Response Translate into Practicable Policy? Post-Flood Provincial-First Nations Housing in Alberta' in M. Papillon and A. Jeneau (eds), *Canada: The State of the Federation 2013: Aboriginal Multi-Level Governance* (MQUP 2015) 267.
80 Tawaak Housing Association, 'Housing Urban Aboriginal Peoples from Tawaak Housing Association' (2014) <https://tawaakhousing.org/>.
81 Belanger (n 79).
82 Alberta, Indigenous Off-Reserve Affordable Housing Engagement (2023) <www.alberta.ca/indigenous-affordable-housing-engagement.aspx> (accessed 1 September 2023).

reliant 'on quickly moving people experiencing homelessness into independent and permanent housing and then providing additional supports and services as needed'.[83] Working from the principle that, once housed, people can move forward with their lives, a Winnipeg (MB) study revealed that Indigenous Housing First participants 'were more likely to report high housing stability and community functioning relative to individuals accessing traditional community services'.[84] Housing First participants described experiencing feelings of detachment common to Indigenous people living in cities practising Indigenous erasure: deleting the Indigenous sense of place and home from historic narratives and contemporary policy.[85] Housing First programmes seek to address these forces[86] while working from a localized understanding of the Indigenous population, their stories, and their strengths.[87]

The lack of federally coordinated homelessness programmes consigns Indigenous homelessness to ad-hoc policymaking. When funding is allocated, Indigenous communities, the third sector, and independent organizations remain responsible for delivery. Innovation is possible, as shown with Housing First. The patchwork of federal and provincial programmes offers potential, but Indigenous communities must carefully monitor federal policy developments. Communities and organizations with capacity can sway policy creation, but this does not guarantee them or other indigenous communities universal programme access, which demands seeking out 'best fit' options. As the totality of programme funding is not directed to service delivery and is often used to reimburse communities and organizations for the associated servicing, only a portion of programme funding is dedicated to operations. Unsuccessful applicants regularly absorb substantial transaction costs without seeing any benefits.

Homelessness Law and Policy: Problems, Opportunities, and Challenges

Canada's institutional colonial approach shaped and preserves a jurisdictional quagmire that guarantees Indigenous peoples will remain vulnerable to 'intersecting sites of oppression' that 'increases the risk of . . . homelessness'.[88] Ongoing governmental reluctance to acknowledge its legal and policy failings then forecloses on any potential to instigate effective systems planning. Identified as an integrated system response that contemplates governance, policy, and programmes, systems planning is challenging. When one factors in Canada's ongoing civilization approach that finds its expression in separate laws and

---

83 Homeless Hub, 'Housing First' <www.homelesshub.ca/solutions/housing-accommodation-and-supports/housing-first>.
84 T. DeBoer, 'Falling Forward into New Selves and Spaces: Transitions from Homeless to Housed for Individuals with Mental Illness' (DPhil thesis, University of Manitoba 2018).
85 Ibid.
86 D. Alaazi and others, 'Therapeutic Landscapes of Home: Exploring Indigenous Peoples' Experiences of a Housing First Intervention in Winnipeg' (2015) 147 *Social Science & Medicine* 30. For the discussion about municipal erasure, see S. Nejad and others, ' "This Is an Indigenous City; Why Don't We See It"? Indigenous Urbanism and Spatial Production in Winnipeg' (2019) 63 *Canadian Geographer – Le Géographe canadien* 411.
87 M. Firestone and others, 'Using Concept Mapping to Define Indigenous Housing First in Hamilton, Ontario' (2022) 19 *International Journal of Environmental Research and Public Health* 12374.
88 A. Alberton and others, 'Homelessness Among Indigenous Peoples in Canada: The Impacts of Child Welfare Involvement and Educational Achievement' (2020) 111 *Children and Youth Services Review* 104846.

policies seeking to assimilate 'Indians', one begins to appreciate why mainstream planning consistently disappoints Indigenous peoples.[89]

Take the recent Indigenous requests to harmonize building codes to mitigate potential harm from house fires, in which First Nations people are ten times more likely to die due to historic/ongoing overcrowding in dilapidated housing in communities lacking emergency services.[90] Pursuant to the *Constitution Act 1867*, First Nations oversight is a federal concern, whereas provinces remain responsible for enforcing building codes that consequently do not apply to First Nations construction projects. The *Indian Act* permits First Nations to fashion by-laws to regulate construction. Repair and upkeep costs for aged housing stock surpass most communities' financial capabilities.[91] In 2019, the Ontario Chief Coroner's Table scrutinizing First Nations fire deaths concluded that '[d]isputes between federal and provincial governments over their respective jurisdictions has contributed to chronic underfunding and fragmented and inadequate services being delivered to Indigenous communities'.[92] Remaining in crowded and substandard housing therefore offers a non-choice: continue to live in inadequate, dangerous shelter or exit into homelessness.

Building on this discussion, the Truth and Reconciliation Commission (TRC, 2015) and the Murdered and Missing Indigenous Women's Inquiry (MMIWI) concluded that, as in the case of the nuance in determining building code jurisdiction, Canada reinforces structural deficits that have the potential to keep Indigenous individuals locked into a cycle of homelessness.[93] Homelessness accordingly needs to be recognized as both a symptom and outcome of colonialism that finds its expression in institutional racism.[94] Absent a thoughtful government response, both the federal and provincial refusal to act and embrace system changes in lieu of applying band-aid schemes reek of a calculated abandonment of responsibility.

Enter Prime Minister Justin Trudeau, who, in 2015, proclaimed, 'It is time for a renewed, nation-to-nation relationship with First Nations peoples, one that understands that the constitutionally guaranteed rights of First Nations in Canada are not an inconvenience but rather a sacred obligation'.[95] Note the emphasis on First Nations, which reveals an origi-

---

89 See generally N. Nichols and C. Doberstein (eds), *Exploring Effective Systems Responses to Homelessness* (Canadian Observatory on Homelessness 2016).

90 J. Migneault, 'People from First Nations 10 Times More Likely to Die in a Fire, Says Indigenous Fire Marshal' *CBC News* (2 February 2023).

91 See G. York, *The Dispossessed: Life And Death in Native Canada* (Vintage 1990).

92 Ontario, 'Ontario Chief Coroner's Table Examining First Nations Fire Deaths' (July 2021) 3 <www.firefightingincanada.com/wp-content/uploads/2021/07/Ontario-Chief-Coroners-Table-on-Understanding-Fire-Deaths in First Nations-final-June-20211.pdf> (accessed 1 September 2023).

93 Truth and Reconciliation Commission of Canada (n 37); National Inquiry into Missing and Murdered Indigenous Women and Girls, *Reclaiming Power and Place: The Final Report of the National Inquiry into Missing and Murdered Indigenous Women and Girls*, Vols. 1a–1b (Canada 2019) <https://www.dgwlaw.ca/national-inquiry-into-missing-and-murdered-indigenous-women-and-girls-releases-final-report/>.

94 Alberton and others (n 88); S. Kidd and others, 'A National Study of Indigenous Youth Homelessness in Canada' (2019) 176 *Public Health* 163–71; R. Caplan and others, 'Indigenous and Non-Indigenous Parents Separated from Their Children and Experiencing Homelessness and Mental Illness in Canada' (2020) 48 *Journal of Community Psychology* 2753.

95 Canada, 'Statement by the Prime Minister of Canada After Delivering a Speech to the Assembly of First Nations' (2015) <https://pm.gc.ca/en/news/statements/2015/12/08/statement-prime-minister-canada-after-delivering-speech-assembly-first> (accessed 1 September 2023).

nalist belief that Canada's responsibilities extend to some Indigenous peoples[96] that clash with the Supreme Court of Canada's in *Daniels* (2015), which pointed to Canada's need to engage with *all* Indigenous peoples. The advocated engagement is essential to ending Indigenous homelessness, due to the fact that it is the product of a complex matrix of relationships linking First Nations, Métis, and Inuit communities; urban Indigenous peoples; and federal, provincial, territorial, and increasingly, municipal governments. Consequently, the Prime Minister's words resonate with Indigenous leaders.

The nation-to-nation relationship is considered by Indigenous leaders to signify Canada's recognition of an Indigenous inherent right to self-determination, and here is where they take their inspiration. Indigenous self-determination can be defined as pursuing the broad goal of autonomy, with self-government offering the institutional expression of these principles.[97] Self-determination is unmistakable in two fundamental Indigenous demands related to homelessness programming in Canada: (1) ensure Indigenous participation in policymaking that directly impacts their people and communities, and (2) ensure improved housing to combat homelessness. Indigenous leaders contend that their inherent self-determination emphasizing these two pathways would lead to the creation of locally and culturally responsive interventions strategies. The formation of multi-level and multi-jurisdictional regimes of co-governance that privilege local decision-making appears to be the preferred model. In sum, in their demands that Canada abandon its reliance on institutionalized jurisdictional divides when fashioning homelessness policies, Indigenous leaders are promoting systems innovation through self-determination.[98]

This starts with integrating Indigenous understandings into federal policy to best respond to Indigenous homelessness distinctiveness. Regrettably, the limited attempts at policy co-production related to Indigenous homelessness programming have been ineffective due to their regressive nature (i.e. federal bureaucratic refusal to acknowledge Indigenous self-determination sets programme proposals up to fail), which continues to undermine efforts being made to end Indigenous homelessness. Governments instead take their lead from policymakers, who choose to address 'the urgent "problem" of Aboriginal poverty essentially managing this margin of society in pursuit of greater social cohesion', which preserves government's paternalistic tendencies.[99] The Urban Aboriginal Strategy (UAS) established in 1997 to nurture partnerships between 'willing provinces and municipalities [to] address the disproportionate socio-economic hardship experiences within the urban Aboriginal population'[100] flopped for similar reasons as well as others anticipated by the RCAP in 1996.[101]

---

96 J. Borrows, '(Ab)Originalism and Canada's Constitution' (2012) 58 *Supreme Court Law Review* 351.
97 J. D. Crookshanks, 'Urban Housing and Aboriginal Governance' in D. Newhouse and others (eds), *Well-Being in the Urban Aboriginal Community: Fostering Biimaadiziwin, a National Research Conference on Urban Aboriginal Peoples, a National Research Conference on Urban Aboriginal Peoples* (Thompson 2012).
98 The language was drawn from the following chapter title: H. Johnson, D. Behn Smith and L. Beck, 'Systems Innovation through First Nations Self-Determination' in M. Greenwood and others (eds), *Introduction to Determinants of First Nations, Inuit, and Métis Peoples' Health in Canada* (CSP 2022) 250.
99 R. Walker, 'Social Cohesion? A Critical Review of the Urban Aboriginal Strategy and Its Application to Address Homelessness in Winnipeg' (2005) 25 *The Canadian Journal of Native Studies* 410.
100 Ibid. 404.
101 Hanselmann (n 77).

In sum, well-meaning attempts to manage the existing legal-policy environment, or to implement modest institutional changes to the 'current patchwork of short-term, overlapping, and inefficient urban Aboriginal programs and policies', complicate an unwieldy 'jurisdictional maze'.[102] Indigenous leaders contend that these failures result from a federal refusal to engage in nation-to-nation discussions, and they have several additional ideas regarding how to move forward.

Indigenous leaders contend that improving our understanding of the Crown's obligations for housing begins with revisiting the treaties. Based in Section 35(1) of the Constitution Act 1982, '[t]he existing [A]boriginal and treaty rights of the [A]boriginal peoples of Canada are hereby recognized and affirmed'. Treaties are joint-governance arrangements where Indigenous leaders agreed to help protect '[their] way of life, livelihood, and governance'.[103] The pre-Confederation treaties contain Crown promises of homes and residential construction, reflecting housing's importance that were expressed in historic dialogues prior to and during the negotiations for the 11 numbered treaties (1871–1877, 1899–1921) (the treaties written terms were not adjusted to reflect these dialogues).[104] Treaties provide a lawful foundation for Crown sovereignty to co-exist with Indigenous sovereignty, a founding principle of the North American Treaty Order, 'a transnational, pluralistic, covenantal framework'[105] that preserved the various parties pre-existing laws while shaping new jurisdictional borderlines.[106] Canada continues, however, to rely on British common law and international (imperial) law to assert legal jurisdiction within its territorial borders, which, as has been demonstrated, remains a source of the jurisdictional divide and an ongoing distal social determinant of health that, as argued earlier, intensifies Indigenous homelessness.[107] Housing's absence from the more prominent Peace and Friendship Treaties (Nova Scotia, 1752, 1761), the Huron Superior Treaties (Ontario, 1850), and the Douglas Treaties (BC, 1854) demands re-consideration.

The AFN's rights-based approach to housing maintains that Crown negotiators assured First Nations shelter as part of its guarantees to protect their economies and way of life. Accordingly, homelessness can be partially countered with new house construction and by renovating existing housing stock, a strategy that heralds Canada's early forays into the welfare state of the 1930s and 1940s, when homelessness strategies were linked with home construction and repair. A renewed treaty dialogue would also likely benefit Métis and urban Indigenous peoples as well, for numerous Métis and a tremendous percentage of urban Indigenous peoples count themselves as treaty members. As the AFN contends,

---

102 C. Andersen and J. Strachan, 'Urban Aboriginal Programming in a Coordination Vacuum: The Alberta (Dis)Advantage' in E. Peters (ed), *Urban Aboriginal Policy Making in Canadian Municipalities* (MQUP 2011) 127.
103 J. Henderson, 'The Constitutional Right of an Enriched Livelihood' (2004) 4 *The Journal of Aboriginal Economic Development* 43.
104 D. Opekokew, *The Nature and Status of the Oral Promises in Relation to the Written Terms of the Treaties* (Royal Commission on Aboriginal Peoples 1996); J. R. Miller, *Compact, Contract, Covenant: Aboriginal Treaty-making in Canada* (UTP 2009).
105 J. Henderson, *Treaty Rights in the Constitution of Canada* (Thomson Carswell 2007) 479.
106 J. Henderson, 'Empowering Treaty Federalism' (1994) 58 *Saskatchewan Law Review* 301; J. Borrows, 'Ground Rules: Indigenous Treaties in Canada and New Zealand' (2006) 22 *New Zealand Universities Law Review* 188.
107 J. Borrows, *Recovering Canada: The Resurgence of Indigenous Law* (UTP 2002).

'[t]hese rights are ... informed by and substantiated through various international declarations such as the United Nations Declaration on the Rights of Indigenous Peoples'.[108]

On 21 June 2021, Canada ratified into law the *United Nations Declaration on the Rights of Indigenous Peoples Act*, described as 'universal international human rights instrument with application in Canadian law'.[109] Historically critical of the colonial state's disregard for Indigenous housing, the UN, in 2019, pronounced Indigenous housing conditions as 'overwhelmingly abhorrent and too often violate the right to adequate housing, depriving them of their right to live in security and dignity'.[110] The Declaration explicitly identifies an Indigenous right to housing, which is Canadian law. In Article 21(1), for example, improving economic and social conditions is tied to housing, and Article 23 conveys that Indigenous peoples have the right to be actively involved in developing and determining housing in relation to exercising a right to development. These articles must be read in conjunction with Article 3, providing for the recognition of the rights of Indigenous peoples to self-determination; Article 4, guaranteeing self-governance; and Article 26, recognizing the Indigenous right to land and resources.[111]

The *Act* has application in Canadian law and provides a framework for the federal government to ensure its laws are consistent with the Declaration.[112] As the Declaration did not distinguish between urban Indigenous peoples and First Nations, Métis, Inuit, and status and non-status Indians, the housing provisions apply to all Indigenous peoples, who may now claim self-determining rights.[113] The *UNDRIP Act* preamble, in principle, already commits the government of Canada to reject 'all forms of colonialism and is committed to advancing relations with Indigenous peoples that are grounded in the principles of justice, democracy, equality, non-discrimination, good governance and respect for human rights'.[114] Canada's civilization agenda that plays an integral role in fostering and perpetuating Indigenous homelessness should therefore be rescinded, and the ensuing constitutional distinctions disallowed.[115] The UN further supports Indigenous arguments that housing is a treaty right and a right that relates to 'the specific historical, cultural and social circumstances of Indigenous peoples'.[116]

Shelter and community have always grounded Indigenous economic and political experiences that do not recollect homelessness. Through the *UNDRIP Act*, Canada has created an institutional pathway to institutional change; its success must be measured through reduced Indigenous homelessness rates.

---

108 Assembly of First Nations (n 66).
109 J. Borrows, 'Revitalizing Canada's Indigenous Constitution' in J. Borrows and others (eds), *Braiding Legal Orders: Implementing the United Nations Declaration on the Rights of Indigenous Peoples* (CIGI 2019).
110 United Nations, 'Report on the Right to Adequate Housing of Indigenous Peoples' UN Doc A/74/183 (Special Rapporteur on the Rights of Indigenous Peoples 2019).
111 J. Henderson, *Indigenous Diplomacy and the Rights of Peoples: Achieving UN Recognition* (Purich 2008).
112 Department of Justice, Canada, *Backgrounder: United Nations Declaration on the Rights of Indigenous Peoples Act* (Department of Justice 2021).
113 Y. Belanger, 'The United Nations Declaration on the Rights of Indigenous Peoples and Urban Aboriginal Self-Determination in Canada: A Preliminary Assessment' (2011) 1 *Aboriginal Policy Studies* 143.
114 Library of Parliament, *Legislative Summary: Bill C-15: An Act Respecting the United Nations Declaration on the Rights of Indigenous Peoples Publication*, Publication No. 43-2-C15-E (Canada 2021).
115 Borrows (n 109).
116 M. Davis, 'To Bind or Not to Bind: The United Nations Declaration on the Rights of Indigenous People Five Years on' (2012) 19 *Australian International Law Journal* 17.

Conclusion

Indigenous homelessness has generated a strikingly low level of attention in Canada, and federal and provincial responses have had a minor effect on First Nations, Métis, Inuit, and urban Indigenous trends. This despite reminders to political officials of their need to address the issues within the context of Canada's historic relationship with Indigenous peoples, reflecting the government's obligation to establish progressive and inclusive programming and policies.[117] The *Indian Act* and the differentiation policy that isolate Indigenous peoples for distinctive treatment remain the mechanisms and context through which policy as a social determinant continues to negatively affect Indigenous outcomes (economic, social). The discussed policy assemblage propagates 'the collective burden of a repressive colonial system [that] has created conditions of physical, psychological, economic and political disadvantage' that frequently finds its expression as homelessness.[118] Distal determinants, as presented, remain the source of the widespread Indigenous 'lack', they act to constrain access to improved healthcare and economic and educational outcomes, and they remain ever-present barriers to policy changes that have been identified as indispensable to systems overhauls.[119]

It is safe to conclude that racism underscores some of the state's Indigenous policy responses. As an example, the state has segregated and isolated Indigenous people from the housing market, yet it refuses to engage in actions that would help Indigenous peoples to successfully participate. This despite the *National Housing Strategy Act* (2019) identifying housing as a fundamental human right that is key to ensuring individual dignity and the well-being of individuals who may seek to build sustainable and inclusive communities. Similarly, federal policy responses to the drastic surge in urban Indigenous homelessness remain deficient, notwithstanding the growing body of research highlighting the promise of several frontline and policy interventions. The Indigenous leadership's definitions of homelessness fittingly emphasize structural and procedural inequities that Canada and its provincial partners appear to understand but still refuse to address. Institutional pathways like the *UNDRIP Act* and Indigenous self-determination offer hope for transformative change, but the state remains path-dependent by addressing problems with conventional policy levers. Nowhere is this more evident than in the way that Canada seeks to create Indigenous add-on space rather than pursuing a *sui generis* approach that may lead to more effective solutions.

Despite the general Canadian willingness to tolerate Indigenous homelessness and the ongoing deterioration of First Nations, Métis, and Inuit housing, Canadians are dissatisfied with the current situation. In 2021, an Environics Poll showed that 37% felt that Canadian government policies were the biggest obstacles to Indigenous peoples looking to achieve economic and social equality (up from 26% in 2016).[120] Trends like these suggest systems

---

117 R. Walker, 'Engaging the Urban Aboriginal Population in Low-Cost Housing Initiatives: Lessons from Winnipeg' (2003) 12 *Canadian Journal of Urban Research* 99.
118 Reading and Wien (n 10) 22.
119 Ibid. 18.
120 Environics Institute, 'Focus Canada: Fall 2021: Canadian Public Opinion about Indigenous Peoples and Reconciliation' (2021) <www.environicsinstitute.org/docs/default-source/default-document-library/fc2021-indigenous-peoples-final-sept-29d44baa3c6d8147c787937fa72130c28b.pdf?sfvrsn=c6caed70_0> (accessed 1 September 2023).

innovation through self-determination to be both timely and hold the potential for improving Indigenous homelessness programming.[121] Indigenous leaders endorsing self-determination support joint partnerships guided by mutual respect and recognition, embracing treaty relationships, constitutional arrangements, and continuing group rights.[122] To end Indigenous homelessness, then, Canada must embrace systems innovation through self-determination. To do otherwise is to remain reliant on outdated ideas that lead to and perpetuate Indigenous homelessness through institutional racism.

---

121 Y. Belanger, 'Breaching Reserve Boundaries: Canada v. Misquadis and the Legal Evolution of the Urban Aboriginal Community' in E. Peters and C. Andersen (eds), *Indigenizing Modernity: Indigenous Identities and Urbanization in International Perspective* (UBC Press 2013).
122 J. Henderson, *First Nations Jurisprudence and Aboriginal Rights: Defining the Just Society* (Native Law Centre 2005); P. Macklem, *Indigenous Difference and the Constitution of Canada* (UTP 2001).

15
HOMELESSNESS IN THE UNITED STATES OF AMERICA
Dreams of a Shining City, Realities of Homelessness

*Maria Foscarinis and Eric S. Tars**

Introduction

In 1944, after the Great Depression had left one-third of the nation 'ill-clothed, ill-housed, and ill-fed', President Franklin D. Roosevelt called for a 'Second Bill of Rights', including the right to a decent home. While never enshrined in law, much of this social contract held for decades, at least for many White Americans. But in the early 1980s, the contract was broken, and modern American homelessness began exploding across the country. Now, with a deficit of millions of affordable homes, more people fall into homelessness every day than exit it, and encampments of people with no place to live have become the norm in communities large and small. Many jurisdictions have adopted laws criminalizing essential survival activities like sleeping and sheltering in public, despite the absence of adequate alternatives. This chapter reviews developments that led to this crisis, responses by advocates and government, and future challenges and opportunities.

Background and Causes of Homelessness in the United States

Before the explosion of the 1980s, visible homelessness primarily affected a limited population – single White males, often older and alcoholic – living on the skid rows of big cities. Then, seemingly suddenly, it reached a much broader cross section, including families with children, working people, and racial and ethnic minorities. Geographically, homelessness expanded to suburban and rural communities.[1] Several causes drove it.

In 1963, President Kennedy launched an initiative to allow mentally disabled people to live and be treated in their communities with the help of newly developed medications, instead of in state-run psychiatric hospitals, whose often-inhumane conditions were then being exposed. The plan called for 2,000 new community mental health centres to support

---

* The authors are grateful to Lauren Kranzlin for her excellent research and editorial assistance.
1 K. Hopper and N. G. Milburn, 'Homelessness Among African Americans: A Historical Contemporary Perspective' in J. Baumohl (ed), *Homelessness in America* (Oryx Press 1996) 123.

the discharged patients, often low-income and unable to afford private care. But of these, fewer than 800 were funded, and in the absence of other options, many former patients found inexpensive housing in single-room occupancy (SRO) hotels, then prevalent in cities around the country.[2]

Gentrification led to the loss of an estimated 1 million SRO units in the 1970s, and the displacement of their tenants, including the former residents of mental institutions, pushed many into homelessness.[3] Currently, a significant minority – but by no means a majority, contrary to common stereotype – of the homeless population also experiences mental illness.[4]

Coming into office in 1981 vowing to shrink the federal government,[5] President Reagan spearheaded massive cuts to social safety net programmes, and housing took an enormous hit.[6] In 1979, federal low-income housing programmes funded over 347,000 new units of housing affordable to poor people, but by 1982, that number had been slashed to 2,630.[7] While the following decades saw some increases in funding, the huge gaps left by these deep cuts have never been filled. Today, only one in four of those who are poor enough to be eligible receives housing assistance.[8]

The Reagan administration also targeted income support programmes. Plants were closing, and manufacturing jobs were being replaced by poorly paid service jobs.[9] But despite this new reality, the administration eliminated public service employment, reduced unemployment benefits, and tightened eligibility requirements for public assistance. New policies terminated assistance for hundreds of thousands of poor people unable to work due to disability or age, and the application process was made much more onerous.[10] Legal services programmes were cut, leaving poor people even more vulnerable.[11]

The Reagan cuts triggered the start of contemporary mass homelessness.[12] Supported by a blame-the-victim narrative that called homelessness a 'lifestyle' choice and a divisive,

---

2 See US Gen Accounting Office, GAO-85-40, HRD, *Homelessness: A Complex Problem and the Federal Response* (HRD 1985) 4.

3 Ibid. 20–21, 23, 29.

4 National Alliance to End Homelessness, 'What Causes Homelessness' *NAEH* (31 August 2012) <https://endhomelessness.org/homelessness-in-america/what-causes-homelessness/health/> (accessed 1 September 2023).

5 Reagan.com, 'Ronald Reagan and Small Government: Reducing the Size' *Reagan.com* (25 June 2018) <www.reagan.com/ronald-reagan-small-government-reducing-the-size> (accessed 1 September 2023).

6 Unlike the across-the-board cuts tied to deficit reduction that began at the end of the Carter administration; M. Wakin, *Otherwise Homeless; Vehicle Living and the Culture of Homelessness* (First Forum Press 2014) 34.

7 Both fell short of the annual goal of 600,000 new units set by Congress in the 1968 Housing Act. Oksana Mironova and Thomas J Waters, 'Social Housing in the U.S' *Community Service Society* (18 February 2020) <www.cssny.org/news/entry/social-housing-in-the-us> (accessed 1 September 2023).

8 W. Fischer, 'Housing Investments in Build Back Better Would Address Pressing Unmet Needs' *Center on Budget and Policy Priorities* (10 February 2022) <www.cbpp.org/research/housing/housing-investments-in-build-back-better-would-address-pressing-unmet-needs> (accessed 1 September 2023).

9 In a 1985 study in New York City, up to 90% of men entering shelter for the first time had been in 'unskilled or low-skilled jobs offering neither decent pay nor job security.' K. Hopper, E. Susser and S. Conover, 'Economies of Makeshift: Deindustrialization and Homelessness in New York City' (1985) 14(1) *Urban Anthropology and Studies of Cultural Systems and World Economic Development* 183, 207.

10 J. L. Palmer and I. V. Sawhill, 'Perspectives on the Reagan Experiment' in J. L. Palmer and I. V. Sawhill (eds), *The Reagan Experiment* (The Urban Institute 1982) 17.

11 F. Barbash, 'White House Wants to Cut Off Federal Legal Aid for the Poor' *Washington Post* (Washington, DC, 6 March 1981).

12 Following the federal lead, state governments also cut or eliminated programs, known as 'general assistance', that provided modest cash aid to single people who were down on their luck. GAO (n 2) 24.

racist trope that demonized poor people as 'welfare queens', these cuts set the stage for punitive and discriminatory policies for decades to come.

A second major wave of homelessness came with the foreclosure crisis and the 'Great Recession', beginning in 2007. Communities across the country reported large increases in families entering shelters, and national data indicated a 30% increase overall,[13] including many experiencing homelessness for the first time. In the wake of that crisis, investors increasingly began buying residential property; by the final quarter of 2021, institutional investors accounted for over 18% of homes sold in the United States.[14] Private equity firms sought to extract as much profit as possible – signalling the increasing 'financialization' of housing, a vehicle for investment and wealth, rather than a social good and human right.[15]

The impact of these developments was not borne equally by all. The New Deal enacted by Franklin D. Roosevelt (FDR) had largely and explicitly excluded African Americans, furthering racial segregation and inequality.

The Reagan cuts exacerbated the impact of this exclusion[16] while also promoting racist narratives. Subprime mortgages predatorily targeted Black, Indigenous, and other People of Colour.[17] Collectively, these contributed to the disproportionate representation of People of Colour, and especially Black people, in the homeless population, even as compared to the poverty population. Research indicates that because of the cumulative effect of racial segregation and discrimination, Black and other minority communities suffer from 'network impoverishment', meaning, that their social networks are so poor that those networks are hard-pressed to help in times of economic need, increasing the likelihood of homelessness.[18] Today, Black people make up some 40% of the homeless population, compared to 28% of the poverty population and 12% of the total US population.[19]

---

13 B. Sard, 'Recovery Package Should Include New Housing Vouchers and Other Measures to Prevent Homelessness' *CBPP* (8 January 2009) <www.cbpp.org/research/number-of-homeless-families-climbing-due-to-recession> (accessed 1 September 2023); National Coalition for the Homeless and others, 'Foreclosure to Homelessness: The Forgotten Victims of the Subprime Crisis' *NCH* (June 2009) <www.nationalhomeless.org/factsheets/foreclosure.html> (accessed 1 September 2023); I. Gould Ellen and S. Dastrup, *Housing and the Great Recession* (Stanford Center on Poverty and Inequality October 2012) <https://furmancenter.org/files/publications/HousingandtheGreatRecession.pdf> (accessed 1 September 2023).

14 D. Anderson and S. Bokhari, 'Real Estate Investors Are Buying a Record Share of U.S. Homes' *Redfin News* (16 February 2022) <www.redfin.com/news/investor-home-purchases-q4-2021/> (accessed 1 September 2023).

15 See The Office of the High Commissioner for Human Rights, 'States and Real Estate Private Equity Firms Questioned for Compliance with Human Rights' *Office of the High Commissioner* (26 March 2019) <www.ohchr.org/en/news/2019/03/states-and-real-estate-private-equity-firms-questioned-compliance-human-rights?LangID=E&NewsID=24404>. The stage had been set with the advent and growth of mortgage-backed securities in the 1980s and 90s. See I. Leijten and K. De Bel, 'Facing Financialization in the Housing Sector: A Human Right to Adequate Housing for All' (2020) 38(2) Netherlands Quarterly of Human Rights 94.

16 R. Rothstein, *The Color of Law: A Forgotten History of How Our Government Segregated America* (W.W. Norton & Company 2017). See also M. Desmond, 'Housing' (2017) *Pathways Magazine* 16–17.

17 U.S. Department of Housing and Urban Development, 'Unequal Burden: Income and Racial Disparities in Subprime Lending in America' *HUD* (22 February 2008) <www.huduser.gov/publications/pdf/unequal_full.pdf>.

18 See J. Olivet and others, *Phase One Study Findings* (Center for Social Innovation 2018) <https://c4innovates.com/wp-content/uploads/2019/03/SPARC-Phase-1-Findings-March-2018.pdf> (accessed 1 September 2023) 4, 12. See also K. Hopper, *Reckoning with Homelessness* (Cornell UP 2003) 165.

19 NAEH, 'Racial Inequalities in Homelessness, by the Numbers' *NAEH* (1 June 2020) <https://endhomelessness.org/resource/racial-inequalities-homelessness-numbers/> (accessed 1 September 2023).

Definitions of Homelessness in the United States: Early Debate and Continuing Controversy

The two main definitions of homelessness currently in use in the United States originated from the McKinney–Vento Homeless Assistance Act of 1987, the first major federal response to homelessness.[20]

The Act's broad formulation of 'an individual who lacks a fixed, regular, and adequate nighttime residence' reflected the reality that people typically move in and out of a variety of makeshift arrangements.[21] But the agencies charged with implementing the new law adopted different interpretations, later codified in law and regulation.[22]

The United States Department of Housing and Urban Development (HUD), which administers the law's shelter and housing programmes, adopted a narrow definition focused on people living in shelters and public places, largely leaving out people who have lost their housing and moved in temporarily with friends or relatives, a common arrangement. The Department of Education (ED) adopted a broader definition that includes this 'doubled up' population in its definition of homeless children.

The difference led to ongoing controversy. Proponents of the narrow definition argue that it is better to target federal funds – which all agree are clearly insufficient – to a smaller population. Proponents of the broader definition counter that it better reflects the reality of homelessness; some also argue it better positions advocates to build a larger coalition to seek more funding, obviating this dilemma.

The choice of definition directly affects the estimated size of the population. Because of this, as well as methodological differences, the two agencies have very different estimates.[23]

---

20 See M. Foscarinis, 'The Federal Response: The Stewart B. McKinney Homeless Assistance Act (1996)' in J. Baumohl (ed), *Homelessness in America* (Oryx Press 1996) 160.
21 As originally enacted, the definition read:
'For purposes of this Act, the term "homeless" or "homeless individual" includes –

(1) an individual who lacks a fixed, regular, and adequate nighttime residence; and
(2) an individual who has a primary nighttime residence that is –
    (A) a supervised publicly or privately operated shelter designed to provide temporary living accommodations (including welfare hotels, congregate shelters, and transitional housing for the mentally ill);
    (B) an institution that provides a temporary residence for ^ individuals intended to be institutionalized; or
    (C) a public or private place not designed for, or ordinarily used as, a regular sleeping accommodation for human beings.'

42 USC 11301 § 103 (a) (1987). It explicitly excluded prisoners: 'For purposes of this Act, the term "homeless" or "homeless individual" does not include any individual imprisoned or otherwise detained pursuant to an Act of the Congress or a State law.' 42 USC 11301 § 103 (c) (1987). This formulation was based on language developed by one of the authors in consultation with Kim Hopper. Congress, of course, had the final word; one result was the exclusion of prisoners.
22 HUD Exchange, 'HUD's Definition of Homelessness: Resources and Guidance' *hudexchange* (8 March 2019) <www.hudexchange.info/news/huds-definition-of-homelessness-resources-and-guidance/> (accessed September 2023); US Interagency Council on Homelessness, 'Key Federal Terms and Definitions of Homelessness Among Youth' *usich.gov* (February 2018) <www.usich.gov/resources/uploads/asset_library/Federal-Definitions-of-Youth-Homelessness.pdf> (accessed 30 September 2021); NAEH, 'Homeless Children and Youth Act (S. 1469, H.R. 6287)' *NAEH* (21 June 2018) (accessed 1 September 2023); School House Connection, 'The Homeless Children and Youth Act of 2017 (H.R. 1511/S.611)' *schoolhouseconnection.org* (June 2018) <www.schoolhouseconnection.org/wp-content/uploads/2018/06/HCYA-Fact-Sheet-June-2018-One-Pager.pdf> (accessed 1 September 2023).
23 See National Law Center on Homelessness and Poverty, 'Don't Count on It' *NLCHP* (2017).

Currently, HUD requires annual 'point-in-time' counts of the homeless populations by 'Continuums of Care', entities typically made up of non-profit service providers or local government entities that receive and manage HUD McKinney–Vento funds.[24] These counts include both a shelter and a 'street' count that the agency itself acknowledges yields a significant undercount. On a single night in January 2020, the HUD number was approximately 580,000.

The ED count captures students who were homeless at any time during the school year, based on data reported by local school districts, which are required to identify them.[25] Because schools often have difficulty doing this, these numbers also are almost certainly undercounts.[26] The count of homeless K–12 public school students for the 2018–2019 school year was 1,387,573.[27]

Currently, there is no accurate estimate of the US homeless population using any definition. The most accurate remains the 1996 estimate (using the HUD definition) by Martha Burt and colleagues which estimated a one-week number of 842,000 and an annual number of 2.5 to 3.5 million.[28] A 1990 survey found that 7.4 % of all Americans (13.5 million people) reported that they had been homeless – using the narrow definition – at some point in their lives.[29]

Legal and Policy Framework: Background and Current Context

Legal advocacy has played a critical role in responding to the crisis from its inception. A key early case filed in 1979 in New York City, *Callahan v Carey*, led to a consent decree establishing a right to shelter in that city[30] and the creation of the largest – still inadequate – public

---

24 HUD Exchange, 'Point-in-Time Count and Housing Inventory Count' *hudexchange* (27 July 2019) <www.hudexchange.info/programs/hdx/pit-hic/> (accessed 1 September 2023).
25 National Center on Homeless Education, 'Data and Statistics on Homelessness' *NCHE* <https://nche.ed.gov/data-and-stats/> (accessed 1 September 2023).
26 M. Foscarinis, 'Undercounting People Experiencing Homelessness' *Huffington Post* (6 February 2017) <www.huffpost.com/entry/communities-count-people-experiencing-homelessness_b_589494cee4b02bbb1816b96e> (accessed 1 September 2023).
27 The most recent data, for the 2019–2020 school year, showed 1,280,886 homeless K–12 public school students. However, that school year included three months of the pandemic, which may have skewed the numbers. See NCHE, 'Student Homelessness in America: School Years 2017–18 to 2019–20' *NCHE* (December 2021) <https://nche.ed.gov/wp-content/uploads/2021/12/Student-Homelessness-in-America-2021.pdf> (accessed 1 September 2023).
28 Using innovative and sophisticated methodology, Burt and colleagues conducted interviews over a one-month period at a representative sample of soup kitchens across the country and, using extrapolation techniques, estimated total figures. M. Burt and others, *Helping America's Homeless: Emergency Shelter or Affordable Housing?* (The Urban Institute Press 2001).
29 B. G. Link and others, 'Lifetime and Five-Year Prevalence of Homelessness in the United States' (1994) 84(12) *American Journal of Public Health* 1907.
30 Filed in New York state court on behalf of a class of men living on that city's Bowery, the case argued for a right to shelter under state and city law, including a provision in the state's constitution imposing a duty to provide 'aid, care, and support' of 'the needy'. *Callahan v Carey*, Amended Complaint, *Callahan v Carey*, 4582/79 (NY 1979). See also Consent Decree, *Callahan v Carey* (4582/79, NY, Aug 1981), spelling out the terms under which the city would provide emergency shelter to all homeless men in the city. Subsequent litigation expanded the terms of the decree to women, *Eldridge v Koch*, 118 Misc 2d 163 (NY 1983), and families, and the latter included a ruling on the merits establishing that the NY Constitution did in fact protect a right to shelter. *McCain v Koch*, 117 AD 2d 198 (NY 1986).

shelter system in the country. *Callahan* also helped spur the growth of advocacy, including the founding of the Coalition for the Homeless in New York City, coalitions around the country, and the National Coalition for the Homeless.

The newly formed National Coalition established an office in Washington, DC, in 1985 to organize and lead a campaign for a federal response to the national crisis. In 1989, the National Law Center on Homelessness & Poverty, now known as the National Homelessness Law Center, was founded to serve as the legal arm of the national movement to end homelessness. Advocates saw initial success with the enactment of the McKinney–Vento Act in 1987.[31] Authorizing $1 billion over two years – and appropriating $712 million – the Act primarily funded emergency shelter and transitional housing, with small amounts provided for permanent housing and job training, and larger amounts allocated to healthcare.[32] To coordinate federal efforts to address what the Act explicitly named a 'crisis' facing the nation, it created an independent federal agency now known as the US Interagency Council on Homelessness (USICH).[33]

In addition, Title V of the Act created a right of first refusal to 'suitable' vacant federal real property for homeless services providers.[34] Litigation to enforce that right yielded a nationwide injunction (still in effect), multiple enforcement orders, and a slow trickle of properties that now number over 500.[35] Title VII created a right for homeless children to enrol in and attend public school, including a right to continue in their school of origin if that was in their best interest, and to receive transportation to get there.[36] Litigation resulted in a 1995 federal appeals court ruling holding that the rights granted under Title VII are judicially enforceable;[37] this has been reaffirmed on multiple occasions.[38] In at least one case, a federal court held that homeless children's right to education is also protected by the US Constitution.[39] Most recently, litigation led to a consent decree requiring New York City to ensure internet access for homeless children living in shelters during the pandemic.[40]

Funding for the McKinney–Vento Act increased significantly over time, exceeding $3.3 billion in 2022. In 2009, amendments known as the HEARTH Act consolidated

---

31 The National Coalition hired Maria Foscarinis, then a young lawyer, to establish that office and organize the campaign. See M. Foscarinis, 'Strategies to Address Homelessness in the Trump Era: Lessons from the Reagan Administration' (2018) 27(1) *Journal of Affordable Housing and Community Development Law* 161; M. Foscarinis, 'Beyond Homelessness: Ethics, Advocacy, and Strategy' (1993) 12(1) *St. Louis University Public Law Review* 37; Foscarinis (n 20).

32 Much of early advocacy was focused on emergency relief; some advocates prioritized shelter, but for many advocates, this was simply a result of the political constraints of the time. M. Foscarinis, 'Homelessness, Litigation and Law Reform Strategies: A United States Perspective' (2004) 10(2) *Australian Journal of Human Rights* 105.

33 42 USC § 11301 (1987); for an overview, see Foscarinis (n 20).

34 42 USC § 11411.

35 NLCHP, 'Public Property, Public Need' *NLCHP* (2017) <https://homelesslaw.org/wp-content/uploads/2018/10/Public-Property-Public-Need-1.pdf> (accessed 1 September 2023).

36 42 USC § 11431. A litigation strategy was also developed as part of the campaign for a federal response aimed at the federal agencies. For an overview, see also M. Foscarinis, 'Federal Legislative and Litigative Strategies: An Overview' (1990) 1(1) *Maryland Journal of Contemporary Legal Issues* 9.

37 *Lampkin v District of Columbia*, 27 F 3d 605 (DC Cir 1994), *cert denied*, 115 S Ct 578 (1994).

38 *Salazar v Edwards*, 92 CH 5703, Settlement Agreement and Stipulation to Dismiss (IL 21 November 1996); L. M. Heybach and S. E. Platt, 'Enforcing the Educational Rights of Homeless Children and Youth: Focus on Chicago' *Chicago Coalition for the Homeless* (1 May 1998); *National Law Center on Homelessness and Poverty v New York*, 224 FRD 314 (EDNY 23 October 2004).

39 *Lampkin* (n 37).

40 *JT v City of New York*, 20 Civ 5878 (CM) (SDNY 20 November 2020).

programmes administered by HUD and codified a joint application process for the funds by local Continuums of Care.[41] The amendments also required USICH to create a federal plan to end homelessness and to develop strategies to address criminalization.

When the McKinney–Vento Act was passed, advocates and key congressional supporters emphasized it was just a first step, and that longer-term relief was imperative.[42] Advocates developed and pushed for an ambitious consensus agenda for housing, income, services, and civil rights, and a few pieces were adopted. Later, advocacy shifted to efforts to include the needs of homeless people in larger, 'mainstream' anti-poverty programmes, with some success.[43]

But the promised longer-term measures to end homelessness were never enacted; instead, a series of harmful policies were adopted.[44] In 1996, following then-president Clinton's promise to 'end welfare as we know it', a major federal programme, Aid to Families with Dependent Children, was repealed and replaced with a new block grant, removing a key, albeit grossly inadequate, cash entitlement for poor families, many of whom were either homeless or on its brink.[45] Two years later, the Faircloth amendment prohibited any net increase in public housing units.

Meanwhile, emergency assistance systems were standardized. HUD required communities receiving its funds to adopt a 'coordinated entry' system to allocate the limited resources. In some communities, a person experiencing a housing crisis may seek help through a variety of system 'access points', for example, calling a hotline, going to any

---

41 There are now approximately 400 CoCs around the country. HUD Exchange, 'The Continuum of Care Program' *hudexchange* <www.hudexchange.info/programs/coc/> (accessed 1 September 2023).
42 R. Pear 'President Signs $1 Billion Bill to Aid Homeless' *New York Times* (24 July 1987); Foscarinis (2018) (n 31).
43 See, for example, NLCHP, 'Due Credit: Increasing Homeless Workers' Earnings Through the Earned Income Tax Credit' *NLCHP* (1998) (new rule clarifying homeless workers' eligibility for refundable tax credit); a programme to help disabled homeless people sign up for disability benefits; a requirement that conversion of military bases to civilian use address the needs of homeless people, NLCHP, 'Utilizing the Base Closure Community Redevelopment and Homeless Assistance Act: A Toolkit for Non-Profits' *NLCHP* (2007) <https://homelesslaw.org/wp-content/uploads/2018/10/BRACtoolkit.pdf> (accessed 1 September 2023); inclusion of homeless children with special needs in special education programs; NLCHP, 'No Barriers' *NLCHP* (2016) <https://homelesslaw.org/wp-content/uploads/2018/10/NoBarriers-1.pdf> (accessed 1 September 2023) inclusion of all homeless schoolchildren in the major federal education programme for low-income schoolchildren NCHE 'Serving Students Experiencing Homelessness Under Title I, Part A' *NCHE* (2014) <https://files.eric.ed.gov/fulltext/ED574592.pdf> (accessed 1 September 2023), automatic eligibility of homeless children for free school lunches, Child Nutrition and WIC Reauthorization Act of 2004, PL 108–265, 118 Stat 729 (2004), and inclusion of homeless preschoolers in Head Start and other early education programs. Housing protections were added to the Violence Against Women Act to help prevent survivors from becoming homeless; see, for example, NLCHP, 'Fact Sheet: The Impact of the Violence Against Women Reauthorization Act of 2013 on the Housing Rights of Survivors of Domestic Violence' *NLCHP* (2013) <https://homelesslaw.org/wp-content/uploads/2018/10/VAWA_Fact_Sheet.pdf> (accessed 1 September 2023). Following the 2007–2008 foreclosure crisis and the resulting sharp increase in homelessness, advocates pushed for, and Congress passed, the Protecting Tenants at Foreclosure Act. See, for example, NLCHP and NLIHC, 'Without Just Cause: A 50 State Review of the (Lack of) Rights of Tenants in Foreclosure' *NLCHP and NLIHC* (2009); K. Johnson, 'Protecting Tenants at Foreclosure' *NLIHC* (6 June 2021) <https://nlihc.org/sites/default/files/AG-2021/06-06_PTFA.pdf> (accessed 1 September 2023).
44 See M. Foscarinis, 'Congress Is 35 Years Overdue on Its Promise to End Homelessness' *The Hill* (23 July 2022).
45 The Personal Responsibility and Work Opportunity Reconciliation Act, PL 104–193, 110 Stat 2105 (1996).

shelter in the area, or engaging with street outreach; in others, they may go to a single central location to seek help.[46]

Despite the plethora of HUD rules and guidance on the 'coordinated entry' process and its advantages, the reality remains that the help available is woefully insufficient. In 2022, HUD's annual count estimated the gap between the number of people experiencing homelessness on a single night and available shelter to be over 160,000 beds. In many communities, there are waiting lists for *emergency* shelter.

The failure to enact long-term solutions, the continued cuts to social welfare programmes, and the ongoing lack even of emergency aid all increased the risk of homelessness for poor people. These developments have also furthered harmful and racist laws and stereotypes directed at those experiencing homelessness.

Local Responses in the Absence of Adequate Housing: Criminalization

A public narrative of 'compassion fatigue' emerged in the 1990s, falsely portraying homeless people as 'service-resistant', or simply unwilling to accept help.[47] The stage was set for a destructive new trend – the criminalization of homelessness –[48] which unfolded primarily at the city level and paralleled the growth of punitive responses to poverty at all levels of government.[49]

With roots in colonial poor laws and in later efforts to control newly freed enslaved persons,[50] laws regulating public space evolved to target homeless people. They included bans on camping, sleeping, vehicle habitation, panhandling, loitering, public urination, and property storage,[51] and laws regulating would-be helpers, such as restrictions on offering food to people in public places.[52] With the increasing prevalence of

---

46 HUD, 'Notice Establishing Additional Requirements for a Continuum of Care Centralized or Coordinated Assessment System' (23 January 2017) <www.hud.gov/sites/documents/17-01CPDN.PDF> (accessed 1 September 2023).
47 The media reported 'compassion fatigue'; see E. Goodman, 'Compassion Fatigue' *Washington Post* (3 February 1990). Public opinion polls during this time did not reflect diminution of compassion. P. O. Buck, P. A. Toro and M. A. Ramos, 'Media and Professional Interest in Homelessness Over 30 Years (1974–2003)' (2004) 4(1) *Analyses of Social Issues and Public Policy* 151, 154.
48 See NLCHP, 'Go Directly to Jail' *NLCHP* (1991), the first of what became a series of national survey reports documenting this trend and advocating for its reversal in favour of constructive solutions.
49 At the national level, these included the 'Contract with America', promoted by Newt Gingrich, and Bill Clinton's pledge to 'end welfare as we know it'. State-level repeal of or limitations on general assistance programs has severely eroded that extremely limited and inadequate source of aid. See L. Schott, 'State General Assistance Programs Very Limited in Half of States and Nonexistent in Others, Despite Need' *CBPP* (2 July 2020) <www.cbpp.org/research/family-income-support/state-general-assistance-programs-very-limited-in-half-the-states> (accessed 1 September 2023). City-level addition of time limits and other restrictions on shelter – including the repeal of Washington, DC, of a right to shelter – removed even that emergency support. M. Ellen Hombs 'Reversals of Fortune: America's Homeless Poor and Their Advocates in the 1990s' (1992) 17 *New Formations* 109.
50 See Hopper and Milburn (n 1); P. Edelman, *Not a Crime to Be Poor* (New Press 2017).
51 See NLCHP, 'Housing Not Handcuffs: Ending the Criminalization of Homelessness in US Cities' *NLCHP* (2019).
52 See Grace Guarneri, 'Why It's Illegal to Feed the Homeless in Cities Across America' *Newsweek* (16 January 2018) <www.newsweek.com/illegal-feed-criminalizing-homeless-america-782861> (accessed 1 September 2023).

criminalization,[53] resistance to these laws became a primary focus for advocates on both the local and national levels.

Litigation challenging such laws as violative of the US Constitution has been a leading form of that advocacy.[54] Recently in *Martin v Boise*, the Ninth Circuit affirmed that criminally punishing a person for sleeping in public in the absence of an indoor alternative is cruel and unusual punishment, in violation of the Eighth Amendment to the US Constitution. In *Johnson v Grants Pass*, the Ninth Circuit affirmed and further clarified that decision.[55] Over the past decade, courts have increasingly, but not always, found in favour of homeless plaintiffs, striking down such laws or requiring notice before an encampment is swept.[56] In January 2024, the US Supreme Court agreed to review the Ninth Circuit's decision in *Grants Pass*, and a judgment is expected in summer 2024.[57]

Some state legislatures have enacted Homeless Bills of Rights, which protect the rights of people experiencing homelessness to use public space.[58] More recently, however, some have enacted statewide measures criminalizing homelessness.[59] But thanks to decades of advocacy, including advocacy with international human rights mechanisms, federal engagement has grown, with increasingly clear guidance from USICH, HUD, and Department of Justice (DOJ).[60] In addition, the federal DOJ filed a statement of interest brief in *Bell v Boise* (later styled *Martin v Boise*).[61] In 2016, the National Homelessness Law Center and National Coalition for the Homeless, in partnership with a steering committee made up of a majority of people with lived experience of homelessness, launched the Housing Not Handcuffs Campaign to bring together groups

---

53 See NLCHP, 'Go Directly to Jail: A Report Analyzing Anti-Homeless Ordinances' *NLCHP* (1991). The most recent such report, NLCHP (n 51), tracked the same 187 cities since 2006, allowing for trend analysis.
54 For an overview, see M. Foscarinis, 'Downward Spiral: Homelessness and Its Criminalization' (1996) 14(1) *Yale Law and Policy Review* 1; see NLCHP, 'Housing Not Hand Cuffs: A Litigation Manual' *NLCHP* (2017) for an overview of more recent litigation.
55 50 F.4th 787 (2022), cert. granted, 92 USLW 3174 (2024).
56 See NLCHP (n 54) 6; NLCHP, 'Housing Not Handcuffs: Supplement to Litigation Manual' *NLCHP* (2022) 5.
57 92 USLW 3174 (2024).
58 Rhode Island was the first state to enact such a law in 2012, followed by Illinois and Connecticut in 2013; Puerto Rico preceded them in 1998. NLCHP, 'From Wrongs to Rights: The Case for Homeless Bills of Rights Legislation' *NLCHP* (2014).
59 NLCHP, 'Housing Not Handcuffs: State Law Supplement' *NLCHP* (2022).
60 In the 1990s, advocacy led to favourable actions by the US Department of Justice, including amicus briefs in two cases. Brief for the United States as *Amicus Curiae*, *Joyce v City and County of San Francisco*, No 95–16940 (9th Cir, 29 March 1996) (DOJ); Brief for the United States as *Amicus Curiae*, *Tobe v City of Santa Ana*, No 803850 (Cal 9 June 1994). After advocates won a congressional directive to USICH to develop constructive alternatives to criminalization, the Council and the DOJ published a report, USICH, 'Searching Out Solutions: Constructive Alternatives to the Criminalization of Homelessness' *USICH* (June 2012); NLCHP, 'Scoring Points: How Ending the Criminalization of Homelessness Can Increase HUD Funding to Your Community' (2018). See also E. Tars and others, 'Challenging Domestic Injustice Through International Human Rights Advocacy: Addressing Homelessness in the United States' (2021) 42(3) *Cardozo Law Review* 913; J. Olivet and others, 'A Brief Timeline of Race and Homelessness in America' *Community Solutions* (March 2019), impact of CERD shadow report and committee's response on public awareness of, and activism aimed at, the disproportionate racial impact of homelessness.
61 Ibid. *Bell v Boise*. See also DOJ, Office of Public Affairs, 'Justice Department Files Brief to Address the Criminalization of Homelessness' (2015) <www.justice.gov/opa/pr/justice-department-files-brief-address-criminalization-homelessness>.

around the country advocating *against* criminalization – and to link explicitly the call against criminalization to the call for housing.[62]

The United States and Housing as a Human Right

The United States does not explicitly include a right to housing in its Constitution.[63] While some scholars have argued for an interpretation that includes minimum subsistence rights,[64] as it is currently understood by most scholars and courts, the US Constitution does not protect economic rights for all. Rather, it protects rights for those who already possess them.

Federal housing programmes were created statutorily by FDR's New Deal following the Great Depression and the mass homelessness of that era.[65] As documented by Richard Rothstein and others, they intentionally excluded Black, Indigenous, and other People of Colour (BIPOC). In the 1949 Housing Act, Congress stated a 'goal' of a 'decent home and a suitable living environment for every American family'[66] but did not guarantee it as a right. Current federal income tax law subsidizes homeownership as a matter of right, while renters (disproportionately BIPOC) have no right to assistance. Local zoning laws that require single-family homes on lots of specified size exclude those who cannot afford them – disproportionately, and sometimes explicitly, minoritized communities. Discrimination pervades housing as well as employment, healthcare, public benefits, and civic participation.

The Universal Declaration of Human Rights incorporated FDR's view that political and economic rights are interdependent. The United States ratified one of two treaties implementing the Declaration: that protecting civil and political rights. The other, enshrining economic, social, and cultural rights, was signed by President Carter but not ratified by the Senate.[67] Policies affirming the human right to housing were adopted in several local jurisdictions,[68] as US advocates working on homelessness began promoting

---

62 NLCHP, 'Housing Not Handcuffs Justice Network: About the Network' *NLCHP* (24 July 2022) <https://homelesslaw.org/housing-not-handcuffs/> (accessed 1 September 2023).
63 NLCHP, 'Homelessness in the United States and the Human Right to Housing' *NLCHP* (2004). See also M. Foscarinis and others, 'The Human Right to Housing: Making the Case in US Advocacy' (2004) 38(3–4) *Clearinghouse Review* 97; E. Tars and others, 'The Champagne of Housing Rights: France's Enforceable Right to Housing and Lessons for U.S. Advocates' (2012) 4(2) *Northeastern University Law Journal* 429. A 1972 US Supreme Court case, *Lindsey v Normet* 405 US 56 (1972), commonly cited for the proposition that there also no implicit right to housing in the US Constitution, falls short of such a clear holding; but the current prospects of federal judicial recognition of such a right are bleak.
64 C. L. Black Jr, 'Further Reflections on the Constitutional Justice of Livelihood' (1986) 86(6) *Columbia Law Review* 1103; A. R Amar, 'Forty Acres and a Mule: A Republican Theory of Minimal Entitlements' (1990) 13 *Harvard Journal of Law and Public Policy* 37; F. I. Michelman, 'Welfare Rights in a Constitutional Democracy' (1979) 3 *Washington University Law Quarterly* 659; J. H. Ely, *Democracy and Distrust: A Theory of Judicial Review* (Harvard UP 1980).
65 Wakin (n 6) 8–9, 15–16; History.com Editors, 'Hoovervilles' *history.com* (5 March 2010) <www.history.com/topics/great-depression/hoovervilles> (accessed 1 September 2023). NLCHP, '"Simply Unacceptable": Homelessness and the Human Right to Housing in the United States' *NLCHP* (2011).
66 Housing Act of 1949, PL 81–171 (1949); M. Foscarinis, 'Advocating for the Human Right to Housing: Notes from the United States' (2006) 30(3) *NYU Review of Law & Social Change* 447.
67 NLCHP (n 65) 19.
68 Cook City Res 04-R-105 (IL, 23 March 2004). Los Angeles included the right to housing in 'Bring LA Home', its ten-year plan to end homelessness. M. Foscarinis and E. Tars, 'Housing Rights and Wrongs: The U.S. and the Right to Housing' in C. Soohoo, C. Albisa and M. F. Davis (eds), *Bringing Human Rights Home: Portraits of the Movement* (Praeger 2008); P. Schneider, 'Grass Roots: Madison Recognizes Housing

the human right to housing[69] and incorporating models from other countries in their recommendations for US policy.[70]

As the affordable housing crisis intensified, commanding greater public attention, key members of Congress as well as President Biden began speaking of housing as a right and including that formulation in policy proposals.[71] Aspects of Biden's agenda on housing, such as a proposal to make housing vouchers an entitlement, would further that right.[72] The right to counsel in eviction cases, an important protection that prevents homelessness, is also gaining momentum.[73]

Current Policy Proposals

The affordable housing crisis means that more precariously positioned renters enter homelessness than exit it into housing, and homelessness continues to grow.[74] Through the advocacy of People's Action, a grassroots housing platform known as the 'Homes Guarantee' or 'People's Housing Platform' was launched in January 2020 as a series of seven bills, with the goal of making housing a human right in the United States. Several of these as well as other promising approaches are discussed next.

---

as a Human Right' *Capital Times* (2 December 2011); Dane County Recognizes Housing as a Human Right, Res 292, 11–12 (WI, 12 July 2012).

69 M. Foscarinis, 'Homelessness and Human Rights: Towards an Integrated Strategy' (2000) 19(2) *Saint Louis University Public Law Review* 327; Foscarinis and others (n 68); Foscarinis (n 66); M. Foscarinis, 'The Grown of a Movement for the Human Right to Housing in the United States' (2007) 20 *Harvard Human Rights Journal* 35.

70 See Tars and others (n 63); E. Tars and C. Egelson, 'Great Scot!: The Scottish Plan to End Homelessness and Lessons for the Housing Rights Movement in the United States' (2009) 16(1) *Georgetown Journal on Poverty Law & Policy* 187. During the Universal Periodic Review, conducted by the UN Human Rights Council (UNHRC), a coalition of organizations submitted reports to the UNHRC on the status of the human right to housing in the United States, Beyond Shelter and others, 'A Report to the UN Human Rights Council on the Right to Adequate Housing in the United States of America' (19 April 2010); NLCHP and Chair, US Human Rights Network UPR Housing Working Group, 'Housing and Homelessness in the United States of America' (14 September 2014); NLCHP, 'Housing and Homelessness in the United States of America' NLCHP (3 October 2019).

71 K. Robillard and A. Delaney, '2020 Democrats Think the Rent Is too Damn High' *Huffington Post* (21 March 2019) <www.huffpost.com/entry/2020-democrats-housing_n_5c92788be4b01b140d34a891> (accessed 1 September 2023); E. Badger, 'Renters are Mad. Presidential Candidates Have Noticed' *New York Times* (23 April 2019); E. Rosen, 'If Housing Is a Right, How Do We Make It Happen?' *New York Times* (17 February 2021).

72 W. Fischer and E. Gartland, 'Housing Vouchers in Economic Recovery Bill Would Sharply Cut Homelessness, Housing Instability' *CBPP* (23 September 2021) <www.cbpp.org/research/housing/housing-vouchers-in-economic-recovery-bill-would-sharply-cut-homelessness-housing> (accessed 1 September 2023); Possible future funding increases enacted by Congress is currently unclear. J Stein, 'White House Confronts Grueling Choices as It Debates Major Cuts to Biden Economic Plan' *Washington Post* (2 October 2021) <www.washingtonpost.com/us-policy/2021/10/02/biden-agenda-budget-cuts/> (accessed 1 September 2023).

73 National Coalition for a Civil Right to Counsel, '2021/2022 Federal/State Civil Right to Counsel Bills' NCCRC <http://civilrighttocounsel.org/legislative_developments/20212022_bills> (accessed 1 September 2023).

74 In Los Angeles, for example, an average of 207 people exit homelessness every day – while 227 people become homeless. Los Angeles Homeless Services Authority, '2020 Greater Los Angeles Homeless Count Results' *Los Angeles Homeless Services Authority* (12 June 2020) <www.lahsa.org/news?article=726-2020-greater-los-angeles-homeless-count-results> (accessed 1 September 2023).

Helping People Currently Homeless

Ending Criminalization

Two bills, Representative Waters's *Ending Homelessness Act* and Representative Jayapal's *Housing Is a Human Right Act*, prioritize federal funding to local governments that have taken steps to decriminalize homelessness, creating an incentive for them to do so.[75] Other bills, such as Representative Cori Bush's *People's Response Act* and Senator Michael Bennet's *Supporting Mental Assistance Responder Teams (SMART) Community Policing Act*, provide funding for communities to have social workers and mental health professionals respond to people experiencing homelessness rather than police.[76]

During the pandemic, following advocacy by the Law Center and others, the Centers for Disease Control and Prevention (CDC) issued guidance recommending individual housing for people living unsheltered and, if unavailable, recommending against clearing encampments,[77] citing the potential of sweeps to spread the virus, risking public health harms to the entire community. Federal Emergency Management Agency (FEMA) reimbursed communities to offer individual housing in vacant hotel rooms to people experiencing homelessness for the duration of the pandemic.[78] Though tragically under-utilized in much of the country, California housed more than 50,000 persons experiencing unsheltered homelessness through its Project Roomkey programme, with some, though not all, then transitioning to permanent housing.[79]

Increased Funding for Housing First and Permanent Supportive Housing

The *Ending Homelessness Act* and *Housing Is a Human Right Act* would address the immediate needs of people experiencing homelessness by dramatically expanding investments in funds distributed to local Continuums of Care under the McKinney–Vento Act, as amended by the HEARTH Act, as well as provide grants for infrastructure needs related to homelessness and to library programmes for people experiencing homelessness.

---

75 HR 3772, 117th Cong (2021); P. Jayapal, 'Jayapal and Meng Lead Lawmakers in Introducing the Housing is a Human Right Act' *Pramila Jayapal* (8 June 2021) <https://jayapal.house.gov/2021/06/08/housing-is-a-human-right-act/> (accessed 1 September 2023).
76 HR 4194, 117th Cong (2021); C. Adams, 'Rep. Cori Bush Wants to Transform Policing and Public Safety with New Bill' *NBC* (28 June 2021) <www.nbcnews.com/news/nbcblk/rep-cori-bush-wants-transform-policing-public-safety-new-bill-n1272490> (accessed 1 September 2023); S 4513, 117th Cong (2022); M. Benet, 'Bennet Unveils Legislation to Support Law Enforcement and Strengthen Community Policing' *Michael Bennet* (13 July 2022) <www.bennet.senate.gov/public/index.cfm/2022/7/bennet-unveils-legislation-to-support-law-enforcement-and-strengthen-community-policing> (accessed 1 September 2023).
77 Centers for Disease Control and Prevention, 'Interim Guidance on Unsheltered Homelessness and Coronavirus Disease 2019 (COVID-19) for Homeless Service Providers and Local Officials' *CDC* (May 2020); NLIHC, 'FEMA Changes Policy to Approve Non-Congregate Shelter Reimbursement for Duration of Emergency' *NLIHC* (22 December 2020) <https://nlihc.org/resource/fema-changes-policy-approve-non-congregate-shelter-reimbursement-duration-emergency> (accessed 1 September 2023).
78 Ibid.
79 See V. Rancano, 'Last Days at the Radisson: As State Shelter Program Shutters, Formerly Unhoused Residents in Oakland Brace for Next Steps' *KQED* (2 August 2022) <www.kqed.org/news/11921155/last-days-at-the-radisson-as-state-shelter-program-shutters-formerly-unhoused-residents-in-oakland-brace-for-next-steps> (accessed 1 September 2023).

Preventing Evictions to Prevent Homelessness

In response to the pandemic, the CARES Act created a temporary national eviction moratorium,[80] later extended by the CDC,[81] and replicated, with varying additional protections, by states and cities across the country.[82] The CARES Act and American Rescue Plan also funded billions of dollars of emergency rental assistance that helped millions of Americans stay in their homes.[83] Unfortunately, as the political urgency of the pandemic waned, these programmes were left to expire.

The *A Place to Prosper Act*, introduced by Representative Alexandria Ocasio-Cortez (D-NY), would create a national framework for rent control, the first ever. It would also create national 'just cause' eviction protections,[84] ban source of income discrimination to protect voucher holders, and provide funding for communities that offer a right to counsel in eviction cases.[85]

Ending Homelessness by Increasing Affordable Housing

Re-Establishing a Commitment to Public Housing

Representative Maxine Waters's *Housing Is Infrastructure Act* would invest $70 billion to repair America's crumbling public housing infrastructure – which leaves many units vacant even as people are homeless – and would repeal the Faircloth Amendment.[86] With a goal of targeting those with the greatest needs first, Representative Waters's *Ending Homelessness Act* would expand the number of housing vouchers over eight years to ultimately achieve a universal voucher programme. It would also ban source of income discrimination and fund fair housing awareness and enforcement.[87]

Representative Ilhan Omar's *Homes for All Act* would also repeal the Faircloth Amendment, authorize construction of 8.5 million new public housing and 3.5 million private permanently affordable rental units,[88] and shift public housing operating and capital expenses from the discretionary to the mandatory side of the federal budget.

---

80 Coronavirus Aid, Relief and Economic Security Act, PL 116–136, Sec 4024 (2020).
81 Temporary Halt in Residential Evictions to Prevent the Further Spread of COVID-19, 85 Fed Reg 55292 (4 September 2020).
82 See Eviction Lab, 'COVID-19 Housing Policy Scorecard' *Eviction Lab* (2021) <https://evictionlab.org/covid-policy-scorecard/> (accessed 1 September 2023).
83 NLIHC, 'Treasury Emergency Rental Assistance Dashboard' *NLIHC* (2021) <https://nlihc.org/era-dashboard> (accessed 1 September 2023); C. Aiken and others, 'Emergency Rental Assistance (ERA) During the Pandemic: Implications for the Design of Permanent ERA Programs' (The Housing Initiative at Penn and NLIHC March 2022) <https://nlihc.org/sites/default/files/HIP_NLIHC_2022_3-10_FINAL.pdf> (accessed 1 September 2023).
84 HR 5072, 116th Cong (2019); P. Sisson, 'Alexandria Ocasio-Cortez's Latest Legislation? Housing Justice for All' *Curbed* (25 September 2019) <https://archive.curbed.com/2019/9/25/20882120/aoc-alexandria-ocasio-cortez-just-society-legislation-housing> (accessed 1 September 2023).
85 Ibid. Several other bills have also been introduced to fund the right to counsel, including the Eviction Prevention Act, HB 3580, 117th Cong (2021); the HELP Act, HB 6696, 117th Cong (2022); and the Affordable HOME Act, HB 5385/ SB 2234, 117th Cong (2021).
86 HR 4497, 117th Cong (2021).
87 HR 4496, 117th Cong (2021).
88 HR 6989, 117th Cong (2022); I. Omar, 'Rep. Omar Reintroduces Homes for All, Manufactured Housing Legislation' *Ilhan Omar* (24 March 2022) <https://omar.house.gov/media/press-releases/rep-omar-reintroduces-homes-all-manufactured-housing-legislation> (accessed 1 September 2023).

Renters' Tax Credits

Multiple bills have been introduced in the past few years that would create a refundable tax credit to ensure renters pay only 30% of their income on housing costs.[89] A renter's tax credit would avoid the annual funding battles over discretionary funding, ensuring everyone who is eligible gets it, moving policy closer to a right to housing. It would also avoid the discrimination perpetrated against voucher holders, making it easier for them to find a place to rent.

National Housing Trust Fund

The National Housing Trust Fund (NHTF), created in 2008, is the first new housing resource since 1974, targeted to the building, rehabilitating, preserving, and operating of rental housing for extremely low-income people. Funded by a fee on federally backed mortgages, it has distributed millions of dollars to states through block grant programmes but still falls far short of meeting the need. Representative Waters's *Ending Homelessness Act* provides substantial new investments in the NHTF to build and preserve deeply affordable rental housing.

Challenges and Opportunities

The crisis of homelessness in America sits at a tipping point. On the bright side, there are many legislative proposals explicitly grounded in housing as a basic human right, a right acknowledged for the first time since FDR by a president and HUD secretary. Organizing pressure is strong: 'end the criminalization of homelessness and implement solutions that treat housing as a right' was the top recommendation from the field to USICH for its next federal plan to end homelessness.[90]

But the pressure is strong because the need is dire. As temporary funding measures and moratoria spurred by the pandemic have expired, evictions are rebounding, hotel programmes are ending, and homelessness is growing. Because many shelters are still at reduced capacity due to Covid prevention measures, even more people are on the streets, where highly visible encampments fuel efforts to criminalize, rather than help, homeless people.

Challenge: Breakdown of Bipartisan Support for Housing First

Alarmingly, the evidence-based practice of Housing First, which emphasizes providing housing and then offering services, has now come under attack from right-wing ideologues, eroding long-standing bipartisan support. Although highly effective in ending homelessness,

---

89 See S 1106, 116th Cong (2019); S 3342, 115th Cong (2018); S 2554, 117th Cong (2021); HR 8357, 117th Cong (2022); NLIHC, 'Representatives Davis, Gomez, Peters, and Panetta Introduce the "Rent Relief Act of 2022" to Establish a Renters' Tax Credit' NLIHC (18 July 2022) <https://nlihc.org/resource/representatives-davis-gomez-peters-and-panetta-introduce-rent-relief-act-2022-establish> (accessed 1 September 2023).

90 A. Vandenberg, 'What We're Hearing from YOU About the Federal Strategic Plan to Prevent and End Homelessness' USICH News (6 January 2022) <www.usich.gov/news/what-were-hearing-from-you-about-the-federal-strategic-plan-to-prevent-and-end-homelessness> (accessed 1 September 2023).

Housing First programmes are not nearly to scale given the need. But some politicians are arguing that the continued growth of homelessness means that Housing First has failed. President Trump's administration attacked the policy, and others on the political right have followed suit.[91] In right-wing American media, the term 'Housing First' has become a negative buzzword, linked to 'critical race theory' and 'racial equity', and made politically toxic for Republicans to support.[92] But even liberal politicians are desperate for 'quick fix' criminalization measures to address visible homelessness without taking steps that are unpopular with real estate developers and other high-dollar donors, such as rebalancing the housing market.[93]

Challenge: Promotion of Short-Term Measures and Criminalization

Of particular concern is template legislation being promoted by a so-called 'think tank' known as the Cicero Institute that promotes short-term measures to address the visible symptoms of street homelessness.[94] Founded in 2016 in Austin, Texas, by Joe Lonsdale, a controversial tech billionaire and venture capitalist with investments in private prisons,[95] Cicero produces slick video and social media messaging to portray homelessness as about drug use and a failure of individual accountability.[96]

Following a successful effort to pass a statewide camping ban in Texas,[97] Cicero drafted template legislation that calls for the diversion of all homeless services funding to short-term measures, such as legal encampments and time-limited emergency shelters, with a grant of immunity for liability to encampment operators for all but grossly negligent conduct; a

---

91 R. E Little and B. Wintrode, 'Trump Administration Proposes Step Back from "Housing First" Homeless Policy' *Howard Center for Investigative Journalism* (23 October 2020) <https://cnsmaryland.org/2020/10/23/trump-administration-proposes-step-back-from-housing-first-homeless-policy/> (accessed 1 September 2023).

92 T. Carlson, 'Tucker Carlson Tonight' *Fox News* (18 January 2022) <https://video.foxnews.com/v/6292476962001#sp=show-clips> (accessed 1 September 2023).

93 See, for example, the recent embrace of California governor Newsom's 'CARE Court' proposal by the overwhelmingly Democratic legislature, which paves the way for putting people experiencing homelessness with mental health disabilities into forced institutionalization. O. Ensign and J. Raphling, 'Op-Ed: "CARE Court" Is No Solution for Unhoused People in California' *Los Angeles Times* (27 May 2022) <www.latimes.com/opinion/story/2022-05-27/care-court-california-mental-illness-homeless-treatment> (accessed 1 September 2023).

94 Cicero Institute, 'Reducing Street Homelessness Act Model Bill' *Cicero Institute* (November 2021) <https://ciceroinstitute.org/wp-content/uploads/2021/11/Reducing-Street-Homelessness-Act-Model-Bill.090821.pdf> (accessed 1 September 2023).

95 J. Lonsdale, 'Align Incentives to Solve Recidivism' *Medium* (15 May 2018) <https://medium.com/8vc-news/the-healing-game-3faa3eb79379> (accessed 1 September 2023); N. Mascarenhas, 'VC Joe Lonsdale's Tweets About "Woke" Tech Diversity Spark Investor Pushback' *TechCrunch* (3 January 2022) <https://techcrunch.com/2022/01/03/vc-joe-lonsdales-tweets-about-woke-tech-diversity-spark-investor-pushback/> (accessed 1 September 2023); J. Lonsdale (@JTLonsdale), 'My AmericanOptimist.com Team Hacked . . . ' *Twitter* (15 December 2021) <https://twitter.com/i/status/1471176120741638147> (accessed 1 September 2023).

96 PragerU, 'Homelessness: The Reality and the Solution' (16 March 2022) <www.prageru.com/video/homelessness-the-reality-and-the-solution?cmid=2f975094-7332-4fc6-afcf-e55071143f37> (accessed 1 September 2023).

97 R. Oxner, 'Texas Likely to Ban Homeless Encampments in Unapproved Public Places After Bill Is Sent to Governor' *Texas Tribune* (28 May 2021) <www.texastribune.org/2021/05/28/camping-ban-bill-approved/> (accessed 1 September 2023).

statewide anti-camping ban and denial of all homeless assistance and public safety funding to any refusing jurisdiction; lowering of due process protections to commit persons experiencing homelessness involuntarily to state psychiatric institutions and threat of jail or $5,000 fines for non-compliance with out-patient treatment; and the creation of 'homeless outreach teams' – law enforcement, funded by homelessness dollars – to force people experiencing homelessness into state-run encampments under threat of enforcement of the anti-camping ban.[98]

Missouri passed a version of this template in May 2022,[99] and with Cicero Institute support, Tennessee has made it a felony to camp on public property statewide.[100] Other versions of Cicero's template were introduced in Arizona,[101] Georgia,[102] Oklahoma,[103] Wisconsin,[104] and Multnomah County (Portland, OR).[105]

Challenge: Further Efforts to Evade Constitutional Protections

Responding to the Ninth Circuit's decision in *Martin v Boise*, some communities are attempting to frame legalized encampments as adequate alternatives in order to enable criminalization. Although legalized encampments based on a harm-reduction approach can provide a safer interim space while longer-term housing solutions are developed,[106] serving as part of a continuum of resources that can help people living unsheltered,[107] some are promoting them not to reduce harm but rather to enable enforcement of criminalizing ordinances. In one egregious example, the city of Chico presented a legal camping area on an unused airport tarmac with no water, electricity, and minimal shade in a city with temperatures that routinely reach over 100 degrees Fahrenheit (38 degrees Celsius) as an adequate alternative.[108]

Other communities are turning to laws governing civil commitments, with California leading a push to remove homeless individuals with mental disabilities from public view

---

98 Cicero Institute (n 94).
99 HB 1696, 101st Gen Assem, 2nd Reg Sess (Mo 2022).
100 SB 1610, 112th Gen Assem, Reg Sess (Tn 2022); Maggie LaMere, 'State Senate Passes Bill That Makes Camping on Public, State Property Illegal' *Fox17* (13 April 2022) <https://fox17.com/news/local/state-senate-passes-bill-that-makes-camping-on-public-state-property-illegal> (accessed 1 September 2023).
101 SB 1581, 55th Gen Assem, 2nd Reg Sess (Az 2022).
102 SB 535, 2021–22 Reg Sess (Ga 2022).
103 SB 1560, 58th Leg, 2nd Reg Sess (Ok 2022).
104 AB 604, 2021–22 Reg Sess (Wi 2022).
105 R. Ellis, 'People for Portland Proposes Ballot Measure to Eliminate Outdoor Camping' *OPB* (25 March 2022) <www.opb.org/article/2022/03/25/people-for-portland-proposes-ballot-measure-to-eliminate-outdoor-camping/> (accessed 1 September 2023).
106 See NLCHP, 'Tent City, USA: The Growth of America's Homeless Encampments and How Communities Are Responding' *NLCHP* (2017).
107 See M. Oak, '"There's a Mission Out Here" Why Residents, Staff Say the State's Homeless Camp Is Working' *KVUE* (17 May 2021) <www.kvue.com/article/news/local/homeless/austin-state-sanctioned-homeless-camp-update/269-1ad3ba51-aa31-46a9-925a-ac41ab4a623b> (accessed 1 September 2023); *Warren v City of Chico*, 2:21-CV-00640-MCE-DMC (ED Cal July 8, 2021); N. Cahill, 'Anti-Homeless Law Put on Ice in California College Town' *Courthouse News* (9 July 2021) <www.courthousenews.com/federal-judge-freezes-california-college-towns-anti-homeless-law/> (accessed 1 September 2023).
108 The judge roundly rejected this, ibid. *Warren*.

through institutionalization. Governor Newsom's proposed 'CARE Court',[109] framed as 'helping those who can't help themselves', will make it easier to place people into coerced, court-ordered treatment and conservatorships, stripping them of all decision-making power. Although acknowledging housing is a primary need, the proposal *prohibits* courts from ordering housing, making it likely that individuals would either remain homeless or end up in state institutions.[110] Because homelessness in California has a significant racially disparate impact[111] and Black, Indigenous, and People of Colour have been historically over- and mis-diagnosed with psychiatric disorders,[112] they will be disproportionately affected.

Challenge: Communications

Promoters of criminalization and other punitive and short-term measures argue that those who advocate long-term housing ignore the immediate plight of those living on the streets.[113] Adopting the language of harm reduction, they argue that any shelter or legal encampment is better than the streets, while ignoring[114] the lack of appropriate – or any – housing and services options. They call those who refuse inappropriate service or housing options 'service resistant' and deem criminalization and forced institutionalization necessary 'tools'.[115] Unlike the costs of housing and services, which must be addressed up front, the costs resulting from criminalization – though typically more – are often not acknowledged. This enables elected officials more easily to pass a ban on camping than allocate funds for affordable housing.[116]

Opportunity: Linking to Broader Movements for Racial Equity and Human Rights

Despite the preceding challenges, the long, patient work to educate advocates and policymakers about the human right to housing framework is coming to fruition, with people chanting in the streets and policymakers grappling with what the right looks like in

---

109 SB 1338, 2021–22, Reg Sess (Ca 2022).
110 Ensign and Raphling (n 93).
111 K. Cimini, 'Black People Disproportionately Homeless in California' *Cal Matters* (5 October 2019) <https://calmatters.org/california-divide/2019/10/black-people-disproportionately-homeless-in-california/> (accessed 1 September 2023).
112 Task Force to Study and Develop Reparation Proposals for African Americans: Interim Report (AB 2121), Op Att'y Gen (Ca DOJ June 2022); R. C. Schwartz and D. M. Blankenship, 'Racial Disparities in Psychotic Disorder Diagnosis: A Review of Empirical Literature' (2014) 4(4) *World Journal of Psychiatry* 133.
113 Office of Governor Gavin Newsom, 'Governor Newsom's CARE Court Proposal Cleared First Legislative Hurdle with Broad Support' *CA.gov* (27 April 2022) <www.gov.ca.gov/2022/04/27/governor-newsoms-care-court-proposal-cleared-first-legislative-hurdle-with-broad-support/> (accessed 1 September 2023).
114 Recovery Research Institute, 'Harm Reduction: Policies, Programs, and Practices That Aim to Reduce the Harms Associated with the Use of Alcohol and Other Drugs' *Recovery Research Institute* (25 September 2018) <www.recoveryanswers.org/resource/drug-and-alcohol-harm-reduction/> (accessed 1 September 2023).
115 C. Dulaney and D. Dawson, 'Mayor Gloria's Push for Homeless "Progressive Enforcement" Leads to Eight-fold Spike in Arrests' *KPBS* (13 June 2022) <www.kpbs.org/news/local/2022/06/13/mayor-glorias-push-for-homeless-progressive-enforcement-leads-to-eightfold-spike-in-arrests> (accessed 1 September 2023).
116 See NLCHP (n 58).

practice.[117] Comprehensive plans, built by people with lived expertise, such as the Homes Guarantee, elaborate what policies are necessary to ensure the right. Meanwhile, elected officials in California and Connecticut have been working to pass statutory or constitutional recognition of the human right to housing, laying a legal basis for further policies to implement the right.[118]

By providing grassroots movements with the legal frameworks offered by the internationally recognized human right to housing, legal advocates are helping to make the demands of activists concrete.

Conclusions

The authors remain cautiously optimistic about the future. The growth of the movement for housing as a human right in the United States and the increasing integration of people with lived experience of homelessness, as well as intersectional racial, gender, disability, and other forms of discrimination into policymaking, bodes well for the future. The pandemic showed that when there was a will, there was a way, to dramatically expand resources available to prevent homelessness. But with major funded threats from organizations like the Cicero Institute, with the active efforts to erase the bipartisan consensus around Housing First, and with pandemic subsidies expired and housing and other costs of living rising, we see the threat of much more homelessness. With more people forced to live on the streets, criminalization and other bad policies have the potential to snowball. The extent to which criminalization continues to increase may depend on the outcome of the Supreme Court's review in *Johnson v Grants Pass*. America, at its best, is a country that can use its ample resources to ensure no one is homeless. But at its worst, it can consolidate wealth for those who have it and use the criminal legal system to further marginalize those who do not. Our cautious optimism ultimately means we believe that by joining our voices and advocacy with those of many others, we can tip US law and policy in the right direction.

---

117 Tars and others (n 60).
118 Ibid. State of California Housing Agency Act, AB 2506, Reg Sess (Ca 2020); SB 194, 2020 Reg Sess (Ct 2020); Saud Anwar, 'Connecticut Should Become the "Right to Housing State"' *Hartford Courant* (9 January 2020) <www.courant.com/opinion/op-ed/hc-op-anwar-housing-0109-20200109-djs67wckuva7f-gvteglywqwsim-story.html> (accessed 1 September 2023).

16
INNOVATIVE POLICY RESPONSES TO HOUSING NEED IN THE UNITED STATES

Case Studies on Safe Parking, Tiny Homes, and Direct Cash Transfers

Daniel Brisson, Katherine Hoops Calhoun, and Jennifer Wilson

Introduction

Homelessness is a significant issue in the United States, impacting, by some estimates, over a million people every year. With no discernible end in sight, this chapter explores the need for innovative approaches to supplement and even disrupt the current housing and homelessness service system. We begin with an overview of the issue of homelessness in the United States, including common definitions and approaches to measurement, influential policy responses in the last few decades, and presenting challenges in affordable housing. We then provide a summary of studies being conducted in the United States on three innovative responses to homelessness: (1) safe parking as an alternative short-term sheltering option, (2) tiny home communities as an alternative long-term sheltering and housing option, and (3) direct cash delivered to unhoused adults as a supplement to existing public assistance programmes. We conclude with implications for homelessness policy responses.

Prevalence of Homelessness in the United States

Estimates of the number of people experiencing homelessness in the United States range between 580,000 people and 1.5 million people.[1] This variation in estimation can be attributed to several factors, one being the varied and dynamic experience of homelessness itself.

---

1 L. Kilduff and B. Jarosz, 'How Many People in the United States Are Experiencing Homelessness?' *PBR* (2020) <www.prb.org/how-many-people-in-the-united-states-are-experiencing-homelessness/> (accessed 1 September 2023). 'The State of Homelessness: 2021 Edition' (National Alliance to End Homelessness 2021) <https://endhomelessness.org/homelessness-in-america/homelessness-statistics/state-of-homelessness-2021/> (accessed1 September 2023).

Kuhn and Culhane categorized homelessness in three distinct experiences: transitional, episodic, and chronic. The most common experience of homelessness is *transitional*, where individuals exit homelessness in days or weeks and, in most cases, do not return to homelessness.[2] Others experience *episodic* homelessness, where they cycle in and out of experiences of homelessness.[3] The minority of people experiencing homelessness are those who experience *chronic* homelessness. People who are chronically homeless are individuals who fit the stereotypical profile of homeless, living unsheltered or in emergency shelters for long periods of time.[4] The US Department of Housing and Urban Development (HUD) has formally defined *chronic homelessness* as being continuously homeless for at least a year or have had at least four episodes of homelessness in the past three years *and* having a disabling condition.[5] The dynamic experience of homelessness can influence the way agencies and individuals categorize what is an experience of homelessness and what is not. Additionally, because most people enter and exit homelessness in a short period of time, the prevalence of homelessness can be difficult to estimate.

Apart from the dynamic experience of homelessness, different homelessness-serving organizations in the United States define *homelessness* differently, which can also influence the variation in estimation of people experiencing homelessness. Often, when people think of homelessness, they think of people who are experiencing literal and chronic homelessness, meaning, those who are on the street; living in cars, bus stations, or tents; or staying in emergency shelters at night.[6] However, definitions of *homelessness* can also include people who are precariously housed, meaning, individuals living in motels, in temporary or transitional housing, or with another family due to economic hardship.[7] The two primary sources that are used to gauge the prevalence of homelessness in the United States use these two different definitions of *homelessness*. The US Department of Housing and Urban Development (HUD) uses the more restrictive, literal *homelessness* definition, and the US Department of Education uses the broader definition that includes individuals who are precariously housed. These differing definitions of what it means to be homeless have impacted our ability to understand the true nature of the issue. Next, we provide a more in-depth discussion of both definitions of homelessness.

HUD Point-in-Time Count

In 2005, HUD began requiring communities that access federal funds for housing and homelessness services to conduct a Point-in-Time Count (PIT) of homelessness every two

---

2 R. Kuhn and D. P. Culhane, 'Applying Cluster Analysis to Test a Typology of Homelessness by Pattern of Shelter Utilization: Results from the Analysis of Administrative Data' (1998) 26(2) *American Journal of Community Psychology* 207. D. P. Culhane, 'Non-Chronic Adult Homelessness: Background and Opportunities' (Presented at the National Alliance to End Homelessness Annual Conference 29 July 2014).
3 Kuhn and Culhane (n 2).
4 Ibid.
5 United States Department of Housing and Urban Development, 'Defining Chronic Homelessness: A Technical Guide for HUD Programs' (Office of Community Planning and Development 2007) <https://files.hudexchange.info/resources/documents/DefiningChronicHomeless.pdf> (accessed 1 September 2023).
6 M. Shinn and J. Khadduri, *In the Midst of Plenty: Homelessness and What to Do About It* (Wiley Blackwell 2020).
7 Ibid.

years. The PIT has become the primary method of assessing the prevalence of homelessness in the United States.[8] The PIT takes place on a single night in late January and includes counting the number of people who are staying in emergency shelters, are in transitional housing, and are sleeping unsheltered.[9] People are considered unsheltered if they are sleeping anywhere that is not meant for long-term human habitation, including abandoned buildings, tents, cars, or the street.[10] To count individuals who are unsheltered, service providers and volunteers go to known areas where people experiencing homelessness spend time and either interview or simply count the people they see.[11]

Many homelessness researchers and advocates argue that the way in which the PIT is designed and implemented varies greatly in communities across the country, resulting in a gross undercount of people experiencing homelessness.[12] People who are unsheltered need to be visible to be counted, and one study in New York City found that between 31% and 41% of people who were unsheltered slept in a location that was not visible, and they were therefore not counted in the PIT.[13] Additionally, people in hospitals and jails are also not counted.[14] In this light, some argue that numbers reported by HUD should be thought of instead as the minimum number of people experiencing homelessness in the country.[15]

According to the 2020 PIT count, more than 580,000 people were experiencing homelessness on a single January night in the United States.[16] This reflects a 2.2% increase from 2019, where roughly 565,000 people were experiencing homelessness.[17] The 2020 PIT showed that more individuals experiencing homelessness were unsheltered (51%) than in shelter (49%) for the first time since the PIT count began.[18] These data were collected prior to the start of the Covid-19 pandemic, so although hesitation to staying in congregate

---

8 T. D. Morgan, *Counting the Homeless: Unsheltered and Sheltered* (Nova Science Publishers 2010). National Alliance to End Homelessness, 'What Is a Point-in-Time Count?' (2012) <https://endhomelessness.org/resource/what-is-a-point-in-time-count/#:~:text=The%20first%20of%20these%20counts,the%20eradication%20of%20the%20problem> (accessed 1 September 2023).

9 R. Addo and P. Gerstenblatt, 'Housing First: A Policy Analysis of the Hearth Act' (2021) 2 *Journal of Policy Practice and Research* 90. Shinn and Khadduri (n 6).

10 United States Department of Housing and Urban Development, 'A Guide to Counting Unsheltered Homeless People' (2004) <www.hudexchange.info/sites/onecpd/assets/File/Guide-for-Counting-Unsheltered-Homeless-Persons.pdf> (accessed 1 September 2023).

11 Shinn and Khadduri (n 6).

12 M. Schneider, D. Brisson and D. Burnes, 'Do We Really Know How Many Are Homeless? An Analysis of the Point in Time Homelessness Count' (2016) 97(4) *Families in Society* 321 <https://doi.org/10.1606/1044-3894.2016.97.39> (accessed 1 September 2023). Shinn and Khadduri (n 6).

13 K. Hopper and others, 'Estimating Numbers of Unsheltered Homeless People Through Plant-Capture and Post Count Survey Methods' (2008) 98(8) *American Journal of Public Health* 1438 <https://doi.org/10.2105/AJPH.2005.083600> (accessed September 2023).

14 National Law Center on Homelessness & Poverty, 'Don't Count on It: How the HUD Point-in-Time Count Underestimates the Homelessness Crisis in America' (2017) <https://homelesslaw.org/wp-content/uploads/2018/10/HUD-PIT-report2017.pdf> (accessed 1 September 2023).

15 Kilduff and Jarosz (n 1).

16 'The State of Homelessness' (n 1).

17 'Federal Funding for Homeless Programs' (National Alliance to End Homelessness 2020) <https://endhomelessness.org/ending-homelessness/policy/federal-funding-homelessness-programs/> (accessed 1 September 2023).

18 'The State of Homelessness' (n 1).

shelters was highlighted following the onset of Covid-19,[19] the 2020 PIT suggests that individuals were hesitant to staying in shelters prior to the onset of Covid-19. Finally, as Kuhn and Culhane suggest in their categorization of experiences of homelessness, of the more than 580,000 people in the 2020 PIT, the minority (19%) were considered chronically homeless.[20]

Though the number of people counted as homeless is expected to grow because of the Covid-19 pandemic, many communities were unable to carry out the 2021 PIT.[21] The Metro Denver area in the United States conducted a version of the PIT in 2021 where people staying in shelters and transitional housing were counted, but people who were unsheltered were not counted.[22] This abridged PIT found that the number of people experiencing homelessness for the first time in Metro Denver doubled between 2020 and 2021, suggesting that the Covid-19 pandemic has had an impact on housing stability and homelessness for people with no history of homelessness.[23]

While the PIT is imperfect and most likely underestimates the true nature of homelessness in the United States, it does provide yearly information that can be used to understand community trajectories of homelessness.

McKinney–Vento Homeless Assistance Act

The McKinney–Vento Homeless Assistance Act requires that public schools provide specific assistance to children and families who are unstably housed, including covering the cost of school supplies, school fees for extracurricular activities, and transportation to their school of origin if their housing situation changes mid-year so they do not have to change schools.[24] This means that schools must collect information from families about housing status to identify those who qualify for assistance. This information is also sometimes used to estimate the number of people experiencing homelessness in the United States.[25]

The definition of *homeless* used by McKinney–Vento is much broader than the one used by HUD's PIT. McKinney–Vento's definition includes families who are 'doubled up', meaning, they are living with another family due to financial hardship, families living in motels and trailer parks, in addition to families who would meet HUD's definition of *homelessness*, living in shelters, cars, or other dwellings not meant for human habitation.[26] According to most recent data, there are roughly 1.3 million children and youth experiencing homelessness

---

19 E. Mosites and others, 'Assessment of SARS-CoV-2 Infection Prevalence in Homeless Shelters: Four U.S. Cities, 27 March–15 April 2020' (2020) 69(17) *Morbidity and Mortality Weekly Report* 521 <https://doi.org/10.15585/mmwr.mm6917e1> (accessed 1 September 2023).
20 Kuhn and Culhane (n 2). 'The State of Homelessness' (n 1).
21 J. Moses, 'COVID-19 and the State of Homelessness' (National Alliance to End Homelessness 2020) <https://endhomelessness.org/covid-19-and-the-state-of-homelessness/> (accessed 1 September 2023).
22 'Metro Denver 2021 Regional Report' (Metro Denver Homeless Initiative 2021) <https://static1.squarespace.com/static/5fea50c73853910bc4679c13/t/612681556bd65364787f25b5/1629913429534/PIT+2021+Metro+Denver+Regional+Report.pdf> (accessed 1 September 2023).
23 Ibid.
24 McKinney–Vento Homeless Assistance Act, s 11302.
25 Kilduff and Jarosz (n 1).
26 'The McKinney–Vento Definition of Homeless' (National Center for Homeless Education n.d.) <https://nche.ed.gov/mckinney-vento-definition/> (accessed 1 September 2023).

who are enrolled in a public school in the United States.[27] The majority of these children (77%) are doubled up and living with another family due to economic hardship, which would not meet HUD's definition of *homeless*.[28] While this number only includes children and youth enrolled in public schools who are experiencing homelessness, the vast difference between it and HUD's reported numbers gives context to the contentious issue of the seemingly simple task of estimating the number of people experiencing homelessness in the United States.

Next, we review the major homelessness policy landscape in place in the United States over the last several decades.

Policy Responses to Homelessness in the United States

The McKinney Act of 1987

The loss of manufacturing jobs, closure of single-room-occupancy units, inflation, and reduction of funding for public housing and other social services all influenced the rise of homelessness beginning in the 1970s and increasing greatly through the 1980s.[29] The increase of people living and sleeping in public spaces increased media attention and public awareness of the issue of homelessness, which spurred government response.[30] The McKinney Act of 1987 was the first piece of federal fiscal legislation to address homelessness in the United States.[31] It created federal funding to address immediate needs of individuals experiencing homelessness, such as emergency shelters, as well as treatment for substance use and mental health.[32] While the McKinney Act of 1987 has been amended over the years, it continues to be the primary federal funding mechanism to address homelessness.[33]

Staircase Model of Care

The McKinney Act of 1987 provided funding to services delivering substance use and mental health treatment, so treatment was an important piece of homeless service provision in what is known as early staircase model of care programmes, sometimes called 'treatment-first' or 'housing readiness'.[34] The staircase model of care consists of a series of steps that begin with entering an emergency shelter and moving towards permanent housing.[35] Most often, substance use or mental health treatment are required and incorporated into

---

27 Ibid.
28 'National Overview' (National Center for Homeless Education 2021) <http://profiles.nche.selservices.com/ConsolidatedStateProfile.aspx> (accessed 1 September 2023).
29 M. Jones, 'Creating a Science of Homelessness During the Reagan Era' (2015) 93(1) *The Milbank Quarterly* 139.
30 K. Kyle, *Contextualizing Homelessness: Critical Theory, Homelessness, and Federal Policy Addressing the Homeless* (Routledge 2005).
31 Shinn and Khadduri (n 13).
32 Jones (n 29).
33 'Federal Funding for Homeless Programs' (n 17).
34 Kyle (n 30). Shinn and Khadduri (n 13).
35 D. Padgett, B. Henwood and S. Tsemberis, *Housing First: Ending Homelessness, Transforming Systems, and Changing Lives* (Oxford Scholarship Online 2015).

the structure of the programme, hence the name 'treatment-first'.[36] These programmes typically require abstinence from substances, participation in treatment, and/or medication compliance as conditions for housing.[37] As such, service providers determine whether clients are ready for housing based on participation in programming and treatment.[38] Individuals are placed in transitional housing when they meet certain treatment goals, such as obtain sobriety or medication management, and then advance towards more permanent housing as they maintain sobriety, participate in treatment, and meet additional goals.[39] If individuals stop participating in treatment or relapse at any time, they are moved back down a step or removed from the programme completely, depending on what the service provider deems appropriate.[40]

The staircase model of care can be beneficial for some, but for many, the strict guidelines regarding treatment can lead to an institutionalized cycle of homelessness with no way out, and for others still, treatment may not be the most pressing issue to exiting homelessness.[41] Refusing to comply with treatment, regardless of the reason, can be considered evidence of poor decision-making and, therefore, a lack of readiness to move into permanent housing.[42] This institutionalized cycle of homelessness led service providers in New York City in the early 1990s to rethink the staircase model of care and create the Housing First model.

Housing First

The Housing First model has become a popular and accepted response to homelessness in the United States and other countries.[43] It has shown positive outcomes in exiting homelessness and maintaining housing stability among people experiencing homelessness, including individuals experiencing chronic homelessness and individuals with mental health conditions.[44,] The Housing First model provides low-barrier permanent housing, offers flexible services with an emphasis on choice, and does not require treatment or sobriety as a

---

36 D. Watson, 'From Structural Chaos to a Model of Consumer Support: Understanding the Roles of Structure and Agency in Mental Health Recovery for the Formally Homeless'(2012) 12(4) *Journal of Forensic Psychology Practice* 325. Padgett, Henwood and Tsemberis (n 35).
37 Ibid.
38 Watson (n 36). Padgett, Henwood and Tsemberis (n 35).
39 Watson (n 36).
40 Padgett, Henwood and Tsemberis (n 35).
41 Ibid.
42 Ibid.
43 Shinn and Khadduri (n 13).
44 S. Tsembaris, L. Gulcur and M. Nakae, 'Housing First, Consumer Choice, and Harm Reduction for Homeless Individuals with a Dual Diagnosis' (2004) 94(4) *American Journal of Public Health* 651.D. Padgett, L. Gulcur and S. Tsemberis, 'Housing First Services for People Who Are Homeless with Co-Occurring Serious Mental Illness and Substance Use' (2006) 16(1) *Research on Social Work Practice* 74 <https://doi.org/10.1177/1049731505282593> (accessed 1 September 2023). J. Woodhall-Melnik and J. Dunn, 'A Systematic Review of Outcomes Associated with Participation in Housing First Programs' (2016) 31(3) *Housing Studies* 287 <https://doi.org/10.1080/02673037.2015.1080816> (accessed 1 September 2023). J. Somers and others, 'A Randomized Trial Examining Housing First in Congregate and Scattered Site Formats' (2017) 12(1) *PLOS One* 1 <https://doi.org/10.1371/journal.pone.0168745> (accessed 1 September 2023).

precursor to housing.[45] Two common programmes that use the Housing First model are permanent supportive housing and rapid rehousing.[46] Permanent supportive housing provides permanent housing and supportive services for individuals with complex needs, while rapid rehousing programmes consist of short-term rental subsidies and short-term case management, meant to get individuals and families with less complex needs out of the shelter system as quickly as possible.[47]

Housing First is compatible with trauma-informed care in that it allows for greater control over one's environment, fosters collaboration between client and service provider, and has a focus on safety and security before attending to other needs. Additionally, Housing First is a harm-reduction approach. In contrast to the staircase model of care, which typically requires sobriety and treatment engagement, Housing First offers choice in treatment and does not require sobriety to receive services. Instead, service providers work with clients to reduce negative consequences of substance use through the conceptual framework that, once housed, individuals are better suited to address underlying substance use issues.[48]

The federal government under the Obama administration embraced the Housing First model, and the passage of the Homeless Emergency Assistance and Rapid Transition to Housing Act (HEARTH) in 2009 shifted the federal homelessness response from treatment-first interventions and emergency sheltering toward interventions that used the Housing First model.[49] Through the HEARTH Act, the federal government increased funding opportunities for homeless service providers using the Housing First model instead of temporary or transitional housing options.[50] HUD suggests the following guidelines for Housing First programming: (1) few to no programmatic prerequisites to permanent housing entry; (2) low-barrier admission policies; (3) rapid and streamlined entry into housing; (4) supportive services to be voluntary but can and should be used to persistently engage tenants to ensure housing stability; (5) tenants having full rights, responsibilities, and legal protections; (6) practices and policies to prevent lease violations and evictions; and (7) applicable in a variety of housing models.

Homelessness responses using a Housing First model are now the most common type of homelessness assistance, with 41% of beds categorized as such.[51] However, emergency shelter beds continue to be a common intervention. Emergency shelter beds are the second most prevalent type of response to homelessness, and the number of emergency shelter beds has increased by 38% since 2007.[52] Although the Housing First model is the most common response to homelessness and HUD provides Housing First guidelines, there is room for

---

45 Padgett, Gulcur and Tsemberis (n 44). D. Srebnik, T. Connor and L. Sylla, 'A Pilot Study of the Impact of Housing First-Supported Housing for Intensive Users of Medical Hospitalizations and Sobering Services' (2013) 103(2) *American Journal of Public Health* 316. Padgett, Henwood and Tsemberis (n 35).
46 Shinn and Khadduri (n 13).
47 Ibid.
48 Padgett, Gulcur and Tsemberis (n 44).
49 Addo and Gerstenblatt (n 9).
50 Shinn and Khadduri (n 13).
51 'Federal Funding for Homeless Programs' (n 22).
52 Ibid.

interpretation of HUD's Housing First guidelines that can lead to varied implementation of the Housing First model.

Coordinated Entry

The Housing First model, and its emphasis on housing and choice in treatment, has become a common response to homelessness and has been a successful intervention in helping individuals gain and maintain housing stability.[53] However, many communities across the country are experiencing a severe lack of affordable housing, which is considered the primary cause of homelessness.[54] Because of the overall lack of housing, HUD requires communities have a coordinated entry process, intended to coordinate services across agencies, break down barriers, and determine who is in need of permanent supportive housing.[55]

As the number of people experiencing homelessness in the United States increases, homeless service providers and governmental agencies have started working together more closely to address access to housing and housing-related services. The collaboration across the homelessness services sector is thought to increase equity in services and allow for innovation for new services. In fact, collaboration between agencies is a requirement for communities to receive federal funding for housing services. To ensure collaboration among service providers in communities, HUD initiated a Continuum of Care system, where all service providers (including governmental agencies, non-profits, and faith-based organizations) in a geographic region must coordinate services, policies, and procedures and apply for federal funding together. The size of a region's Continuum of Care varies from community to community. There are over 400 Continuums of Care in the United States; some represent a single city, others a county or region made up of several cities, and some are state-wide. Regardless of the size, each Continuum of Care is required by federal law to have a uniform coordinated entry process to assess and prioritize individuals for housing and housing-related services. The coordinated entry process allows agencies to triage the limited supply of housing for the growing number of individuals experiencing homelessness and is meant to break down barriers to services, including housing, for people experiencing homelessness.

The main purpose of using the coordinated entry process is to determine risk for continued homelessness and prioritize housing for individuals who are considered the most vulnerable, or those with the most complex needs.[56] Guiding principles of the coordinated entry process include having a person-centred approach, access to appropriate and timely services, reducing stress of people experiencing homelessness by limiting the assessment process, standardization of tools and processes, and sharing information across services. The assessment process in coordinated entry is meant to determine the need and vulnerability of individuals. Through assessment, individuals are recommended to receive one of three

---

53 Padgett, Gulcur and Tsemberis (n 44). Shinn and Khadduri (n 13).
54 Ibid. K. M. O'Regan, I. G. Ellen and S. House, 'How to Address Homelessness: Reflections from Research' (2021) *Annals of the American Academy of Political and Social Science* 322.
55 US Department of Housing and Urban Development (n 10).
56 C. Balagot and others, 'The Homeless Coordinated Entry System: The VI-SPDAT and Other Predictors of Establishing Eligibility for Services for Single Homeless Adults' (2019) 28(2) *Journal of Social Distress and Homelessness* 149 <https://doi.org/10.1080/10530789.2019.1622858> (accessed 1 September 2023).

housing options: (1) permanent supportive housing for people with high vulnerability; (2) rapid rehousing for people scoring in the moderately vulnerable range; or (3) mainstream affordable housing[57] for people scoring as minimally vulnerable.[58]

Challenge of Housing Affordability

A significant gap in policy and programmatic responses to homelessness in the United States is the challenge of housing affordability. Some service models, such as housing navigation and housing stabilization, attempt to address housing affordability for people experiencing homelessness. However, a lack of affordable housing units in the United States is one of the major barriers to stable housing for people experiencing homelessness.

To house all those experiencing homelessness in Denver, Colorado, where the authors of this chapter live, would require the development of approximately 5,000 homes overnight. At the median home price of approximately 600,000 US dollars, that would mean an investment of approximately 3 billion US dollars today. Thinking about the scope of the homelessness and housing affordability crisis in these terms leads us to believe that we need innovation, new approaches, new investments and partnerships, and a rethinking of housing and homelessness.

Innovative Approaches to Housing and Homelessness

As the housing affordability crisis radiates across the United States and rates of homelessness continue to increase and diversify, there is growing recognition of the need to re-evaluate and disrupt existing homeless service systems. These new approaches can be categorized as social innovations, which describe mechanisms by which novel solutions are devised to answer complex social challenges that have not been adequately addressed by existing approaches.[59] These housing and homelessness social innovations are capable of effecting change at both the individual and systems level, potentially transforming our policy and programme approaches to housing and homelessness.[60]

Additionally, social innovations have the potential to introduce new partners and investments to the issue at hand. Often viewed as an interdisciplinary approach, social innovation celebrates the problem-solving potential of diverse perspectives, knowledge, and skills working in concert. In doing so, new sources of capital present opportunities to finance the exploration of new solutions.

---

57 M. Brown and others, 'Reliability and Validity of the Vulnerability Index – Service Prioritization Decision Assistance Tool (VI-SPDAT) in Real-World Implementation' (2018) 27(2) *Journal of Social Distress and Homelessness* 110 <https://doi.org/10.1080/10530789.2018.1482991> (accessed 1 September 2023).

58 Ibid.

59 G. Mulgan and others, *Social Innovation: What It Is, Why It Matters and How It Can Be Accelerated* (Skoll Centre for Social Entrepreneurship 2007) <http://eureka.sbs.ox.ac.uk/761/1/Social_Innovation.pdf> (accessed 1 September 2023). 'Social Innovation Theory and Research: A Guide for Researchers' (TEPSIE 2014) <https://iupe.files.wordpress.com/2015/11/tepsie-research_report_final_web.pdf> (accessed 1 September 2023); J. van Wijk and others, 'Social Innovation: Integrating Micro, Meso, and Macro Level Insights from Institutional Theory' (2019) 58(5) *Business & Society* 887 <https://doi.org/10.1177/0007650318789104> (accessed 1 September 2023).

60 'Social Innovation Theory and Research' (n 59).

The Center for Housing and Homelessness Research has been working with leaders in the field, innovating novel responses to homelessness here in Colorado. Three case studies evaluated by the Center for Housing and Homelessness Research and featured here describe promising social innovations. First, we provide a case study of safe parking as an alternative short-term sheltering option. Then we review tiny home communities as an alternative long-term sheltering and housing option. Then, third, we describe our work, providing direct cash as a supplement to existing public assistance programmes for people experiencing homelessness.

Case Studies

Case Study #1: Vehicle Homelessness and Safe Parking

Vehicle Homelessness

Vehicle homelessness is defined as the utilization of a vehicle (compact cars, vans, RVs, etc.) as one's primary shelter in public spaces.[61] Though little is known about the prevalence or characteristics of vehicle homelessness, one study in Seattle found that there was a 46% increase in vehicle homelessness between 2018 and 2019.[62] Most people experiencing vehicle homelessness report sheltering in vehicles due to financial insecurity and a lack of access to affordable housing,[63] and individuals report that sheltering in their vehicle is a survival tactic that allows for accessing resources while avoiding risks associated with street homelessness and staying in traditional emergency shelters.[64] Individuals report that they prefer their vehicles over emergency shelters due to lack of street parking around emergency shelters, shelter rules such as family separation of males over the age of 12, and that shelters were perceived as less safe.[65]

However, people experiencing vehicle homelessness also report challenges to sheltering in their vehicles. Individuals sheltering in their vehicles can be at risk for break-ins and losing property, unsanitary living conditions, and a growing number of laws that criminalize sheltering in vehicles. Communities across the United States have enacted laws and ordinances that target people experiencing homelessness with criminal penalties for actions such as sleeping in public, camping, and asking for charity.

In addition to laws that target people experiencing homelessness broadly, there has also been an increase in laws that criminalize vehicle homelessness more specifically. The

---

61 G. Pruss, 'A Home Without a Home: Vehicle Residency and Settled Bias' (ProQuest Dissertations Publishing 2019).
62 Ibid.
63 G. Wehman-Brown, 'Home Is Where You Park It' (2015) 19(3) *Space and Culture* 251.
64 M. Wakin, 'Not Sheltered, Not Homeless: RVs as Makeshifts' (2005) 48(8) *The American Behavioral Scientist* 1013; Pruss (n 61).
65 Pruss (n 61).

criminalization of vehicle homelessness includes laws and ordinances that increase parking citations and restrictions. According to the National Law Center on Homelessness and Poverty, there was a 213% increase in the number of cities in the United States that criminalized sleeping in vehicles between 2006 to 2019. Examples of laws criminalizing vehicle homelessness include prohibiting the parking of large vehicles, prohibiting parking inoperable or abandoned vehicles, prohibiting parking in one location for more than 72 hours, and prohibiting sleeping in vehicles. One response to the criminalization of vehicle homelessness and the associated barriers is the popularization of safe parking lots, which now exist in several cities in the United States.[66]

Safe Parking Lots

Safe parking lots provide overnight parking for individuals experiencing vehicle homelessness without fear of being ticketed or forced to move their car in the middle of the night. Safe parking lots also offer an alternative for individuals who may not feel safe or comfortable in shelters, individuals who have pets, or individuals and families who do not have access to shelter at all. Safe parking lots attempt to meet individuals where they are and provide low-barrier access to services, which is consistent with a trauma-informed approach.

Often, safe parking lots provide participants access to community resources and aim to address other common barriers to sheltering in vehicles, such as access to bathrooms, showers, and waste disposal, in addition to a place to park overnight. Many safe parking programmes require a valid driver's license, up-to-date car registration, vehicle insurance and might run background checks to screen out people with a history of criminal sex offense or violent offense. Some safe parking lots have set time limits for length of stay, typically between 30 and 90 days, that may be renewed depending on use of case management services. As with many interventions addressing homelessness, the primary goal of safe parking lots is for participants to eventually be able to move out of the lot and into stable housing.

Evaluation of the Colorado Safe Parking Initiative

Setting

Founded by community members in 2019 as a grassroots community coalition, the Colorado Safe Parking Initiative (CSPI) applied for 501c(3) status in 2020. CSPI has been a critical part of the growth and success of establishing safe parking in the seven-county Denver, CO, metro area. CSPI does not directly provide safe lots but works to expand the network of safe parking lots and provides technical assistance and implementation support for organizations operating safe parking lots.

---

66 M. Wakin, *Otherwise Homeless: Vehicle Living and the Culture of Homelessness* (First Press Forum 2014).

Research Design

In collaboration with CSPI, our Center for Housing and Homelessness Research (CHHR) developed an exploratory, mixed-methods research design to answer the following research questions: (1) Who are safe parking lots serving? (2) Do safe parking lots have an impact on housing stability?

Data were collected between June 2020 and April 2021 in two distinct ways: (1) intake and interim or exit surveys of lot guests, and (2) semi-structured interviews with participants. All safe lot guests were invited to complete an intake survey upon entering a safe lot. Additionally, guests were invited to complete an exit survey when leaving a safe lot. As the research came to an end, it was determined that individuals who completed an intake survey but who had not yet left a safe lot should be offered the opportunity to complete a follow-up survey. These individuals were invited to complete an interim survey to share their experience since entering the safe lot.

Sample Characteristics

At the end of data collection in April 2021, 37 participants completed intake surveys, 12 participants completed interim surveys, and 18 participants completed exit surveys, meaning, of the 37 individuals who completed intake surveys, 30 completed some form of follow-up survey. Most of the participants identified as White, 8% of the participants identified as Black or African American, 5% identified as Native American or American Indian, 5% identified as Latino or Hispanic, 8% identified as having multiple racial and ethnic identities, and 3% indicated that their identity was not listed on the survey. There were slightly more males (51%) in the safe lots than females (43%), and 6% of participants identified as transgender. On average, people reported experiencing vehicle homelessness for ten months prior to joining a safe lot.

Findings

Research Question 1: Who are the lots serving? Because so little is known about people experiencing vehicle homelessness, our first research question sought information about the population. We gathered information about the circumstances that led to vehicle homelessness and education level and employment status. Figure 16.1 describes circumstances that led to vehicle homelessness. The two most frequently reported reasons for sheltering in a vehicle were the inability to pay rent or mortgage (54%) and the loss of a job (41%). Participants were invited to choose all situations that apply, so responses are not mutually exclusive.

Participants reported a range of employment status. Most participants reported having some form of employment, either full-time (8%), part-time (24%), or self-employment (8%), and 19% of participants reported that while they were not currently working, they were actively looking for employment. Five participants reported being unable to work (14%), and six reported receiving Social Security Disability Insurance (SSDI) (16%).

Research Question 2: How does safe parking impact well-being? Table 16.1 describes the average length of time spent at a safe lot and the reported reasons for leaving the safe lot for the 18 participants who completed an exit survey. The average time participants stayed at the

Innovative Policy Responses to Housing Need in the US

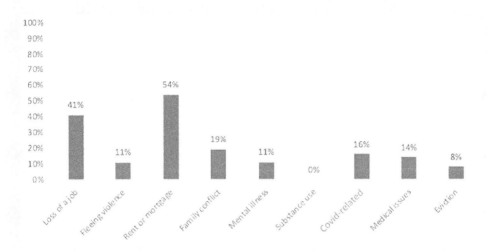

Figure 16.1 Reported circumstances for sheltering in vehicle.
Source: Authors' own analysis.

Table 16.1 Reported reason for leaving safe lot

	Exit n = 18
	Mean (SD) or % (Total)
Average time in lot, months	2.95 (1.9)
Secured long-term housing	28% (5)
Secured temporary housing	17% (3)
Found other parking	6% (1)
Asked to leave	11% (2)
The lot location was inconvenient	17% (3)
No longer wanted to stay at the lot	28% (5)

Source: Authors' own work.

lot was 2.95 months. Almost half (45%) of participants left a safe lot because they secured either long-term housing (28%) or temporary housing (17%). Almost a third (28%) reported leaving because they no longer wanted to stay at the lot. Three participants (17%) left the lot as it was an inconvenient location for them, while 11% were asked to leave the lots. Participants were invited to choose all situations that were relevant, so responses are not mutually exclusive.

Safety indicators included self-reported feeling of general safety as well as worrying about belongings and physical safety when going to sleep. These were presented on a Likert scale of 1 to 5, where 1 is *strongly disagree*, 3 is *neutral*, and 5 is *strongly agree*. Paired-sample t-tests show a statistically significant improvement in perceived safety from intake to follow-up. Participants reported feeling safer when going to sleep while at the safe lot ($t = -1.48$, $df = 26$, $p < .001$).

Participants reported worrying less about their belongings when going to sleep while at a safe lot ($t = 1.25$, $df = 27$, $p = .001$). Additionally, participants reported worrying less about their physical safety while at a safe lot ($t = 1.45$, $df = 28$, $p < .001$).

Wrap-Up

Safe parking lots are a promising response to the criminalization of vehicle homelessness as a short-term alternative option to traditional emergency sheltering. Participants in our study reported improved perception of safety, and nearly half of participants accessed either temporary or long-term housing while staying at a safe lot. While it is promising, participants also report challenges to vehicle homelessness, such as the cost of car maintenance and meeting basic needs, even when they had access to a safe parking lot. Tiny homes are another innovative response to homelessness that offer an alternative to emergency shelter while providing shelter that is not offered in safe parking lots.

Case Study #2: Tiny Home Communities Addressing Homelessness

Introduction

The use of tiny houses as an innovative response to homelessness is a relatively new phenomenon, formally launching in 2000 with Dignity Village in Portland, Oregon.[67] As of July 2019, an inventory of US-based tiny home communities addressing homelessness identified 115 villages across 39 states in varying stages of development and operations.[68] According to the inventory, the average house size was 205 square feet, and the average number of homes in a village was 35.[69]

Tiny Home Communities

It is important to note that each tiny home community presents its own unique characteristics. Some homes are built on trailers, allowing structures to be mobile to comply with restrictive building and zoning codes enforcing minimum space and location requirements.[70] However, trailers tend to be the costliest component of a tiny home; therefore, lower-cost

---

67 C. A. Mingoya, 'Building Together: Tiny House Villages for the Homeless: A Comparative Case Study' (MA thesis, Massachusetts Institute of Technology 2015).
68 K. Evans, 'Tackling Homelessness with Tiny Houses: An Inventory of Tiny House Villages in the United States' (2020) 72(3) *The Professional Geographer* 360 <https://doi.org/10.1080/00330124.2020.1744170> (accessed 1 September 2023).
69 Ibid.
70 L. Furst, *Finding Space: Assessing How Planning Responds to Tiny Houses for Homeless Populations* (McGill University 2017); A. Heben, *Tent City Urbanism: From Self-Organized Camps to Tiny House Villages* (The Village Collaborative 2014); Emily Keable, 'Building on the Tiny House Movement: A Viable Solution to Meet Affordable Housing Needs' (2017) 11(2) *University of St. Thomas Journal of Law and Public Policy* 111.

options are often built on simple foundations of cinderblocks and wooden beams.[71] Some villages have been master-planned and professionally constructed on meticulously landscaped sites, while others have developed more organically with homes constructed from largely recycled and reclaimed materials.[72] Some villages and homes are connected to electricity and running water, while others rely on solar panels, composting or portable toilets, and portable showers.[73] There are sites that feature 24-hour security services, microbusinesses, gardens, hired support staff, and communal spaces ranging from kitchens and bathhouses to libraries, chapels, and yoga studios.[74] In some of these communities, residents are expected to contribute a portion of their income towards rent or membership dues, while other villages require sweat equity (i.e. non-monetary contributions, such as physical or mental labour).[75]

Evaluation of 'Beloved Community Village', Denver's First Tiny Home Community

Setting

Construction of Beloved Community Village (BCV or the Village), Denver's first tiny home community, was completed in July 2017 as a 180-day pilot project for individuals experiencing homelessness. It was launched as an experiment to provide a partial solution to the housing crisis facing the Denver metropolitan area with the specific intent of serving those individuals experiencing homelessness whose needs were not being met by the traditional shelter system. BCV resulted from a combined effort carried out by the Colorado Village Collaborative, the Barton Institute for Community Action, and several other non-profit and for-profit groups and independent community members. Inspired by similar tiny home villages across the country, BCV operates as a shared-governance, transformational community that seeks to provide a safe and dignified alternative sheltering solution that bridges the gap between living on the streets and stable housing.

BCV was initially constructed on a parcel of land in Northwest Denver, Colorado, with a total of 11 tiny homes, a makeshift community structure, a bathhouse, and portable toilets. The community has relocated three times since 2017 and is now comprised of 19 homes and a community building with three full bathrooms and a shared kitchen.

---

71 Furst (n 70), Heben (n 70).
72 Heben (n 70).
73 'Tiny Communities with Wood Sleeping Cabins to House Homelessness People' (Amikas 2017) (accessed 1 September 2023); Furst (n 70).
74 L. T. Alexander, 'Tiny Homes for the Homeless: A Return to Politically Engaged Community Economic Development Law?' (2017) 26(1) *Journal of Affordable Housing and Community Development Law* 39; 'Tiny Communities with Wood Sleeping Cabins to House Homelessness People' (n 73); L. Deaton, 'Creating Community: Housing Insecurity & the Tiny-House Village Model' (presented at the Architectural Research Centers Consortium, European Association for Architectural Education at Tempe University/Drexel University 2018); Heben (n 70); Mingoya (n 67).
75 E. Brown, *Overcoming the Barriers to Micro-Housing: Tiny Houses, Big Potential* (University of Oregon, Scholar's Bank 2016).

One of our evaluation goals was to assess if living in the Beloved Community Village resulted in changes to employment, financial capabilities, and well-being. Results from this evaluation question are presented here.

Research Design

CHHR established a partnership with the Colorado Village Collaborative and the Barton Institute for Community Action to evaluate BCV from 2017 to 2020. Employing a mix of quantitative and qualitative data, the evaluation sought to compare individual outcomes among BCV residents with a group of people experiencing homelessness who had not lived in BCV.

Sample Characteristics

This study drew from a body of quantitative and qualitative data collected among two participant groups: (1) current and former residents of BCV (BCV residents), and (2) individuals on the wait list for a tiny home with CVC (comparison group).

Of the 32 residents in the history of BCV, a total of 24 (75%) participated in study data collection at some point between 2017 and 2020. BCV residents completed surveys at move-in as well as 6 months, 12 months, 24 months, and 36 months following their move into BCV. The average reported age of residents was 39. A majority of residents identified as White (75%), 13% as Black or African American, 4% as Latino or Hispanic, and 8% indicated that their identity was not listed on the survey. Forty-eight percent of BCV residents identified as male, 43% as female, and 9% as transgender, genderqueer, gender fluid, agender, or an identity not listed on the survey. Sixty-eight percent of residents identified as straight or heterosexual, and 32% identified as lesbian, gay, bisexual, queer, asexual, questioning, or unsure. The majority of residents (63%) identified as single, while 21% reported being divorced, and 17% reported being married or in a domestic partnership.

A total of 25 individuals from the comparison group completed the initial survey. Of the 25, 17 (68%) completed a follow-up survey six months later. The average reported age of residents was 48. Forty percent of the comparison group identified as White (40%), 20% as Black or African American, 20% as Latino or Hispanic, 4% as Native American or American Indian, and 16% indicated that their identity was not listed on the survey. More participants identified as female (52%) than male (40%) or transgender, genderqueer, gender fluid, agender, or an identity not listed on the survey (8%). Eighty-eight percent of the comparison group identified as straight or heterosexual, and 12% identified as lesbian, gay, bisexual, queer, asexual, questioning, or unsure. Lastly, 48% of participants identified as single, while 28% reported being divorced, 20% widowed, and 4% married or in a domestic partnership.

Findings

BCV Residents

Upon move-in, all interviewed residents reported sleeping outside at some point over the last six months. However, six months later, no BCV residents interviewed reported sleeping outside. Of note, four former residents participated in the evaluation and were asked where they slept the night before completing the survey, how long they had been sleeping at that location, and how long they can stay there. The average length of time that former residents reported being at their current location was 365 days. Two of the four former residents who completed a survey in evaluation 2 reported sleeping in their own home the night before completing the survey, while one former resident reported sleeping in their partner's home, and one reported sleeping in their RV. Three of the four former residents stated that they viewed their current sleeping location as permanent, whereas one of the four reported that while their sleep location was not permanent, they could stay there as long as they needed to.

Analysis revealed positive impacts of BCV related to employment. To assess employment, employment categories were collapsed into working or not working. The working category includes the following options: working full-time, working part-time, self-employed, and student. The 'not working' category includes the following options: not working and currently applying for work/school, not working and not applying for work/school, unable to work, and retired. Using logistic regression and controlling for work and school at move-in/initial recruitment, BCV residents demonstrated a 3.9 times greater likelihood to be in the working category at the six-month follow-up than the comparison group (Exp(B) = 4.9, $p < .10$), as depicted in Figure 16.2. There appeared to be two factors influencing this finding. The first was that BCV residents more consistently reported being able to maintain part-time employment than individuals in the comparison group. The second, and possibly more complex factor, was that individuals in the comparison group more frequently reported being unable to work.

Positive outcomes were also demonstrated among BCV residents pertaining to finances. From move-in to the most recent survey completed, BCV residents reported an increase in being able to save money, pay bills, and make payments on debt in the last six months. The average number of times BCV residents reported having their belongings stolen in the last month decreased from an average of 1.8 times at move-in to zero times at the most recent survey completed.

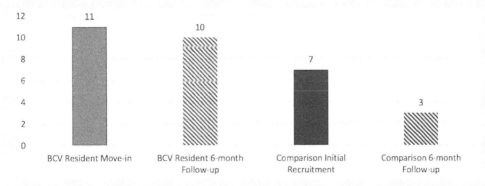

Figure 16.2 BCV resident and comparison group working or in school.
Source: Authors' own analysis.

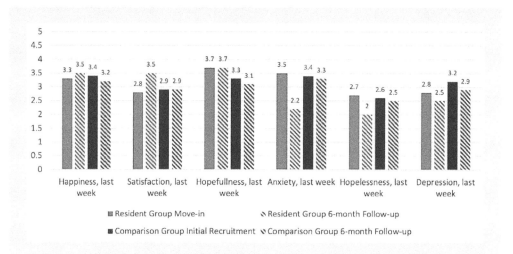

Figure 16.3 BCV resident and comparison group average frequency of emotional states. (Note: Participants reported frequency of various emotional states on a scale of 1 to 5, with 1 corresponding to a response of 'none of the time' and 5 corresponding to a response of 'all of the time'.)

Source: Authors' own analysis.

Evaluation findings show that BCV residents experienced positive impacts in the areas of health and well-being. From move-in to the six-month follow-up, BCV residents reported increased happiness and satisfaction as well as decreased anxiety, hopelessness, and depression compared to people experiencing homelessness who were on the BCV wait list. Furthermore, paired sample t-tests show a statistically significant decrease in anxiety ($t = 3.0$, $p < .05$) among BCV residents from move-in to the six-month follow-up. Additionally, a comparison of BCV residents and the comparison group demonstrates that residents experienced statistically significant improvements in anxiety when compared to the comparison group ($t = -2.64$, $p < .05$). Anxiety change scores were -1.3 for BCV residents and -0.1 for the comparison group.

Using a measure of social isolation, BCV residents reported a decrease in feeling left out and lacking companionship from move-in to six-month follow-up, while comparison group participants reported an increase in all three indicators of social isolation over a six-month period. Additionally, using a measure of sense of control, BCV residents reported an increase in personal mastery six months following move-in, while comparison group participants' scores decreased.

During each survey, BCV residents were asked to establish and provide status reports on personal goals. Of the 47 goals set by BCV residents over the course of the study, 14 (30%) were reported as completed, and 8 (17%) were reported as significant progress made, for a total of 47% reported as either completed or significant progress made as of the most recent survey completed.

Qualitative feedback was collected from residents about their experience living at BCV. Qualitative responses offered a wide range of views and perspectives on BCV. Aspects of

BCV that participants cited as satisfactory included overall safety and peace of mind, security for their belongings, a place to keep pets, village cleanliness, a new community building, a supportive resident and staff community, and the opportunity to use BCV as a stepping stone for achieving other goals. Residents also acknowledged that, like many groups (including family), relationships at BCV are ever-evolving, interpersonal differences are to be expected, and there is always room for improvement. Some critiques raised by residents about their experience at BCV included power dynamics between staff and residents, lack of decision-making power, needed attention to trauma-informed practices, needed mediation support for resident conflicts, and too little enforcement of BCV standards.

Wrap-Up

The results of this evaluation provide an encouraging picture of the BCV resident experience as well as an account of the impact of BCV on the surrounding neighbourhood. Study findings show that BCV residents reported increased rates of being sheltered, increased likelihood of employment, improved financial well-being (including saving money, paying bills, and paying off debt), increased happiness and satisfaction, and decreased anxiety, hopelessness, and depression compared to unhoused individuals on the BCV wait list.

While a continuum of services is critical for addressing immediate sheltering and other basic needs, large-scale structural change and policy responses are needed to address economic inequalities that maintain systems of homelessness, housing precarity, and working poverty. Direct, unrestricted cash transfers have been identified as a promising response to homelessness that both promote the agency and dignity of individuals while practically reducing administrative costs for oversight of standard cash transfer programmes. One such programme studying direct cash as a dedicated and scalable response to homelessness is the Denver Basic Income Project, explored in greater detail as Case Study #3.

Case Study #3: The Denver Basic Income Project

What Is GBI?

Unconditional cash transfers like Universal Basic Income (UBI) and Guaranteed Basic Income (GBI) are responses to poverty and, more recently, homelessness in the United States. Leaders of the National Welfare Rights Organization argue that work requirements for welfare, and waged work more generally, led to 'institutionalized poverty', forcing individuals into jobs when their skills could be more valuable in their own home and in their own communities.[76] Their main argument for a guaranteed adequate income is that individuals know what is best for themselves and their family.[77]

---

76 W. Sherwin and F. Fox Piven, 'The Radical Feminist Legacy of the National Welfare Rights Organization' (2019) 47(3–4) *Women's Studies Quarterly* 135 <www.jstor.org/stable/26803267> (accessed 1 September 2023).
77 Ibid.

Basic income has become popular again in the United States. During the Covid-19 pandemic, cash transfers were delivered to every family with children earning less than $400,000 per year.[78] Current rationale for unconditional cash transfer challenge the moral construction of poverty theory that assumes that people living in poverty, including those experiencing homelessness, are unable or not trustworthy to spend money responsibly.[79]

GBI is meant to supplement income and other cash and non-cash benefits. Most often, eligibility criteria for GBI are based on income and poverty level.[80] If an individual meets a particular income criterion, they qualify for the cash transfer. A critical element of GBI is that the cash transfer is unconditional, meaning, that once an individual is eligible to receive the cash transfer, there are no requirements that need to be met to receive the cash.[81] Recipients do not need to participate in financial literacy courses or maintain sobriety, for example, and there are no restriction on the use of the money. This unrestricted cash allows individuals and families the flexibility needed to address the concerns they find most important.[82]

GBI is not always an approach to address homelessness. However, some projects are now being specifically designed to test the impact of GBI on homelessness. At the time of this writing, CHHR is evaluating the Denver Basic Income Project (DBIP) in Denver, CO. DBIP is a GBI designed to support people experiencing homelessness.

The Denver Basic Income Project (DBIP)

DBIP was started with the vision of the founder, Mark Donovan, an entrepreneur based in Denver, Colorado, that envisioned direct cash to people experiencing homelessness as a potential solution to the homelessness experience. Mark Donovan self-funded a pilot GBI programme with ten hand-selected recipients and then initiated the full DBIP launch to 820 people experiencing homelessness.

DBIP is a 12-month programme providing unconditional cash transfers to unhoused people living in Denver. The aims of the programme are to test the feasibility and impact of guaranteed income for unhoused people. One primary goal of DBIP is to increase housing stability for people experiencing homelessness. DBIP is also interested in the impact of guaranteed income on health, family well-being, locus of control, hopefulness, and other outcomes.

The study uses a mixed-methods randomized controlled trial (RCT) design to test the impact of receiving a guaranteed basic income compared to receiving typical care and services. Homelessness Service Providing Organizations (HSPOs) will be recruited to partner on the

---

78 The White House (2022) <www.whitehouse.gov/child-tax-credit/#:~:text=These%20people%20qualify%20for%20at,else%20with%20income%20under%20%24200%2C000> (accessed 1 September 2023).
79 'Cash Payments to People Experiencing Homelessness' (Homelessness Policy Research Institute 2021) <https://socialinnovation.usc.edu/wp-content/uploads/2021/05/Cash-Payments-Lit-Review_final.pdf> (accessed 1 September 2023).
80 A. Castro Baker and others, 'Mitigating Loss of Health Insurance and Means Tested Benefits in an Unconditional Cash Transfer Experiment: Implementation Lessons from Stockton's Guaranteed Income Pilot' (2020) 11 *SSM – Population Health* 100578 (accessed 1 September 2023).
81 Ibid.
82 'About MGI' (Mayors for Guaranteed Income, 2021) <www.mayorsforagi.org/> (accessed 1 September 2023).

study, and individuals screened at HSPOs who meet study sample criteria will serve as study participants and be randomly assigned into one of three groups:

- Study Group A: Participants will receive 12 consecutive monthly cash transfers of $1,000 on the 16th of each month.
- Study Group B: Participants will receive a one-time cash transfer of $6,500 during the initial enrolment month and then will receive 11 consecutive monthly cash transfers of $500 on the 16th of each month.
- Study Group C: Study Group C will be considered the control condition for the study. Participants in Study Group C will receive 12 consecutive monthly cash transfers of $50 on the 16th of each month and will continue to receive treatment as usual.

DBIP Theory of Change

Figure 16.4 provides an illustration of the projected changes for individuals and families experiencing homelessness as a result of DBIP.

As seen in Figure 16.4, DBIP is delivered to people experiencing homelessness guided by anti-oppressive, self-determination, social stress, and street-level bureaucracy theories. DBIP expects that unrestricted cash will allow people experiencing homelessness to make their own decisions about (1) securing material needs; (2) moving away from harmful relationship and harmful ecological conditions; (3) safety; (4) feeling in control of one's life; (5) addressing short-term stress; (6) confidence in decision-making; and (7) stability. As seen from the

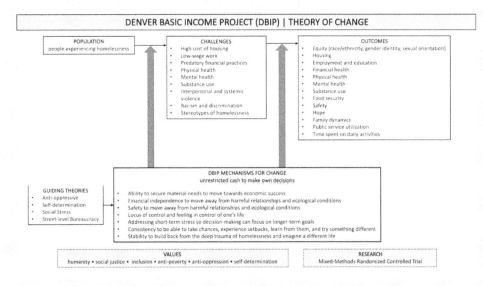

Figure 16.4 Denver Basic Income Project theory of change.
Source: Authors' own analysis.

theory of change, there will be challenges. However, if effective, DBIP has the potential to impact a wide range of outcomes for people experiencing homelessness.

Preliminary DBIP Results

Full results from the DBIP study will be available in 2024. However, we do have some preliminary results from pilot studies of the project.

DBIP participants report having used the money to pay off debt, respond to family needs, create a safety net, and cover unexpected expenses. Direct deposits of cash into a debit card have generally worked well, and participants report few issues accessing funds. Interviews with pilot study participants revealed that the ending of guaranteed income creates a kind of 'cliff effect' for participants who have come to rely on the funding, implying that exiting out of a guaranteed basic income project may cause challenges for participants who have come to rely on the direct cash.

DBIP provides a hopeful innovation to address homelessness. However, challenges persist. Implementation of guaranteed income into existing systems remains a challenge. This includes implementation as a public or private endeavour and the capacity of the existing HSPO system to take on an additional service demand for people experiencing homelessness. Additionally, homelessness is directly related to the affordable housing crisis in the United States. Providing guaranteed income is important for people experiencing homelessness – and assuring that there are affordable dwelling units available is paramount for achieving housing stability for all. Also, currently, guaranteed income is unique and likely experienced as special for recipients. If guaranteed income is no longer special for recipients, it is likely that expected outcomes will change. Next, we provide overall conclusions for the role of innovation to address issues related to homelessness in the United States.

Conclusions

Homelessness continues to grow in communities across the country. While addressing homelessness has become a priority for many of these communities, the current systems in place do not meet the need. Communities with high rates of income and wealth inequality see the largest numbers of people experiencing homelessness, largely due to high rent and renter and lack of affordable housing. The issues of affordable housing and access to affordable housing must be confronted to adequately address homelessness. In addition to addressing affordable housing, social innovation presents an opportunity to consider new possibilities to address the varied needs of people experiencing homelessness. Social innovations bring in new partners that may not have been previously engaged in the work, such as builders and entrepreneurs, which can help address the oversized scope of the issue. New external partners also provide an educational component on homelessness that can help change the narrative from homelessness as an individual moral issue to one to be addressed by the greater community.

The three case studies outlined in this chapter illustrate the need for policy responses that address housing and economic inequalities across a broad continuum, as there is no single solution for the intractable issue of homelessness. While safe parking lots address an immediate and ideally temporary sheltering need, tiny home communities provide a longer-term shelter and, in some cases, permanent housing option. Direct, unrestricted cash transfers support basic needs beyond shelter by providing individuals with monetary resources to exercise greater economic choice. Many other housing and homelessness responses are emerging to fill remaining gaps in the United States and globally. Some of these innovations include a convertible winter coat/sleeping bag/duffel bag; mobile shower and laundry units; portable sleeping pods using recycled, inflatable, and solar-powered materials; construction of pallet shelters, 3D-printed prefab homes, and shipping container apartments; technologies facilitating contactless donations, optimizing public health messaging, and generating free legal aid using artificial intelligence; and policies supporting vacancy taxes on empty homes and accessory dwelling units on single-family lots. Together, these novel approaches raise critical questions about the role and potential of social innovations in this space. Do these ideas divert attention and resources away from the central fact that people need affordable, permanent housing? Is there a place for innovations that do not create long-term housing solutions – those that fill gaps and raise awareness? Is there a role for innovations to excite and inspire – does the experimental, inventive nature of some innovations compromise the dignity of the discussion? Can novel approaches both supplement existing services while calling for a rethinking and restructuring of the entire system? Like so many wicked issues, the answer to all these questions is likely a combination of yes and no, and sometimes, it depends, highlighting the challenges inherent in homelessness policy response.

Regardless, in the United States, we need to take action to address the growing issue of homelessness. The increase in visible homelessness has people from every political persuasion, people from rural and urban areas, and people living with vast wealth, or near poverty, all now agreeing that the issue needs to be addressed. One way to act is to catalyze the interests of people from diverse backgrounds and vocational sectors to find common ground on the best way to support our unhoused community members. This may mean considerable increased investment in affordable dwelling units for people who struggle with the exorbitant cost of housing. Or thinking about systems change, it may mean rethinking land ownership as a root cause of our community members and neighbours living without a home.

PART III
South America

17

'NOTHING ABOUT US WITHOUT US'

How Homeless People Protagonism Has Shaped the Law and Public Policy on Homelessness in Brazil

Kelseny Medeiros Pinho, Luiz Tokuzi Kohara, and Erminia Maricato

Homelessness: A Definition Caught Between Two Frontiers

There is no consensus on a definition of 'homelessness' amongst different countries and socio-cultural contexts, whether in the Global North or the Global South.[1] The process of developing a homeless categorization is understood, by several researchers, as a social construction,[2] a process of intense theoretical dispute, situated and politically oriented.[3] This process involves building public and political awareness about the fact that there are people living on the streets, that is to say, transforming it into a social question,[4] which has concrete consequences in formulating public policies for this section of society.

In Brazil, the official and widespread definition of the 'homeless population' is provided for in the *Política Nacional da População em Situação de Rua* – PNPSR (National Policy

---

1 O. Olufemi, 'Barriers That Disconnect Homeless People and Make Homelessness Difficult to Interpret' (2002) 19 *Development Southern Africa* 455.
2 I. Anderson, 'Synthesizing Homelessness Research: Trends, Lessons and Prospects' (2003) 13 *Journal of Community & Applied Social Psychology* 197.
3 T. Melo, 'Politics of the "Improbable": Activists Engagement Pathways in the National Homeless Population Movement (*MNPR*)' (PhD dissertation, Fluminense Federal University 2017); D. De Lucca Reis Costa, 'The Moving Street: Urban Experiences and Social Games around Homeless Population' (Thesis, University of Sao Paulo 2007).
4 According to De Lucca (n 3) 115: 'The constitution of the homeless population as a social question is the result of plural bundles of motivations, actors, institutions and events that historically were chaining irregularly, unpredictably, not linear or determined. However, it was the interaction of these actors (and many others), which allowed a language constitution capable of naming and dealing with this universe of relationships. The trajectories and displacements that they narrated and lived, wove the network of intelligibility that made visible and make it sayable what is homeless population.'

for Homeless Population Law 2009), reflecting the national scientific production and political mobilization on this theme:

> [T]he homeless population is considered to be the heterogeneous population group that has in common extreme poverty, interrupted or weakened family ties, that experience inexistence of regular conventional housing, and uses the public streets and degraded areas as a place to live and sustain themselves, temporarily or permanently, as well as shelters for temporary overnight stays or as provisional housing.[5]

This perspective, therefore, emphasizes this population's various vulnerabilities aggravated by living in extreme poverty, but it does not give centrality to housing exclusion.[6] In concrete terms, homeless people are considered as being only those who experience life on the streets directly and those who are temporarily sheltered through a public service provider. While we use the term 'homeless' to align with international literature, terms like 'people experiencing homelessness' or 'people living on the streets' better reflect Brazilian categorization. The homeless are a larger category, involving not only those living in shelters and on the streets but also those that are unhoused,[7] meaning, those being forcibly evicted, those squatting, or people living in precarious housing conditions.

People living on the streets, in contrast to those who are simply in precarious housing conditions, carry with them 'the street' as a mark or signifier of 'irreducible difference' – this results in claims that go beyond the housing sphere, such as those relating to basic forms of survival (shelter, water, food, protection from violence on the streets). In the Brazilian political field, the homeless and the unhoused have developed quite separate and distinct social movements. Likewise, there is an unequal value and importance ascribed to this differentiation between 'house vs street'. The social movements focused on 'street' are associated with the homeless, and with 'greater need and vulnerability, both in terms of the precariousness of family ties, housing, the world of work, and the current attribution given to the fragility of their subjective and bodily conditions'.[8] Conversely, social movements focused on 'house/home' precarity are 'more organized, articulated and have the family unit – or the discourse about it – as an important positive reference'.[9]

In a context of extreme social inequality and overtaken by strong meritocratic beliefs, the homeless are perversely stigmatized by a large portion of Brazilian society that sees them as unproductive and socially ill-adjusted people.[10] They are considered 'disposable,

---

5 This definition was included in Article 1, sole paragraph of the National Policy for the Homeless Population Law, which is the main law in Brazil on the rights of the homeless population. This law was issued by Brazil's president in the form of a decree, and it does not need to be approved by the legislative body to come into force. It will be better addressed in the 'National Policy for the Homeless Population' section.
6 Melo (n 3). Housing exclusion is considered one but not the main cause of homelessness.
7 Hereafter, to construct a proper differentiation in the Brazilian context, we will use the term 'the homeless' when referring to people living on the streets and shelters, and the term 'unhoused' when referring to other situations of housing exclusion.
8 De Lucca (n 3) 175.
9 Ibid 156.
10 L. Kohara, 'Housing Is the Structural Basis for Life and Social Inclusion of the Homeless Population' (PhD dissertation, Federal University of ABC 2018).

despicable and undesirable urban residents'.[11] These social stains can be detected in repressive medical and what we might call 'hygienic' practices present in many public administrations and in pronouncements all used to reduce them to an inferior category of human being.

In conclusion, the Brazilian definition of homelessness aims to address a wide range of meanings, spatialities, and experiences, responding to a 'semantic plurality'[12] of homelessness. However, this broad approach may overlook 'borderline alterities',[13] groups such as collectors of recyclable materials or those emerging from the criminal justice system or psychiatric institutions. For the purposes of this chapter, it is important to note that the line between those living on the streets and those in precarious housing conditions is not always clear. To fully understand homelessness, it is necessary to embrace the complexity and continuum between these two frontiers.

As will be detailed later, public policies for the homeless in Brazil recognize homelessness as a state of multiple vulnerabilities. However, these policies do not focus on housing stability. Municipalities provide various forms of care on the streets, including outreach from multidisciplinary teams offering emergency shelter and free health checks. Public centres near areas with high concentrations of homeless individuals provide daytime services, such as showers and meals. However, transitional housing is scarce, and permanent housing is unavailable. These policies are outlined in laws and secondary legislation set by the central government and adapted by local governments to their specific needs.

The Homelessness Debate: The Brazilian Historical Perspective

The debate on homelessness in Brazil has spanned multiple disciplinary fields since the 1970s. Until the 1980s, studies referred to people living on the streets as 'beggars'. However, the term 'homeless population' emerged in more contemporary analyses to encompass a broader range of social marginalities, which includes but is not limited to begging.[14]

During the 1990s, 'homeless population' and 'population experiencing life on the streets' became more common terms, emphasizing the transitoriness of homelessness rather than viewing it as a natural condition. The Marxist concept of 'lumpenproletariat' was prominent throughout the 1990s, shifting the perception of begging from a moral and pathological perspective to a structural consequence of capitalist society. At this stage, some studies define homelessness as the 'maximum example of social exclusion' and a state of absence or disengagement from social ties. Others see it as an intense process of disqualification or disaffiliation from social bonds. In both cases, the homeless population is defined by their losses, particularly in relation to housing and employment.[15]

The shift in understanding homelessness is more than just a theoretical dispute. It involves significant political transformation. Starting in the mid-1970s, grassroots movements

---

11 Ibid 25. According to the author's model, the homeless population in Brazil is often perceived as disposable from an economic standpoint, despicable from a social perspective, and irrecoverable from a public policy viewpoint.
12 S. Miziara Frangella, 'Wandering Urban Bodies: A Corporality's Ethnography of People Living in the Streets of Sao Paulo' (PhD dissertation, University of Campinas 2004) 115.
13 De Lucca (n 3) 174.
14 Melo (n 3) 74.
15 De Lucca (n 3) 173.

based on Paulo Freire's concept of 'popular education' and inspired by 'liberation theology' emerged in cities such as Sao Paulo and Belo Horizonte.[16] These movements were led by social organizations and religious groups, with significant participation from homeless individuals. This process produced leaders who actively worked to change the terminology and status of homeless people in society.

In 1975, the *'Organização de Auxílio Fraterno'* (OAF)[17] began its work with the homeless. This marked a significant departure from the predominant forms of intervention at that time. Instead of relying on institutionalized intervention based on 'assistencialism',[18] OAF preferred emancipatory and community-based practices. This approach allowed excluded individuals to participate as agents of social change. In other words, OAF shifted from 'working for the poor' to 'working with the poor.'[19] This new approach challenged many welfare practices and highlighted economic and structural contradictions. It also reinforced the state's responsibility towards social problems.

Across Sao Paulo's central region, communities integrating the homeless and OAF's participants were organized, leading to annual large-scale mobilization activities such as protests which were held to render the homeless more visible as a collective struggling for rights. Open letters were made public, denouncing injustices suffered in work, but also reporting the lack of access to public services and cultural activities. These were relevant public spaces where the homeless could express their stories in their own words.

In 1982, some members of civil society who had been working with waste pickers[20] began organizing homeless individuals as a political group, mobilizing them to advocate for their rights and interests beyond just receiving community services. This effort led to the creation of Brazil's first recyclable material collectors' cooperative, COOPAMARE, which provided an alternative income for homeless individuals by allowing them to negotiate as a group with buyers, instead of doing it individually. COOPAMARE also offered a more organized and structured approach to work. During this time, homeless individuals began to squat in empty properties in downtown Sao Paulo. Additionally, some homeless individuals were able to access housing by rent, with OAF's support, on a small scale.

---

16 M. da Glória Gohn, 'Paulo Freire and the Formation of Sociopolitical Subjects' (2009) 4 *Caderno de Pesquisa Pensamento Educacional* <https://app.utp.br/cadernosdepesquisa/pdfs/cad_pesq8/2_paulo_freire_cp8.pdf> (accessed 1 September 2023). According to Gohn's work, popular education and liberation theology were part of a paradigm in which social movements developed social action throughout the 1970s and 1980s. This paradigm focused on building fairer social relations and emphasized the connection between knowledge and politicization, education, and social movements.
17 The Fraternal Aid Organization (OAF) is an NGO founded in 1955 with a mission to help the most destitute. OAF worked to bridge the social gap between vulnerable individuals and society. Its support was aimed at single mothers, women in prostitution, homeless children, and homeless and street dwellers.
18 In the sense of helping only to meet emergency needs, such as food or blankets.
19 G. Castelvecchi, *We Are a People Who Want to Live* (Paulines 1982).
20 Waste pickers are a large segment of the homeless population in Brazil. Although they are organized in different social movements, they are brotherly social movements. The *'Movimento Nacional dos Catadores de Materiais Recicláveis – MNCR'* (National Recyclable Material Collectors Movement) has campaigned throughout the years to replace the use of the term 'waste pickers' by the term 'collectors of recyclable materials' as a way to value the profession. Because of this political re-reading, we will not apply 'waste pickers' in this work.

Figure 17.1 Sufferers from the Street Community marching on their thirteenth mission (1981), holding posters with the slogan 'We are a people who want to live'.

Source: Photo by and reproduced with the permission of Alderon P. da Costa.

By the early 2000s, the efforts of organizing homeless individuals into a political group led to the establishment of the *Movimento Nacional da População de Rua* – MNPR (National Homeless Population Movement) after the 'Sé Square massacre'.[21] Studies began to focus on the construction of a social identity for the homeless, defining them not just by their needs and shortages but also by positive characteristics present in their discourse and political identification. The Sé Square massacre brought attention to the killing of homeless people, making their pain and suffering visible in the public space. This event created new meaning and understanding around the injustice of homelessness and deaths on the streets. As a result, researchers and other individuals involved in addressing homelessness were able to expand their field of study and collective action to unearth new perspectives.[22]

It is noteworthy that the emergence of a new social movement, spearheaded by homeless people on a national scale, was surprising to some researchers in the area, leading researcher Tomás Mello to refer to their political activity as the 'politics of the improbable'.[23] Despite

---

21 Between 19 and 22 August in 2004, a massacre of homeless people occurred in Sé Square in downtown São Paulo. The attacks resulted in seven deaths and six people suffering irreversible injuries. Despite the passage of time, the crime remains unsolved, and none of the victims' families have received compensation. This tragic event sparked a series of demonstrations and marked a political turning point regarding the visibility of deaths on the streets. It also led to the emergence of the National Homeless Population Movement.
22 D. De Lucca Reis Costa, 'Death and Life in the Streets of Sao Paulo: Biopolitics Seen from the Center' (Anthropology of Law National Meeting – ENADIR – conference, Sao Paulo 2009).
23 Melo (n 3).

The Homeless as Part of the Wider Dramatic Housing Problem in Brazil

Although numerically small compared to wider sections of society that do not have access to the right to decent housing in Brazil, the homeless population is a social phenomenon that reflects perhaps the cruellest face of this socio-economic system:

> The social phenomenon of homeless people is a synthesis of multiple determinations, whose characteristics, even with historical variations, make it an element of extraordinary relevance in the composition of poverty in capitalist societies.[24]

The homeless population is primarily an unhoused population that lives in conditions of extreme social vulnerability. It cannot be treated separately from the national and international socio-economic structure, which is directly responsible for the production and reproduction of severe social problems in Brazil. In this sense:

> The increasingly significant presence of people living in public spaces in large- and medium-sized Brazilian cities is not an isolated issue from the problems occurring internationally, in the last two decades, regarding the intense changes in the world of work and in the scope of the state. It is also closely linked to the way in which Brazilian society is organized in a process of income concentration, marked by social inequalities, economic circumstances of recession and unemployment, and the worsening of urban life poor conditions reproduction, such as housing and health, for example.[25]

It is worth observing that spaces in Brazilian cities are distributed according to social class and reflect and perpetuate existing social and racial inequalities, captured by socio-territorial segregation of low-income working families. There is no way to understand precarious housing in Brazil without acknowledging these processes. As Lúcio Kowarick demonstrates:

> The housing problem cannot be analyzed in isolation from other broader socio- economic and political processes, even though a set of specific contradictions is condensed in it. Thus, in the first instance, it is necessary to verify the productive modalities from which housing is made.[26]

Brazilian economic development has been oriented towards capitalist interests and wealth accumulation for the few, thereby widening socio-economic inequality for centuries. The Brazilian state's structure and public resources are subordinated to these interests. Lower-income

---

24 M. Lúcia Lopes Silva, *Labor and Homeless Population in Brazil* (1st edn, Cortez 2009) 91.
25 C. Moreno Maffei Rosa, *Street Lives* (Hucitec 2005) 29.
26 L. Kowarick, *The Urban Spoliation* (Paz e Terra 1993) 59.

workers form large, segregated areas of poverty in urban peripheries, creating antagonistic cities with different urban spaces designated by social class:

> Urban evolution in Brazil has contradicted the expectations of many in overcoming backwardness, archaic and marginality, by the capitalist modern. The urbanization process, accelerated and concentrated, marked by the 'modern development of backwardness', charged a high price from the 1980s onwards, after a few decades of intense economic growth in the country, through predation on the environment, low quality of life, gigantic social misery and its corollary, violence.[27]

Most urban housing in Brazil is not generated by the formal real estate market or the state's public social housing policy. Access to housing offered by the formal market is only available to families who can afford a private mortgage or rent. Between 60% and 80% of the population in Brazilian metropolises do not have the income to meet market demands and do not find solutions in public policies.[28]

Hence, in Brazil, housing is typically constructed through auto-construction, which involves residents building their own homes without architectural or engineering plans, proper licensing, or adherence to urban planning laws.[29] This type of construction lacks security of tenure,[30] physical safety,[31] and proper sanitation[32] and often involves the use of illegal actors, such as land grabbers and organized crime factions in accessing informal settlements. Even the middle classes participate in this informal market. Evidence of this can be seen in the booming real estate production in the outskirts of the Rio de Janeiro Metropolitan Region, where housing is created and overseen by militias with the collaboration of municipal and metropolitan authorities.[33] Brazil's informal housing production is not an exception but rather the norm of how our cities are built.

In 2019, the *João Pinheiro Foundation* (FJP)[34] used data from the National Household Sample Survey (PNAD) by the Brazilian Institute of Geography and Statistics (IBGE)[35] to determine the size of Brazil's housing problem. They drew a distinction between *housing deficit*

---

27 E. Maricato, *Metropolis on the Periphery of Capitalism: Illegality, Inequality, and Violence* (Hucitec 1996) 31.
28 E. Maricato and P. Colosso, 'The Urban Crisis in Brazil: From the Neodevelopmentalist Experiment and the Rise of Bolsonarismo' in B. Bianchi and others (eds), *Democracy and Brazil Collapse and Regression* (Routledge 2020).
29 Construction codes, zoning laws, environmental laws among others.
30 It usually does not have registration of land ownership.
31 It can be subject to slips, flooding.
32 According to our SISTEMA NACIONAL DE INFORMAÇÕES SOBRE SANEAMENTO – SNIS (National Sanitation System), more than 100 million people in Brazil do not have access to sewage by public network, and more than 30 million do not have access to drinking water network, without health (insalubrity), housing congestion. Data <www.snis.gov.br/> (accessed 1 September 2023).
33 Observatório das Metrópoles, 'GENI UFF' <https://br.boell.org/sites/default/files/2021-04/boll_expansao_milicias_RJ_v1.pdf?dimension1=no&fbclid=IwAR2o-KXcWgiA6BhTcYVshvWorVq0jk7Y21QwUVx-7sXfvquSzfqdVb7ERf30> (accessed 1 September 2023).
34 Housing Deficit in Brazil – 2016/2019 <https://fjp.mg.gov.br/deficit-habitacional-no-brasil/> (accessed 1 September 2023).
35 The Brazilian Institute of Geography and Statistics – IBGE is the main provider of geographic information and statistics in Brazil. More information can be accessed at <www.ibge.gov.br/> (accessed 1 September 2023).

and *home inadequacy* using data from each municipality. The housing deficit includes precarious housing, cohabitation, and excessive rent burden. In 2019, a need for 5.876 million new homes was identified. The deficit was made up of 89% of families with less than three minimum wage incomes, and 60% were households with women in charge of the family. Home inadequacy, by contrast, includes lack of urban infrastructure, building inadequacy, and land inadequacy. In 2019, 24.893 million households exhibited at least one housing inadequacy component.[36]

As regards the homeless population in Brazil, data analysis was conducted separately. The only national survey[37] was conducted in 2008 in 71 cities.[38] It showed 31,922 homeless people living in Brazil, predominantly male (82%), aged between 25 and 44 years (53%), and Black (67%). According to the data, 70.9% had paid work but with low income; the majority (52.6%) received between R$20.00 and R$80.00 per week. In terms of education, 74% could read and write, while 17.1% could not write and 8.3% could only sign their own name.

In December 2022, a technical study conducted by the *Instituto de Pesquisa Econômica Aplicada* – IPEA[39] estimated that there were 281,472 homeless people in Brazil based on federal government Social Assistance Ministry[40] data.[41] Through both the Covid-19 pandemic and economic crisis, there is still no official data on how many people are currently homeless in Brazil. It is noteworthy that the homeless population is not counted in the national census conducted by IBGE or included in the housing deficit.

Always Searching for Legal Rights: The Struggle of the National Homeless Population Movement

The legal and policy framework for the homeless population in Brazil is closely tied to the activism of homeless people themselves, who serve as leaders representing their own experiences and demand recognition as citizens with rights and public policies claims. Prioritizing the establishment of legal rights as a form of activism reflects the predominant

---

36 Household Inadequacy in Brazil – 2016/2019 <www.gov.br/mdr/pt-br/assuntos/habitacao/relatorio_iInadequacao_2016_2019_versao_2.pdf> (accessed 1 September 2023).
37 *Rua: aprendendo a contar. Pesquisa Nacional sobre a População em Situação de Rua* (2009) <www.mds.gov.br/webarquivos/publicacao/assistencia_social/Livros/Rua_aprendendo_a_contar.pdf> (accessed 1 September 2023).
38 The criteria were cities with over 300,000 inhabitants and States capitals.
39 IPEA is a federal public foundation linked to the Ministry for Economics. Technical note n. 103 of IPEA, which presents the estimate of the homeless population in Brazil for the whole period from September 2012 to December 2022 <https://repositorio.ipea.gov.br/bitstream/11058/11604/4/NT_103_Disoc_Estimativa_da_Populacao.pdf> (accessed 1 September 2023).
40 The Social Assistance Ministry can be understood as the Social Care Department, but the use of the word 'assistance' instead of 'care' has a political and academic background in Brazil. Social workers have long battled to distinguish social policies based on rights strengthening from charitable providers action, which also uses the terminology 'care' rooted in religious meaning. Consequently, 'assistance' would characterize a more neutral word, separating social services carried out by the state.
41 The data was extracted from CadÚnico and Censo SUAS. CadÚnico is the social assistance single registry for accessing all government benefits, and Censo SUAS is a census conducted by the Ministry for Social Development on every municipality's social services.

socio-legal tradition[42] in Brazil, seen not only in the struggle for homeless people's rights but also, more broadly, in housing social movements that use constitutional rights rhetoric to legitimize their direct action, such as occupying buildings and vacant land.[43]

It was precisely this form of socio-legal mobilization approach that created the political conditions for including the homeless in the public policy agenda and as a legislative priority during the rise of left-wing governments in Brazil. There were isolated experiences in the 1990s in some cities and, more broadly, on a national scale in the first decade of the 21st century. The first examples of including homeless people within specific public programmes took place during Mayor Luiza Erundina's democratic administration in Sao Paulo, undertaken by the *Partido dos trabalhadores* – PT (Workers' Party) from 1989 to 1992.

The Brazilian Federal Constitution of 1988 was established with the help of various popular movements, social organizations, and progressive sectors. It aimed to promote social justice, enshrine citizenship, human dignity, and equality as fundamental principles. One example of this can be seen in Article 6, which recognizes housing as a fundamental social right and assigns responsibility for its provision to the union, states, and municipalities. Other social rights, including education, health, food, work, transport, leisure, security, social security, protection of motherhood and childhood, and assistance to the destitute, are also outlined in the Constitution.

Articles 182 and 183 of the Federal Constitution,[44] related to urban policy, are regulated by '*Estatuto da Cidade*'[45] (City Statute Act), which establishes norms for public order, social interest, and the collective good. The law aims to ensure citizens' security, well-being, and environmental equilibrium, as well as to provide instruments for the social functioning and urban property development of cities to facilitate the use and expansion of urban land for social housing purposes.

President Luiz Inácio Lula da Silva, who held office from 2003 to 2010 under the Workers' Party, recognized the homeless population and recyclable material collectors as social priorities. This led to the development of legal frameworks and public policies coordinated by the federal government, acknowledging homelessness as a public policy issue of national importance affecting cities all over Brazil. While civil society representatives, including leaders of the MNPR, emphasized that tackling homelessness required an intersectoral and multidisciplinary approach encompassing human rights, housing, work, health, social assistance, education, culture, and leisure, it was the social assistance sectoral policy that took centre stage in addressing the issue. This will be further developed later.

With the establishment of MNPR in 2004, the 'politics of the improbable'[46] began to occupy institutional spaces, focusing on public policies and legislation. People who were homeless gained a new political status and a new life:

> Deprivation lived individually and fragmentarily is now staged as a collective experience of the whole category. With this, they stop, or try to stop, speaking on their

---

42 D. Culhane and others, 'Contrasting traditions in homelessness research between the UK and US' in L. Teixeira and J. Cartwright (eds), *Using Evidence to End Homelessness* (Bristol UP 2020).
43 L. Earle, 'From Insurgent to Transgressive Citizenship: Housing, Social Movements and the Politics of Rights in São Paulo' (2012) 44 *Journal of Latin American Studies* 97.
44 Constituição Federal Brasileira 1988 (BR).
45 Lei 10.257 de 2001 (BR).
46 Melo (n 3).

own behalf, because they speak on behalf of others in an attempt to build a broader proposition, based on their experiences, on the knowledge they have acquired, and on the social spaces through which they have passed.[47]

It is in this setting that important advances in the legal framework and public programmes aimed at the homeless population were made. It is worth listing the most significant of these here.

The Organic Social Assistance Act and the National Social Assistance Policy Regulation

The Brazilian Social Assistance System was established in 1993 by the *Lei Orgânica da Assistência Social* – LOAS[48] (Organic Social Assistance Act). However, it was not until 2004 that the *Política Nacional da Assistência Social* – PNAS[49] (National Social Assistance Policy Regulation) was issued, which created specific public services, established parameters for their functioning, and defined the responsibilities of national and local governments. Homelessness was identified as one of the target populations in the PNAS, which considers homelessness as part of a special social protection policy aimed at groups experiencing social risk and weak or broken social bonds. PNAS provides temporary shelter in various forms[50] and creates the Social Approach Program (SEAS), led by teams that establish relationships with unsheltered homeless individuals to connect them with the social assistance network.

In 2005, Law No. 11.258[51] was drafted to amend Article 23 of LOAS to insert a single paragraph requiring Social Assistance public services to create programmes that support the homeless in an intersectoral way. The following year, Regulation 381[52] of the Ministry for Social Development and Fight against Hunger was issued to establish co-financing between federal entities to provide continuous services of institutional shelter for homeless individuals in municipalities with more than 250,000 inhabitants.

The Participatory Process Behind the National Policy for the Homeless Population Law (PNPSR)

In 2005 and 2009, the federal government funded the first and second National Meetings on Homelessness. These events brought together experts from various ministries and civil society professionals to work with people experiencing homelessness. According to Melo,[53] public

---

47 De Lucca (n 22) 12.
48 Lei 8.742 de 1993 (BR).
49 The PNAS is a secondary legislation <www.mds.gov.br/webarquivos/publicacao/assistencia_social/Normativas/PNAS2004.pdf> (accessed 1 September 2023), which can be compared to a statutory instrument (SI) in the UK. In this case, it was issued by a minister and approved by the National Social Assistance Council (CNAS). All regulations and resolutions mentioned in this chapter are also secondary legislation that have been issued either by a ministry or a participatory council in accordance with a previous act.
50 Besides traditional institutional shelters, PNAS informs about *Repúblicas*, which is a type of supported transitional housing, foster care for homeless children and teenagers, among other forms of temporary accommodations.
51 Lei 11.258 de 2005 (BR). It is an Act of Brazilian Congress, therefore primary legislation. Throughout this chapter, whenever the word 'Law' is used before a specific number, we are indicating a primary legislation.
52 The Regulation 381 can be found at <http://blog.mds.gov.br/redesuas/portaria-no-381-de-17-de-novembro-de-2009/> (accessed 1 September 2023).
53 Melo (n 3).

funding played a crucial role in ensuring the direct participation of homeless individuals and consolidating the leadership of the National Homeless Population Movement (MNPR). In October 2009, President Lula established an Inter-Ministerial Group tasked with developing the National Policy for the Homeless Population Law (PNPSR). MNPR leaders were included in this working group and contributed directly to creating guidelines that formed the basis of PNPSR.

The National Social Assistance Services Regulation

In 2009, the National Social Assistance Council (CNAS) established Resolution No. 109,[54] which created the National Social Assistance Services Regulation. This regulation defined the parameters for the human and physical resources and practices offered in homeless services throughout the country.

The National Policy for the Homeless Population Law

On 23 December 2009, Presidential Decree No. 7.053[55] established the *Política Nacional da População em Situação de Rua* – PNPSR (National Policy for the Homeless Population Law) and its Intersectoral Committee for Monitoring and Evaluating (CIAMP-RUA).[56] This new law is the most significant at a national level on homelessness and represents a new model of state attention to the homeless population.[57]

The PNPSR's priorities include adopting a legal definition of homeless people; laying down principles, guidelines, and national goals on policies aimed at the homeless; binding federal entities to foster intersectoral management committees integrated by civil society representatives; establishing a National Centre of Human Rights Defence for the Homeless Population, aimed at promoting and defending their rights, monitoring complaints, preparing research and social indicators, in addition to encouraging local human rights defence centres; and creating CIAMP-RUA to monitor PNPSR's implementation.

Unified Registry, Social Assistance Specialized Reference Centres (CREAS), and Homeless Population Specialized Reference Centres (Centros Pop)

In 2010, Joint Operational Regulation No. 07[58] by the National Secretariat of Social Assistance (SNAS) and the National Secretariat of Income and Citizenship (SENARC) was published. It provides guidelines for municipalities and the federal district to include homeless

---

54 The resolution formulated by the Ministry for Social Development and Fight Against Hunger and approved by CNAS <www.mds.gov.br/webarquivos/public/resolucao_CNAS_N109_%202009.pdf> (accessed 1 September 2023).
55 Decreto n 7053 de 2009 (BR) <www.planalto.gov.br/ccivil_03/_Ato2007-2010/2009/Decreto/D7053.htm> (accessed 1 September 2023). A presidential decree in Brazil is a legal instrument issued by the president of the republic to regulate or discipline specific issues related to the functioning of the state or the implementation of public policies. For a presidential decree to be legally valid, it must comply with the Federal Constitution of Brazil and other applicable laws and regulations.
56 *Comitê Intersetorial de Avaliação e Monitoramento da Política Nacional da População em Situação de Rua*.
57 L. Valesca Pimentel, 'Public Policies to Assist Homeless: Reflections on Rights Effectiveness in the Fortaleza Municipality' (2018) 8(20) *Conhecer: debate entre o público e o privado*.
58 Joint Operational Regulation No. 07 can be found at <www.justica.pr.gov.br/sites/default/arquivos_restritos/files/migrados/File/Capacitacao/centropop/01.ppt> (accessed 1 September 2023).

people in the *Social Assistance Unified Registry* (CadÚnico), an instrument for monitoring the homeless and a requirement to access social assistance benefits.

That same year, Regulation No. 843[59] was produced by the Social Development Ministry, providing federal co-financing of social assistance services offered by *Social Assistance Specialized Reference Centres* (CREAS) and *Homeless Population Specialized Reference Centres* (Centros POP). These centres are managed by multi-professional teams that must know their territories in depth and serve as a gateway for homeless people to access services, care, and provide them a reference address.[60] Although they have the same attributions, the Centros POP units are focused on homelessness in high-concentration areas and thus more specialized. In 2012, Regulation No. 139[61] complemented Regulation No. 843 and provided parameters for federal co-financing of social assistance services delivered by Centros POP.

The Street Clinics (CnR)

In January 2011, the Ministry for Health instituted Resolution No. 122,[62] which introduced the policy of *Consultórios na Rua* – CnR (Street Clinics). CnRs are made up of multidisciplinary teams that provide on-site healthcare (including examinations, medical appointments, vaccinations, etc.), facilitating the access of homeless people to health and mental healthcare, bridging, and referring them on to the other services of the Brazilian Universal Health System, which is a public and free national health system.

Resolution No. 40 from the National Council on Human Rights (CNDH)

Recently, the National Human Rights Council (CNDH) issued Resolution No. 40,[63] providing guidelines to promote and protect the human rights of homeless people. The resolution addresses challenges not sufficiently developed in over ten years of National Policy validity. It is innovative in addressing housing as a gateway to other rights and mentions Housing First[64] as a model to be implemented by the state. The resolution also addresses public security policies and violence against homeless people. It places obligations on institutions

---

59 The Regulation is online at <http://blog.mds.gov.br/redesuas/portaria-no-843-de-28-de-dezembro-de-2010/> (accessed 1 September 2023).
60 For homeless people who need to declare an address for referrals to access services, receive documents/receipts, or even to obtain employment.
61 The complementary Regulation <http://blog.mds.gov.br/redesuas/portaria-no-139-de-28-de-junho-de-2012/> (accessed 1 September 2023).
62 Resolution 122 can be found at <https://bvsms.saude.gov.br/bvs/saudelegis/gm/2012/prt0122_25_01_2012.html> (accessed 1 September 2023).
63 <www.in.gov.br/web/dou/-/resolucao-n-40-de-13-de-outubro-de-2020-286409284> (accessed 1 September 2023).
64 *Moradia Primeiro* refers to Brazilian initiatives that implement the Housing First (HF) model, an evidence-based intervention approach that aims to address chronic homelessness by providing immediate and unconditional access to housing. This model was developed by Pathways to Housing and is being disseminated internationally. It is a departure from traditional public policies for homeless individuals, which typically involve a staircase approach that requires temporary shelter and several steps before the individual can access permanent housing. The Housing First model instead prioritizes the provision of permanent housing as the first intervention. For more information, see S. Tsemberis's book, *Housing First: The Pathways Model to End Homelessness for People with Mental Health and Substance Use Disorders* (Hazelden 2015).

to collaborate, including public agencies and the Brazilian justice system, ensuring access to justice for the homeless population.

Resolution No. 425 from the National Council of Justice (CNJ)

Resolution No. 425 of 2021[65] by the National Council of Justice establishes the National Judicial Policy of Attention to Homeless People and their intersectionalities. The resolution recognizes institutional barriers for homeless people in accessing the justice system and identifies measures to provide better inclusion and integration. It creates obligations to prioritize assistance for homeless people, reduce bureaucracy to access the justice system,[66] conduct training with justice officials for the humane treatment of homeless people, and consider itinerant justice activities, that is, taking the justice system to the places where homeless people live.

***

This section has demonstrated that Brazil regulates the social phenomenon of homelessness and the homeless 'problem' through various means. It is regulated not only through a global, national policy, the National Policy for the Homeless Population, but also through multiple services and rights provided to the homeless population in diffuse legislation within different sectoral policies, particularly social assistance, and health policies.

The legal framework on homelessness in Brazil is, however, mostly based on weak instruments, such as regulations and decrees that can be easily altered. Nevertheless, there are also more stable laws developed through complex legislative procedures. All these policies and regulations have been extensively discussed and reviewed with the homeless population, either through representatives in participatory councils or through events and training sessions. Moreover, there are several laws at the state and municipal levels that are aimed at the homeless.

The Promotion of Homeless People Protagonism as the Basis for Developing Effective Practices to Improve the Lives of the Homeless in Brazil

When considering public policy responses to homelessness in Brazil that foster homeless protagonism, it is important to highlight the Social Approach Program (SEAS)[67] and the Street Clinics *(CnR)*.[68] Both initiatives require their professional teams to include people who have experienced life on the streets. This assists in ensuring dialogue between homeless people and policy teams, bringing them closer to the values, lifestyles, and culture of policy beneficiaries.

Institutionalized participatory councils, however, best reflect the Brazilian approach to homeless social participation. At the national level, CIAMP-RUA[69] is a council with five

---

65 <https://atos.cnj.jus.br/files/original1447482021101161644e94ab8a0.pdf> (accessed 1 September 2023).
66 Avoiding the need for previous scheduling meetings with authorities or the obligation to exhibit personal documents, often lost in the streets.
67 It is a public service characterized by the continuous and active presence of professionals in public spaces to identify and get to know the real demands and needs of people and families at personal and social risk in public spaces. See 'The Organic Social Assistance Law and The National Social Assistance Policy' section earlier for more.
68 See 'The Street Clinics (CnR)' section above for more information.
69 About the Council <www.gov.br/mdh/pt-br/navegue-por-temas/populacao-em-situacao-de-rua/ciamp-rua> (accessed 1 September 2023).

civil society representatives appointed by organizations that assist the homeless, including the National Movement for the Homeless Population. On the government side, there are ministries such as Women, Family, and Human Rights; Justice; Public Security; Education; Citizenship; Health; and Regional Development.

Among the responsibilities of CIAMP-RUA are key activities, such as developing periodic action plans for implementing the National Policy for the Homeless Population; developing indicators for monitoring and evaluating PNPSR; proposing measures to ensure intersectoral federal public policies articulation; proposing ways to disseminate the National Policy; cataloguing information on homeless policy delivery in states, federal districts, and municipalities; encouraging local participatory committees' creation and strengthening; and organizing periodic national meetings to consolidate PNSR.

Melo points out that CIAMP-RUA allows MNPR leaders to gather every 45 days in the federal district, facilitating dialogue between regional leaders and articulating national guidelines that subsequently reverberate at the local level. This transit of leaders between local and national levels allows for informed dialogue and learning for all parties as discussions move from national to political to local bases and vice versa.[70]

The Intersectoral Committee for Monitoring and Evaluating PNSR is a valuable instrument for structuring federal government actions tackling homelessness. It ensures that the homeless voice is active and heard while reforming outdated models, practices, and discourses surrounding the homeless population. Recently, the committee has worked to popularize a new policy model centred on immediate access to housing for the homeless combined with other intersectoral policies (including welfare, health)[71] that help them stay housed. This advocacy resulted in Resolution No. 2.927 of 2021[72] establishing the Housing First Project under the Ministry of Women, Family, and Human Rights and authorizing federal funding for the programme.[73]

The creation of participatory councils to discuss intersectoral policies for the homeless is mandatory for any federal entity that agrees with and operates under the Homeless National Policy Law (PNPSR).[74] According to data from the Ministry of Social Development,[75] up to 2020, six states and 18 cities had implemented local participatory committees. Although small in number, it demonstrates that participation is slowly gaining ground and influence.

In Sao Paulo, Act No. 17.252 (2019) consolidates the Municipal Policy for the Homeless Population and introduces an obligation for all services offered to the homeless to provide spaces for their participation. This ensures their right to have a voice and vote on issues related to their daily life in public services. Although not yet in force because of a lack of secondary enacting legislation, it is an attempt to go beyond councils and assure participation directly where public policies are implemented.

---

70 Melo (n 3) 40.
71 R. Bichir and P. Canato, 'Intersectorality and Social Networks: The Implementation of Programs for Homeless People in são paulo' (2021) 55 *Revista de Administracao Publica* 995 <http://dx.doi.org/10.1590/0034-761220200688> (accessed 1 September 2023).
72 The full text can be found at <www.gov.br/mdh/pt-br/acesso-a-informacao/institucional/portaria-no-2-927-de-26-de-agosto-de-2021> (accessed 1 September 2023).
73 Ministry of Women, Family and Human Rights, 'Is it possible Housing First in Brazil? Housing experiences for homeless in Europe and Brazil' (MMFDH 2019).
74 Pimentel (n 57).
75 Data <www.google.com/maps/d/u/0/viewer?ll=-13.811708863141298%2C-2.78968668750003&z=3&mid=1GqTJ22kqRgvSFZRjvQ7eRog3e8NH4JqX (accessed 1 September 2023).

It is necessary to point out that participatory spaces where social movements like MNPR interact with the state are replete with tensions.[76] Several problems already recognized in literature include asymmetry of information and power among members;[77] lack of training and continuing education for participants; low coercivity of guidelines developed by councils in relation to government; and the elitist profile of many participants, among other concerns. As for recent challenges, during the Covid-19 pandemic, the migration of meetings into the virtual sphere underlined the digital exclusion of the homeless and impacted their direct participation.[78]

Overall, the presence of social movements within institutional spaces like participatory councils could lead to a loss of autonomy of those movements and even imply loss of their imaginative potential to project another possible world beyond state limits.[79] Tatagiba suggests that institutional participation creates contradictions between political effectiveness (the ability to influence public policies for their group) and autonomy (the ability to retain control over their own priorities) for these social movements.

However, tensions and asymmetries in institutional spaces must be considered in light of material and symbolic homeless rights violations in Brazilian society. The homeless are a population whose political status is constantly infringed or at risk,[80] making their silence an important dimension of exclusion.[81] Despite difficulties permeating participatory practices and spaces in Brazil, these compel the state to listen directly to the homeless, breaking from their historical invisibilization. This change and legacies built over years in participatory spaces make the homeless struggle in Brazil distinct from the social experience of homelessness in other countries.

Assessing Homelessness in Brazil: Building Exit Doors or Revolving Doors?

As this chapter has shown, Brazil has made advances in developing a legal framework and public policies to meet the needs of the homeless population. However, there is an increase in the number of people living on the streets in Brazilian cities.[82] The failure to overcome homelessness is not due to lack of law or regulation but rather the absence of its effective application.[83]

---

76 Luciana Tatagiba, 'Challenges of the Relationship between Social Movements and Political Institutions: Housing Movements Case in Sao Paulo' (2010) 71 *Colombia Internacional* 63.

77 Ibid; R. Neaera Abers and others, 'Social Movements and Public Policy: Rethinking Actors and Political Opportunities' (2018) 105 *Lua Nova* <https://doi.org/10.1590/0102-015046/105> (accessed 1 September 2023); C. Almeida and others, 'Balance of Studies on Public Policy Councils in the last Decade' (2015) 94 *Lua Nova* <https://doi.org/10.1590/0102-64452015009400009> (accessed 1 September 2023).

78 B. Calheta and others, 'Political Participation as a Space for Listening: The Advisors to Sao Paulo's Homeless Council Actions during the Pandemic' (2022) 7(32) *Cadernos da Defensoria Pública do Estado de São Paulo* 139.

79 E. Maricato, 'We Have Never Been So Participative' in *Urban Policy Impasse in Brazil* (Editora Vozes 2014).

80 De Lucca (n 22).

81 J. Dantas Germano Gomes, 'Hearing as a Human Rights Practice: Reflections on Luiz Gama Human Rights Clinic Activities' in C. Nicácio and others (eds), *Human Rights Clinics and Legal Education in Brazil: From Criticism to the Practice That Renews* (Arraes Editora 2017).

82 M. Antônio Carvalho Natalino and others, 'Estimate of the Homeless Population in Brazil' (Technical Note No. 73, IPEA June 2020).

83 Maricato (n 79).

From constitutional rights to infra-constitutional and secondary legislation, the legal issues around homelessness are widely established and generally very protective of homeless rights. Kohara suggests that in a capitalist system, especially in a peripheral capitalism environment, legal advances are often 'allowed' but prove not to be effective:

> Capital's socio metabolic system allows advances in the legal frameworks, but prevents their effectuation or implementation. Thus, in order for the contradiction between the written and the concrete life not to become a fighting force, the system allows the 'the poor and miserable class' to have only the illusory crumbs and leftovers. Legal norms have failed to effectively place them as citizens and for the economic system they are unproductive.[84]

From a public policy point of view, since the 1990s, the homeless have been targeted for constant experimentation[85] in Brazil with numerous policies in various fields. However, these policies have not addressed the increase in homelessness due to failure to build strong intersectorality[86] and a constant discontinuity between different governments preventing durability and coherence.[87]

According to Benjaminsen and Dyb, homelessness should be understood at the intersection between housing and welfare policies as both shape interventions directed towards the homeless population.[88] In Brazil, however, homelessness was introduced into the government agenda through social assistance, with a focus on institutional shelter policies. This model characterizes support for the homeless as palliative and introduced emergency measures that became permanent techniques for treating the issue.[89] This disarticulation has contributed to the absence of preventive measures on forced evictions and an increase in families living on the street.

Once on the street, the homeless individual is hostage to shelter availability and the time they can stay there. It is common for individuals to move successively between different temporary accommodation in a 'continuous circulation' mode[90] without securing stable housing conditions to overcome homelessness. Nakagawa points out that shelter supply has always been below demand.[91] In this context, shelters may represent state control over people living in poverty in urban public spaces, offering a backstop for the police, welfare, and

---

84 Kohara (n 10) 25.
85 D. De Lucca Reis Costa, 'Neither Inside Nor Outside The Shelter: Transformations and Uses of an Assistance Device' (ANPOCS Sao Paulo, 2010) (accessed 1 September 2023).
86 R. Bichir and P. Canato, 'Solving Complex Problems? Challenges of Implementing Intersectoral Policies' in R. Pires (ed), *Implementing Inequalities: Reproduction of Inequalities in Public Policies Implementation* (Rio de Janeiro IPEA 2019). In the authors' perspective, 'intersectorality' is a concept that can be defined as 'the interaction of different government sectors to deliver services in an articulated manner to the same group of beneficiaries who have diverse demands'.
87 P. Canato, 'Intersectorality and Social Networks: An Analysis of Projects Implementation for the Homeless Population in Sao Paulo' (Thesis, University of Sao Paulo 2017).
88 L. Benjaminsen and E. Dyb, 'The Effectiveness of Homeless Policies-Variations among the Scandinavian Countries' (2008) 2 *European Journal of Homelessness* 45.
89 De Lucca (n 85).
90 Frangella (n 12).
91 C. Teixeira Nakagawa, 'The Housing Right and Homelessness' (2020) 27 *Ponto-e-Vírgula*.

interventions aiming to ban the homeless from the public sphere. In other words, shelters are operating far beyond their official role of welcoming vulnerable people but instead are a place to which unwanted people in the city's public space are referred.[92]

In contrast, the homeless population's relationship with housing policy is one of almost absolute exclusion. Despite national and municipal guidelines ensuring the right to housing, services for this section of the community have occurred only occasionally as a result of social pressure, with only a small fraction receiving help. Therefore, it can be said that in Brazil the homeless population is 'without a place' in housing policy.[93]

It is precisely the fact that there is in Brazil a national social movement led by the homeless that presents the possibility and potential to address challenges faced by the homeless population. To give visibility and to strengthen their fight for housing, the National Pastoral of the Homeless Population[94] chose housing as their main action plan and launched the campaign 'Chega de Omissão, queremos habitação!' ('No more Omission! We want housing now!') in 2015. Additionally, in 2016, MNPR defined the right to housing as their main goal.[95] These initiatives have contributed to awareness among society and government sectors about the importance of housing rights for this group.[96]

Taken together, the significant challenge facing homelessness in Brazil is to overcome a model centred on emergency shelter that fails to address the root causes of homelessness. This requires redefining homelessness to acknowledge the critical role of housing exclusion processes and breaking down political barriers that separate people living on the streets from those unhoused. However, a housing policy for the homeless population, including 'Housing First', must consider the difficulty of accessing formal, decent housing with security of tenure for most Brazilians. The demand for housing by homeless individuals is further complicated by the structural fragility of wider housing and urban policies.[97]

The nature of this fragility can be illustrated by Lima's research on the Social Renting Housing Program's selection process for *Empreendimento Asdrúbal do Nascimento*, the only building project targeted at helping the homeless in Sao Paulo city with 34 flats. Lima found that 93.9% of the homeless in Sao Paulo were excluded from selection due to income criterion.[98] In addition to income barrier, there is an institutionalized stigma serving as a further barrier for the homeless to access housing based on the belief that only institutional shelter is suitable.[99]

When addressing homelessness in Brazil, it is important to reconsider the approach to housing programmes and the emphasis on private property ownership. The social right to housing involves more than just receiving a house key; it requires a sustainable process of

---

92 De Lucca (n 85).
93 Over the years, homeless individuals have made progress in health and welfare policies through their participation in councils. However, housing councils were occupied by unhoused individuals. As a result, homeless individuals never had the same strength to discuss housing policies as unhoused individuals.
94 Homeless Pastoral is a sector in the Brazilian Catholic church dedicated to the homeless.
95 Pimentel (n 57).
96 Kohara (n 10).
97 Maricato (n 28).
98 J. Carvalho Ferreira Barbosa Lima, 'Phase I Evaluation on Asdrúbal do Nascimento II Development implementation: Pilot Project of Social Rental Housing for the Homeless Population in Sao Paulo' (Public Management Specialist Final Project, Insper 2020) 40.
99 Kohara (n 10) 42.

social inclusion. Social work before and after housing is essential and should be comprehensive and intersectoral (work and income, health, education, social assistance, human rights, culture).[100] Public managers in the housing field must be prepared for property, condominium, and social management.

Decent housing should be recognized as a social right, and access should not depend on payment capacity.[101] As the homeless population is diverse, different programme modalities should be available. Access to and sustainability of housing should be guided by equity. Housing for homeless people should be a continuous public service that provides a structural basis for sustainable social inclusion and an exit from homelessness[102] and not a revolving door.[103]

The MNPR has opened up a national debate on the Housing First model, which is well-known in North America and Europe. The difference in the Brazilian setting is that this debate has engaged intense and direct homeless participation. It goes beyond discussing public policies models by academics or public managers, reaching directly politically organized homeless people themselves. The homeless population has claimed the right to live with dignity, demonstrating that the challenge of tackling homelessness in Brazil is already underway.

Conclusions

This chapter has sought to present the ways in which Brazil has approached the growing social phenomenon of the homelessness social question, with its particular Brazilian context distinguishing between those who are homeless and those who are unhoused, in a country where these two groups have been treated very differently in the political field, legislation, and in public policies. As has been emphasized, the striking distinction in the Brazilian account of homelessness is the fact of intense social participation and protagonism of the homeless population, a practice which has produced a homelessness social movement on a national scale. More importantly, this movement is led by activists with a life on the streets and their own homelessness journey. This is the common thread that runs through and explains much of the various national legislation, regulations, and practices pertaining to the homeless population in Brazil.

The prevailing understanding and approach to homelessness in Brazil have resulted in extensive social assistance interventions while excluding the homeless from housing policies. Homeless individuals have replied to this challenge by rejecting institutionalized temporary accommodation policies as a naturalized response and by striving to challenge barriers to access to housing policies, thereby redefining traditional interpretations of homelessness in Brazil.

---

100 Ibid.
101 Brazil has a public educational system and a universal health system, both of which are free of charge for citizens and foreigners living in the country.
102 Fórum da Cidade de Defesa da População em Situação de Rua de São Paulo, 'A Proposal for a Housing Program for Homeless Population' (2022) 7(32) *Cadernos da Defensoria Pública do Estado de São Paulo* 173.
103 Kohara (n 10).

To combat this exclusion and promote the public character of social housing, the homeless must overcome the commodification of housing and the state's oppressive guardianship paradigm over them. This transformation requires more than just technical assistance or policy changes but a shift in theoretical-conceptual, ethical-political-legal, and sociocultural perceptions of the homeless. Building housing for the homeless entails not just providing shelter but also elevating their social status in Brazil and affirming their right to live with dignity, regardless of income or barriers to autonomy.

18
PUBLIC POLICIES FOR THE HOMELESS IN CHILE
A Shifting Picture

Ignacio Eissmann and Felipe Estay

Introduction: Homelessness in Latin America and the Chilean Context

Homelessness ('personas en situación de calle' in Spanish)[1] is a global problem that affects a significant number of individuals across the world.[2] Despite the efforts of governments and private organizations, the number of homeless individuals remains high. For instance, Europe has seen an increase in homelessness over the past five years.[3] The situation is similar in North America, where Canada has an estimated 25,000 chronically homeless individuals,[4] and the United States has over 580,000 homeless individuals, according to the 2020 Annual Homeless Assessment Report to Congress.[5]

In the context of Latin America, most countries lack systematic information and data on their homeless populations. Chile and Uruguay stand out as exceptions, having established procedures to measure homelessness over the past 15 years.[6] Uruguay conducted

---

1 In Chile and other Latin American countries, the concept of 'people in a street situation' is commonly used to refer to, what in many other countries, would be termed homeless people. Within the chapter, both concepts will be used synonymously.
2 V. Busch-Geertsema, D. P. Culhane and S. Fitzpatrick, 'Developing a Global Framework for Conceptualizing and Measuring Homelessness' (2016) 55 *Habitat International* 124; L. Farha, *Report of the Special Rapporteur on Adequate Housing as a Component of the Right to an Adequate Standard of Living, and on the Right to Non-Discrimination in This Context* (United Nations 2018); D. Finfgeld-Connett, 'Becoming Homeless, Being Homeless, and Resolving Homelessness among Women' (2010) 31(7) *Issues in Mental Health Nursing* 461; K. Johnson, M. McGreevy and M. Seeley, 'An Overview of Global Homelessness and Strategies for Systemic Change' (2018) *Institute of Global Homeless* <https://vfhomelessalliance.org/wp-content/uploads/2018/10/Briefing-IGH-Overview-of-Global-Homelessness-ENG.pdf> (accessed 1 September 2023).
3 FEANTSA and Foundation Abbé Pierre, *Third Overview of Housing Exclusion in Europe* (FEANTSA and Foundation Abbé Pierre 2018); FEANTSA and Foundation Abbé Pierre, *Fifth Overview of Housing Exclusion in Europe* (FEANTSA and Foundation Abbé Pierre 2020).
4 Government of Canada, *Canada's National Housing Strategy* <www.placetocallhome.ca/-/media/sf/project/placetocallhome/pdfs/canada-national-housing-strategy.pdf> (accessed 1 September 2023).
5 US Department of Housing and Urban Development, HUD, *The 2020 Annual Homeless Assessment Report (AHAR) to Congress*, US Department of Housing and Urban Development (2021) 1.
6 Busch-Geertsema and others (n 2).

one-night counting from 2006 to 2020, with the number of homeless people counted rising from 739[7] to 3,917.[8] Chile, which is the focus of this chapter, conducted counts (using different methodologies) in 2005, 2011, and since 2016 has implemented a permanent homeless register via administrative data. The first count was not conducted nationally and only considered the three regions with the largest populations, recording 7,254 homeless people.[9] The second, national count recorded at least 12,255 homeless people;[10] 11,623 people were recorded as homeless in August 2017,[11] a number that had risen to over 19,000 by October 2022.

Homelessness in Chile was not widely recognized as a public or social issue until the turn of the 21st century. Throughout the 20th century, it was mainly viewed as begging or vagrancy and received little attention from the government or society.[12] However, the growing recognition of the issue has led to greater engagement with the term 'homelessness (Situación de Calle)' in Chile as a way to describe this population without stigma and to raise awareness of their needs.[13] This shift in perspective acknowledges that homelessness is not only a result of a lack of housing but is also caused by exclusion and vulnerability resulting from various, complex, and contributing factors.[14]

The 20th century saw social interventions in Chile aimed at homeless individuals by Catholic Church–linked civil society organizations. These institutions offered housing assistance, mainly for children and the elderly, through charitable foundations. In the late 1990s, new non-profit organizations joined in, mainly through volunteer efforts. Chile's deep neoliberal reforms in the 1980s, imposed under a dictatorship, established a unique approach to public policy design and implementation that influenced subsequent decades. Like many other Latin American nations, Chile reduced poverty but failed to address inequality. This prompted the implementation of a social protection system and sparked discussions on poverty, vulnerability, and public policy response, with a focus on ensuring social minimums, equal access to services, and a rights-based approach.[15]

---

7 Ministerio de Desarrollo Social, MIDES, *Primer Conteo y Censo de personas en situación de calle y refugios de Montevideo 2006. Informe preliminar de resultados* (MIDES 2006)
8 MIDES & Dirección Nacional de Transferencias y Análisis de Datos, DINTAT, *Evolución y caracterización de las personas en situación de calle en Uruguay. Principales resultados de los relevamientos de personas sin hogar realizados en 2020 y 2021* (MIDES and DINTAT 2021).
9 Ministerio de Planificación, *Habitando la Calle. Catastro Nacional de Personas en Situación de Calle* (Ministerio de Planificación 2005).
10 Ministerio de Desarrollo Social, *En Chile Todos Contamos. Segundo Catastro Nacional de Personas en Situación de Calle*, Colección Observatorio Social (Universidad Alberto Hurtado 2012)
11 Ministerio de Desarrollo Social, *Política Nacional Política Nacional de Calle Nacional de Calle Balances y proyecciones de una política pública para Personas en Situación de Calle* (Ministerio de Desarrollo Social 2017).
12 I. Celic, 'La multidimensionalidad de la Situación de Calle en Chile: Mucho más que no tener techo. Análisis Cualitativo de los programas del Estado y la sociedad civil que abordan el problema' *(Master thesis, University of Chile 2016)*; Ministerio de Planificación (n 9); J. Wong, 'Análisis Crítico a las Políticas Públicas para Personas en Situación de Calle en Chile' (Master thesis, Alberto Hurtado University 2017).
13 I. Eissmann, 'Claves para Observar la Situación de Calle en Chile' (2021) 1(1) *Revista Situación de Calle* 123.
14 Celic (n 12); Eissmann (n 13); M. Weason, 'Personas en Situación De Calle: Reconocimiento e Identidad en Contexto de Exclusión Social' (Undergraduate thesis, Alberto Hurtado University 2006); Wong (n 12).
15 C. Robles, 'Persistencias de la pobreza y esquemas de protección social en América Latina y el Caribe' (Colección CLACSO-CROP 2013).

In response to these challenges, Chile established the *Chilean Solidarity Social Protection System*[16] in 2002. Within this system, the *Calle Program*[17] was created, providing psychosocial support for 24 months to homeless individuals.[18] In 2012, the Ministry of Social Development introduced the *Dignified Night Program*[19] (PND) to ensure that people experiencing street homelessness have access to basic social services and opportunities to improve their situation.[20] In 2018, the *Housing with Support*[21] programme was established based on the Housing First model, targeting individuals over 49 years of age who have been homeless for at least five years.[22] These programmes are largely carried out by civil society organizations through a bidding process, where the government finances policies but does not implement them directly. Instead, local government and non-profit organizations are selected to do so.

The Current State of Homeless People in Chile

In Chile, there are currently more than 19,000 people living without a home, distributed throughout the country. To address this issue, the government offers a range of social services that homeless people can access for help (these services are detailed later in this chapter). These services primarily provide two resources: (1) psychosocial support, mainly from social workers and psychologists, and (2) temporary and emergency accommodation. However, the capacity of these services is limited and not available in all cities across the country. As a result, there are many areas where homeless people exist, but there are simply no social services for them, or services are scarce. At the local government level, while universal services are available for homeless people, they are not specialized and do not offer housing solutions. Only a few local governments have managed to implement social programmes specifically for the homeless.

When individuals become homeless and lack social networks to address their housing situation, their main recourse is to seek help from emergency shelters or civil society organizations such as NGOs and foundations. These organizations provide basic services and connect individuals with specialized social services for homeless people provided by central government and universal social services provided by local governments. However, the main problem with these services is their limited coverage, and most of them do not have any legal guarantee ensuring their long-term existence. Only the Street Program, which offers psychosocial support, is underpinned by a law that ensures its budget each year, while the remainder of public programmes pertaining to homelessness depend on ongoing action and support from the government, which could be withdrawn at any time. Additionally, access to housing is not guaranteed as a constitutional right for all citizens in Chile. Consequently, public policies for homeless people in Chile are

---

16 Sistema de Protección Social, Chile Solidario.
17 Programa Calle in Spanish. More information at <www.desarrollosocialyfamilia.gob.cl/programas-sociales/personas-en-situacion-de-calle/programa-calle> (accessed 1 September 2023).
18 Ministerio de Desarrollo Social (n 11).
19 Programa Noche Digna in Spanish.
20 Ministerio de Desarrollo Social (n 11) 46.
21 Programa vivienda con apoyo in Spanish.
22 Ministerio de Desarrollo Social y Familia, *Viviendas con Apoyo para Personas en Situación de Calle* (Ministerio de Desarrollo Social y Familia 2020).

fragile, and civil society organizations remain the most permanent resource for addressing homelessness.

This chapter aims to examine the evolution of public policies for the homeless in Chile from 2006 to 2021. It conducts a literature review on homelessness conceptualizations in Chile and assesses the key social programmes implemented during this period. The chapter is structured in three parts. The first part analyzes the conceptualization and problematization of homelessness in Chile, comparing it to international definitions, especially in Latin America. The second part focuses on the development of key social programmes for homeless individuals, particularly those focused on housing, and highlights major accomplishments in this area from 2006 to 2021. The final part offers a critical discussion of and draws conclusions on the evolution of public policies on homelessness in Chile, addressing the central question of the chapter.

The Conceptual Framework of Homelessness

Understandings of Homelessness: The Global North and Global South Compared

The theoretical and conceptual framework regarding homelessness has been more extensively developed in North America and Europe compared to Latin America. In Chile, much of the conceptual development has been based on literature from these countries. Therefore, it is relevant to review the global discussion to understand and contextualize the issue of homelessness in Latin America and, in particular, in Chile. The literature defines *homelessness* in various ways with different approaches and categories. Some categories define *homelessness* as sleeping solely on the street, while others acknowledge more complex processes with different contexts.[23] These categories create operational definitions for the homeless and those at risk of homelessness.[24] In the 1990s, debates arose about whether the causes of homelessness were at the individual or structural level,[25] but now there is consensus on the need for an integrated analysis of both.[26] This integrated analysis helps to effectively address the root causes of homelessness.

Homelessness has been a subject of keen focus in recent decades, particularly in relation to the challenge of accessing and maintaining adequate housing.[27] The problematization of homelessness is based on a human rights perspective, not just acknowledging the material

---

23 F. Ciapessoni, 'Recorridos y desplazamientos de personas que habitan refugios nocturnos' (Master Thesis, The Republic University 2013); Eissmann (n 13); D. Levinson and M. Ross, *Homelessness Handbook* (1st edn, Berkshire Publishing Group LLC 2007).

24 Canadian Observatory on Homelessness, *Canadian Definition of Homelessness* (Canadian Observatory on Homelessness Press 2012); Johnson and others (n 2); United States Interagency Council on Homelessness, *Opening Doors Federal Strategic Plan to Prevent and End Homelessness* (United States Interagency Council on Homelessness 2015).

25 Ciapessoni (n 23); D. Clapham, 'Pathways Approaches to Homelessness Research' (2003) 13(2) *Journal of Community and Applied Social Psychology* 119; S. Fitzpatrick, 'Explaining Homeless' (2005) 22(1) *Housing, Theory and Society* 1; Levinson and Ross (n 23).

26 Clapham (n 25).

27 Johnson and others (n 2); D. Padget, B. Henwood and S. Tsemberis, *Housing First Ending Homelessness, Transforming Systems, and Changing Lives* (1st edn, OUP 2016).

aspect of homelessness but also recognizing its impact on individuals' rights.[28] To conceptualize homelessness, important frameworks have been developed in the Global North which have influenced Chile's debate. Three frameworks have been deemed useful in analyzing homelessness as a global social issue, as they provide operational definitions to delimit the problem: (1) the right to adequate housing, (2) the European Typology of Homelessness and Housing Exclusion (ETHOS), and (3) the Global Framework. These frameworks offer a comprehensive understanding of homelessness from different perspectives and can be applied in different contexts.

The right to adequate housing is a fundamental human right that ensures access to a home that is secure, accessible, and suitable for living.[29] It encompasses various aspects, such as security of tenure, non-discrimination, community involvement, maintenance, availability of services, accessibility, habitability, connectivity, and cultural adaptation.[30] This right is interdependent with other basic human rights, including the right to work, health, social security, privacy, and education. The deprivation of this right can have negative effects on individuals and communities.[31] The European Typology on Homelessness and Housing Exclusion (ETHOS) categorizes homelessness based on three domains: physical, social, and legal. The *physical* domain refers to the availability of adequate living space, the *social* domain refers to the ability to maintain privacy and form social relationships, and the *legal* domain refers to the legality and security of tenure.[32] If a person lacks any of these domains, they can be classified as homeless or experiencing housing exclusion.[33] The Global Framework on Homelessness, developed by the Institute of Global Homelessness (IGH),[34] is a new typology based on ETHOS. It incorporates the social and physical domains from ETHOS and adds a third domain of security, which encompasses the concept of accessibility to housing.[35] The framework categorizes homelessness into three groups: those without a place to live, those living in temporary places, and those living in inadequate and insecure housing.[36]

In Latin America, homelessness is often referred to as a 'street problem', with a focus on the population affected by it and the social exclusion and vulnerability they experience. The emphasis is on the processes that lead to homelessness, rather than just the lack of a permanent and adequate place to live.[37] In Chile, the investigation of homelessness

---

28 K. Amore, M. Baker and P. Howden-Chapman, 'The ETHOS Definition and Classification of Homelessness: An Analysis' (2011) 5(2) *European Journal of Homelessness* 19; Busch-Geertsema and others (n 2); FEANTSA, *ETHOS – Taking Stock* (FEANTSA 2006); Johnson and others (n 2).
29 L. Farha, *Report of the Special Rapporteur on Adequate Housing as a Component of the Right to an Adequate Standard of Living, and on the Right to Non-discrimination in This Context* (United Nations 2015); Leilani Farha, *Report of the Special Rapporteur on Adequate Housing as a Component of the Right to an Adequate Standard of Living, and on the Right to Non-discrimination in this Context* (United Nations 2018); Johnson and others (n 2); Office of the United Nations High Commissioner for Human Rights, *The Right to Adequate Housing: Fact Sheet (21)* (United Nations 2009).
30 Office of the United Nations High Commissioner for Human Rights (n 29) 3–4.
31 Ibid 9.
32 FEANTSA (n 28).
33 Amore and others (n 28) 24–25.
34 Busch-Geertsema and others (n 2).
35 Ibid.
36 Johnson and others (n 2).
37 I. Eissmann and C. Cuadra, *El potencial de las Estrategias Residenciales para Superar la Situación de Calle: Aportes desde la Experiencia Chilena* (Moviliza. Unidad de Investigación y Desarrollo 2018); Ciapessoni (n 23); Celic (n 12); Eissmann (n 13); Weason (n 14).

has primarily centred on three dimensions: (1) Official measurements and data collection undertaken by the government. These measurements are mainly used by policymakers to inform the design of social programmes, but they lack the ability to capture the variations and individual experiences of the homeless population over time. (2) Characterization studies of the homeless population have been conducted through the review and analysis of primary and secondary data. These studies examine participants in social programmes, the identity and construction of specific groups such as migrants or local populations, families, demographic profiles, complexity levels, resource usage, and other analyses. However, these studies are limited by a lack of long-term analysis and widespread dissemination, academic discussion, and follow-up. (3) Finally, there are reports and studies on public policies and social programmes addressing homelessness in Chile.

This consensus on official definitions has resulted in a shared understanding of homelessness and has allowed for effective identification and targeting of homeless individuals through public policy. The development of these definitions has been driven by a political and social framework that aims to name this population in a non-stigmatizing manner and prioritize their needs in public policy. The government has taken this framework into consideration and has responded by developing policies and programmes aimed at addressing the needs of homeless individuals. By adopting these definitions, a common understanding of homelessness has been established, enabling a more effective response to the issue through public policy.[38]

How Has the Homeless Problem Been Understood by the Chilean State?

The official definitions of *homelessness* in Chile have been established by the government, specifically the Ministry of Social Development, serving as a benchmark both for researchers and those who work directly with the homeless population.

Table 18.1 Official definitions of homelessness in Chile

Official definitions of the state of Chile	Definiciones Oficiales del Gobierno de Chile
Inhabiting the Street. National Registry for Homeless People (2005).	**Habitando la Calle. Catastro Nacional para Personas en Situación de Calle (2005).**
'(It) is considered a homeless person who is spending the night in public or private places, without having an infrastructure such that it can be characterized as housing, even if it is precarious. In this situation are the people who are on public roads and coves. Also included in the definition are those who, due to the lack of fixed, regular, and adequate accommodation to spend the night, find a night residence, paying or not for this service, in accommodation run by public, private or private entities, and that provide shelter. temporary. In this situation are the people who are in solidarity hostels or	'(se) considera persona en situación de calle a quien se halle pernoctando en lugares públicos o privados, sin contar con una infraestructura tal que pueda ser caracterizada como vivienda, aunque la misma sea precaria. En esta situación se encuentran las personas que están en la vía pública y caletas. Asimismo, se incluye en la definición a quienes, por carecer de alojamiento fijo, regular y adecuado para pasar la noche, encuentran residencia nocturna, pagando o no por este servicio, en alojamientos dirigidos por entidades

(Continued)

---

38 Eissmann (n 13).

Table 18.1 (Continued)

Official definitions of the state of Chile	Definiciones Oficiales del Gobierno de Chile
commercial hostels. Lastly, homeless people were also considered to be those who, with a proven track record of being homeless, receive temporary accommodation or for significant periods from institutions that provide them with bio-psycho-social support.'[39]	públicas, privadas o particulares, y que brindan albergue temporal. En esta situación se encuentran las personas que están en hospederías solidarias u hospederías comerciales. Por último, también se consideraron como personas en situación de calle aquellas que, con reconocida trayectoria de situación de calle, reciben alojamiento temporal o por períodos importantes de instituciones que les brindan apoyo bio-psico-social.'[40]
In Chile we all count. Second National Registry of Homeless People (2012). 'People who spend the night in public or private places, without having an infrastructure that can be characterized as housing, even if it is precarious. This excludes families and people living in camps. People who, due to the lack of a fixed, regular, and adequate accommodation to spend the night, find a night residence – paying or not for this service – in places run by public, private or private entities, which provide temporary shelter. They belong to this group who stay in residences and hostels, solidarity or commercial.'[41]	**En Chile Todos Contamos. Segundo Catastro Nacional de Personas en Situación de Calle (2012).** 'Personas que pernoctan en lugares públicos o privados, sin contar con una infraestructura que pueda ser caracterizada como vivienda, aunque esta sea precaria. Esto excluye a las familias y personas que viven en campamentos. Personas que por carecer de un alojamiento fijo, regular y adecuado para pasar la noche, encuentran residencia nocturna – pagando o no por este servicio – en lugares dirigidos por entidades públicas, privadas o particulares, que brindan albergue temporal. Pertenecen a este grupo quienes alojan en residencias y hospederías, solidarias o comerciales.'[42]
Law Decree 29. 'Person in a Homeless Situation: persons and/or families, who lack a fixed residence and who spend the night in places, public or private, that do not have the basic characteristics of a home even though they fulfill that function (does not include camps). Likewise, those people who, in accordance with a recognized trajectory of homelessness, as determined by the executor of the axis program, receive temporary accommodation or for significant periods, provided by institutions that provide biopsychosocial support.'[43]	**Decreto de Ley 29.** Persona en Situación de Calle: personas y/o familias, que carecen de residencia fija y que pernoctan en lugares, públicos o privados, que no tienen las características básicas de una vivienda aunque cumplan esa función (no incluye campamentos). Asimismo, aquellas personas que de conformidad con una reconocida trayectoria de situación de calle, según determine el ejecutor del programa eje, reciben alojamiento temporal o por períodos significativos, provisto por instituciones que les brindan apoyo biopsicosocial[44]

39 Ministerio de Planificación (n 9) 136.
40 Ibid.
41 Ministerio de Desarrollo Social (n 10) 20.
42 Ibid.
43 <www.bcn.cl/leychile/navegar?idNorma=1053855>.
44 Ibid.

Official definitions of the state of Chile	Definiciones Oficiales del Gobierno de Chile
Annex Questionnaire for Homeless People. Social Registry of Homes. '[A homeless person shall be considered one who] is spending the night in public or private places, without having an infrastructure that can be characterized as housing, even if it is precarious (a precarious home implies, at least, walls and ceilings that provide some privacy, allow to house belongings, and generate a relatively stable situation). [And in turn] He lacks fixed, regular, and adequate accommodation to spend the night and finds night residence in accommodation run by public, private or private entities that function as commercial inns (paying or not for this service) and that provide temporary shelter.'[45]	**Cuestionario Anexo para Personas en Situación de Calle. Registro Social de Hogares.** '[Se considerará persona en situación de calle a aquella que] se encuentre pernoctando en lugares públicos o privados, sin contar con una infraestructura que pueda ser caracterizada como vivienda, aunque la misma sea precaria (una vivienda precaria supone, al menos, paredes y techos que otorguen cierta privacidad, permite albergar pertenencias y generan una situación relativamente estable). [Y a su vez] Carece de alojamiento fijo, regular y adecuado para pasar la noche y encuentra residencia nocturna en alojamientos dirigidos por entidades públicas, privadas o particulares que funcionan como hospederías comerciales (pagando o no por este servicio) y que brindan albergue temporal.'[46]

These definitions facilitate a comprehensive examination of homelessness in Chile by acknowledging that homelessness can occur at different times and spaces in a person's life. Despite this, official studies and statistics on homelessness often only consider individuals who are sleeping on the street, in shelters, or in transitional housing as forming part of the homeless population.

Development of Social Programs for Homeless People in Chile

After the return of democratic governments, the centre-left coalition governments managed to considerably reduce poverty in Chile. Despite this, inequality persisted, as well as a percentage of people who remained persistently below the indigence line, which led Chile – as well as other countries of the region – to implement social protection systems that addressed vulnerability and poverty from public policies and with a rights-based approach.[47] With the return of democratic governments in Chile after the fall of the military dictatorship, the government of President Ricardo Lagos created the Chile Solidario Social Protection System in 2002. Notwithstanding this progress, homeless people were not initially included in the programmes that make up this system. It was not until 2005

---

45 Ministerio de Desarrollo Social, *Cuestionario Anexo para Personas en Situación de Calle Manual de Aplicación* (Ministerio de Desarrollo Social 2017) 5.
46 Ibid.
47 One of the first programs that began in this decade are the Conditional Transfer Programs (PTC) in Mexico and Brazil, which are mainly oriented towards generating income and articulating with the basic security and promotion networks: Robles (n 15). This, under the logic of social protection, is understood as 'a set of public and private policies and programs adopted in the face of contingencies in order to compensate for the absence or fall in labor income, provide assistance to families with children and provide access to health and housing:' Robles (n 45) 39.

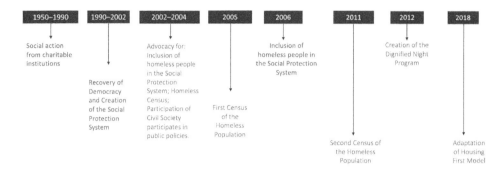

Figure 18.1 Evolution of public policy on homelessness in Chile.
Source: Authors' own presentation.

when a count of homeless people was conducted,[48] and in 2006 that the first public social programme for homeless people was established, called the Street Program.[49] This programme provides psychosocial support for a period of 24 months.[50] From 2006 to 2010, in addition to the Street Program, various short-term initiatives were implemented with the goal of providing socio-labour support, promoting entrepreneurship, and addressing mental health needs. These initiatives also included training opportunities for the teams delivering these programmes, which were primarily composed of non-government organizations (NGOs).

The Dignified Night Program was established in 2012 as a result of the second count of homeless individuals in 2011.[51] Its aim is to provide basic social services to people living in a street situation, to protect them and offer opportunities for them to improve their circumstances.[52] This programme has two main elements: the Winter Plan and the Temporary Centres for Improvement (CTS). The Winter Plan operates during periods of lower temperatures, offering alternative housing and basic care in public areas, to alleviate the adverse effects of homelessness during these times. On the other hand, the Centres for Improvement provide temporary housing and basic services,[53] including day centres, hostels, improvement residences, shared homes, and supportive housing.

The Dignified Night Program focuses on implementing interventions aimed at aiding people who are homeless to overcome the difficulties they face while living on the streets and protect them from potential harm caused by their surroundings, particularly weather conditions. Although these programmes were rolled out gradually starting in 2012, they have not been supported by longitudinal studies that would enable the monitoring of the

48 Ministerio de Planificación (n 9) 136.
49 Celic (n 12); Wong (n 12).
50 Ministerio de Desarrollo Social (n 11).
51 Ministerio de Desarrollo Social (n 10).
52 Ministerio de Desarrollo Social (n 11) 46.
53 Ibid.

programmes' outcomes. However, there are case studies and evaluations that provide insights into the development of the programmes so far.[54]

An evaluation commissioned by the Budget Directorate of the Ministry of Finance of the Chilean government, covering the period from 2012 to 2014, showed that the Winter Plan component achieved its goal of protecting people's lives, as there were fewer deaths during winter compared to previous years. However, the temporary centres component failed to achieve its main objective, and it was not possible to observe the effective implementation of the proposed intervention approach. The 'overcoming ladder' model of the temporary centre component of the Dignified Night Program is advertised as a series of social services designed to help homeless individuals progress out of their homelessness situation. The idea is that as individuals move from less complex services to more complex ones, they will overcome their homelessness. However, the model is implemented as a series of increasingly specific and complex interventions, rather than a linear process with successive steps. The model does not suggest that individuals will move through the system in a sequential manner.[55]

Another similar study highlighted the need for more structured and consistent implementation of the intervention model in the Dignified Night Program in order to effectively address the needs and challenges faced by homeless people in Chile. Additionally, this emphasised the need for further research and monitoring of the programme in order to assess its effectiveness and make necessary improvements to better serve the homeless population in Chile.[56] This meant that although the design of the interventions followed the idea of a ladder for improvement, it was not carried out as a coordinated and connected set of services that could build an upward progression for people. Instead, the interventions were carried out as separate, individual projects, with varying levels of complexity and specificity, and the full range of services was only available in a few areas. The study concluded that while the interventions had some individual successes, they did not make up a comprehensive, integrated programme.[57]

However, other studies conducted in Chile have shown that temporary residential care, despite criticism, has been able to interrupt trajectories of homelessness and generate significant changes for a proportion of homeless people.[58] In 2015, a survey identifying key factors to tackling homelessness through housing interventions[59] pointed out that housing services themselves improved biopsychosocial well-being, which tended to give people greater levels of autonomy and independence to develop daily life. Thus, housing services allow a pause in the critical stages of homelessness towards interventions designed to

---

54 I. Eissmann and I. Lacalle 'Programa Vivienda con Apoyo: Aproximación a los primeros resultados de la experiencia Chilena' (2022) 10 *Revista de Políticas Sociales Urbanas. Ciudadanías* 1.
55 V. Monreal, S. Saldivia and J. Bravo, *Evaluación Programas Gubernamentales (EPG) Informe Final De Evaluación. Programa Noche Digna* (Ministerio De Desarrollo Social. Subsecretaría de Servicios Sociales 2015) 36.
56 Instituto de Sociología, Universidad Católica, *Estudio de caracterización y levantamiento de buenas prácticas, programa noche digna* (ISUC 2014).
57 Eissmann and Cuadra (n 37).
58 I. Eissmann, M. Weason, C. Cuadra and E. Merdech, *Buenas Prácticas de Metodologías de Superación de la Situación de Calle en Residencias* (Moviliza 2015); Eissmann and Cuadra (n 37).
59 Ibid 45–50.

improve the quality of life and to contribute in the long term to tackling homelessness.[60] Various experiences reviewed in these studies showed some critical factors to consider: (1) the processes of adapting work methodologies to the specific situations of people, (2) promoting the development of emotional openness in the work process, (3) providing spaces for more comprehensive personal development beyond access to housing and work activity, (4) integrating failures as part of the intervention process, (5) recognizing motivational states and integrating them into the work process, and (6) strengthening personal capabilities as the key resource for autonomy and well-being.[61] Despite these results, the long-term success of these interventions is often uncertain as maintaining momentum and continuity of positive outcomes is not guaranteed. In this way, one of the main gaps or problems in the programmes is the absence of territorial articulation of services that connect homeless people within local communities and local government articulated services.[62]

Recognizing these gaps, the Ministry of Social Development and Family assumed the centrality of guaranteeing housing and implemented the Supported Housing Program in 2018,[63] which was based on the Housing First model.[64] This model changed the strategy from providing shelters and temporary accommodation to providing permanent housing access, opposing the 'staircase model or continuum of care'.[65] The Housing First model has become the benchmark of excellence for solving homelessness, as it has been proven effective in maintaining housing and improving the health and social integration indicators of previously homeless individuals.[66]

The Housing First model has several key features, including: (1) emphasis is put on individual autonomy and decision-making, with immediate and permanent access to housing and accompanying clinical and social support services; (2) access to housing is not contingent upon completing treatment;[67] (3) support is geared towards recovery and well-being and adopts a harm reduction approach; (4) the model primarily targets the chronic homelessness of people with severe issues[68] but can be adapted to other homeless groups or profiles;[69] and (5) the model is guided by a set of clear principles that inform intervention.[70]

The Supported Housing Program is based on the main characteristics of Housing First, building an intervention model that seeks to solve the problem of homelessness for older

---

60 Ibid.
61 Ibid.
62 Eissmann and Cuadra (n 37).
63 Ministerio de Desarrollo Social y Familia (n 22); Ministerio de Desarrollo Social y Familia, *La Vivienda es lo Primero* (Ministerio de Desarrollo Social y Familia 2021).
64 FEANTSA, *Guía Housing First Europa* (Feantsa 2016); Padget and others (n 27); L. Polvere, T. Macleod, E. Macnaughton, R. Caplan, M. Piat, G. Nelson, S. Gaetz and P. Goering, *Canadian Housing First Toolkit: The At Home/Chez Soi Experience* (Calgary and Toronto: Mental Health Commission of Canada and the Homeless Hub, Canada 2014).
65 Ibid.
66 FEANTSA (n 62); Polvere and others (n 62).
67 Polvere and others (n 62).
68 *Harm reduction* refers to a public health strategy to minimize the negative effects of substance use. In this sense, the objective of harm reduction is to reduce both the risk and the effects associated with substance abuse and addiction at the level of the individual, community, and society without the need for abstinence; Polvere at al (n 62).
69 Polvere and others (n 62) 9.
70 FEANTSA (n 62); Padget and others (n 27); Polvere and others (n 62).

adults without disabilities and who have homelessness trajectories equal to or greater than five years. Although the focus is on housing, the understanding of the problem assumes that many other problems are present including:[71] (1) there is a negative impact on the general health of people, both physically and mentally; (2) people's abilities to perform basic activities of daily living and instrumental activities of daily living are reduced; (3) active participation in neighbourhood and community activities declines; and (4) the quality and quantity of primary support networks are diminished. Additionally, although they do not appear formally and explicitly in the definitions of the programme, it is clear that lack of housing increases homeless people's exposure to risks of suffering harm at the individual level as a result of the context in which they live and progressively increases the barriers that they must face to access social services, as a result of social exclusion, as well as the decision not to use or adhere to the processes and procedures that social services establish.

The solution to the problems associated with homelessness starts with a focus on access to housing. The programme's design and interventions aim to provide services that have a positive impact on the individual's well-being. Through access to housing and tailored support services, it is expected that participants will be able to (1) interrupt or break their cycle of homelessness by accessing a home and adapting to it, living with one or two other people; (2) improve their overall health, excluding chronic or degenerative diseases that should already be adequately treated; (3) increase their ability to perform basic and instrumental activities of daily living; (4) increase their participation in neighbourhood and community activities, leading to an improvement in their social integration; and (5) increase the quantity and quality of their primary support networks, contributing to overall individual well-being.[72]

The Supported Housing Program aims to not only provide access to housing but also to encourage participants to take responsibility for reducing the risks and harms associated with homelessness, particularly those related to substance abuse. The programme aims to support individuals in engaging with and accessing the social services they need, with the ultimate goal of helping them maintain stable housing over time. By addressing both the immediate need for housing and promoting individual responsibility and self-sufficiency, the programme strives to end the cycle of homelessness and promote long-term well-being for those it serves.[73]

Four years after the start of the programme, it can be concluded that the supported housing programme has effectively managed to end street homelessness for the majority of participants, greatly improving the living conditions of those who engage with the programme and enhancing their subjective well-being. The success of the programme presents a unique opportunity to develop a sustainable strategy to combat homelessness in Chile, ensuring that permanent housing is secure, and that each person has access to support services based on their needs and abilities.[74]

Therefore, it is important to continue collecting long-term data and conducting studies with mixed-method designs to evaluate the programme's effectiveness in terms of housing

---

71 Moviliza, *Sistematización Programa Vivienda con Apoyo 2020–2021* (Moviliza 2021); Nuestra Casa, *Sistematización Programa Vivienda con Apoyo 2020–2021* (Nuestra Casa 2021).
72 Ibid.
73 Ibid.
74 Eissmann and Lacalle (n 52).

maintenance, social integration, health, and the subjective experiences of participants. This will allow for a more comprehensive understanding of the programme's impact and help determine if it truly offers a permanent solution to homelessness or if it only provides temporary relief. It is crucial to take into account the perspectives and experiences of homeless people themselves in order to identify the key factors that contribute to positive change in their lives.[75]

In conclusion, the Chilean supported housing programme offers valuable insights into addressing homelessness through access to housing and tailored services. However, it is too early to fully assess its long-term success, and more research and data collection is needed to fully understand the impact of the programme and its potential for replication in other countries. The Chilean experience serves as a valuable learning opportunity and provides a basis for further analysis and reflection on the development of effective public policies on homelessness in Latin America. Further research is needed to adapt the Housing First model to the specific needs and conditions of the region.

An Assessment of the Effectiveness of Public Policies on Homelessness in Chile

The review of the experience of public policies for homeless people in Chile in this chapter reveals that there has been a significant increase in the recognition of homelessness as a public issue in the country in the past 15 years, and the government and various organizations have come to understand the magnitude of the problem and its consequences for the lives of those affected. Despite this recognition, the limited scope of social programmes for the homeless and the fragile progress made thus far indicate that a stable public policy has not yet been established. The impact of these conclusions will be further analyzed in this section.

The Last 15 Years of Public Policy for Homeless People in Chile: An Important Step Forward

The last 15 years have seen significant advancement in the way public policy approaches homelessness in Chile and Latin America. Previously, homeless people were not considered a priority by social programmes for vulnerable populations; however, there has been a shift towards providing psychosocial support and housing-centred services using both the staircase model and the Housing First philosophy. It is noteworthy that these advancements have been achieved at the national level, with increased coverage being made available year after year. Despite the limitations in terms of coverage and resources for social programmes aimed at homeless people and the lack of information systems to accurately measure their impact, the progress that has been made has placed homelessness as a priority for the government and has led to the creation of strategies and methodologies for working with homeless individuals. This has also led to the growth of a significant number of civil society organizations that are dedicated to working with and researching homelessness.

---

75 Ibid.

Intervention According to a Public–Private Working Model

In the past, only non-government organizations (NGOs) were responsible for addressing the needs of homeless people in Chile. As a result, the understanding and experience of working with this population were largely concentrated within these NGOs. The 'Street Program' was the first psychosocial programme aimed at addressing the issue of homelessness in Chile. Even though the financing for this programme came from the government, it was considered crucial to involve the participation of NGOs from civil society. This approach created a working model where the Chilean government provides funding for social programmes, but private and public organizations are also actively involved in implementing these programmes. For example, if the government aims to establish ten shelters in the city of Santiago, it might receive 20 proposals from various organizations, from which the 10 best will be selected for implementation.

Based on this model, from 2006 to 2021, NGOs have been heavily involved in implementing social programmes designed to help homeless people. Some of the positive effects of this are better engagement between social workers and customers, especially when many NGOs have gone from volunteer to becoming professional organizations. However, this modality has meant that the government develops a subsidiary role in social interventions and does not make an investment that ensures robust social protection for the homeless population. Thus, public financing does not cover the actual cost of the social programmes but only those of direct social intervention and minimal administration costs. Moreover, it does not assume the risks generated by the market, especially in housing-centred services. For example, those services that provide temporary accommodation cannot meet increasing housing rental costs. This situation has created a fragility within these organizations, questioning their sustainability and long-term reliability. This has strained the public–private relationship, which was initially seen as effective and virtuous, but today presents a serious problem.

Limitations on the Scope of Public Actions[76]

Despite advances in public policies aimed at addressing homelessness in Chile, their implementation has been limited. The programmes are only available in cities with the largest homeless populations, and their absence in much of the country has led to an increase in the number of homeless people over the past decade. This highlights the need for more widespread and effective social programmes. Additionally, it is essential to consider the varying needs of different regions and communities to develop more tailored solutions that can effectively address homelessness. Moreover, continued monitoring and evaluation of these programmes are crucial to ensure their efficacy and make necessary adjustments.

The Fragility of Public Policy Design for Homeless People

In this chapter, all social programmes for homeless individuals in Chile are referred to as 'public policies for homeless people'. These programmes are institutionally located in

---

76 Eissmann and Cuadra (n 37).

two systems: the Street Program and the Dignity Night Program. The Street Program is part of the social protection system and is supported by a law ensuring its continuity over time, regardless of changes in government. The remaining programmes, under the Dignity Night Program, do not have a legal basis and depend on annual approval of their budget. As this chapter has shown, these programmes, which offer various accommodation options, are crucial in addressing homelessness and providing emergency aid. It is important to note that the success of these programmes also depends on their effective implementation and coordination with other relevant stakeholders, such as non-profit organizations and local communities.

The current model for addressing homelessness in Chile is vulnerable due to insufficient funding for the associated costs of homeless programmes, which puts both non-profit organizations and local governments at risk. This lack of stability and resources could result in the loss of accumulated knowledge and human capital in the medium to long term. Moreover, as has been noted, the lack of nationwide coverage leaves a significant portion of the homeless population without adequate assistance. It is crucial to address these issues and ensure that adequate resources and support are available to effectively address homelessness in Chile.

Conclusions

The development of public policy for homeless people in Chile is relatively recent, but it has made significant advances in recent years and offers valuable lessons that should be shared with other countries in Latin America. There has been a methodological evolution in the approach to addressing homelessness, allowing for continuous improvement in intervention programmes and design. Furthermore, the human rights approach has been incorporated through the adoption of the Housing First philosophy, creating a new standard for advancing this type of programme.

To further improve and address the challenges facing homelessness in Chile, the authors of this chapter recommend the following steps be taken by the Chilean government: (1) Enact a law that ensures the permanence of public policy programmes for homelessness and makes it a formal duty of the state. (2) Increase public investment in social programmes and improve the public–private partnership model, providing better operating conditions for non-profit organizations involved in the design and implementation of these programmes. (3) Implement a monitoring and evaluation system to measure the impact of these programmes and ensure their effectiveness. Additionally, it is important to recognize and address the intersections of homelessness with other social issues, such as forced human mobility and gender violence. To effectively tackle homelessness in all its complexities, a comprehensive and integrated approach is needed. Furthermore, regular reassessment and adaptation of the programmes and policies should be carried out, responding to new information and changes in the social and economic landscape in Chile.

PART IV

Africa

19
HOMELESSNESS IN NIGERIA
Issues and the Way Forward

*Andrew Ebekozien, Clinton Ohis Aigbavboa,
Wellington Didibhuku Thwala,
Mohamad Shaharudin Samsurijan,
and Rex Asibuodu Ugulu*[*]

Introduction

Housing the masses is a pertinent agenda for nations like Nigeria, with economic urbanization and a fast-growing population. Housing is a basic need and vital in enhancing the well-being of humankind.[1] This is because housing provision is significant to humanity and enhances the positive impact on the labour force, education, and public health outputs.[2] Article 25 of the Universal Declaration of Human Rights acknowledges housing as a right to an adequate standard of living.[3] The UN Habitat[4] enshrined in the Habitat Agenda the right to an adequate shelter for all that is inexpensive, available, healthy, secure, and safe. The aim is to ensure good and adequate housing for every citizen. Moore[5] has affirmed that housing is one of the best indicators to define a person's status in

---

[*] Special thanks to the anonymous reviewers who helped hone and strengthen the quality of this manuscript during the blind peer-review process. Authors thank the following institutions for their support. This includes Auchi Polytechnic, Auchi, Nigeria; Faculty of Engineering and the Built Environment and CIDB Centre of Excellence (05–35–061890), University of Johannesburg, South Africa; University of South Africa, Pretoria, South Africa; and School of Social Sciences, Universiti Sains Malaysia, Malaysia.

[1] United Nations, *Urbanisation and Development: Emerging Future World Cities Report* (United Nations 2016); S. Shuid and M. F. M. Zamin, 'Maqasid Al-Syariah and Human Well-Being: A Study on Melaka's Public Housing' (2018) 16(2) *Journal of the Malaysian Institute of Planners* 236; W. C. Herbert, 'Squatting for Survival: Precarious Housing in a Declining U.S. City' (2018) 28(5) *Housing Policy Debate* 797; A. Ebekozien, 'A qualitative approach to investigate low-cost housing policy provision in Edo State, Nigeria' (2021) 26(2) *International Planning Studies* 165.

[2] World Bank Press Release, *World Bank Approves New Financing to Support Affordable Housing in Indonesia* (The World Bank 20 March 2017) <https://www.worldbank.org/en/news/press-release/2017/03/20/world-bank-approves-new-financing-to-support-affordable-housing-in-indonesia> (accessed 1 September 2023).

[3] UN General Assembly, *Index to proceedings of the general assembly* (United Nations General Assembly 1968).

[4] United Nations Habitat, *National Trend in Housing Production Practices* (United Nations Centre for Human Settlements, Vol. 4 2001).

[5] E. A. Moore, 'Addressing Housing Deficit in Nigeria: Issues, Challenges, and Prospects' (2019) 57(4) *Economic and Financial Review* 200.

society. Similarly, Abraham Maslow identified housing as one of the most fundamental, basic needs of citizens.[6] It implies that shelter availability is germane to the population's welfare. Also, Moore asserted that the housing sector is a key variable in measuring a nation's health. Ekpo[7] and Oyediran[8] affirmed that successful housing provision would assist in achieving Goal 11 (sustainable cities and communities) of the 17 Sustainable Development Goals (SDGs).[9] The housing sector thus plays a critical role in the economy, especially for developing countries. It is an economic growth stimulator. Despite the relevance of housing provision to humanity, a large population in developing countries lives in dilapidated houses, which should prompt widespread concern. Ebekozien[10] reported that by 2050, the United Nations has projected that about 68% of the world's population will live in urban locations. Similarly, the United Nations[11] projected that by 2050, 2.5 billion people would be added to the world population, and 90% of this new addition would be from Asia and Africa,[12] found that sub-Saharan Africa is leading the way in terms of urban population living in slums.

Access to affordable shelters in Nigeria remains an unrealized dream, especially for low-income earners (LIEs) and disadvantaged citizens. Disadvantaged citizens include LIEs in the informal sector, internally displaced persons (IDPs), self-employed artisans, market traders, unemployed young adults, and under-employed persons. Housing accessibility and the affordability deficit have grown from bad to worse in Nigeria in recent years even with past governments' efforts for over six decades since independence. The exponential population growth has hampered government efforts. Population in urban locations is increasing in Nigerian cities, including a growing challenge of the IDPs across the country. Are Nigerian cities prepared to shelter this high population with the extra demand it places on infrastructure facilities? How prepared are the stakeholders, especially government and housing developers? These are questions searching for satisfactory answers and feasible solutions. The worst-hit group are low-income earners (LIEs) in Nigerian cities. This is a worldwide issue, but especially pertinent in Nigeria. The United Nations reported that not less than half of the world's population resides in urban locations, growing to 73 million yearly. If not well managed, Nigeria's cities may be overtaken by homelessness. Future social challenges (in particular homelessness) may be inevitable if a concerted effort is not made. Adetokunbo and Emeka[13] have opined that the Nigerian government should provide

---

6 Ebekozien (n 1) 165.
7 A. Ekpo, 'Housing Deficit in Nigeria: Issues, Challenges, and Prospects' (2019) 57(4), *Economic and Financial Review* 177.
8 O. S. Oyediran, 'Institution and Housing Development: Mirage, Magic, and Miracle of Low-cost Housing in Nigeria' (2019) 57(4) *CBN Economic and Financial Review* 37.
9 A. Ebekozien, A-R. Abdul-Aziz and M. Jaafar, 'Low-cost Housing Policies and Squatters in Nigeria: The Nigerian Perspective on Possible Solutions' (2021) 21(11) *International Journal of Construction Management* 1088.
10 A. Ebekozien, C. Aigbavboa, M. Aigbedion, I. F. Ogbaini and O. Awe, 'Housing Finance Inaccessibility: Evidence from the Nigerian Pensioners' (2022) 40(5) *Property Management* 671.
11 United Nations, *Sustainable Cities and Human Settlements, United Nations Sustainable Development Knowledge Platform* (2018) [online] <https://sustainabledevelopment.un.org/topics/sustainablecities> (accessed 1 September 2023).
12 Ebekozien and others (n 9) 1088.
13 I. Adetokunbo and M. Emeka, 'Urbanisation, Housing, Homelessness and Climate Adaption in Lagos, Nigeria: Lessons from Asia' (2015) 15(2) *Journal of Design and Built Environment* 15.

more low-cost housing (LCH) to curb homelessness, which impacts most strongly the poor population. This chapter seeks to understand homelessness from Nigeria's context and offer insights into policy and programme interventions to tackle, prevent, and mitigate homelessness. Pison Housing Company[14] found that there were about 10.7 million houses in Nigeria, with the most acute housing shortage being more pronounced in the LIEs groups. Moore highlights that it is the Federal Mortgage Bank of Nigeria that is responsible for providing housing loans to LIEs via the National Housing Trust Fund.[15] However, the National Housing Trust Fund has experienced several financial issues that significantly affected their effectiveness.

This chapter strategically reviews the literature on housing and homelessness in Nigeria. It explores how to tackle, prevent, and mitigate homelessness in the country via integrated and all-inclusive policies and programmes. The chapter is divided into six sections. Section 1 offers an introduction, with Section 2 reviewing how the concept of 'homelessness' is defined in the Nigerian context. A third section explores the root causes of homelessness in Nigeria. Next, in Section 4, past and current initiatives, policies, and programmes to prevent or mitigate homelessness in the country are examined. Section 5 proffers a way forward to mitigate or eliminate homelessness across major Nigerian cities before, in Section 6, the chapter concludes. This chapter argues that in a fast-growing sub-Saharan African country like Nigeria, all-inclusive and 'pro-poor' policies and programmes of interventions are vital is homelessness is to be tackled effectively.

Housing Deficit and Homelessness in Nigeria

This section discusses Nigeria's housing deficit and homelessness. Reliable statistics and data on the number of homeless people in Nigeria are not available, and estimates vary widely. Some have suggested that as many as 24.4 million people may be homeless in the country, accounting for around 13% of the nation's overall population. The issue is particularly prevalent in the capital, Lagos, where 70% or more may reside in so-called 'informal settlements'.[16] An estimated 8.6 million orphaned children in Nigeria are living under bridges, railway stations, and markets. Clearer data is, however, available as to housing deficit. The Affordable Housing Investment Summit put existing housing stock at 23 per 1,000 inhabitants and estimated a staggering 18–22 million deficits with an estimated population of 185–200 million people.[17] Moore[18] found that about NGN21 trillion is needed to finance the housing deficit, and barely 10% of intending home owners in Nigeria can afford it (purchase or direct construction) as against 92% in Singapore, 54% in Korea, 60% in China, 72% in the USA, and 78% in the UK. Similarly, Nigeria is top of the list of countries with an estimated housing deficit as of 2019 across Africa. In Ghana, it is 1.7–2.6 million units, in Kenya it is 2 million units, in Uganda it is 1.7–2 million, and in South Africa it is 2.5 million units.[19] The housing and building sector

---

14 Pison Housing Company, *Overview of the Housing Finance Sector in Nigeria* (Commissioned by EFInA and FinMark, Finmark Trust 2010) 1, 15–20.
15 Moore (n 5).
16 See, for example, estimates provided by the Borgen Project <https://borgenproject.org/homelessness-in-nigeria/> (accessed 1 September 2023).
17 Moore (n 5) 200.
18 Ibid.
19 In Affordable Housing Investment Summit, cited in Moore (n 5).

accounts for 3.1% of rebased GDP, and housing production is about 100,000 units annually. This is insufficient for a country of over 200 million people. Moore suggested about 1,000,000 additional units annually are needed to bridge the housing deficit gap and mitigate urban homelessness in the future. The Nigerian government and the private sector have not contributed enough in this regard, especially in LCH delivery for the masses. Moore[20] found that formal housing production falls significantly below levels required to meet housing demand in Nigeria.

In Nigeria, there is no universally accepted definition of *homelessness*. The definition varies even within the country because of differing criteria used by various government agencies. Homelessness describes an individual in an emergency shelter or transitional housing (unsheltered). An example are the IDPs camps across the country and abandoned buildings. These locations were not designed to accommodate people to sleep or used as residential accommodations. There should be evidence of no safe alternative for the person to be homeless, as established for the 2.7 million IDPs. Homelessness has direct and indirect impacts on neighbourhoods in Nigeria. This includes increased banditry, kidnapping, child trafficking, prostitution, religious extremism, child abandonment, 'baby factories', and fraudsters.

Informal settlements, a significant factor that contributes to homelessness, is 'ballooning' in Nigeria, and conditions in these settlements are routinely found to be 'inhumane'. Successive Nigerian governments have added to this ballooning by failing to tackle or by actively causing greater economic inequality, allowing inequality to reach extreme levels in the country, as evident in the housing sector. However, and in contrast, newly built luxury dwellings are springing up throughout urban locations across the country, and many remain vacant. The majority of these newly built buildings in cities were only made possible through the forced eviction of poor communities without providing any suitable compensation or alternative housing for them. The violent insurgency in the northeast of Nigeria for over 15 years, population increases (expected to double by 2050), and rural–urban migration have compounded the homelessness issue in Nigeria. The relevant government authorities (national and state levels), such as the National Emergency Management Agency and Minister of Humanitarian Affairs, Disaster Management, and Social Development are key bodies responding to homelessness yet are overwhelmed. Thus, the homeless, especially the elderly, are left to their own fates by the state. When citizens become homeless, whether through forced eviction or otherwise, they often find themselves residing in informal settlements with little or no provision from the state. This lack of homelessness provision is notable and should be a wake-up call to the relevant government authorities to ensure the disadvantaged can access alternative shelter and support.

Root Cause of Homelessness in Nigeria

The principal causes of homelessness in Nigeria are abject poverty[21] and chronic unemployment (which hit 41% in 2023),[22] but also the failure of the Nigerian government's interventions via policies and programmes to meet housing goals for its citizens, which also

---

20 Moore (n 5).
21 B. Komolafe, v. Ahiuma-Young, E. Elebeke, J. Alechenu and E. Adegbesan, '133 Million Nigerians Poor-NBS' *Vanguard* (18 November 2022) <www.vanguardngr.com/2022/11/133-million-nigerians-poor-nbs/> (accessed 1 September 2023).
22 A. Egole, 'Nigerian Unemployment Rate to Hit 41% in 2023 – KPMG' *Punch* (11 April 2023) <https://punchng.com/nigerian-unemployment-rate-to-hit-41-in-2023-kpmg/> (accessed 1 September 2023).

contributes to homelessness. Busch-Geertsema et al[23] classified the causes of homelessness into structural and individual factors. In the Nigerian context, Moore has identified the main drivers of homelessness as the exclusion of low-income earners (LIEs) by planners in housing design and development, inadequate basic infrastructure, slow bureaucratic procedures, the inability of LIEs to afford equity contribution and repay mortgage loans, high building input cost and labour, inaccessibility to credit facilities, poor motivation by and concessions made to housing developers, poor mortgage penetration, and high land cost in cities. The housing deficit increased from 4–7 million from a population of 104 million in 2007 to 18–22 million from an estimated 184 million population in 2017–2019. Further contributing factors include mortgage inefficiency, slum demolition, urban migration, overpopulation, urban expansion, increased poverty, lax incentives provided to institutional agencies, political interference, and stakeholders' self-interest. Oyo-Ita[24] found slow bureaucratic procedures, high cost of building inputs, lack of basic infrastructure, high land cost in cities, low incentives and concessions to investors, inadequate access to the credit facility, and exclusion of LIEs in the design as key related factors driving unsuccessful housing initiatives. The main encumbrances impacting the availability of low-cost housing (LCH) include:

1. **Housing Finance Inaccessibility and Paucity of Long-Term Funds.** Besides the high prime lending rate (as high as 17.5%) in the mortgage institutions (CIA World Factbook, as cited in Moore),[25] mortgage accessibility by LIEs is quite challenging in developing countries like Nigeria. It is not encouraging to use a high lending rate for housing development. This threatens affordable housing development, especially for LIEs and disadvantaged citizens. Housing provision is a capital investment; about US$363 billion is needed to curb the housing deficit in Nigeria and is ever increasing.[26] The Nigerian government is reviewing the process of accessing housing finance.
2. **Urbanization and Rural–Urban Migration.** There is increased movement of people from rural locations to cities for greener pastures. Inability to plan for migration and accommodation is a main cause of homelessness.
3. **Unemployment and Poverty.** Unemployment and poverty are correlated.[27] These variables influence homelessness. In Nigeria, the National Bureau of Statistics reported that 63% (133 million people) of Nigerians are suffering from unspeakably stifling multidimensional poverty as of the end of 2022.[28] This implies that two out of every three Nigerians are poor, including in relation to housing and living standards. The H1 2023 report released by KPMG shows that unemployment in Nigeria will rise to 40.6% in 2023 because of the inability of the economy to fully engage the 4–5 million new entrants into the Nigerian job market yearly and the hindrance of slower-than-required economic growth.[29]

---

23 V. Busch-Geertsema, W. Edgar, E. O'Sullivan and N. Pleace, *Homelessness and Homeless Policies in Europe* (European Commission 2010).
24 E. W. Oyo-Ita, 'Tackling the Housing Affordability Challenge: Nigeria Experience' (2017) *Proceedings from the 30th International Union for Housing Finance World Congress* (held in Washington DC, USA, 27 June 2017).
25 Moore (n 5).
26 Ibid.
27 Ekpo (n 6).
28 Komolafe and others (n 18).
29 Egole (n 19).

4. **Lack of Basic Infrastructure.** Inadequate infrastructure, such as electricity, pipe-borne water, internet connection, and roads impacts housing developers' motivation to construct houses in certain locations, thus reducing the number of housing units available.
5. **Systematic Corruption.** The housing sector is not exempted from the alleged epidemic of corruption which has long bedevilled the country. One consequence is Nigeria's poverty trajectory, including depriving eligible LIEs of their allocated houses and increasing homelessness. Corruption has caused deepening underdevelopment, with Nigeria poorly ranked 158th out of 189 countries on the human development index.[30] Nigerian social-economic conditions with widespread poverty and dilapidated economic superstructures, including housing scarcity, are key causes for concern.
6. **High Construction and Development Costs.** The inflation in construction labour and materials over a five-year period has increased to over 100%. This inflation discourages housing developers and other investors from investing in LCH because of the reduced purchasing power of intending buyers (LIEs).
7. **Security Issues.** For the past ten years, the security crisis in the Northeast has generated over 2.7 million IDPs. It is complicated because the Nigerian government is yet to plan holistically for IDPs' resettlement. Thus, many IDPs become homeless.[31]
8. **Enforcing Foreclosure.** Housing market trends and policies directly affect homelessness levels. Lack of housing supply and worsening affordability negatively impact lower-income earners, such as the LIEs and the disadvantaged, leading to homelessness.[32] Increases in housing unaffordability and inaccessibility, especially within the LIEs group, also increases homelessness.
9. **Property Registration and Title Documentation.** The bureaucracy involved can increase the cost of the property, to the detriment of LIEs.
10. **Land Use Act.** The Land Use Act discouraged housing developers and investors because of the fear of abuse of by the state governor, who is mandated to reserve the right to cancel title to any land under the state dominion. The consequence is an increase in the housing deficit in the sector.
11. **Taxation.** Sometimes, the housing sector is exposed to multiple forms of taxation. This also serves as a disincentive for potential investors.
12. **Construction Permits Issue.** The bureaucracy in pre-construction administration can often be tedious and expensive for developers and thus works to the detriment of LIEs.
13. **Urban Slums.** Urban slums are prevalent in many Nigerian cities. Ajegunle in Lagos,[33] Abuja, and Port Harcourt are good examples of this. Slums contribute to present and future homelessness if provision via slum upgrading is not implemented and/or alternative accommodation is not provided.

---

30 R. O. S. Dauda and O. Iwegbu, 'Human Development and Macroeconomic Shocks in Nigeria: An Empirical Investigation' (2022) 16(1) *Journal of Social, Behavioural, and Health Sciences* 371.
31 C. P. Ekoh, O. U. Okoye, O. E. George, E. Chukwuemeka and U. P. Agbawodikeizu, 'Resettlement of Internally Displaced Persons (IDPs) in Nigeria: The Housing Problems Facing IDPs in Abuja Camps and the Risk of Homelessness and Secondary Displacement' (2022) *Journal of Social Distress and Homelessness* 1.
32 V. Lima, R. Hearne and P. M. Murphy, 'Housing Financialisation and the Creation of Homelessness in Ireland' (2022) *Housing Studies* 1.
33 E. Daniel, O. Oreoluwa, H. U. Abubakar, A. Opeyemi and A. Ekpenyong, '"Of What Use Is the Counting to Us?" An Account of the (De) Motivations of Homeless Persons Ahead of Census in Nigeria' (2023) *Journal of Social Distress and Homelessness* 1.

Nigerian Government Housing Policies and Programmes

Table 19.1 Summary of Nigerian housing policies, programmes, and performance of public housing, 1928 to 2018

Period	Policy and programme	Programme target	Achievement level
1928–1979	The Lagos Executive Development Board (LEBD) was established in 1954. It was formed after the Lagos bubonic plaque of 1928. The LEBD initiated various Nigerian housing programmes[34] including the formation of the Nigerian Building Society (NBS) in 1955.[35]	The aim of the NBC was to provide access to housing mortgages.	The NBS failed because the government was the sole funder of it.[36]
	The 1st National Development period (1962–1968).	A total of 61,000 housing units were planned for construction.	Less than 1% of the planned units were developed, possibly because of the civil war (1966–1970) and associated political pandemonium.
	The 2nd National Development period (1970–1974): In 1972 and 1973, the National Council of Housing and the Federal Housing Authority, via Promulgation of Decree No. 40 of 1973, were established respectively.[37]	A total of 59,000 LCH units were planned for development across the country.	About 12% of the planned units were constructed.
	The 3rd National Development period (1975–1980): The period saw introduction of the	The Land Use Act (1978) introduced for the first time in the whole of Nigeria	About 15% (around 30,000 LCH units) of the planned units were built.

(*Continued*)

---

34 A. Aribigbola, 'Housing Policy Formulation in Developing Countries: Evidence of Programme Implementation from Akure, Ondo State, Nigeria' (2008) 23(2) *Journal of Human Ecology* 125.
35 A. F. Ibimilua and O. A. Ibitoye, 'Housing policy in Nigeria: An overview' (2015) 5(2) *American International Journal of Contemporary Research* 53.
36 G. A. Waziri and R. Roosli, 'Housing Policies and Programmes in Nigeria: A Review of the Concept and Implementation' (2013) 3(2) *Business Management Dynamics* 60.
37 Ibimilua and Ibitoye (n 32).

Table 19.1 (Continued)

Period	Policy and programme	Programme target	Achievement level
	National LCH scheme.[38] In 1977 the NBS metamorphosed into the Federal Mortgage Bank of Nigeria (FMBN). The military government made the Land Use Decree in 1978.[39] The Land Use Act of 1978 vested all land comprised in the territory of each State in the Federation in the Governor of that State.	a uniform system of land titles and land control.[40] The primary objective of the 1978 Act was that "all land comprised in the territory of each State in the Federation are hereby vested in the Military Governor of that State and such land' shall be held in trust and administered for the use and common benefit of all Nigerians". In this period, 202,000 LCH units were planned for development across the nation.	
1980–1989	The 4th National Development period (1981–1985): In 1980, the Federal Housing Authority (FHA) was launched. The FHA operated under the National Housing Programme (NHP). The federal government allocated NGN1.9 billion (US$ 5.28 million) to develop the first phase.[41] Also, between 1980–1983, NGN1.9 billion was made available for housing construction to the 20 states of Nigeria existing at that time.	A total of 160,000 LCH units were planned for the first phase and 20,000 units for the second phase.	The first phase constructed 47,234 units, while the second phase was cut-short because of the political instability of the military coup of 1983. From the NGN1.9 billion, NGN600 million (37.5%) was spent to complete 32,000 units by June 1983, yielding only 20% of the planned delivery.[42] Overall, the scale and impact of housing construction was insignificant.[43]

(Continued)

38 E. O. Ibem, M. N. Anosike, and D. E. Azuh, 'Challenges in Public Housing Provision in the Post-independence Era in Nigeria' (2011) 8(2) *International Journal of Human Sciences* 421.
39 Waziri and Roosli (n 33).
40 A. N. Allott, 'Nigeria: Land Use Decree, 1978' (1978) 22(2) *Journal of African Law* 136–160.
41 C. Aigbavboa and W. Thwala, *Residential Satisfaction and Housing Policy Evolution* (Routledge 2019).
42 Federal Republic of Nigeria, *National Housing Policy* (Federal Ministry of Works and Housing, Lagos 1991).
43 Moore (n 5).

Table 19.1 (Continued)

Period	Policy and programme	Programme target	Achievement level
1990–1999	In 1991, the Nigerian Military Government launched the 'Housing for All by the Year 2000', as the projected housing need at that time was about eight million units. In 1993, Decree No. 82 empowered the FMBN to assemble, supervise and administer contributions to the National Housing Fund (NHF). The NHF emerged from the 1992 Housing Policy.[44]	A total of 121,000 LCH units were planned by the National Housing Programme.	5,500 LCH units were built, about 5% of those planned.
2000–2018	Between 2000–2004, the policy focus shifted to the private sector as the channel for housing provision in Nigeria with various housing reforms via the established Federal Ministry of Housing and Urban Development. Examples are the National Prototype Housing Programme (2000–2003), the Presidential Housing Mandate Scheme (PMHS) (2004–2006), and the public–private partnership (PPP) housing schemes.[45]	A total of 10,271 housing units were planned via the PPP arrangement. Planned development of 500 units in the PMHS across the 36 state capitals and the federal territory.	The PPP achieved 4,440 housing units while the PMHS began in a few states, for example, Edo State. In Ogun State, only 100 housing units were built against the 500 units planned. Most of the policies during the 2000–2004 period did not effectively capture nor respond to the fate of homeless urban Nigerians.
	The 1991 housing policy was reviewed because of the inability to meet the set goals, which in turn gave rise to the Nigerian National Housing Policy (NHP) of 2006. This policy developed transition strategies from public to privately developed housing.[46]	2,736 housing units under the NHP's pilot projects are under construction in 33 states nationwide.[47]	Project on-going. However, findings show that the houses developed under the NHP of 2006 must be made more affordable to the target group.

(Continued)

44 Ibimilua and Ibitoye (n 32).
45 Ibem, Anosike and Azuh (n 35); Ebekozien (n 1).
46 Aribigbola (n 31).
47 D. Dimeji-Ajayi, 'Federal Government of Nigeria Set to Deliver 2,736 Housing Units' (2018) *Property Proinsider* (25 April 2018) <www.propertypro.ng/blog/federal-government-of-nigeria-set-to-deliver-2736-housing-units/> (accessed 1 September 2023).

Table 19.1 (Continued)

Period	Policy and programme	Programme target	Achievement level
	One of the peculiarities of the 2012 NHP was the emphasis placed on bringing in private sector involvement in LCH construction and investment[48] while Ebekozien[49] findings show that implementation of the NHP is less than 10%. This calls for concern.	Attempts to bring in the private sector sought to increase LCH construction.	Despite efforts to bring in the private sector, construction output was low during this period.
	In late 2017, the Central Bank of Nigeria (CBN) launched a PPP programme called 'My Own Home'. World Bank, Works and Housing, Federal Ministry of Justice, Federal Ministry of Finance, Federal Ministry of Power, Mortgage Banking Association of Nigeria, and Primary Mortgage Banks jointly fund this. In 2015, the Federal Integrated Staff Housing (FISH) Programme was introduced.	The 'My Own Home' scheme was aimed at providing mortgages, mortgage guarantees and insurance as well as housing microfinance to the wider Nigerian population. The FISH programme sought to address the acute accommodation challenges facing Federal Civil Servants by delivering quality and affordable housing units through provision of loan and mortgage facilities with long-term repayment periods.	Some state governments are yet to provide land for the commencement of the 'My Own Home' programme. Both this and the FISH programme are PPP schemes and thus not pro-poor urban housing policies. It does nothing to help LIEs in Nigeria who are the most impacted by homelessness. It has been questioned where in the world PPPs are successfully used to provide homes for the LIEs without subsidies and grants from the state government?[50] Ajayi[51] has found that 32 of the 55,000 civil servants that subscribed to FISH programme have received keys to a new home as of December 2018.

(Continued)

48 D. Akintomide, 'Only 5% of Nigerian Housing Stock Affordable; Building for LIE Not Profitable, Experts React' *Nigerian News Direct* (3 December 2021) <https://nigeriannewsdirect.com/tag/only-5-of-nigerian-housing-stock-affordable-building-for-low-income-earners-not-profitable/> (accessed 1 September 2023).
49 A. Ebekozien, 'Community Participation in Affordable Housing Provision in Developing Cities: A Study of Nigerian Cities' (2020) 30(7) *Journal of Human Behaviour in the Social Environment* 918.
50 O. Ajimotokan, 'Nigeria: Chinese Investors Plough N108 Billion into FISH Project' *This Day* (7 June 2018) <https://allafrica.com/stories/201806080744.html> (accessed 1 September 2023).
51 I. S. Ajayi, 'Addressing Housing Deficit in Nigeria: Issues, Challenges, and Prospects' (2019) 57(4) *CBN Economic and Financial Review* 223.

Table 19.1 (Continued)

Period	Policy and programme	Programme target	Achievement level
2017–2020	Economic Recovery and Growth Plan set up a Family Homes Fund to stimulate the building sector via social housing provision. The main goal was to ensure an increase in available housing loans and the construction of housing units for the masses. This includes recapitalising the Federal Mortgage Bank of Nigeria from NGN2.5 billion to NGN500 billion (US$1/NGN462) to address the housing demands.[52]	2,700 housing units to increase to 10,000 housing units/annum from 2020 are planned and construction of 20,000 pilot social housing units.	Project on-going.

Source: Authors' own compilation.

The Way Forward

In Nigeria, as this chapter has shown, housing policies and programme initiatives have failed to adequately meet LIEs' and disadvantaged citizens' housing demands. This will become a 'time-bomb' for urban homelessness in Nigeria in the future if not addressed now. The chapter has exposed that there is no single recognized legal, institutional framework to define and manage a Nigerian citizen who becomes homeless, and in addition, owning a habitable home is still an unachievable goal for many LIEs and disadvantaged citizens in Nigeria. Mortgage finance inaccessibility and unaffordability are the key encumbrances hindering LIEs and disadvantaged citizens from moving onto and up the housing ownership ladder in Nigeria. The housing need in Nigeria is enormous, as the chapter exposes. As such, mechanisms to respond to and redress the housing deficits, especially for urban LCH provision, should be developed and founded on all-inclusive pro-poor policies to promote homeownership for the most disadvantaged and low-income earners. Public and private sector participation should be encouraged by key housing stakeholders, and learning from selected developed and developing countries' models of housing delivery is vital. Provided below is a series of suggestions for the way forward via policies and programme interventions designed to tackle, prevent, and mitigate homelessness in Nigeria:

1. **Revamp Nigeria's Government Role in LCH Provision.** Political will and unwavering commitment by government would go a long way to addressing Nigeria's housing and homelessness crisis. Malaysia and Morocco provide examples of how restructuring the housing delivery system and engaging the private sector can accelerate advancement in

52 Moore (n 5).

easing the housing crisis, especially regarding LIEs' housing demands. The political will demonstrated by the Singaporean government in LCH delivery via pro-poor policies and programmes to enhance homeownership for LIEs is a notable example of government support. It creates an enabling environment that induces private sector participation in LCH provision. Many countries, including Chile, have successfully employed the enabling method to reform their housing policies and programmes. An enabling mechanism demands an overhaul of government housing interventions, institutions, legal frameworks, and regulations to support an integrated and functioning housing market. The mechanism would change the government role from a housing provider to a facilitator and co-developer. In Malaysia, the State Economic Development Corporation, an agency of the government, is engaged in housing delivery, and the State Government Housing Department is engaged in policy formulation.

2. **Policy and Regulation.** Administrative amendment to the Land Use Act to delegate authorization of consent to the director of lands at the national and commissioner at state levels is long overdue. This would ease bottlenecks, time wastage, and high charges associated with title deeds and procuring consents for transfers. Land title simplification is germane to reducing housing costs and encouraging housing development. This policy would mitigate against barriers to homeownership for LIEs. A government role in land and/or building material subsidies and incentives aimed at the LIEs group becoming homeowners should also established. The Nigerian government should urgently develop an all-inclusive institutional framework to address homelessness in various internally displaced populations and policy regarding resettlement and integration via resilience and self-sustaining resources, that is, based on the provision of employment opportunities. Amending and adopting the revised document of the 2003 National Policy on Internal Displacement is long overdue to address the estimated 2.7 million Nigerians displaced as of 2020.[53]

3. **Housing Finance Reform.** Review of the established Nigeria Mortgage Refinance Company and resuscitation of the Federal Mortgage Bank of Nigeria to make housing finance facilities available to LIEs and disadvantaged citizens is critical in tackling homelessness now and in the future. The government should summon the political will to formulate a formal approach to ensuring LIEs have access to housing finance and supervised by the apex bank. As part of statutory obligations, the apex bank (Central Bank of Nigeria) should encourage mergers and acquisitions among primary mortgage institutions. This would enhance institutionalization of the Code of Corporate Governance for primary mortgage institutions. Strengthening the financial and operational capabilities of the Federal Mortgage Bank of Nigeria cannot be over-emphasized. In addition to an upward review of the National Housing Fund savings scheme contribution from 2.5% to 15% of the basic salary, other financial-related matters such as decent incomes to enhance savings and eligibility for housing loans and incremental building loans should be addressed by government to mitigate urban homelessness, especially among Nigerian LIEs in the future.

4. **Collaboration and Capacity Building.** Collaboration and capacity building are instruments that some countries, such as Malaysia and Singapore, have employed to achieve their LCH delivery recorded success. The authors of this chapter would encourage

---

53 Moore (n 5).

relevant government housing agencies in Nigeria, such as the Mortgage Bankers Association of Nigeria, Housing Finance Professionals Association of Nigeria, Real Estate Developers Association of Nigeria, Federal Mortgage Bank of Nigeria, and the Central Bank of Nigeria, to collaborate to institutionalize reskilling and upskilling of experts in the mortgage sector, leading to professional certification in the housing finance sectors in Nigeria. It is hoped the outcome would be the development of higher education academic programmes, such as a BSc/BTech/HND degrees in housing finance. Also, training and retraining of housing finance experts in real estate should be sustained through regular local and international programmes, study visits, workshops, seminars, and conferences.
5. **Sustainable City Planning.** Less than a decade since the creation and identification of the Sustainable Development Goals (SDGs), sustainable city planning is a key tool used by regulatory agencies for guiding urbanization and growth. The planning policy defines land use, city infrastructure design, internet, and provisions that protect the natural environment. The mechanism offers city expansion and makes development land available for housing delivery. The application of this tool is missing in many Nigerian cities. Many Nigerian cities lack up-to-date urban plans. This has increased urban sprawl, urban slums, and unplanned housing developments in many Nigerian cities. Thus, to improve sustainable cities in Nigeria, the government, via the regulatory agencies, should regularly update its feasible city plans to ensure well-located land is made available for housing and infrastructure.
6. **Private Sector Engagement in LCH.** The private sector should become the 'engine' and partner with government (federal, state, and local governments) in increasing the supply of LCH. In countries like Malaysia, the housing developers (private sector) are at the forefront of constructing and financing LCH development for LIEs. This construction is done simultaneously with other high-cost buildings within the same development layout. Thus, the imposition of LCH quotas on housing developers in urban locations should become a key part of their contribution to corporate social responsibility to mitigate urban homelessness. This is the practice in Malaysia, Singapore, and other countries that have recorded success in mass housing delivery. Also, incentives such as tax waivers and urban land allocations to encourage private organizations to develop LCH for their LIEs that have served a minimum of ten years should be encouraged. A clear and effective housing and homelessness framework deeply rooted in the Nigerian experience should be developed.

Summary and Conclusions

This chapter has provided a platform to identify and address the scale of homelessness in Nigeria and offer insights into policy interventions that could be implemented to combat housing scarcity in the country. The chapter has exposed that there is no legal, institutional framework to manage a Nigerian citizen who becomes homeless, and owning a habitable home is still an unachievable goal for many LIEs and disadvantaged citizens in Nigeria. Besides the uncertainty of homelessness of 2.7 million IDPs across Nigeria's cities with little and slow progress regarding resettlement and reintegration, many LIEs and disadvantaged Nigerians in urban locations are living in slums because of housing scarcity. This is a cause of concern and requires recognition and action. This chapter has argued that designing policy interventions to tackle, prevent, and mitigate Nigeria's homelessness is long overdue.

Thus, the government should create an enabling environment for the housing sector (private and public/governmental bodies working in collaboration) to respond to the housing deficits. Achieving this requires a political will and commitment from policymakers and political appointees. Politicians always use housing provision promises as a strategy during election campaign yet fail to fulfil them after being elected – as Table 19.1 earlier in the chapter amply reflected. Homelessness is a global social problem and will worsen in developing countries like Nigeria if no concerted effort is taken. Poverty, unemployment, rural–urban migration, urbanization growth, insecurity, low household income, and urban land shortages are identified as key driver factors for homelessness if not addressed and challenged. This chapter has revealed that LCH paucity in semi-urban and urban locations and poverty are key components influencing homelessness in Nigeria. The chapter has identified the root causes of homelessness and reviewed Nigeria's affordable housing policies and programmes to date. The chapter has argued for integrated and all-inclusive 'pro-poor' home policies and revamping existing interventions via public housing institutions at all government levels, focusing on the sustainability of LCH programmes across Nigerian cities. The chapter ultimately contends that stakeholders, especially governments at all levels and housing developers, should improve their level of LCH delivery for LIEs and disadvantaged citizens. Only if this is done can the phenomenon of homelessness in Nigeria be tackled. The approach should be resilient and all-inclusive, including upgrading urban slums, creating better job prospects, and advocating an inclusive and global economy that works for all in Nigeria.

20
PREVENTING AND ENDING HOMELESSNESS IN SOUTH AFRICA

Fusing Research, Policy, and Practices – Lessons from the City of Tshwane

Stéphan de Beer

Introduction

This chapter offers a reflection on attempts to prevent and end homelessness in the city of Tshwane, the administrative capital of South Africa. It is done against the backdrop of diverse faces of homelessness and the inability of South African cities to undo the apartheid spatial fabric.

The city of Tshwane adopted its Street Homeless Policy in 2019.[1] Flowing from research on street homelessness in the city, and oriented towards practices that could facilitate sustainable pathways out of homelessness, there has been a real sense, among some, of the importance of fusing research, policy, and practices, in our attempts to prevent and end street homelessness in the city. An important, recent collaboration in the city has sought to integrate direct interventions; litigation, legal advice, and policy work; and evidence-based research in advancing a progressive agenda to end homelessness. This chapter provides a critical reflection on this collaboration and related interventions in the city of Tshwane as an example of effective approaches that could represent a blueprint for the future of tackling homelessness across the whole of South Africa.

Homelessness and the Failure of Socio-Spatial Transformation in South African Cities

The apartheid city was the result of deliberate urban planning to segregate urban populations in South African cities racially. In the process, the urban poor was mostly restricted to the fringes of cities, far from the concentration of economic opportunity, with little or no access to quality services such as health, recreation, and education, and with long

---

1 City of Tshwane, *Street Homeless Policy for the City of Tshwane* (City of Tshwane Metropolitan Municipality 2019).

traveling times to and from work, due to the nature of public transport. Twenty-nine years after the formal collapse of apartheid, the apartheid city is still reproducing itself in different forms. Although there are various causes of street homelessness in South Africa today, one of the critical causes not adequately accounted for by policymakers or considered in strategic interventions is how ongoing socio-spatial apartheid hinders people from opportunities to break cycles of poverty and exclusion. A large proportion of the homeless are new migrants into the city coming from rural and marginalized urban communities to locate themselves in proximity to more desirable employment opportunities. The suburbanization of homelessness attests to this, as people seek out nodes of economic concentration. As these nodes seldom offer affordable and diversified housing options, people are then forced to become homeless. A growing number of street-based persons[2] in South Africa are the so-called 'working homeless'. These are people who work, and who actually have accommodation elsewhere, unlike the majority of street homeless people, but they opt to live in parks, in river beds, or on construction sites, as restrictive commuting costs to and from their family homes would absorb all they earn. Instead, they choose to use their incomes rather to sustain the livelihoods of their family or children, returning home more infrequently.

Government officials routinely suggest that people should return to where they come from, since there they must have homes 'somewhere else'. Even non-governmental organizations offering homeless services reinforce this discourse by concentrating much of their efforts on reintegrating homeless people back into their families. This is not always successful due to conflict or violence at home, the inability of families to deal with mental health issues, or desperate poverty and even hunger. Without addressing these circumstances, people cannot be expected to simply return 'home'. The structural causes of homelessness in South Africa are also denied. Homelessness is not only a psycho-social issue, or an issue of family reconciliation, but also an issue of economics, sustainable livelihoods, access to affordable housing, and a question of the right to the city. People opt to exercise their right of access to the city and its resources by locating themselves in ways that make the possibility of employment or sustenance more likely. This is not necessarily an ideological choice but an existential one.

The argument in this section is that homelessness and its diverse expressions in South Africa must be read and understood against the backdrop of the apartheid city and recurrent failures to transform it socio-spatially. Appropriate housing and economic solutions need to be designed and offered, not only in places where homelessness traditionally is concentrated, but also in every sphere of opportunity. Cross and others[3] have made the essential link between housing and economics. They argued

> that spatial access to street livelihoods and access to the metro core zones are critical factors linking housing access to poverty economics, and it questions

---

2 As used by M. J. Stowe, 'No One Should Have to Suffer Through This: Covid-19 Experiences of Street-Based People Who Use Drugs in South Africa' *Talking Drugs* (15 April 2020) <www.talkingdrugs.org/no-one-should-have-to-suffer-through-this-covid-19-coronavirus-experiences-of-street-based-people-who-use-drugs> (accessed 1 September 2023).

3 C. Cross, J. Seager, J. Erasmus, C. Ward and M. O'Donovan, 'Skeletons at the Feast: A Review of Street Homelessness in South Africa and other World Regions' (2010) 27(1) *Development Southern Africa* 5.

whether in South Africa's situation street homelessness can be eliminated in the foreseeable future.

Building on Cross and others, it is argued here that we should refrain from pessimistic or cynical conclusions that lead to paralysis and, instead, rethink our approaches to homelessness entirely: shifting from a welfare approach to a housing, economic, and infrastructure approach, from an approach that pathologizes or criminalizes people who are homeless to an understanding that acknowledges the structural causes of homelessness, requiring interventions and solutions (socio-spatial, economic, and institutional) that are concrete, measurable, and evidence-based. Socio-spatial transformation remains an elusive imperative, but much bolder interventions should be optimistically engaged.

Homelessness in South Africa Today: Definitions and Descriptions

There is no standardized, global definition of *homelessness*, and the same is true in South Africa. In the city of Tshwane, there is a working definition, contained in the policy and strategy on street homelessness, of *street homelessness* as people 'who live on the streets (on pavements, under bridges, in bushes or next to rivers or spruits), who fall outside a viable social network of assistance, and who are therefore not able to provide themselves with shelter at a given time or place'.[4] In Tshwane's first homeless count conducted in October 2022, 4,177 persons were counted being homeless in all seven regions of the city.[5] There is an estimated 200,000 homeless person across South Africa.[6] Whereas this definition provides a good starting point, street homelessness must be regarded as just one expression of precariousness, in addition to informal settlements,[7] backyard dwellings,[8] occupied buildings,[9] hijacked buildings,[10] and other forms of precarious housing. A large

---

4 City of Tshwane (n 1) 23.
5 In the count, we excluded people living in backyard dwellings or informal settlements: see S. De Beer, *Everyone Counted, Counts: The First Homeless Count in the City of Tshwane, October 2022. Research Report* (Unit for Street Homelessness 2023).
6 See E. E. Obioha, 'Addressing Homelessness Through Public Works Programmes in South Africa' (2019) Discussion Paper, Presented at the Expert Group Meeting on the Priority Theme 'Affordable Housing and Social Protection Systems for all to Address Homelessness' organised by Division for Inclusive Social Development, United Nations on 22–24 May 2019 at United Nations Office Gigiri, Nairobi, Kenya <www.un.org/development/desa/dspd/wp-content/uploads/sites/22/2019/06/Prof-Emeka-E-Obioha-Emeka-Obioha-ADDRESSING-HOMELESSNESS-THROUGH-PUBLIC-WORKS-PROGRAMMES-IN-SOUTH-AFRICA.pdf> (accessed 1 September 2023). This is not based on reliable enumeration, and my own estimate, based on a narrow working definition of *street homelessness*, would estimate the total number of people living without any form of shelter at no more than 100,000.
7 In the city of Tshwane, there are 221 informal settlements, with an estimated population of 1,053,642, which means 29.7% of the total population of 3.6 million people: see Municipalities of South Africa, 'City of Tshwane Metropolitan Municipality (TSH)' (2021–2023) <https://municipalities.co.za/demographic/3/city-of-tshwane-metropolitan-municipality> (accessed 1 September 2023).
8 Backyard dwellings – built in the backyards of formal dwellings – have increased by 700% in the city of Tshwane over 20 years, currently estimated at 201,956 dwellings.
9 *Occupied buildings* are referred to as privately or state-owned buildings being unutilized and then occupied by unhoused people. Sometimes, building occupations are a deliberate political strategy, but at times simply a last resort for very precarious people. These buildings usually do not have any form of payment to a central institution or person.
10 *Hijacked buildings* are referred to as privately or state-owned buildings being unutilized and taken over by individuals or syndicates who benefit by letting out space for accommodation, receiving in return a monthly

proportion of people are perpetually at risk of becoming homeless due to insecure housing tenures and ongoing forced removals from land or buildings they informally occupy. Informal settlements are precarious, either unrecognized by local government, erected on flood land, or earmarked for other purposes. These communities regularly face eviction, and where alternative housing is not provided, many people become homeless. Similarly, backyard dwellers often pay exorbitant sums for the right to erect a structure on someone else's property, often far in excess of what could be afforded in social housing units in the city, with perpetually insecure tenure.[11]

Apart from the 4,177 people enumerated during the Tshwane homeless count, either living on the streets or in buildings not suitable for habitation, there is therefore a much larger population that is 'near homeless', as evictions from buildings, informal settlements, and backyard dwellings are daily occurrences in South African cities. It must be recognized that homelessness is rarely recognized as a strategic issue of concern in African cities because of the relatively small number of street homeless people in South African and other African cities as compared to the very large number of urban dwellers residing in informal urban settlements or backyard dwellings. With 62% of African urban dwellers living in informal settlements, or urban slums, the real magnitude of the human settlement challenges in African cities cannot be denied.[12] The street homeless are often, in the words of Cross et al., the real skeletons at the feast – rendered invisible in the cityscape at worst or, at best, an unfortunate consequence of how the city works – the ultimate 'waste of capital'.[13]

The faces of homelessness in the city of Tshwane and other South African cities are diverse and constantly changing.[14] This is due to a variety of factors that cause street homelessness, including poverty, unemployment, a lack of affordable housing, spatial inequities, evictions, deinstitutionalization from correctional facilities or psychiatric hospitals, chronic psycho-social illnesses, harmful use of substances, and transnational migration. For this reason, a 'one-size-fits-all' strategy, still peddled by most cities and non-profit organizations in South Africa, is inappropriate in providing the context-aligned support homeless people need. By way of an extreme anecdotal example, a homeless person of 70 years is expected to live in temporary shelters and, if unable to find income or be reintegrated into her family, will be evicted. For those with no relatives, networks of social support, or prospect of gainful employment, safe and secure permanent housing provided by the state must be the only viable option here, and tackling homelessness demands close collaborative and holistic approaches between state, homelessness, and social housing organizations – examples of this approach in the city of Tshwane are discussed in the next section.

---

rental payment/protection fee in exchange for the right to stay there, mostly without the income being used to maintain the property.
11 In neighbourhoods across the city, backyard dwellers might pay rent of between R 1,500 and R 3,500 per month, which is similar or higher than the cost of a self-contained unit of 32 square metres in newly developed social housing.
12 UN-Habitat Discussion Note 3, *A New Strategy of Sustainable Neighbourhood Planning: Five Principles* (2014) <https://unhabitat.org/sites/default/files/documents/2019-05/five_principles_of_sustainable_neighborhood_planning.pdf> (accessed 1 September 2023).
13 Z. Baumann, *Wasted Lives: Modernity and Its Outcasts* (Polity 2004).
14 City of Tshwane (n 1) 13–14.

Examples of Institutional Mechanisms and Collaborative Processes Tackling Homelessness in the City of Tshwane

Over the past decade, various collaborative processes have been initiated in the city of Tshwane to address more effectively the challenge of street homelessness in particular. This section explores a number of these.

The Tshwane Homelessness Forum

The Forum was created in the 1990s as an attempt to coordinate services offered to homeless communities. The Forum has contributed significantly over the years, despite ebbs and flows in its effectiveness.[15] It has continuously kept homelessness on the agenda of local government, lobbying for facilities that could be used as shelters and challenging the violation of homeless people's rights. It was instrumental in engaging Mayor Kgosientso Ramokgopa during 2014/2015 on several issues related to homelessness, which resulted in the mayor requesting revisioning of the city's draft policy on homelessness that up to then was not implemented. With the onset of the Covid-19 and a hard lockdown in the city of Tshwane, the local municipality was slow in its response to the reality of homeless people, and it was again the Forum that gathered partners to challenge the city's apathy of approach. Today, with a reconstituted executive committee, the Forum has 30 formal member organizations representing the concerns of homeless communities and providing services in support of the homeless. Over the years, the presence and voices of people with lived experience of homelessness have been central to and have helped shape significantly the agenda of the Forum.

Successful Outcomes of the Forum and Its Partners: 2015 and Beyond

A number of successful outcomes resulted from the meeting of the Forum and then-mayor Kgosientso Ramokgopa. The mayor's request to revise and draft a new policy on homelessness for consideration by the city was adhered to, and researchers from the University of Pretoria and University of South Africa collaborated with the Tshwane Homelessness Forum and the city of Tshwane in this effort. The process began with crafting the *Pathways Out of Homelessness Research Project*, which became a multi-year project, now in its third phase.[16] This research generated new knowledge and informed the draft of the Tshwane Homelessness Policy. The research culminated in the first-ever *Tshwane Homelessness Summit*, hosted in 2015 and engaging a highly participatory approach. There was a requirement that 200 participants be homeless or had lived experiences of homelessness, and another 200 participants representatives from government, non-profit organizations, the research community, law enforcement agencies, or religious groups. Research findings were shared, and the draft policy presented for discussion.

---

15 Being a voluntary organization, the Forum sometimes faced institutional challenges, such as transition of leadership, internal organizational politics, or disregard by local government. In spite of such challenges, it steadily kept homelessness on the city's agenda.
16 S. de Beer and R. Vally, *Pathways Out of Homelessness* (Research Report, University of Pretoria 2015).

In 2016, the partners that participated in the development of the research, the Summit, and the draft policy signed a joint social contract expressing their shared commitment to end homelessness in the city of Tshwane.[17] This was an important moral commitment which is still intermittently referenced by partners when needed during periods of dwindling support for the homelessness agenda. At the same time, fleshing out the meaning of this commitment requires constant renewal. Although the Homelessness Policy was drafted in 2015 and presented to the city in early 2016 for adoption, the process of adoption dragged on, and the city only adopted the *Street Homelessness Policy for the City of Tshwane* in 2019.[18] This was done without the provision of a budget to accompany the policy's implementation. Nevertheless, the existence of a policy has been critical, especially during the Covid-19 crisis, to keep all stakeholders engaged and accountable, but also as a catalyst to enable a number of collaborative interventions which, without the policy framework, would not have been delivered.

Although the city did not start out well in its response to Covid-19 and hard lockdown,[19] through the intervention of the Tshwane Homelessness Forum and activist academics, the city soon recovered, and under the leadership of Mr Tich Mekhoe, then group head of Community and Social Development Services in the city of Tshwane, a *Tshwane Homelessness Task Team* was formed. The task team consisted of key individuals from various social partners and provided an effective and collaborative Covid-19 response, guided by a risk reduction strategy[20] that, as the author of this chapter, I was asked to draft, in conjunction with partners. In ten days, the task team was able to secure 27 temporary Covid-19 shelters, accommodating 2,000 people safely, whilst providing associated psycho-social and health services. The result was that post-Covid, in Tshwane, there are 600 sorely needed new bed spaces for homeless people only in existence as a result of Covid-19 shelters becoming formalized beyond the hard lockdown.[21]

The Community-Oriented Substance Use Programme (COSUP)

Another important element in the city's work tackling homelessness is the existence of the Community-Oriented Substance Use Programme (COSUP),[22] which is a partnership between the University of Pretoria's Faculty of Health Sciences and the City of Tshwane Metropolitan Municipality. The focus of COSUP is to roll out harm reduction programmes with substance users across the city, marking a critical shift away from a punitive to a therapeutic approach. During the hard Covid-19 lockdown, when homeless users could not access substances as previously, COSUP proved a critical intervention. It has since

---

17 The social contract to end homelessness was entered into by the city of Tshwane, the Tshwane Homelessness Forum, the University of Pretoria, and the University of South Africa.
18 City of Tshwane (n 1).
19 This process is recorded in a research report titled *Homelessness and Covid-19 in the City of Tshwane* (2021).
20 The city requested us to draft a risk reduction strategy that would support homeless individuals during the period of hard lockdown with temporary shelters, access to psycho-social and health services, access to vaccinations, and options for self-isolation if they were testing positive with Covid-19.
21 Data through a survey of shelter providers done quarterly by the Pathways Operational Centre (2022).
22 University of Pretoria, *Community-Oriented Substance Use Programme* (2023) <www.up.ac.za/up-copc-research-unit/article/2934203/cosup> (accessed 1 September 2023).

expanded to include general access to primary healthcare for all homeless people in shelters and transitional housing programmes across the city and in specific areas of particular homelessness concentration.

The Pathways Operational Centre

The impact of the work done through the collaborative approach of the Tshwane Homelessness Task Team led to key officials in the city requesting the University of Pretoria to consider formalizing the task team, to mirror the partnership the city had with the Faculty of Health Sciences to roll out harm reduction programmes. At the same time, the Senate at the University of Pretoria approved the establishment of a Unit for Street Homelessness at the university, dedicated to research, advocacy, and policy related to street homelessness. As a result, the *Pathways Operational Centre* (POC)[23] was established as an institutional vehicle through which both the city and the homeless sector could be provided with technical, capacity-building, and research support. The POC, as a central project of the Unit for Street Homelessness, provides strategic support to the homelessness sector through capacity-building workshops, a community of practice, dissemination of data and information, and making connections between available resources and housing needs.

The Tshwane Homeless Count

The national census conducted by Statistics South Africa has acknowledged that their own count of homeless populations is unreliable, deeming this one of their so-called 'hard-to-count' populations. To ensure greater accuracy in terms of the numbers of homeless people in Tshwane, and disaggregating the information in order to facilitate more strategic interventions in particular subgroups of the homeless population, the Unit for Street Homelessness at the University of Pretoria, in partnership with the Tshwane Homelessness Forum and the city of Tshwane, decided to spearhead the first-ever *Tshwane homeless count* for October 2022.[24] Further expertise was volunteered by individuals from Statistics South Africa, and Bloomberg Associates in New York City provided helpful advice during the process, based on their experiences of similar counts in a number of cities around the world. The October 2022 count recorded 4,177 homeless people, and the specific data captured is currently being processed.[25] The intention is that the results will inform more appropriate strategic and budgetary investment going forward, distribution of resources, and provision of homelessness services across the city. It is hoped that the methodology developed for the

---

23 Centre for Faith and Community, *Pathways Operational Centre* (2023) <www.home-less.net/street-homelessness> (accessed 1 September 2023).
24 S. de Beer, 'First City-wide Tshwane Homeless Count Set for 19 October, Activists Appeal for Volunteers' *Maverick Citizen* (25 September 2022) <www.dailymaverick.co.za/article/2022-09-25-first-city-wide-tshwane-homeless-count-set-for-19-october-activists-appeal-for-volunteers/> (accessed 1 September 2023); C. Gilili and W. Mabona, 'Homeless: Hundreds Volunteer to Count Homeless People across Tshwane' *GroundUp* (21 October 2022):www.groundup.org.za/article/homeless-hundreds-volunteer-to-count-homeless-people-across-tshwane/ (accessed 1 September 2023).
25 De Beer (n 5).

count will be refined and shared, for possible replication in other South African cities, and for consideration by Statistics South Africa as they contemplate enumeration of this apparent 'hard-to-count' population.

Legal and Policy Environment in Local and National Government: Disparate Government Approaches to Homelessness

Approaches to homelessness differ from city to city right across South Africa. Sometimes even within a particular city, distinct departments follow different, and sometimes conflicting, approaches, not synergized, not coherent, and often not congruent with official policy or strategy documents. Different approaches have particular foci, which are not always mutually exclusive, although they can be rather divisive. Tshwane is offered in this chapter as an example of how one city seeks to tackle this social phenomenon and lessons for best practice.

A *social welfare approach* to homelessness can lack appreciation of the structural causes of homelessness and deals with homelessness predominantly as a matter of individual pathology, victimhood, or choice. A *law enforcement approach* tends to criminalize people who are poor, and in some cities in South Africa (as the Stellenbosch example shows), this approach has been developed to staggering levels of sophistication, punishing people without addressing the fundamental causes of people's homelessness. A *structural approach* acknowledges that many people are homeless because of structural and institutional failures: lack of affordable housing; lack of access to primary health care; lack of appropriate, accessible mental healthcare in communities; deinstitutionalization from correctional services or psychiatric hospitals without adequate community infrastructure to meaningfully integrate people; and lack of vocational support and employment.

In the city of Tshwane, there has been a marked shift away from a narrowly defined law enforcement approach. Arguably, its policy on homelessness has assisted in curbing the use of stringent and criminalizing by-laws to address homelessness, as there are less frequent by-law infringement cases reported in Tshwane than in some other South African cities.[26] The Tshwane approach formalized in its policy and strategy seeks to enable interventions designed to address the structural – physical, psycho-social, health, economic, and institutional – constraints and gaps in communities. Street outreach and street medicine teams meet homeless persons where they are, whilst drop-in centres and temporary shelters are scattered across different parts of the city. Should a person who is homeless present to local government, they would ordinarily be referred to some of the services offered by non-profit organizations.

In addition to the formally adopted 2019 homelessness policy in Tshwane, there are also other policies and by-laws that either complement the homelessness policy,[27] stand in opposition to the policy,[28] or have not yet been considered as potentially useful instruments to be applied in tackling homelessness constructively. Tshwane's *indigent programme*

---

26 This is based on anecdotal witness from conversations in the National Homelessness Network, representing different cities across South Africa.
27 The city of Tshwane adopted a harm reduction programme to deal with substance use and homelessness; see A. Scheibe and others, 'Harm Reduction in Practice – the Community-Oriented Substance Use Programme in Tshwane' (2020) 12(1) *African Journal of Primary Health Care and Family Medicine* 2285.
28 City of Tshwane Metropolitan Municipality, 'By-laws Relating to Public Amenities' 11(42) *Gauteng Provincial Gazette* 265 s 8(1)(u): (accessed 1 September 2023).

warrants mention here.[29] This programme is intended to support people who lack access to 'basic necessities for an individual to survive',[30] such as water, sanitation, food and clothing, health, or housing. Officially, it states that the programme is targeted at 'anyone who does not have access to these goods and services'.[31] In reality, the indigent programme provides poor households with rebates on water and electricity and refuse removal; free provision and connection of prepaid electricity metres; and writing off of municipal debt arrears arising prior to registration in the programme. Sadly, people who live on the streets or in temporary shelters and who technically fall within the definition of the 'indigent' population do not benefit from the provisions of this programme because they lack a physical address in their own name.

At a national level, the Department of Social Development has set up the South African Social Security Agency (SASSA) to administer a cluster of social grants. These include an Older Persons Grant for people 60 years and older who have no other means of income, a War Veterans Grant, a Social Relief of Distress Grant that was instituted during Covid-19, a Disability Grant, and a Child Support Grant.[32] Of the 4,177 homeless people recorded in the recent Tshwane homeless count, early indications are that only 8.94% of these people have access to any form of social grant. Older homeless people who are eligible for the Older Person Grants often do not access it, either because of lack of information or a mismatch between services rendered to them and their actual needs. Even where people access these grants, the monetary value is so low it can hardly secure any form of safe and permanent housing. There should be greater emphasis on increasing access of eligible people to available social grants.

Even though a national Social Housing Policy (2003) exists,[33] the city of Tshwane has been far from proactive in its social housing delivery, lacking a localized social housing policy and strategy. In addition, homelessness has never been regarded as a key element in South African social housing policy. Yeast City Housing,[34] a faith-based social housing institution established in 1997, and their founding organization, the Tshwane Leadership Foundation,[35] have interpreted and implemented the social housing policy creatively over the years, developing (with subsidy from provincial government) various special needs housing options for homeless and near homeless people. Innovative housing options include accommodation for at-risk women and children, people with chronic psycho-social illness, terminally ill or frail older people from the streets, as well as older homeless people.

---

29 City of Tshwane, *The Indigent Policy* (City of Tshwane Metropolitan Municipality, 2012).
30 Ibid.
31 Ibid.
32 For more information, see South African Social Security Agency (SASSA) <www.sassa.gov.za/#> (accessed 1 September 2023).
33 Government of South Africa, *Social Housing Policy for South Africa: Towards an Enabling Environment for Social Housing Development* (Government of South Africa July 2003) <www.gov.za/sites/default/files/gcis_document/201409/social-housing-policy.pdf> (accessed 1 September 2023).
34 Yeast City Housing, (2022) <www.yeastcityhousing.org.za> (accessed 1 September 2023).
35 Tshwane Leadership Foundation <www.tlf.org.za> (accessed 18 September 2022).

Unfortunately, rather than supporting initiatives such as the ones mentioned earlier proactively, local government focuses much of its energy on preventing 'illegal' occupation of city land. Sipho Stuurman,[36] spokesperson for the city of Tshwane, said:

> The City of Tshwane has consistently taken a zero-tolerance approach to land invasion and will continue to implement or support the implementation of eviction orders against individuals who unlawfully occupy public land in all areas of the municipality.
> *(3SMedia 2021)*

Enforcement across the city is patchy, often determined by public pressure in local neighbourhoods. The Prevention of Illegal Eviction and Unlawful Occupation of Land Act of 1998 (Government of South Africa 2014)[37] makes such evictions difficult for local municipalities, as the Act provides very specific guidelines as to eviction processes that must be followed by the authorities. Usually, it requires the provision of alternative accommodation, which is often not available. Examples exist in Tshwane of housing lawyers relying on the provisions of this Act to prevent homelessness.[38]

Before concluding this section, a critical word on the adoption of the Tshwane homeless policy is perhaps necessary. This policy's implementation has been a mix of success and missed opportunities. On the one hand, a policy without budgetary commitment can arrive stillborn. Equally, local government has not proactively provided leadership for the policy. That said, because of the vigilance of the civic and charitable sector, the policy has become a powerful instrument for implementing organizations in framing their own interventions. When Covid-19 struck, the policy became a critical document, and the nature of its development also serves as a learning tool, a blueprint for crafting future provincial and even national policies on homelessness.

The Absence of a National Legal and Policy Framework on Homelessness

Currently in South Africa, there is no national policy on tackling homelessness. This leaves provinces and local municipalities to develop their own approach and policies. No specific budgetary provisions are allocated by the National Treasury to the provinces or municipalities for homelessness.

When President Ramaphosa announced the hard Covid lockdown, only one sentence in his speech required that temporary shelters had to be set up in all municipalities for people living on the streets. The president's announcement set in motion a comprehensive process in many larger cities, and significant interventions in secondary cities and smaller towns.

---

36 3SMedia, 'Informal Waste Recycling Site in Tshwane Removed' *Infrastructure News* (8 December 2021) <https://infrastructurenews.co.za/2021/12/08/informal-waste-recycling-site-in-tswane-removed/> (accessed 1 September 2023).

37 Government of South Africa, *Prevention of Illegal Eviction and Unlawful Occupation of Land Act of 1998* (Government of South Africa June 1998) <www.gov.za/sites/default/files/gcis_document/201409/a19-98.pdf> (accessed 1 September 2023).

38 A recent example is the prevention of eviction from a temporary city-managed homeless shelter in the suburb of Lyttleton, which the city wanted to close down, unless the city provided an alternative facility in the same proximity. Other examples include the prevention of the eviction of shack dwellers in the neighbourhoods of Salvokop and Woodlane Village, arguing that an eviction would render them homeless.

Yet that was in the absence of any national strategy guiding such interventions. Every municipality and province were forced to act independently.

Subsequently, the Policy Unit in the National Presidency invited policy inputs from South African academics, based on learnings during Covid-19 that related to implementing the Sustainable Development Goals. With my colleague in the Faculty of Health Sciences Jannie Hugo, we drafted recommendations for the creation of a national policy platform involving diverse stakeholders to debate and construct a national homelessness policy. Recommendations were presented both to the Policy Unit in 2020 and the National Department of Social Development in 2021.[39] In November of 2021, the National Department of Social Development convened the first national roundtable to kickstart the process around policy development. Unfortunately, this was done in great haste, and on very short notice, excluding significant role players, such as members of the National Homelessness Network, the only organized platform that brings together practitioners and those with lived experience of homelessness to share lessons learned. Preceding the national roundtable, Strategic Analytics and Management, a research organization focused on public health issues, was commissioned to do a high-level and initial diagnostic report on the status of homelessness in South Africa to frame the conversation and the process.[40] The final report is yet to be published. In July 2022, the National Department of Social Development put out a call for proposals from interested parties for drafting a national policy on street homelessness. The Department has not yet appointed anyone to lead this process.

It is argued here that lessons learned from Covid-19 as well as the existing policy framework in the city of Tshwane provide a strong basis from which to draft a national homelessness policy. The policy vacuum that currently exists nationally, but also in many provinces and local municipalities, created local paralysis and a tendency to pass the buck from one level of government to another. It also allows for illegal and even criminal interventions by local governments and law enforcement agencies to be implemented in unchecked ways, including regular confiscation and even destruction of people's property and documents, which have been deemed illegal and unconstitutional in a number of precedent cases across the country.[41] Yet local law enforcement agencies continue with this practice, often without accountability.[42]

In considering a national policy on homelessness, its interface with other policy documents is critical. How will such policy interface, for example, with the Social Housing Policy, a proposed Special Needs Housing Policy, the social grants on offer by the South

---

39 S. de Beer and J. Hugo, 'Ensuring Pathways Out of Street Homelessness: Policies, Processes and Practices' (A response to the SA SDG Hub Policy Support Initiative Call for Proposals. Policy submission to the Policy Unit of the National Presidency, Republic of South Africa, September 2020).
40 Strategic Analytics and Management, 'Diagnostic Study to Understand Homelessness in South Africa' (Strategic Analytics and Management November 2021 – June 2022) <www.strategicanalyticsmx.co.za/our-work-project/diagnostic-study-to-understand-homelessness-in-south-africa> (accessed 1 September 2023).
41 One example is the so-called Ngomane case: *Ngomane and Others vs City of Johannesburg Metropolitan Municipality and Another* (734/2017) (2019) ZACSA 57; (2019) 3 All SA 69 (SCA); 2020 (1) SA 52 (SCA) (3 April 2019): (accessed 1 September 2023).
42 In cities and towns where the homeless community and service providers are well-coordinated and following a rights-based approach, local governments are held accountable. Where that is not the case, local governments are often able to get away with actions against homeless people that are undignified, illegal, or unconstitutional.

African Social Security Agency, and multiple pieces of legislation pertaining to healthcare, refugees, and asylum seekers? All these have an important bearing on homelessness, and national policy formation must be cognizant of this to ensure optimized alignments and synergies. One example is the national Special Needs Housing Policy, which has been in development for more than ten years. This policy, once adopted and implemented, will provide a framework for housing provision to a much broader array of people with special housing needs, including people who experience homelessness and people who are destitute as a result of substance use.

In the absence of a national legal and policy framework on homelessness, we look to the major cities. Currently in South Africa, only three cities have policies on homelessness. As discussed earlier, the city of Tshwane has had its street homelessness policy since 2019. Beyond this, the city of Cape Town has, in light of Covid-19, placed its street homelessness policy under review.[43] The Inkathalo Conversations[44] took the form of public hearings on street homelessness during the period after the lockdown in Cape Town. This resulted in a 447-page document with specific recommendations for policy and strategy, which, sadly, have to date not been implemented or considered.

The Homeless Action Coalition[45] is a new formation recently formed in Cape Town, merging the old Street People's Forum, mostly made up of people providing services to homeless communities, with the Strandfontein Crisis Committee, formed by street-based people in response to the city's ineffectual approach to homelessness during the Covid-19 lockdown. There is much potential in this coalition, which brings together people with lived experience, service providers, and activists, offering a real chance to engage and develop policy processes more critically and robustly in the city of Cape Town.

The third municipality with a homelessness policy is the smaller city of Stellenbosch.[46] Here, by-laws to manage street homelessness have been systematically implemented. People who are homeless receive warnings for sleeping on the street, as it is deemed illegal under municipal by-laws.[47] If they remain on the street, they are issued a fine. If they do not pay the fine, which obviously they are mostly unable to do, they receive a warrant of arrest. If they still fail to comply, they are arrested and kept in a cell for the night. But then, to 'soften' this process, the city speaks of a 'restorative justice' approach, sentencing

---

43 City of Cape Town 2013, *Street People Policy* (Cape Town, 4 December 2013) <https://resource.capetown.gov.za/documentcentre/Documents/Bylaws%20and%20policies/Street%20People%20-%20(Policy%20number%2012398B)%20approved%20on%2004%20December%202013.pdf> (accessed 1 September 2023).

44 Inkathalo Conversations, *Inkathalo Conversations: Phase 1. Comprehensive Report* (Submission into the review of the Street People Policy 2013 [Policy number 12398b] and the development of a citywide strategy, 2021) <www.groundup.org.za/media/uploads/documents/Inkathalo-2021-compressed.pdf> (accessed 1 September 2023).

45 C. Mesquita, 'Hope for the Homeless' *Cape Argus* (13 October 2021) <www.iol.co.za/capeargus/opinion/hope-for-the-homeless-of-cape-town-8329cf27-cbab-43e4-9ad4-850b7260321d> (accessed 1 September 2023).

46 Stellenbosch Municipality, *Street People Policy Revised October 2018(2)* (Stellenbosch Municipality 2020) <https://stellenbosch.gov.za/download/street-people-policy-revised-oct-2018-2/> (accessed 1 September 2023).

47 Homeless persons in Stellenbosch are fined in terms of the Roads and Streets By-Law that was approved by the city council on 23 February 2022; see A. De Lilly, 'Stellenbosch Homeless Now Face Fines for Sleeping on the Streets' *Stellenbosch Media Forum* (8 March 2022).

people to undertake odd jobs for a number of hours, after which people are once again released to the streets. The same people get recycled through this system repeatedly, as evidently it is not designed to break the cycle of homelessness. Even the magistrate responsible for overseeing cases in the municipal court has stated in a recent platform to revisit the city's homeless policy that there had to be a different and more effective way of doing things.[48]

The city of Johannesburg now also has a draft homelessness policy, hopefully coming into full effect shortly, and taking its cue from the provincial homelessness policy.[49] Currently, the Gauteng Province is the only one of nine South African provinces that has a formal policy on homelessness, accompanied by an action plan and budget.[50] In the Western Cape, the bulk of funds to address homelessness is concentrated in the city of Cape Town. Smaller cities in the Southern Cape, such as George and Knysna along the beautiful garden route coast, have between 100 and 300 people each night living on the streets. These smaller cities can make a big impact through relatively small interventions but are often excluded from the provincial fiscus and other government-supported infrastructure. A few examples will demonstrate this. A local pastor in the city of George has spoken of how law enforcement would drive homeless people across the Outeniqua Pass to drop them inland, only for the very same people to resurface just a few days later in George. Moreover, Waleed Grootboom, the politician responsible for community services in Knysna, has recounted how the notorious Red Ants, a private security company specializing in forced evictions from government-owned and private land and property, dealt with homeless people in their town. Grootboom noted that 'they were treated like animals', including anecdotally a man being beaten up by private security officers next to his wife whilst sleeping on the street at night.[51] The point is that where there is a lack of homelessness policy, these sorts of behaviours can occur undeterred. Municipalities often rely on local municipal by-laws in law enforcement of this kind, actions which might be unconstitutional if tested in the courts.

Looking Ahead: Considering Homelessness in Relation to Other Macro-Challenges and Policies

At this point, three final considerations from a national policy perspective are explored. Each of these three relates directly or indirectly to homelessness and, it is argued, requires examination.

---

48 In a plenary discussion organized by the Stellenbosch Municipality on 18 August 2022, titled 'Conversations on Homelessness'.

49 City of Johannesburg, *City of Johannesburg Policy on Street Adult Homelessness Draft 2* (City of Johannesburg 2022) <www.joburg.org.za/documents_/Documents/POLICIES/Social%20Development/HOMELESSNESS%20DRAFT%202%20POLICY%20(As%20at%2003%2003%202022).pdf> (accessed 1 September 2023).

50 Y. Sobuwa, 'Gauteng Social Development Set Aside over R 87 Million for Homeless People' *City Press* (5 September 2022) <www.news24.com/citypress/news/gauteng-social-development-set-aside-over-r87-million-for-homeless-people-20220905> (accessed 1 September 2023).

51 From a conversation the author had with the MMC for community services in the Knysna Municipality.

First, there is the on-off debate in South Africa about the possibility of a Universal Basic Income Grant (UIBG). Hein Marais[52] engages with the various competing arguments and develops his own position. A secure monthly source of income, he argues, would ensure 'income for poor households ... reduce people and widen people's life choices'. In addition, it would 'increase demand for basic goods and services, which would boost growth and, especially, local production and jobs'. Individuals who are homeless would equally benefit from a stable source of income.

A second consideration is access to *National Health Insurance* (NHI). With significant pushback from private healthcare providers and medical aid schemes, the bill on a National Health Insurance scheme has been in development for more than ten years now. People who experience homelessness and fall through the cracks in terms of accessing primary healthcare services would benefit greatly from a bill intending to ensure 'universal access to quality health care for all South Africans as enshrined in the Constitution'.[53] Attempts are already being in Tshwane to give expression to the aspirations of the NHI, through connecting healthcare services directly to those who are homeless.[54]

A third consideration is the challenge of work. Marais speaks of the dearth of employment in South Africa today, and how traditional ways of thinking about work are unfit to solve the challenge of national unemployment.[55] Dominant approaches of shelter care, for example, strongly link the provision of support services to people's ability to secure employment. This is based on a faulty assumption that jobs are readily available in the employment market in South Africa. When an individual then fails to secure a job, blame is often placed on the individual instead of the economic and structural impediments to securing employment. Policies and practices intended to support people's sustainable exit from homelessness need, therefore, to consider this challenge much more sensitively and creatively if cycles of exclusion are to be permanently broken.

Homelessness Policymaking in South Africa: Promises, Pitfalls, and Processes

In this section, by way of a brief diversion, questions about the processes of constructing homelessness policy are explored. Much of what is wrong with policy lies not in the actual products but in the initial processes of policy construction; the question of who 'owns' implementation; the lack of synergy and alignment between different sets of policy, different spheres of government, or different government departments; and the lack of accountability by key custodians of policy for the failure to deliver effective implementation.

Social policymaking should not be regarded as a technocratic endeavour but as an instrument for deeper liberative and transformative interventions to achieve a just, democratic,

---

52 H. Marais, 'The High Stakes of a Universal Basic Income' *Maverick Citizen* (24 October 2022) <www.dailymaverick.co.za/article/2022-10-24-the-high-stakes-of-a-universal-basic-income/> (accessed 1 September 2023).

53 Parliament of the Republic of South Africa, 'The National Health Insurance (NHI) Bill' <www.parliament.gov.za/project-event-details/54> (accessed 1 September 2023).

54 R. Mahope, 'UP Professors Help Structure NHI to Tackle Homeless Healthcare' *Rekord* (13 October 2022) <https://rekord.co.za/?p=434424> (accessed 1 September 2023).

55 H. Marais, 'The Crisis of Waged Work and the Option of a Universal Basic Income Grant for South Africa' (2019) 17(2) *Globalizations* 1.

and environmentally sustainable society. This makes assessment of policy processes – construction, adoption, and implementation – crucial.

The new resolve to create a national policy on street homelessness provides a unique opportunity to forge a social contract between diverse stakeholders, from those with lived experience, practitioners providing housing and social services, and researchers, to government officials and politicians. Participatory spaces need to be created to capture the experiences and wisdom of all who want to contribute. In crafting a national policy, those engaged in this task need to have one foot in local contexts, drinking from the well of practices that have unfolded over many years, but another foot in the global networks of people concerned to bring about an end to homelessness. Existing best practice needs to be heeded, but also because local interventions provide important lessons for both successes and failures for national policy development. It is important, too, to consider the United Nations resolution on homelessness.[56] It would be wise to consider the language and commitments of this resolution, as well as the epistemic and conceptual frameworks within which this commitment was made, considering how best to align a national policy on homelessness in South Africa to such a global commitment.

The National Homeless Network in South Africa has become an important platform for developing a united voice as they liaise with government and other stakeholders, but also as a learning space between different South African cities.[57] It is important for this network to take its rightful place in processes of policy formation.

A final note in this section will draw from what is known as deliberative public administration (DPA).[58] Elsewhere, I explored this in relation to participatory research and policymaking processes on homelessness in the city of Tshwane.[59] Baccaro and Papadakis[60] are sceptical about 'the problem-solving capacities of the state', and they advocate 'the devolution of as many decision-making prerogatives as possible from centralised bureaucracies to policy-making fora in which citizens participate either directly or (more frequently) through their representative bodies'.[61] I subsequently asserted:

> This echoes strongly with the rationale behind the participatory research on homelessness in our city, the Tshwane Homeless Summit, as well as collaborative engagement to forge a Covid-19 homelessness plan, and a post-lockdown operational plan.[62]

Equally, such collaborative policy fora should be insisted upon, not only for crafting national policy, but also for the ongoing implementation and impact assessment of national,

---

56 UN General Assembly passed Resolution (resolution 76/133) on Homelessness in December 2021 <www.ohchr.org/en/special-procedures/sr-housing/homelessness-and-human-rights> (accessed 1 September 2023).
57 U-Turn, 'National Homeless Network' (2023) <https://homeless.org.za/national-homeless-network/> (accessed 1 September 2023).
58 L. Baccaro and K. Papadakis, *The Promise and Perils of Participatory Policy-making* (International Labour Organisation 2008).
59 S. de Beer, 'Homelessness and Covid-19 in the City of Tshwane: Doing Liberation Theology Undercover – A Conversation with Ivan Petrella' (2020) 76(1) *HTS Theological Studies* a6209.
60 Baccaro and Papadakis (n 58) 5.
61 Ibid.
62 de Beer (n 59).

provincial, and local policies. That could aid in reducing possible pitfalls and in actualizing the promise of good social policy. People who are homeless deserve policies that will ensure their freedom, in concrete terms.

Case Study in Collaborative Action: Bringing Together a Grassroots Service Provider, a Public Interest Law Organization, and University-Based Research

This section explores an example of an innovative new partnership that demonstrates the benefits of collaborative action in shaping policy. Since 2019, with external donor support, an innovative new partnership has been formalized between the Tshwane Leadership Foundation, a faith-based organization providing servicing and support to homeless communities since 1993; Lawyers for Human Rights, a public interest law organization offering legal support and litigation services in the areas of land and housing rights, migration, and refugees; and the Centre for Faith and Community, an activist research centre based at the University of Pretoria. This collaboration became an important learning process for how best to fuse research (knowledge generation and dissemination), practices (the development of prototypes), and policy work (including litigation, intervention, and prevention). Practices are not always developed in ways that take notice of good research, whilst research should be more deliberate about retrieving and documenting good practices. Similarly, policymaking processes are sometimes oblivious to some innovative practices that exist, which is a failure to appreciate and capitalize on important local knowledge. The partners in this innovative partnership were of the view that a deliberate and synergetic fusion of research, policy, and practices could enhance the ways in which we seek to address and overcome homelessness. Policy and practices will be designed and implemented based on evidence, whereas research will be made accessible to policymakers and practitioners alike. Similarly, best practice will be documented in ways that can disrupt dominant discourses about homelessness that, at times, seem mythical, and shape policy formation in ways that can ensure deeper impact.

The collaborative partnership had a number of very concrete objectives: (1) to reduce the number of older homeless people and people with chronic mental illness living on the streets by 50% by 2021; (2) to facilitate the reintegration of 1,100 homeless people into society through holistic support; (3) to advance the land and housing rights of urban dwellers living in precarious housing and the homeless; (4) to strengthen organizational and management infrastructure for ending homelessness; and (5) to support the preceding interventions and changes through evidence-based research and data gathering. A number, but not all, of these stated concrete outcomes have been achieved. It was identified, for example, that Lawyers for Human Rights had far too little capacity to deal with all cases of possible or pending eviction. Instead, communities had to be equipped with the knowledge and skills to understand their own land and housing rights, to be able to organize themselves for joint action, and to build campaigns that would ensure the protection and advancement of their right to the city. As a result, the Tshwane Urban Activist School was launched, so far having equipped three cohorts of community activists from nine different communities; forming a community of solidarity; and continuing to journey together on issues affecting these communities. The rationale is that communities will be aware of and understand their rights and be able to engage local government accordingly.

During the Covid-19 lockdown, Lawyers for Human Rights created a helpline through which more than 1,000 people were supported to avoid eviction from their places of residence. They also took up cases of waste reclaimers and other vulnerable communities, either seeking to prevent their eviction from land or property they were occupying or seeking relief in cases where eviction had taken place. As a custodian and advocate for the rights of all people, but particularly those most vulnerable in our cities and towns, Lawyers for Human Rights monitors in how far policies are rights-based and, if they are, if such policies are implemented. Sometimes they use existing policies to frame their cases, reminding government of the commitments they have already made to vulnerable communities, and some of their cases become legal precedents directly impacting policy.

Again, during the hard lockdown, the growing reality of older homelessness – first made clear during the Pathways Out of Homelessness research process – became even more evident. The Tshwane Leadership Foundation advocated for vacant units in one of the social housing projects of Yeast City Housing to be made available for accommodating older people coming from homelessness or at risk of becoming homeless. As a result, an innovative 'Housing First'[63] project was created for 36 older people fully integrated into a social housing project now known as the Inn.[64] A second facility for 18 frail older people was created in the Tau Village. The Centre for Faith and Community backed these interventions with evidence-based research, documentation of processes, and capacity-building spaces for homeless practitioners and housing activists to develop their own agency for action.

What emerges from the collaborative partnership is that homelessness can be much more effectively addressed at the intersections of knowledge generation, legal support or litigation, and the development of housing prototypes. What makes this particular collaborative effort different from many other partnerships is its intentionality about being embedded in action-oriented, evidence-based research whilst creating tangible interventions across disciplinary, professional, and institutional boundaries, both to prevent and end homelessness. It advanced an understanding of the homelessness research agenda and advocacy, which includes (1) embracing the responsibility to reframe how we define, describe, and assess homelessness; (2) debunking myths, stereotypes, and generalized assertions of what constitutes homelessness; (3) giving appropriate visibility to a population ordinarily rendered invisible; (4) centring solutions to homelessness in ways that make them real and deliverable, through advancing contextually appropriate policies, strategies, and investment possibilities; (5) helping broader society to recognize homelessness as a symptom of our collective failure; and (6) ensuring the lived experiences of (former) homeless people are drawn from in generating means for transforming the status quo.

---

63 The Inn is a 54-unit social housing project; 36 bed spaces are offered in 18 of the units, integrating older people who depend solely on government old-age subsidies into a social housing project. The other 36 rooms are for any member of the public who qualifies for social housing.

64 G. Tlhabye, 'Desire to Provide Affordable Housing for Tshwane's Homeless' *Pretoria News* (3 October 2020) <www.iol.co.za/pretoria-news/news/desire-to-provide-affordable-housing-for-tshwanes-homeless-21517663-0d63-4c13-857c-61d2e554554b> (accessed 1 September 2023).

Conclusion: Lessons and Recommendations for Homelessness Reform in South Africa and Beyond

This chapter concludes by summarizing lessons learnt and offering recommendations. Whilst these are necessarily rooted in the South African context, in key respects it is hoped, they will also have a broader, global relevance:

1. Apart from its other causes, homelessness is an expression of continued socio-spatial fragmentation of the South African city.
2. Homelessness in the African context is one expression of the precarious city, alongside informal settlements, backyard dwellings, and urban slums.
3. The diverse faces of homelessness require diversified strategies of intervention, tailor-made funding mechanisms, and broad-based, holistic collaborations.
4. The city of Tshwane has a rich and layered narrative to draw from in terms of policy formation, practical interventions, and diverse institutional mechanisms.
5. The lack of alignment between various policy frameworks hinders optimized impact of the Tshwane homeless policy, and clearer political, moral, and administrative will from local government in the city of Tshwane can distinguish this as a city of best practice.
6. The absence of South African national policy on homelessness allows for inaction at best, and unconstitutional treatment of homeless individuals at worst, in cities and towns across South Africa.
7. The promise of crafting a new national homelessness policy provides an opportunity to forge a new social contract between government, civil society, people with lived experience of homelessness, and the research community, with the view of achieving optimized impact.
8. Learning from deliberative administration theory, the necessity for participatory and collaborative policy formation, implementation, and assessment processes, through creating broad-based policy must be recognized.
9. There is value in fusing (evidence-based) research, action (producing prototypes), and litigation/policy work as we seek to address homelessness. Such fusion acknowledges immediate needs whilst working towards structural change.
10. It is vital to engage in self-critical reflection on policies and practices, asking whether what we do is innovative and impactful, preventing homelessness, breaking cycles of homelessness, or perpetuating the status quo.

In summary, in seeking to tackle homelessness, policy frameworks should be enabling, allowing space and providing direction for innovative and bold attempts at ending homelessness sustainably and collaboratively, for as many people as possible. This bold aim could be better served if research, practices, and policy were synergistically fused, as the example of the city of Tshwane demonstrates.

21

THE HOUSING CRISIS AND HOMELESSNESS IN ZIMBABWE

Examining the Exclusionary Nature of Urban Legislation and Planning Practice in Harare

George Masimba

Introduction: Overview of Homelessness in Zimbabwe

Homelessness in urban Zimbabwe is manifested through the existence of a range of precarious housing conditions under which land tenure is typically insecure. Homelessness signifies lack of adequate access to affordable and quality housing facilities.[1] This implies that exorbitant costs triggered by hyper-inflationary conditions in the context of Zimbabwe have mostly hindered improved access to decent housing. In the same vein, land tenure insecurity has often been associated or resulted in realities of homelessness. This latter position underscores the centrality of land tenure security as a determinant of housing precarity. Another dimension of homelessness that is crucial to examine relates to how urbanization has contributed towards informal urban growth.[2] That is, due to rapid increase in urban population, significant parts of cities have tended to grow informally, and this holds for land and housing markets. Yet informal urban developments have been classified as illegal, thereby outlawing their existence in the urban environment.[3] The net result has often been swift responses by urban authorities to counter such unsanctioned urban spatial activity through either demolitions or evictions. A classic example in the history of urban Zimbabwe is Operation Murambatsvina of 2005 – a countrywide eviction and demolition exercise ostensibly carried out to institute urban order. The characterization of urban informality in Zimbabwean cities has been premised and informed by legal considerations, thereby centring the role of urban legislation in general and more precisely that of town planning laws.

---

1 UN-Habitat, *Homelessness and the Sustainable Development Goals. Housing Unit Presentation* (2018) <www.un.org> (accessed 1 September 2022).
2 A. Le Roux and M. Napier, 'Southern Africa Must Embrace Informality in Towns and Cities' *ISS* (13 April 2022) <https://issafrica.org/iss-today/southern-africa-must-embrace-informality-in-its-towns-and-cities#:~:text=Rather%20than%20ignoring%20slums%20in,incrementally%20address%20the%20massive%20challenges> (accessed 1 September 2023).
3 E. Fernandes, 'Law and the Production of Urban Illegality' (2001) 13(1) *Land Lines* 1.

Zimbabwe's housing deficit has been pegged at over a million, with Harare's homeless population constituting approximately 50% of this total backlog. In principle, low-income residents in need of housing are expected to register on the local authority waiting list. Yet estimates indicate that only half of Harare's home-seekers are on the waiting list, on account of manifold reasons. The City of Harare, for instance, levies residents an annual fee of US$12 for the housing waiting list registration. Diminished delivery by the city authorities in Harare on the housing front has also resulted in a trust deficit towards the official housing production mechanisms. Whilst the 2013 National Constitution incorporates shelter under Section 28, it is important to note that it is only captured as a mere national objective.[4] Meanwhile, Section 81(1)(f) only stipulates a right to shelter under the 'rights of children'. Section 81(1)(f) not only restricts the 'right to shelter' to children but also highlights that, for everyone, the 'right to shelter' can only be vicariously claimed through children.[5] These constitutional realities demonstrate that there is no right to housing that is explicitly provided for every individual in Zimbabwe's constitution. The net effect of this legal lacuna is that it significantly limits the justiciability of the right to housing in Zimbabwe. At the local authority scale, this means there is no institutional eagerness to prioritize housing or robustly respond to the growing demand given the legal laxity. This chapter deploys Harare as a case study and explores homelessness while juxtaposing it beside existing exclusionary urban planning legislation and practice in Zimbabwe.

Cities are often conceived as orderly spatialities.[6] Therefore, urban laws, policies, and plans are all consistently deployed as instruments to achieve and maintain that degree of predictability and stability in the urban environment. A multiplicity of legislative instruments is in place to guide urban development in Zimbabwe. However, the Regional, Town and Country Planning Act and the Urban Councils Act are possibly the most referenced pieces of legislation that authorities routinely invoke. Urban legislation helps define what is acceptable and that which is condemned and, thus, considered intolerable in cities. Planning and plans, in turn, become the physical translation of urban town planning regulations into spatial and material constructions, such as housing, road network, water, and sanitation systems. In practice, urban legislation may outline the procedures for land and housing development, for example, insistence on full infrastructure installation prior to occupation of residential plots. On the infrastructure side, urban legal frameworks may indicate service options that are recognized in urban areas, such as reticulated waterborne sewerage systems in the case of sanitation. In terms of land access, unauthorized land occupations through, for example, invasions are not recognized, setting the stage for confrontations between illegal settlers and the landowner. Often, the end result is forced displacement and, therefore, homelessness.

Yet such tendency to weaponize town planning legislation against the urban poor culminating in varied forms of homelessness has not been spared from considerable criticism

---

4 2013 National Constitution – Zimbabwe.
5 Supreme Court Case, *Zimbabwe Homeless People's Federation, Pesiwe Gonye and Six Others v The Minister of Local Government and National Housing and Three Others*, Case Number SC541/2019 and Judgement Number SC94/2020
6 G. Boeing, 'Urban Spatial Order: Street Network Orientation, Configuration, and Entropy' (2019) 4(1) *Applied Network Science* 1.

within urban scholarship.[7] Planning legislation has been accused of being too elitist and hence less inclined to serve the interests of the urban poor. Mbiba bemoans what he terms a *fetish* with modernity motivated by the need to achieve 'world-class cities'.[8] While this fetish with planned cities constitutes an agenda for attaining First World status, this chapter highlights how it ends in homelessness for the majority of the urban poor. That is, in a bid to promote Western-type urban environments, planning legislation renders illegal a majority of spatial practices by the urban poor. Typically, slums are frowned upon as they are considered illegal spatialities that depart from the acceptable urban schema. Evictions and demolitions, therefore, become means by which such aberrations are corrected by urban managers. Yet in reality, such official responses usually exacerbate housing precarity through pushing slum dwellers into conditions of homelessness. Additionally, town planning legislation has been culpable for making lofty requirements for the emplacement of infrastructure and subsequent construction of housing for aspiring urban residents. Urban studies literature has criticized Zimbabwe's urban legislation as being embedded in colonial legacy, thereby lacking contextual relevance.[9] This chapter acknowledges these colonial continuities in planning legislation but further contends that this has not been purely accidental. Rather, this chapter argues that there has been a deliberate intention to re-create an apartheid-like city, albeit premised on economic principles.[10] This analysis is key in unmasking the instrumentality of planning in furthering elitist city programmes; hence, legislation merely serves as a tool for serving this agenda. This resonates with what Roy refers to as exposing planning's complicity with neoliberal globalization.[11] This chapter draws on critical urbanism arguments to conceptually frame subaltern practices from Harare amidst what appears to be a neoliberal city.

Homelessness in Zimbabwe: A Review of Literature

Globally, cities continue to experience a myriad of challenges amidst growing urbanization. Yet these challenges have been more pronounced in the Global South, where typically the phenomenon of urbanization has coincided with intractable crises of urban services delivery gaps coupled with growing urban informality. Homelessness has been one form by which urban services lacunae have manifested through proliferation of slums. However, often, such insurgent subaltern spatial practices have been met with evictions or demolitions, with urban planning legislation criticized for playing a key role in the resultant arbitrary displacements.

---

7 A. Y. Kamete, 'In the Service of Tyranny: Debating the Role of Planning in Zimbabwe's Urban "Clean-Up" Operation' (2009) 46(4) *Urban Studies* 897; M. Mbiba, 'Planning Scholarship and the Fetish about Planning in Southern Africa: The Case of Zimbabwe's Operation Murambatsvina' 2019 24(2) *International Planning Studies* 97; V. Watson, ' "The Planned City Sweeps the Poor Away . . .": Urban Planning and 21st Century Urbanisation' (2009) 72(3) *Progress in Planning* 151.
8 Mbiba (n 7).
9 A. Chigudu, 'Influence of Colonial Planning Legislation on Spatial Development in Zimbabwe and Zambia' (2021) 147(1) *Journal of Urban Planning and Development* 04020057.
10 E. Bandauko and G. Mandisvika, 'Right to the City? An Analysis of the Criminalisation of the Informal Sector in Harare, Zimbabwe' (2015) 4(3) *Journal of Advocacy, Research and Education* 184; A. Chigwenya, 'Contestations for Urban Space: Informality and Institutions of Disenfranchisement in Zimbabwe – the Case of Masvingo City' (2020) 85(5) *GeoJournal* 1277.
11 A. Roy, 'Praxis in the Time of Empire' (2006) 5(1) *Planning Theory* 7.

Homelessness has been widely accepted as a function of the massive gaps between supply and rising demand for housing in cities.[12] Premised on this logic, this chapter conceptualizes homelessness either as total lack of decent housing facilities or any housing efforts by the urban poor that fail to meet the basic standards for habitable accommodation. Moving further with this reasoning, informal settlements signify an unmet housing need and, therefore, qualify to be characterized as an indicator of homelessness. Centred on the assumption that at some point supply interventions must either equate or offset demand, tackling homelessness has thus been preoccupied with quantitative targets. Alongside this rationality, a programmatic thrust has evolved, advancing production of more housing units as the panacea to addressing homelessness. Yet Zami and Lee, in a contribution aptly focused on outlining forgotten dimensions of Zimbabwe's housing crisis, argue that such tendency to atomize homelessness obscures important elements underlying sustainable housing responses. They posit, for instance, that such a stance misses an analytical scrutiny of the contextual factors as well as potential for a clearer framing and understanding of the housing situation in Zimbabwe.[13] Kamete has also echoed similar sentiments cautioning against this fixation with statistics, as 'this leaves some problems untouched'.[14] Consistent with this interpretation, debates about homelessness are then associated with housing waiting lists to further amplify the numerical disparities between supply and demand. Considering the volatile Zimbabwean socio-economic context, this emphasis on merely pushing numbers does appear to be misleading. This, however, is not to presume that a quantitative stance is not helpful. Rather, it is an acknowledgement of the shortcomings of such an approach in contributing towards relevant policy and practice insights.

Significant literature on the housing crisis and homelessness in Zimbabwe has also attended to the affordability gap as a key consideration in the sector.[15] Broadly, these studies have observed that the country's unstable macro-economic environment has severely undermined both institutional and individual-led housing provision efforts. That is, recurrent budget deficits have hamstrung government service delivery programmes, and housing, in particular, has not escaped the predicament. For instance, in its 2022 budget statement, the city of Harare reported constrained fiscal space and no specific provision for housing development.[16] At the local level, accompanying widespread poverty conditions have also triggered acute low-cost housing shortages. The role of affordability issues in contributing to the housing crisis in Zimbabwe has to be viewed within the context of the state's withdrawal from social services and the subsequent entry of market-oriented approaches under the auspices of the economic structural adjustment programme (ESAP). Post-ESAP, housing programmes were adversely affected by the principle of cost recovery, which

---

12 A. Y. Kamete, 'Revisiting the Urban Housing Crisis in Zimbabwe: Some Forgotten Dimensions?' (2006) 30(4) *Habitat International* 981.
13 M. S. Zami and A. Lee, 'Forgotten Dimensions of Low-Cost Housing Crisis in Zimbabwe' (The 8th International Postgraduate Research Conference, June 2008) 26–27.
14 Kamete (n 12) 982.
15 Chigwenya (n 10); I. Chirisa, 'Building and Urban Planning in Zimbabwe with Special Reference to Harare: Putting Needs, Costs and Sustainability in Focus' (2014) 11(1) *Consilience* 1.
16 City of Harare, *2022 Budget Speech and Proposals* (Presented to City of Harare on the 9th of November 2021 at 09:30hrs by the Chairperson of Finance and Development Committee Councillor Tichaona Mhetu, 2022).

essentially entailed recapturing of all project costs from target communities.[17] The 'cost-recovery turn' was necessitated by the need for ensuring replicability and sustainability of the housing projects. Yet against the backdrop of deepening poverty conditions, cases of defaulters culminating in repossessions or evictions spiked, rendering low-income housing an investment risk.

Urban planning legislation has been a subject of sustained contestation, with different scholars adopting equally varied conceptual positions.[18] Some authors have insisted that planning legislation is a prerequisite for order in the built environment, while others have countered that it has merely served a neoliberal exclusionary agenda. Fernandes has advanced an argument centred on urban legal reforms challenging law for its contribution in producing urban illegality.[19] Urban planning legislation is the collection of policies, laws, decisions, and practices that mediate the management of the built environment in the city.[20] Urban planning or town planning legislation has been promoted and considered as a tool for instituting order in the urban environment. Glasser observes that, at its best, urban legislation lends some level of predictability to urban existence.[21] In this regard, zoning regulations are an example of planning instruments that assist in regulating lot sizes, densities, and acceptable land uses and hence contribute towards some form of urban order. The net effect of such zoning arrangements is such that typically everything that departs from this prescribed urban form is deemed illegal. Yet notwithstanding criminalization of such spatial aberrations, reality in cities still reflects prevalence of unapproved developments, often in the form of informal settlements. Rauws concurs with this analysis while positing that cities occasionally follow uncertain trajectories, and proceeds to argue that what is required is to swiftly promote the responsiveness of the urban environment.[22] Thus, uncertainty is not necessarily incompatible with urban planning ethos and statutes. City authorities have also been accused of inheriting colonial planning legislation which has proved to be out of sync with current socio-economic realities.

Analysis of Homelessness in Harare: Theoretical Underpinnings

This chapter deploys the 'right to the city' and 'urban modernism' as key theoretical lenses for generating crucial analytical insights and understandings of the urban poor's housing experiences in Harare. The 'right to the city' approach was developed and popularized by Henri Lefebvre in the 1960s during the period of working-class and students uprisings

---

17 A. Y. Kamete, 'The Practice of Cost Recovery in Urban Low-income Housing: A Discourse with Experiences from Zimbabwe' (2000) 24(3) *Habitat International* 241.
18 Fernandes (n 3) 1–3; Kamete (n 7); D. Muchadenyika and J. J. Williams, 'Social Change: Urban Governance and Urbanization in Zimbabwe' (2016) 27 *Urban Forum* 253; D. Potts, 'We Have a Tiger by the Tail': Continuities and Discontinuities in Zimbabwean City Planning and Politics' (2011) 4(6) *Critical African Studies* 15; Watson (n 7); K. H. Wekwete, 'Physical Planning in Zimbabwe: A Review of the Legislative, Administrative and Operational Framework' (1989) 11(1) *Third World Planning Review* 50.
19 Fernandes (n 3).
20 UN-Habitat, *Rules of the Game: Urban Legislation* (2020) <www.unhabitat.org> (accessed 1 September 2023).
21 M. Glasser, 'Land Use Law and the City: Toward Inclusive Planning' (2013) 5 *World Bank Legal Review* 351.
22 W. Rauws, 'Embracing Uncertainty without Abandoning Planning: Exploring an Adaptive Planning Approach for Guiding Urban Transformations' (2017) 53(1) *DisP-The Planning Review* 32.

that were confronting capitalism in Paris. At the core of the slogan were political claims to belong to and co-produce urban spaces. In other words, the 'right to the city' formulation is a political quest by marginalized and alienated groups in the city to meaningfully contribute towards urbanization processes. Lefebvre posited that urbanization provided conditions for surplus accumulation and hence furthering capitalist agendas. This, therefore, means that the city constitutes a site of dialectical tensions, an arena for class struggles. For instance, he contended that state-led planning emphasized the exchange value of the city as opposed to its use value, leading to cities becoming venues of expropriation rather than participation. Unlike conventional Marxists, who looked upon industries as potential places of triggering uprisings, Lefebvre believed that the city represented an appropriate locus of revolution. It is within that logic that the right to the city constituted a political tool for dismantling neoliberal cities and, thus, capitalism. Elaborating Lefebvre's postulations, Harvey introduces notions such as 'creative destruction' and 'accumulation by dispossession' to illustrate how capitalistic urbanization processes are preoccupied with orchestrating displacements and appropriations of land settled by the marginalized urban poor in the city.[23] However, notwithstanding the utility of the right to the city as advanced by Lefebvre and Harvey among other critical urban scholars, Purcell has argued that the theoretical framing is fluid and not very clear regarding what constitutes the right to the city and how it challenges urban disenfranchisement. The fixation with the urban scale has also been questioned, considering how other layers, such as regional, national, and global, mediate how urban space is produced.[24]

The notion of informal housing practices or informal settlements that are a manifestation of the housing crisis in Harare as explored in this chapter has theoretical relevance for the 'right to the city' approach. That is, such 'insurgent urban tactics' could be understood as part of what Lefebvre postulates as political claims by the marginalized urban poor to co-produce the city. In this case, informal housing becomes subaltern arrangements through which the urban poor respond to homelessness in a city that has failed to meet their housing needs. Drawing on this 'right to the city' theoretical logic, informal settlements, therefore, represent a way through which marginalized groups are reshaping the city. In the same vein, the capitalistic conceptions of 'creative destruction' and 'accumulation by dispossession' rationalized under the right to the city appear to directly relate to evictions and demolitions that are considered in this contribution as key dynamics resulting in homelessness and the housing crisis in Harare. Thus, in this regard, the right to the city accurately reflects the contested visions about urban land in Harare, whereby city authorities insist on value capture arguments to dismiss insurgent urban practices by the urban poor. Another 'right to the city' dimension that is observable in Harare relates to appropriation of space as depicted through the example of housing social movements pushing hegemonic ideologies on urban inclusion through slum upgrading. The right to the city as an analytical lens is not new to Harare. In a related study, targeting informal economic and housing practices examining secondary sources, Bandauko and Mandisvika have also deployed the 'right to the city' approach to help advance the argument for socially just cities.[25]

---

23 D. Harvey, 'The Right to the City' (2008) 6(1) *The City Reader* 23.
24 M. Purcell, 'Excavating Lefebvre: The Right to the City and Its Urban Politics of the Inhabitant' (2002) 58 *GeoJournal* 99.
25 Bandauko and Mandisvika (n 10).

Urban modernism constitutes an approach to planning that prioritizes urban design, aestheticization of urban space, renovation, urban order, high-rise buildings, zoning, market interests, and prioritization of the city's tourism potential, among other town planning and design considerations.[26] Urban modernism as a planning project gained theoretical referencing against the backdrop of the social crises and disorder generated by industrial capitalism in Europe.[27] In this regard, Holston proceeds to state that modernist planning sought to transform the 'unwanted present by a means of an imagined future'.[28] It contends that transforming city conditions can be achieved by either obliterating the current city so as to change its form, which entailed demolishing existing dilapidated urban developments. The modernist project, however, constituted a top-down exercise, through which urban planners were thought to be always acting in the best interests of the common good. In line with zoning, urban modernism represents a quest to institute order, whereby everything in the urban environment is positioned in its rightful territory.[29] Urban modernism postulations have, however, been questioned, especially regarding how the approach assumes a unidirectional relationship through which the built environment shapes the citizens and not vice versa. Yet the presence of 'insurgent spaces and practices' in the form of informal housing and markets could be interpreted as a means through which people reshape the city form to suit their aspirations of urbanity.[30] Critiques have further doubted urban modernism's commitment to confronting the city's social relations, considering how it concentrated on the physical reorganization of the urban form.[31]

Notwithstanding its theoretical limits, urban modernism does appear to have relevance for contextualizing Harare's housing crisis and the attendant conditions of homelessness. The formulations of urban order and aestheticization of urban space, for instance, that loom large within urban modernism seem to mirror how state authorities have justified evictions and demolitions on the pretext of instituting order and cleanliness in Harare. The launch of a countrywide demolitions named 'Operation Restore Order' by the Zimbabwean government in 2005 provides an instructive example. Furthermore, the continued fixation with envisioning attainment of 'world-class status' in Harare could be equated with urban modernism's inclination towards the use of 'western cities as reference points for modernity'.[32] The prominence assigned to planning in Harare insofar as it is mandated to guide city-making processes could be related to the centrality of planners as professionals that will always act in the best interest of the general public within urban modernism. This position, though, is in sharp contrast with the 'right to the city' theory, which emphasizes participation of marginalized urban groups in co-producing the urban environment.

---

26 L. Leontidou, 'Alternatives to Modernism in (Southern) Urban Theory: Exploring in-between Spaces' (1996) 20(2) *International Journal of Urban and Regional Research* 1/8.
27 J. Hobson, 'New Towns, the Modernist Planning Project and Social Justice: *The Cases of Milton Keynes*, UK and 6th October, Egypt' (Working Paper No.108, Development Planning Unit, UCL, 1999).
28 J. Holston, 'Spaces of Insurgent Citizenship' in L. Sandercock (ed), *Making the Invisible Visible: A Multicultural Planning History* (University of California Press 1998) 40.
29 D. Harvey, 'Between Space and Time: Reflections on the Geographical Imagination' (1990) 80(3) *Annals of the Association of American Geographers* 418.
30 J. Holston and A. Appadurai, 'Introduction: Cities and Citizenship' in J. Holston (ed), *Cities and Citizenship* (Duke UP 1998) 1–18.
31 D. Harvey, *Rebel Cities: From the Right to the City to the Urban Revolution* (Verso Books 2012).
32 P. Dibazar and others, 'Questioning Urban Modernity' (2013) 16(6) *European Journal of Cultural Studies* 643.

Applicable studies referencing the modernist planning school of thought have also been undertaken in Harare by Mbiba and Kamete. Kamete observes that a planning fetish with order explains the knee-jerk displacements by authorities and cites Operation Murambatsvina as a classic example.[33]

Homelessness in Zimbabwe: Harare Case Study – Methodology

The Harare case study which informs this chapter examined the contribution of urban planning practice and legislation to homelessness and, hence, the housing crisis in Harare. The investigation employed a qualitative research approach, and housing and planning experiences from Harare were selected as a relevant case study for investigating the research questions. A purposive sampling procedure was utilized to narrow down the study area to five settlements, namely, New Park, Epworth, Crowborough Paddocks, Boko Haram, and Churu Farm. Evidence for the study was gathered from both primary and secondary sources. Harare, as the capital, has been one of the cities where land-related contestations have resulted in a massive housing crisis manifesting through land and housing precarity and displacements. Most of the urban growth in Zimbabwe has been witnessed in Harare whilst, at the same time, producing a range of urban informalities. The city's housing waiting list is reported to be approximately 1.3 million, although this has often been challenged as understating the magnitude of demand, considering how residents have lost confidence in the system due to constrained delivery and land-related corruption.[34] A citywide informal settlement profiling conducted in 2014, for example, enumerated 63 informal settlements.[35] The subject and tradition of displacements has typically been focused on Harare, with obstinate city officials insisting on reclaiming the city's sunshine status as an overarching urban agenda. Operation Murambatsvina, which displaced an estimated 700,000 people in 2005, is a relevant reference. More recently, widespread evictions and demolitions were unleashed in Harare as part of the Covid-19 pandemic–induced, state-led containment measures.[36] These eviction and demolition experiences in the capital, therefore, present Harare as an ideal site for examining how authorities fronted by planning have contributed towards amplifying homelessness and housing crisis in Zimbabwe.

Homelessness in Zimbabwe: Harare Case Study – Findings

This section presents results from the case study and in so doing engages with three emerging dimensions from the gathered data. First, the study reflects on the scope and nature of homelessness and housing crisis in Harare, and this is realized based on the varied characterizations of the land and housing context in the capital. Secondly, this section provides diverse understandings from both planners and informal settlement residents on the

---

33 A. Y. Kamete, 'On Handling Urban Informality in Southern Africa' (2013) 95(1) *Geografiska Annaler: Series B, Human Geography* 17.
34 D. Muchadenyika, 'Slum Upgrading and Inclusive Municipal Governance in Harare, Zimbabwe: New Perspectives for the Urban Poor' (2015) 48 *Habitat International* 1.
35 Dialogue on Shelter Trust, Zimbabwe Homeless People's Federation and City of Harare. Harare Slum Profile Report (2014).
36 Dialogue on Shelter Trust and Cities Alliance, *Housing and Land Tenure Strategies That Help the Urban Poor Fight the Covid-19 Pandemic. Policy Brief* (Harare 2021).

Qualifying and Quantifying Homelessness and the Housing Crisis in Harare

The scope and nature of homelessness, and hence the housing crisis affecting the urban poor in Harare, have been well-documented. City authorities have typically considered homelessness in terms of official demand expressed through the housing waiting list. The housing waiting list constitutes a demand management tool through which home-seekers register with Harare City Council's Housing Department to join the queue for either land or housing allocation. Applicants are required to present four requirements to successfully register on the housing waiting list, namely, national registration documents, marriage certificate, current payslip, and registration fee of US$12 per annum.[37] City of Harare is estimated to have a housing deficit of 1.3 million, with approximately 500,000 residents registered on the housing waiting list.[38] The mismatch between the quantum of demand and those on the official housing waiting list register was also corroborated by a resident who indicated that:

> It's pointless to re-register on the housing waiting list as it no longer serves its purpose. Besides that, city has not been providing housing as much as it used to, the allocation system is also heavily politicised and characterized by massive corruption.[39]

While official council-led assessments of homelessness and housing crisis have tended to rely on the housing waiting list, urban housing social movements have directed attention at slums as an expression of the housing challenges in Harare.[40] The Zimbabwe Homeless People's Federation has led, for example, a citywide process through which 63 informal settlements were documented in and around the city of Harare in 2014. The exercise entailed the physical counting of the actual slums coupled with detailing the nature and type of urban services existing in these slums. Urban services gaps in the profiled slums were also being captured. A community enumeration leader observed that the citywide slum profiling exercise was conducted as a way of increasing visibility on the reality and magnitude of land and housing informality in Harare as well as getting council to acknowledge the challenge.[41] An additional and yet significant dimension to the citywide slum profiling practice relates to how the process is used to mobilize and organize slum communities building much-needed social cohesion facilitating engagements with city authorities. The latter, for instance, have included negotiations for land tenure security and improved access to basic services.[42]

---

37 City of Harare Housing Waiting List Form.
38 T. Chitagu, 'ED Petitioned over Looming Demolitions' *NewsDay* (2 March 2021) <www.hic-mena.org/news.php?id=qGpmaQ==> (accessed 1 September 2023).
39 Interview with Dzivarasekwa Extension settlement resident.
40 Dialogue on Shelter Trust (n 35).
41 Interview with Zimbabwe Homeless People's Federation community-led enumeration leader.
42 Accountable Democratic Action 4th Semi-Annual Report Project Year Two.

In a move that potentially extends the conceptualization of homelessness and the housing crisis in Harare, urban social movements–led citywide slum profiling exercises have also targeted conditions in the council's dilapidated hostel accommodation. A majority of the hostels in Harare were built prior to independence in 1980 as part of accommodation facilities for laborers. After independence, when colonial restrictions were lifted, hostels started to accommodate entire families, placing an enormous strain on existing facilities. A Covid-19 impact assessment, for example, revealed how overcrowding and the attendant living space challenges in Mbare hostels adversely affected physical distancing measures.[43] Overcrowding is rampant in the hostels, and in some instances, a single room accommodates 13 people, underlining the housing crisis.[44] Illegal subletting is also widespread in the council-built Mbare hostels, further exposing an unmet housing need in Harare's oldest high-density suburb.[45] Besides overcrowding, hostels in Mbare are also typified by infrastructure decay, exemplified by dysfunctional water and sanitation systems.[46] Additionally, the nature of land tenure relations for council's hostel accommodation also presents some level of uncertainty and, hence precarity, for tenants. For instance, due to polarization in the country's political landscape, especially in Harare, some hostel occupants have been arbitrarily evicted by ruling party youth militias following accusations that they are aligned to the opposition.[47] This means that despite hostel housing being allocated by the council and, thus, with some degree of tenure security, politics in Harare often interferes with residents' peaceful occupancy. The net effect of these uncertainties, brought about by the political dynamics of Harare, is that social housing is viewed less favourably.

Built-Environment Legislation and Practice: Problem or Panacea?

The practice of urban planning has classically been associated with the quest for order and aesthetics in cities. *Order*, in this regard, is considered to be key in contributing towards the city's aesthetic appeal. Consequently, slums are then regarded a spatial inconvenient to the tidy and orderly urban environment. This inclination towards order was echoed during a workshop with City of Harare officials where strong positions about how 'slums disrupt urban sanity' were expressed.[48] It is within this rationality that city authorities then undertake arbitrary evictions and demolitions on unsanctioned residential developments

---

43 Dialogue on Shelter Trust and International Institute of Environment and Development, *Covid-19 Impact Assessment Report: Counting the Covid-19 Costs in Slums of Harare* (2021).
44 P. Manomano, 'Zimbabwe: Plans Afoot to Decongest Mbare Flats' *The Herald* (2 August 2021) <www.herald.co.zw/plans-afoot-to-decongest-mbare-flats/> (accessed on 1 September 2023).
45 Investigations Editor, 'Subletting of Council Flats Rampant' *The Herald* (12 July 2021) <www.herald.co.zw/subletting-of-council-flats-rampant/> (accessed 1 September 2023).
46 M. Matenga, 'Harare Council to Demolish Mbare Hostels' *NewsDay* (4 January 2016) <www.newsday.co.zw/news/article/94959/harare-council-to-demolish-mbare-hostels> (accessed 1 September 2023).
47 C. Mazorodze, 'Zimbabwe: Mbare Hostels Occupants Must Be Vetted – Harare Residents Trust' *The Standard* (21 July 2012) <https://allafrica.com/stories/201207230921.html> (accessed 1 September August 2023).
48 Dialogue on Shelter Trust Workshop with City of Harare built environment practitioners. Conducted on 13 October 2022.

that emerge in the city.[49] Demolitions, therefore, serve to erase and remove slums from the urban landscape and restore spatial order and sanity. The arguments for Operation Murambatsvina (Operation Restore Order), which was launched countrywide in 2005, largely fit this logic. Yet the efficacy of this displacement-oriented strategy has often resulted in the same slums resurfacing either in the same location or elsewhere, reinforcing the futility of such a policy response. The continued re-emergence of Gunhill informal settlement following a series of state-led evictions provides a pertinent example.[50] While arbitrary displacements evidently destroy housing investments by the urban poor, the implications also encroach into the livelihoods sphere. That is, such displacements tend to disrupt established economic configurations, typically plunging households into financial chaos. One community member confirmed this, indicating that housing for the urban poor constitutes more than residential facilities as it provides critical space for home-based business enterprises.[51]

While advancing the notion of urban order, city authorities have deployed urban legislation to operationalize and actualize this ideal city. Typical statutes that are relevant for the built environment that have been invoked by urban managers in Harare to implement evictions and demolitions include the Regional Town and Country Planning Act (RTCP Act), Urban Councils Act, and the Public Health Act.[52] An urban planner working for Dialogue on Shelter Trust observed that whereas in the past the council would unceremoniously demolish illegal residential structures, nowadays

> [i]t appears the city is now more methodical when it comes to evictions and demolitions hence their responses to urban informality are being guided by the RTCP Act. Now, they systematically secure all the relevant court rulings prior to effecting evictions.[53]

In addition to the RTPC Act, authorities have also relied on the Public Health Act to carry out and order evictions and demolitions. In particular, a Public Health Act's Sections 104, 105, 106, and 107, which all consider slums as a public nuisance, have been frequently invoked to legally support evictions and demolitions. Further, emphasizing how built-environment legislation has become instrumental in the execution of evictions, the city of Harare is reported to have pending 103 court cases, 11 cases executed, and secured 25 court rulings sanctioning evictions and demolitions but still awaiting execution.[54] These legal realities may mean that authorities in Harare have now largely shifted from carrying out arbitrary evictions to more systematically executed displacements through due process. In a majority of these scenarios, the informal settlements would have been established on the council's institutional sites, especially schools. A classic case is the Negidi housing cooperative, which has been illegally occupying a school site for three years in Budiriro 4, a high-density suburb in Harare. An eviction court order is still pending in the courts. These results reinforce the centrality of urban planning legislation in displacements.

---

49 Dialogue on Shelter Trust and Cities Alliance, *Housing and Land Strategies That Help the Urban Poor Fight Covid-19 Pandemic* (2021).
50 Dialogue on Shelter Trust (n 35).
51 Interview with Zimbabwe Homeless People's Federation community leader.
52 Interview with Dialogue on Shelter Trust official with urban planning experience.
53 City of Harare List of Eviction Court Cases.
54 Ibid.

World-Class City Visioning and Displacements in Harare

Another important finding from the study with implications on evictions and demolitions and, therefore, homelessness in the city of Harare relates to 'world-class city visioning' processes. As discussed earlier in this chapter, 'world-class city visioning' describes the quest to establish cities that have iconic architecture premised on the ideal of Global North cities. The study revealed that at the core of Harare's Strategic Plan 2012–2025 is 'city greening and beautification'.[55] Further to this, it also emerged that the city of Harare is guided by a strategic thrust known as 'Vision 2025', whose agenda is achieving a 'world-class city by 2025'.[56] Under the same vision, the study further revealed that Harare also imagines 'first-class service delivery' as a strategic priority area. This strengthens the argument regarding how Harare is preoccupied with attaining First World urban conditions in the city. This continued push towards world-class status evident in city pronouncements and strategic documents is meant to establish a competitive city that not only has tourism potential but also attracts global business investment. City-to-city twinning arrangements also appear to betray that proclivity towards referencing Western cities as ideal templates for city-making. Thus, any built-environment developments outside what constitutes the desired urban schema, in this case, the sister city from the Global North, are considered a spatial anathema that ought to be corrected through, at worst, demolitions and, at best, slum improvement. The city of Harare's website shows that the council has multiple twinning agreements with such cities as Munich in Germany, Nottingham in England, Winnipeg in Canada, and Columbus in the United States of America.[57] In the context of the Global South, there are collaboration initiatives with what may be perceived as model cities, and a classic case is the partnership arrangement with Kigali in Rwanda around what has been termed the 'Expanded Beautification Programme'.[58] These findings demonstrate how capital and tourism agendas help influence displacements, especially when set in the context of a series of evictions and demolitions at the Gunhill informal settlement located in the midst of the affluent Gunhill high-come suburb.[59]

The Commodification of the City and the Eviction Crisis in Harare

The study revealed how the notions of profit extraction and capital accumulation now dominate both the practice and conception of urban space in Harare. This essentially means that the city increasingly is being viewed as an investment vehicle that should maximize revenue and minimize costs. Presenting at a launch of the Harare Urban Renewal Programme in 2019, the then town clerk remarked:

> There is a lot of urban decay especially in the Central Business District which is driving out business to other investment centers, some outside the country. Our objective

---

55 City of Harare Strategic Plan 2012–2022 (City of Harare 2012).
56 City of Harare, *Vision 2025* (City of Harare 2022) <www.metropolis.org/sites/default/files/2022-02/harare-presentation.pdf> (accessed 1 September 2023).
57 See City of Harare website <www.hararecity.co.zw> (accessed 1 September 2023).
58 City of Harare Facebook Page (5 August 2019) <www.facebook.com/cohsunshinecity/photos/council-to-launch-expanded-beautification-programmestaff-reporterrwandan-ambassa/2425665244192509/> (accessed 1 September 2023).
59 Dialogue on Shelter Trust (n 35).

with this project is to return the city to its Sunshine City status as well as a gear up towards our vision of achieving a World Class City Status by 2025. A beautiful and well combed city attracts investors and tourists and is also boon for business. The Urban Renewal Programme will see council carrying out various initiatives such as the Mbare Renewal Project in partnership with Central government.[60]

Yet regardless of how desirable and noble this business-oriented agenda may be, there is a risk of translating this approach into an exclusionary project that precludes pro-poor considerations in urban management. A 'well-combed beautiful city' here, for instance, is understood as a city free from urban slums and other informal constructions that are thought to drive away investors. The current developments towards the north-west of Harare, where the proposed new US$500 million Cyber City will be built, also reinforces the centrality of tourism and business opportunities as the guiding urban planning logic. It emerged through the study that an iconic US$200 million new Parliament Building has been built in the same vicinity through a Chinese government grant.[61] The subsequent eviction threats for slums within and around the confines of the 'New City' location emphasize how profit and tourism interests supersede housing considerations for the urban poor. For instance, it was discovered that informal settlements such as Robrick, Lumader, and Chigomo have all been issued with eviction notices to pave way for the 'New City'.[62] The city of Harare is currently charging extortionate penalty fees for informal residential developments in high-density neighbourhoods as a pre-condition for regularization. One city of Harare policymaker stressed during a workshop that informal settlers have to accept the reality that an urban existence has costs tied to it. He further pointed out that those in informal settlements should be ready to pay US$2,000 as penalty for the council to activate the regularization process, or else, demolitions would be effected. This appears to demonstrate how the exchange value of the city has taken centre stage in Harare.

Homelessness in Zimbabwe: Harare Case Study – Discussion and Policy Pathways

The results in the preceding section indicate that the housing crisis in Harare continues to grow, as illustrated by the burgeoning numbers on official waiting lists and housing records. The study, however, also illustrated that official demand management tools also fail to capture the proliferation of slums in Harare as an expression of housing need. The built-environment legislation presented under the findings section of this chapter showed how it influences exclusionary urban practice stifling housing aspirations of the urban poor in Harare. An inclination towards profit and capital as an overarching planning philosophy informing urban practice in Harare has also been revealed through the results. The study examined the extent and nature of the housing crisis in Harare, and findings revealed that the quantum of demand continues to grow, highlighting an ever-expanding unmet

---

60 City of Harare Town Clerk's Speech on the official launch of the Urban Renewal Programme on the 30th of August 2019.
61 E. Ziwira and Z. Murwira, 'Iconic New Parliament Building Complete' *The Herald* (28 June 2022) <www.herald.co.zw/iconic-new-parly-building-complete/> (accessed 1 September 2023).
62 Interview (n 41).

need. While housing demand estimates have typically been understood in terms of council housing waiting lists, the study extended such conceptualization by bringing onto spotlight informal settlements as a clear articulation of the city's housing deficit, especially for low-income groups. This proliferation of informal settlements chimes with Lefebvre's theoretical postulations on informality as an expression of the urban poor's political interest to participate in urbanization processes. This finding matters, as it also has wider implications for cities other than Harare by providing potential policy pathways that enable local authorities, in particular, to comprehensively enumerate and capture citywide demand for housing products. Furthermore, documenting informal settlements as an integral component of understanding housing need also has scope for transforming policy responses, from exclusionary displacements to catalyzing participatory slum upgrades. However, even though citywide informal settlement profiling and enumeration processes help provide a fuller picture of housing need in the city, it is important to note that urban informality is inherently a contested terrain. That is, unless authorities are meaningfully involved and the requisite political buy-in secured, there is a tendency towards challenging the very existence and extent of informal settlements.

The study discovered that the notion of urban order has been a key defining philosophy guiding urban practice in Harare. In this instance, urban planning becomes the instrument by which this urban order is achieved and maintained. This means that any urban developments produced outside the agreed parameters of urban planning constitute a challenge to urban order and should, thus, be eliminated from the cityscape. Planning regulations help 'correct' these spatial disruptions to urban order through either prohibition or demolition orders. This reinforces the culpability of urban planning as a discipline that has contributed to displacements in Harare. This institutional appetite for a well-planned city resonates with the modernist urban planning theory's preoccupation with orderly cities. In the same vein, the blameworthiness of urban planning regarding deploying evictions in the pursuit of urban order which is emerging from the results echoes similar discoveries by Mbiba, Watson, and Kamete.[63] Watson, for instance, contends that planning systems are the central problem contributing to spatial exclusion.[64] Watson's study, however, appears not to consider the potential contribution of other built-environment disciplines, such as architecture and engineering, which might equally be said to be fixated on producing orderly cities. This means that the charges against urban planning should be approached with some degree of caution. As a matter of fact, it may actually be counterargued that what planners are simply doing is operationalizing existing legislation, whose formulation is well outside the purview of their responsibilities.

This academic contribution argues that urban practice in Harare betrays elitist, world-class visioning ideologies. Yet socio-economic realities in Harare depict deepening urban poverty expressed through informal settlements among other social manifestations. These results suggest that the pursuit of a world-class city agenda in Harare is inversely related to the pervasive poverty conditions in the city, forcing authorities to practice exclusionary programmes that artificially try to foist an untenable elitist reality. This modernistic inclination is often motivated by the need to create a city that is pushing towards either regional or global competitiveness. It may also be posited that

---

63 Mbiba (n 7); Watson (n 7); Kamete (n 33).
64 Watson (n 7).

world-class city visioning reflects an anti-poor agenda. In this regard, the prevalence of urban poverty in all its forms, including informality, is seen as an indictment of city authorities. The implications of such a finding from this study appear to point towards the need for reality-check interventions that help reconcile city policy responses with current experiences in Harare. City managers need to be persuaded to re-imagine an alternative urbanism separated from the idyllic Western urban planning algorithms. Urban social movements such as the local Slum Dwellers International affiliate in Harare, for instance, have since started similar pro-poor policy engagements that seek to address these contradictions.

The revelations emerging out of this study concerning the commodification of the city are instructive for understanding the housing crisis and homelessness in Harare. Essentially, this means prioritization of profit continues to frustrate land and housing struggles of the urban poor in the city. That is, land and housing-related financial obligations such as planning approval fees, inspection fees, and regularization end up disenfranchising the poor out of the city. The sum effect of this is that the city has become a very unaffordable place for vulnerable groups. These scholarly discoveries on commodification tendencies resonate with Harvey's 'right to the city' arguments challenging how capitalistic urbanization processes produce urban realities that emphasize the exchange value of the city at the expense of use value.[65] This raises the need for reorienting the city policies and programmes towards more inclusive trajectories, such as housing subsidies or levies exemptions. Current process focusing on the formulation of a 'pro-poor water policy' for the city of Harare could be discerned as a very significant starting point. However, it is also important to observe that what is interpreted as commodification propensity could also be a reflection of deepening hyperinflationary conditions in Harare.

Conclusion

Even though the dynamics behind homelessness and, thus, the housing crisis in Harare remain contested, this chapter has sought to illustrate the culpability of urban planning practice and the attendant built-environment legislation. This analytical contribution has argued that modernistic exclusionary planning and regulatory frameworks account for demolitions and displacements, which, in turn, disenfranchise the urban poor, frustrating their attempts to actualize their 'right to the city' as imagined by Lefebvre. Yet the study also revealed insurgent and subaltern spatial struggles by the urban poor through qualifying and quantifying extensive informal land, housing, and infrastructure self-provisioning in Harare. The chapter proceeded to posit that these informal spatial experiences have scope to inform pro-poor policy formulation, and SDI-led efforts were cited as potential pathways towards a more inclusive Harare. The magnitude and scope of informal settlements presented in this chapter have policy relevance and highlight the need for the city of Harare to acknowledge the reality of urban informality and institute appropriate frameworks that reorient local authorities towards trajectories of inclusion. While the chapter has constructed an argument exposing the liability of urban planning practice and legislation, there is scope for spotlighting opportunities for innovation and advancement of an inclusion agenda even within the confines of the same existing regulatory mechanisms in

---

65 Harvey (n 23).

Harare. Furthermore, the study has also provided insights that have the potential to inform housing practices in urban Zimbabwe more widely. This chapter closes by presenting the following key lessons that, the author argues, can be learned for housing policy in the city of Harare and across Zimbabwe more broadly:

- **Realigning demand management tools to suit changing forms of homelessness.** The chapter has shown that current demand management mechanisms are not sufficient. In short, the housing waiting list was demonstrated to be an inadequate tool, especially considering that few have confidence in it. Additionally, homelessness is no longer finding expression through tenancy. Instead, slums have become a serious testament to the housing crisis in cities. Yet councils continue to rely on housing waiting lists to quantify housing demand. The author, therefore, proposes the need for local authorities to embrace commissioning comprehensive data collection processes in low-income neighbourhoods, including in slums, to capture the full extent of housing demand and homelessness across Zimbabwe.
- **Forging collaborative research processes with housing social movements is key.** This contribution has amply illustrated the need for informal settlement data as a way of establishing the comprehensive housing demand in Harare. Yet it may also be true that currently councils may not have the requisite expertise and technical capacity to produce slum data. The chapter, thus, recommends further collaborative arrangements with housing social movements in the mould of partnerships that have been established between the Zimbabwean SDI affiliate and the city of Harare. Such a partnership has been used to co-produce informal settlement data, helping the city to leverage the expertise of local SDI affiliates in Zimbabwe.
- **Innovative municipal financing systems are critical for affordable cities.** This chapter has demonstrated that the exchange value of the city increasingly mediates the experience of urbanity. This commodification of the urban environment has turned out to be exclusionary and hence pushes the urban poor into homelessness. Innovative municipal financing instruments are, thus, required to make housing and infrastructure development more affordable. The city of Harare has piloted the Harare Slum Upgrading Finance Facility – a co-financed and co-governed funding mechanism that pools together upgrading resources from the city, urban poor groups, and civil society. This helps institute inclusive governance processes and has the potential to be replicated in other jurisdictions with some modifications.
- **Adaptive application of urban planning legislation is crucial.** The chapter has highlighted the limits of current urban planning laws in Harare. In their present form, the various pieces of urban planning legislation are evidently exclusionary, as supported by the proliferation of slums and endless arbitrary evictions and demolitions. While repealing elitist town planning laws is surely a protracted endeavour, councils are able and should be encouraged to flexibly apply these statutes in ways that allow specific experimentations around alternative inclusive housing and infrastructure options. Eventually, such flexible approaches may become rooted in co-designed urban upgrading pilots, for example, in the form of the Harare Slum Upgrading Programme, which has scope for catalyzing inclusive urban legislation reform processes.

PART V

Asia

22
HOMELESSNESS AND RESIDENTIAL POLICY IN JAPAN

Yoshihiro Okamoto

Introduction

After World War II (1945), Japanese society was hit by a housing shortage of 4.2 million housing units (30% of all units at the time) but the Korean War (1950–1953) triggered economic recovery and led to rapid economic growth from the 1960s onwards. Despite experiencing the oil shocks in the early 1970s and a recession in the 1980s, due to the strong yen, Japanese society remained on the cusp of economic growth until the 'bubble economy' peaked around 1990 and Japan entered economic stagnation under what has become known as the 'lost 30 years'. During the oil crises of the 1970s, the problem of people living on the streets was highlighted, but it was not really seen as a problem in light of the economic growth that followed. The economic recession after 1990, however, the Great Hanshin–Awaji earthquake in 1995, the 1997 Asian financial crisis, and other economic downturns again brought to the fore the issue of people living on the streets, in parks, and in station buildings.[1]

In 2002, the Law on Special Measures to Support the Independence of the Homeless (2002) (hereinafter referred to as the Homeless Independence Support Act) was enacted, reducing the number of people living on the streets from over 25,000 in 2003 to around 3,000 by 2022. At the same time, Japan's GDP per capita began falling, with Japan slipping from 2nd in the world in 2000 to 24th in 2020.[2] As economic conditions declined, residential

---

1 On homelessness and housing precarity in Japan, see, amongst others, Y. Okamoto, *The Creation Process of Residential Deprivation and Residential Welfare* (Toshindo 2022); M. Iwata, 'What Is the Problem of Homelessness in Japan? Conceptualisation, Research, and Policy Response (2021) 1(1) *International Journal on Homelessness* 2021, 98; Y. Hirayama and R. Ronald (eds), *Housing and Social Transition in Japan* (Routledge 2006); Y. Hirayama, *Temporary Housing and Postwar Japan* (Seidosha 2020); Y. Kakita, S. Yamada, H. Goto, D. Culhane and N Nakano, 'Homelessness and Housing Exclusion in Japan from an International Perspective' *16th European Research Conference on Homelessness* (23 September 2022) <www.feantsaresearch.org/public/user/Observatory/2022/16th_Research_Conference/Presentations/WS_16_Kakitaetal.pdf> (accessed 1 September 2023).
2 *International Monetary Fund World Economic Outlook* (2020); for more recent data, see <www.imf.org/en/Countries/JPN> (accessed 1 September 2023).

deprivation spread, and the number of people living in poor or precarious housing conditions increased. The number of households unable to achieve adequate housing increased due to the loss of housing following the Hanshin–Awaji earthquake (1995) and other severe disasters that have occurred frequently in the country. As housing is allocated through the housing market, it is difficult for people to secure housing if they cannot afford the housing costs and provide a guarantor. It is therefore believed that an increasing number of people are forced to live in poor living conditions and precarious housing, such as free and low-cost accommodation, internet cafés, comic book cafés, demolished houses, and 24-hour shops.[3]

This chapter therefore explores the relationship between homelessness and housing policy by examining the actual situation of people living on the streets and changes in homelessness policy in Japan. First, the definition of *homelessness* and changes in homelessness policy are considered to demonstrate that homelessness policy consists of measures in the welfare and housing sectors, and that the concept of 'employment independence' exists at its foundation. Secondly, through the results of the *National Survey of Homelessness* conducted by the government to date, the 'attributes of homeless people'[4] in Japan are clarified, and the challenges of homelessness policy are emphasized. Thirdly, changes in homelessness policy in recent years are examined from the welfare policy field and the housing policy field. Finally, the challenges of homelessness policy in Japan are analyzed from the perspective of 'housing security'.

Definition of Homelessness and Overview of Homelessness Policy in Japan

Definition of Homelessness

Homeless people in Japan are defined in the Homeless Independence Support Act 2002 under Article 2 as follows: ' "homeless" means a person who, without reason, carries out their daily life in urban parks, rivers, roads, station buildings or other facilities as his or her place of residence'.[5] When compared to the European Typology of Homelessness and Housing Exclusion (ETHOS), the Japanese definition of *homelessness* clearly falls into the 'roofless' category of the four conceptual categories that make up ETHOS and/or the operational category 'people living rough'. This makes the definition deployed by the Japanese government extremely narrow, calling into question the reliability of homelessness data for assessing the true scale of broader homelessness in the country.[6] Article 1 of the 2002 Act notes:

> The purpose of this Act is to contribute to the resolution of problems related to homelessness by clarifying the responsibilities of the national government, etc. with regard

---

3 A television documentary by Hiroaki Mizushima, 'Net Café Refugees and Poor Japan' (Broadcast by NTV started a major conversation in Japan on so-called 'internet café refugees', 2007).
4 In this chapter, the term 'homeless' is used to denote homelessness in the broadest sense. The term 'street' or 'street dweller' is used to refer to homelessness in a narrower sense. The use of the terms 'homeless' and 'living on the street' was distinguished as follows. *Homelessness*: a state of being unable to obtain housing and living in poor living conditions. Includes precarious residential conditions, such as living in dwellings. Living on the street: a situation where a person has no residence and lives in parks, streets, river beds, station buildings, etc.
5 See <https://elaws.e-gov.go.jp/document?lawid=414AC1000000105> (accessed 7 November 2023).
6 Iwata (n 1).

to support for the self-reliance of homeless persons and assistance in living to prevent them from becoming homeless, and by taking necessary measures in consideration of their human rights and with the understanding and cooperation of local communities.

The 2002 law additionally provides 'measures to support people in their daily lives to prevent them from becoming homeless' and those 'who may be forced to become homeless'. Japan's homelessness measures are targeted at 'homeless people with the will to be self-reliant'. Article 3 explains that the 'objectives of the measures to support the self-reliance of homeless persons' include 'preventing these persons from becoming homeless by securing employment opportunities for them, providing consultation and guidance on daily life, and other daily life support, mainly in areas where there are many persons who are likely to become homeless'.[7]

Overview of Homelessness Policy in Japan

Background to the Enactment of the Homeless Independence Support Act 2002

Against the backdrop of intensifying economic competition due to the economic stagnation and progress in economic globalization, many Japanese companies pursued a short-term profit and expenditure balance. It was difficult for companies to continue to employ young people who needed vocational training and middle-aged and older workers with higher salary levels, as they were not cost-effective. They therefore dismissed middle-aged and older employees and hired younger workers as temporary, precarious, low-paid labour. When it became clear that the bubble economy, which peaked in 1990, had entered its downturn (1992–1993), the cardboard houses lining the underpass about 300 metres from the west exit of Shinjuku Station began to attract public attention, and the homeless problem became a visible social issue.[8]

At the same time, *yoseba*, or open-air labour markets, were formed in large Japanese cities during periods of strong economic growth. *Yoseba* are gathering places featuring cheap accommodation, where day workers trade their labour with recruiters on a short-term, day-by-day basis. When the economy was good and demand for work was high, jobseekers could easily find work in *yoseba*. Prior to the 1990s, these yoseba-based workers were the main street dwellers. Since the 1990s, however, economic globalization has led to a variety of low-paid jobs, and the recruitment function of *yoseba* and the number of workers in *yoseba* has consequently declined. In addition, unemployment among middle-aged and older workers has become ubiquitous, so that street dwellers can now be seen in areas far from the *yoseba*. Life on the streets, which had not previously been seen by society in general, came to be recognized as a new social problem.[9]

In response to calls for more radical and effective action on homelessness, in February 1999, the Liaison Conference on the Homeless Problem was established and comprised central government departments, including the Cabinet Office for Domestic Policy, Ministry

---

7 See <https://elaws.e-gov.go.jp/document?lawid=414AC1000000105> (accessed 7 November 2023).
8 K. Kasai, 'The So-Called "Homeless" Problem: From Shinjuku, Tokyo' (1995) 8 *Yoseba* 5, Gendai Shokan, Japan Yoseba Society.
9 Tokyo Metropolitan Government, Planning and Deliberation Office, Research Department, *New Urban Problems and the Direction of Responses: On 'Street Life' Tokyo* (Tokyo Metropolitan Government 1995).

of Health and Welfare, Ministry of Labour, National Police Agency, Ministry of Construction, Ministry of Home Affairs, as well as representatives from the Tokyo Metropolitan Government, Yokohama City, Kawasaki City, Nagoya City, Osaka City, and Shinjuku Ward, Tokyo. The aim was to exchange views on the current homelessness problem and measures that could be taken to tackle it. In May 1999, the Liaison Conference on Homelessness published 'Immediate measures to deal with the homeless problem'.[10] It classified homeless people into three categories (those who are willing to work but are unemployed due to lack of work, those in need of medical and welfare assistance, and those who refuse to live in society) and set out specific directions for measures to combat homelessness, including: (1) establishment of a comprehensive consultation and self-reliance system; (2) stability of employment; (3) enhancement of healthcare; (4) securing housing for those in need; and (5) development of a safe and secure regional environment. In other words, the aim was to return those who had lost their place of employment and become homeless to the path of 'employment and self-reliance'. The policy was that homeless people who could not return to the 'work and independence' route would be supported via medical and welfare assistance. This policy has remained the backbone of homelessness policy in Japan ever since. In July 1999, the Ministry of Health and Welfare established the Study Group on Measures to Support the Independence of Homeless People, as the number of homeless people in Japan exceeded 20,000.[11] On 8 March 2000, the Japanese government compiled 'Measures to Support the Independence of the Homeless'[12] and published reports including 'The Current State of the Homeless Problem' and 'Issues to Promote the Independence of the Homeless'. In August 2002, the 'Homeless Independence Support Act' was enacted, originally with a ten-year time limit, but this was subsequently extended until 2027. Importantly, while the 2002 Act centred on 'homeless' people (and the Japanese government using the foreign loan-word 'homeless' at that time), the measures contained are not based on loss of home or anti-poverty but instead concerned with citizens' independence realized through employment.

Composition of Homelessness Policy

The Homeless Independence Support Act 2002 sets out the essential framework for homelessness policy in Japan, including conducting surveys to identify the actual situation and scale of homelessness, establishing a basic policy based on the results of the survey, and formulating a local implementation plan and a municipal implementation plan again based on the results of the survey. Since then, a cycle of surveys, formulation of basic policies, and of implementation plans has been carried out every four or five years.

The first National Survey on Homelessness was conducted in 2003, with an estimated number of 25,296 people living homeless. The second survey was conducted in 2007, with 18,564 people; the third in 2012, with 9,576 people; the fourth in 2016, with 6,235 people; and the fifth in 2021, with 3,824 people identified as living homeless. A 2023 survey conducted by the Ministry of Health, Labour, and Welfare of the number of homeless people in the country's parks and riverside areas found 3,065 homeless people.[13]

---

10 Liaison Conference on Homelessness (1996), 'Immediate Measures for the Homeless Problem Wages and Social Security' late June (1252) 40–44.
11 According to the Ministry of Health, Labour, and Welfare at the end of October 1999.
12 <www.mhlw.go.jp/www1/houdou/1203/h0308-1_16.html> (accessed 1 September 2023).
13 The study only explored parks and riverside areas, however, so the statistics do not capture the whole complete picture of homelessness in the country.

The Basic Policy on Supporting the Independence of Homeless People was formulated in 2003, 2008, 2013, and 2018. The basis of the policy is a system of 'employment independence' which aims to achieve economic independence through employment and 'independence through welfare response' (via the welfare office) if the person is unable to find work.

Measures to support the self-reliance of homeless people are stipulated in Article 3 of the Homeless Independence Support Act, which notes key objectives as being 'securing a stable place of employment', 'securing employment opportunities (by developing vocational skills)', 'securing a stable place to live (by moving into housing and providing support)', 'securing health and medical care (by providing health check-ups and medical care)', 'consultation and guidance on daily life', 'provision of temporary accommodation', 'livelihood protection', 'protection of the human rights of the homeless', and 'support for living in the community.' Specific provisions and interventions provided include 'consultation and guidance on daily life', 'temporary provision of accommodation', 'provision of goods necessary for daily life (to meet daily needs) and emergency assistance', 'livelihood protection', 'protection of the human rights of the homeless', and 'improvement of the living environment and securing the environment in the community'.

The operation of these specific measures to support the self-reliance of homeless people is best explained by reference to the approach in Japan's major cities. Nagoya City is used here an example. Figure 22.1 shows the basic structure of support for homeless people to become self-reliant by reference to the 4th Nagoya City Implementation Plan for Supporting the Independence of the Homeless Evaluation Report.[14] First, people living on the street are classified according to their potential for employment independence. The homeless are classified into three categories: (1) those who are willing to work but are unemployed; (2) those in need of medical, welfare, and other assistance; and (3) those who are judged as refusing to live in society. Specifically, homeless persons and persons who are at risk of being forced into homelessness are assessed through patrol activities, counselling, and consultation services. Homeless people categorized in category 1 will proceed along the path to employment independence, with the aim of securing employment opportunities. They are provided with accommodation and meals in temporary housing and emergency accommodation services (shelters). There, they are assessed for homelessness through lifestyle and health counselling, and a decision is made about the extent and location of support. Those who are classified as capable of working independently receive accommodation and meals at the self-support project, while receiving advice on living, health, debt, and other issues. In parallel, public housing and residential support councils are used to secure housing. To secure employment opportunities, they receive skills training, work experience training, and counselling. Once employment opportunities and housing have been secured, the person will achieve employment independence, but to ensure this, follow-up services are implemented to check employment status and provide employment guidance and lifestyle support as necessary. Those in category 2, who are judged to be in need of medical, welfare, or other assistance, live on social welfare and with other therapeutic measures. This decision is made through outreach and consultation services, temporary protection services, and self-reliance counselling services. This route is linked to existing welfare measures. Homeless people in category 3 are those who have either rejected homelessness assistance or are judged to be refusing to live in society. The reasons for this are age, physical

---

14 Study Group on the Evaluation of the Homeless Implementation Plan, *Evaluation Report of the 'Third Phase of the Implementation Plan on Supporting the Independence of the Homeless in Nagoya City'* (2018).

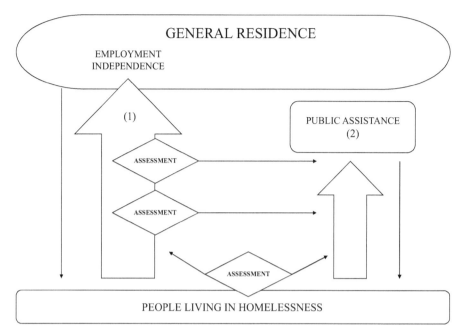

Figure 22.1 Basic homelessness self-reliance support scheme structure.
Source: Author's own presentation.

condition or health problems that make it unlikely that they will be able to find employment opportunities, or the accommodation provided being multi-bedded or having strict rules and residence conditions. Homeless people in category 3 do not receive homeless services from central or local governments. However local governments do, nevertheless, provide basic, outreach services for rough sleepers. This means that, generally, the most that people in category 3 will receive are outreach services provided by social workers who visit rough sleeping sites. NGOs working in the area of rough sleeping may also provide food and drink at the roadside or in parks.

Changes in the Demographics of Homeless People in Japan

Background to Life on the Street

Based on the results of the *National Surveys on Homelessness (Survey of Living Conditions)* conducted by the Ministry of Health, Labour, and Welfare of Japan, this section of the chapter tracks the changes in the attributes of people living on the street in Japan. The results of the surveys reflect and reveal the effect of measures implemented to support the self-reliance of homeless people. Using this survey data, consideration is given to the reasons for living on the street, the occupation of people before becoming homeless, the characteristics/demographics of the homeless, employment status, and homeless people's expectations for the future.

Reasons for Living on the Street

Table 22.1 shows the composition of reasons for homelessness by survey year. The top five reasons for homelessness were almost exclusively connected to loss of employment opportunities. This was followed by reasons connected to rent arrears. The loss of employment opportunities made it difficult to earn an income and led to an inability to maintain housing. The reasons for loss of employment opportunities include direct loss of employment opportunities, such as 'bankruptcy or unemployment'; loss of physical functions, such as 'illness, injury, or old age'; and 'relationship problems' in the workplace that prevent maintaining a working environment. However, the proportion has gradually declined, falling below 50% in 2021. Reasons related to physical function, such as 'illness, injury, or old age', are on a downward trend but still account for around one in seven. The proportion of 'loss of employment opportunities' citing 'relationship problems' is increasing, which contrasts sharply with the decline in the proportion for 'physical function'.

The main reasons given for living on the street related to housing included 'leaving home due to debt collection', 'could no longer pay rent on the flat', 'left accommodation due to expiry of contract', 'could no longer pay hotel or accommodation fees', 'evicted due to foreclosure', 'left hospital or institution and have no place to stay'. The total percentage citing these reasons fell from around 30% up to 2012 to around 25% between 2016 and 2021. Of these, economic reasons such as rent arrears and foreclosure accounted for around 80% of the responses relating to housing, making it easy for those involved to believe that they would not have ended up living on the streets if only they had improved their financial circumstances.

While the majority of reasons for living on the street related to loss of employment opportunities, one-third of the reasons for living on the street were 'illness, injury, or old age' and 'relationship problems', which are not simple problems that can be solved even if employment opportunities are available.

Table 22.1 Reasons for living on the street

Reasons for living on the street	2003	2007	2012	2016	2021
Bankruptcy/unemployment	32.9%	26.6%	27.1%	26.1%	22.9%
Job losses	35.6%	31.4%	34.0%	26.8%	24.5%
Sick, injured, or too old to work	18.8%	21.0%	19.8%	16.9%	14.3%
Quit their jobs due to poor working conditions	–	5.0%	6.1%	5.0%	5.5 %
Quit job because of a bad relationship	–	15.0%	15.4%	17.1%	18.9%
Decrease in work for reasons other than those listed	–	2.3%	3.0%	1.8%	1.6%
Left home due to debt collection	4.3%	6.5%	4.3%	3.3%	3.0%
Can no longer afford to pay rent on flats, etc.	15.2%	12.9%	16.9%	11.0%	13.2%
Left accommodation at the end of the contract period	–	2.4%	3.1%	1.8%	2.7%

(*Continued*)

Table 22.1 (Continued)

Reasons for living on the street	2003	2007	2012	2016	2021
Can no longer pay for hotels and accommodation	8.2%	5.1%	4.8%	4.2%	5.3%
Evicted by foreclosure	0.6%	0.7%	0.1%	0.4%	1.1%
Discharged from hospital or institution and have nowhere to stay	1.9%	2.4%	2.7%	1.7%	1.5%
Domestic disputes	7.4%	7.5%	7.2%	7.4%	Separation and bereavement (8.5%) 7.9%
Drinking alcohol (sake) or gambling	5.8%	6.8%	7.6%	8.9%	6.9%
Other	19.3%	17.8%	19.6%	16.7%	21.2%

Source: The author, using raw data from Ministry of Health, Labour and Welfare, *Results of the National Survey on the Actual Situation of Homeless People (Survey of Actual Living Conditions)*.[15]

Occupation Immediately Before Living on the Street

The availability of work opportunities depends on economic trends, but informal, non-regular employees are more likely to be dismissed than formal, regular employees. A worker's employment status, therefore, has a significant impact on the degree of stability in his or her life. Although informal employment is increasing in Japanese society in general (now accounting for around 40%), looking at the employee status (Table 22.2) immediately before becoming homeless, the proportion of regular employment such as 'full-time or permanent employee' is consistently around 40%, reaching 45.8% in 2021. The fact that the proportion of homeless people in full-time employment remains in the 40% range is low compared to the proportion of workers in full-time employment overall (60%), indicating that informal workers with precarious employee status are more likely to end up on the street. In 2021, the year of the coronavirus pandemic, even workers in formal employment were more likely to lose their job opportunities and end up on the street than in other survey years. Regularly employed workers were also at increased risk of ending up on the street.

Table 22.3 shows that the occupations immediately prior to people becoming homeless were concentrated in the construction sector (a peak of 55.2% in 2003), which is a more precarious form of employment than white-collar jobs. The proportion gradually declined, reaching 36.3% in 2021, partly due to the coronavirus pandemic. According to a report by the Ministry of Health, Labour, and Welfare (Ministry of Health, Labour, and Welfare, *Information on the impact on employment caused by new coronavirus infection*), the coronavirus disaster caused workers in the accommodation, restaurant, wholesale and retail, labour dispatch, road passenger transport, manufacturing, service, and entertainment industries to lose their jobs. It is assumed that the proportion of 'construction and mining workers' has decreased in the official surveys due to the fact that they have ended up living on the streets.

---

15 See <www.mhlw.go.jp/toukei/list/64-15.html> (accessed 7 November 2023).

Table 22.2 Employee status immediately before living on the street

Immediate previous employee position	2003	2007	2012	2016	2021
Full-time (permanent)	39.8%	43.2%	42.0%	40.4%	45.8%
Temporary/part-time/daily	36.1%	26.2%	25.8%	26.7%	20.7%

Source: The author, using raw data from Ministry of Health, Labour, and Welfare, *Results of the National Survey on the Actual Situation of Homeless People (Survey on the Actual Situation of Living Conditions).*[16]

Table 22.3 Immediate previous occupation

Immediate previous occupation	2003	2007	2012	2016	2021
Construction and mining workers	55.2% (construction)	29.5% (work) 18.3% (skills)	46.2%	48.2%	36.3%
Production process workers	10.5% (manufacturing sector–related)	12.2%	14.5%	13.0%	12.9%

Source: The author, using raw data from Ministry of Health, Labour, and Welfare, *Results of the National Survey on the Actual Situation of Homeless People (Survey of Actual Living Conditions).*[17]

Table 22.4 Immediate previous residence

Last residence	2003	2007	2012	2016	2021
Own house	8.1%	8.2%	9.1%	9.0%	11.3%
Privately rented housing	37.5%	38.0%	41.1%	39.5%	45.7%
Public housing	3.2%	3.0%	1.8%	1.8%	2.3%
Public subsidized housing		0.6%	0.6%	1.0%	0.6%
Dormitories and company housing	13.8%	17.3%	17.4%	17.3%	15.7%
Relatives' and acquaintances' homes	3.1%	4.0%	5.3%	4.8%	5.3%
Live-in accommodation	3.5%	3.3%	2.8%	3.0%	2.7%
Catering and workers' accommodation	13.9%	13.5%	13.2%	12.5%	6.3%
Simple lodging	11.8%	7.9%	5.9%	6.6%	4.9%
Business hotels, capsule hotels, saunas, and 24-hour shops	1.9%	1.7%	2.0%	2.3%	1.6% 1.1% (24-hour shops)
Hospital	0.7%	0.2%	0.0%	0.1%	-
Rehabilitation facilities	0.6%	0.2%	0.3%	0.4%	0.5%

(*Continued*)

16 Ibid.
17 Ibid.

Table 22.4 (Continued)

Last residence	2003	2007	2012	2016	2021
Self-support centres	-	0.4%	0.2%	0.0%	0.1%
Other	1.9%	1.6%	0.5%	1.7%	2.1%

Source: The author, using raw data from Ministry of Health, Labour, and Welfare, *Results of the National Survey on the Actual Situation of Homeless People (Survey of Actual Living Conditions)*.[18]

The increasing trend of citizens moving from stable living to living on the street is also reflected in the data. As shown in Table 22.4, private rented accommodation was the most common type of housing immediately prior to the transition to living on the street, accounting for between the high 30% and mid 40% ranges, reaching 45.7% in 2021. The share of owner-occupied dwellings (8.1% (2003) and 11.3% (2021)) is also gradually increasing. Other types of residences have halved, including the share of 'catering/worker dormitories' (13.9% (2003), 6.3% (2021)) and 'simple lodging facilities' (11.8% (2003), 4.9% (2021)), indicating a marked decrease in the number of work-based residences. In particular, in 2021, the availability of catering and workers' accommodation is thought to have decreased due to the reduction in the number of construction projects as a result of the coronavirus pandemic.

Characteristics of People Living on the Street

Homeless people in Japan are perceived as middle-aged and elderly single men, but in fact, the demographics of homeless people is changing due to support measures related to assisting homeless people to become self-reliant.

Duration of Homelessness, Age, and Gender

The ageing of people living on the streets and the lengthening of the period of time spent on the streets are shown in the trends in the results of the *National Survey on the State of Homelessness*. The proportion of people who have been on the streets for 'more than 10 years' increased from 15.6% in 2007 to 27.0% in 2012, 34.6% in 2016, and 40.0% in 2021, indicating an increase in homelessness duration.

As Table 22.5 shows, the average age of homeless people continues to rise from 55.9 in 2003 to over 60 in 2016 and reached 63.6 in 2021. The proportion of elderly people has also increased, with the proportion of people aged 65–69 increasing from 10.5% in 2003 to 20% in 2021, and the proportion of people aged 70 and over increasing from 4.6% in 2003 to 34.4% in 2021. From the increase in the average age of people living on the street, the increase in the number of elderly people, and the decrease in the number of homeless people overall, it can be inferred that it is becoming ever more difficult for older people to escape homelessness. The ratio of job vacancies to applicants is consistently shown to be higher for younger people than for older people, which may account for this trend in increasing elder homelessness.

On the other hand, as Table 22.6 shows, with regard to gender, the composition is consistently around 95% men and around 4% women.

18 Ibid.

Table 22.5 Age distribution of homeless people

Age distribution	2003	2007	2012	2016	2021
65–69 years	10.5%	13.6%	16.6%	23.1%	20.0%
70 years and over	4.6%	7.4%	12.9%	19.7%	34.4%
Average age	55.9 years	57.5 years	59.3 years	61.5 years	63.6 years

Source: The author, using raw data from Ministry of Health, Labour and Welfare, *Results of the National Survey on the Actual Situation of Homeless People (Survey on the Actual Living Conditions)*.[19]

Table 22.6 Gender of homeless people

Gender	2003	2007	2012	2016	2021
Men	95.2%	96.4%	95.5%	96.2%	95.8
Women	4.8%	3.6%	4.5%	3.8%	4.2%

Source: Ministry of Health, Labour, and Welfare, *Results of the National Survey on the Actual Situation of Homeless People (Survey of Actual Living Conditions)*.[20]

Employment Status

It is generally perceived that people living on the street are not currently working, cannot work, or do not work, but the majority of people living on the street are actually employed, because the concept of 'employment independence' has permeated the general public consciousness. Many homeless people are walking the city collecting cardboard boxes, empty cans, and other waste materials, which are then sold to waste collectors (see Table 22.7). The purchase price of empty cans and cardboard is, however, low (for example, 70 350 ml aluminium cans weighing about 1 kg are purchased for 50–200 yen).[21] The homeless must collect large quantities of cans and boxes to sustain their existence.

Future Outlook and Expectations

The future prospects and expectation of the homeless are thought to reflect the environment created by homelessness policies. According to interview responses recorded in the Ministry of Health, Labour, and Welfare, *Results of the National Survey on the Actual Situation of Homeless People*,[22] almost half (49.7%, 2003) of the respondents at the time of the first survey said they wanted to 'get a proper job and work', which is close to the homelessness policy goal. The positive ambition/intention to 'live in a flat, find a job, and support [one]self' (the objective of support for homeless people to become self-sufficient, etc.) has declined with each successive survey: 35.9% (2007), 26.3% (2012), 21.7%

---

19 Ibid.
20 Ibid.
21 According to the website of Mitsui Metal Ltd, viewed 26 April 2023.
22 See <www.mhlw.go.jp/toukei/list/64-15.html> (accessed 7 November 2023).

Table 22.7 Employment status of the homeless

Employment status	2003	2007	2012	2016	2021
Percentage of employed homeless people	64.7%	70.4%	60.4%	55.6%	48.9%
Percentage of homeless people collecting scrap metal	73.3%	75.5%	77.7%	70.8%	66.4%
Average monthly salary	-	Approx. 40,000	Approx. 35,000	Approx. 38,000	Approx. 58,000

Source: The author, using raw data from Ministry of Health, Labour, and Welfare, *Results of the National Survey on the Actual Situation of Homeless People (Survey of Actual Living Conditions)*.[23]

(2016), and 17.5% (2021). On the other hand, 'I want to find light work while receiving welfare support in a flat' remained almost constant at 11.9% (2012), 12.8% (2016), and 12.0% (2021). 'I want to live on welfare because I cannot find a job' also remained relatively stable at 8.6% (2003), 10.8% (2007), 11.2% (2012), 10.1% (2016), and 7.6% (2021). The perception of accepting the current situation, that life in the future will be 'just as it is', has increased year by year: 13.1% (2003), 18.4% (2007), 30.5% (2012), 35.3% (2016), and 40.9% (2021). From these responses on future prospects, it can be inferred that the likelihood of finding employment among homeless declines with age and that homeless people are increasingly giving up on achieving 'employment independence'.

Structural Changes in Homelessness Prevention

As homelessness, in the narrow sense of the term, decreases, measures to support people who are at risk of homelessness and to prevent those who have exited homelessness from returning to homelessness are attracting attention as a solution to the homelessness problem. In Japan, there are measures under the jurisdiction of the Ministry of Health, Labour, and Welfare (MHLW) to support employment and livelihoods, and the Ministry of Land, Infrastructure, Transport, and Tourism (MLITT) also has policies to secure and maintain housing before homelessness occurs (see [3] and [4] on Figure 22.2). MHLW has enacted the Law for Supporting the Independence of the Needy (2013), which provides advance support to those who are at risk of becoming homeless and thus brings preventive action into the remit of initiatives combatting homelessness. It provides direct rent subsidies to those with housing problems. The benefit is granted for a period of three months. There are strict eligibility requirements, including that recipients are limited to those who have become unemployed, are actively seeking employment, and have registered at a public employment centre. It is not, therefore, a universal housing allowance system but again based on employment status. In the housing sector, the Law on the Promotion of the Supply of Rental Housing for People

23 n 19.

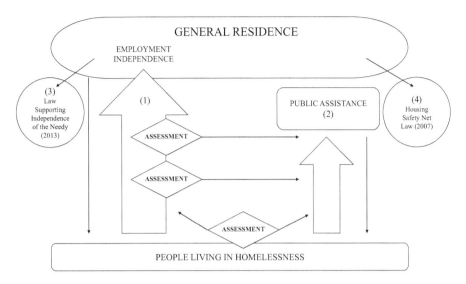

Figure 22.2 Expanded homelessness prevention.
Source: Author's own presentation.

in Need of Housing Security (hereinafter referred to as the Housing Safety Net Law) (2007) was enacted as a measure by MLITT. This was in response to concerns that the elderly, low-income earners, foreigners, women, and households with children were being noticeably and particularly excluded from the housing market and becoming homeless because they could not secure housing.

New Measures and Challenges in the Employment and Welfare Sectors

Preventing homelessness requires support for those most at risk of losing their housing due to lower or falling incomes and increased expenditure. Through repeated amendments to the Law for Securing the Proper Operation of Worker Dispatching Undertakings and Protection of Dispatched Workers, enacted in 1985, the system of dispatching workers with advanced vocational/occupational skills has been replaced with one in which general workers are dispatched.[24] Unstable and temporary employment proliferated. As a result, the loss or reduction of employment opportunities has led to a decline in income and an increase in the number of people losing their homes. Possible countermeasures include temporary housing cost supplementation, the development of vocational skills that provide employment, and the introduction of work placements. The increase in household consumption is thought to be due to difficulties in managing household finances as well as behaviours linked to gambling, drugs, and alcohol.

The Law for Supporting the Independence of the Needy was enacted in 2013 as a project to support those who are at risk of falling into homelessness, and under this law, the

---

24 Y. Mizuno, 'Dispatch Labour in Japan' (2012) 4(2) *Social Policy* 105.

Self-Reliance Counselling and Support Services for the Indigent, Housing Security Benefit for the Needy, and Temporary Living Support Services for the Needy have begun to be implemented. The number of new consultations for self-reliance counselling for the needy has more than tripled, from 248,398 in 2019 to 786,163 in 2020, due to the coronavirus disaster. The number one consultation topic, regardless of gender, was 'financial hardship', while for those aged 20 and over, the second most common concern was 'housing insecurity'. The number of applications for 'Housing Security Benefit' rose dramatically from 4,270 in 2019 to 153,007 in 2020, while the number of benefit decisions rose from 3,972 in 2019 to 134,946 in 2020, an almost 34-fold increase. Another key scheme is the Temporary Livelihood Support for the Needy project, which provides accommodation, clothing, and food for a certain period of time to those who do not have a home or are in unstable forms of housing, such as living in internet cafés. It also provides support for self-reliance, such as employment support.[25]

New Measures and Challenges in the Housing Policy Sector

Need for Housing Safety Net Schemes

An increasing number of people are finding it difficult to secure housing due to ageing and other demographic changes. Key factors are the lack of suitable housing stock and exclusion from the housing market. The first is the decline in low-rent housing. The *Housing and Land Statistics Survey* shows that the number of rented houses with a rent of less than 40,000 yen was 7,787,000 in 1993, accounting for 49.9% of all rented houses, but by 2018, this had fallen to 5,336,600, or 28.0%. Public housing has also fallen from 2,183,000 units in 2003 to 1,922,000 units in 2018 and salaried or issued housing has fallen from 2,051,000 units in 1993 to 1,100,000 units in 2018.

Secondly, there is a lack of housing stock suitable for habitation. Barrier-free access to stairs, steps, and elevators in buildings to which people with disabilities and the elderly are relocated is essential if they are forced to move out of their original home, but more than 95% of rental housing is not barrier-free,[26] making finding barrier-free accommodation increasingly difficult. Furthermore, visits to clinics and hospitals for treatment are essential on a daily basis for the elderly and disabled. In addition, the elderly need shopping streets and other facilities in easily accessible locations for their daily needs but finding barrier-free housing in such locations is extremely challenging.

Thirdly, there is the issue of the elderly, disabled people (including the mentally or mentally disabled as well as the physically disabled), single-parent families, child-rearing households, foreign nationals, and people with low income who are excluded from the private rental housing market and thus from secure housing. The reason for this exclusion is landlords' fears such as the negative impact of these occupants on rental housing management. Landlords' concerns include the inability to immediately detect the death of an elderly resident and the property becoming a crime scene, difficulties in disposing of leftover items, accidents and fires due to the

---

25 On the Temporary Livelihood Support for the Needy project see < (accessed>www.mhlw.go.jp/stf/seisaku-nitsuite/bunya/0000073432.html> (accessed 21 November 2023)
26 According to data provided by Ministry of Land, Infrastructure, and Transport, *2020 Housing Economy Related Data* (2020).

residents' physical disabilities, as well as conflicts with neighbouring residents. Other anxieties are that foreign nationals will not assimilate into the neighbourhood's lifestyle and waste collection and disposal issues due to differences in language and customs and, finally, concerns of rent arrears due to low incomes. Furthermore, the demand from lenders that a guarantor is provided, serves as an obstacle to securing housing for needy people, for whom such guarantor relationships and connections may be difficult to source.

Measures in the Housing Policy Area

The Basic Act on Housing and Living Conditions (2006) was enacted with a view to maintaining stable residence conditions for those people living in housing. Article 6 of the Act provides for the need to 'ensure stable housing', and Article 14 stipulates the implementation of 'the supply of necessary housing'. In response to these provisions, the Housing Safety Net Law was enacted in 2007, and the law was amended in 2017. This law is aimed at 'those with difficulty in securing housing', which is defined as follows: (1) low-income earners, (2) disaster victims,[27] (3) the elderly, (4) those with disabilities, and (5) households in which there are dependent children. In order to achieve this ambition, the law implemented a range of initiatives, including (1) a registration system for private rental housing that actively accepts tenants from the target groups noted earlier (this group is traditionally locked out of such housing, as explored previously due to landlords' concerns); (2) financial support for registered housing to upgrade their accommodation and to offer reduced rents; (3) matching those in the target groups with private rental housing. Furthermore, in view of the fact that a contract for rented housing cannot be concluded without a guarantor being able to be presented, guarantee companies are now used to act on behalf of the guarantor. In addition, organizations that provide housing support to help people realize stable accommodation are officially registered as housing support corporations. The hope is that landlords' concerns will be allayed with the involvement of these support corporations. In addition, 'Residential Support Councils' have been established in most prefectures and major cities to ensure the appropriate distribution of housing and residential resources are made available and to match those 'with difficulty securing housing' with housing. A critique of these housing policy measures is offered in the next section as the chapter explores these and wider challenges for housing and homelessness policy in Japan.

Challenges for Housing and Homelessness Policy in Japan

Japan's housing and homelessness policies must be seen in the specific context of the country and its past. These policies, as this chapter has shown, emphasize the need for greater inter sectoral coordination and housing security. As has been discussed, key challenges for Japan are, therefore, the ageing of its population, those giving up on or being unable to realize employment independence (which is so prominent in the country's approach to tackling housing and homelessness measures), and the lack of accommodation for those in 'difficulty of securing housing'.

In relation to the Housing Safety Net Law explored earlier, there are limitations and ongoing issues. First, the measures involve the promotion of the supply of rental housing to

---

27 Within three years of the disaster having taken place.

persons in need of housing security, not only through new construction, but also through the use of vacant housing. However, the promotion of the supply of rental housing has not sufficiently considered the relationship with residential life, and even if people with housing security needs are able to live in safety-net housing, it is difficult for them to realize their housing needs, as there is no connection made with medical institutions, purchasing facilities, social and friendship networks, and acquaintances, and residential support necessary for citizens to succeed in daily life. Secondly, there are only relatively few safety-net registered houses, which do not cover all areas, where people with housing needs can live. Thirdly, the scheme is heavily landlord-orientated, and the registered houses that do exist do not necessarily accommodate all people with housing needs. Landlords involved in the scheme do not always accept tenants from all five identified groups noted in the previous section. They are able to select which tenants to engage with, and many choose the elderly as they are perceived as generally less-problematic tenants. Fourthly, the Safety Net scheme does not provide direct housing allowance to tenants, but instead, it is provided in the manner of subsidies to landlords for reduced rent. Fifthly, many ordinary landlords in the Japanese housing market are not involved in the scheme,[28] and finally, much of the provided housing is shared housing, meaning, many dilapidated boarding houses and empty properties are renovated under the scheme. The result is that tenants often reside in shared, group homes as opposed to independent residences.[29]

More broadly, the need for inter-sectoral coordination is an issue between legal systems, from homelessness prevention measures to housing policy. The Homeless Independence Support Act 2002 targets the 'homeless' and those who are at risk of becoming 'homeless' but mainly targets 'homeless people'. Those who have the potential to work and become self-supporting are given the opportunity to work and become self-supporting, while those who do not have the potential to work and become self-supporting are given 'welfare' under the Public Assistance Act (1950) to live independently. In doing so, Article 4 stipulates that it is 'a requirement that persons in need utilise their available assets, abilities and all other things for the maintenance of their minimum standard of living'. On the other hand, in the housing sector, the Basic Act on Housing and Living Conditions (2006) has been established to 'comprehensively and systematically promote measures to ensure stability and promote the improvement of housing and living conditions' (Article 1). In particular, the Act covers 'ensuring the stability of housing for low-income earners, disaster victims, the elderly, families raising children and other persons who require special attention in securing housing' (Article 6). This law is based on the premise that people are already established in housing and does not cover those who have lost their homes.

Of the other measures that exist to provide housing and homelessness support, as explored in this chapter, there are key challenges. First, only those with very limited living and residential conditions are eligible for support; otherwise, they would have to choose to live in poor living conditions or in precarious housing. Secondly, there is a need for coordination housing and residential support. The transition from homelessness to shelter and then to employment independence (living in a flat and working) is the basis of homelessness support measures in Japan. Once employment is obtained and housing is established, the maintenance of the residence is, however, left to the person concerned. Even though there are visits from follow-up services,

---

28 Hirayama (n 1) 250–252.
29 Ibid.

there is no link with the residential sector to provide housing in a place where former street dwellers do not have to feel lonely and isolated. Adequate living space is not guaranteed, making it difficult for the elderly and other homeless people to find a safe place to live. For example, sheltered accommodation is multi-bed and does not ensure privacy for residents. Adequate facilities are not provided, the capacity of old people's homes is low, and it takes several years to be admitted to a special nursing home even if one applies for admission.[30]

Furthermore, as already mentioned, in the private rental housing market, people with housing security needs are excluded from the market due to requirements such as guarantors and are forced to choose between live-in work that leads to unstable housing or irregular housing with inappropriate living conditions.[31]

'Housing security' and 'employment independence' are mutually complementary, and thus a lack of employment independence inhibits housing security. Without appropriate employment, this leads to housing difficulties. There are three challenges to the 'employment independence' mechanism. The first issue is the challenge of making 'employment independence' a social norm. Article 25 of the Constitution of Japan provides for the right of citizens to lead a healthy and cultural life, and it is the responsibility of the government to ensure the environment and conditions for such a life. Generally, the age at which people can work is set, and pre-work (children) and post-retirement elderly people cannot work. Therefore, the government has an obligation to guarantee their housing before work, after retirement, or if they are unable to work. 'Employment independence' makes it harder to recognize this. The realization of housing based on employment status alone is therefore only possible for a very limited period of life.

Secondly, employment is affected by work status and household status. Non-regular or informal employment is not included in social security schemes such as health insurance. Non-regular employees have to shoulder larger financial burdens, such as healthcare, and their households have less leeway and financial headroom from which to fund their housing. In the first place, it is difficult for non-regular employees to take out mortgages, and in any event, due to high house prices, the term of a Japanese mortgage is longer than 30 years, and it is difficult to imagine that they will continue to earn a stable income during that period. Non-regular employees are more exposed to lower incomes and the risk of redundancy. In Japan, where there is no general housing subsidy, declining incomes are also likely to result in mortgage default, bankruptcy, and rent arrears.

Employment status is affected by reduced capacity to work due to illness, injury, or disability, or leaving work or working shorter hours to care for a parent, spouse, or other family member. Children may not be able to complete their schoolwork due to caregiving and may not be able to find a job that provides sufficient income. Mechanisms are needed to ensure adequate housing regardless of income.

A third challenge is demographic and industrial structural changes. After retirement, many will have no income and will support themselves on savings and pension benefits. If

---

30 According to the Institute for Healthcare Economics, *Research on the Actual Situation of Applications for Admission in Special Nursing Homes for the Elderly*, there were 3.4 times as many applicants for admission than there were places available.

31 For example, 'At Least 4 Tenants Killed in Fire at Kobe Apartments for the Needy' *The Asahi Shimbun* (23 January 2023) <www.asahi.com/ajw/articles/14821400> (accessed 1 September 2023).

they cannot pay off their mortgages before retirement, they will have to give up on owning a home and will be forced to live in rented accommodation.

In the past, it was common for elderly people to live with their eldest child's household, but with the increasing sophistication of industry and the expanding global scope of corporate activities, it has become rare for the younger generation to live in the same area as their parents. As a result, it has become common for elderly couples and single people to live alone, both in rural and in urban areas. A major challenge in rural areas is to support the livelihoods of couples and elderly people living alone, while in urban areas, it is a major challenge to support the housing of elderly people more generally.[32]

The various changes in ways of working and lifestyles as described previously have weakened the mechanisms for sustained stable employment. Thus, in large part, the mechanism of 'employment independence' as a means of ensuring support housing has ceased to function. This has created conditions conducive to the proliferation of homelessness in Japan beyond the narrow definition of *rooflessness* but in the broadest sense of the term.

Conclusion

This chapter has examined the issue of homelessness and housing policy in Japan from the perspective of 'housing security' and, in so doing, has identified the following issues.

First, because 'employment independence' is the basis of homelessness measures, many homeless people are older people who have difficulty finding work, and many have given up on realising employment independence altogether.

Secondly, the types of people at risk of being forced into homelessness have diversified, increasing the need for preventative support.

Thirdly, Japanese housing policy is divided into two systems: employment and welfare and living in housing. The former does not consider the issue of securing housing as a given and implements measures focusing mainly on the acquisition of employment, with welfare benefits as a secondary consideration. The latter is based on the premise of living in a house and does not target those who do not live in housing or those who will not be able to live in housing. Therefore, comprehensive housing policies have not been developed for everyone, from those living on the street and those who are no longer able to live in housing to those living in poor living conditions.

Fourthly, due to changes in employment practices and demographics, it is difficult to maintain employment, and people are easily forced to live on the street or in precarious accommodation in poor living conditions. These informal and poor living conditions become home for those excluded from the housing market and not living in formal facilities, such as foreign nationals, low-income earners, single-mother households, people with disabilities, and the elderly.

Ultimately, Japan's housing system is centred on employment independence and requires continued stable employment and income security. Looking to the future, housing must be guaranteed to prevent vulnerable people, who have lost these two conditions, from falling into homelessness.

---

32 On urban poverty and social exclusion, see K. Yamaguchi and H. Aoki (eds), *Urban Poverty in the Midst of Globalisation* (Minerva Shobo 2020).

23

'POSITIVE NON-POLICY': HOMELESS SERVICES AND TRANSITIONAL REHOUSING INITIATIVES IN HONG KONG AND MALAYSIA

Geerhardt Kornatowski and Constance Ching

Introduction

The government has classified certain locations to be unfit for living.... Sarcastically, it is quite true. The rental rate for per square feet of the sub-divided flats paid by the grassroots are even higher than the rent of the luxury mansions. However, the grassroots people still cannot find places that are 'suitable for living'. It is no wonder that the population of homeless people has been rising in recent years. They can be seen sleeping on the streets, at internet cafes and twenty-four hours fast food shops.[1]

This chapter provides an overview of homeless services in the Hong Kong Special Administrative Region (HKSAR) and in brief reference to Malaysia. By analogy with Hong Kong's long-standing economic ideology of 'positive non-intervention', in which the government 'weighs up carefully the arguments for and against an act of intervention . . . and . . . comes to a positive decision as to where the balance of advantages lies',[2] we propose the conceptual framework of 'positive non-policy' to guide the review. Such a framework is helpful because both the HKSAR and Malaysia do not have (and do not wish to have) a legislative framework to guide comprehensive homeless policy – one that could be used to mandate government responsibilities and officially recognize the rights of citizens in this regard. However, this does not mean that there is no policy at all, but it does mean that the role of the voluntary sector (i.e. NGOs and charities) is crucial to the provision of any form of service.

For practical reasons, we will start by looking at the Hong Kong case in detail. Over the past 20 years, as homelessness services have been delivered through an 'integrated service

---

1 Society for Community Organisation (SoCO), *Life Stories of the Homeless* (SoCO 2019) 199.
2 D. Tsang, 'Big Market, Small Government' (*Chief Executive Press Release*, 18 September 2006) <www.ceo.gov.hk/archive/2012/eng/press/oped.htm> (accessed 18 February 2023).

Table 23.1 Number of registered street sleepers in Hong Kong (1980–2021)

1980	1981	1982	1983	1984	1985	1986	1987	1988
702	842	935	880	971	1,152	1,333	1,319	1,343
1989	1990	1991	1992	1993	1994	1995	1996	1997
1,133	1,009	1,073	1,131	n/a	1,030	n/a	1,023	1,019
1998	1999	2000	2001	2002	2003	2004	2005	2006
726	783	819	1,150	785	529	463	n/a	n/a
2007	2008	2009	2010	2011	2012	2013	2014	2015
335	358	421	392	487	555	718	787	881
2016	2017	2018	2019	2020	2021			
908	1,075	1,270	1,423	1,580	1,564			

Source: Raw data from Social Welfare Department (SWD).

system'[3] organized and managed through a partnership between the Social Welfare Department (SWD) and the voluntary sector (NGOs), there has been a noticeable shift in emphasis from re-employment to rehousing. This links to the Malaysian case in that the need for rehousing resources is high on the agenda (see the latter part of this chapter).

Homelessness in Hong Kong is narrowly defined as 'street sleeping'.[4] Street sleepers are registered in the SWD's Street Sleeper Registry (SSR), which is a computerized registration system of street sleepers' personal details and the services they receive. To be registered, a person must have been sleeping rough for more than seven consecutive days. Registration is managed by the SWD and its funded partner NGOs, who register and deregister cases on a monthly basis. When a street sleeper is housed or leaves the service (i.e. becomes untraceable), they are deregistered. The SSR itself is the source of official statistics on the number of street sleepers (Table 23.1). However, the voluntary sector and academic researchers have frequently stated that it is an inappropriate method for determining the total number of street sleepers.[5]

In Hong Kong, street sleeping is seen primarily as a welfare issue and therefore falls under the purview of the SWD. In each district, the SWD manages 'Integrated Family Service Centres' (IFSCs), which are run directly by the SWD or by NGOs through outsourcing, and act as frontline help desks. If a person is experiencing economic difficulties that could lead to homelessness, he or she should seek help from the ISFC in his or her district. The IFSC will carry out an assessment and may provide an emergency fund and/or assistance

---

3 G. Kornatowski, 'Partnerships and Governance: Struggle, Cooperation, and the Role of NGOs in Welfare Delivery for the Homeless in Hong Kong' (2010) 1(3) *City, Culture and Society* 155, 164.
4 The Audit Commission (2022) defines *street sleepers* as 'people sleeping by the roadside, in rear lanes, at bottom of flyovers, in common staircases, in parks and playgrounds, on vehicles and in toilets, and those staying in 24-hour fast food shops' (5). This definition is used by the SWD, yet it is not part of any legislation. In practice, it is registration in the SSR that makes one eligible for homeless services.
5 S. C. E. Au-Liu and C. Ching, *H.O.P.E. Hong Kong 2013: City-Youth Empowerment Project* (Department of Applied Social Studies of the City University of Hong Kong, The Salvation Army, The Society for Community Organization, and St. James' Settlement, 2014); G. Kornatowski and H. Wong, 'Homelessness in Hong Kong: The Evolution of Official Homeless Assistance and the Context of Housing' in C. Zufferey and N. Yu (eds), *Faces of Homelessness in the Asia Pacific* (Taylor and Francis 2017); Homeless Outreach Population Estimation (H.O.P.E) survey report (H.O.P.E. Project 2015).

in applying for benefits (see next section). The IFSC may also refer cases to partner NGOs funded by the SWD that provide a mix of shelter and social services. However, these NGOs often encounter street sleepers who are unfamiliar with social welfare resources and do not know where to go for help. It may also be the case that communication with the IFSC social workers is not smooth, or that the social stigma attached to applying for social services discourages people on the brink of homelessness from approaching an IFSC.[6]

Worldwide, however, homelessness is now recognized as a condition which goes beyond simply sleeping on the streets.[7] By focusing on rehousing services for unstably housed people, Kornatowski[8] has provided an account of a broader definition of *homelessness* and related policies in the context of Hong Kong. Here, *homelessness* includes a specific form of unstable (and unsafe) housing, namely, 'bedspace apartments', also popularly known as 'cage homes'. More recently, the scope of unstable housing has been expanded to include so-called 'subdivided flats' (or 'subdivided units – SDUs').[9] While the act of subdividing itself is not illegal, safety regulations are often violated in order to save on materials and (re)construction costs. Bedspace apartments are the most extreme form of subdivision: they are stacked like bunk beds to make full use of vertical space. As with the large-scale resettlement of squatter communities into public housing in post-war Hong Kong,[10] deadly fires would become the main cause of government intervention, leading to rehousing programmes in the form of 'singleton hostels'.[11] However, unlike social housing, this is temporary accommodation overseen by the Home Affairs Department (HAD), with management outsourced to the voluntary sector. Nowadays, hostels can also accommodate street sleepers if they are referred. In the following section, we provide a more detailed breakdown of homeless services for street sleepers in line with our positive non-policy framework.

(Non-)Policy Framework, Regulations, and the Role of the Voluntary Sector in Hong Kong's Post-Colonial Context

Capitalist Ideology, Colonialism, and 'Positive Non-Policy'

Before examining the regulatory framework for homeless services, we must first contextualize Hong Kong's approach to welfare services in relation to its colonial past. As Chan

---

6 Based on personal communication with a partner NGO.
7 K. Amore, M. Baker and P. Howden-Chapman, 'The ETHOS Definition and Classification of Homelessness: An Analysis' (2011) 5(2) *European Journal of Homelessness* 19, 37.
8 G. Kornatowski, 'The Reconceptualization of Homelessness Policy and the Social Welfare Response of Non-governmental Organizations in Hong Kong' (2008) 6 *Japanese Journal of Human Geography* 53; see also C. Blundell, *Hong Kong's Hidden Homeless: Street Sleepers and Cage House Men* (City Polytechnic of Hong Kong 1993).
9 Kornatowski and Wong (n 5); Society for Community Organization (SoCO) *Sojourning as Tempura* (2012); Society for Community Organization (SoCO) *Trapped* (2016). If we include the number of people living in SDUs in the broad definition of homelessness, we will have a homeless population of more than 217,000 people in 2021: Census and Statistics Department, *Thematic Report: Persons Living in Subdivided Units* (Population Census Office, 2023) <www.censtatd.gov.hk/en/data/stat_report/product/B1120113/att/B11201132021XXXXB0100.pdf> (accessed 17 February 2023). In 2015, the number was around 200,000 (SoCO 2016).
10 A. Smart, *The Shek Kip Mei Myth: Squatters, Fires and Colonial Rule in Hong Kong, 1950–1963* (Hong Kong UP 2006).
11 Kornatowski (n 8).

explains in detail,[12] welfare (including homeless services, we would argue) has historically been conditioned by fiscal constraints, co-optive politics, and extreme capitalist ideology. As such, welfare is subservient to Hong Kong's economic needs and essentially operates as a function of economic growth. In other words, economic prosperity is seen as 'the best way of dealing with poverty'.[13] Ideologically, this has remained unchanged in the post-handover era. After the 1997 handover, Hong Kong was transformed from an English colony into a Chinese 'Special Administrative Region (HKSAR)'. Institutionally distinct from mainland China's system of government, the colonial fiscal, economic, housing, and social welfare systems were left intact as a pragmatic way of supporting China's own modernization project.[14] This means that Hong Kong still adheres to a residual welfare system, in which the bare minimum of public resources is provided to those deemed most in need of services. The cornerstone of the HKSAR's social security programme is the Comprehensive Social Security Assistance (CSSA) scheme, which provides benefits in the form of a living and rent allowance. However, the level of the CCSA barely provides sufficient income to meet basic needs and is considered insufficient to lift people out of poverty.[15] Therefore, (re-)entry into the labour market is the primary solution to improve one's fate.

It is this ideological background that forms the basis of our conceptual framework of 'positive non-policy': during the post-war colonial period, the government was adamant that the market (read: big business interests in the form of cartels and monopolies co-opted into the government board) should sort out the socio-economic composition of Hong Kong, except in times of structural disruption. As Goodstadt mentions,[16] there was a strong element of self-reliance that 'went hand-in-hand with a deep reluctance among [colonial government] officials to become involved in social development, combined with a market preference for leaving Chinese society to manage its own affairs'. However, a thriving market economy can only be realized through public investment in infrastructure. Goodstadt[17] goes on to argue that public sector intervention in economic and social development has been a strategy of last resort. In other words, the state is a facilitator of market-led economic growth, and any intervention in socio-economic matters would have the ultimate goal of sustaining that growth. Even in the post-colonial era, Lui[18] points out that Hong Kong has always been perceived as an 'economic city', where there is no room for politics. Large public investments, such as in public housing and social service programmes, have therefore functioned as 'indirect but important subsidies that helped to compensate for the low wages of the labour force and to contain potential social discontent'.[19] Overall, the colonial government's approach of positive non-interventionism represented a political

---

12 K. C. Chan, *Social Security Policy in Hong Kong: From British Colony to China's Special Administrative Region* (Lexington Books 2011).
13 Ibid 23.
14 T. L. Lui, 'The Unfinished Chapter of Hong Kong's Long Political Transition' (2020) 40(2) *Critique of Anthropology* 270, 276.
15 K. W. Choi, 'Poverty Eradication and Social Welfare in Hong Kong' in D. T. L. Shek and others (eds), *Advances in Social Welfare in Hong Kong* (The Chinese UP 2002).
16 L. F. Goodstadt, *Uneasy Partners: The Conflict Between Public Interest and Private Profit in Hong Kong* (Hong Kong UP 2005) 3.
17 Ibid 6.
18 Lui (n 14) 273.
19 Goodstadt (n 16) 6; F. Mizuoka, *Contrived Laissez-Faireism: The Politico-Economic Structure of British Colonialism in Hong Kong* (Springer 2018) but also see Smart (n 10). Rather, archival research into colonial

pragmatism through which capitalist ideals of continuous economic growth could be secured through strategic intervention in socio-economic matters.

Since its inception, Hong Kong's negative approach to welfarism has only been possible because of its vibrant voluntary sector, which has traditionally taken the lead in providing (human) poverty alleviation and rudimentary forms of welfare.[20] However, the relationship between the public and voluntary sectors has been rather dynamic, with the balance of power between the two sectors often fluctuating. Ho[21] explains that the changing political context in the 1980s, which involved a democratic overhaul of district-level institutional structures, provided an opportunity for grassroots organizations and pressure groups to enter the political arena in both direct (elections) and indirect (alliances with political parties) ways. This transformation was partly the result of an emerging middle class that became more politically vocal, but at the same time, the voluntary sector had to seek closer links with the government as foreign donations declined (especially in the case of church-related organizations). The relationship between the public and voluntary sectors could well be described as uneasy but interdependent. It is important to note that as Hong Kong moved into its developed economic status, community groups – often with the help of professionalized social workers and student groups – became increasingly concerned with the 'left out', who were not benefiting from Hong Kong's accumulated wealth. Thus, there was a strong urban element to the community movement, which, although primarily issue-based, engaged in social conflicts over housing and social justice for the vulnerable.[22] Again, frontline service delivery would be undertaken by the voluntary sector, but in an increasingly professionalized and advocacy-based environment.

Positive non-policy, such as the regulatory framework for homeless services, was largely a response to the harsh social reality after the handover. The timing coincided with the economic turmoil caused by the International Monetary Fund (IMF) crisis, which was eventually followed by the East Asian SARS pandemic in 2003. Goodstadt,[23] in his analysis of Hong Kong's deliberate trajectory of mismanaged prosperity (benefiting only the elite but not the poor), noted that '*no one in government* had experience in responding to a serious economic recession, a slump in the labour market and a fall in wages'.[24] Soon, however, Hong Kong would face its 'first' homelessness crisis, in the form of able-bodied people being priced out of the labour and housing markets. The government could not stand by and watch but had to take action, and it turned to the voluntary sector.

The IMF Crisis and the Consolidation of Homeless Services

While the plight of overcrowding in substandard housing began to attract public attention in the late 1970s,[25] it was not until the 1980s that systematic care/advocacy services for

---

documents suggests that public investment in social services was designed to prevent the local population from sympathizing with communist ideology.

20 Kornatowski (n 3).
21 D. K. L. Ho, *Polite Politics: A Sociological Analysis of Urban Protest in Hong Kong* (Ashgate Publishing Limited, 2000).
22 Ibid 48.
23 L. F. Goodstadt, *Poverty in the Midst of Affluence: How Hong Kong Mismanaged Its Prosperity* (Hong Kong UP 2013).
24 Ibid 173 (emphasis added).
25 Kornatowski (n 3) 158.

the homeless began to emerge. In particular, the emergence of services was framed around structural causes, namely, the inner-city redevelopment projects that were gradually transforming the built environment and housing landscape into the modern high-rise landscape for which Hong Kong is known today.[26] While it is not clear whether the encroaching regeneration projects directly pushed vulnerable tenants into homelessness, the link was useful for voluntary organizations in lobbying and making the case for rehousing, which eventually materialized in the form of temporary accommodation (hostels). However, it took an international event (the UN International Year of Shelter for the Homeless in 1987) for the SWD to take an explicit role in the provision of services to street sleepers. This included night-time outreach, statistical surveys, street sleeper registration (SSR), and the establishment of emergency and temporary shelters.[27] The HAD, for its part, had begun to explore ways of rehousing rough sleepers following a dramatic fire incident in a bedspace apartment in 1990. The SWD had been conducting its own surveys since 1983, but because housing (safety) and social policy were (and still are) administratively separate, the issue of bedspace housing was brought under the purview of the HAD. Initially, the HAD chose to fund an 'urban hostel' programme in which voluntary organizations would manage temporary accommodation for displaced bedspace tenants. Eventually, it would also fund the construction of two large hostels, one on Hong Kong Island and one in Kowloon, and outsource the day-to-day management to voluntary organizations through competitive bidding. This was an important but still somewhat-neglected milestone in the development of 'third sector housing' (see section on social housing that follows). The SWD would eventually copy this transitional housing programme to house street sleepers.

As noted earlier, the IMF crisis marked a turning point in the organization of homeless services. Whereas street sleepers had largely been perceived and treated as vagrants, drug addicts, and vulnerable elderly single people, the crisis revealed the existence of a different type of homeless, namely, the precariously employed and housed. These were able-bodied men who were relatively younger and more diverse than the traditional 'vagrant population' but who had become highly visible in Hong Kong's (prime) public spaces.[28] It was not necessarily a numbers game: SSR data showed that the number of street sleepers had hovered around 1,000 throughout the 1990s. This number would peak at around 1,300 in 2001, but voluntary organizations estimated the number to be almost three times higher. Kornatowski[29] explained that the loss of cheap but easily accessible jobs prevented any real opportunity for reintegration into the labour market. Consequently, the ideological mantra

---

26 The 1989 Hong Kong Metroplan and the establishment in 1988 of the Land Development Corporation, the forerunner of the current Urban Renewal Authority, would significantly accelerate the pace of urban redevelopment in the old urban areas, that is, the city centre and inner-city areas (see R. Y. W. Kwok, 'Last Colonial Spatial Plans for Hong Kong: Global Economy and Domestic Politics' (1999) 7(2) *European Planning Studies* 207).
27 Kornatowski (n 3) 159.
28 It is useful to draw a comparison with other East Asian cities at that time, as a similar trend had fuelled public concern about the rapidly growing numbers of an invisible homeless population. Aoki describes this population as 'bottom workers', living in precarious housing and extremely vulnerable to economic shocks: H. Aoki, *The Bottom Worker in East Asia: Composition and Transformation Under Neoliberal Globalization* (Brill Academic Pub 2023); see also T. Mizuuchi, G. Kornatowski, and T. Fukumoto, *Diversity of Urban Inclusivity: Perspectives beyond Gentrification in Advanced City-Regions* (Springer Nature 2023) for case studies of Tokyo, Osaka, Taipei, Seoul and Hong Kong.
29 Kornatowski (n 8).

of self-reliance through the market economy could no longer be relied upon, although the government would remain reluctant to make CSSA more accessible.[30] A different approach would therefore be needed to tackle the problem of homelessness, whether it was to solve the problems of public nuisance, as complained about by the business sector and the public, or to provide decent and effective forms of care, as demanded by the voluntary organizations providing frontline support.

The government's response, through the SWD, came in the form of a 'Three Year Action Plan to Help Street Sleepers'. It was a welfare-inspired intervention aimed at understanding the new phenomenon of 'economic homelessness', from which homelessness services could be properly institutionalized.[31] It involved a strategic approach to maximize the resources of the voluntary sector (through funding) and strengthen assessment channels to other departments. One of these channels is the Compassionate Rehousing Scheme, through which the SWD can recommend cases in need of long-term housing solutions to the Housing Department. If the case is successful, the applicant is allocated to a public rental flat.[32]

The Action Plan was initiated in 2001 following field research by SWD in collaboration with the City University of Hong Kong, which oversaw the evaluation of this pilot project. It would form the basis of the current service landscape, defining the responsibilities and service formats of partner NGOs. The SWD appointed three core partner NGOs as 'Integrated Services Teams (ISTs)'. These ISTs were experienced organizations that had already been running shelter and outreach programmes, as well as providing counselling, employment guidance, and emergency funds. The emergency funds are mostly provided in the form of loans to street sleepers who need temporary or one-off financial assistance (such as rent deposits and food expenses). Importantly, these funds also serve as an alternative to applying for CSSA.

It is worth noting that the NGOs (and SWD) have developed their services, including transitional housing, from the local Hong Kong context. In addition to the personal motivation and expertise of the NGO leaders, the availability of highly trained social workers in Hong Kong has been crucial. In the case of the ISTs, each organization has its own service area, which is: (1) Hong Kong Island and the outlying islands (including Hong Kong International Airport), (2) the Yau Tsim Mong core area in the Kowloon peninsula, and (3) all other areas, including the former Now Kowloon area (including the poor inner-city area Sham Shui Po) and the New Territories. Social workers sometimes have experience of working in more than one IST or other homeless service organization through internships. As a result, there is a rich pool of knowledge and expertise, not only about service provision, but also about the locality in which the organization is based. This knowledge

---

30 Goodstadt (n 23).
31 The LegCo Panel on Welfare (2003) provided the following profile of the new homeless: 71.7% are under 50 years old, 87.5% are in normal health, 95.5% have formal education, and 75.5% have been sleeping rough for one year or less: see LegCo Panel on Welfare Services, *Final Report on the 'Three-year Action Plan to Help Street Sleepers' and the Way Forward* (Paper No. CB(2)1609/03–04(13) 2004) <www.legco.gov.hk/yr03-04/english/panels/ws/papers/ws0308cb2-1609-13e.pdf> (accessed 8 November 2022).
32 The number of successful cases is low, partly due to the chronic undersupply of public housing in Hong Kong: LegCo Commission, 'Support Measures for the Homeless in Selected Asian Places' (*Essentials* 26 August 2021) <www.legco.gov.hk/research-publications/english/essentials-2021ise25-support-measures-for-the-homeless-in-selected-asian-places.htm> (accessed 8 November 2022). The scheme prioritises the rehousing of people with severe disabilities and those experiencing family breakdown.

was helpful not only in identifying outreach routes but also in identifying the local private rented housing stock (see next sections).

Upon completion in 2004, the Action Plan was positively evaluated, as the number of street sleepers had more than halved. This prompted SWD to continue its funded partnership model with the ISTs and to consolidate their services into 'one-stop integrated services'. The ISTs would handle CSSA applications and SSR registration, and each would streamline its services around a continuum of intake (including outreach), accommodation (free and on a nightly basis), transitional housing (low-rent short-/medium-term hostels), and follow-up services (to prevent relapse). In addition, the SWD funds a number of other NGOs that provide transitional housing services and also provides rent-free premises to NGOs that run drop-in centres. The SWD sees itself as responsible for providing social support services to street sleepers, but this provision mainly involves funding the NGOs. The funding is organized through the 'Lump Sum Grant Subvention System', through which the SWD monitors and evaluates the quality of services provided according to Funding and Service Agreements (FSAs). The FSAs set annual performance targets for NGOs in the areas of casework, temporary accommodation, and relapse prevention. While the targets are agreed by mutual agreement, the data management required to produce the target reports requires a significant number of staff hours, which are ultimately taken from service hours. In addition, the FSA essentially prohibits experimentation with new services, as salaries are calculated on the basis of target achievement, meaning, that there is practically no room for social workers to allocate time to services other than those specified in the targets.[33]

The one-stop integration service model has remained the basic norm since 2004. Only a few additions have been made, especially since the Covid-19 pandemic. In 2021–2022, SWD expenditure on homeless services was approximately HK$30 million.[34] The SWD has provided additional staff resources to each IST, namely, two social workers, a registered nurse, and a motor vehicle with a driver. The addition of a nurse is to assist with outreach: medical examinations can be carried out on the streets, and drug use can be monitored in a safe manner.

Overall, social services in general and homelessness services in particular rely heavily on partnership models between the SWD and the voluntary sector. We have already noted that the voluntary sector has been the main driver of welfare service provision, while the state has kept its responsibilities to a minimum. As a result, there has been a continuing role for community organizations (i.e. NGOs) to solve social problems through community-based social work. Together with the official emphasis on self-reliance, this model serves as a justification for minimal government intervention.[35] Positive non-policy is intrinsically linked

---

33 For this reason, one IST has decided to end its funding contract with the SWD in 2023 and become fully self-funded. One manager remarked: 'In the beginning we were partners with the government, now we are just like employees under a boss' (interview, March 2023). The time gained from ceasing data reporting was used to experiment with new forms of long-stay accommodation (see next section). For SWD, this was a great loss, as a stable partnership of 20 years ended abruptly. The authors do not know whether the SWD issued a call for tender, but it is known that this service territory has been allocated to another IST.
34 Audit Commission, 'The Report of the Director of Audit on the Accounts of the Government of the Hong Kong Special Administrative Region for the Year Ended March 31, 2022' (*Report No 79*, 31 November 2022) <www.aud.gov.hk/eng/pubpr/pubpr_press.htm> (accessed 15 December 2022).
35 See K. K. Fung and S. T. Hung, 'Community Work in Hong Kong: Changing Agenda in the Recent Phase of Economic Globalization' (2011) 46(4) *Community Development Journal* 458.

to this context: although there is a regulatory framework for service delivery, there has not been a legal framework that clearly defines government responsibilities. This remains a source of dissatisfaction for the voluntary sector, as there would be virtually no recourse if the SWD decided to withdraw funding.[36] This dissatisfaction is also evident when other departments step in to deal with homelessness as a public nuisance.

Managing Homelessness in an Unequal City: Bottom-Up Housing Strategies

Punitive Responses and Invisible Homelessness

Hong Kong's rise to prosperity did not come with a solution to entrenched poverty and deprivation.[37] While the post-war era of high economic growth and large-scale public housing projects brought much optimism for the future, Hong Kong's structural transformation into a (financial) services-driven economy in the 1980s would soon be marked by social polarization (especially in terms of income and occupation) and striking inequality.[38] In the aftermath of the 2008 global financial crisis, homelessness would re-emerge as an issue of inequality, not least in relation to housing. This is reflected in the following comment by the director of a semi-funded NGO:

> For twenty years, society's economic upturn has surpassed that in the past, to the extent that the government has accumulated tens of billion dollars in consecutive years. However, the gap between the wealthy and the poor has deteriorated to the worst in the last forty-five years. Now, it has reached the dangerous level of 'caution' and is on par with that of developing countries in Africa. As the society becomes more prosperous and wealthy, the care for grassroots and marginalized groups has been receding incessantly. *The government sheds its responsibility*. The homeless can only help themselves or rely on donations from kind-hearted persons to get their meals now and then[39] [emphasis added].

---

36 Since the 2000s, there has been frequent interaction between homeless service organizations (NGOs) in East Asia. Interaction with Japanese counterparts has been an important inspiration, as Japan has clearly defined its responsibilities in the 2002 Act on Special Measures concerning Assistance in Self-Support of Homeless Persons. South Korea and Taiwan also have similar legislation. Another factor was the perceived Japanese tolerance of the use of public spaces (such as parks) by street-sleeping communities (see: M. Wong, 'Homeless Find New Hope from Osaka Visit' *South China Morning Post* (Hong Kong, 13 July 2001) <www.scmp.com/article/352240/homeless-find-new-hope-osaka-visit> (accessed 19 January 2023). The SWD has also organized study tours to, among others, Japan. Around 2012, Singapore's former Ministry of Social and Family Development organized a study tour to Hong Kong (and Australia) to study transitional housing schemes for the homeless.
37 Goodstadt (n 23).
38 S. Chiu and T. L. Lui, *Hong Kong: Becoming a Chinese Global City* (Routledge 2009). The HKSAR government was aware of the problem and had set up the Commission on Poverty in 2005, which was disbanded in 2007, only to be re-established in 2012. However, the government's approach to inequality would not deviate from its anti-welfare approach: 'In a free, open and mature capitalist economy, the wealth gap can hardly be eradicated' (D. Tsang, 'Cost of Living' (*Policy Address*, 12 October 2011) <www.policyaddress.gov.hk/11-12/eng/p82.html> (accessed 18 February 2023) quoted in Goodstadt (n 16) 152.
39 Society for Community Organisation (SoCO) (n 1) 6.

As the number of street sleepers began to return to previous highs, the homeless themselves had become more diverse and their overall situation bleaker.[40] NGOs were finding it more difficult to reach the homeless, many of whom were seeking refuge in places other than public spaces. This led to the need for a new survey on the state of 'street sleeping', which was realized through a collaboration between universities and NGOs (mainly the ISTs), called the Homeless Outreach Population Estimation (HOPE) survey.[41] The 2015 survey found that the actual number of homeless people was almost twice as high as the SSR data. Moreover, only half of this number had taken refuge on the streets: one-sixth of the total number slept in 24-hour fast-food outlets (the so-called 'McRefugees/McSleepers'), while more than one-third were temporarily housed in night shelters and transitional housing.[42] Compared to the 2013 survey, the duration of homelessness had increased for many respondents, suggesting that access to housing (whether private or public) had become more difficult. It is not clear how many of the medium- to long-term homeless decided to seek shelter in the fast-food outlets. However, a 2018 NGO survey found that a higher percentage (11.2%) of this population were women. They preferred to stay overnight 'in the outlets because they felt safer [and were] air-conditioned and clean'.[43] But the survey also (re)confirmed that a significant number of street sleepers, in fact, rent accommodation. The problem, however, is that these flats, while affordable, are extremely substandard and practically uninhabitable, especially during the hot summer months.[44] Indeed, the 2015 HOPE survey found that prior to becoming homeless, almost half of respondents had lived in unstable housing, mainly SDUs, and had moved home in the two years leading up to their predicament.[45] As with long-term homelessness, addictive behaviours (ranging from alcoholism to gambling) were the primary personal cause.[46]

The 2015 survey also mentions that there is a minority of non-Chinese street sleepers among the homeless, half of whom are Vietnamese long-term homeless men and Nepalese refugees. As they do not have Hong Kong citizenship, they are ineligible for government-funded homeless services, leaving them in a limbo. Crucially, their presence has also been instrumental for the voluntary sector in problematizing and challenging the government's punitive measures. These measures range from evicting street sleepers and resorting to anti-homeless architecture to exclude them from certain public spaces[47] to evicting street sleepers from their dwelling structures and unjustifiably removing personal belongings left in

---

40 The official figure had risen to 1,270 in 2018.
41 See Au-Liu and Ching (n 5); Kornatowski and Wong (n 5).
42 Kornatowski and Wong (n 5) 103.
43 X. Su, 'Hong Kong's McSleeper Trend Rises 50 Per Cent in Three Years, as NGO Highlights Vulnerability of Women in the Group: Survey Findings Come Alongside Calls for Government to Adapt Vacant Sites for Social housing' *South China Morning Post* (Hong Kong, 4 March 2018) <www.scmp.com/news/hong-kong/community/article/2135647/hong-kongs-mcsleeper-trend-rises-50-cent-three-years-ngo> (accessed 19 January 2023).
44 See also J. Ngo, 'Sleeping in McDonald's Better Than in a Bug-infested Bed at Home, says Hong Kong McSleeper' *South China Morning Post* (Hong Kong, 1 November 2015) <www.scmp.com/news/hong-kong/education-community/article/1874477/sleeping-mcdonalds-better-bug-infested-bed-home> (accessed 19 January 2023).
45 Kornatowski and Wong (n 5) 106.
46 Ibid 108.
47 Kornatowski (n 8).

public spaces,[48] and sealing off 'hot spots for refuge'.[49] The departments responsible would be other than the SWD, such as the Leisure and Cultural Services Department (in charge of tourist spaces and parks), the Lands Offices and the Highway Department (in charge of unused spaces under flyovers, etc.), the Transport Department (in charge of pedestrian spaces), and even the HAD (public safety).

The unwarranted removal of personal belongings in public space has sparked a discussion on the policy of removal procedures. Legal retaliation by an NGO for three different incidents in 2012 (a street), 2015 (tunnel), and 2019 (street park) resulted in the obligation of the responsible department to post notices and/or verbal notifications two weeks before any removal operation. While the first two incidents were settled out of court with fair compensation, the third was settled in court with almost no compensation for the homeless people whose belongings were removed and destroyed. The department representatives were also forced to apologize for their actions. Crucially, for the third incident, the affected street sleepers and representatives of the NGO utilized the 'Public Health and Municipal Services Ordinance' to challenge the unlawful removal of personal belongings as litter or waste.

Evictions from public spaces are seen as ineffective because there is no responsibility to rehouse. Evictions in old inner-city areas are also seen as part of the housing affordability crisis. The case of eviction of Nepalese street sleepers was part of 'greening works' under and along a highway flyover in Yau Ma Tei, following new upper-class housing developments that took place from 2012 to 2015.[50] The scene soon became symbolic for charitable organizations to show their concern and for advocacy groups to criticize the unilateral punitive measures.[51] The NGOs tried to mediate between the officials and the street sleepers, but no structural solution could be found. Promises were made to work more effectively with the SWD, but the only option in sight was to refer those eligible for services to temporary accommodation. This short-term solution was not accepted by the street sleepers concerned.

Recent Experiments with Alternative Forms of Transitional Housing

As noted earlier, rehousing options, whether at the end of services or during services, have been a prominent key issue in ending homelessness. There are three main reasons for this:

---

48 Society for Community Organisation (SoCO) (n 1) 6.
49 Ibid 198.
50 On which see, ibid., but also J. Ho, 'Down, Out and Waiting to Be Evicted: Many of the 17 Homeless People Living under a Flyover Have Ignored a Notice to Leave' *South China Morning Post* (Hong Kong, 10 July 2013) <www.scmp.com/news/hong-kong/article/1278978/down-out-and-waiting-be-evicted?module=perpetual_scroll_0&pgtype=article&campaign=1278978> (accessed 19 January 2023); G. Chan and A. Chen, ' "I'd Rather Live on the Streets than in a Filthy Subdivided Flat": Action Needed to Tackle Hong Kong's Homeless' *South China Morning Post* (Hong Kong, 5 January 2015) <www.scmp.com/lifestyle/families/article/1674176/id-rather-live-streets-filthy-subdivided-flat-action-needed> (accessed 19 January 2023). These works included the placement of heavy flowerpots, which were perceived as anti-homeless objects, to prevent sleeping. Other open spaces were used to install a dog park and a mini-car racing track.
51 In response, district counsellors and social welfare officers denounced all the public attention, which in their view acted as a disincentive for street sleepers to seek proper services and accommodation (see Chan and Chen (n 46)). On the other hand, NGOs pointed out that due to skyrocketing rental prices, 'in no more than half a year, they resume the life of street sleepers again': SoCO (n 1) 199.

(1) a private housing market that has failed to provide affordable and adequate housing; (2) inadequate access to and supply of public rental housing (PRH); and (3) a highly regulated system of temporary accommodation that is avoided by the medium- and long-term homeless. We will discuss the first two reasons in the next section, but here we present recent initiatives in the field of transitional housing as examples of good practice.

One problem with government-funded temporary accommodation has been its short-term nature. By referral, people can only stay for between three and six months,[52] and there are many rules to follow, from visiting hours to confiscation of personal belongings to mealtimes. Rents are calculated according to the maximum amount of the CSSA rent allowance,[53] but rents may vary according to the location of the bed (e.g. next to a window or not), etc. Rooms are shared with other clients, which can lead to conflicts. To overcome these 'organizational barriers', NGOs have recently experimented with self-funded longer-term facilities.[54] Long-term hostels are better equipped to provide continuous care, including personal counselling, housing planning, employment services, combined with health and behavioural monitoring. The aim of these services is individualized but broadly to promote self-sufficiency (preferably through employment), resolve family conflicts, and bridge the waiting time for PRH accommodation. Ng et al[55] discuss the advantages and disadvantages of a self-funded project that allows stays of up to three years. While self-funded projects lack predictable stability and capacity, long-term engagement with clients allows these facilities to function as 'integrated homeless service hubs' through which social networks can also be formed.[56]

Similar projects run by a former IST are funded through church networks and rely on forms of 'housing philanthropy' in which landlords rent their properties to vulnerable people at below market rates.[57] Here we briefly introduce two projects that differ in architecture but share the same goal of providing decent living conditions suitable for homemaking.[58] The first is the social housing project, where the flat is rented from the landlord at an agreed price below market value through a five-year contract (Figure 23.1). The NGO, in turn, has renovated the flat, which is divided into four rooms with a shared kitchen, toilet/shower, and laundry room. The NGO's staff monitor the residents, but because of the co-living arrangement, the residents are asked to manage the unit themselves. There are no specific rules. Instead, social interaction becomes the basis of the co-living arrangement. The concept of self-care plays an important role. Like a healing process, the aim is to gradually prepare for reintegration into society, but without time pressure. If the resident receives CSSA, the rent is set at the maximum rent allowance, while for others, the rent is

---

52 Most hostels allow their clients to extend their stay if absolutely necessary (usually only up to one year), but extensions have a negative impact on performance targets.
53 In January 2023, the rent allowance for a single household will be HK$2,515.
54 F. S. K. Ng, Y. Y. H. Chung, W. T. Ng, J. K. Chan, and Y. C. Wong, 'Long-Stay Hostels as an Alternative Pathway out of Homelessness: Prospects and Challenges' (2022) 55(1/2) *The Hong Kong Journal of Social Work* 21, 22.
55 Ibid.
56 Ibid 37.
57 B. Yung, 'Third Sector Housing as a Social Innovation in Hong Kong: A Qualitative Study' (2022) 14(2) *Voluntary Sector Review* 314.
58 G. Kornatowski and C. Ching, 'Home-making While Homeless: Livelihood and Intervention of Hong Kong Street Sleepers under Extreme Inequality' *RC21* (Antwerp 14–16 July 2021).

Figure 23.1 The Co-Living Capsule Hostel project (left) and the Social Housing project (right). While living spaces are minimal, both projects stand out in cleanliness and brightness, which are so often lacking in a subdivided flat environment.

Source: Authors' own photographs.

set at 25% of their income. The rental incomes from the four tenants are sufficient to pay the monthly rent to the landlord.[59] Another project is the Co-living Capsule Hostel, which operates on a two-year cycle to rehouse street sleepers. At first glance, the sleeping units look like refurbished bedspaces, but the same living arrangements address the social isolation associated with substandard housing. There is plenty of open communal space, and (like the other project) the accommodation is located in an old inner-city community where local food, etc., is most affordable and social interaction is easy in Hong Kong.

The intensity of interaction between residents is crucial to reintegration, and hostels provide an enabling environment for this. Kornatowski and Ching[60] discuss the positive effects on residents. Because of the co-living arrangement, there was a strong sense of ownership and belonging, which was fostered by the sharing of chores. The fact that the environment does not feel like a mere shelter, where there is a constant sense of transience and self-protection, encourages residents to treat the place as their own and keep it as decent and clean as possible. There is a sense of camaraderie that comes not only from working together but also from age differences and seniority: older, more 'experienced' street sleepers tend to take on a mentoring role for younger residents, 'showing them the ropes' of successful hostel life. For residents who have been involved in family conflict and have led a secluded life, the opportunity to engage in dialogue is greatly appreciated. In addition, the availability of a support and care network, including contact with social workers, creates an atmosphere in which even failures (such as gambling and alcohol binges) can be discussed and forgiven. Even though the accommodation is (relatively) long-term, the residents are aware that it is not a permanent solution: there is plenty of time to 'recover', but the act of homemaking tends to happen on the fly and would have to be repeated if they moved to private or public accommodation, which would often be seen as a downgrade.

---

59 An extra HK$ 300–400 is charged for electricity and water.
60 n 58.

Transitional Social Housing as the Way Forward? Putting Welfare and Housing Together . . . in a Community Framework

The long-term hostels are part of a larger movement seeking a 'third solution' to Hong Kong's housing crisis, namely, the voluntary sector–led 'transitional social housing' movement. This section zooms out from the practice of long-term hostels and looks at post-2017 initiatives for alternative forms of housing for inadequately housed households. Crucially, this recent development in housing is another example of positive non-policy: the third sector is taking the lead and managing it, while the government intervenes selectively as a financial backstop with a minimum of regulatory underpinning. It is important to note, however, that the current upscaling and expansion of these initiatives has provided the impetus for a policy framework, namely, the HKSAR's 'Light Public Housing' programme. This is a temporary public housing scheme that operates within the same operational framework as transitional social housing but is funded from the public budget under the official housing policy.[61] As the programme is still under development, it will not be discussed here, but its potential future contribution to the prevention and/or treatment of homelessness in a broader sense will be highlighted.

The term 'transitional social housing' (TSH) is a somewhat generic one, broadly referring to temporary accommodation run by the third sector, outside but not unrelated to the traditional PRH system. Other terms such as *social housing*, *transitional housing*, and *community housing* are often used.[62] The TSH initiative is primarily a response to the SDU phenomenon, which came to public attention in the early 2010s. As noted earlier, SDUs are an important but mostly inadequate housing resource in the private rental market for the poor, including street sleepers. However, it is the systematization of the substandard housing market, even for lower-middle-class households, that has been the subject of intense criticism from social movements and the public at large. When the SDU market became popular as 'affordable' self-contained apartments, there were many profits to be made, but the rush to subdivide brought with it a series of collapses and fires due to inadequate construction work, such as re-laying water and waste pipes, and electricity lines. As mentioned earlier, traditional forms of SDUs such as 'cubicles' and 'cage homes' (both with shared toilets and kitchens) had long existed, but they were hidden away in the old urban communities.[63] After the 2000s, the number of SDUs increased rapidly, and most units are found in old tenement buildings, especially the *tong lau*. Often built in the 1960s and 1970s, these buildings are favoured for subdivision as they create new value and (conveniently) often lack access security.

According to Lau,[64] the reasons for the rapid proliferation of SDUs are related to (1) the large increase in the number of low-income migrants from China after the 2000s (about 220,000 new arrivals between 2006 and 2010); (2) a decline in PRH supply (around 2010,

---

61 Housing Bureau, 'Light Public Housing' (*Chief Executive's Policy Address*, 2022) <www.hb.gov.hk/eng/policy/housing/policy/light_public_housing/index.html> (accessed 5 May 2023).
62 H. M. M. Lau, 'Community-based Housing Solutions in Hong Kong: How and Why Have They Emerged?' (2020) 20(2) *International Journal of Housing Policy* 290; B. Yung and A. Chan, 'Third Sector Housing in 21st- Century Hong Kong: Opportunities and Challenges' (2020) 11(3) *Voluntary Sector Review* 337; Yung (n 57).
63 While vacant SDUs are displayed and advertised in real estate offices, access to cubicles, etc., is through informal points of contact in old urban communities.
64 Lau (n 62).

the waiting period had doubled from about two years to more than four years); and (3) a sharp rise in private housing prices (mainly due to inflows of Chinese investment capital – from 2007 to 2017, average property prices tripled). In this context, not only the remaining *tong lau* in old urban areas but also abandoned factory flats in inner-city areas became the target of subdivision and increasingly took on the role of absorbing the 'new poor.'[65] There is a common perception that *tong lau* owners are mostly locals (often with a migrant background) who bought these aging properties when they were still affordable.[66]

The initial phase of TSH in Hong Kong is generally considered to have started around 2010, when a local social enterprise began to provide low-cost housing to low-income households living in extremely substandard SDUs.[67] Their business model quickly inspired Hong Kong's voluntary sector to experiment with their own forms of social housing, making the current format rather complex. Nevertheless, two practices are instructive, namely, the reuse of vacant public spaces, such as abandoned school buildings and dormitories, and the establishment of personal contacts with 'benevolent landlords' (as seen in the previous section). Acting as a social realtor, the social enterprise operates on the promise of a relatively low but stable return and takes care of the actual management of the apartments (including the recruitment of tenants). In terms of tenants, there is a clear focus on households with a strong sense of (self-)responsibility but who are held back by poor housing conditions. Tenants are therefore expected to work on their social mobility, mainly by saving money during their stay, but also by 'mixing' with other residents and community members. This is facilitated by shared living arrangements and by encouraging residents to organize events with each other in the communal areas.

The initiative attracted a lot of media attention and praise. As a result, the voluntary sector became interested, as the sector had been trying to address the housing poverty issue, but mostly by putting pressure on the HKSAR government (i.e. housing policy). Concern movements seriously questioned the proliferation of SDUs after a fatal fire in a local market street in 2011, following media reports on how the design of one of the SDU flats had hindered rescue efforts. Concerned groups were opposed to the further proliferation and deterioration of the SDU market and had therefore lobbied for the reintroduction of rent control (abolished in 1998) and tenancy control (tenant protection – abolished in 2004). However, such regulation was seen as critical to any change in the housing situation.[68] In response, however, the HKSAR government denounced the reintroduction of regulation as it could lead to disinvestment in the private market. Moreover, when it released its Long-Term Housing Strategy (LTHS) in 2014, it rejected the idea of social housing on the grounds that all vacant land and disused industrial sites should be reserved for public housing. For the concern movement, this was a major blow, but also an opportunity to change course.

The change of course came in the form of practical experiments. Having been defeated as a protest movement, the movement shifted its energy to pragmatism, partly because this

---

65 Goodstadt (n 16).
66 C. Cheng, 'Sham Shui Po: The Centre of Poverty in Hong Kong' (2013) 53(7) *Journal of the Royal Asiatic Hong Kong Branch* 30.
67 See also Lau (n 62).
68 H. M. M Lau, 'Lobbying for Rent Regulation in Hong Kong: Rental Market Politics and Framing Strategies' (2018) 56(12) *Urban Studies* 2515; see also Lau (n 62).

was the only remaining chance to bring about change in Hong Kong's housing landscape. A crucial factor was the entry of the Hong Kong Council of Social Services (HKCSS) in 2017.[69] The HKCSS drew on the local 'community connection approach', in which 'community', 'mutual aid', and 'co-housing' are important keys. However, it also organized study tours to Europe and Taiwan to study supply and management models. Finally, it launched a three-year pilot project called the Community Housing Movement (CHM). However, because CHM was set up outside the general housing policy framework, it had to rely on third-party resources and donations for funding. To this end, a joint injection of HK$5.8 million from the Community Chest of Hong Kong and the Social Innovation and Entrepreneurship Development Fund (SIE Fund) kick-started the initiative. With the available funding, a total of 14 NGOs, ranging from grassroots organizations (including some specializing in homeless services) to large welfare groups, were recruited as Service Operator NGOs. Each was to set up and manage its own project, including defining tenant profiles and renovation styles.

The main challenge in operationalizing the CHM was access to available housing units and land. Gradually realizing the potential of this movement, the HKSAR government set up a task force under the Transport and Housing Bureau (THB) to identify and secure potential units.[70] The answer was to be found in the HKSAR's land banks and inner-city areas with buildings earmarked for redevelopment, where the Task Force could support and facilitate transitional social housing projects by tapping into vacant government and privately owned vacant land (the new-build method) and privately owned vacant residential and non-residential buildings for temporary use (the renovation method). It is the new-build method that has attracted the most attention. Called 'modular integrated housing', it uses techniques similar to those in the Netherlands to provide fast-to-build and easy-to-dismantle units by stacking containers. The pilot project was launched in 2020 in the symbolically poor area of Sham Shui Po. It was dismantled in 2023, and the land has already been returned to the private developer.

The HKCSS has set basic guidelines for the use and purpose of PRH: (1) NGOs will target households living in SDUs who have been waiting for more than three years to move into PRH; (2) Eligible households who have gone through the application and interview process will be accommodated for only two years. The responsible NGO manages its units using funds from the Community Chest to renovate the housing (mostly on a co-living basis); (3) The NGO assists the household in preparing to move into PRH (ideally, the PRH unit is accessible upon discharge from the SDU).

The temporary and effective reuse of vacant land and buildings earmarked for redevelopment has been a critical factor in government support, as it represents a socially innovative achievement and does not interfere with existing housing policy and the status quo in the private housing market. It could be argued that this pragmatism has given the government sufficient leeway to intervene at its own time and convenience. Another factor is that the CHM resonates with the mantra of self-reliance: tenant households are expected to reinvigorate their social mobility by forming/strengthening their own mutual support networks

---

69 The HKCSS is an umbrella organization that coordinates social service NGOs. The organization is an important driver of social innovation, including the social housing movement.
70 In 2022, the THB was split into the Transport and Logistics Bureau and the Housing Bureau (HB). The HB will oversee the Light Public Housing Scheme in the future.

and capacities. TSH serves as a facilitator of this process and thus makes it a perfect target for positive non-policy.

The social impact assessment report of the CHM pilot project[71] reported significant changes in tenant households' family relationships, social participation, and neighbourhood interaction. A critical, but somewhat underemphasized, factor in this scheme is that the household gains access to the welfare resources of active NGOs in the neighbourhood. In this sense, social housing also acts as a service hub for other related services. Following the perceived success, the HKSAR government increased the budget in 2020 with a commitment to increase the total number of social housing units to 15,000 by 2024. By mid-2022, it had identified sufficient land to provide about 21,700 units.[72]

Homelessness in Malaysia: Ambiguous Definitions

Introduction to Public Policy and Service Landscape

Like Hong Kong, homelessness in Malaysia has emerged as a visible social issue in the urban ecosystem. However, there is no official definition of *homelessness*. The lack of a definition of *homelessness* in Malaysia has allowed stakeholders such as government officials, policymakers, researchers, and homeless people themselves to interpret the issue in a variety of ways. Groups and organizations that provide assistance and support to the homeless generally understand homelessness as a condition of not having regular shelter or a private space to sleep, wash, and carry out daily activities.[73] However, similar to Hong Kong, the understanding of homelessness in Malaysia is limited to the most visible form, where homeless people live or spend time in public spaces such as parks and on the streets – often seen in urban areas such as Kuala Lumpur and Penang.[74]

Due to the lack of an official definition of *homelessness*, relevant government agencies have their own position on what constitutes homelessness and how it should be addressed. Matters relating to the homeless are administered by the Ministry of Women, Family, and Community Development (MWFCD), enforced by the Department of Social Welfare (DSW), and grouped together as part of the broader category of displaced and marginalized groups. The MWFCD is responsible for implementing four key national policies: (1) the National Social Policy, (2) the National Women's Policy, (3) the National Policy on the Elderly, and (4) the National Social Welfare Policy. However, none of these policies directly address homelessness.[75] There are a number of government initiatives through which homeless people can access services and support, as explained later.[76] Under the

---

71 HKCSS, *Community Housing Movement Brief Report on Social Impact Assessment 2017–2020* (Hong Kong Council of Social Service 2021) <www.socialhousing.hkcss.org.hk/en/content/community-housing-movement> (accessed 13 January 2023).
72 Ibid.
73 M. Adib, N. Amalina, and Y. Ahmad, 'How Effective Are the Current Initiatives in Dealing with Homelessness in Malaysia?' (2018) 15(3) *Journal of Administrative Science*.
74 W. Y. Ghee and R. N. B. R. Omar, 'Homelessness in Malaysia: Victims of Circumstance or by Choice?' (2015) 1(1) *Asian Journal for Poverty Studies (AJPS)* 26.
75 S. M. Alhabshi and A. K. Abdul Manan, 'Homelessness in Kuala Lumpur, Malaysia: A Case of Agenda Denial' (2012) 1(2) *International Journal of Social Science Tomorrow* 1.
76 E. Michael and T. B. Teck, 'Understanding Homelessness in Malaysia: Effects and Solutions' (2023) 7(3) *International Journal of Advanced Natural Sciences and Engineering Researches* 178.

DSW, the government agency Desa Bina Diri (DBD) runs a transitional housing programme ('Transit Centre') that provides protection, care, and recovery plans for destitute people, with the aim of helping them reintegrate into society. It also provides vocational training. Only Malaysian citizens aged 18–59 with no family, no income, and no illness are eligible for its services. DBD is available in the urban areas of Johor, Pahang, Sarawak, Sabah, and Selangor. Here, the *homeless* are classified as needy and impoverished beggars and vagrants. They have no fixed abode or regular employment and move from place to place, living by begging for money or food.

Also at the city-region level, Anjung Singgah was launched in April 2011 in Kuala Lumpur to provide temporary shelter. It is a collaboration between the MWFCD and the National Welfare Foundation (NWF). Apart from Kuala Lumpur, Anjung Singgah also operates in Kuching in Sarawak, Johor Bahru in Johor, Penang, and Ipoh in Perak. Anjung Singgah helps the homeless by providing them with a place to live that is less restrictive than DBD. In addition, Pusat Transit Gelandangan Kuala Lumpur is operated by DSW and follows the establishment of Anjung Singgah. Three main agencies are involved in the establishment of this centre, namely, the Malaysian Resources Corporation Bhd (MRCB), Kuala Lumpur City Hall (KLCH), and the Ministry of Federal Territory.

Although there is no legislative framework that guides homelessness policy in Malaysia, the MWFCD has long taken the position that the Destitute Persons Act 1977 (the Act), a federal vagrancy law, can be used to enforce control over the homeless. This position was confirmed when the department announced plans to criminalize begging by amending the Destitute Persons Act. The punitive and criminalizing framing of homelessness is reflected in the government's attempt to ban soup kitchens in the business distrct of Kuala Lumpur serving the homeless.[77] On the other hand, the DSW has labelled homeless people as 'vagrants' and 'troublemakers', but since many are considered 'healthy and have jobs', they cannot be regulated under the law and are considered a public nuisance to law enforcers and business owners.[78] Under the Act that allows for enforcement of homelessness as vagrancy,[79] homeless people are ordered to stay in welfare homes for up to three years. During this time, they are provided with basic care and are under strict control and discipline. Escape from these institutions is considered illegal and can result in up to three months' imprisonment.[80]

In line with this approach, in 2014, the MWFCD introduced the 'Ops Qaseh' channel for placing homeless people in transit shelters, with the aim of eliminating begging. The initiative aims to help homeless people by providing support and assistance, including temporary accommodation at DBD. The initiative is a collaboration with DBD centres in the towns of Mersing, Jerantut, Kota Kinabalu, and Sungai Buloh, each with a capacity of 200 people.[81] As part of this collaboration, homeless people are placed in the DBD for at least six months before being transferred to the National Anti-Drug Agency (NADA) if drug addiction is

---

77 R. M. Rusenko, 'Imperatives of Care and Control in the Regulation of Homelessness in Kuala Lumpur, Malaysia: 1880s to Present' (2018) 55(1) *Urban Studies* 2123.
78 Ghee and Omar (n 74); Alhabshi and Abdul Manan (n 75).
79 R. M. Rusenko and D. Y. M. Loh, 'Begging, the Destitute Persons Act 1977, and Punitive Law: An Exploratory Survey' in *Paper presented by the University of Malaya Seminar on Homelessness in Kuala Lumpur, Malaysia* (2014).
80 R. M. Rusenko, 'Homelessness, Begging, and The Destitute Persons Act 1977' *Policy Paper* (2015).
81 BERNAMA, 'Ops Qaseh to Address Problems of the Homeless' *New Straits Times* (Kuala Lumpur 11 June 2014).

involved. Other categories of homelessness include the mentally ill, the homeless with jobs, the homeless without jobs, and those who have no place to live.[82] Also at the town level, the MWFCD established the Rumah Ehsan (RE) care centres in 1996 for the elderly who have no family to take care of them. RE provides shelter, medical care, and physiotherapy and is located in Dungun, Terengganu, and Kuala Kubu Bahru, Selangor. In order to be admitted, patients must prove that they are unable to carry out their daily activities and responsibilities on their own, have been diagnosed with an illness, and have no family or carers. They must also be certified as destitute patients by government medical officers.[83]

Homeless Numbers and Geography in Kuala Lumpur

There is no reliable data on the size of the homeless population in Malaysia, as empirical studies undertaken to address this issue are limited.[84] Although homeless individuals are included in the National Population and Housing Census collected in 14 cities in the nation – and in 2012, the homeless were categorized as a separate group in the census – the statistics have never been made publicly available, as government statistics representatives cited lack of reliability on collection methodology as the main reason.[85] Information obtained from the MWFCD showed that as of 2010, the number of homeless individuals was 1,646, with most of them concentrated in the capital region of Kuala Lumpur. There have also been wider estimates of 1,500 homeless people across 15 hot spots in Kuala Lumpur, where there is the highest concentration of homeless people in the country, signalling a rise in human insecurity. They congregate at populated places, such as the Puduraya bus terminal, the Dayabumi complex, Petaling Street, Central Market, Klang Bus Stand, Jalan Tuanku Abdul Rahman, and Chow Kit Road Market. Some of them also live underneath or around bridges, such as under the Syed Putra and Jalan Kinabalu Roundabouts and below the bridges along Jalan Istana and Brickfields, as those areas provide some degree of shelter and privacy away from the public and enforcement authorities.[86]

According to surveys conducted by NGOs that provide aid and support on the ground, the number of homeless people in Malaysia had increased to 2,000 by 2015.[87] No updated data on the homeless population in Malaysia is available, but it can be assumed that the numbers have increased due to the Covid-19 pandemic. During the Movement Control Order in April 2020, roughly 800 homeless individuals in Kuala Lumpur were placed in temporary shelters to avoid the spread of infections.[88] A study on homelessness conducted in 2012 indicates that close to 90% of the homeless at that time were male, and close to 40% of them had completed secondary or tertiary education.[89] Apart from Malaysian citi-

---

82 Ibid.
83 Ghee and Omar (n 74).
84 Adib, Amalina and Ahmad (n 73).
85 J. Foong and S. Ho, 'Homeless in KL' *The Star* (Kuala Lumpur 4 June 2016) <www.thestar.com.my/Travel/Malaysia/2010/07/19/Homeless-in-KL/> (accessed 24 September 2023).
86 Penang Institute, 'Homelessness in Our Cities' *A Report by Penang Institute* (2015).
87 Homeless World Cup Organisation, 'Global Homelessness Statistics' (Homeless World Cup 2016) <www.homelessworldcup.org> (accessed 4 June 2016).
88 S. Azahar, 'Tackling the Problem of Homelessness' *MalaysiaNow* (22 January 2021) <www.malaysianow.com/opinion/2021/01/22/tackling-the-problem-of-homelessness> (accessed 15 September 2023).
89 Alhabshi and Abdul Manan (n 75).

zens, homeless individuals also consist of immigrants from Indonesia, Vietnam, Thailand, Bangladesh, Myanmar, Cambodia, and others.[90]

A study on homelessness in Malaysia[91] revealed the multifaceted nature of homelessness. The study found that most homeless experiences were directly related to stressful events, such as poverty, unemployment, substance abuse, and family violence. Low and unstable income and poverty were found to be contributing factors to homelessness, while the breakdown of family relationships or social support networks was also highlighted as connected to homelessness. Such breakdown represents much more than the loss of a partner or family member, as it also represents a loss of stability, security, and a sense of home. A history of abuse within the family was also identified as a factor leading to homelessness. Behaviours such as drug use and gambling were also associated with the breakdown of family and support networks, job loss, and ultimately, loss of stable housing. Drug use in particular was associated with chronic health conditions such as HIV/AIDS among homeless people. People who are homeless have been found to have a much higher risk of developing chronic diseases than people who are housed.[92]

Non-Governmental Support

As in Hong Kong, NGOs have been very active in raising awareness and providing services and support to the homeless. Among the many organizations, some of the more prominent and active ones include Pertubuhan Tindakan Wanita Islam (PERTIWI) Soup Kitchen, Kechara Soup Kitchen (KSK), Dapur Jalanan, Need to Feed the Need (NFN), Kaseh4U, and Food Not Bombs.[93]

Pertubuhan Tindakan Wanita Islam (PERTIWI) Soup Kitchen

PERTIWI Soup Kitchen was established and is managed by the Pertubuhan Tindakan Wanita Islam. PERTIWI Soup Kitchen is a well-recognized NGO that provides aid services such as meals at various city centre locations around Kuala Lumpur (e.g. Masjid India, Chow Kit, and Kota Raya). Together with other NGOs, they provide help generally to those who are in need, including those who are poor. Around 700 packs of food are distributed each round, with a few rounds each week. They also provide basic healthcare and assistance with daily activities such as free haircuts. Assistance and aid are mostly short-term.

Kechara Soup Kitchen (KSK)

Founded by His Eminence Tsem Rinpoche, Kechara Soup Kitchen is another well-known NGO that provides food and other aid to the homeless guided by their motto, 'Hunger Knows No Barriers'. Other than food, they also provide medical care, counselling, aid such as clothes, referring services for employment, and accommodation. They engage homeless people at a number of 'hot spots' in the Kuala Lumpur city centre area, including Bukit

---

90 Ghee and Omar (n 74).
91 Alhabshi and Abdul Manan (n 75).
92 Ibid.
93 Adib, Amalina and Ahmad (n 73).

Bintang, Jalan Ipoh, Chow Kit, Pudu Raya, Pudu Market, Masjid Jamek, Penang, Johor Bahru, Petaling Jaya, and Sentul. Kechara's mission is to provide practical and systematic solutions, with a longer-term aim to reduce the number of people living on the streets. To establish a Nurture Centre is part of their long-term goal.

Dapur Jalanan

The founder of Dapur Jalanan, Mastura Mohd, established the Nasi Lemak Projek in 2012. It is a volunteer-based soup kitchen service which operates every week at Jalan Panggong, Kuala Lumpur. Many of the volunteers are university students, due to the social networks of the founder and methods of recruitment (tapping into university platforms).

Need to Feed the Need (NFN)

A community-run initiative, Need to Feed the Need (NFN) was established in 2013 with the aim of providing meals to 'the unfortunate' in the Kuala Lumpur city areas. As they are not a registered NGO, the operation is less formal, leaning toward a 'social network group' approach. Due to their flexibility, they sometimes collaborate with other social groups such as Free Market, Tamak Pahala, and Street Interview, groups that mainly provide material aid to people living on the streets. Their ultimate aim is to improve living conditions of the poor and reduce the number of homeless people. They focus on building personal rapport with their 'street clients', as they believe connections and relationships are key to initiating change.

Kaseh4U

Kaseh4U regularly distributes food and drinks to those in need around Kuala Lumpur. Providing aid is their main aim, and they serve around 400 people each week with their food and provisions.

Food Not Bombs

Food Not Bombs Kuala Lumpur (FNBKL) was founded over two decades ago. Their focus is organizing among active individuals to help provide free food for homeless people on the streets of Kuala Lumpur. They have coined the term 'home free' to refer to the state of homelessness, as the term *homeless* refers to a kind of lacking that may carry stigma.

Short-term Support & Street Shelter

Although some of these above-mentioned organizations act as a bridge between the government (MWFCD and DSW) and homeless population to communicate the need for services and assistance, one of the most prominent services provided to the homeless by NGOs and charities is free food on the streets or in designated locations.

Whether these 'NGOs' are the more formal organizations that are registered with the Registry of Societies of Malaysia (a department under the Ministry of Home Affairs handling non-governmental organizations and political parties), or the less-formal, self-organized voluntary groups, most of them tend to focus on providing short-term help, such as food and provisions, rather than policy advocacy.

The distribution of food and provisions has raised concerns about food waste, hygiene, and enabling a 'charity' culture, as well as the wider question of how far the provision of food and other supplies is constructively addressing the problems of homelessness. Authorities also receive complaints from local businesses because of the perception that areas where groups of homeless people congregate are seen as unsafe. These factors have led to more punitive responses, involving strategies such as containment, criminalization, and eradication of homeless people in public spaces (e.g. arrest or removal of homeless people from the city or to camps under the Destitute Persons Act). While smaller NGOs and groups provide assistance in a more ad hoc manner, there is some coordination between larger organizations, but overall coordination in terms of times and locations of food distribution and other types of services is lacking.[94]

Although there are currently Anjung Singgah and Pusat Transit Gelandangan, which provide shelter, food, and employment in major cities, including Kuala Lumpur, the expected length of stay is short (two weeks), and the focus is solely on reintegration into the workforce.[95] The establishment of Anjung Singgah focuses on short-term implementation, demonstrating a lack of awareness of the complexities of homelessness and the political will to create longer-term changes to restructure the problem. Homeless people who enter these shelters are often released back onto the streets.[96] Often, homeless people are also reluctant to engage with government programmes, for fear of being 'sent away' to government institutions and shelters, where they will be deprived of their freedom.[97]

Discussion: Moving Forward

Recognizing the symbiotic relationship between containment and control, and sustenance and care,[98] and the crucial role of the voluntary sector in guiding policy initiatives, we address three main areas for propelling further change in the HKSAR and Malaysia.

A Working Definition of Homelessness in Preparation of a Homeless Law

Definitions have shaped public policy, influenced public opinion, and defined responses and solutions. Homelessness is one of the most complex social problems, and the lack of a consistent definition of *homelessness* makes it difficult to develop a comprehensive policy framework. *Homelessness* in Hong Kong is too narrowly defined as sleeping on the streets in certain public spaces, and current policy in Malaysia is guided only by a legally enforceable Vagrancy Act, which equates homelessness with either begging and vagrancy or destitution. While the establishment of a homelessness law is a political matter (which is not easily accessible in the HKSAR and Malaysia), the development of a working definition can lead to clearer service and policy objectives and provide an opportunity to formulate longer-term solutions. This, in itself, requires further insight into the complex causes of homelessness

---

94 Think City, *Homelessness – Finding a Novel Way Forward* (2018) <https://documents.pub/document/homelessness-in-kuala-lumpur-think-city-homelessness-in-kuala-lumpur-page-4.html?page=1>.
95 Penang Institute (n 86).
96 Alhabshi and Abdul Manan (n 75).
97 Ghee and Omar (n 74).
98 G. DeVerteuil, M. Matthew Marr, and D. Snow, 'Any Space Left? Homeless Resistance by Place-type in Los Angeles County' (2009) 30(6) *Urban Geography* 633.

but also recognizes the role of structural factors beyond traditional welfare questions, such as shortcomings in employment and housing policies. A working definition of *homelessness* could therefore provide an opportunity to move beyond the confines of social assistance and tap into other public resources.

To (Re-)Examine the Causes or Factors Leading to Homelessness

Understanding causes that contribute to homelessness can bring to light more effective responses and solutions that address, and possibly prevent, homelessness. Studies on homelessness in Hong Kong[99] and Malaysia[100] have identified factors that contribute to homelessness and predicted that a new form of homelessness will emerge following the global economic uncertainty. However, many of those studies lack theoretical underpinning, which runs the risk of conflating superficial symptoms of homelessness with causes.[101] The voluntary sector can offer unique insight into the struggles, barriers, and capacity of people who experience homelessness. Further to that, the voluntary sector can build upon the positive relationships with homeless individuals and help support and facilitate the rapport and trust-building process between researchers and homeless communities.

This will enable researchers to engage in in-depth studies that apply or generate theoretical frameworks to examine beyond the dichotomized causes (individual vs structural).[102] With the voluntary sector as the bridge, researchers, NGOs, and homeless individuals can be active participants to co-examine the pathways that lead into homelessness[103] and propose pilot service models based on the findings.

To Propose Constructive and Effective Service and Support Models

Immediately after the 2013 Homeless Outreach Population Estimation (HOPE) survey in Hong Kong, a rapid rehousing model, which includes an Assertive Community Treatment Approach, was proposed as a solution in the survey report.[104] In 2019, the 'Housing First Support First' model was proposed by Think City, a Malaysian think tank. Although the proposals have not been officially implemented in Hong Kong and Malaysia, the model recognizes the complex nature of homelessness and is based on the understanding that pathways to homelessness are made up of a dynamic interplay of causal factors that span four main areas: housing structures (lack of access to housing), economic structures (factors such as lack of employment skills and insufficient income), interpersonal characteristics (such as domestic violence and family breakdown), and personal characteristics (such as

---

99 J. Kwok and R. Chan, 'Street Sleeping in Hong Kong' (1998) 41(4) *International Social Work* 471; Au-Liu and Ching (n 5); Homeless Outreach Population Estimation (H.O.P.E) survey report (H.O.P.E. Project 2015).
100 Alhabshi and Abdul Manan (n 75); Adib, Amalina and Ahmad (n 73).
101 See C. Ching, 'Structurational Perspectives on the Resilience of Homeless People in Hong Kong' in T. Mizuuchi, G. Kornatowski and T. Fukumoto (eds), *Diversity of Urban Inclusivity: Perspectives Beyond Gentrification in Advanced City-Regions* (Springer 2023) 137.
102 See J. Neale, 'Homelessness and Theory Reconsidered' (1997) 12(1) *Housing studies* 47; S. Fitzpatrick, 'Explaining Homelessness: A Critical Realist Perspective' (2005) 22(1) *Housing, Theory and society* 1; Ching (n 101).
103 Fitzpatrick (n 102).
104 Au-Liu and Ching (n 5).

gambling or mental illness). Some factors may cut across more than one area, and they may also reinforce each other.[105] The model is adapted from the Housing First (HF) model[106] that encompasses, with equal importance, housing and comprehensive supportive services that address barriers in each of the four areas. It suggests that in order to effectively address the complex nature of homelessness, policy and programme frameworks must adequately address these four key factors. In the HKSAR, the CHM initiative is moving in this direction with the help of a highly organized voluntary sector. The next step would be to integrate personal care services, such as those provided by the home help sector. The voluntary sector is already exploring this direction. The question remains, however, whether the Light Public Housing Scheme will go the same way. At present, the burden of care resources is still shared at the community level.

In Malaysia, although a proposal was developed, the plan never materialized because there was insufficient awareness and understanding of the causes of homelessness – let alone policy and programme responses. NGOs can use their knowledge of the specific needs of homeless people to advocate for a more comprehensive approach to homelessness in Malaysia. The government's non-policy stance, without any legal framework to clearly define government responsibilities and citizens' rights, potentially provides 'space' for the voluntary sector to act not only as a short-term aid provider but also as an advocate, mediator, and communicator between the homeless and the government, and as an agent to help reframe the narrative of homelessness from vagrancy and passive service-receiving to agency and resilience.

Conclusion

This chapter has introduced the concept of positive non-policy to describe the development of homeless services in Hong Kong and Malaysia. Positive non-policy allows both governments to intervene in homelessness, often at times of crisis, without being constrained by legal obligations. In practice, the government directs services through the funding of voluntary agencies and thus the outsourcing of services. In theory, this allows policy to be made on the fly, but the absence of any legal obligations implies a certain fragility, as funding could be withdrawn at any time. This is unlikely, however, as the partnership between the public and voluntary sectors is not a one-way power relationship, and service delivery without the accumulated expertise of NGOs would be an unworkable proposition.

The chapter began with the case of Hong Kong, where we introduced the category of 'street sleepers' as a population in need of social services. Services are organized under the Integrated Service System, which is a one-stop service run by appointed NGOs (the Integrated Teams). The NGOs are bound by Funding and Service Agreements (FSAs) which specify the number of street sleepers to be served from outreach to aftercare. Here we see that the colonial background and ideology of anti-welfarism has given rise to the current service system, where NGOs take responsibility for caring for underprivileged people. However, in Hong Kong's political economy, this has proved to be no easy task, especially

---

105 Fitzpatrick (n 102).
106 S. Tsemberis, L. Gulcur, and M. Nakae, 'Housing First, Consumer Choice, and Harm Reduction for Homeless Individuals with a Dual Diagnosis' (2004) 94(4) *American Journal of Public Health* 651.

during the current housing crisis. Nevertheless, the recent Community Housing Movement initiative is a hopeful sign of pragmatic intervention in the housing problem. Again, the NGO expertise built up over the past two decades has been crucial in organizing this initiative.

As in HKSAR, Malaysia's colonial past plays a role in the organization of homeless services. The punitive attitude of treating homelessness, begging, and vagrancy as a set under the Vagrancy Act in Malaysia has its roots in the 19th-century British colonial period.[107] The overarching framework of legal paternalism behind the Vagrancy Act combines punishment and care – disciplinary and compassionate at the same time, depending on whether the homeless person is deemed a 'vagrant' or 'destitute'. These two seemingly opposing yet complementary forces have historically functioned as two sides of the same coin of state control that continues to alienate the rights and interests of homeless people today. The control apparatus that imposes decisions, whether care or punishment, on homeless people on the basis of perceived incapacity is an obstacle to constructively addressing homelessness.[108]

However, it is also important to recognize that within punitive governance, many of the 'sites of control' such as hostels and transit centres are also 'sites of resistance' for homeless people. The very structures used to control, contain, and criminalize are also spaces where homeless people demonstrate their resilience and agency to cope with structural barriers and hardship – and where NGOs and volunteers provide genuine care and build relationships and alliances.[109] The HKSAR's CHM initiative now offers opportunities to build the resilience and agency of vulnerable people.

In conclusion, it is the resilience and resourcefulness of the voluntary sector that are the real positive sides of positive non-policy. It has made up for the colonial legacy of anti-welfare and has been a crucial link both in steering policy (often, but not exclusively, through advocacy) and in innovating the content and delivery of care services. On the other hand, positive non-policy is characterized by insufficient political will to address homelessness in a legally-binding way. Nevertheless, it provides space for the voluntary sector to experiment with novel solutions, albeit to varying degrees in the cases of HKSAR and Malaysia. But here, at a pragmatic level, the reliance on community resources has been critical. This has been done out of necessity, even to the dismay of many organizations seeking greater public sector involvement. In the discussion, we identified three main areas of further opportunity in the HKSAR and Malaysia. We conclude with a call for further research into workable solutions in the context of positive non-policy.

---

107 Rusenko (n 77).
108 Ibid.
109 Ching (n 101).

24
HOMELESSNESS IN INDIA
A State Legislative and Civil Society Perspective

Kalpana Goel, Mohd Tarique, Meenu Anand, and Elvis Munyoka

Introduction

Homelessness is growing in many parts of the world and has become a worldwide pressing phenomenon. Homelessness has a significant impact on communities and individuals in both developing and developed countries.[1] However, India is one of the countries with the world's highest number of homeless people.[2] Today, there are 1.8 million homeless people in India, with 52% of the homeless population living in metropolitan areas.[3] The Indian Census in 2011 highlighted that there were 1.77 million homeless people in the country, accounting for 0.15% of the total population.[4] According to more recent statistics, India has over 4 million homeless people.[5] There is currently a shortage of 10 million urban residential units, with another 25 million required by 2030.[6] The extent and magnitude of homelessness in India have risen enormously in the past few decades. The outbreak of the Covid-19 pandemic has also exacerbated the calamity of homelessness and led to many deaths, owing to the lack of access to health services and adequate shelter.[7] Despite India's stable economic growth over the past four decades, it is home to a quarter of the world's undernourished people, as the

---

1 S. Roy, A. Bose, and I. R. Chowdhury, 'Darkness under the City Lights: A Qualitative Study on the Life of Urban Homelessness, Evidence from Siliguri City of West Bengal, India' (2023) 88 *GeoJournal* 2263.
2 N. Singh, P. Koiri, and S. Kumar Shukla, 'Signposting Invisibles: A Study of the Homeless Population in India' (2018) 3 *Chinese Sociological Dialogue* 179.
3 Action, *Housing Is a Human Right. Homelessness Is a Violation of That Right* (Action 2009).
4 K. Goel and R. Chowdhary, 'Living Homeless in Urban India: State and Societal Responses' in C. Zufferey and N. Yu (eds), *Faces of Homelessness in the Asia Pacific* (Routledge 2017).
5 Z. Siffiqui and S. Kataria, 'Some of Us Will Die': India's Homeless Stranded by Coronavirus Lockdown' *Reuters* (1 April 2020).
6 S. Mitra, P. Priya, and A. Venkatesh, *The Bass Model: Demand Forecasting for Affordable Housing in India* (SAGE Publications: SAGE Business Cases Originals 2022).
7 D. Banerjee and P. Bhattacharya, 'Coronavirus Disease 2019 (COVID-19) and Homelessness: Global Perspectives on the "Dual Pandemic"' (2021) *Homelessness and Mental Health* 167.

minimum dietary diversity[8] has decreased and the gap between the rich and poor has grown.[9] Over the last two decades, the total number of people living in shanty houses in India has more than doubled.[10] This chapter examines homelessness in India, including statistics, drivers, types of homelessness, challenges, policy and legal provisions, initiatives, and recommendations from the government and from a civil society perspective.

Defining Homelessness

There is no universally accepted definition of *homelessness*. The Indian Census defines a *homeless person* as someone who does not reside in a census house – a census house is a structure with a roof which is either self-rented or owned – but instead lives in a houseless household, for example, on the roadside, on railway platforms; spends nights at transit homes, under staircases or flyovers; or lives in temporary shelters without walls and roofs, in common areas or parks.[11] This definition, however, exempts the attribution of adequate housing provided for in the Universal Declaration of Human Rights, making it difficult to record the actual numbers of homeless people in India.

Due to the steady increase in homelessness in India, civil society organizations recently developed a more comprehensive definition of *homelessness* as part of their advocacy for a national policy for the urban homeless to capture previously unrecognized people living in homeless conditions. The homeless are conceptualized to mean such people who, as individuals or families, do not have a house, either self-owned or rented, or do not have a settled place to stay, or live and sleep in park boundaries, over bridges, on flyover edges, on pavements, in railway and bus stations, in places of worship, outside shops, over shop roofs, in Hume pipes, inside flyovers, on road medians, in garbage dumps, on river beds, on river embankments, near cremation grounds or graveyards, in underpasses, in memorials of eminent people, and other places under the open sky.[12]

Under this definition, *homelessness* includes people who live in temporary structures, including under plastic sheets on the roadside or on pavements, also referred to as pavement dwellers in many states, or spend their nights sleeping in places of work, like shops (comprising *dhabas*), factories, construction sites, or spend their nights in or on their means of livelihood, such as hand- or pushcarts, and rickshaw, or spend their nights in night shelters, transit homes, homes for children, or any short-stay home.[13] All this indicates severely inadequate, insecure, and temporary shelter, which can be classified as homelessness. This is a much broader definition that includes aspects that unequivocally typify homelessness, such as including people who live alongside other family members, but in crudely crowded circumstances.

---

8 The intake of 4 or more of the 7 food categories to improve dietary quality and fulfil the daily nutritional and energy needs of the 7 suggested food groups like legumes and nuts, roots and tubers, grains, flesh foods, and dairy products.
9 WFP, *UN WFP India Annual Country Report 2021* (WFP 2021).
10 J. F. Keenan and M. McGreevy, *Street Homelessness and Catholic Theological Ethics* (Orbis 2019).
11 Office of the Registrar General and Census Commissioner, *Census India 2011* (2011).
12 Government of India Ministry of Housing and Urban Affairs, *The National Policy for the Urban Homeless* (2021).
13 Ibid.

Statistics on Homelessness: An Indian Outlook

India is a densely populated country. Located in South Asia between Myanmar and Pakistan, India has a population of 1.3 billion people. Mumbai is one of India's most populous cities, having a population density of 20,692 persons per km^2.[14] The informal sector employs most of Mumbai's population, with an average monthly salary of 6,000 rupees. Due to low income in rural regions, Mumbai's population increased dramatically in the 1970s. Employers prefer migrant workers over local workers because they are less expensive and more willing to work in hazardous conditions for long periods.[15] Approximately 60% of the homeless in Mumbai are migrant labourers.[16] Migrant labourers travel to the city in search of a better way of life, better food, better healthcare, and clean drinking water, as well as to escape the caste-based violence that has deprived them of any chance of making a good living.[17] Living in slums has become a temporary remedy to the otherwise exorbitant expense associated with metropolitan life. Mumbai's slums are home to around 5.5 million people yet occupy only 8% of the overall, total land mass. Squatters reside in filthy, overcrowded conditions with inadequate lighting and power. To address the issue of inadequate housing, particularly in slums, the Maharashtra government created the Maharashtra Slum Areas Improvement, Clearance, and Redevelopment Act in 1971.[18]

Despite this and other attempts by the Indian government to improve the homeless situation in metropolitan areas, homelessness remains widespread, owing in part to increasing urban growth.[19] Therefore, the Indian government must exercise extreme caution to guarantee equal opportunity to all residents in line with the Universal Declaration of Human Rights, specifically the right to adequate housing for all. At present, the Indian government is incapable of providing these basic services to all citizens. Another issue is that there is significant social inequality between the oligarchy and the impoverished classes.[20] The poverty of the 21st century is unlike any other in Indian history. It is not the result of natural scarcity but of a set of priorities imposed upon the rest of the world by the rich.[21] Consequently, the modern poor are not pitied but are written off as disposable – essentially as trash.[22]

Employers tend to hire only those they believe are suitable or of their class, ignoring those who are less privileged.[23] As a result of unemployment, people are pushed into greater

---

14 P. Deokar, 'Homelessness in India: Causes and Remedies' *Leagle Samiksha* (19 June 2022) <https://leaglesamiksha.com/2022/06/19/homelessness-in-india-causes-and-remedies/> (accessed 1 September 2023).
15 Internal Displacement Monitoring Centre, *Country Profile India* (Internal Displacement Monitoring Centre 2021).
16 M. K. Jha and P. Kumar, 'Homeless Migrants in Mumbai: Life and Labour in Urban Space' (2016) *Economic and Political Weekly* 69.
17 Ibid.
18 Ibid.
19 J. Castaldelli-Maia, A. Ventriglio, and D. Bhugra (eds), *Homelessness and Mental Health* (OUP 2021).
20 C. Olaf Christiansen and S. L. B. Jensen, 'Histories of Global Inequality: Introduction' in C. Olaf Christiansen and S. L. B. Jensen (eds), *Histories of Global Inequality: New Perspectives* (Springer International Publishing 2019).
21 S. Fitzpatrick, G. Bramley, and S. Johnsen, 'Pathways into Multiple Exclusion Homelessness in Seven UK Cities' (2012) 50 *Urban Studies* 148.
22 Castaldelli-Maia, Ventriglio, and Bhugra (n 19).
23 H. Munthe-Kaas, R. Berg, and N. Blaasvær, 'NIPH Systematic Reviews' (2016) *Report from the Norwegian Institute of Public Health* No. 2016–02.

poverty, which leads to destitution. Prices for food, clothing, and shelter have soared to the point where even the most basic goods are no longer affordable to the poorest in society.[24] Furthermore, the have-nots are frequently compelled to choose between two square meals and long-term shelter. Due to the high cost of housing, the homeless are forced to live in a temporary shelter made of scraps than buy or rent a proper home.[25] Recent statistics projected that over 20 million houses are needed in India.[26] Family migrants, moving to urban areas from rural areas due to loss of property and in search of employment and better opportunities, are frequently left homeless due to high rents (a basic apartment costs around 3,000 rupees) and a lack of houses to accommodate them. When faced with homelessness, these migrants resort to making a shelter out of cardboard, tin, plastic, and wood.[27]

Difficult circumstances force many impoverished people to reside in shanty houses. A significant number of deaths have occurred because of inadequate protection from the winter season weather. For example, the death of 164 people because of a lack of protection from cold conditions from 2015 to 2016 led to improvements in the night shelter scheme provided by the government of India.[28] Due to extraordinarily harsh winter conditions, 200 individuals died in Delhi during the winter season of 2022, because the city's homeless shelters could only house around 9,300 people.[29] Shanty houses, makeshift houses, and tenements accommodate 78 million people, accounting for 17% of the global slum population.[30] Over the past two decades, the total number of people living in shanty houses has more than doubled in cities across India. According to the Housing and Land Rights Network in India report, which was presented to the United Nations Human Rights Council, some of the cities with the highest numbers of homeless people include Mumbai, which has an approximate population of 200,000 homeless individuals. Another city with a large number of homeless people is Delhi, which has a rough population of 150,000 to 200,000 people, while Ahmedabad has an estimated population of 100,000 homeless persons.[31]

Types of Homelessness in India

There are several types of homelessness recognized in India. There is seasonal homelessness, which consists of regular families who migrate interstate and intrastate for a few months each year in pursuit of work;[32] occupational homelessness, which consists of both interstate and intrastate migrant families who migrate for a specific job and, once the task is completed, move on to another area or state; and distress homelessness, which comprises families who have temporarily migrated from the source area because of social ostracization, floods, poverty, and riots that rendered it impossible for them to continue residing in

---

24 S. Malik and S. Roy, 'A Study on Begging: A Social Stigma – An Indian Perspective' (2012) 18 *Journal of Human Values* 187.
25 Deokar (n 14).
26 Reuters (n 5).
27 S. Valson, *Prevention of Homelessness: How Is the Problem Treated Legally* (2022) <https://blog.ipleaders.in/prevention-homelessness-problem-treated-legally/> (accessed 1 September 2023).
28 Factbook, *The World Factbook*.
29 Aljazeera, *In India's Capital, the Homeless Are Suffering a Record Winter* (1 February 2022).
30 Roy, Bose, and Chowdhury (n 1).
31 Housing and Land Rights Network, 2015.
32 Ministry of Housing and Urban Affairs, *The National Policy for the Urban Homeless* (Government of India 2021).

the source area. They may choose to either move out of the source area on a permanent or temporary basis or remain in a city for a short period, making their homelessness more dynamic. Thus, their homelessness is complicated since it is not a cultural transition but rather a manifestation of a lack of accessibility to any place of residence when they travel from one location to another in pursuit of greener pastures.[33]

Other forms of homelessness include chronic homelessness, which involves persons who have been homeless for a long period. Chronically homeless people are mostly senior citizens who are unable to work due to physical or mental impairments. Such people make up a small but significant hidden percentage of the homeless population often overlooked in policy initiatives.[34] Finally, *episodic homelessness* refers to those who are homeless regularly and have behavioural, physical, and medical issues, as well as persistent unemployment. However, there appears to be a glaring absence in the framing of homelessness of the penniless elderly, those deserted by their spouses, children, or relatives, people with disabilities, and sexual and gender minorities. Since their circumstances differ from those of the rest of the population, these vulnerable groups demand that the concept of homelessness be expanded to include the language of violence, sporadicalness, and fluidity.[35] This dilemma in policymaking promotes inequality rather than reducing the crippling consequences that it seeks to eliminate.

Drivers of Homelessness in India

Homelessness in India can be seen as caused by several complex issues, including discrimination, a persistent shortage of affordable housing, family and domestic violence, multigenerational poverty, unemployment, and severe mental illness.[36] Independent factors like low academic achievement, employment status, domestic violence, and trauma may increase the likelihood of becoming homeless.[37] However, the causes of homelessness may be divided into two broad categories: structural and personal, familial conditions.[38] Structural factors include inequality, poverty, limited access to affordable housing motivated by the commodification of housing, forced eviction, lack of social protection, and lack of access to land or financing.[39]

Personal and familial causes of homelessness include circumstances like chronic sickness, mental illnesses, substance addiction, impairments, or domestic violence, which render individuals and families more prone to homelessness.[40] Women and children are the most vulnerable demographic, frequently afflicted by a cocktail of structural and personal factors that contribute to homelessness, such as domestic abuse or human trafficking.[41]

---

33 Ibid.
34 Valson (n 27).
35 Ibid.
36 A. Steen, 'The Many Costs of Homelessness' (2018) 208 *Medical Journal of Australia* 167.
37 Fitzpatrick, Bramley, and Johnsen (n 21).
38 Ibid.
39 G. Wood and others, *The Structural Drivers of Homelessness in Australia 2001–11* (Final Report No. 238, Australian Housing Urban Research Institute 2015).
40 D. Banerjee and P. Bhattacharya, 'The Hidden Vulnerability of Homelessness in the COVID-19 Pandemic: Perspectives from India' (2021) 67(1) *International Journal of Social Psychiatry* 3.
41 B. A. Lee, K. A. Tyler and J. D. Wright, 'The New Homelessness Revisited' (2010) 36 *Annual Review of Sociology* 501.

Breaking the intergenerational cycle of homelessness is critical to rescuing children from the pattern of homelessness and destitution. For example, children who become orphans or lose their breadwinner parents because of homelessness may end up homeless later in their own lives.

Homelessness is not a transient phenomenon caused only by natural disasters. It is the result of several push factors that compel people to leave their homes.[42] The reasons for homelessness differ according to various segments of the population in India. Studies have indicated that violence is one of the major causes of homelessness among women, as well as social banishment for people belonging to the LGBTQIA community. Similarly, demolitions, forced evictions, communal rights, and lack of proper rehabilitation after big developmental plans are some of the other reasons that cause homelessness. Rapid urbanization, increased living costs, and economic downturns, for example, have all contributed to the increase in homelessness in India.[43] Fast human population growth and ongoing migration of individuals from rural to urban areas have worsened homelessness in major cities, particularly among the poor. Big metropolitan cities such as Delhi (31,181,377 people), Mumbai (20,667,655 people), Kolkata (14,974,073 people), and Bangalore (12,764,935 people) are struggling to strike a balance between rapid growth and the substantial pressure to provide commercial and residential infrastructure.[44]

In some cases, government projects are blamed for causing homelessness. For example, evictions throughout urban and rural India in 2017 demonstrated a disturbing reality of state-sponsored de-housing and obliteration of the country's poorest homes and property. In addition, during the Covid-19 pandemic from March 2020 to July 2021, state authorities displaced over 257,000 individuals from their houses in India for different environmental and infrastructural projects.[45] According to one report[46] conducted between January and December 2021, around 173,000 individuals were evicted and 36,812 houses were bulldozed across India.[47]

Most of the people who were displaced by infrastructural projects did not receive any rehabilitation or assistance from the government; they had to search for alternative accommodation, rendering them homeless. The way programmes are administered demonstrates insufficiency in terms of respecting people's fundamental human rights, particularly the right to adequate housing, which has been severely harmed by the eviction of residents from their houses, an issue that has been raised and lobbied for by several human rights organizations in India, such as the Housing and Land Rights Network. The reality that

---

42 G. Johnson and others, *Entries and Exits from Homelessness: A Dynamic Analysis of the Relationship Between Structural Conditions and Individual Characteristics* (Final Report No. 248, Australian Housing Urban Research Institute 2015).

43 S. Johnsen, S. Fitzpatrick, and B. Watts, 'Homelessness and Social Control: A Typology' (2018) 33 *Housing Studies* 1106.

44 S. Verma and V. Srivastava, 'Urban Homelessness and Baseras/Shelters: An Evaluative Study Conducted During Winter in NCT Delhi' (2020) 29 *Journal of Social Distress and Homelessness* 110; Statistics Times, 'Population of Cities in India' *Statistics Times* (2021).

45 R. Chitlangia, '257,000 People Evicted during Pandemic, Shows Report by Housing Rights Body' *Hindustan Times* (9 September 2021).

46 Forced Evictions in India in 2020: A Grave Human Rights Crisis During the Pandemic, Housing and Land Rights Network, 2021.

47 See Chitlangia (n 45).

is underscored in all this is that being homeless is not a deliberate choice but rather is the result of desperation due to multiple factors, including poverty and violence.[48]

Challenges Faced by Homeless People in India

Homeless people face a variety of challenges, which include healthcare, gender-specific issues, denial of human rights, and mental health conditions. Each of these challenges is discussed in the following subsections.

Healthcare

Access to healthcare in India is incredibly challenging for homeless people. Many homeless shelters do not provide any type of healthcare to their occupants, including women. Homeless people, notably women and the elderly, suffer from a variety of illnesses because of poor living circumstances and inclement weather.[49] Homeless people are susceptible to heat, rain, and cold and lack adequate clothing and shelter. This lowers their immunity and makes them more vulnerable to a variety of health problems. Often, their illnesses go untreated or are detected too late, leaving them vulnerable to infection and even death.[50] The scarcity of adequate medical and mental health assistance aggravates homelessness, as many homeless people will go on to develop mental illnesses.

Gender

Homeless women and children typically struggle to gain access to basic services, resulting in a feeling of hopelessness. Women and children are frequently classified as hidden homeless, with inadequate housing impacting them twice as much as it does men.[51] Without stable housing, they often rely on informal support networks to avoid sleeping on the street. Homeless women and mothers are usually victims of domestic abuse. Homeless women, particularly young women, face the most severe forms of violence, and they are vulnerable to sexual exploitation and trafficking.[52] Incidences of rape, harassment, molestation, and women spending restless nights guarding their teenage daughters are all typical among homeless women in India. For example, in India, civil society organizations working on homelessness have estimated that there are between 0.15 and 2 million homeless people in the capital city of Delhi alone, with at least 0.01 million of them being women.[53] There have been several reports in India of women being denied care and being sent away from hospitals. As a result, homeless mothers have been forced to deliver children on the roadside, heightening their and their infants' mortality.[54] Shel-

---

48 Roy, Bose, and Chowdhury (n 1).
49 Munthe-Kaas, Berg, and Blaasvær (n 23).
50 Housing and Land Rights Network, *Shelters for Homeless Women: Working Paper with a Focus on Delhi* (Housing and Land Rights Network 2017).
51 Ibid.
52 Action (n 3).
53 Ibid.
54 Keenan and McGreevy (n 10).

ters and places of safety for homeless women, particularly pregnant and breastfeeding mothers, remain scant and inadequate.[55]

Denial of Human Rights

Homelessness violates the principle of human dignity enshrined in Articles 1 and 22 of the *Universal Declaration of Human Rights* and in the *International Covenants on Civil and Political Rights and Economic, Social, and Cultural Rights*. The United Nations special rapporteur on the right to adequate housing has stated that:

> Homelessness is a profound assault on dignity, social inclusion, and the right to life. It is a prima facie violation of the right to housing and violates several other human rights in addition to the right to life, including non-discrimination, health, water and sanitation, security of the person, and freedom from cruel, degrading, and inhuman treatment.[56]

The right to adequate housing is also recognized as a fundamental human right under the Indian Constitution. The Supreme Court, on the other hand, has recognized Articles 14, 19, and 21 as decisive criteria in defining a person's dignity. States must safeguard an individual's dignity by providing housing for the homeless.[57] Despite these legal provisions, homeless people largely remain invisible to society and are not stakeholders in any decision-making processes in India. Their lack of identity and status means that they get little chance to determine aspects of their living conditions. The homeless lack power to such a degree that many are effectively non-persons, without documents, rights, or the right to vote. In India, they are the nearest approximation to being hidden in society.[58]

Mental Health Conditions

Homeless people with mental health conditions constitute one of the most disadvantaged groups in the international health stage.[59] Homelessness is viewed as both a cause and a result of a psychiatric condition. Although not all homelessness is caused by or results from a mental health condition, when they co-exist, a lack of support makes it more difficult for homeless mentally ill people to break free from the destructive cycle of homelessness.[60] In a country of around 1.8 billion people, with a mental illness frequency of at least 5% (55 million), and with the number of psychiatrists just slightly above 3,000,[61] the result is a 90% treatment gap. Only 43 government mental institutions are functioning,

---

55 Action (n 3).
56 *UN Special Rapporteur on the right to adequate housing (A/HRC/43/43, 30)*.
57 Deokar (n 14).
58 M. Mabhala and A. Yohannes, 'Being at the Bottom Rung of the Ladder in an Unequal Society: A Qualitative Analysis of Stories of People without a Home' (2019) 16(23) *International Journal of Environmental Research and Public Health* 4620
59 Ibid.
60 Ibid.
61 V. Patel, 'The Future of Psychiatry in Low-and Middle-Income Countries' (2009) 39 *Psychological Medicine* 1759.

with three psychiatrists for one million people, and psychologists and psychiatric social workers are far fewer. There are, in addition, only 25% or 11 mental health hospitals in rural India, yet rural India is home to more than 70% of the country's population. In the context of the Covid-19 pandemic, homeless persons with mental health conditions were among the most vulnerable people to the disease, and those with medical or psychological problems were more likely to develop Covid-19.[62] The outbreak of the pandemic has also worsened the pre-existing discrimination of persons suffering from mental illnesses through, for example, the segregated administration of vaccines. Many people suffered from anxiety because of a life devoid of basic needs, prolonged stress, and little hope during the pandemic in India. Homeless people without access to mental health treatments were forced to live on the streets, worsening the challenges presented by homelessness. Homelessness may be either a cause or an effect of mental illness; thus, the link between the two is complex.

Policy and Legal Provisions in India

There exists a variety of fundamental rights, guiding principles of state policy, and treaties that require India to provide appropriate housing for citizens, including homeless children, women, disabled people, refugees, and asylum seekers. To begin, Article 21 of the Indian Constitution explicitly stipulates that '[n]o person shall be deprived of his or her personal liberty except according to procedures established by law'.[63] Although Article 21 does not include housing, Indian courts, through various judgements, have found that the right to life encompasses, among other things, the right to housing or shelter, clean water, power, sanitation, and livelihood.[64] Therefore, any legislation, or administrative action, that violates a person's right to life, such as forcible eviction without the provision of alternative housing, might be challenged in the respective state high courts or the Supreme Court of India through petitions.[65]

In addition, Article 14 of the *Constitution of India* further proclaims that '[t]he state shall not deny to any person equality before the law or equal protection of the laws within the territory of India'.[66] These clauses are interpreted to mean that every citizen of India is equal before the law and must have access to basic needs of life to ensure the protection of their personal liberty.[67] The controversy stems from the fact that there is no direct provision in the Indian Constitution for providing adequate housing for citizens, although interpretations of Articles 14 and 21 imply that the right to shelter or decent accommodation is a basic human right derived from the Constitution. Many decisions by the Indian Supreme

---

62 M. Narasimha Vranda, J. Ranjith, and P. Shaji Sreelakshmi, 'Reintegration of Homeless Patients with Mental Illness (HPMI) in the Community – Challenges Faced During COVID-19 Pandemic' (2021) 43(3) *Indian Journal of Psychological Medicine* 257.
63 Article 21 of the Constitution of India.
64 High Court Cases on the Human Right to Adequate Housing: Compendium and Analysis of Important Judgments.
65 Action (n 3).
66 Article 14 of the Constitution of India.
67 P. Bhattacharya and K. Priya, 'Stakeholders Facilitating Hope and Empowerment Amidst Social Suffering: A Qualitative Documentary Analysis Exploring Lives of Homeless Women with Mental Illness' 68(4) *International Journal of Social Psychiatry* 908.

Court testify to the linkage between the right to housing and the right to life, as contained in Article 21, but an unambiguous provision is required.

At the international level, India is a signatory to several international human rights laws relating to the right to adequate housing and land. For example, India ratified binding international instruments, such as the *Universal Declaration of Human Rights* 1948 Article 25[1], which states that:

> Everyone has the right to a standard of living adequate for the health and well-being of himself and his family, including food, clothing, housing and medical care, and necessary social services, and the right to security in the event of unemployment, sickness, disability, widowhood, old age, or other lack of livelihood in circumstances beyond his control.[68]

Moreover, India accepted Article 14 [2] of the 1979 *Convention on the Elimination of All Forms of Discrimination Against Women*, which states that:

> States Parties shall take all appropriate measures to eliminate discrimination against women in rural areas to ensure, on a basis of equality of men and women, that they participate in and benefit from rural development and, in particular, shall ensure to such women the right: [a] To participate in the elaboration and implementation of development planning at all levels . . . [h] To enjoy adequate living conditions, particularly in housing, sanitation, electricity and water supply, transport, and communications.[69]

Aside from these international legal instruments, India has ratified various guidelines and declarations on homelessness. These include the United Nations General Assembly Resolution 43/181; United Nations Global Strategy for Shelter to the Year 2000; housing and property restitution in the context of refugees and other displaced persons, Sub-Commission on Human Rights Resolution 2002/7; the Right to Adequate Housing Article 11 [1] of the Covenant, Commission on Human Rights Resolution 2005/25; and the United Nations Declaration on the Rights of Indigenous Peoples 2006.

Begging and Destitution: The Rights, Laws, and the State

Notwithstanding India's tremendous economic progress, begging has existed in the country since the dawn of human civilization and continues to exist even after government attempts to eliminate it through a variety of laws.[70] Beggary regulations are still in place in Indian law, despite any proof of exploitation and with no assumption of criminal behaviour among an already-vulnerable part of society. It is concerning that the unjustified limitation on begging imposed by anti-begging legislation in India deprives the homeless who

---

68 Universal Declaration of Human Rights 1948 Article 25(1).
69 Convention on the Elimination of All Forms of Discrimination Against Women 1979 Article 14 (2).
70 S. Shivansh, *Beggary Laws in India: A Constitutional Analysis*, (2022) *Legal Service India E-Journal* <www.legalserviceindia.com/legal/article-1367-beggary-laws-in-india-a-constitutional-analysis.html (accessed 1 September 2023).

rely on begging as their only source of livelihood and violates their fundamental human rights.[71] Begging is a growing social and legal issue that exists practically all over the globe. Every country has its unique begging population, and persons in beggary are a familiar occurrence in India today.[72] The problem cannot be reduced to a mere state of deprivation, or exclusion, but must also be viewed as a refusal of citizenship, the right to live in dignity, and the ability to work.[73]

The *Bombay Prevention of Begging Act* of 1959 is one of the major laws against beggary which was established to change the mindset of the individuals begging. However, the major flaw of the provisions is their penalizing nature on people who either do not make conscious decisions to be beggars or who have no other choice.[74] No one chooses to be living in poverty. In that regard, this aspect of the law violates the right to freedom of speech granted by Article 19 [1] of the Constitution, as well as the right to life and liberty provided by Article 21 of the Constitution. The following is an extract from a victim of the anti-begging legislation that demonstrates the extent of the repercussions for victims who are penalized because of the government's incompetence and failure to fulfil its constitutional duty of providing basic needs to its citizens. When asked about his detention under the Bombay Prevention of Begging Act of 1959, Daya Rathore (pseudonym), 65, expressed his helplessness. Knowing that arrest is a legal step taken against criminals, he pondered why he had been arrested since he had done nothing wrong:

> [I] have been sentenced to 1 year of detention? My children abandoned me a few years ago and since then I have been living on the streets. I do odd jobs for my survival. I do not know why I was arrested.[75]

What is evident from this paragraph is that incarceration has induced mental illness in an already-vulnerable individual. The notion of poverty as a cause of crime is within the purview of the law. In this case, the impoverished bear the blame for their poverty, which becomes an offence.[76] The most serious feature of homelessness is that it violates fundamental human rights such as freedom of expression and assembly, as well as access to food. The shocking reality is that, because of this controversial punitive legislation, state governments appear to be targeting the poor, particularly those experiencing homelessness. This is made evident by the legislative structure in place to address homelessness and poverty, especially in urban areas.

Most Indian states have anti-begging legislation, which can be viewed simply as a legal instrument to punish poverty.[77] This includes states like Punjab, Chandigarh, and Hary-

---

71 Ibid.
72 B. Kaushik and M. Gupta, 'An Analysis of Anti-Begging Policy in India' (2022) 43(1) *Specialusis Ugdymas* 7965.
73 A. Goel, 'Indian Anti-Beggary Laws and Their Constitutionality Through the Prism of Fundamental Rights, with Special Reference to Ram Lakhan V. State' (2010) 11 *Asia-Pacific Journal on Human Rights and the Law* 23.
74 S. Menka and T. Hassan, 'Begging Is a Curse on Society: An Empirical Study' (2013) 2(7) *International Journal of Advanced Research in Management and Social Sciences* 44; Shivansh (n 70).
75 Goel (n 73).
76 U. Ramanathan, 'Ostensible Poverty, Beggary and the Law' (2008) 43(44) *Economic and Political Weekly* 33.
77 Shivansh (n 70).

ana – even appearing poor in these states is enough to have you detained on the basis that begging is considered a crime.

Hundreds of individuals face the prospect of incarceration across the country, wherever beggary law is in effect. In what could be easily understood as a mockery of human rights and constitutional guarantees, many states in the country have anti-begging legislation that criminalizes homeless people. Beggary laws illustrate how law can be created, sustained, and practised in circumstances in which the constituency affected by those laws is defenceless, because of the unlawfulness that the law imposes on them, the gap between privilege and poverty, and the state's failure to fulfil its obligations.[78]

Article 41 of the Indian Constitution provides that the state shall 'make effective provision for securing the right to work, education, and public assistance in case of unemployment, old age, sickness, and disablement'.[79] However, what most states have adopted is completely contrary. Instead of securing people's rights, all that states do is criminalize these contexts of vulnerability. These state laws are, broadly, versions of the *Bombay Prevention of Beggary Act* 1959, which grant powers to officials to detain people presumably engaged in begging in government-run custodial centres.[80]

Although there are government schemes, including pensions, for the welfare of groups like the elderly, persons with disabilities, and widows, people in beggary rarely get any access to these programmes due to the legal identity of a beggar being constructed under the beggary law.[81] In fact, some of these schemes, like the Pension Scheme in Delhi, contain a clause that if any action has been taken against a person under the beggary law, then the person is not eligible to receive a pension under the scheme.[82] Even a wrongful arrest would amount to action and therefore mean disqualification from the much-needed scheme. Emphasizing this exclusion based on the assumption of crime, Tarique and Raghavan argue that 'a central assumption underlying and legitimising the penal treatment of the poor [by the State] is that most people who beg are part of organised gangs and criminal networks'.[83]

The Law and Its Coverage

The Bombay Prevention of Begging Act of 1959, though a state law, is a piece of legislation that has been adopted and adapted more widely by several other states.[84] So it is appropriate and sufficient to use and analyze this piece of legislation as a way of understanding the nature and coverage of the anti-beggary laws in India more broadly. The Act defines 'beggary' in such a manner that a homeless person with mental illness, a small-time vendor, a person wandering about, or even an elderly person can legally be considered a beggar. While defining *beggary*, Section 2 [1](d) of the Act says: '[H]aving no visible means of subsistence and wandering about or remaining in any public place in such condition or manner,

---

78 Ramanathan (n 76).
79 India Constitution Article 41.
80 V. Raghavan and M. Tarique, 'Penalising Poverty: The Case of the Bombay Prevention of Begging Act 1959' (2018) 53(22) *Economic & Political Weekly* 27.
81 Kaushik and Gupta (n 72).
82 Menka and Hassan (n 74).
83 Ibid.
84 Ibid; Shivansh (n 70).

as makes it likely that the person doing so exist soliciting or receiving alms.'[85] This clause alone is enough to make a large section of the population vulnerable under the law. Several groups in India have traditionally engaged in activities such as fortune-telling, singing, dancing, and street shows. All such communities are equally susceptible to falling foul of this draconian legislation.[86]

While the way beggary has been defined technically renders every homeless person a potential beggar, it also gives extreme powers to the police, as there is a lot of discretionary power provided under the law.[87] Surprisingly, there is no strict necessity for a warrant for imprisonment to take place. There is no requirement of proof for the offence to be made out in court. On the contrary, the accused must demonstrate that he or she earns a living other than by begging. The trial court will send the accused on remand for the investigation to be completed. If charges against the person are not proven, then the person would be released. There is no need to be concerned about a breach of a person's liberty. If the allegations of beggary are proven, the individual can be imprisoned for one to three years for a first offence, and up to ten years for a second offence.[88]

What is vital to understand in the context of human rights is how implementation has been designed. The law grants powers to state agencies to keep any person in detention for a period between one and ten years as punishment for beggary, which could arise from nothing more than merely a situation of destitution.[89] The implications of this law need to be understood from the context of the structure of an offence and how *beggary* has been defined. Since the definition of *beggary* includes different vulnerable circumstances, punishing begging is equivalent to punishing those circumstances. This is a most extreme example of the poor being punished by the state for its failure to protect or provide for its poor citizens.[90] Let us examine a few more sections of this law here. Section 9 of the Act says that the 'court may order the detention of persons wholly dependent on beggar'.[91] This makes family members who may not have begged themselves as vulnerable as the person committing the offence. Furthermore, there is a section that provides for indefinite detention. Section 10 provides that the state has the power to detain the person for an indefinite period – after the completion of ten years of detention.[92] Though there is a clause and certain procedural requirements governing this, the fact remains that a person accused of beggary can be detained for an indefinite period.

Government of India Programs to Eradicate Homelessness

The Indian government has implemented several initiatives to help homeless people in the country. Despite frightening homelessness statistics, India is making progress in combating homelessness and poverty. It is said that 44 individuals are lifted out of homelessness every

---

85 The Bombay Prevention of Begging Act of 1959 Section 2 [I] (d).
86 Goel (n 73).
87 Raghavan and Tarique (n 80).
88 Ibid.
89 Kaushik and Gupta (n 72).
90 Ibid.
91 Shivansh (n 70).
92 Goel (n 73).

day because of government programmes.[93] The Indian government is currently working to establish affordable, low-cost homes. The Jawaharlal Nehru National Urban Renewal Mission (JNNURM) is one such policy to deal with the problem of inadequate shelter in cities. This policy aims to ensure efficiency in urban infrastructure and service delivery systems, community involvement, and parastatal institution accountability to people.[94] In addition, the government is desiring to reduce traffic congestion in Indian cities and give universal access to essential services. The JNNURM necessitates that densely populated towns demand essential utilities such as sanitation and power from their landowners.

To combat homelessness, one of the JNNURM's priorities was to create cheap housing for the urban poor, shanty dwellers, and those from poor backgrounds. This initiative was able to construct several dwellings, yet the condition of the shelters was criticized for not reaching appropriate housing standards. The Indian government has spent Rs 21,482 crores[95] on housing for the urban poor during the last decade. The JNNURM built 224,000 of the 238,448 unoccupied dwellings, while the Rajiv Awas Yojana built the other 14,448.[96] This means that 93.9% of the houses lying vacant were built under the JNNURM. Since these dwellings lack adequate facilities, the urban poor were unwilling to relocate. It is also because these residences were constructed in places where employment was limited. Poor people cannot afford to commute longer distances due to low income levels.

The Indian government has also launched Night Shelter programmes to offer temporary accommodation to the country's homeless. The Housing and Urban Development Corporation initially implemented Night Shelters between 1992 and 1997.[97] The scheme aimed to provide communal night shelters with a water supply and sanitary facilities for the people who are homeless in metropolitan areas and other big cities on a pay-and-use basis. Following that, in 1992, the Ministry of Urban Development launched a scheme called Shelter and Sanitation Facility for street dwellers in metropolitan areas to provide night shelters to the completely homeless habitats in major cities until they were qualified for low-cost housing provided by any of the state-level schemes.[98] However, most shelters were found to be vacant of homeless people. The government and non-governmental organizations conducted several studies, which found a lack of basic facilities and shelter upkeep, resulting in impoverished people abandoning shelters.[99] Since then, provisions have been changed, and the names of schemes have been changed from Shelter and Sanitation Facilities to Night Shelters for the Urban Shelterless. These programmes had inadequate implementation at the state level as a result of poor administration and mismanagement of funds.[100]

---

93 S. Chari, 'A View into Homelessness in India' *The Borgen Project* (2020) <https://borgenproject.org/homelessness-in-india/> (accessed 1 September 2023).
94 M. Moiz, 'Homelessness in India' *Cauf Society* (2023) <https://caufsociety.com/homelessness-in-india/> (accessed 1 September 2023).
95 Equivalent to USD 2,541,468.3.
96 Shanu, 'All You Need To Know About JNNURM' *Makaan IQ* (1 July 2016) <www.makaan.com/iq/news-views/all-you-need-to-know-about-jnnurm> (accessed 1 September 2023).
97 P. Ghosh, G. Goel, and M. Ojha, 'Homeless Shelters in Urban India: Life Sans Dignity' (2018) 13 *International Journal of Housing Markets and Analysis* 4.
98 Ibid.
99 Ibid.
100 Ibid.

Initiatives by Civil Society Organizations to Support the Homeless in India

Various civil society organizations are partnering with the government to assist homeless people in India. For example, the Society for Promotion of Youth and Masses (SPYM) runs government-funded night shelters in Delhi City and provides basic amenities such as drinking water, toilet facilities, and bedding to the homeless. They also have provisions for basic health services.[101] Other civil society organizations have been founded specifically to assist homeless women. The URJA Trust in Mumbai is one among them. The URJA Trust is an organization dedicated to protecting the rights of homeless women. The organization has helped more than 400 women transition from homelessness to safe environments, provided mental health services to over 300 women, and promoted public awareness of women's homelessness.[102]

The URJA Trusts have also made great strides in providing shelters specifically for women who have escaped domestic violence, as often state agencies providing accommodation rarely consider the plight of women fleeing from domestic violence. Homeless women are housed in a shelter when they come in but are later shifted to group homes as soon as they start becoming financially independent. The URJA non-profit organization houses roughly 50 women and girls each year and has successfully rehabilitated 250 women in the last four years.[103]

Some civil society organizations are striving to assist homeless children who are vulnerable to a variety of issues such as abuse and a lack of shelter. For instance, Salaam Baalak Trust, located in New Delhi and Mumbai, is a non-profit organization that helps homeless children. The group runs several programmes aimed at improving the lives of homeless children, such as educational activities. So far, they have helped a total of 108,014 young people in India. The Salaam Baalak Trust has been in operation in Delhi since 1989 and runs four community centres that are available 24 hours a day, seven days a week, and can house up to 220 children at any given time.[104] Salaam Baalak Trust has consistently provided free clothing, food, education, and rehabilitation services to homeless children in India.

Moreover, the Tata Institute of Social Sciences in Mumbai founded Koshish, a civil society organization, to combat the illegality of poverty under beggary legislation. Koshish focused on developing a comprehensive framework to help individuals get out of poverty by addressing numerous vulnerabilities.[105] Started in Mumbai in 2006, the initiative was expanded to Delhi in 2009 and to Bihar in 2012. The initiative was implemented in conjunction with state governments in each of these states. Koshish is sceptical of and resistant to the state's response to poverty and destitution, yet as an institution, it also recognized that the solution must come from the state and hence is working closely with the government to abolish the criminalization of beggars.[106]

---

101 S. Ghosh, 'Understanding Homelessness in Neo-Liberal City: A Study from Delhi' (2020) 55(2) *Journal of Asian and African Studies* 285.
102 Ibid.
103 Gayatri Manu, *This Garment Factory Turned Shelter Home Has Supported More Than 250 Women in the Past 4 Years* (2016) https://www.thebetterindia.com/72883/urja-trust-mumbai-homeless-women-runaway/.
104 S. Gardner, 'Homelessness during India's Rainy Season' *The Borgen Project* (2020) <https://borgenproject.org/homelessness-during-indias-rainy-season/> (accessed 1 September 2023).
105 S. P. K. Jena, *Homelessness: Research, Practice, and Policy* (Taylor & Francis 2020).
106 Raghavan and Tarique (n 80).

Koshish created national-level coalitions and collaborated with many organizations working on issues of urban poverty to create a support structure for the wider Indian community.[107] The overarching objective has been to replace the punitive approach with a non-punitive one. Koshish developed a solid community-level preventative campaign to accomplish this.[108] As part of the community-based framework, several concerns including mental health difficulties, family repair, vocational training, supporting livelihoods, education, and questioning the conventional acceptability of vagrancy are all addressed.[109] A special focus was also given to children's education. These are the children from the communities that have traditionally had recourse to begging or to vocations that are considered as begging under the law, like selling small articles or rag picking. Koshish provides close handholding and support to these children and seeks to prepare them to understand and resist the historical discrimination that these communities have long faced.[110] Today, more than 90% of the children in each of the communities in which Koshish works go to school. This has led to extremely positive changes in their parents, as most parents desire for their children to avoid the risks and vulnerabilities the streets present.

Since 2006, the Koshish-Tata Institute of Social Sciences (TISS) Field Action Project on Homelessness and Destitution has been working with several state governments to raise the problem of criminalization under the Beggary Prevention Laws.[111] Gradually, states like Maharashtra and Delhi have begun discussing the possibility of decriminalizing beggary through amendments to the law. Both states constituted committees to recommend amendments to the law. The state of Rajasthan also brought in a pilot scheme in two districts of the state where rehabilitation was the central focus. In a progressive development, the state of Bihar launched a pilot intervention in 2012 where, for the first time, the amendment to the Beggary Prevention Laws was made. This flagship programme by the Social Welfare Department in the state is known as *Mukhya Mantri Bhikshavriti Nivaran Yojana*.[112]

The Way Forward for Homelessness in India

Homelessness is a major challenge affecting millions of people globally, with a substantial proportion of those impacted in India, a nation that has so much potential. Homeless people in India encounter abuse, discrimination, and starvation. Although having minimal resources and power, civil society organizations play an important role in addressing homelessness in India. They campaign for the rights of the homeless and work to better their lives. The government is also involved in tackling India's homeless dilemma. The government intends to provide homes for every citizen in India within the next few years. While these initiatives may or may not be as successful as one wishes, they do give some optimism that the deplorable state of homeless Indians may be remedied.

---

107 R. Thara, 'NGOs and Mental Health: Initiatives and Progress' in J. Kumar Trivedi and A. Tripathi (eds), *Mental Health in South Asia: Ethics, Resources, Programs and Legislation* (Springer 2014).
108 A. Mitra, 'Food security in South Asia: A Synthesis Paper' (2010) <https://idl-bnc-idrc.dspacedirect.org/bitstream/handle/10625/45094/131551.pdf?sequence=2&isAllowed=y> (accessed 1 September 2023).
109 A. L Hall and J. Midgley, *Social Policy for Development* (Sage 2004).
110 Kaushik and Gupta (n 72).
111 M. Malik, 'Street Begging in Delhi: A Study of Anti-Begging Act and Institutional Arrangements for Homeless People' (Researching Reality Summer Internship Working Paper, Centre for Civil Society 2012).
112 Hall and Midgley (n 109).

Despite the promising initiatives implemented by the Indian government and civil society organizations to address the country's homelessness problem, however, the emphasis has been primarily on providing emergency temporary accommodation, for decades, to alleviate the plight of millions of people who are homeless in urban and regional areas. The Indian government has recently focused its efforts on providing permanent shelter to the homeless, but the state has failed to offer the facilities considered necessary for decent shelter. Underlying the problem is the state's failure to develop effective systems for maintaining the facilities after they are built.

The long-term solution to India's homelessness problem, which has existed for decades, is to plan for the provision of permanent housing for the homeless with adequate facilities so that the housing provided will be occupied permanently by homeless people. Since the homeless are unable to access many services due to a lack of documentary proof such as residence and birth certificates, shelter should serve as a hub for various social security programmes, and all homeless people living in government-arranged housing must be given priority access to food, health, and social security entitlements. Increased housing investment has proved to be a significant solution to keeping up with population growth in crowded cities like Delhi and Mumbai. However, increased investment must be accompanied by accountability in the use of resources to ensure the success and timely completion of projects, as these are just some of the challenges crippling the government's attempts to reach its aim of providing adequate housing for all.[113]

On the other hand, housing governance in India has usually concentrated on national initiatives. Policy guidance and technical aid at the national level are critical, but there is an urgent need to scale up sub-national assistance. This requires determining what kind of housing delivery systems have been established by governmental institutions to address local housing requirements. To carry out such initiatives, there is a need for reliable and disaggregated data on people who are homeless to develop and implement context-appropriate and holistic strategies, as well as to assess whether those solutions are effective in achieving the desired outcomes. This would also help achieve the Sustainable Development Goals, with the objective that everyone have access to appropriate and adequate housing by 2030, with priority given to the most vulnerable in society. This is consistent with the UN-Habitat Convention Resolution mandating member states and local governments to develop integrative programmes and policies spanning multiple sectors such as physical and mental health, housing, and employment, as well as measures ensuring access to digital technology and finance.[114] Sustainable homelessness practices that should be recommended include preventative policies aimed at addressing the fundamental causes of homelessness, such as better access to affordable housing, greater social protection measures, and discrimination prevention.[115] India must also standardize the measurement, collection, and disaggregation of statistics on homelessness, which is crucial, given the paucity of accurate data on the homeless population in the country.

In terms of the *Bombay Prevention of Begging Act* of 1959, the primary law on destitution, there is no doubt that unless the Act is repealed and criminalization is eliminated,

---

113 Ghosh, Goel, and Ojha (n 97).
114 UN-Habitat, *Priorities 2022–2023: Adequate Housing, Cities and Climate Change, and Localising the Sustainable Development Goals* (UN-Habitat 2022).
115 Ibid.

little will change. Vulnerable people will continue to be punished for their poverty.[116] To solve this problem, all stakeholders must unite and work together. Reviewing the draft bill created by the Ministry's special committee and enacting it as law might be one significant step toward systemic change. Effective collaboration between the state and civil society, as well as a shift in the government's attitude towards the urban poor, may be harnessed by signing the *Persons in Destitution Model Bill* into law. Until impoverished people are acknowledged as equal citizens and their rights are respected in the spirit and essence of constitutional provisions, as they are for all other citizens, India will continue to be haunted by legislation like the 1959 *Bombay Prevention of Begging Act*. Affirmative action from states is desperately needed to help people who are already entangled in the vortex of homelessness and misery. As things stand today, the government's ability to accomplish this is not just constrained but nearly non-existent. Homeless people in India, as in other countries, must be regarded as citizens equal with all others and as people deserving of the necessary support and assistance to ensure they can stabilize their circumstances and pursue meaningful lives.

---

116 Menka and Hassan (n 74); Kaushik and Gupta (n 72).

25
CENTRALITY OF THE HOME AND HOMELESSNESS IN SINGAPORE

Poh Leng Teo

Introduction

This chapter examines the issue of homelessness in Singapore, a small city state of 730 km² with a resident population of 4.07 million. It begins with a historical explanation of Singapore's national housing policy and its success, with special mention on what public housing means and how it is different from other countries. This will be useful for readers unfamiliar with Singapore's housing situation and provides the context to understand why being homeless is considered odd in Singapore. The chapter then discusses the 're-emergence of contemporary homelessness' and the nature of homelessness in Singapore. The remaining sections delve into the policies and strategies to address homelessness. The chapter ends with some thoughts on the ecosystem to address homelessness and contextual variations to consider.

As in many other countries, homelessness is a complex issue in Singapore. There are different manifestations of homelessness, one of which is living in open spaces like the streets or parks, or even in public areas with physical shelter (like a covered carpark or a pavilion). However, a person who stays temporarily with friends in their homes (doubling up) or shares living spaces with strangers in a shelter, though having a place of residence, can be defined as homeless. Research has highlighted that homelessness is not just based on the presence or absence of a roof over one's head or a physical abode. Homelessness (with 'home' being its flipside) has been posited to be a psycho-social-spatial entity. While the homeless have been assisted with accommodation and social services, the lived experience of the homeless has been associated with the lack of comfort, privacy, independence, autonomy, and control over one's daily activities. Homelessness is also associated with poverty, emotional health, lack of access to services, unemployment, and other concerns.[1]

---

1 U. Anucha, 'Housed but Homeless? Negotiating Everyday Life in a Shared Housing Programme' (2010) 91(1) *Families in Society: The Journal of Contemporary Social Services* 67; V. Busch-Geertsema, D. Culhane and S. Fitzpatrick, 'Developing a Global Framework for Conceptualising and Measuring Homelessness' (2016) 55 *Habitat International* 124; S. Mallett, 'Understanding Home: A Critical Review of the Literature' (2004) 52(1) *The Sociological Review* 62; C. Parsell, 'Home Is Where the House Is: The Meaning of Home

It is equally difficult to define who the homeless are due to the heterogeneity of the homeless population(s). This is also the case in Singapore. The homeless can be classified based on their demographic characteristics, such as homeless singles, homeless families headed by single parents, nuclear families that are homeless, the homeless who are employed, the homeless with mental health conditions, those who are homeless due to domestic violence, rough sleepers who live on the streets versus the 'sheltered homeless', and so on. Even within each specific homeless population, there is differentiation, as each group has unique needs, like a homeless individual with some kin support or one without any support, a homeless person who is employed vis-à-vis one who is unemployed. Notwithstanding the different homeless populations, studies show that there are similarities in terms of their lived experiences being homeless, especially when co-sharing living spaces and not having a place they can call their own.[2]

In terms of the pathways to homelessness, discussions have been along the lines of agency-vs-structural causes. However, the polarity between agency and structural causes is artificial, as neither exists on its own and both influence each other. There is synergistic interaction between micro-level and macro-level factors. For instance, personal risk factors like poor health, which affects one's employment and, consequently, financial ability to pay for housing, can intersect with fluctuating home mortgage interest rates due to the effects of globalization and precipitate homelessness. Likewise, strategies to exit homelessness involve intervening at both individual and structural levels. To add to this argument, people can be rendered homeless due to unanticipated events at different scales, like an earthquake in a geographical region or the Covid-19 pandemic, which has affected people globally.[3]

---

for People Sleeping Rough' (2012) 27(2) *Housing Studies* 59; P. Sommerville, 'Homeless and the Meaning of Home: Rooflessness or Rootlessness' (1992) 16(4) *International Journal of Urban and Regional Research* 529; P. L. Teo, 'Experiences of Homeless Families on the Interim Rental Housing Scheme in Singapore' (Doctoral thesis, National University of Singapore 2015) <http://scholarbank.nus.edu.sg/handle/10635/126245> (accessed 1 September 2023); P. L. Teo and Y. L. Chiu, 'An Ecological Study of Families in Transitional Housing – "Housed but Not Homed"' (2016) 31(5) *Housing Studies* 560; V. Tischler, '"I'm Not Coping, I'm Surviving": Understanding Coping in a Marginalised Population' (2009) 6 *Qualitative Research in Psychology* 191.

2 H. Easthope, 'A Place Called Home' (2004) 21(3) *Housing, Theory and Society* 128; J. W. Schiff, 'Homeless Families in Canada: Discovering Total Families' (2007) 88(8) *Families in Society: The Journal of Contemporary Social Services* 131; M. L. Shier, M. E. Jones and J. R. Graham, 'Perspectives of Employed People Experiencing Homelessness of Self and Being Homeless: Challenging Socially Constructed Perceptions and Stereotypes' (2010) 37(4) *Journal of Sociology and Social Welfare* 13; B. Teater, 'A Place to Call "Home: Exploring the Experiences of Section 8 Housing Choice Voucher Program Recipients in Their Efforts to Find Housing' (2009) 90(3) *Families in Society: The Journal of Contemporary Social Services* 271; Teo (n 1); Teo and Chiu (n 1); P. A. Toro, 'Toward an International Understanding of Homelessness' (2007) 63(3) *Journal of Social Issues* 461; S. Williams and T. Stickley, 'Stories from the Streets: People's Experiences of Homelessness' (2011) 18(5) *Journal of Psychiatric Mental Health Nursing* 432.

3 Hansard Parliament 13 session 2 vol 94 sitting 131 *Assistance for Rough Sleepers and Measures to Help Them Cope with COVID-19 Circuit Breaker Conditions* (4 May 2020) <https://sprs.parl.gov.sg> (accessed 1 September 2023); Hansard Parliament 14 session 1 vol 95 sitting 49 *Requests by Homeless and Rough Sleepers for Temporary Accommodation or Shelters in 2022 and Options Available* (18 February 2022) <https://sprs.parl.gov.sg> (accessed 1 September 2023); Ministry of Social and Family Development (MSF), *Report on the Street Count of Rough Sleepers 2022* (Ministry of Social and Family Development, Republic of Singapore 2023); K. H. Ng and J. S. Sekhon Atac, 'Seeking Shelter: Homeless During the COVID-19 Pandemic in Singapore' (2022) Singapore: Lee Kuan Yew School of Public Policy <https://lkyspp.nus.edu.sg/

Singapore – A City State of Homeowners

Homelessness is not entirely a new issue in Singapore, as the city state has had to address poor living conditions and people living in public places in the past. However, the issue had not been discussed openly or seen as a national problem for decades until the years 2007–2008 onwards. It began in 2007, with a few news reports of families with young children who made their homes in parks and on beaches. This came as a surprise as it was assumed that everyone should have a home. This can be attributed to Singapore's unique housing policy and conditions, where the government plays a leading role in providing public housing. Unlike in other countries, public housing in Singapore is for the masses and not just for lower-income households. The national housing programme has rehoused Singaporeans from squalid housing conditions of the 1960s till today, where almost everyone has a roof over their head. Singapore has a consistently high homeownership rate, close to 90%. This is a remarkable achievement by world standards.[4]

The national public housing programme for Singaporeans was born out of the vision to promote homeownership in 1964, under the leadership of then prime minister Lee Kuan Yew, who stated, 'I wanted a home-owning society [so that citizens] could have a stake in Singapore', and he believed that 'if every family owned its home, the country would be more stable'.[5] Singapore's housing authority, the Housing and Development Board (HDB), a statutory board under the Ministry of National Development (MND), has been providing a spectrum of subsidized national public housing (on 99-year leasehold) for the upper-middle-, middle-, and low-income groups since the 1960s.[6]

Through the Public Home Ownership Program, 80% of Singapore's resident population, or about 3.04 million people, live in HDB flats, of which 90% own their homes. For lower- income citizen households who are not able to afford their own homes, there is a social safety net for them to rent smaller HDB flats at heavily subsidized rates through the Public Rental Scheme.[7] HDB public rental flats constitute about 4% of all HDB flats. As of 2020, there were 50,000 households under the Public Rental Scheme. These flats, though not owned by the families, are akin to permanent housing.[8]

---

research/social-inclusion-project> (accessed 1 September 2023); Toro (n 2); L. Weinreb, D. J. Rog and K. A. Henderson, 'Exiting Shelter: An Epidemiological Analysis of Barriers and Facilitators for Families' (2010) 84(4) *Social Service Review* 597.

4 Department of Statistics (DOS), 'Households' <www.singstat.gov.sg/find-data/search-by-theme/households/households/latest-data> (accessed 1 September 2023). T. K. Liu and A. S. Tuminez, 'The Social Dimension of Urban Planning in Singapore' in D. Chan (ed), *50 Years of Social Issues in Singapore* (World Scientific Publishing 2020) 97.

5 K. Y. Lee, *From Third World to the First. The Singapore Story: 1965–2000. Memoirs of Lee Kuan Yew*. (Singapore Press Holdings 2000); B. Yuen, 'Squatters No More: Singapore Social Housing' (2007) 3(1) *Global Urban Development* 1.

6 Housing and Development Board (HDB), 'About Us' (n.d.a) <www.hdb.gov.sg/cs/infoweb/about-us> (accessed 1 September 2023); Liu and Tuminez (n 4); Teo (n 1); Teo and Chiu (n 1).

7 Housing and Development Board (HDB), 'Public Rental Scheme' (n.d.b) <www.hdb.gov.sg/residential/renting-a-flat/renting-from-hdb/public-rental-scheme> (accessed 1 September 2023).

8 Ministry of National Development (MND), 'Written Answer by Ministry of National Development on Households Living in HDB Rental Flats' (2020) <www.mnd.gov.sg/newsroom/parliament-matters/q-as/view/written-answer-by-ministry-of-national-development-on-households-living-in-hdb-rental-flats> (accessed 1 September 2023).

There are also public rental schemes to assist lower-income individuals. For example, the HDB Joint Singles Scheme (JSS), where two or more singles can apply for an HDB rental flat at heavily subsidized rates. HDB recently implemented the Joint Singles Scheme Operator-Run (JSS-OR) Pilot in December 2021 to offer single rooms with shared facilities (using converted disused facilities like vacant schools). Singles can apply for rental housing without first having to find flatmates. Instead, applicants will be matched with flatmates by an operator appointed by HDB, who will consider factors like age, ethnicity, sex, and living habits. This is another housing option that the homeless or those at risk of homelessness can consider.[9]

Meaning of Homelessness in Singapore

No Legal Definition of Homeless

Unlike some countries, for example, Japan, the UK, and most states in America, which have a legal definition of *homelessness*, Singapore does not have a legal definition of *homelessness*.[10] The closest to a legal meaning or definition of a *homeless person* can be found in the Destitute Persons Act (1989), and even then, the term 'homeless' is not used.[11] The Act also does not address the specific issue of an entire family being homeless. The Act (Section 2) defines a *destitute person* as:

> Any person found begging in a public place in such a way as to cause or be likely to cause annoyance to persons frequenting the place or otherwise to create a nuisance; or any idle person found in a public place, whether or not he is begging, who has no visible means of subsistence or place of residence or is unable to give a satisfactory account of himself.

The roots of this legislation can be traced to Singapore's state of socio-economic development in the 1960s. This Act was enacted in 1965, when poverty was rampant in the early days of nation-building. It was a means to assist with persons who were destitute, with little subsistence and without a place to stay, so that they could be admitted into a residential facility for their care.[12] Based on this definition, a destitute person who has no place to stay or is roofless can be regarded as being homeless. It is possible that a destitute person may have a home or a family but choose to live in public spaces for various reasons. The Act is under the ambit of the Ministry of Social and Family Development (MSF), the government

---

9 Housing and Development Board (HDB), 'Eligibility Criteria and Schemes' (n.d.c) <www.hdb.gov.sg/residential/renting-a-flat/renting-from-hdb/public-rental-scheme/eligibility> (accessed 1 September 2023).
10 L.-C. Cheng and Y.-S. Yang, 'Homeless Problems in Taiwan: Looking Beyond Legality Towards Social Issues' (2010) 1 *City, Culture and Society* 165; H. Goto, D. Culhane and M. Marr, 'Why Street Homelessness Has Decreased in Japan: A Comparison of Public Assistance in Japan and the US' (2022) 16(1) *European Journal of Homelessness* 81.
11 <https://sso.agc.gov.sg/Acts-Supp/8-1989/Published/19900315?DocDate=19890303> (accessed 1 September 2023).
12 B. L. Ang, 'The Soul of National Building in Singapore: Contributions from Social Work' in D. Chan (ed), *50 Years of Social Issues in Singapore* (World Scientific Publishing 2015) 133.

Definition(s) of Homelessness and Types of Homelessness in Singapore

Homeless Singles

While there is no legal definition of *homelessness*, the Singapore government has defined a *homeless person* as one who does not have access to housing. This would include those who do not have a home, rough sleepers who have homes but are sleeping in the streets due to difficulties returning to their homes, and those who are living temporarily in shelters.[14] There are also homeless singles who live temporarily with relatives and friends. This policy definition is broad and similar to the European Typology of Homelessness and Housing Exclusion (ETHOS) developed by the European Federation of National Organizations Working with the Homeless and the European Observatory on Homelessness,[15] as it takes into account different types of homelessness and homeless groups.

In terms of homeless singles, one group would be destitute persons who can be admitted into welfare homes for care and rehabilitation. Most of the destitute in the homes are single middle-aged or elderly males in need of accommodation and assistance. A number of them also have mental health conditions.[16] 'Rough sleepers' are another homeless group. The government is cognizant that not all persons may have slept rough (that is, living in public areas), as they may be living in shelters, whilst working towards getting permanent housing. In a recent report released by MSF on a single night street count conducted on 11 November 2022, it was found that there were 530 rough sleepers. Most of the rough sleepers are middle- to older-age males who tend to have low education, are in low-paying occupations, and lack social support. Fifty-seven of the 530 rough sleepers who took part in a survey reported having strained family relationships as well as housing and money difficulties. About half (28 persons) of the 57 rough sleepers had health concerns, and half (24) were unemployed.[17] The number of rough sleepers is small compared to data collected from street counts done in other countries like America or Japan.[18] This is likely due to Singapore's national housing policy, as well as its smaller geographical and population size.

---

13 Ministry of Social and Family Development (MSF), 'Mission and Values' (n.d.) <www.msf.gov.sg/who-we-are/mission-values> (accessed 1 September 2023).
14 Hansard Parliament 13 session 2 vol 94 sitting 115 *Addressing Homelessness Problem as Reported in Study of Over 1,000 People Sleeping in the Rough* (6 January 2020) <https://sprs.parl.gov.sg> (accessed 1 September 2023).
15 FEANSTA, 'ETHOS Typology on Homelessness and Housing Exclusion' (2011) <www.feantsa.org/en/toolkit/2005/04/01/ethos-typology-on-homelessness-and-housing-exclusion> (accessed 1 September 2023).
16 Hansard Parliament 13 session 1 vol 94 sitting 10 *Approach in Tackling Homeless Cases* (24 March 2016) <https://sprs.parl.gov.sg; Hansard Parliament 13 session 2 vol 94 sitting 105 *Number of Displaced Persons in Shelters* (8 May 2019) <https://sprs.parl.gov.sg> (accessed 1 September 2023); Hansard, 4 May 2020 (n 3).
17 Hansard, 6 January 2020 (n 13); Hansard, 4 May 2020 (n 3); Ministry of Social and Family Development (MSF) (n 3). Ministry of Social and Family Development. Republic of Singapore.
18 Goto and others (n 10).

Homeless Families

Homeless families refers to single-parent families or nuclear families with children without stable and permanent housing.[19] The issue of contemporary family homelessness 'resurfaced' in Singapore in late 2007 and 2008, with media reports of families with children making their homes, sleeping in tents or sheltered area, in the parks, and beaches. This was also during the economic recession. An investigation into the families' housing histories revealed that many of them had homes. Three in four were previously HDB flat owners. Some of these families were not literally roofless; they had options like staying with other family members or were listed as owners, tenants, or occupiers of flats but chose not to stay in them. Some homeless families were previously homeowners who had benefitted from housing subsidies provided by the government in the past to buy their own HDB home. Some of them had purchased and sold their HDB homes twice. They had sufficient amounts from the sales of their homes to buy or rent another home from the open market. Interestingly, some of these families who had sold their homes said that they could not afford to buy or rent a home from the open market as it was too expensive or they had spent the sale proceeds.[20]

Under HDB regulations, families who have benefitted from government-subsidized flats and sold their flats are debarred from public rental housing for 30 months. These families found themselves edged out of the private property market and yet are not defined as being poor to qualify for public rental housing. Some of the homeless families had weak social support and preferred to make their homes in a way that gave them a sense of control and independence. These cases illustrate the intersection of personal and structural factors.[21]

There are no official reports on the total number of homeless people in Singapore. However, MSF reported in 2016 that between the years 2005 and 2015, it had provided assistance to an average of 300 homeless individuals each year.[22] Most of the homeless in Singapore have financial issues and weak family support, and they tend to have low incomes. Some of the homeless individuals also exhibit anti-social behaviour or addiction-related problems. Among the homeless families were cases where they sold their HDB homes to clear debts or for other purposes. Some of the families found themselves without a home after selling their flat following a divorce. Working with homeless individuals and families is challenging as they have preferences (for example as to the type of financial assistance or accommodation)

---

19 E. L. Bassuk and S. Geller, 'The Role of Housing and Services in Ending Family Homelessness' (2006) 17(4) *Housing Policy Debate* 781; Teo (n 1).
20 Hansard Parliament 11 session 1 vol 85 sitting 6 *Defaulters of HDB Mortgage Loans* (18 November 2008) <https://sprs.parl.gov.sg> (accessed 1 September 2023); Hansard Parliament 12 session 1 vol 89 sitting 5 *Number and Profile of Homeless Persons* (13 August 2012) <https://sprs.parl.gov.sg> (accessed 1 September 2023); Hansard Parliament 12 session 1 vol 91 Sitting 1 *Homeless Families Who Camp by Beach* (20 January 2014) <https://sprs.parl.gov.sg> (accessed 1 September 2023); *The Straits Times* (28 January 2007); Teo (n 1); Teo and Chiu (n 1).
21 Hansard, 18 November 2008 (n19); Hansard, 13 August 2012 (n 19); Hansard, 20 January 2014 (n 19); Teo (n 1).
22 Hansard Parliament 13 session 1 vol 94 *HDB Rental Flats for Displaced and Homeless Families* (1 March 2016) <https://sprs.parl.gov.sg> (accessed 1 September 2023). Hansard Parliament 13 session 1 vol 94 9 *Approach in Tackling Homeless Cases* (24 March 2016) <https://sprs.par.gov.sg> (accessed 1 September 2023).

Singapore's Approach to Tackling Homelessness

The issue of homelessness with HDB housing being ubiquitous has gained traction over the years, with the topic being discussed in Parliament on the extent of homelessness and adequacy of the social safety net. This section examines the Singaporean approach to tacking homelessness, including a description of support measures during the Covid-19 pandemic (between 2020 and 2021) to assist those who were homeless or inadvertently found themselves homeless.[24] Tackling homelessness is challenging due to the diverse homeless population groups and their different needs, as well as the reality that government agencies and stakeholders handle different aspects of homelessness. For example, if a member of the public sees a homeless person sleeping in the open in a housing estate in Singapore, what should that member of the public do? The possibilities are to call the police, who can respond quickly, especially if there are security concerns, or call MSF so that the person may be admitted to a welfare home while a social investigation (to gather information on the person's circumstances, needs, risks, and support systems) is being done, or to contact the housing estate's town council that controls and maintains the common facilities in the area.[25]

Policy Principles and Policy Leads

The government adopts a so-called 'Whole of Society' approach to address national issues, and this is similarly used to manage homelessness. As articulated by Mr Desmond Lee, then minister for family and community development (MSF), the approach means 'all Singaporeans come together, when we look out not only for ourselves, but our families, neighbours, and fellow Singaporeans in need'.[26] This is very much a Singaporean approach, also known as 'Many Helping Hands'. This approach emphasizes self-reliance, followed by the role of the family to support its members who are in need, and the role of the community in meeting the needs of the disadvantaged and vulnerable, with the government setting the framework for policies and service models and standards, funding parameters, and connecting service providers with beneficiaries. Singapore's social compact is not just about the state doing more but different segments of society (social service agencies, community agencies like ethnic self-help groups, and religious bodies, donors, and volunteers) coming together to provide support and assistance.[27]

---

23 Hansard, 18 November 2008 (n 19); Hansard, 8 May 2019 (n 15); Hansard, 4 May 2020 (n 3); Hansard, 8 February 2022 (n 3); Ng and Sekhom Atac (n 3); Teo (n 1); Teo and Chiu (n 1).
24 Hansard, 4 May 2020 (n 3); Ng and Sekhom Atac (n 3); Teo (n 1); Teo and Chiu (n 1).
25 Ministry of National Development (MND), 'Functions of Town Councils' (n.d.) <www.mnd.gov.sg/our-work/regulating-town-councils/about-town-councils> (accessed 1 September 2023).
26 *The Straits Times* (5 March 2020) <www.straitstimes.com/politics/parliament-whole-of-society-approach-key-to-address-social-challenges-build-stronger> (accessed 1 September 2023).
27 Ang (n 12); Hansard Parliament 11 session 2 vol 86 sitting 17 *Problem of Homelessness in Singapore* (2 March 2010), Hansard, 13 August 2012 (n 19); Hansard, 24 March 2016 (n 15); Hansard, 4 May 2020 (n 3).

Looking at how Singapore has approached the issue of homelessness over time, it is observed that there has been consistency in policy principles, as well as a shift in the role and responsibility of the state vis-à-vis social service agencies, community agencies, as well as the public. Based on a review of parliamentary speeches from 2008 to 2022 on homelessness by the author, the principles that undergird Singapore's approach to dealing with homelessness can be encapsulated as follows: multi-level and multi-pronged, comprehensive and coordinated, and timely and targeted:

- *Multi-level and multi-pronged*. Government, social service agencies, community partners (like grassroots bodies, ethnic self-help groups, secular and religious groups, etc.), and the public collaborating, albeit at different levels, in policy planning and implementing programmes and services that are preventive and remedial in nature.
- *Comprehensive and coordinated*. Provision of programmes and services to address short-term and long-term needs. This encompasses information and referral services, counselling and casework, healthcare support, financial assistance, stable accommodation, training and employment, childcare, education support for children, and so on.
- *Targeted and timely*. The unique needs of each homeless person or family are recognized and addressed, taking into consideration their immediate needs and issues that require more time to address.

The main authorities that oversee homelessness are MSF (social safety net – setting policy directions, service models, and funding framework on social services) and MND and HDB (housing), while being cognizant that intervention straddles different government bodies. At the policy level, there were two task forces formed to look into homelessness. There was a task force formed in 2007 to strengthen inter-agency coordination on the issue of rough sleepers after reports of more single men being sighted sleeping in the open. About a decade later, in May 2018, another inter-agency task force was set up, building on the work done by the earlier task force. The second task force comprised representatives from 11 government agencies – indicating the multifaceted nature of homelessness and reiterating the need for a whole-of-government approach. The task force reviewed protocols and programmes and looked into upstream work to support the homeless, including rough sleepers.[28]

Upstream and Downstream Schemes, Programmes, and Services

Homeownership and Managing Housing Loans/Mortgage Payments

At its core, Singapore promotes homeownership. This national priority since the 1960s has enabled the city state to keep the number of homeless cases low. Consequently, there is a strong culture of homeownership in Singapore. One of the key ways of promoting homeownership has been to keep the prices of HDB flats affordable, with HDB housing being heavily subsidized by the government. At the same time, aspiring homeowners are encouraged to exercise personal responsibility, to ensure that they can upkeep their mortgage payments. They are advised to plan for contingencies like retrenchment or a serious illness which can affect their ability to pay housing mortgages. In its upstream work, HDB

---

28 Hansard, 6 January 2020 (n 13).

has included website advice as well as financial tools to assist potential HDB flat owners to review their finances, calculate their mortgage payments and interest rates, so that repayment of housing loans remain manageable, and that homeownership will not be a financial burden in the long run. The other option is public rental housing, which has been explained. Implicitly, these prevent homelessness.[29]

Another upstream measure focuses on financial prudence or discipline for homeowners as well as by financial institutions. The Total Debt Servicing Ratio (TDSR) framework was introduced by the government in 2012. The intention behind the framework is to ensure that there is holistic assessment of the debt servicing ability of borrowers when applying for property loans. Financial institutions must consider potential homeowners' ability to pay their property loans, by looking into these persons' other outstanding debt obligations. Currently, there is a mortgage servicing ratio (MSR) cap of 30% of a borrower's gross monthly income for the purchase of an HDB flat.[30]

Comprehensive and Coordinated Social Assistance

For individuals and families who are at risk of homelessness or already experiencing homelessness and other associated difficulties, there is a national hotline, known as the ComCare hotline, they can call. They can get advice and be referred to other agencies for housing, financial, employment, medical, or counselling services. Members of the public can also call the hotline if they know of anyone who requires assistance, including reporting those who are sleeping in public areas so that social services can reach out to them.[31]

Individuals and families can also approach community-based agencies providing social services for advice and support. There are 24 Social Service Offices (SSOs) and 46 Family Service Centres (FSCs) located in different housing estates in Singapore. The staff at these agencies will assess their needs and provide support to them. The SSOs, which are under MSF, administer financial assistance schemes, assist in developing care plans, and refer individuals and families to relevant agencies, like FSCs, for other services. FSCs provide casework and counselling, supporting individuals and families with housing concerns, emotional issues, and underlying social challenges in life. SSOs and FSCs also refer the homeless or those at risk of homelessness to transitional shelters.[32]

Transitional Shelters for Homeless Individuals and Families

MSF appoints and funds social service agencies and community partners to run transitional shelters. There are currently six transitional shelters. The shelters provide temporary

---

29 Housing and Development Board (HDB), 'Ability to Pay' (n.d.d) <www.hdb.gov.sg/cs/infoweb/residential/buying-a-flat/working-out-your-flat-budget/ability-to-pay> (accessed 1 September 2023).
30 Monetary Authority of Singapore (MAS), 'Rules for New Housing Loans' (2021) <www.mas.gov.sg/regulation/explainers/new-housing-loans/msr-and-tdsr-rules> (accessed 1 September 2023).
31 Hansard Parliament 11 session 2 vol 86 sitting 17 *Problem of Homelessness in Singapore* (2 March 2010); Hansard, 13 August 2012 (n 19); Hansard Parliament 13 session 1 vol 94 sitting 46 *Applications for Shelter for the Homeless* (8 May 2017) <https://sprs.parl.gov.sg> (accessed 1 September 2023).
32 Hansard, 18 February 2022 (n 3); Ministry of Social and Family Development (MSF), 'Standing Together: Lifting Lives' (2019) <www.msf.gov.sg/media-room/article/Standing-Together-Lifting-Lives> (accessed 1 September 2023).

housing and social services to individuals and families who have not been able to find accommodation, despite their personal efforts, and are also not eligible for HDB housing options. The shelters are usually repurposed older HDB flats. There is co-sharing of common spaces in the shelters. The shelters have a capacity to house 500 homeless individuals and 180 homeless families. As of 2022, the occupancy rate in the shelters was 50% for homeless individuals and 60% for homeless families. There are no immediate plans to develop more transitional shelters given the current occupancy rate.[33]

Most applicants requiring shelter are admitted within a week after social assessments (of their needs, risks, health conditions, and support systems) are completed and provided they are found to be suitable for independent living within the communal setting of the shelter. While they are in the shelter, the shelter's care staff as well as social workers provide the homeless with counselling and casework assistance and financial aid and assist them to find long-term accommodation. The homeless clients pay a nominal rent for their stay in the shelter, much lower than market rental rates. The average period of stay in a shelter is about six months, which can be extended if more time is needed to deal with complex issues.[34]

Interim Rental Housing Scheme for Homeless Families

In 2009, the Interim Rental Housing Scheme (IRHS), a temporary housing scheme for needy families facing housing transitions and requiring urgent accommodation, was started by HDB. This new scheme supplemented the Public Rental Scheme and is a form of low-cost housing to assist vulnerable families. In the early days of its implementation, about 1,000 flats, located in different parts of Singapore, were allocated to the IRHS. Homeless families can be considered for the IRHS after exhausting all other avenues for accommodation. The rental period for the IRHS flats was revised in 2011 – it was extended from six months to a year, and renewable up to two years, to cater for families who require more time to find their own homes. The IRHS is not open for the public to apply, and it is offered on a case-by-case basis (after an assessment is done by social workers or HDB officers) to those who have no other temporary housing options.[35]

Under the IRHS, two needy families (who are unrelated) co-rent a two- or three-room public housing flat (an IRHS flat is typically about 54–60 m², with two bedrooms, and each family occupies one of the two bedrooms and co-shares common spaces like the living room, kitchen, and toilets) at a lower individual rental cost (below the private market rate). HDB, through its managing agents, will match the families as co-tenants, taking into consideration the families' profiles. The rental would depend on their financial circumstances. While on the scheme, the families work through their housing and other issues with social workers.[36] As of 2016, about 4,600 families were assisted through this scheme. Families on

---

33 Hansard Parliament 11 session 2 vol 86 sitting 17 *Problem of Homelessness in Singapore* (2 March 2010) <https://sprs.parl.gov.sg> (accessed 1 September 2023); Hansard 13 August 2012 (n19); Hansard, 24 March 2016 (n15); Hansard Parliament 13 session 1 vol 94 sitting 33 *Number of Homeless Individuals* (7 February 2017) <https://sprs.parl.gov.sg> (accessed 1 September 2023); Hansard, 6 January 2020 (n 13).
34 Hansard, 2 March 2010 (n 33); Hansard 13 August 2012 (n 19); Hansard Parliament 14 session 1 vol 95 sitting 68 *More Transitional Shelters for Homeless Persons and Rough Sleepers* (13 September 2022) <https://sprs.parl.gov.sg> (accessed 1 September 2023).
35 Teo (n 1); Teo and Chiu (n 1).
36 Ibid.

the scheme have reported that co-sharing with strangers was uncomfortable and conflicts occurred between the tenant families. The families also shared concerns as to the loss of control, lack of privacy, conflicts with tenants, among other issues. The challenge of living with strangers is not peculiar to the IRHS, as this has been noted in overseas studies on the homeless living in shelters and other shared housing arrangements.[37]

Welfare Homes for the Destitute

Welfare homes have been in existence in Singapore for close to five decades – this is a 'traditional' social service. There are 11 welfare homes established under the Destitute Persons Act (DPA), and MSF appoints social service agencies to manage these government homes and regulates them. Admission into welfare homes is an option for the destitute.[38] Rough sleepers who lack family support and are unable to care for themselves can be considered destitute and may be admitted into welfare homes. Nevertheless, one is not admitted into a welfare home simply based on the legal definition of being 'destitute'. The general principle is to first provide social work services which include financial aid, counselling and casework services, accommodation, etc. within the community. Admission into to a welfare home is a last resort, after it has been assessed that the destitute person has risk and safety issues (for instance, they are not able to care for themselves due to mental health conditions). As of 2020, there were about 1,900 destitute persons in the 11 welfare homes.[39] The welfare homes provide the residents with casework and counselling services, training and employment programmes, as well as medical care. This is especially important for those with mental health issues. Residents who are medically fit will be assisted to find employment, and by law, they can be asked to pay a sum towards their stay. There is a review board that assesses the care plans and discharge plans for persons admitted into the welfare homes, working towards the goal of re-integration back into the community.[40]

Partners Engaging and Empowering Rough Sleepers Network (PEERS Network) and Safe and Sound Sleeping Places (S3Ps)

There has generally been an expectation and a strong reliance on the government to do more for the homeless, such as providing public rental housing, other forms of accommodation, financial aid, counselling services, and support for the educational needs of children affected by homelessness. While the government plays a major role at the macro-level, there seems to have been a shift over the years, with the community playing an increasingly active role in helping the homeless in Singapore. The principles of 'multi-level and multi-pronged' and 'comprehensive and coordinated' are evident in the 'Partners Engaging and Empowering Rough Sleepers' Network, or PEERS Network, a ground-up initiative that was established in July 2019. This collaboration among social service agencies, community groups, and government bodies, with representatives from 26 different agencies, collectively examines

---

37 Anucha (n 1); Y. He, B. O'Flaherty and R. A. Rosenheck, 'Is Shared Housing a Way to Reduce Homelessness? The Effect of Household Arrangements of Formerly Homeless People' (2010) 19(1) *Journal of Housing Economics* 1–12; Teater (n 2); Teo (n 1); Teo and Chiu (n 1).
38 Ang (n 12).
39 Hansard, 4 May 2020 (n 3).
40 Ang (n 12).

ways to support rough sleepers, manage shelters, and provide social intervention for the homeless. For instance, PEERS Network's volunteers (from various agencies) conduct outreach to befriend the homeless, namely, rough sleepers; provide them with information on services; and through the connections built, encourage the homeless to be more open to seeking formal help.[41]

Another new ground-up community initiative is the Safe and Sound Sleeping Places (S3Ps), operated by agencies in the PEERS Network. Set up in 2020, S3Ps, which are not funded by the government, are an option for the homeless who are not ready to be admitted to welfare homes or transitional shelters or to receive formal assistance. Community partners in the S3Ps open their premises to the homeless who sleep rough, providing them with a safe place to rest. These premises include temples, churches, or social service agencies. These places add to the existing range of housing options for the homeless. The homeless are referred to S3Ps by the PEERS Network. Those who are not eligible to be admitted to S3Ps due to mental health or issues like addiction are referred to more appropriate services and facilities.[42]

During the Covid-19 pandemic (years 2020–2021), more community agencies responded to offer their premises as temporary lodging and to provide meals for homeless Singaporeans and non-citizens who lost their jobs and were unable to return to their country of residence due to international travel restrictions. More people sought assistance from the PEERS Network during the early period of the pandemic – about 300 persons were given shelter and other forms of support, compared to July 2019, when the PEERS Network was first set up, when less than half of the 65 people who were engaged were willing to accept help. In 2020, there were 7 S3Ps, and the number increased to 35 S3Ps during the pandemic. HDB also provided vacant rental flats to community partners to operate S3Ps during this period. In 2020, about 300 homeless people received assistance from 3SPs, with 400 spaces still available. In 2021, about 165 people were in S3Ps.[43]

As the Covid-19 pandemic subsided and with the resumption of normalcy of daily life, the number of S3Ps was reduced to 20 S3Ps (as of the end of May 2021). The S3Ps had nevertheless played an important role in supporting the homeless during the pandemic, as evident in the high occupancy rate of 93%. For those who stayed in S3Ps, about 45% sought shelter at these places regularly for at least six months. Post Covid-19, S3Ps continue to be important touch points for PEERS Network befrienders and social service providers to connect with the homeless, to provide them with advice and services.[44]

Conclusion

The issue of homelessness is unique and fairly well managed in Singapore, largely because it has been predicated on the success of its national public housing policy. Homeownership has been the norm in Singapore for more than five decades, with in excess of 90% owning

---

41 Hansard, 4 May 2020 (n 3); Ministry of Social and Family Development (MSF), *Report on the Street Count of Rough Sleepers 2022* (Ministry of Social and Family Development, Republic of Singapore 2023).
42 Hansard, 4 May 2020 (n 3); Hansard 8 February 2020 (n 3).
43 Ibid.
44 Ng and Sekhon Atac (n 3); Hansard, 4 May 2020 (n 3); Hansard Parliament 14 session 1 vol 95 sitting 33 *Utilisation Rates and Profile of Residents at Safe and Sound Sleeping Places* (26 July 2022) <https://sprs.parl.gov.sg> (accessed 1 September 2023).

their homes. Subsidized housing for the masses as an investment for its citizens can be regarded as both an effective and practical approach in preventing homelessness and raising the quality of life.[45] There is no official dataset on homelessness in Singapore. The number of homeless cases is low, relative to the resident population of 4.07 million, and the number is based on available information on homeless individuals and families who are recipients of housing and social assistance at a single point in time (a proxy of homelessness). As discussed in previous sections, MSF had indicated that an average of 300 homeless cases per year (from 2005 to 2015) were assisted, and about 1,900 people are residing in welfare homes. The single night street count conducted on 11 November 2022 found that there were 530 rough sleepers. These numbers may or may not include those who received help from the PEERS Network and S3Ps, which were services that were developed later.[46] There could be other homeless people who have found ways to cope without receiving formal support from social services or HDB. Nevertheless, the issue is important to address, given the deleterious effects of homelessness on the person and family and costs to society as a whole.

Research has shown that the quality of life and life chances of persons are affected by homelessness as well as risks that accompany homelessness. The homeless experience is negative for both adults and children, with vulnerabilities in the spheres of physical, cognitive, mental, emotional, and relational health.[47] The multi-agency and targeted approaches adopted in Singapore, with the provision of housing support and myriad of social services, are elements of a comprehensive approach to address homelessness and its associated issues. To address homelessness effectively, these service provisions cannot be viewed as distinct or isolated. The implication for social workers is that they need to be well-versed with housing and other policies relevant to the needs of their homeless clients, as well as being competent and adept at integrating micro-, mezzo-, and macro-levels of practice.

Tackling homelessness is an ongoing process, and strategies will evolve. For instance, when contemporary homelessness re-emerged as an issue, parliamentarians had raised concerns about the plight of homeless individuals, especially families with children. The media also highlighted these cases, raising awareness of the issue. The authorities did not anticipate that there would be such cases, and the system to tackle homelessness seemed to be inadequate at that time. The government responded by developing the IRHS in 2009, setting up more shelters that better cater to the needs of homeless families, and working with community partners to reach out to rough sleepers. For instance, there were two shelters for the homeless in 2010, and the number increased to six transitional shelters by 2022, and shelters are still not at full capacity.[48]

An interesting observation is that while Singapore is not a welfare state, the government plays a major role at the macro-level in policy planning, funding programmes and services, and ensuring that social services are accessible, available, and adequate for its citizens. By

---

45 Department of Statistics (DOS), 'Households' <www.singstat.gov.sg/find-data/search-by-theme/households/households/latest-data> (accessed 1 September 2023); Liu and Tuminez (n 4); I. Sim and others, *The Social Service Sector in Singapore: An Exploratory Study on the Financial Characteristics of Institutions of a Public Character (IPCs) in the Social Service Sector* (National University of Singapore 2015).
46 Hansard, 24 March (n 15).
47 Anucha (n 1); Parsell (n 1); M. Kirkman and others, '"Are We Moving Again This Week?" Children's Experiences of Homelessness in Victoria' (2010) 70(7) *Australia: Social Science Med* 994; Schiff (n 2); Shier, Jones and Graham (n 2); Teater (n 2); Teo (n 1); Teo and Chiu (n 1).
48 Hansard, 2 March 2010 (n 33); Hansard 13 September 2022 (n 33).

and large, the ecosystem to address homelessness is aligned with the 'Many Helping Hands' principles of *self-reliance* (support is temporary, and the homeless are assisted to regain stability and independence), *family support* (the family is seen as the basic unit of society and the first line of support to help family members facing housing-related and other issues), and *community partnership* (social service agencies running FSCs, religious groups or other agencies providing social services, donors, volunteers, etc.),[49] and working with the *government*. While self-reliance and seeking and receiving family support are positive qualities, expending time and effort to get help from family members (given that research has shown that the homeless lack family support or are estranged or have difficult family relationships), and having to exhaust other housing options first, for example, living with family or friends, or renting from the open market, can be stressful for the homeless.[50] This is an area that perhaps should be re-evaluated as it is counterintuitive to the benefits of early help-seeking and being responsive to the needs of the homeless in a timely way.

On the positive side, there seems to be a slight shift in the social compact and civic society involvement at the mezzo-level, with community agencies collaborating to develop and implement ground-up initiatives – such as the PEERS Network and S3Ps - in response to a pressing national issue. As aptly put by Mr Masagos Zulkifli, minister for MSF, these initiatives 'have embodied Singapore's Together spirit'.[51] There is also potential for this form of social innovation and community development to be replicated further and more widely to address other social issues.

In conclusion, social challenges are never static, and there is no universal approach to dealing with homelessness. The Singapore approach to tackling homelessness is an interesting case study. This chapter has shown how homelessness was put on the government agenda for action. It explained how the unexpected number of homeless cases set against the backdrop of high homeownership, increased political pressure, public reactions, and stakeholder responses, pushed the issue of homelessness to the forefront. In addition, this chapter has noted that the approach taken in Singapore is deeply influenced by, but not limited to, historical, political, legal, and socio-cultural and economic factors. No government can address social issues on its own, and a partnership approach with the community can reap greater success, as the example of Singapore demonstrates.

---

49 Ang (n 12); Sim and others (n 45).
50 Teo (n 1); Teo and Chiu (n 1).
51 Hansard Parliament 14 session 1 vol 95 sitting 33 *Utilisation Rates and Profile of Residents at Safe and Sound Sleeping Places* (26 July 2021).

PART VI

Oceania

26

FROM VAGRANCY TO PUBLIC NUISANCE IN 200 YEARS

Is It Still a Crime to Be Homeless in Australia?

Tamara Walsh

Introduction

People experiencing homelessness are amongst the most criminalized of all population groups in Australia.[1] They are vulnerable to being questioned, searched, moved on, and 'banned' from certain areas, as well as being arrested, charged, sentenced, and detained, for reasons intimately connected with their homeless status. They are both more likely to come to the attention of police officers and less likely to be treated leniently by the courts when charged.

People experiencing homelessness are highly visible to police and experience regular – often daily – interactions with police officers as a result.[2] They may be forced to commit crimes to obtain necessary items such as food and clothing. People experiencing homelessness tend to carry their belongings with them, so those who have addictions are likely to have drugs on their person if they are stopped and searched by the police. Those who have alcohol dependency are forced to drink alcohol in public, making them vulnerable to public drinking charges. Behaviour associated with mental ill health, intoxication, or anger at being interfered with by police can result in additional charges for disorderly and 'anti-social' behaviour or offensive language.

In Australia, many offences committed in public space are punishable by way of infringement notice.[3] It is not uncommon for people experiencing homelessness to accumulate thousands of dollars' worth of fines that will never be paid, and enforcement action may be taken against them as a result. If they do receive criminal charges, people experiencing homelessness often receive harsher sentences. They may fail to appear in court because the

---

1 See generally A. Young and J. Petty, 'On Visible Homelessness and the Micro-Aesthetics of Public Space' (2019) 52(4) *Australian & New Zealand Journal of Criminology* 444; A. Clarke and C. Parsell, 'The Ambiguities of Homelessness Governance: Disentangling Care and Revanchism in the Neoliberalising City' (2020) 52(5) *Antipode* 1624; T. Walsh, *Homelessness and the Law* (Federation Press 2011).
2 Young and Petty (n 1).
3 G. Lansdell and others, 'Infringement Systems in Australia: A Precarious Blurring of Civil and Criminal Sanctions?' (2012) 37(1) *Alternative Law Journal* 41.

chaotic nature of their life makes it difficult to remember and keep appointments. People experiencing homelessness are less likely to receive bail because they lack a fixed address, and if they are found guilty and sentenced, they are less likely to receive community-based orders because they are unable to comply with the conditions.[4] Ultimately, magistrates may sentence people who are homeless to a period of imprisonment, believing that this is 'for their own good'.[5]

Problem-solving courts targeted at people experiencing homelessness have been trialled in some Australian jurisdictions, with the goal of applying a therapeutic jurisprudential approach to their offending behaviour. However, these initiatives have been judged expensive and inefficient, and they have not been universally embraced by people experiencing homelessness or their advocates.[6]

The very purpose of the criminal justice system is to discourage, and thereby reduce, individuals' offending behaviour. Yet the 'criminal' behaviour of people experiencing homelessness poses a profound challenge to the foundational principles underlying the criminal justice system. A criminal charge is generally symptomatic of a complex mix of legal and non-legal concerns in a person's life. If these underlying problems remain unaddressed, the offending will continue. According to people who are homeless, what they need for rehabilitation to occur is a home.[7]

Definitions of Homelessness in Australia

Australian definitions of *homelessness* have focused on the 'houselessness' aspect of homelessness rather than those aspects of homelessness that relate to culture, safety, and stigma.[8] The most widely accepted definition of *homelessness* in Australia is the Australian Bureau of Statistics (ABS) definition, which conceives of homelessness as the state of living in a dwelling that is inadequate, has no tenure or only tenure that is short and not extendable, or does not allow the person to have control of or access to space for social relations, and the person does not have a suitable accommodation alternative.[9] Within this broad definition, categories of homelessness are specified to include living in an improvised dwelling or 'rough sleeping', living in supported accommodation (including shelters and refuges), staying temporarily in another household ('couch surfing'), staying in a boarding house, staying in other temporary lodgings, and living in a severely crowded dwelling.[10]

---

4 K. Boyle, ' "The More Things Change . . .": Bail and the Incarceration of Homeless Young People' (2009) 21(1) *Current Issues in Criminal Justice* 59; E. Baldry and others, 'Ex-Prisoners, Homelessness and the State in Australia' (2006) 39(1) *Australian & New Zealand Journal of Criminology* 20.
5 T. Walsh, *A Special Court for Special Cases* (UQ 2011) 38.
6 T. Walsh, 'Defendants' and Criminal Justice Professionals' Views on the Brisbane Special Circumstances Court' (2011) 21(2) *Journal of Judicial Administration* 93.
7 C. Parsell, 'Home Is Where the House Is: The Meaning of Home for People Sleeping Rough' (2012) 27(2) *Housing Studies* 159.
8 C. Chamberlain and D. Mackenzie, 'Understanding Contemporary Homelessness: Issues of Definition and Meaning' (1992) 27(4) *Australian Journal of Social Issues* 274.
9 Australian Bureau of Statistics (ABS), *A Statistical Definition of Homelessness: Information Paper* (Commonwealth of Australia 2012).
10 Australian Bureau of Statistics (ABS), *Census of Population and Housing: Estimating Homelessness* (Commonwealth of Australia 2016).

Defining *homelessness* according to a person's quality of accommodation or living standards has limitations.[11] Many people who fulfil the ABS definition of *homelessness* would not consider themselves to be homeless. In particular, Aboriginal and Torres Strait Islander peoples may sleep outside by choice, especially on certain lands and during certain times of the year.[12] Refugees and asylum seekers may choose to reside in overcrowded dwellings because this is culturally appropriate for them.[13] Other people may consider themselves to be homeless even though they do not meet the ABS definition. In particular, women and children who are victims of family violence, and young people who have been victims of abuse or neglect, may technically have a 'suitable accommodation alternative' but remain practically homeless because they are unsafe at home.[14]

Having said this, research suggests that people experiencing homelessness themselves do associate having a 'home' with being housed.[15] They recognize that having housing brings safety, stability, privacy, and control over one's environment, whereas hostels and homeless accommodation are not 'a "normal" place where authority and control [can] be exercised'.[16] Judicial officers have interpreted 'home' in a similar way, considering aspects that relate to shelter, as well as those related to safety and security. Tribunals in Australia have considered 'home' to be 'where the centre of gravity of one's domestic life is to be found' or 'a place where persons ordinarily eat, morning and night, and where they sleep'.[17] Judicial officers have noted the role that subjective experience plays in the concept of home, finding that whilst a 'home' will usually require 'an affinity to its location and usage by the occupier', it 'need not be a structure of four walls and a roof'.[18]

Trends in Homelessness in Australia

In 2023, around 123,000 people were classified as being homeless in Australia on census night.[19] This equates to a rate of 48 per 10,000 of the population, around 10% higher than the rate recorded ten years prior.[20] Most of the increase in homelessness has occurred

---

11 C. Chamberlain and G. Johnson, 'The Debate About Homelessness' (2001) 36(1) *Australian Journal of Social Issues* 35; J. Minnery and E. Greenhalgh, 'Approaches to Homelessness Policy in Europe, the United States and Australia' (2007) 63(3) *Journal of Social Issues* 641.
12 P. Memmott and D. Nash, 'Indigenous Homelessness: Australian Context' in E. Peters and J. Christensen (eds), *Indigenous Homelessness: Perspectives from Canada, Australia and New Zealand* (Wiley 2016); D. Habibis, 'A Framework for Reimagining Indigenous Mobility and Homelessness' (2011) 29 *Urban Policy and Research* 401.
13 D. Smith, F. H. McKay and K. Lippi, 'Experiences of Homelessness by People Seeking Asylum in Australia: A Review of the Published and "Grey" Literature' (2019) 54 *Social Policy Administration* 441, at 450.
14 R. Martin, 'Gender and Homelessness' in Chris Chamberlain, Guy Johnson and Catherine Robinson (eds), *Homelessness in Australia: An Introduction* (UNSW Press 2014).
15 Parsell (n 7).
16 Ibid. 167.
17 *Dickeson and Secretary Department of Social Security* (1989) 18 ALD 58, 59, 61; cited in *Trevillien and Secretary, Department of Social Services* [2018] AATA 2279; *Mitchell v Xu* [2020] ACAT 110; *Zakariya v Chief Commissioner of State Revenue* [2003] NSWADT 26.
18 Ibid.
19 Australian Bureau of Statistics (ABS), *Census of Population and Housing: Estimating Homelessness* (Commonwealth of Australia 2023).
20 ABS (n 10), Data table 1.1.

amongst those living in improvised dwellings or sleeping out and those living in severely overcrowded dwellings.[21]

Older people, particularly older women, constitute the fastest-growing cohort of homeless people in Australia – there was a 50% increase in the number of people aged 55 and over who were counted as homeless between 2006 and 2016.[22] Aboriginal and Torres Strait Islander people remain substantially over-represented amongst those experiencing homelessness, comprising 20% of the homeless population.[23] Whilst this is considerably less than the rate of Indigenous homelessness recorded in 2006 – when Aboriginal and Torres Strait Islander people comprised 29% of the homeless population – it is still shamefully in excess of Indigenous peoples' prevalence in the community, which is around 3%.[24]

The rate of homelessness amongst women and children also seems to be increasing in Australia. Presently, around one-third of all people experiencing homelessness are young people aged 12 to 24 years, compared with around one quarter in 2006.[25] Indeed, this is likely to be an under-estimate, since young people are more likely to couch surf and may therefore be classified as 'visiting' rather than 'homeless' on census documents.[26] Similarly, census data suggests that women comprise 44% of all people experiencing homelessness,[27] but women escaping violent relationships are also likely to be undercounted as they, too, tend to 'visit' with friends and family until they find something more permanent.[28]

Policing of Public Space: Safety and Risk

Whilst it is true that people experiencing homelessness are highly vulnerable to criminalization, not all homeless individuals or cohorts are policed to the same extent or in the same way. It is those who dwell in public places – on the streets, in marginal housing, or in vehicles – who are most visible and vulnerable to criminal law responses.

The manner in which public spaces are policed is underpinned by community conceptions of 'safety' and 'risk'. Marginalized public space users are often stereotyped as being dangerous and presenting a threat to law-abiding citizens when, in fact, they are likely to have been victims of crime themselves, and they, too, have concerns about their safety in public spaces.[29] In Australia, 'law and order commonsense' and 'public punitivism' are dominant paradigms within the community, fuelling the belief that crime rates are soaring

---

21 Ibid.
22 Ibid. See further M. Petersen, 'Addressing Older Women's Homelessness: Service and Housing Models' (2015) 50(4) *Australian Journal of Social Issues* 419.
23 ABS (n 19).
24 ABS (n 10).
25 Ibid; ABS (n 19).
26 P. Flatau and others, *Lifetime and Intergenerational Experiences of Homelessness in Australia* (AHURI 2013) 29.
27 ABS (n 19).
28 A. Sharam and K. Hulse, 'Understanding the Nexus Between Poverty and Homelessness: Relational Poverty Analysis of Families Experiencing Homelessness in Australia' (2014) 31(3) *Housing, Theory and Society* 294.
29 Young and Petty (n 1); Petersen (n 22); Chris Middendorp, 'Homelessness and Public Space: Unwelcome Visitors' (2002) 15(1) *Parity* 18.

and the criminal justice system does not provide adequate protection to average members of the public, even though crime rates overall are in decline.[30]

In the early 2000s, there was a surge in law and order policing in Australia reflected in the rise of mandatory sentencing, zero-tolerance approaches to policing public spaces, and the introduction of police 'move-on' powers. 'Preventative' policing was normalized, and under the pretence of making public spaces safe for the average citizen, behaviour that was merely undesirable or anti-social was classified as criminal.[31] False assumptions about risk meant that laws and policies failed to clearly distinguish between the policing of nightclub districts during peak times and the policing of the same spaces during the day when they provide a home for marginalized people with nowhere else to go. The tacit assumption of law and order policy was that both groups posed an identical threat to public safety. The entrenchment of the 'broken windows theory'[32] in law, policy, and discourse contributed to a policing approach that prioritized 'street sweeping', despite the fact that often the only evidence of 'brokenness' was destitute human beings.

Of course, this perspective has its roots in British vagrancy laws which Australia inherited and later replicated in its own legislation. Nineteenth-century Vagrancy Acts characterized people experiencing homelessness as deliberately deviant and victims of their own idleness.[33] The *Vagrants, Gaming, and Other Offences Act 1931* (Qld), for example, criminalized having 'no visible means of support' and 'being an habitual drunkard', and the *Neglected and Criminal Children's Act 1864* (Vic) criminalized children who were 'found wandering about' or 'sleeping in the open air'. At around the same time, concerns regarding the 'welfare' of Aboriginal people were used to justify laws that removed them to government-controlled reserves.[34] Aboriginal and Torres Strait Islander peoples were systematically removed from their lands and placed in institutions with the purported aims of providing them with 'care and protection' and removing them from the 'insanitary or undesirable conditions' in which they were living.[35] Despite the apparent benevolence of their stated goals, these Acts had a devastating effect on Aboriginal and Torres Strait Islander peoples, promoting an 'unacceptable'

---

30 L. Schaefer and L. Mazerolle, 'Predicting Perceptions of Crime: Community Residents' Recognition and Classification of Local Crime Problems' (2018) 51(2) *Journal of Criminology* 183; B. Davis and K. Dossetor, '(Mis)perceptions of Crime in Australia' (2010) 396 *Trends and Issues in Crime and Criminal Justice* 1; D. Brown and R. Hogg, 'Law and Order Commonsense' (1996) 8(2) *Current Issues in Criminal Justice* 175.

31 A. Pennay, E. Manton and M. Savic, 'Geographies of Exclusion: Street Drinking, Gentrification and Contests Over Public Space' (2014) 25(6) *International Journal of Drug Policy* 1084; E. Methven, 'Commodifying Justice: Discursive Strategies Used in the Legitimation of Infringement Notices for Minor Offences' (2020) 33 *International Journal for the Semiotics of Law* 353.

32 J. Q. Wilson and G. L. Kelling, 'Broken Windows: The Police and Neighbourhood Safety' (1982) 3 *The Atlantic Monthly* 29.

33 See T. Walsh, 'Waltzing Matilda One Hundred Years Later: Interactions Between Homeless Persons and the Criminal Justice System in Queensland' (2003) 25(1) *Sydney Law Review* 75–77; A. McLeod, 'On the Origins of Consorting Laws' (2013) 37(1) *Melbourne University Law Review* 103.

34 See, for example, *Aboriginal Protection Act 1869* (Vic); *Aboriginal Protection and Restriction of the Sale of Opium Act 1897* (Qld); *Aborigines Act 1905* (WA); *Native Administration Act 1905–1936* (WA); *Aborigines Protection Act 1909* (NSW); *Aborigines Act 1911* (SA) s 38(1)(i), (j); *Aboriginals Ordinance 1918* (NT); *Aborigines Act 1934–1939* (SA).

35 See further L. Behrendt, 'Meeting at the Crossroads: Intersectionality, Affirmative Action and the Legacies of the Aboriginal Protection Board' (1997) 4 *Australian Journal of Human Rights* 25; R. Kidd, 'Abuse of trust: The government as banker in Queensland and the United States' [2003] *Indigenous Law Bulletin* 48.

level of intrusion into their lives, families, and culture.[36] Many have argued that their legacy remains in the shape of criminal laws that prohibit sleeping, gathering, or drinking alcohol in public places, and police powers that allow people to be moved away or banned from certain areas.[37]

Move-on Powers, Banning Notices, and Search-and-Seizure Powers

People who are homeless in urban centres, particularly those who sleep rough, report that their interactions with police occur on a daily basis – they describe being stopped, questioned, woken up, moved on, and harassed by police officers. Extensive police powers in all Australian jurisdictions allow police to approach, interfere with, and issue directions to people in public places.[38]

Police in all Australian jurisdictions have the power to issue 'move-on' directions in situations where a person is reasonably suspected to be causing anxiety to others, interfering with trade, or acting in an offensive or disorderly manner.[39] Move-on powers became popular amongst Australian legislators in the early 2000s, despite early evidence that they were impacting disproportionately on people experiencing homelessness.[40] Australian move-on powers allow police to issue a direction to a person or group to move away from a particular area for a certain period of time, generally between 4 and 24 hours. Research has suggested that rough sleepers are amongst those most likely to be moved on, as well as young people, Indigenous people, and sex workers.[41]

A more recent development has been the introduction of banning notices in some Australian states and territories.[42] These laws empower the police to exclude a person from a particular public space for a specified period time – months in some instances – because

---

36 This has been judicially recognized: see *Kruger and Others v Commonwealth* (1997) 190 CLR 1, 36 (Brennan CJ).
37 K. Menzies, 'Forcible Separation and Assimilation as Trauma: The Historical and Socio-Political Experiences of Australian Aboriginal People' (2019) 17(1) *Alienation Theory and Research in Education and Social Work* 1; A. Nettelbeck, 'Creating the Aboriginal Vagrant: Protective Governance and Indigenous Mobility in Colonial Australia' (2018) 87(1) *Pacific Historical Review* 79.
38 J. J. J. Wang and D. Weatherburn, 'The Effect of Police Searches and Move-On Directions on Property and Violent Crime in New South Wales' (2021) 54(3) *Journal of Criminology* 383; J. Murphy, 'Homelessness and Public Space Offences in Australia – A Human Rights Oriented Case for Narrow Interpretation' (2019) 7(1) *Griffith Journal of Law and Human Dignity* 103.
39 *Crimes Act 1900* (ACT) s 175; *Law Enforcement (Powers and Responsibilities) 2002* (NSW) s 197; *Summary Offences Act 1923* (NT) ss 47A-47B; *Police Powers and Responsibilities Act 2000* (Qld) ss 46–48; *Summary Offences Act 1953* (SA) s 18; *Police Offences Act 1935* (Tas) s 15B; *Summary Offences Act 1966* (Vic) s 6; *Criminal Investigation Act 2006* (WA) s 27.
40 T. Walsh and M. Taylor, ' "You're Not Welcome Here": Police Move-On Powers and Discrimination Law' (2007) 30(1) *University of New South Wales Law Journal* 151, 160.
41 Ibid. 152; NSW Ombudsman, *Policing Public Safety* (NSW Government 1999) 229, 235; P. Spooner, 'Moving in the Wrong Direction: An Analysis of Police Move-On Powers in Queensland' (2001) 20(1) *Youth Studies Australia* 27; C. Goldie, 'Indigenous People and Public Space: The Use of Move-On Powers in Darwin, Northern Territory and Associated Legal Challenges' (2004) 17(1) *Parity* 86.
42 C. Farmer, 'Should Australia's Police-Imposed Public Area Banning Powers Be Subject to Independent Oversight and Review?' (2019) 38(6) *Drug and Alcohol Review* 630; C. Farmer, A. Curtis and P. Miller, 'The Steady Proliferation of Australia's Discretionary Police-Imposed Patron Banning Powers: An Unsubstantiated Cycle of Assertion and Presumption' (2018) 18(4) *Criminology and Criminal Justice* 431.

they are considered to have disrupted or interfered with 'the peaceful passage, or reasonable enjoyment of other persons'.[43]

Whilst receiving a move-on direction or banning notice is not a criminal offence, contravening the direction or notice is.[44] Since people experiencing homelessness can rightly become distressed and angered when they are told to move away from a place that is home to them or is proximate to the services they require, contraventions do occur, and it is not uncommon for exchanges between police and homeless people to result in other charges, particularly obstruction or assault of a police officer.[45] Transient Indigenous people are particularly vulnerable to charges that are associated with the person's presence in public space.[46] This has long been the case; indeed, in 1991, the Royal Commission into Aboriginal Deaths in Custody concluded that non-Aboriginal people seem unable to tolerate the 'essentially public nature of Aboriginal life'.[47]

People who are homeless also report being constantly searched by police, which they say may be because they have a criminal record or otherwise are 'known' to police.[48] Police officers in Australia have the power to search people without a warrant if they 'reasonably suspect' that the person has committed or is about to commit a criminal offence, has something in their possession that has been or may be associated with criminal activity (such as stolen property, drugs, or weapons), or has failed to comply with a direction or requirement.[49] Police also have the power to seize objects that may provide evidence of the commission of an offence or that the person may use to cause harm to themselves or another.[50] In many jurisdictions, police are granted an explicit power to confiscate and dispose of alcohol in public places.[51] Since people experiencing homelessness tend to carry their belongings with them, a police search will commonly result in the seizure of prohibited items, particularly alcohol, drugs, and utensils, but also objects that people experiencing homelessness need to survive, such as knives.[52]

---

43 *Liquor Act 2019* (NT) ss 212, 218; *Police Powers and Responsibilities Act 2000* (Qld) ss 602B-602F; *Liquor Licensing Act 2015* (Tas) ss 81, 81A ('barring' order); *Liquor Control Reform Act 1998* (Vic) s 148A.
44 *Crimes Act 1900* (ACT) s 179; *Law Enforcement (Powers and Responsibilities) 2002* (NSW) s 199; *Summary Offences Act 1923* (NT) ss 47A(2), 47B(4); *Police Powers and Responsibilities Act 2000* (Qld) ss 602Q, 791; *Summary Offences Act 1953* (SA) s 18(2); *Police Offences Act 1935* (Tas) s 15B(2); *Summary Offences Act 1966* (Vic) s 6(4); *Criminal Investigation Act 2006* (WA) s 153; *Criminal Code* (WA) s 64(2).
45 R. Lees, 'Place and Displace in Cairns: The Use of Banning Orders' (2019) 32(4) *Parity* 20. For a case example, see *Rowe v Kemper* [2008] QCA 175.
46 C. Cunneen, *Conflict, Politics and Crime: Aboriginal Communities and the Police* (Routledge 2020); L. Boon-Kuo and others, 'Policing Biosecurity: Police Enforcement of Special Measures in New South Wales and Victoria During the COVID-19 Pandemic' (2021) 33 *Current Issues in Criminal Justice* 76, 80.
47 E. Johnston, *Royal Commission into Aboriginal Deaths in Custody: Overview and Recommendations* (Commonwealth of Australia 1991) [13.2.23].
48 T. Walsh, *No Vagrancy* (UQ 2007).
49 *Criminal Code 2002* (ACT) ss 207, 227; *Law Enforcement (Powers and Responsibilities) Act 2002* (NSW) ss 21, 31; *Police Administration Act 1978* (NT) s 119; *Police Powers and Responsibilities Act 2000* (Qld) ss 29–30; *Summary Offences Act 1953* (SA) s 68; *Criminal Investigation Act 2006* (WA) ss 33, 69.
50 *Law Enforcement (Powers and Responsibilities) Act 2002* (NSW) ss 21, 23; *Police Powers and Responsibilities Act 2000* (Qld) ss 29(2), 197; *Police Offences Act 1935* (Tas) s 6B; *Criminal Investigation Act 2006* (WA) ss 43–44, 68, 146.
51 *Local Government Act 1993* (NSW) ss 632A, 642; *Police Powers and Responsibilities Act 2000* (Qld) ss 53, 53A; *Police Offences Act 1935* (Tas) ss 13(3B), 21A(2).
52 Young and Petty (n 1); Walsh (n 48).

Additional police powers were created in the late 2010s in response to the 'tent cities' that emerged in several Australian capital cities.[53] The new laws allowed authorities to evict people from public lands by taking down their tents and seizing personal belongings.[54] These laws did not result in a high number of arrests; however, they did result in the seizure of personal items, as well as the displacement of significant numbers of homeless people who found comfort, safety, and warmth within these communities.[55] Efforts were made to provide alternative housing to evicted residents, yet many residents of the tent cities reported that other forms of accommodation were unsuitable for them, often because they were accompanied by a partner or pet or because they were unable to comply with the strict behavioural rules in social housing.[56] The response of the community and mainstream media to Australian tent cities tended to emphasize their unsightliness, uncleanliness, and inconvenience caused to pedestrians, consistent with broader narratives about homeless people that suggest homelessness is the result of poor life choices and individual failings.[57]

Homeless Persons as 'Offensive' and a 'Public Nuisance'

Conceptions of homeless individuals as unhygienic, dangerous, or annoying can result in charges for offensive, threatening, or disorderly behaviour. Offensive behaviour is criminalized in all Australian states and territories.[58] These provisions have operated as 'catch-all' offences, granting police extremely wide discretionary powers to charge people for all kinds of behaviour.[59] The High Court of Australia has held that their scope should be limited to behaviour that is 'serious' enough to justify the imposition of a criminal penalty.[60] However, in practice, a wide range of innocuous behaviours are routinely prosecuted under these provisions, including behaviours associated with mental illness, like shouting and acting in a 'bizarre' manner.[61] Laws that criminalize offensive language and offensive behaviour tend to be justified on public order and public safety grounds, yet research

---

53 Young and Petty (n 1); J. Decouto, 'Tent City: A Public Space "Hot Spot" Response to Problematic Drug Use and Homelessness' (2006) 19(8) *Parity* 47.
54 *Sydney Public Reserves (Public Safety) Act 2017* (NSW); *Forests (Recreation) (Temporary) Regulations 2021* (Vic).
55 R. Cook and C. Hartley, 'Interference with Public Enjoyment? Law Enforcement Responses to Homelessness in Sydney's Central Business District' (2018) 31(3) *Parity* 49.
56 Ibid.; S. Convery, '"Our Spirits Are Being Broken: A Year After Perth's Homeless Tent City Was Cleared, the Crisis Remains' *The Guardian* (20 February 2022).
57 L. Simpson Reeves and others, 'Fulfilling and Desperately Needed: Australian Media Representations of Responses to Homelessness' (2022) 57 *Australian Journal of Social Issues* (online first).
58 *Crimes Act 1900* (ACT) s 392; *Summary Offences Act 1988* (NSW) ss 4, 4A; *Summary Offences Act 1923* (NT) ss 47, 47AA, 53; *Summary Offences Act 1953* (SA) ss 6A, 7, 22, 58; *Police Offences Act 1935* (Tas) ss 12, 13(1), 21; *Summary Offences Act 1966* (Vic) ss 17, 17A; *Criminal Code Act Compilation Act 1913* (WA) s 74A.
59 Murphy (n 38); T. Walsh, 'Offensive Language, Offensive Behaviour and Public Nuisance: Empirical and Theoretical Analyses' (2005) 28(1) *University Of Queensland Law Journal* 122.
60 *Coleman v Power* (2004) 220 CLR 1, 29, 74, 87. See also *Nelson v Mathieson* [2003] VSC 451; *Normandale v Brassey* [1970] SASR 177 at 182.
61 T. Walsh, 'Public Nuisance, Race and Gender' (2018) 26(3) *Griffith Law Review* 334; *Cash v Commissioner of Police* [2017] QDC 38.

confirms that people who are homeless are likely themselves to be victims of violent crime in public spaces.[62]

Swearing, particularly at police officers, is the behaviour most likely to form the basis for an offensive behaviour charge. Research suggests that Indigenous people, and particularly Indigenous women, disproportionately receive charges for swearing at police officers.[63] This has long been the case; in fact, offensive language charges were noted by the Royal Commission into Aboriginal Deaths in Custody to be a factor contributing to the over-criminalization of Indigenous people more than 30 years ago.[64] The fractious relationship between Indigenous people and police is well-documented, and these low-level discretionary offences often act as 'gateway offences' for Indigenous people, particularly Indigenous young people.[65] The Royal Commission recommended that offensive language should not generally result in arrest or charge and that the use of offensive language charges against Indigenous people should be closely monitored; however, this has not occurred.[66] In the case of *Coleman v Power*, the High Court reiterated that insulting words directed at police officers should not, in the absence of aggravating circumstances, attract a criminal charge, because police officers are expected to be 'thick skinned and broad shouldered in the performance of their duties'.[67] Yet these arguments are seldom raised successfully in lower courts, even where the is evidence that police themselves used offensive language towards the defendant.[68]

In the early 2000s, researchers and advocates began drawing attention to the high rate of arrest for offensive behaviour offences amongst homeless individuals. At this time, in some jurisdictions, these offences were still criminalized under Vagrancy Acts, and advocates called for the repeal of these antiquated laws.[69] The Vagrancy Acts were repealed, but they were replaced by laws that had the same effect. Indeed, in Queensland, prosecutions increased under the new offence of 'public nuisance'.[70]

At around the same time, 'ticketing' – that is, the issuing of infringement notices – was introduced for public nuisance and related offences in several Australian states and

---

62 H. Menih, '"Come Night-Time, It's a War Zone": Women's Experiences of Homelessness, Risk and Public Space' (2020) 60 *The British Journal of Criminology* 1136; S. Larney and others, 'Factors Associated with Violent Victimisation Among Homeless Adults in Sydney, Australia' (2009) 33(4) *Australian and New Zealand Journal of Public Health* 347.

63 E. Methven, 'A Little Respect: Swearing, Police and Criminal Justice Discourse' (2018) 7(2) *International Journal for Crime, Justice and Social Democracy* 58; Australian Law Reform Commission, *Pathways to Justice: Inquiry into the Incarceration Rate of Aboriginal and Torres Strait Islander Peoples* (Commonwealth of Australia 2018) [12.171]; Walsh (n 61).

64 Johnston (n 47) Recommendation 86.

65 R. White, 'Indigenous Young Australians, Criminal Justice and Offensive Language' (2002) 5(1) *Journal of Youth Studies* 21; E. Methven, 'A Death Sentence for Swearing: The Fatal Consequences of the Failure to Decriminalise Offensive Language' (2020) 29 *Griffith Law Review* 73.

66 Johnston (n 47); T. Anthony and others, '30 Years on: Royal Commission into Aboriginal Deaths in Custody Recommendations Remain Unimplemented' (2021) 140 *CAEPR Working Paper* 1.

67 *Coleman v Power* (2004) 220 CLR 1, 26–27 (Gleeson CJ) 79 (Gummow and Hayne JJ) 99 (Kirby J).

68 See for example *Ferguson v Walkley* (2008) 17 VR 647; *Heanes v Herangi* [2007] WASC 175; *Atkinson v Gibson* [2010] QCA 279; see further Walsh (n 61).

69 Those Acts were: *Vagrants, Gaming and Other Offences Act 1931* (Qld); *Vagrancy Act 1966* (Vic). See further McLeod (n 33).

70 *Summary Offences Act 2005* (Qld) s 6. In Tasmania, there is an equivalent offence of 'public annoyance': *Police Offences Act 1935* (Tas) s 13.

territories.[71] Reviews found that the use of ticketing resulted in a substantial decrease in the number of offensive behaviour charges reaching the courts.[72] However, this masked the total number of penalties being issued – when the number of infringement notices was added to the number of arrests, it was found that prosecutions had actually increased.[73] Whilst defendants may prefer to receive a ticket for an offence rather than being required to appear in court, they may not appreciate the long-term consequences of incurring multiple fines for minor offences.[74] The accumulation of fines can result in enforcement action being taken, such as suspension of driver's licence, income quarantining, property seizure, and conversion of unpaid fine amounts to community service orders.[75] In some jurisdictions, fine default can result in a warrant being issued for the person's arrest, or a period of imprisonment being imposed.[76]

Crimes of Survival: Begging, Trespass, Theft, and Substance Use

People experiencing homelessness in Australia describe a lifestyle where much of their time and effort is directed towards providing themselves with the necessities of life. Many of the 'crimes' they commit are a direct result of not having those necessities. For example, people experiencing homelessness can be charged with trespass for inhabiting public spaces or squatting in abandoned buildings,[77] or evading public transport fares for seeking shelter on trains.[78]

Australian research has confirmed that people who are homeless report feeling forced to steal to provide themselves with the necessities of life.[79] The most common item stolen by people who are homeless is food.[80] Whilst some people who are homeless report that food is easy to come by, through food vans and other charitable organizations, newly homeless people may be unaware of the existence or location of such services. Some

---

71 New South Wales Ombudsman, *On the Spot Justice? The Trial of Criminal Infringement Notices by NSW Police* (NSW Government 2005); Queensland Crime and Misconduct Commission, *Policing Public Order: A Review of the Public Nuisance Offence* (Queensland Government 2008) 130.
72 New South Wales Law Reform Commission, *Penalty Notice Offences* (NSW Government 2012) 7; P. Mazerolle and others, *Ticketing for Public Nuisance Offences in Queensland: An Evaluation of the 12-Month Trial* (Queensland Government) 130–31.
73 T. Walsh, 'Ten Years of Public Nuisance in Queensland' (2016) 40(2) *Criminal Law Journal* 59; New South Wales Law Reform Commission (n 72) 294.
74 New South Wales Law Reform Commission (n 72) 103.
75 S. Forell, E. McCarron and L. Schetzer, *No Home, No Justice? The Legal Needs of Homeless People in NSW* (NSW Law and Justice Foundation 2005) 96.
76 G. Lansdell and others, 'Exposing the Injustice of Imprisonment for Fine Default: The *Taha* Case and Achieving Social Justice' (2013) 38(3) *Alternative Law Journal* 160.
77 *Crimes Act 1900* (ACT) ss 151, 154; *Inclosed Lands Protection Act 1901* (NSW) ss 4–6; *Trespass Act 1987* (NT) ss 4, 6–7; *Summary Offences Act 1923* (NT) s 46A; *Summary Offences Act 2005* (Qld) s 11; *Summary Offences Act 1953* (SA) ss 17, 17A; *Police Offences Act 1935* (Tas) s 14B; *Summary Offences Act 1966* (Vic) s 9(1)(d), (e); *Criminal Code* (WA) s 70A.
78 P. Hughes and K. Maroske, 'Fare Evasion in Queensland: Compounding Inequity and the Need to Improve Social Inclusion on Public Transport' (2019) 32(2) *Parity* 18–19.
79 J. A Heerde and S. A Hemphill, 'Stealing and Being Stolen from: Perpetration of Property Offences and Property Victimisation Among Homeless Youth – A Systematic Review' (2016) 48(2) *Youth and Society* 265; E. Chew and B. Midgley, 'Justice for the Homeless' (2004) 17(9) *Parity* 17.
80 S. Booth, 'Eating Rough: Food Sources and Acquisition Practices of Homeless Young People in Adelaide, South Australia' (2006) 9(2) *Public Health Nutrition* 212.

people who are homeless report feeling too ashamed or embarrassed to approach these services, whilst others say that visiting food vans at night poses a threat to their physical safety.[81]

Begging remains an offence in many Australian jurisdictions despite the repeal of vagrancy legislation.[82] The extent to which prohibitions against begging are enforced vary over time as police respond to shifts in community sentiment.[83] The problem with begging offences in Australia is that they are framed very broadly. No circumstances of aggravation, such as aggressive or threatening behaviour, are required for a person to be charged. An individual's state of destitution, coupled with the absence of a relationship between the parties, seems to provide the legal foundation for a begging charge. Other requests for assistance – such as that of a motorist who has been in an accident, or an individual who needs a small coin for a shopping trolley or parking meter – have been distinguished by the courts as situations where a 'relationship [is] temporarily created by emergency or a commonly shared experience'.[84] Yet the vast majority of those who beg do so because they have no other way of obtaining the necessities of life, and Australian research has established a clear link between homelessness, particularly rough sleeping, and begging.[85] Those who beg report doing so as an alternative to stealing, and they describe the experience as humiliating and dangerous.[86] Regardless, calls to repeal or amend begging offences have been largely ignored.[87]

There are other behaviours that become unlawful only when conducted by people who are homeless. For example, in many Australian states and territories, there are separate offences for drinking alcohol in public[88] and camping or sleeping in public,[89] all of which are lawfully conducted by housed individuals for leisure. People experiencing homelessness commonly observe that whilst they may be charged or moved on for drinking alcohol with friends or sleeping in parks, people who are housed commonly picnic and camp in parks

---

81 S. Booth and others, 'Gratitude, Resignation and the Desire for Dignity: Lived Experience of Food Charity Recipients and Their Recommendations for Improvement, Perth, Western Australia' (2018) 21(15) *Public Health Nutrition* 2831; Menih (n 62).
82 *Summary Offences Act 1923* (NT) s 56(1)(c); *Summary Offences Act 1953* (SA) s 12(1); *Police Offences Act 1935* (Tas) s 8(1)(a); *Summary Offences Act 1966* (Vic) s 49A(1).
83 P. Hughes, 'The Crime of Begging: Punishing Poverty in Australia' (2017) 30(5) *Parity* 32–33.
84 *Begg v Daire* (1986) 40 SASR 375, 388.
85 P. Lynch, 'Understanding and Responding to Begging' (2005) 29(2) *Melbourne University Law Review* 518; T. Walsh, 'Defending Begging Offenders' (2004) 4(1) *Queensland University of Technology Law & Justice Journal* 58; M. Horn and M. Cooke, *A Question of Begging: A Study of the Extent and Nature of Begging in the City of Melbourne* (Hanover Welfare Services 2001).
86 Horn and Cooke (n 85); Lynch (n 85).
87 Note, however, that in 2023, the offence of begging was repealed in Queensland following the recommendations of a parliamentary inquiry: see Queensland Parliamentary Committee (Community Support and Services), *Towards a healthier, safer, more just and compassionate Queensland: decriminalising the offences affecting those most vulnerable* (Queensland Parliament, 2022).
88 See for example *Summary Offences Act 1923* (NT) s 45D. See further P. D'Abbs, 'Controlling "Rivers of Grog": The Challenge of Alcohol Problems in Australian Indigenous Communities' (2010) 37(3) *Contemporary Drug Problems* 499.
89 See for example *Sydney Harbour Federation Trust Regulation 2021* (NSW) s 29; *Brisbane City Council Public Land and Council Assets Local Law 2014* (Qld); *Melbourne City Council Activities Local Law 2009* (Vic) s 2.8; *City of Perth Local Government Property Local Law 2005* (WA) cl 30(3); *Darwin City Council By-Laws 1994* (NT) s 103.

without such interference.[90] Public urination is another offence that may be committed in public spaces by people who are homeless as a matter of necessity.[91]

Charges for drug possession and drug use may also be associated with a person's homeless status. Substance use is common, perhaps even rampant, amongst people experiencing homelessness, and the causal relationship between homelessness and drug use is complex.[92] Some people experiencing homelessness suggest that drug use makes homelessness more bearable, whilst others report that they became homeless as a result of their addiction.[93] Regardless, without a private space in which to store or use drugs, the substance use of people who are homeless is easily detected by police and therefore more likely to result in criminal charges. The drug-related offences that homeless individuals are most often charged with involve consumption of a prohibited substance or possession of a prohibited substance (in small quantities),[94] possession of a prohibited item which is used in drug taking (such as a pipe or other implement),[95] and failure to dispose of a syringe.[96] Chroming – that is, inhaling volatile solvents such as paint – is also prevalent amongst young people who are homeless, particularly those in regional and remote areas.[97] In some Australian jurisdictions, there are specific laws that target chroming, providing police with the power to confiscate volatile substances, and in some areas, the possession of volatile substances is an offence.[98]

In most states and territories, police are empowered to take a person into protective custody if they are intoxicated.[99] Whilst such laws are intended to reduce arrests and ensure

---

90 See for example Walsh (n 48).
91 *Crimes Act 1900* (ACT) s 393A; *Summary Offences Act 2005* (Qld) s 7; *Summary Offences Act 1953* (SA) s 24; *Police Offences Act 1935* (Tas) s 8(1A) (wilful exposure).
92 M. Bower, J. Perz and E. Conroy, 'What Role Does Substance Use Play in the Social World of Australian People Who Have Experienced Homelessness? A Critical Realist Mixed-Methods Exploration' (2021) 31(1) *Journal of Community and Applied Social Psychology* 68–82; N. Thomas and H. Menih, 'Negotiating Multiple Stigmas: Substance Use in the Lives of Women Experiencing Homelessness' (2021) 20 *International Journal of Mental Health and Addiction* (online first).
93 G. Johnson and C. Chamberlain, 'Homelessness and Substance Abuse: Which Comes First?' (2008) 61(4) *Australian Social Work* 342.
94 *Drugs of Dependence Act 1989* (ACT) ss 169, 171, 171AA; *Drug Misuse and Trafficking Act 1985* (NSW) ss 10, 12; *Misuse of Drugs Act 1990* (NT) ss 7B, 13; *Drugs Misuse Act 1986* (Qld) ss 9, 9A; *Controlled Substances Act 1984* (SA) ss 33L, 33LB; *Misuse of Drugs Act 2001* (Tas) ss 24–25; *Drugs, Poisons and Controlled Substances Act 1981* (Vic) ss 73, 75; *Misuse of Drugs Act 1981* (WA) ss 6(2), 7(2) 14.
95 *Drug Misuse and Trafficking Act 1985* (NSW) s 11; *Misuse of Drugs Act 1990* (NT) s 12(1); *Drugs Misuse Act 1986* (Qld) ss 9A, 10, 10A, 10B; *Controlled Substances Act 1984* (SA) ss 33L(1)(c), 33LA; *Misuse of Drugs Act 2001* (Tas) s 23; *Misuse of Drugs Act 1981* (WA) s 14.
96 *Misuse of Drugs Act 1990* (NT) s 12(4), (5); *Local Government Act 1993* (NSW) s 630; *Drugs Misuse Act 1986* (Qld) s 10(4A); *HIV/AIDS Preventative Measures Act 1993* (Tas) s 35.
97 R. Fairbairn and D. Murray, 'Chroming – Legislative Change and Practical Dilemmas' (2003) 5(25) *Indigenous Law Bulletin* 19; S. MacLean, ' "It Might Be a Scummy-Arsed Drug but It's a Sick Buzz: Chroming and Pleasure' (2005) 32(2) *Contemporary Drug Problems* 295.
98 See *Volatile Substance Abuse Prevention Act 2005* (NT); *Police Powers and Responsibilities Act 2000* (Qld) s 603; *Police Offences Act 1935* (Tas) s 21A(2); *Controlled Substances Act 1984* (SA) s 19. Chroming is occasionally prosecuted under offensive behaviour provisions, although note that in *Nelson v Mathieson* [2003] VSC 451, the defendant argued successfully before the Victorian Supreme Court that chroming was not in itself 'offensive'.
99 *Law Enforcement (Powers and Responsibilities) Act 2002* (NSW) s 206(1); *Police Administration Act 1978* (NT) s 128; *Protective Custody Act 2000* (WA) s 6; *Public Intoxication Act 1984* (SA) s 7(1); *Intoxicated People (Care and Protection) Act 1994* (ACT) s 4.

the safety of intoxicated persons, concerns have been raised regarding the number of people, particularly Indigenous people, who have died whilst being held in protective custody under intoxicated persons provisions.[100] Coroners have concluded that police cells are not appropriate places in which to hold intoxicated persons, and have argued that intoxicated persons would be better cared for in hospital.[101]

The injustice of criminalizing behaviour that is directly associated with poverty and homelessness has been recognized by the Australian courts.[102] Regardless, such laws remain on the Australian statute books, and many homeless people find themselves in a 'revolving door' of arrests and court appearances for offences that they consider were necessary or unavoidable.

Specialist Courts for People Experiencing Homelessness

Some jurisdictions within Australia have experimented with problem-solving courts in response to the high prevalence of vulnerable people appearing on low-level criminal charges. In some locations, specialist lists have been introduced especially for people who are homeless or at risk of homelessness.

Problem-solving courts expand the role of the criminal court beyond the adjudication of guilt and sentencing to address the causes of defendants' offending behaviour. The principles of therapeutic jurisprudence underpin problem-solving courts, transforming the court's focus from penalizing defendants to promoting their rehabilitation.[103] Criminal justice practitioners – including the magistrate, prosecutor, defence lawyer, and court liaison officers – work together to bring about positive changes in defendants' lives by linking defendants with required services and monitoring their progress through regular court appearances.[104] In problem-solving courts, all cases coming within the eligibility criteria are transferred to a separate docket to be dealt with by a judicial officer, or officers, dedicated to that particular list. Problem-solving courts employ a deferred sentencing approach to capitalize on this moment of crisis in the life of the defendant. Defendants are told that if they do not take this opportunity to access treatment and support, their matter will be sent back to the mainstream court, which may result in a more severe sentence.

Drug courts are the oldest and most well-known of all problem-solving courts, and several Australian jurisdictions have drug courts in operation.[105] Most Australian drug courts

---

100 Commonwealth Ombudsman, *Australian Federal Police: Use of Powers Under the Intoxicated People (Care and Protection) Act 1994* (Commonwealth of Australia 2008); L. Collins and J. Mouzos, 'Deaths in custody: A Gender-Specific Analysis' (2002) 238 *Trends and Issues in Crime and Criminal Justice* 1, 6.
101 See for example Coroners' Court of Victoria, *Finding into Death with Inquest: Tanya Louise Day* (Coroners' Court of Victoria 2020); Coroners' Court of the Northern Territory, *Inquest into the Death of Mark Corbett* (NTMC 2003) 044.
102 *Moore v Moulds* (1981) 7 QL 227 (Shanahan DCJ).
103 See generally D. B. Wexler and B. J. Winnick, *Law in a Therapeutic Key: Developments in Therapeutic Jurisprudence* (Taylor and Francis 1997).
104 L. Schaefer and M. Beriman, 'Problem-Solving Courts in Australia: A Review of Problems and Solutions' (2019) 14(3) *Victims and Offenders* 344; M. S. King, 'Judging, Judicial Values and Judicial Conduct in Problem-Solving Courts, Indigenous Sentencing Courts and Mainstream Courts' (2010) 19 *Journal of Judicial Administration* 133; A. Freiberg, 'Problem-Oriented Courts: Innovative Solutions to Intractable Problems?' (2001) 11 *Journal of Judicial Administration* 8.
105 R. Kornhauser, 'The Effectiveness of Australia's Drug Courts' (2018) 51(1) *Journal of Criminology* 76.

were introduced by state and territory governments as part of their law and order strategies, unlike problem-solving courts targeted at homeless people, which were initiated by judges. Judicial officers were frustrated about the criminal law system's 'revolving door' and believed that using the coercive power of the court to link homeless defendants to services might be a more effective response to their offending.[106]

The 'Special Circumstances Courts' introduced by the Melbourne and Brisbane Magistrates Courts were loosely based on the drug court model.[107] The Melbourne Special Circumstances Court commenced in 2002, and the Brisbane Special Circumstances Court was established in 2006.[108] These were specialist lists for defendants who were experiencing, or were at risk of, homelessness or had impaired decision-making capacity where these circumstances contributed to their offending. They dealt with low-level offences only, and defendants were required to plead guilty, or indicate a willingness to plead guilty, to the offences as charged. The focus of proceedings was on the defendant's rehabilitation. The magistrates who presided over these lists worked closely with defendants to find practical solutions to the difficulties they faced. Defendants were granted bail on the condition that they participated in activities such as working with service providers to secure accommodation, attending drug or alcohol treatment, or participating in counselling and other self-help activities. Defendants were required to appear regularly before the court, often on a weekly or fortnightly basis, so that their compliance could be monitored. Prosecutors and defence lawyers worked as a team to agree on an appropriate case plan for each defendant, and service providers were present in court on sitting days to participate in case planning and accept referrals. Magistrates oversaw defendants' case plans with assistance from court liaison officers, who acted as the defendants' case manager. Defendants generally spent a number of months within the programme, and some remained involved for years.

Defendants generally spoke positively about their involvement with the Special Circumstances Courts.[109] Many defendants said they developed close relationships with court personnel, including the magistrate, and that they felt respected, valued, and humanized.[110] This, they said, meant they respected the court and its processes and made them want to stop offending. Some even said the court saved their lives and gave them a sense of hope. However, other defendants said they felt the process was intrusive of their privacy, and that the regular court appearances were burdensome.[111] Some said they would rather receive a

---

106 J. Popovic, 'Homelessness and the Law: A View from the Bench' (2004) 17(1) *Parity* 53; Judge Marshall Irwin, 'Disabled Justice: People with Disability in the Criminal Justice System' Speech delivered at the Banco Court, Supreme Court of Queensland, 22 May 2007.
107 They were also influenced by the proliferation of community courts and homeless courts in the United States: see S. R. Binder, *Taking the Court to the Streets: Homeless Court* (American Bar Association Commission on Homelessness and Poverty 2001); S. Kundu, 'Privately Funded Courts and the Homeless: A Critical Look at Community Courts' (2004/2005) 14 *Journal of Affordable Housing and Community Development* 170; G. Berman, 'What Is a Traditional Judge Anyway? Problem Solving in the State Courts' (2000) 84 *Judicature* 79.
108 Popovic (n 106); T. Walsh, 'The Queensland Special Circumstances Court' (2007) 16 *Journal of Judicial Administration* 223.
109 Walsh (n 6) 93.
110 Ibid.
111 M. Brown and others, ' "I'm Sorry but You're Just Not That Special" – Reflecting on the Special Circumstances Provisions Of the *Infringements Act 2006* (Vic)' (2013) 24(3) *Current Issues in Criminal Justice* 375–93.

fine to get their matter over and done with. Many service providers and advocates agreed, observing that the requirements imposed by Special Circumstances Courts were much more onerous than any sentence the defendant would likely have received from an ordinary court. They also expressed concern that the defendants' personal relationships with the magistrates were inappropriate and noted that magistrates were not trained to engage in case planning or therapeutic interventions.[112]

The Brisbane Special Circumstances Court was discontinued in 2012 on the basis that it was 'costly' and 'inefficient'.[113] Melbourne Special Circumstances Court continued until 2019, but even prior to this, establishing 'special circumstances' had become more difficult as the legislation became increasingly complex.[114] Early evaluations of the Special Circumstances Courts recommended that the successful aspects of these lists be mainstreamed to ensure support could be delivered to as many vulnerable defendants as possible. 'Generic integrated assessment, referral and support schemes' were established in response: the Victorian Magistrates Court introduced the Court Integrated Services Program (CISP), and the Queensland Magistrates Court introduced 'Court Link'.[115] Both CISP and Court Link are bail-based programmes that are available to people experiencing homelessness and other vulnerable defendants. Defendants are assigned a case manager, linked with services, and monitored by magistrates through regular court appearances over a period of months. Their participation in the programme is then taken into account in sentencing.

Attempts at mainstreaming court-based service delivery were embraced by some and rejected by others. Some scholars argued that this was the next step in the implementation of 'incremental improvements' to the traditional criminal court model; however, practitioners doubted that judicial officers in generalist courts would be willing or able, given time and resource constraints, to apply problem-solving methods in every relevant case.[116] Anecdotally, there seems to be less support for these generic integrated referral programmes than there was for the specialist lists.[117] Success of such programmes depends on the support of local social service agencies to take on clients and effectively matching clients with appropriate services and workers.[118]

Specialist lists are an expensive way of delivering services to homeless defendants.[119] However, cost benefits accrue in other areas. If the defendant's health and welfare needs can be met, the ongoing criminal justice and social welfare costs that would otherwise have been incurred are minimized.[120] Regardless, it must be acknowledged that courts cannot provide defendants with housing. By focusing on peripheral service delivery, courts may

---

112 Walsh (n 6).
113 M. Edgely, 'Addressing the Solution-Focused Sceptics: Moving Beyond Punitivity in the Sentencing of Drug-Addicted and Mentally Impaired Offenders' (2016) 39(1) *University of New South Wales Law Journal* 206.
114 Brown and others (n 111).
115 A. Freiberg and others, *Queensland Drug and Specialist Courts Review: Report Summary and Recommendations* (Queensland Government 2016) 17; S. Ross, *Evaluation of the Court Integrated Services Program* (Victorian Government 2009).
116 Freiberg (n 104) 8, 21, 24; Walsh (n 6).
117 H. Blagg, 'A problem shared . . . ? Some reflections on problem solving courts and court innovation in Australia' (2013) 5 *Plymouth Law and Criminal Justice Review* 24, 35.
118 Ibid., 34.
119 A. Freiberg, 'Problem-oriented courts: An update' (2005) 14 *Journal of Judicial Administration* 196, 214–5.
120 Ross (n 115); Edgely (n 113).

actually entrench welfarist responses to criminalization rather than addressing its causes.[121] When asked, people experiencing homelessness report that what they really need to stop offending is a home.[122]

Conclusion

Laws that criminalize activities associated with homelessness are justified either by concerns about 'risk' and public safety or paternalistic notions of 'welfare' and protection. Whilst the crime of vagrancy and the laws that promoted Aboriginal protectionism have been abolished, these same discourses underlie the policing of public spaces in Australia today. People experiencing homelessness are still charged with offences that are intimately connected to their housing status and their poverty. They are still considered threatening and a 'nuisance' when, in fact, they are much more likely to be victims than perpetrators of crime.

The operation of the criminal law makes the difficult and chaotic lives of those who are homeless even more challenging. Being moved on or banned from certain areas can compromise their ability to access services or stay safe. Criminal charges can compound when people miss court dates and accumulate fines that they cannot pay.

Criminal law responses will not address the complex reasons behind homeless persons' offending, and innovative court processes cannot ameliorate the adverse impacts of the criminal law on individuals' lives. Whilst services and support are important and needed, the courthouse may not be the most appropriate venue in which to deliver them. The consistent message from homeless individuals themselves is that if they had adequate, safe, affordable housing, they would have no reason or opportunity to offend. No matter how kind and sympathetic, 'a court is still a court' – and what people need is a home.[123]

---

121 C. Parsell, 'Growing Wealth, Increasing Homelessness and More Opportunities to Exercise Our Care to the Homeless' (2019) 13(2) *European Journal of Homelessness* 13–25.
122 Parsell (n 7).
123 J. Braithwaite, 'Housing, Crises and Crime' (2021) 54(1) *Journal of Criminology* 34, 39; T. Walsh and R. Fitzgerald, *Logan Community Justice Centre: Community Consultation and Design Report* (UQ 2020) 63.

27
HOMELESSNESS PREVENTION IN AUSTRALIAN RESIDENTIAL TENANCIES AND SOCIAL HOUSING LAW

The Case for Reform

Chris Martin and Hal Pawson

Introduction

Australia is generally a well-housed nation, but homelessness is a significant and growing problem. Homelessness services are provided to over 250,000 people every year,[1] at an annual cost to governments exceeding $1 billion.[2] Some 8,200 people were sleeping rough on the 2016 census night.[3]

'Homelessness' is understood by most relevant agencies in a broad sense, encompassing sleeping rough and other insecure, unsatisfactory accommodation arrangements. The breadth of accepted understandings of 'homelessness' is indicated by the definition in a Bill considered by the Australian Parliament in 2013:

Section 5 . . . a person is experiencing *homelessness* if:

(a) the person is sleeping rough or living in an improvised dwelling; or
(b) the person is temporarily living with friends or relatives, has no other usual address and does not have the capacity to obtain other suitable accommodation; or

---

1 Australian Institute of Health and Welfare, *Specialist Homelessness Services Annual Report 2021–22* (AIHW 2022) <www.aihw.gov.au/reports/homelessness-services/shs-annual-report/contents/about> (accessed 1 September 2023).
2 Productivity Commission, *Report on Government Services 2022: Homelessness* (Productivity Commission 2022) <www.pc.gov.au/ongoing/report-on-government-services/2022/housing-and-homelessness/homelessness-services/rogs-2022-partg-section19-homelessness-services-data-tables.xlsx> (accessed 1 September 2023).
3 ABS, *Census of Population and Housing: Estimating Homelessness* (ABS 2018) <www.abs.gov.au/statistics/people/housing/census-population-and-housing-estimating-homelessness/latest-release> (accessed 1 September 2023).

(c) the person has no safe place to live (including because the person is, or is at risk of, experiencing domestic violence); or
(d) the person is living in accommodation provided by a specialist homelessness service; or
(e) the person is living in a refuge, shelter or similar crisis accommodation; or
(f) the person is living in a caravan park, boarding house, hostel or similar accommodation, whether on a short-term or long-term basis, in respect of which the person has no secure lease and the person is not living in that accommodation by choice.

For this chapter, the *Homelessness Bill* 2013 (Cth)[4] is significant for a further reason: it exemplifies the general inadequacy of legislative responses to homelessness. The 2013 Bill did not proceed to a second reading, let alone become enacted in law. Even had it been enacted, the Bill would have had no legal effect beyond mere 'recognition' of homelessness as defined (Section 6). Instead, the Bill expressly stipulated that it would 'not, by its terms or operation, create or give rise to any rights (whether substantive or procedural), or obligations, that are legally enforceable in judicial or other proceedings' (Section 14(1)), and that '[n]o action, suit or proceeding is to be instituted in reliance on [the legislation]' (Section 14(2)).

The double-oddity of never-passed legislation that disavowed any legal effect is, unfortunately, emblematic of Australian governments' approach to homelessness prevention. Homelessness was a high-priority issue late in the first decade of the 2000s, particularly for the Australian government,[5] led by Kevin Rudd (2007–2010), which provided state and territory governments and the non-government sector with funds for new and reformed programmes across the various forms of homelessness. Rudd also pledged a 50% cut in homelessness by 2020, although how it would be achieved was never fully worked through. Under subsequent Commonwealth governments, homelessness slipped quickly down the national political agenda.

Meanwhile, at the level of Australia's states and territories, homelessness is likewise a matter of policy and practice rather than legally defined rights and responsibilities. Two areas of law are a natural domain for legislative action for homelessness prevention: residential tenancies law and social housing law. Neither, however, makes a strong commitment to preventing homelessness.

The present chapter focuses on these two areas of law. First, however, to ground that discussion, we briefly sketch the nature of 'homelessness' in Australia as indicated by the main data sources, and its drivers in the housing system. The chapter's second main section reviews Australian residential tenancies laws, showing how they provide for ready termination by landlords, and how the statutory considerations and discretion vested in tribunals afford only limited scope for preventing homelessness. In the third main section, we review the law relating to social housing specifically, where applicants and tenants have, at best, mere legitimate expectations, rather than legal rights to housing assistance, and access to judicial review is uncertain. The chapter concludes with directions for law reform.

---

4 <www.legislation.gov.au/Details/C2013B00149>
5 Often styled the Federal Government or the Commonwealth Government.

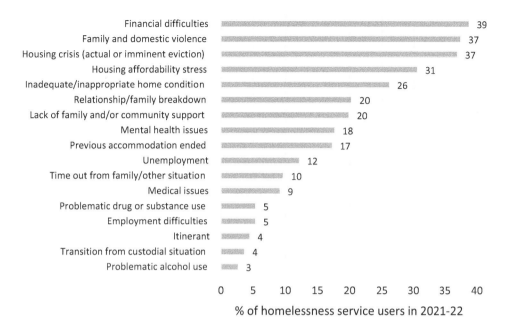

Figure 27.1 Homelessness service users (persons) in 2021–2022: factors cited as contributing to service user decisions to seek assistance – own analysis.

Note: Figures relate to all persons receiving SHS help in 2021–22 (272,700). Service users could cite more than one factor.

Source: The authors, using Specialist Homelessness Services (SHS) data for 2021–2022 released by the Australian Institute of Health and Welfare under a Creative Commons BY 4.0 (CC-BY 4.0) licence.

Homelessness in Australia

Factors contributing to homelessness in Australia are recorded in service user data collected by specialist homelessness services (SHSs), the sector of non-government agencies that work to end and prevent homelessness.

These factors are set out in Figure 27.1. Most cited is 'financial difficulties', reflecting the strong connection between homelessness and poverty established internationally.[6] Domestic violence and relationship breakdown also figure prominently. Just as prominent are housing system–related factors, where housing law could, potentially, mitigate the problem and thereby prevent homelessness. 'Housing crisis', a synonym for 'eviction', was a factor in more than a third of calls for assistance in 2021–2022, and 'inadequate/inappropriate home conditions' in more than a quarter. Challenging a common stereotype, only 5% of 2021–2022 service users sought help due to problematic drug or substance abuse, and only 3% due to alcohol addiction.

Homelessness trends over time may be gauged from the five-yearly ABS Census of Population and Housing; however, as of this writing (January 2023), the latest published census statistics relate to 2016. The SHS data gives a more up-to-date picture, showing in the four years to 2021–2022, SHS service users (a proxy for 'homeless people') increased in number

---

6 G. Bramley and S. Fitzpatrick, 'Homelessness in the UK: Who Is Most at Risk?' (2018) 33(1) *Housing Studies* 96.

by 8% – twice the rate of overall population growth.[7] This continues the trend of rising homelessness numbers recorded over the 2011–2016 period.[8]

Residential Tenancies Law

In Australia's federal system, residential tenancies law is the responsibility of the eight state and territory governments.[9] Each has its own residential tenancies legislation – styled the 'Residential Tenancies Act' (RTA), or similar.[10] While there are numerous differences in the details, these Acts are on a broadly common model. First outlined in reports of the Australian government's Commission of Inquiry into Poverty,[11] RTAs were enacted in all jurisdictions by the late 1990s, combining elements of consumer protection – standard form contracts, prescribed rights and obligations, and accessible dispute resolution – with light regulation of rents, and provision for 'ready but orderly' termination of tenancies.[12] The RTAs apply to private and social housing tenancies, mostly alike. The different terms of occupancy experienced by social renters (generally more secure tenancies and below-market rents) are mostly a matter of policy rather than law.

Tenancy termination is 'ready' because the circumstances in which a tenancy may be terminated are relatively broad, and the process relatively straightforward: the landlord gives a termination notice and, if the tenant has not vacated by the end of the notice period, applies to the jurisdiction's tribunal for an order terminating the tenancy. In most jurisdictions, the tribunal is a statutory agency designed to be quicker and less formal than a court; in two jurisdictions (Tasmania and WA), the tribunal is the Magistrates Court operating in a quicker and less formal mode.[13] And they are quick: the NSW tribunal, for example, finalizes 69% of termination proceedings within four weeks of the landlord lodging the application.[14]

---

7 H. Pawson and others, *Australian Homelessness Monitor 2022* (Launch Housing 2022) <https://cms.launchhousing.org.au/app/uploads/2022/12/AustralianHomelessnessMonitor_2022.pdf> (accessed 1 September 2023).

8 H. Pawson and others, *Australian Homelessness Monitor 2020* (Launch Housing 2020) <https://cityfutures.be.unsw.edu.au/documents/619/Australian_Homelessness_Monitor_2020.pdf> (accessed 1 September 2023).

9 New South Wales (NSW), Victoria (Vic), Queensland (Qld), South Australia (SA), Western Australia (WA), Tasmania (Tas), the Australian Capital Territory (ACT) and the Northern Territory (NT).

10 The *Residential Tenancies Act 2010* (NSW) (NSW RTA); the *Residential Tenancies and Rooming Accommodation Act 2008* (Qld) (Qld RTRAA); the *Residential Tenancies Act 1995* (SA) (SA RTA); the *Residential Tenancy Act 1997* (Tas) (Tas RTA); the *Residential Tenancies Act 1998* (Vic) (Vic RTA); the *Residential Tenancies Act 1987* (WA) (WA RTA); the *Residential Tenancies Act 1997* (ACT) (ACT RTA); the *Residential Tenancies Act* (NT) (NT RTA).

11 A. J. Bradbrook, *Poverty and the Residential Landlord-Tenant Relationship* (Australian Government Commission of Inquiry into Poverty 1975); R. Sackville, *Law and Poverty in Australia: Second Main Report* (Australian Government Commission of Inquiry into Poverty 1975).

12 C. Martin and others, *Regulation of Residential Tenancies and Impacts on Investment* (AHURI Final Report No. 391, Australian Housing and Urban Research Institute Limited 2022).

13 The tribunals are: the NSW Civil and Administrative Tribunal, the Queensland Civil and Administrative Tribunal, the SA Civil and Administrative Tribunal, the Tasmanian Magistrates Court, the Victorian Civil and Administrative Tribunal, the Western Australian Magistrates Court, the ACT Civil and Administrative Tribunal, and the NT Civil and Administrative Tribunal.

14 NCAT, *Annual Report 2021–22* (NSW Civil and Administrative Tribunal 2022).

Termination is 'orderly' in that tenants may be forcibly evicted only by order of the tribunal executed by an authorized officer.[15] Self-help evictions ('lock outs') are prohibited, and the associated penalties are generally the heaviest in the RTAs.

All states and territories provide for landlords to take termination proceedings on prescribed grounds, as well as without grounds.[16] During the fixed term of a tenancy, some grounds for termination are unavailable, and without-grounds termination is available only at the end of the fixed term. As a matter of practice, private sector tenancies typically commence with a fixed term of 6 or 12 months and continue as periodic tenancies or, if the parties agree, are subject to a further fixed term of similar length. Historically, social housing tenancies were offered without fixed terms, and de facto security was provided by social landlords not requiring their properties for other purposes. However, in recent years, most public housing landlords have introduced policies to periodically review tenants' eligibility, and some use fixed terms corresponding to review periods: for example, in NSW, public housing tenants are offered fixed terms of two, five, or ten years, depending on their assessed housing need.

Termination Notices by Landlords: With Grounds and Without

Termination proceedings by landlords generally commence with a termination notice. There is no requirement or facility for notice issuance to be recorded, so the number issued is unknown. In many cases, the matter would proceed no further because the factors underlying the notice are resolved: for example, a breach by the tenant is remedied. Termination notices are sometimes issued with the main intention of warning the tenant or spurring them to engage with the landlord.[17] However, in many cases, tenants respond by vacating the premises, thereby terminating the tenancy without further proceedings.

With Grounds

All RTAs allow landlords (whether the agreement has a fixed term or not) to give a termination notice on the grounds that the tenant has breached a term of the residential tenancy agreement. In most jurisdictions, a notice to remedy the breach is required as a preliminary step; if the breach is not remedied, then a termination notice may be given (Queensland, ACT), or the effect of the notice to remedy becomes that of a termination notice (SA, WA, NT).

According to the limited data available, failure to pay rent is by far the most common ground for termination proceedings before the tribunals.[18] All the RTAs deal with failure to pay rent somewhat differently from other breaches, to reduce the prospect of termination because of merely temporary non-payment. All jurisdictions provide for a short period after

---

15 A sheriff's officer or bailiff; only the NT RTA provides for the tribunal to authorize the landlord themselves to effect an eviction.
16 This is readier termination than envisaged in the Poverty Inquiry reports, which recommended against providing for termination without grounds.
17 C. Martin and others, *Social Housing Legal Responses to Crime and Anti-Social Behaviour: Impacts on Vulnerable Families* (AHURI Final Report No. 314, Australian Housing and Urban Research Institute Limited 2019).
18 C. Martin, 'Australia's Incipient Eviction Crisis: No Going Back' (2021) 46(2) *Alternative Law Journal* 134.

non-payment – ranging between 14 days (Tasmania) and 28 days (NSW and Victoria) – before which landlords can apply to the tribunal. Additionally, in Victoria, Tasmania, and WA, payment of all the arrears before the tribunal hearing makes the termination notice ineffective, while NSW goes further and provides payment of all the arrears at any time before eviction will stop the process. However, termination may proceed where tenants are repeatedly arrears: three times in 12 months in Tasmania, five times in 12 months in Victoria, and 'frequently' in arrears, as determined by the tribunal, in NSW.

Most of the other 'breach' grounds relate to forms of tenant misconduct, such as use of the premises for an illegal purpose, causing nuisance and annoyance, and damage to the property. These generally proceed more quickly (14 days or 21 days to the termination application).

The misconduct grounds are used disproportionately by social housing landlords, though still less frequently than failure to pay rent.[19] The high use of breach termination notices reflects a mix of factors, just one being the disadvantaged profile of social housing's clientele. Another is social housing's profile as a tenancy manager: it is more closely implicated in the lives of individual tenants and in community relations in social housing neighbourhoods. Because tenants in a social housing apartment block or estate have a landlord in common, disputes between neighbours are more apt to become tenancy disputes than in other settings. Social housing landlords also often have closer relations with police, including information-sharing arrangements, and are seen by governments – and themselves – as responsible for responding to crime and anti-social behaviour, often in a 'get tough' or 'zero tolerance' mode. Yet another factor is social housing's use of termination notices with grounds, rather than without, because it is more consistent with the principles of procedural fairness.[20]

All the RTAs provide grounds for termination where the tenant is not in breach, mostly available only at the end of a fixed term or in a periodic agreement. These grounds differ between jurisdictions, but the most common are frustration because the premises have become uninhabitable (all jurisdictions except Tasmania) and sale of the premises requiring vacant possession (all jurisdictions except the NT and not during the fixed term of a tenancy). Numerous other grounds are prescribed in Victoria, SA, Tasmania, and Queensland, including that the landlord or a family member requires the premises for their own housing. In the other jurisdictions, these reasons are implicitly covered by without-grounds terminations. In Victoria and Queensland, where availability of termination without grounds is more restricted (see following), grounds for termination are wider: for example, both provide for termination where a landlord is merely preparing to sell the property.

Without Grounds

All jurisdictions provide for 'without grounds' termination, except the ACT. NSW, SA, WA, and the NT allow termination without grounds at the end of the fixed term of a tenancy and during a periodic tenancy. Notice periods range from 14 days (end of fixed term, NT) to 90 days (periodic tenancies, NSW). Tasmania and Queensland allow without-grounds

---

19 Martin and others (n 17).
20 C. Martin, 'Contracts and Conduct: Using Tenancy Law to Govern Crime and Disorder in Public Housing in New South Wales' (2015) 5 *Property Law Review* 81; Martin and others (n 17).

termination only at the end of the fixed term of a tenancy (i.e. so periodic agreements may be terminated with grounds only). In practice, many landlords and agents there offer tenancies on successive short-fixed terms, thereby keeping open the prospect of termination without grounds. Victoria allows without-grounds termination only at the end of the first fixed term of a tenancy. The Victorian and Queensland limitations are recent amendments, as is the ACT's provision for termination with grounds only; the issue has been prominent in recent reviews of legislation and is an area of increasing divergence.

Tribunals' Considerations and Discretion in Termination Actions

When determining a landlord's termination application, the tribunal decides whether the formal requirements are satisfied (e.g. the period of notice is correct) and whether the ground, if any, is made out. Whether it can consider other factors, such as the tenant's circumstances, and decide, on balance of all the factors, not to terminate varies by jurisdiction and by the type of proceedings.

Where Termination Is Mandatory

In NSW, Queensland, WA, and SA, without-grounds proceedings result in the termination of the tenancy without regard to any factors or circumstances, except where invalidated by a formal defect (e.g. insufficient notice) or where the proceedings are retaliatory.[21] Those exceptions aside, the tribunal has no discretion to decline termination orders in without-grounds termination proceedings, and its discretion is confined to setting the date for possession – making without-grounds proceedings a virtual trump card for landlords. Under its original RTA, the NSW tribunal could decline to terminate considering 'the circumstances of the case',[22] but that discretion was removed in the 2010 RTA. Both Victoria and Tasmania have moved in the other direction, providing new scope for declining termination where it was previously mandatory. This is a result of recent legislative reform (in Victoria) and judicial interpretation (in Tasmania).

In NSW, termination is also mandatory in a range of termination proceedings brought by social landlords. Several categories of 'use of premises for an illegal purpose' (s 154D) attract mandatory termination – manufacture or sale of illegal drugs, keeping illegal firearms, child sexual abuse material offences, and car rebirthing – except where termination would result in 'undue hardship' to a child, a person with a disability, or a person experiencing domestic violence (s 154D(3)). In those exceptional cases, discretion may be exercised. Termination is also mandatory in proceedings on grounds relating to specific features of social housing tenancies, such as being assessed as ineligible for social housing (s 147).

Some consequences of mandatory termination provisions are illustrated by the NSW tribunal's decision in *Aboriginal Housing Office v Corrie* [2013] NSWCTTT 650, in which the NSW public housing landlord sought termination on the grounds that the tenant – a

---

21 Another rare exception in NSW: where the tenancy has existed 20 years or more, the landlord cannot give a termination notice without grounds but can instead apply to the tribunal, which may terminate the tenancy if appropriate in the circumstances of the case (s 94).
22 *Swain v Roads and Traffic Authority* [1995] NSW Supreme Court 30034 (unreported, Rofe J, 22 March 1995).

highly vulnerable person – had had a boyfriend who had conducted several small drug deals at the premises:

> If I had a discretion whether or not to terminate the residential tenancy agreement, I would exercise that discretion in favour of the tenant and I would refuse to make an order of termination, for the reasons appearing below.
>
> The tenant herself did not commit any unlawful act. [The boyfriend's] illegal conduct was relatively minor and took place over a short period of one to two weeks. The tenant ended her relationship with [the boyfriend] following his arrest and assisted police with their enquiries. He has not stayed at the residential premises since.
>
> The tenant has a previously good tenancy history. The tenant has lived in public housing since she was 17. No evidence was presented of any other problems with the present tenancy, or problems arising from any past tenancy.
>
> The tenant is an Aboriginal women with four children aged between 4 and 11. The children are settled at [the local] Public School and, if they are required to move from their home, they will be detrimentally affected. She has no references and no alternative accommodation with family or friends available. The tenant suffers from depression and is a victim of domestic violence.
>
> There was no evidence presented of any serious adverse effects the tenancy has had on neighbouring residents, or other persons. There was no evidence presented indicating that a failure to terminate the agreement would subject neighbouring residents, or other persons, or property, to unreasonable risk.
>
> The tenant has never been in breach of an order of the Tribunal.
>
> Unfortunately . . . I do not have a discretion whether or not to terminate the residential tenancy agreement. As I am satisfied on the balance of probabilities that the tenant permitted the residential premises to be used by [the boyfriend] for the purpose of the sale of a prohibited drug, namely, cannabis leaf, an order of termination is mandatory.

The *Corrie* case was prior to the legislative carve-out from mandatory termination of persons with disability, children, and experiencing domestic violence. The limits of the carve-out should be noted. In *NSW Land and Housing Corporation v O'Reilly* [2021] NSWCATCD 148, the public housing landlord sought termination on the grounds that the tenant's mother had engaged in small-scale drug dealing at the premises; although the tenant was not involved in the offences and her mother had moved out, she had neither children, a diagnosed disability, nor the domestic violence factor, so the mandatory termination order was made. Even where these factors are present, the tenant needs to show 'undue hardship', which is not a given. In *NSW Land and Housing Corporation v Reid* [2019] NSWCATCD, where the public housing landlord sought termination on the grounds that a tenant's son had kept a firearm at the premises, the tribunal found the tenant was disabled and would suffer hardship, but not 'undue' hardship. Despite accepting that 'there is a dire shortage of affordable rental accommodation for people on low income', the tribunal held that it was 'not satisfied that this would result in the tenant becoming homeless'.[23] Accordingly, the exception was not engaged, and mandatory termination orders were made.

---

23 *NSW Land and Housing Corporation v Reid* [2019] NSWCATCD at 46. The tribunal observed (at 45) that it may be possible for the tenant to stay with her adult daughter – herself a public housing tenant with

Where Termination May Be Declined

All state and territory tribunals have discretion to decline termination in most proceedings on grounds of breach by the tenant. In Tasmania, Victoria, ACT, and NT, the discretion to decline termination extends to proceedings without grounds.

Each RTA structures the discretion somewhat differently. In NSW, WA, and Queensland, the tribunal is directed to consider whether the breach, if proven, justifies termination, and in NSW and Queensland, justification is expressly considered in relation to the circumstance of the case (s 87(4) NSW RTA; s 71(2)(b) WA RTA; (s 337(3) Qld RTRAA). In SA, the tribunal may decline termination orders for breach 'where it is just and equitable' to do so (s 80(5)).

In Tasmania, the tribunal must consider whether the landlord's reasons for termination are 'genuine or just' (s 45(3)(b)). This provision was considered by the Tasmanian Supreme Court in *Parsons v Director of Housing* [2018] TASSC 62,[24] in which the public housing landlord sought to terminate, without grounds, the lease of an intellectually disabled tenant. The landlord refused to disclose its reasons, even when pressed by the magistrate. The Supreme Court held:

> The reason for the notice will be the owner's reason and that is the starting point of the evaluation. What is 'just' takes its colour from all the circumstances, including rights of ownership and matters agreed at the commencement of the lease. It is not a consideration focussed solely on the circumstances of the tenant. . . . The provision confers some protection against capricious and arbitrary action by imposing a requirement going beyond checking for compliance with the formal steps for procuring vacant possession, and which directs the Court to make a judgment about the matter which takes account of all the circumstances.[25]

In ACT and NT, each jurisdiction's superior court has found that the tribunal has discretion in termination proceedings generally, based on the permissive language of the legislation (i.e. the tribunal 'may terminate').[26]

In Victoria, the tribunal must terminate if it is 'reasonable and proportionate', considering 'the interests of, and impact on' the landlord, tenant, and other residents (s 330(1)(f)). The tribunal must also have regard to a list of factors at s 330A, including 'the nature, frequency and duration of the conduct of the renter which led to the notice to vacate being given (s 330A(a))', and 'whether any other order or course of action is reasonably available instead of making a possession order' (s 330A(h)). These provisions, which commenced March 2021, apply to proceedings with grounds and without, in the limited

---

a disabled child. Evicting a tenant from public housing in contemplation that she would next reside with another public housing tenant, whose own household and tenancy would likely come under stress, is a bizarre course.

24 *Parsons v Director of Housing* [2018] TASSC 62; upheld *Director of Housing v Parsons* [2019] TASFC 3.
25 It also held that 'genuine or just' meant 'genuine and just': *Parsons v Director of Housing* [2018] TASSC 62 at 58.
26 *Eastman v Commissioner for Housing for the ACT* [2006] ACTSC 52; *Williams v CEO Housing* [2013] NTSC 28.

circumstances where the latter are still allowed in Victoria, and replace more narrowly structured provisions.[27]

Reported decisions on the new provisions are still few and outcomes are mixed, but some show an increased engagement with homelessness prevention. In *Danrell v Morris* [2022] VCAT 1303, the landlord sought to termination on the ground that they intended to prepare the property for sale; the tribunal, having heard that the tenants had made almost 90 unsuccessful applications for alternative premises, declined to terminate:

> There is no doubt that the rented premises is the rental providers' property and they are entitled to sell it. They should also be able to realise the best price possible for their investment – but at what cost to the renters? The reality for the renters, and their family, is that a possession order will make them homeless. The renters are employed locally, their children attend local schools and all their needs are currently being met by local services as they require. A move out of the area is not an option. The renters have also attempted to find alternative accommodation locally, but the rental market, along with the general economic climate, means there is nothing suitable that is available.
>
> Selling the premises with the renters in possession is a course of action that is reasonably available to the rental providers and should be explored. . ... For these reasons it is not reasonable and proportionate to make a possession order at this time and the application for possession is dismissed.[28]

Contrast *Lynch v Manion* [2021] VCAT 1156, where the tribunal terminated the tenancy on the same grounds, observing a ' "tidy-up" would attract a greater number of buyers' and 'it is reasonable that she [the landlord] wants to take advantage of the current market and get the best price possible by selling it with vacant possession'.[29]

In its first major decision on the new provisions, the Victorian Supreme Court has emphasized that the legislation requires an 'active intellectual consideration' of the impact of termination on the tenant, which may include, according to the tenant's evidence and submissions, an assessment of the likelihood that the tenant may be made homeless. In *Hanson v Director of Housing* [2022] VSC 710, the public housing landlord sought termination on the grounds that the tenant had failed to keep the premises reasonably clean; the tenant, who had lived there 22 years, having previously been homeless, gave evidence of several serious medical conditions and low income, but the tribunal had 'failed to make a finding as to the likelihood of [the tenant] becoming homeless, [so] the Tribunal was not then properly able to weigh that possible impact on him in the analysis of whether the possession order was reasonable and proportionate'. It is fair to say that not all of the tribunal's prior decisions on ss 330(1) and 330A include such a deliberate assessment of the likelihood of homelessness, so the Supreme Court's decision signals that more rigorous attention to homelessness, where it is suggested by evidence and submissions, is required by the new provisions.

---

27 Previously, termination was mandatory where a breach was proven, except where a breach was trivial, was remedied, and would not be repeated (s 330).
28 *Danrell v Morris* [2022] VCAT 1303 at 22–23.
29 *Lynch v Manion* [2021] VCAT 1156 at 57.

In NSW and Queensland, special provisions apply to discretion in social housing termination proceedings. These provisions were not introduced to restrict terminations and prevent homelessness but, on the contrary, to overcome perceived reluctance of the tribunal to terminate social housing tenancies. The NSW tribunal is required to consider a special list of factors (s 154E), including 'the effect of the tenancy has had on neighbouring residents'. Queensland's legislation specifies that the tribunal must not decline to terminate merely because a tenant is a social housing tenant (s 349A).

As noted earlier, all jurisdictions also make some provision for the tribunal to decline termination where it is retaliatory. The scope of this protection is limited, because either it applies only where certain actions against the landlord have been taken (especially SA), the onus is on the tenant to prove the retaliatory intent (all but WA), or what is 'retaliatory' is narrowly interpreted. The WA Supreme Court has held that without-grounds proceedings are not retaliatory where taken in response to a tenant defending with-grounds proceedings.[30] Similarly, the Queensland Civil and Administrative Tribunal (QCAT) Appeals Panel has characterized a landlord's use of a without-grounds notice (given two days after the tenant filed a dispute notice) as '[choosing] the path of peace', rather than retaliation.[31] Even where proceedings are found to be retaliatory, in all jurisdictions (except ACT), tribunals can exercise discretion and terminate the tenancy anyway. In *O'Keefe v Davies* [2016] NSWCATCD 7, without-grounds termination proceedings were brought to prepare a property for sale, after a long history of incompetent management by the landlord:

> Even if I were satisfied that the termination notice and/or the application were retaliatory, I would not exercise my discretion in this case to declare that the termination notice has no effect or to refuse to make the termination order. . . . The Landlord is extremely stressed about how he can manage two mortgages and provide for his family. The Landlord's financial position is taking a toll on his health. The Landlord wants to sell the premises, pay down his debt and get on with his life. He is entitled to do so. The Tenant is unemployed and separated from his partner. He cares for his 13-year-old son who attends school near the residential premises. It is coming up to Christmas. The Tenant has nowhere else to go and has limited financial means. . . . The interests of justice require that the residential tenancy agreement be terminated. The residential tenancy agreement is terminated in accordance with s 85 of the Act. Possession of the premises is to be given to the Landlord on 4 January.[32]

The Covid-19 Eviction Moratoriums

The 'ready' termination of tenancies in Australia was disrupted, temporarily, in the early months of the Covid-19 pandemic in 2020. Amongst the extraordinary policy measures introduced during the early 'shutdown' phase of the emergency, Australian state and territory governments implemented an 'eviction moratorium'. In fact, each jurisdiction

---

30 *Re Magistrate Steven Malley; ex parte the Housing Authority* [2017] WASC 193.
31 *De Bruyne v Ray White Waterford* [2020] QCATA 113 at 28.
32 *O'Keefe v Davies* [2016] NSWCATCD 7 at 78–85.

implemented its own measures, of different scope and strength, none of which entirely stopped landlords from taking termination proceedings.[33] In summary:

- Several jurisdictions stopped without-grounds termination proceedings (Queensland, Tasmania, Victoria, WA, and NSW in its second 2021 lockdown moratorium).
- Several jurisdictions introduced or expanded preliminary scrutiny of termination proceedings, with an emphasis on resolving rent arrears with repayment plans and rent variations (NSW, Victoria, WA).
- Two jurisdictions afforded the tribunal discretion to refuse termination, considering the need to avoid homelessness (NSW and SA). These two now-expired emergency measures represent the only express references to homelessness prevention in Australian residential tenancies legislation.

All emergency measures have now ended; however, they continue to offer lessons for law reform, particularly regarding termination grounds and tribunal discretion.

Marginal Rental and the Law

Numerous small categories of rental housing arrangements are excluded from the mainstream provisions of each jurisdiction's RTA: boarders and lodgers, residents of crisis accommodation, and residents of manufactured home estates and caravan parks. The housing rights of these marginal renters vary within and across jurisdictions, but almost all have less protection against eviction than mainstream renters.[34]

ACT's approach to marginal renters is distinctive: generally, all have 'occupancy agreements' and are subject to a set of 'occupancy principles' in the ACT RTA.[35] The occupancy principles are more broadly stated than the prescribed terms and other provisions applying to mainstream tenancies: for example, an occupancy agreement must state 'under what circumstances the occupancy agreement may be terminated' and provide a 'reasonable period of notice' (s 71EK). This allows more variation between individual occupancy agreements, reflecting the diversity of arrangements to which the provisions apply. Occupancy agreements can be terminated without tribunal orders.

In other jurisdictions, the regulation of marginal rental arrangements is piecemeal, with some arrangements covered by specific legislation, while others are left to the common law of lodging.[36] All jurisdictions except WA have legislated with respect to boarding houses (or 'rooming houses' or 'rooming accommodation') where more than a certain threshold number of persons

---

33 For further details, see C. Martin, 'Australian Residential Tenancies Law in the COVID-19 Pandemic: Considerations of Housing and Property Rights' (2021) 44(1) *UNSW Law Journal* 197; C. Leishman and others, *Australia's COVID-19 Pandemic Housing Policy Responses* (AHURI Final Report No. 376, Australian Housing and Urban Research Institute Limited 2022).
34 One exception: in most jurisdictions (NSW, Queensland, SA, Victoria, WA), persons who own a manufactured dwelling and rent the site on which it is installed are covered by specific legislation and have stronger protection against termination than mainstream renters: for example, no termination without grounds, and compensation rights where their agreement is terminated other than on grounds of breach by the resident.
35 Some arrangements, such as crisis accommodation and supported housing, are excluded, unless the agreement expressly states that it is an occupancy agreement (s 71C).
36 Where the accommodation provider is 'in business', the Australian Consumer Law (ACL) also applies and implies into the accommodation agreement a warranty that the accommodation will be 'fit for purpose'. The ACL does not affect the ways in which the accommodation agreement may be terminated.

reside. In most jurisdictions, the legislated notice periods for the termination of boarding house agreements are less than for mainstream tenancies (e.g. in Victoria, a rooming house landlord may, after rent is unpaid for seven days, give two days' notice of termination). In NSW and SA, boarding house landlords can terminate agreements without orders of the tribunal.

Social Housing Law

Like residential tenancies law, social housing in Australia is the responsibility of the states and territories. Each has a statutory corporation empowered to acquire land and housing and provide it to eligible persons for rent (public housing). Each jurisdiction also has not-for-profit NGOs (community housing providers) managing a smaller amount of rental housing for similarly eligible persons; some jurisdictions also have a smaller-still sector of Indigenous housing organizations. Local governments in Australia are very rarely involved in social housing provision.

Aside from residential tenancies legislation, the principal pieces of legislation for the social housing system are those establishing the public housing authorities and the regulatory schemes for community housing providers. The legislation says little about the types of housing assistance that may be provided, or eligibility criteria and other terms of assistance – in contrast to, say, social security legislation. Instead, these are almost entirely matters of policy.[37] All the public housing landlords have published comprehensive manuals or compendiums of operational policies about eligibility, allocations, rental rebate calculations, and termination proceedings. The NSW Supreme Court described their significance in *AA v Vevers* [2013] NSWSC 1799:

> Policies are published not only for the guidance of decision-makers but also of the public, which is entitled to know what the criteria for obtaining social housing are and, accordingly, what their entitlements are. . . . [The NSW public housing landlord] is not a charity; it is an instrument of public policy undertaking a task entrusted to it by the legislature. Thus the Policies are not merely internal guides but govern the interaction of the public with an arm of government and must be construed with that fundamental purpose in mind.[38]

Community housing providers publish similar operational policies, although none are as comprehensive as the public housing policies.[39]

Review of Decisions

In terms of preventing homelessness, the most important types of social housing decisions are those regarding applicants' eligibility and priority and the taking of termination proceedings.

---

37 Where RTAs refer to social housing eligibility, rental rebates, and transfers, it is generally to provide that the legislation does not impinge on social housing policies: for example, provisions about rent increases do not apply to changes in rental rebates.
38 *AA v Vevers* [2013] NSWSC 1799 at 18.
39 A. Powell and others, *The Construction of Social Housing Pathways Across Australia* (AHURI Final Report 316, Australian Housing and Urban Research Institute Limited 2019).

In all jurisdictions, applicants can have eligibility decisions by public housing landlords reviewed through a two-tier process: first internally, and secondly by a dedicated appeals body (Tasmania does not have this second tier). In SA and ACT, the second-tier body is the Civil and Administrative Tribunal; in the other jurisdictions, it is a committee that reports to the jurisdiction's housing executive.[40] Eligibility decisions are also subject to judicial review by each jurisdiction's Supreme Court. An example is *AA v Vevers*, cited earlier, in which the NSW Supreme Court reviewed and overturned a decision of the NSW public housing landlord to deny eligibility to an applicant because he was a convicted child sex offender and, therefore, in the executive's view, unable to sustain a successful tenancy per the eligibility policy. As the Court observed, 'if the Minister decides that the appropriate policy in respect of applicants such as the plaintiff is they should be denied social housing, this should be explicitly state in the relevant Policies'. The minister subsequently did precisely that, revising the policy to expressly exclude persons on the Child Protection Register.

Decisions to take termination proceedings are excluded from the two-tier review process in all jurisdictions. State superior courts have taken different approaches as to whether these decisions are subject to judicial review. The question is complicated by legislative and interpretive changes regarding the ability of tribunals to decline termination in proceedings under the RTAs.

In *Burgess & Anor v Director of Housing & Anor* [2014] VSC 648, which concerned illegal use of termination proceedings against a public housing tenant and single mother who had been convicted of drug offences, the Victorian Supreme Court held that the Victorian public housing landlord was obliged to afford procedural fairness at two decision points in the termination process: the decision to give a termination notice and, after a termination order was made, the decision to apply for an enforceable warrant of possession. At the first decision point, procedural fairness requires informing the tenant that termination is being considered, the general nature of the reasons and the types of matter that may count either way, and inviting the tenant's response; and the decision itself would involve considering 'what other accommodation is available to the tenant if evicted; their family situation; health issues', and 'balancing the extent of the negative impact of eviction on the tenant and the tenant's household, against the aims of ensuring that public housing is a safe and secure environment that supports the health and wellbeing of tenants in residence'. At the second decision point, procedural fairness requires considering any relevant information arising since the decision to give a termination notice.

However, the Court in *Burgess* also found that the scope for challenging defective decisions is limited. Here the public housing landlord had failed to meet its obligations at both points, but the only proper time to seek judicial review of the decision to give a termination notice was prior to the tribunal making a termination order; after that, the decision's legal effect was spent, and it could no longer be quashed. The tenant, therefore, succeeded only in having the decision to seek a warrant of possession quashed. Furthermore, the only forum for judicial review is the Supreme Court – not the tribunal. In the earlier decision in *Director of Housing v Sudi* [2011] VSCA 266, the Victorian Court of Appeal held that the tribunal could not conduct collateral review of the lawfulness of the public housing landlord's

---

40 The NSW Housing Appeals Committee, the Queensland Housing Act Reviews Team, the Victorian Housing Appeals Office, WA's Regional Appeals Committees, and the NT Public Housing Appeals Board.

decision to seek termination. Support for this position was based in the ready-but-orderly nature of termination in Australian residential tenancies law:

> The RTA was intended to establish a scheme under which landlords could seek to evict, by expeditious process consistent with the requirements of natural justice, those in occupation of premises 'without licence or consent'. More obviously than in most other statutory contexts, the role of the Tribunal under this scheme is as an instrument of legislative policy. That is, once satisfied that the conditions for eviction are met, the Tribunal must evict.[41]

Around the same time, the Tasmanian Supreme Court took a different approach in *King v Director of Housing* [2013] TASFC 9, in which a tenant sought an injunction against Housing Tasmania's without-grounds termination proceedings, arguing that they had been denied procedural fairness. The Tasmanian Supreme Court refused the injunction, holding that Housing Tasmania's decision to seek termination was not open to judicial review because, applying *Griffith University v Tang* [2005] HCA 7, the decision did not derive force from a statutory power granted the housing authority but instead from the tenancy agreement as governed by the general law. As discussed previously, the Supreme Court subsequently decided in *Parsons* that Tasmania's RTA does, in fact, require the magistrate to evaluate whether a landlord's reasons for seeking termination are 'genuine and just' (s 45(3)(b)). However, *Parsons* did not over-rule *King* on the point about judicial review and the application of the principle in *Griffith University v Tang*.

Comments in the Victorian Court of Appeal's judgement in *Sudi* appear to be supportive of the reasoning in *King*, although the former does not cite *Tang*, and the later decision in *Burgess* did not develop the comments to deny judicial review there. As Maxwell P observes in *Sudi*, it is under the *Housing Act 1983* (Vic) that 'the Director [of Housing] is . . . authorised to enter into leases of public housing'. However:

> Having entered into a particular lease, the Director's rights and obligations are governed by the RTA as if she were any other landlord. In short, the Director was not here acting in exercise of a power conferred upon her in her statutory capacity as such. Rather, she had standing to apply for a possession order . . . because she was 'a person who claims to be entitled' to possession. Her eligibility to apply for such an order was no different from that of any other person claiming a similar entitlement. The statutory scheme thus operates in exactly the same way for the Director, as a public landlord, as it does for private landlords.[42]

Similarly, the WA Supreme Court has held that the WA Housing Authority is not required to afford procedural fairness when deciding whether to take termination proceedings, because the *Residential Tenancies Act 1987* (WA) allows termination without grounds and affords no discretion to decline termination (*Blanket v the Housing Authority* [2014] WASC 409; reaffirmed this reasoning in *Re Magistrate Steven Malley; ex parte the Housing Authority* [2017] WASC 193). In NSW, no recent decision has squarely addressed the issue. There is

---

41 *Director of Housing v Sudi* [2011] VSCA 266 at 79.
42 Ibid. at 73.

an older decision, *Nicholson v NSW Land and Housing Corporation* [1991] NSW Supreme Court 30027 (unreported, Badgery-Parker J, 24 December 1991), in which the Supreme Court enjoined without-grounds termination proceedings by the public housing landlord because they denied procedural fairness to the tenant, but its authority must now be in doubt; it predates *Tang*, and both *King* and *Blanket* expressly declined to follow it. The availability of without-grounds proceedings to social housing landlords was confirmed by the NSW Court of Appeal in *Coffs Harbour and District Local Aboriginal Land Council v Lynwood* [2017] NSWCA 317, which also confirmed that, in such proceedings, termination is mandatory.

While the law regarding judicial review of termination decisions by public housing landlords is unsettled, there is even greater uncertainty regarding community housing landlords. The Victorian Supreme Court considered the issue in *Durney v Unison Housing Ltd* [2019] VSC 6, in which a tenant sought review of a community housing landlord's decisions to give a termination notice (subsequently withdrawn) and refuse the tenant contact with the landlord's staff following several highly conflictual episodes. The relevant principle, observed the Court, was that set out in *R v Panel on Take-overs & Mergers; ex parte Datafin plc* [1987] QB 815:

> A decision of a private body which was not made in the exercise of a statutory power, may be amenable to judicial review if the decision is in a practical sense, made in the performance of a 'public duty' or in the exercise of a power which has a 'public element'.[43]

The *Datafin* principle has been referred to favourably in Australian superior court decisions, though never expressly adopted by the High Court. In this case, the Court held the principle did not apply because:

(a) Unison is a private body, and was not acting under any statutory power;
(b) Neither decision was made in the performance of a public duty, or in the exercise of a power that had a public element or public law consequences;
(c) The decision to serve a notice to vacate under the RT Act is a decision to take the first step towards the recovery of possession of rented premises under the RT Act;
(d) A right to obtain possession of premises under the RT Act is a private property right, arising from the tenancy agreement. [44]

In doing so, the Court highlighted the point made in *Sudi* that decisions to give termination notices can be characterized as deriving from general property rights, rather than social housing statues.

Human Rights Law and Social Housing

Three jurisdictions – Victoria, ACT, and most recently, Queensland – have enacted human rights charters, with some implications for social housing law. The charters enumerate

---

43 *Durney v Unison Housing Ltd* [2019] VSC 6 at 56.
44 Ibid. at 65.

rights reflecting international human rights conventions and provide that actions by public authorities in conflict with the charter rights are generally unlawful.

The Victorian Charter was invoked in *Sudi* and *Burgess*, particularly its provision, reflecting the UN Convention on the Rights of the Child, that families and the best interests of children are to be protected (s 17). In *Burgess*, the public housing landlord was held to have failed to consider the interests of the tenant's child, and this was a further reason for finding its decisions to be unlawful. However, the Court also confirmed that the Charter 'does not itself create any new remedy' and instead relies on 'pre-existing forms of action' – that is, judicial review – being available.

The ACT's *Human Rights Act 2005* (ACT) is similar. In *Commissioner for Social Housing in the ACT v Massey* [2013] ACAT 41, the tribunal observed that the discretion provided by the RTA admitted some scope for human rights to be considered in the exercise of discretion, but not to amount to a review of lawfulness of the decision. As Bell observes, this is a more restrictive approach to the litigation of human rights in relation to housing than has been taken in Europe and South Africa.[45]

There are no decisions yet regarding the Queensland Charter. In what may be an inauspicious start, shortly after the Charter's commencement, the Queensland housing minister sought to justify retaining without-grounds termination at the end of fixed terms, stating 'a proposal that an owner would not be able to end a tenancy at the conclusion of a lease is actually a breach of Queensland's Human Rights Act', specifically the right to property.[46] The Queensland human rights commissioner, however, stated via a media release that 'given significant housing instability and homelessness in Queensland, there seems a clear justification for limiting the rights of lessors by requiring them to provide a reason to end a tenancy at the end of a fixed term lease'.[47]

The Future of Homelessness Prevention in Residential Tenancies and Social Housing Law

Homelessness policy in Australia has almost entirely neglected to use residential tenancies law and social housing law in the prevention of homelessness. Both areas of law have developed in ways that contribute to the deepening problem of homelessness, providing too readily for the termination of tenancies by landlords generally, and allowing social housing landlords to determine whether an applicant will receive assistance, and whether a tenant will continue to be housed, without sufficient external scrutiny.

From our examination of the many deficiencies in both areas of the law, we suggest the following reform agenda.

Residential tenancies law should be reformed to bring provisions for termination and eviction into alignment with the right to housing recognized at international law, particularly Article 11(1) of the *International Covenant on Economic, Social, and Cultural Rights*.

---

45 K. Bell, 'Protecting Public Housing Tenants in Australia from Forced Eviction: The Fundamental Importance of the Human Right to Adequate Housing and Home' (2013) 39(1) *Monash University Law Review* 14.
46 F. Caldwell, 'Plan to Make It Harder to Kick Tenants Out a "Breach of Human Rights"' *The Brisbane Times* (7 July 2021).
47 Queensland Human Rights Commissioner, 'Human Rights Commissioner Says Rights Must Be Appropriately Balanced in Tenancy Reform Debate' (media release 8 July 2021).

This right has been the subject of comments by the United Nations Committee on Economic, Social, and Cultural Rights elaborating on state obligations: these include ensuring that evictions occur only after accessible legal proceedings to 'ascertain that the measure in question is duly justified', only as a 'last resort', and not to 'render individuals homeless'.[48]

Each principle is a touchstone for reform. To align with them, states and territories should:

- Repeal provisions for landlords to terminate without grounds. This reflects the principle that termination must be 'duly justified'. This has been implemented in the ACT's recent reforms and is the logical extension of the recent reforms restricting, but not eliminating, without-grounds termination in Victoria and Queensland.
- Reduce the scope of some grounds for termination, and repeal unjustifiable grounds altogether. As an example of the former, the 'illegal use' ground should be limited to where the tenant's conduct causes harm or detriment to a neighbour. As an example of the latter, the ground of preparation of a property for sale is unjustifiable and should be repealed.
- Provide that payment of rent arrears stops termination proceedings at any point prior to eviction. This would be an extension of the provisions in NSW, Tasmania, Victoria, and WA and reflects the principle that eviction must be a last resort.

Reforms to the functions and powers of the tribunals are also required. The recent Victorian reforms, and the Covid-19 emergency measures, offer some practical guidance to achieving greater assurance of scrutiny and justification in termination proceedings. In particular:

- Provide that the tribunal must consider whether termination is reasonable and proportionate in the circumstances of the case, including whether other courses of action were or are reasonably available, the best interests of any children in the household, and the risk of the tenant becoming homeless.
- Provide that where the tribunal terminates a tenancy, it must set a date for possession that allows sufficient time to access assistance and find alternative accommodation and will not likely result in the tenant becoming homeless.
- Provide that the tribunal must decline to terminate where it is satisfied that the proceedings are retaliatory.

Regarding marginal renting, the ACT's occupancy principles are a model for achieving broader legislative coverage for all renters outside the mainstream and specific regimes. All jurisdictions should enact occupancy principles for otherwise-excluded rental accommodation arrangements – such as private lodgings and crisis accommodation – and work with stakeholders to draft and road-test occupancy agreements that address their specific

---

48 Committee on Economic, Social and Cultural Rights, Views Adopted by the Committee under the Optional Protocol to the International Covenant on Economic, Social and Cultural Rights with Regard to Communication No 5/2015, 61st sess, UN Doc E/C.12/61/D/5/2015 (21 July 2017) 11 [15.1]–[15.2] ('Djazia and Bellili v Spain'). See also the discussion in P. Kenna, 'Introduction' in P. Kenna and others (eds), *Loss of Homes and Evictions Across Europe: A Comparative Legal and Policy Examination* (Edward Elgar 2018) 1–65.

circumstances and give effect to the principles. Occupancy principles legislation should also go further than the current ACT legislation and provide for all termination proceedings to go through the tribunal, for appropriate scrutiny, as to whether termination is reasonable and proportionate in the circumstances.

In the area of social housing law, the accountability of social landlords to applicants, tenants, and the wider public is an important principle that deserves separate and specific legal enhancement. Accordingly, social housing legislation should be amended to provide expressly that adequate housing is the right of all persons, and where a person needs assistance to access reasonably adequately housing, they are entitled to assistance. Express provision should also be made in the legislation for internal and binding external review of eligibility, priority, rent calculation, and other decisions, including decisions to commence termination proceedings and to execute possession orders. This would override the emerging suggestion in the caselaw that termination decisions in both public and community housing are not reviewable because they do not derive from statutory authority. In practice, however, the need for internal and judicial review of social housing termination decisions would be reduced were the level of protection against homelessness increased for tenants generally.

For a genuine and enduring 'whole-of-government' approach to preventing homelessness, reform of residential tenancies and social housing laws should be high on the Australian government's agenda.

28
A SNAPSHOT OF A FRAGMENTED LANDSCAPE

Homelessness Law and Policy in Aotearoa New Zealand

Brodie Fraser, Clare Aspinall, Elinor Chisholm, Jenny Ombler, Sarah Bierre, Lucy Telfar-Barnard, Ellie Johnson, and Philippa Howden-Chapman

Introduction

Adequate and safe housing is a human right; human rights are universal and inalienable – everyone, regardless of wealth, class, race, ability, sexual orientation, and gender, should be able to access adequate housing. Homelessness is a direct failure of the state to secure this right for its people. In this chapter, we discuss homelessness law and policy in the context of Aotearoa New Zealand (henceforth Aotearoa NZ; Aotearoa is the te reo Māori/indigenous Māori language name for the country), highlighting how policy and service provision has frequently been fragmented across multiple government agencies. We begin by discussing how homelessness is defined and measured in our context, and then move on to provide a brief overview of what is known about homelessness in Aotearoa NZ. We then discuss key legal and policy frameworks as they relate to homelessness in our jurisdiction, which leads into a discussion of several noteworthy initiatives aimed at addressing homelessness in Aotearoa NZ. We end with a look to the future of homelessness law and policy in Aotearoa NZ.

Firstly, some context. Aotearoa NZ is a settler-colonial state which has an uncodified constitution, unicameral parliament, and unitary central government.[1] Our most important founding constitutional document is Te Tiriti o Waitangi – the Treaty of Waitangi. Te Tiriti, signed in 1840 between Māori (the indigenous people of Aotearoa NZ) and the Crown, sees important and significant differences between te Tiriti, the te reo Māori version, and the Treaty, the English version.[2] At the time of writing, the centre-left Sixth Labour–led government is in their second term, having, at the last election, secured an unprecedented majority in the house for the first time since Mixed Member Proportional

---

1 S. Levine, 'Aotearoa New Zealand's System of Government' in J. Hayward, L. Greaves and C. Timperley (eds), *Government and Politics in Aotearoa New Zealand* (OUP 2021).
2 M. Godfery and J. Hayward, 'Te Tiriti o Waitangi' in J. Hayward, L. Greaves and C. Timperley (eds), *Government and Politics in Aotearoa New Zealand* (OUP 2021).

A Snapshot of a Fragmented Landscape

was introduced in 1996.³ Governing parties usually need to enter into coalitions, or confidence and supply agreements, with minor parties. This chapter was written in late 2022; since then a new right-wing Government has been elected with a three-way coalition in place. Although it is early into their term, we expect further significant changes to housing policy. Housing has increasingly become a key policy issue during election campaigns. In terms of the housing context more broadly, unlike other OECD countries, Aotearoa NZ does not have national surveys of housing quality, but there is a wealth of evidence showing that housing is of poor quality – particularly rental housing – resulting in a number of adverse health outcomes and a high burden of disease.⁴ Historically, there have been minimal policy and legislation aimed at addressing housing standards and protecting renters' security of tenure and rights.⁵ Enforcement and compliance monitoring of the legislation that does exist – particularly that aimed at improving standards for rental housing – is relatively minimal in comparison to the scale of the issue.⁶

The Aotearoa New Zealand Definition of Homelessness

Researchers in Aotearoa NZ have developed and tested a rigorous definition of *homelessness*.⁷ Based on this work, the official definition provided by Statistics New Zealand is as follows: 'Homelessness is defined as living situations where people with no other options to acquire safe and secure housing: are without shelter, in temporary accommodation, sharing accommodation with a household or living in uninhabitable housing.'⁸ The official Aotearoa NZ definition of *homelessness* is grounded in the European Typology of Homelessness and Housing Exclusion (ETHOS) typology but has been adapted and changed to suit the context of Aotearoa NZ.⁹ Differing from the ETHOS typology, the Aotearoa NZ definition has been expanded to include those in 'concealed homeless' living situations as well as those in housing considered not suitable for habitation.¹⁰ Homelessness thus includes situations such as rough sleeping, couch surfing, living in shelters and women's refuges, living in severely crowded dwellings, and living in cars, amongst others.¹¹ Those who are considered as meeting the definition of *homelessness* as

---

3 J. Van Veen and others, 'Anniversary of a Landslide' (*The Conversation*, 15 October 2021) <https://theconversation.com/anniversary-of-a-landslide-new-research-reveals-what-really-swung-new-zealands-2020-covid-election-169351> (accessed 1 September 2023).
4 P. Howden-Chapman and N. Pierse, 'Commentary on Housing, Health, and Well-Being in Aotearoa/New Zealand' (2020) 47 *Health Education & Behavior* 802; L. Riggs and others, 'Environmental Burden of Disease from Unsafe and Substandard Housing, New Zealand, 2010–2017' (2021) 99 *Bulletin of the World Health Organization* 259.
5 E. Chisholm, P. Howden-Chapman and G. Fougere, 'Tenants' Responses to Substandard Housing' (2020) 37(2) *Housing, Theory and Society* 139; L. Telfar-Barnard and others, 'Measuring the Effect of Housing Quality Interventions' (2017) 14 *International Journal of Environmental Research and Public Health* 1.
6 Telfar-Barnard and others (n 5).
7 K. Amore, 'Everyone Counts: Defining and Measuring Severe Housing Deprivation (Homelessness)' (PhD thesis, University of Otago 2019).
8 Statistics New Zealand, *New Zealand Definition of Homelessness* (Statistics New Zealand 2009) 6.
9 K. Amore, H. Viggers and P. Howden-Chapman, *Severe Housing Deprivation in Aotearoa New Zealand, 2018* (He Kāinga Oranga 2020).
10 Ibid.
11 K. Amore and others, *Severe Housing Deprivation: The Problem and Its Measurement* (Official Statistics Research 2013).

per the uninhabitable housing category are those whose dwellings lack at least one basic amenity (i.e. drinkable tap water, a kitchen sink, cooking facilities, electricity, a toilet, and/or a bath or shower) *and* are on low incomes and therefore lack the resources to change their circumstances.[12]

This official definition is adapted from the work of Amore and others, which, in turn, is adapted from the ETHOS typology.[13] The ETHOS typology identifies 'three domains which constitute a home, the absence of which can be taken to delineate homelessness'.[14] For this framework,

> having a home can be understood as: having a decent dwelling (or space) adequate to meet the needs of the person and [their] family (physical domain); being able to maintain privacy and enjoy social relations (social domain); and having exclusive possession, security of occupation and legal title (legal domain).[15]

These domains, according to the ETHOS typology, intersect to result in different forms of homelessness and housing exclusion. Homelessness is considered as exclusion from either all three domains or exclusion from the legal and social domains. Exclusion from any other domain and/or their intersections is considered to be housing exclusion. There has been some disagreement around whether this typology of homelessness is adequate – particularly in relation to exclusion from these domains. For example, Amore, Baker, and Howden-Chapman contend that living situations in which people are excluded from two or more of the three essential domains, regardless of which two they are excluded from, should be considered as homelessness.[16] This is the key difference between the ETHOS typology and the official Aotearoa NZ definition of *homelessness*.

These definitions are suitable for quantitative analysis but do not capture the range of experiences related to homelessness, particularly from Indigenous perspectives. A quantitatively oriented definition is necessary for understanding the measurable scale of a problem, but more expansive definitions can provide necessary context for policymaking. As part of the Waitangi Tribunal's Kaupapa Inquiry on Housing Policy and Services, a definition of *homelessness* has been proposed by some claimants to reflect the multiple meanings of homelessness from an Indigenous Māori perspective. The proposed definition begins:

> Homelessness is the absence and loss of kāinga [home], ahi kā roa [continuous occupation], tino rangatiratanga [absolute sovereignty], the capability and capacity to achieve and sustain an enduring state of whānau ora [healthy families], tu mana motuhake [self-determination/autonomy]. Homelessness is the deprivation of the right to determine, in accordance with one's own Tikanga/cultural norms, what a home should be and looks like for whānau and individuals. Homelessness impacts on the

---

12 H. Viggers, K. Amore and P. Howden-Chapman, *Housing That Lacks Basic Amenities in Aotearoa New Zealand, 2018* (He Kāinga Oranga 2021).
13 K. Amore, M. Baker and P. Howden-Chapman, 'The ETHOS Definition and Classification of Homelessness: An Analysis' (2011) 5 *European Journal of Homelessness* 19.
14 B. Edgar, *European Review of Statistics on Homelessness* (European Observatory on Homelessness 2009) 15.
15 Ibid. 15.
16 Amore, Baker and Howden-Chapman (n 13).

dignity, respect, integrity, mana and tapu of all those affected, including their mental, cultural and physical wellbeing, which can result in humiliation and embarrassment.[17]

This qualitative definition describes the experience of homelessness from a Te Ao Māori worldview, as well as accounting for the ongoing impacts of colonization.

Homelessness in Aotearoa New Zealand

Rates of homelessness in Aotearoa NZ are measured using data from the New Zealand Census; rates have been steadily increasing since counts first began.[18] At the 2018 Census, there were over 41,000 New Zealanders, or nearly 0.9% of the population, who were experiencing homelessness.[19] However, these statistics have, until recently, been unable to adequately capture the number of people who are experiencing homelessness by way of living in uninhabitable housing. Further analysis of Census 2018 data has since added an additional 60,000 people to this count under the 'uninhabitable housing' category, making it the most prevalent form of homelessness in Aotearoa NZ.[20] While gender-diverse populations are not yet captured in national statistics, numbers indicate that the rates of homelessness amongst men and women in Aotearoa NZ are almost identical.[21] This differs greatly to other jurisdictions, where men are frequently over-represented.[22] While further research is needed, we believe this anomaly is in large part due to our broad, comprehensive definition of *homelessness* which is able to capture traditionally 'hidden' forms of homelessness, and a liberal welfare state which does not provide sufficient support for single mothers.[23] Children and young people under 25 comprise half of those experiencing homelessness.[24] Māori and Pacific people's rates of homelessness are nearly four and six times higher, respectively, than for Pākehā/New Zealand Europeans.[25] Māori are over-represented in homelessness statistics.[26] This over-representation stems from both historic and current colonization of Māori, which has served to dispossess them from their land, destroy their economic base, and threaten their culture, language, and worldviews.[27]

---

17 Waitangi Tribunal, *Generic Closing Submissions: Homelessness Policy and Strategy 2009–2021* (Wai 2750 2021) #3.3.35 at 33.
18 Amore, Viggers and Howden-Chapman (n 9).
19 Ibid.
20 K. Amore, H. Viggers and P. Howden-Chapman, *Severe Housing Deprivation in Aotearoa New Zealand, 2018: June 2021 update* (He Kāinga Oranga 2021).
21 Amore, Viggers and Howden-Chapman (n 9); Brodie Fraser and others, 'Service Usage of a Cohort of Formerly Homeless Women In Aotearoa New Zealand' (2021) 15 *SSM-Population Health* 1.
22 Fraser and others (n 21).
23 Ibid.
24 Amore, Viggers and Howden-Chapman (n 9).
25 Ibid.
26 K. Amore, *Severe Housing Deprivation in Aotearoa/New Zealand 2001–2013* (He Kāinga Oranga 2016); K. Amore, 'Māori Homelessness' (2016) 29 *Parity* 7; S. Groot and E. Peters, 'Indigenous Homelessness: New Zealand Context' in E. Peters and J. Christensen (eds), *Indigenous Homelessness: Perspectives from Canada, Australia, and New Zealand* (U of Manitoba P 2016).
27 J. Kake, 'Why Are Our People Overrepresented Amongst Te Pani Me Te Rawakore?' (2016) 29 *Parity* 8; K. Lawson-Te Aho and others, 'A Principles Framework for Taking Action on Māori/Indigenous Homelessness in Aotearoa/New Zealand' (2019) 8 *SSM-Population Health* 1.

Other historic and political factors have also contributed to growing levels of homelessness in Aotearoa NZ. The neoliberal political reforms in the 1980s and 1990s that dramatically altered the political, social, and economic landscape of Aotearoa NZ are one significant example. These included deregulating the economy, substantial welfare cuts, tax reform, and changes to the way public housing was operated.[28] These changes meant the welfare state was restructured, poverty became entrenched, rents rose, and there became a shortage of both public and private housing. During this period, a number of changes were made to housing policy: state housing was transferred to a Crown-owned company that was charged with making profit, market rents replaced Income-Related Rents in state housing, the state's mortgage portfolios were privatized, and the Accommodation Supplement was introduced to assist with housing costs.[29] In essence, the state began to withdraw from a number of housing matters in favour of allowing for market provision.[30] This emphasis on market provision has served to further encourage homeownership for investors and the wealthy, which, combined with an under-regulated rental market, has resulted in low-income earners having unmet housing needs, thus pushing them into insecure living situations, such as homelessness in its many forms.[31]

In more recent decades, the Fifth Labour Government (1999–2008) re-introduced Income-Related Rents for public housing tenants and set their rate at 25% of a household's income (meaning, those eligible only pay a maximum of 25% of their income on rent).[32] During this period, the New Zealand Coalition to End Homelessness was established in 2007 by social service organizations and several local governments in response to both a growing awareness of homelessness and a lack of central government policy to address the issue.[33] During the Fifth National Government's (2008–2017) tenure, policy tended to favour homeownership ideals and a resumption in the selling-off of state housing.[34] In addition, the Social Housing Reform Act (2013) further changed the housing landscape, aiming to encourage a competitive public housing market.[35] During this time, the housing crisis worsened, and increasing awareness and visibility, as well as the government's denial of the crisis, was one of the catalysts to a change in government at the 2017 election.[36] Since then, the housing landscape in Aotearoa NZ has contin-

---

28 L. Evans and others, 'Economic Reform in New Zealand 1984–95' (1996) 34 *Journal of Economic Literature* 1856; T. Cheer, R. Kearns and L. Murphy, 'Housing Policy, Poverty, and Culture' (2002) 20 *Environment and Planning C: Government and Policy* 497; J. Boston and C. Eichbaum, 'New Zealand's Neoliberal Reforms' (2014) 27 *Governance* 373.
29 Cheer, Kearns and Murphy (n 28); L. Murphy, 'Reasserting the "Social" in Social Rented Housing' (2003) 27 *International Journal of Urban and Regional Research* 91; L. Murphy, 'To the Market and Back' (2003) 59 *GeoJournal* 119.
30 Ibid.
31 P. Howden-Chapman, 'A Future for Social and Affordable Housing' in S. Bierre, P. Howden-Chapman and L. Early (eds), *Homes People Can Afford* (Steele Roberts Aotearoa 2013).
32 S. Figenshow and K. Saville-Smith, 'Housing' in Graham Hassall and Girol Karacaoglu (eds), *Social Policy Practice and Processes in Aotearoa New Zealand* (Massey UP 2021).
33 C. Leggatt-Cook and K. Chamberlain, 'Houses With Elastic Walls' (2015) 10 *Kōtuitui* 10.
34 B. Schrader, 'Crisis? What Crisis? An Overview of the Fith National Government's Housing Policies' in S. Levine (ed), *Stardust and Substance* (Victoria UP 2018).
35 Ibid.
36 Ibid.

A Snapshot of a Fragmented Landscape

ued to shift; much of what we discuss in this chapter has occurred since this change in government.

Academic scholarship specifically focusing on homelessness in Aotearoa NZ remains somewhat limited compared to other jurisdictions, particularly that which is quantitative. However, that which does exist shows those who are housed frequently have negative conceptions of those who are experiencing homelessness, despite limited interactions with people who are experiencing homelessness.[37] Despite negative public attitudes, people who are experiencing homelessness in Aotearoa NZ have repeatedly been reported to find and create belonging in public spaces, such as libraries, the streets, and within service providers.[38] For rough sleepers, begging and window-washing are another means to claim space and to increase self-worth through self-reliance.[39] Homelessness in Aotearoa NZ has been identified as being the sharp edge of precarity, in which precarity of labour markets and place contribute to pathways into homelessness.[40] In their class analysis of pathways into homelessness, Hodgetts and co-authors argue that there are 'drifters' for whom homelessness is a continuation of their existing hardships and experiences of poverty, and 'droppers' who have higher class backgrounds and have somewhat unexpectedly dropped into a state of homelessness.[41] Other Aotearoa NZ–specific literature of pathways into homelessness explores how people can drop in and out of various forms of homelessness, such as rough sleeping, boarding houses, campgrounds, and informal housing.[42] Previous political rhetoric labelled people experiencing homelessness as 'hard-to-reach'; however, research has shown that these populations have interactions with government services at far greater rates than the wider population.[43] In regards to specific demographics, research reveals that the under-regulated rental market is central in older renters' pathways into homelessness, and that takatāpui, lesbian, gay, bisexual, transgender, intersex, and queer populations commonly experience multiple forms of instability and difficulty in accessing housing and support systems prior to experiencing homelessness.[44] Finally,

---

37 Darrin Hodgetts and others, ' "Near and Far": Social Distancing in Domiciled Characterisations of Homeless People' (2011) 48 *Urban Studies* 1739; Darrin Hodgetts and others, 'The Mobile Hermit and the City' (2010) 49 *British Journal of Social Psychology* 285; S. Groot and others, 'A Māori Homeless Woman' (2011) 12 *Ethnography* 375.
38 Darrin Hodgetts and others, 'A Trip to the Library' (2008) 9 *Social and Cultural Geography* 933; S. Groot and Darrin Hodgetts, 'Homemaking on the Streets and Beyond' (2012) 15 *Community, Work and Family* 255; B. McGovern, 'A Life Lived on the Corner' (PhD thesis, Victoria University of Wellington 2013); L. Dowdell and C. Li Liew, 'More Than a Shelter: Public Libraries and the Information Needs of People Experiencing Homelessness' (2019) 41 *Library and Information Science Research* 1.
39 S. Groot and D. Hodgetts, 'The Infamy of Begging' (2015) 12 *Qualitative Research in Psychology* 349.
40 N. Christensen, 'The Sharp Edge of Precarity' (MA thesis, University of Otago 2017).
41 D. Hodgetts and others, 'Drifting Along or Dropping into Homelessness' (2012) 44 *Antipode* 1209.
42 P. Carroll, 'Capturing Realities of Informal Housing in Aotearoa/New Zealand' (PhD thesis, University of Otago 2009); C. Aspinall 'Anyone Can Live in a Boarding House, Can't They?' (MPH thesis, University of Otago 2013); C. Severinsen, 'Housing Pathways of Camping Ground Residents in New Zealand' (2013) 28 *Housing Studies* 74.
43 Nevil Pierse and others, 'Service Usage by a New Zealand Housing First Cohort Prior to Being Housed' (2019) 8 *SSM-Population Health* 1; Fraser and others, (n 21).
44 B. Fraser, E. Chisholm and Nevil Pierse, ' "You're so Powerless": Takatāpui/LGBTIQ+ People's Experiences Before Becoming Homeless in Aotearoa New Zealand' (2021) 16 *PloS ONE* 1; B. Lorraine James and others, 'Tenure Insecurity, Precarious Housing and Hidden Homelessness Among Older Renters in New Zealand' (2022) 37 *Housing Studies* 483.

some scholars have also explored the relationship between homelessness and policy on both the local and central government scale.[45]

Legal and Policy Framework

Homelessness in Aotearoa NZ has become a growing public and political concern since the early 2000s.[46] This mounting concern, and pressure, resulted in Parliament's Social Services Select Committee holding an inquiry into boarding houses in 2011, and a 2016 cross-party inquiry into homelessness which was jointly conducted by the New Zealand Labour Party, the Green Party of Aotearoa New Zealand, and Te Pāti Māori.[47] There is a range of legislation and government policy (both at a central and local level) which are relevant in efforts to prevent and reduce homelessness, as well as supporting those who *are* experiencing homelessness. We focus here on several key pieces of legislation and policy at the national level. Most are relatively new, having been introduced – or updated – in recent years as rates of homelessness have grown and public pressure increased.

One of the key drivers of homelessness in Aotearoa NZ is the ongoing impacts of colonization, with Māori being more likely to experience homelessness. Te Tiriti o Waitangi, signed in 1840, is the main constitutional grounding for the relationship between Māori and the settler government. Te Tiriti guaranteed sovereignty for Māori nations and afforded Māori the same rights and privileges as British citizens; however, for much of Aotearoa NZ's colonial history, Te Tiriti has not been honoured.[48] The Waitangi Tribunal was established in 1975 as a permanent commission of inquiry to make recommendations to government on claims brought by Māori relating to Crown breaches of Te Tiriti. The Tribunal currently has a Kaupapa (Thematic) Inquiry on Housing Policy and Services, the first stage of which was on contemporary homelessness, with claims and evidence heard during 2021.[49] Much of the evidence heard centred on how many contemporary government policies had failed to address the systemic drivers of homelessness for Māori and had failed to resource and provide services appropriate for Māori, with ongoing intergenerational effects.

Prior to 2016, there was a lack of any coherent and coordinated policy framework to address homelessness per se. Consequently, emergency housing and transitional housing were poorly defined in Aotearoa NZ. These terms were used interchangeably by those working in government agencies and various community organizations working with people experiencing homelessness. Without specific policy and consistent funding, emergency and transitional housing included a range of dwelling types, such as night shelters, women's refuge, marae (cultural meeting spaces), charitable community– and commercial-run

---

45 P. Laurenson and D. Collins, 'Towards Inclusion: Local Government, Public Space and Homelessness in New Zealand' (2006) 62 *New Zealand Geographer* 185; P. Laurenson and D. Collins, 'Beyond Punitive Regulation?' (2007) 39 *Antipode* 649; D. Collins, 'Homelessness in Canada and New Zealand' (2010) 31 *Urban Geography* 932; Leggatt-Cook and Chamberlain (n 33).
46 P. Bellamy, *Homelessness in New Zealand* (Parliamentary Library 2014).
47 Social Services Select Committee, *Inquiry into Boarding Houses in New Zealand, and Briefing into Long-Term Caravan Park and Motor Camp Accommodation* (2011–2014); New Zealand Labour Party, Green Party of Aotearoa New Zealand and Te Pāti Māori, 'Ending Homelessness in New Zealand: Final Report of the Cross-Party Inquiry on Homelessness' (2016).
48 Lawson-Te Aho and others (n 27).
49 Waitangi Tribunal, 'Housing Policy and Services Inquiry' (*Waitangi Tribunal*, 2019) <https://waitangitribunal.govt.nz/inquiries/kaupapa-inquiries/housing-policy-and-services-inquiry/> (accessed 1 September 2023).

boarding houses, hostels, and campgrounds.[50] The then-state housing provider, Housing New Zealand (now Kāinga Ora – Homes and Communities), contributed minimally to emergency and transitional housing supply through Community Group Housing (CGH) by leasing properties to community organizations.[51] Policy and funding for support services were similarly lacking or fragmented across various government agencies, such as Child, Youth, and Family; Department of Corrections; Ministry of Health; Ministry of Social Development; District Health Boards; and local government.[52] Community organizations that worked with people experiencing homelessness frequently reported inadequate and inconsistent funding. As a result, they were unable to employ the number of staff with the skills required to meet people's support needs.[53] To manage demand, community organizations supported the people that they had the capacity to work with. Ultimately, these policies and practices reduced access to emergency and transitional housing for groups who have more complex support needs.[54]

Homelessness policy and provision have, overall, been relatively fragmented in Aotearoa NZ, with several different agencies holding responsibility for different aspects of closely connected policy, funding, and service provision. One of the key guiding documents for addressing homelessness is the cross-agency homelessness action plan (HAP), released by the government in 2020 and active until 2023, when it will be reviewed and updated.[55] Developed across the Ministry of Housing and Urban Development, the Ministry of Social Development, the Ministry of Health, the Department of Corrections, the New Zealand Police, and other central government agencies, the HAP is the first time across-agency policy aimed at preventing and reducing homelessness has been created in Aotearoa NZ.[56] The significance and necessity of this cross-agency commitment will be highlighted in our following discussion of the complex web of support available for those experiencing homelessness. The vision of the HAP is that homelessness in Aotearoa NZ is prevented where possible, or is rare, brief, and non-recurring when it does occur.[57] It outlines a set of actions and accountability measures which are divided into four action areas: prevention, supply, support, and system enablers.[58] Each of these areas has a series of affiliated actions/initiatives with a corresponding lead agency and time frame for implementation.[59] Progress reports are published every six months, and the Plan is due to be reviewed in 2023. Currently, the main aims of the HAP are not well-implemented, with there being a significant lag between high-level policy intention and translation into policy delivery.

---

50 Amore, Viggers and Howden-Chapman (n 9); Aspinall (n 42); Severinsen (n 42); S. Richards, *Homelessness in Aotearoa: Issues and Recommendations* (The New Zealand Coalition to End Homelessness 2008).
51 M. Stringfellow, 'Responding to Homelessness: Housing New Zealand' (2007) 20 Parity 30.
52 Ibid.
53 C. Aspinall, key informat interviews for 'The Implementation of Housing First in Aotearoa New Zealand' (in-progress PhD thesis, University of Otago 2022).
54 Ibid.
55 B. Fraser, 'Housing and the Sixth Labour Government' in Stephen Levine (ed), *Politics in a Pandemic* (Victoria UP 2021).
56 New Zealand Government, *Aotearoa/New Zealand Homelessness Action Plan* (New Zealand Government 2020).
57 Ibid.
58 Ibid.
59 Ibid.

MAIHI Ka Ora, the National Māori Housing strategy, builds on te MAIHI o te Whare Māori – Māori and Iwi Housing Innovation Framework for Action (MAIHI) and runs from 2021 to 2051.[60] Its vision is that all whānau (family group/extended family) have safe, healthy, affordable homes with secure tenure across the Māori housing continuum.[61] MAIHI Ka Ora signals a shift in government strategy, as it relates directly to the articles of Te Tiriti, rather than more vague 'Treaty principles' that have previously been used, and has been developed in direct partnership with Te Matapihi – the national Māori housing advocacy organization – and with iwi (extended kinship group/nation), hapū (kinship group/subtribe), and whānau Māori.[62] The strategy and its implementation plan are focused on by Māori, for Māori solutions, and include plans to make building papakāinga (housing) on Māori land more accessible.[63]

The Government Policy Statement on Housing and Urban Development (GPS-HUD) sets out the government's intentions for housing and urban development and was developed alongside MAIHI Ka Ora.[64] The vision of the GPS-HUD is that everyone in Aotearoa NZ lives in a home, and within a community, that meets their needs and aspirations.[65] Nested below this overarching vision are four 'aspirational' outcomes: thriving and resilient communities, well-being through housing, Māori housing through partnership, and an adaptive and responsive system. It has five focus areas: ensure that more affordable homes are built; ensure houses meet needs; enable people into stable, affordable homes; plan and invest in our places; support whānau to have safe, healthy, affordable homes with secure tenure; and re-establish housing's primary role as a home rather than a financial asset.[66] Regarding homelessness, it aligns closely with the HAP in its goal of preventing homelessness where possible, or that it is rare, brief, and non-recurring when it does occur.[67]

In Aotearoa NZ, homeownership is a deeply embedded cultural norm.[68] Despite this, homeownership rates are at a historic low, seeing a consistent rise in rates of renting.[69] With few exceptions, renting in Aotearoa NZ is regulated by the Residential Tenancies Act 1986 (RTA), which lays out landlord and tenant rights and responsibilities, including specifying how and when landlords may give notice.[70] Recent changes to the RTA have potential flow-on effects for homelessness. The first major amendment in recent years was the Healthy Homes Guarantee Act 2017 (HHGA). The HHGA requires landlords to meet

---

60 Ministry of Housing and Urban Development, *MAIHI Ka Ora* (New Zealand Government 2021).
61 Ibid.
62 J. Kake, 'New Māori Housing Strategy gets Implementation Plan That Delivers' *Stuff* (Wellington, 23 March 2022) <www.stuff.co.nz/business/opinion-analysis/128114865/new-mori-housing-strategy-gets-implementation-plan-that-delivers> (accessed 1 September 2023).
63 Ibid.
64 Ministry of Housing and Urban Development, *Government Policy Statement on Housing and Urban Development* (New Zealand Government 2021).
65 Ibid.
66 Ibid.
67 Ibid.
68 A. Dupuis and D. Thorns, 'Home, Home Ownership and the Search for Ontological Security' (1998) 46 *The Sociological Review* 24.
69 A. Johnson, P. Howden-Chapman and S. Eaqub, *A Stocktake of New Zealand's Housing* (Ministry of Business, Innovation, and Employment 2018); P. Howden-Chapman and others, *Spotlight on Housing* (Royal Society of New Zealand 2021).
70 Residential Tenancies Act 1986.

housing quality standards specified in updated 2019 regulations.[71] In the long term, these requirements may be expected to reduce the likelihood of people experiencing homelessness due to living in 'uninhabitable' housing. However, there is also potential for short-term volatility in housing tenure stability, as investors extend inter-tenancy vacancy periods to carry out improvements or divest non-compliant rental stock and purchase new or previously owner-occupied compliant properties instead. Further major amendments came in 2020. Under previous law, landlords could end a tenancy with 90 days' notice, without having to provide a reason.[72] Now, no cause notice is no longer legal, though tenancies can still be ended due to property sale, the landlord or their family wishing to move into the property, evidence of imminent significant building work, overdue rent, damage to the property, or threatening behaviour by the tenant.[73] While the amendments have improved tenure security overall, tenants whose financial circumstances make it difficult to always meet regular rent payments are still unlikely to feel secure in their tenure, and as the changes are recent, we are yet to observe whether landlords will find ways around them.

While a tenancy can be ended for several reasons with a 90-day notice, the process of eviction in Aotearoa NZ for breach of contract is formalized through a tribunal system. The RTA established a mediation process and the Tenancy Tribunal to enable the affordable and accessible resolution of disputes without the use of advocates or lawyers. In the July quarter of 2022, 40% (2076) of hearings were to terminate a tenancy or seek possession of a property, most often as a result of rent arrears.[74] The high threshold of evidence that is required to avoid the termination of a tenancy for rent arrears means that without the necessary support to navigate the legal system or to access welfare provisions, tenants can have difficulty in using the available provisions in the RTA to maintain their tenancies, and eviction ensues.[75] Eviction is frequently a precursor to homelessness.[76] Qualitative research conducted with people in Aotearoa NZ who had experienced an eviction – broadly understood as a tenancy that ended against the tenant's wishes – found that several participants became homeless when they were not able to find appropriate housing after they moved out of their rental home. They moved into substandard housing – including garages – that were cold and had no electricity source, or they moved in with friends or family or moved into cars or emergency accommodation, including camping grounds. Participants had to pay for storage or dispose of belongings while they were homeless. Participants reported that the period of homelessness following their eviction damaged relationships within the family and with the people they stayed with, worsened respiratory and mental health, and contributed to unhealthy behaviours.[77]

---

71 Healthy Homes Guarantee Act 2017.
72 Ministry of Business, Innovation, and Employment, 'Security of Rental Tenure – Law Changes' (*Tenancy Services*, 2021) <www.tenancy.govt.nz/law-changes/phase-2/security-of-rental-tenure-law-changes/> (accessed 1 September 2023).
73 Residential Tenancies Act 1986.
74 Ministry of Business, Innovation, and Employment, 'Dispute Resolution Statistics 1 July–30 September 2022' (October 2022) <www.tenancy.govt.nz/assets/Uploads/Tenancy/Data-and-statistics/dispute-resolution-stats-2022-q3.pdf> (accessed 1 September 2023).
75 B. Toy-Cronin and Sarah Bierre, 'Sustaining Tenancies or Swift Evictions' (2022) 53 *Victoria University of Wellington Law Review* 105.
76 M. Crane and A. Warnes, 'Evictions and Prolonged Homelessness' (2000) 15 *Housing Studies* 757.
77 E. Chisholm and others, 'That House Was a Home' [2021] *Health Promotion Journal of Australia* 1.

Initiatives to Support People Experiencing, or at Risk of, Homelessness

There are an increasing number of initiatives aimed at supporting those experiencing – or at risk of experiencing – homelessness in Aotearoa NZ. These occur on both a national and local level, and are championed not just by central government but, often, by local government, non-governmental organizations, activists, and in some cases, business. We focus here on national programmes implemented by central government – often in partnership with non-governmental organizations/social service providers.

One key form of support for people experiencing homelessness is Housing First (HF). HF is a holistic approach to addressing homelessness which is premised on the idea that complex issues are best addressed from the starting point of permanent housing.[78] This contrasts with more traditional models of addressing homelessness, in which sobriety or other requirements must be met in order for clients to obtain and maintain housing.[79] The first organization in Aotearoa NZ to provide HF services was the People's Project, located in Kirikiriroa/Hamilton, who began operating prior to any central government funding.[80] Research shows promising outcomes for their clients, with increases in incomes and reductions in health system interactions.[81] The success of this programme was a key catalyst in central government choosing to fund HF. There are now government-funded HF services – provided by social service non-governmental organizations – in most main centres across Aotearoa NZ.[82] It was first funded by the Fifth National–led government in 2017, with $3.7 million given to a HF pilot in March, and a later $16.5 million allocated in Budget 2017.[83] The following Sixth Labour–led government then announced an increase in funding to $63.4 million in Budget 2018.[84] In Aotearoa NZ, HF is aimed specifically at those who are deemed 'chronically homeless' and have experienced homelessness for at least 12 months over the past three years.[85] While contracts allow for a small amount of flexibility in these criteria, some providers have criticized it for being too strict.[86] Those who do not meet these criteria are supported by a 'Rapid Rehousing' trial implemented as part of the HAP, often provided by services also providing HF.[87] As of December 2022, 5,336 households had been accepted into HF, with 1,5477 households successfully housed.[88]

---

78 S. Tsemberis, 'Housing First: Ending Homelessness, Promoting Recovery, and Reducing Costs' in I. Gould Ellen and B. O'Flaherty (eds), *How to House the Homeless* (Russell Sage Foundation 2010).
79 Ibid.
80 Pierse and others (n 43).
81 B. Fraser and others, 'Post-Housing First Outcomes Amongst a Cohort of Formerly Homeless Youth in Aotearoa New Zealand' [2022] *Journal of the Royal Society of New Zealand* 1; Nevil Pierse and others, 'Two-Year Post-Housing Outcomes for a Housing First Cohort in Aotearoa New Zealand' (2022) 16 *European Journal of Homelessness* 121.
82 Ibid.
83 Ibid.
84 Fraser (n 55).
85 Ministry of Housing and Urban Development, *Housing First* (Ministry of Housing and Urban Development 2022) <www.hud.govt.nz/our-work/housing-first/> (accessed 1 September 2023).
86 L. Smith, L. Davies and M. Marama, *Housing First Evaluation and Rapid Rehousing Review* (Ministry of Housing and Urban Development 2022).
87 Ministry of Housing and Urban Development, *Rapid Rehousing* (Ministry of Housing and Urban Development 2022) <www.hud.govt.nz/our-work/rapid-rehousing/> (accessed 1 September 2023).
88 Ministry of Housing and Urban Development, *The Government Housing Dashboard* (Ministry of Housing and Urban Development 2022) <www.hud.govt.nz/stats-and-insights/the-government-housing-dashboard/housing-support/#tabset> (accessed 1 September 2023).

The welfare state has a range of provisions and services that provide housing-related assistance to those experiencing, or at risk of experiencing, homelessness. The two main financial supports are the Accommodation Supplement and Income-Related Rent Subsidy. The Income-Related Rent Subsidy is paid directly to public housing providers and ensures that tenants' rents are tied to their incomes – usually 25% of their net income.[89] However, the subsidy is only available to Kāinga Ora and Community Housing Provider tenants; those in council housing are unable to access the subsidy.[90] The Accommodation Supplement is paid directly to recipients; it is a weekly means-tested payment available to those in the private rental market.[91] These and other housing support are split across three main central government agencies: the Ministry of Housing and Urban Development (HUD), Kāinga Ora, and the Ministry of Social Development (MSD). In brief, Kāinga Ora are the state housing provider. MSD manages the public housing wait list, sets Income-Related Rent rates, helps people access emergency housing, funds Emergency Housing Special Needs Grants, and pays the Accommodation Supplement (as well as other welfare benefits).[92] HUD pays the Income-Related Rent Subsidy to Kāinga Ora and other Community Housing Providers, funds the majority of transitional housing (and provides contracts to approved providers), and contracts Sustaining Tenancies services.[93] This fragmentation and complexity is a key reason as to why the HAP is an explicit cross-agency initiative.

People seek emergency and transitional housing for a range of circumstances, including eviction, family and intimate partner violence, on leaving institutional settings – such as hospital, prison, or state care – and following natural disasters.[94] In attempting to gauge the demand for emergency and transitional housing, there proved to be a lack of consistent and timely administrative data collected by government and community organizations about people's unmet housing and support needs.[95] Only a minority of those seeking help from MSD to find housing were placed on the public housing register. Of those, a smaller proportion on the register noted 'homelessness' as the main application reason.[96] Policy officials used the register data as one proxy for housing demand, despite introducing strict entry criteria for the register in prior years. As a result, they underestimated the demand for emergency and transitional housing. Initially, in June 2017, MSD funded 1,123 transitional

---

89 Ministry of Housing and Urban Development, *Income-Related Rent Subsidy* (Ministry of Housing and Urban Development 2022) <www.hud.govt.nz/funding-and-support/income-related-rent-subsidy/> (accessed 1 September 2023).
90 E. Te Ora, 'There Is a Little-Known Two-Tier System Within Social Housing' *Stuff* (Wellington, 22 July 2021) <www.stuff.co.nz/pou-tiaki/our-truth/125681860/there-is-a-littleknown-twotier-system-within-social-housing-thousands-of-tenants-are-paying-the-price> (accessed 1 September 2023).
91 Work and Income, *Accommodation Supplement* (Ministry of Social Development 2022) <www.workandincome.govt.nz/products/a-z-benefits/accommodation-supplement.html> (accessed 1 September 2023).
92 Work and Income, *Housing* (Ministry of Social Development 2022) <www.workandincome.govt.nz/housing/index.html> (accessed 1 September 2023).
93 Ministry of Housing and Urban Development, *Public and Transitional Housing* (Ministry of Housing and Urban Development 2022) <www.hud.govt.nz/our-work/public-and-transitional-housing/> (accessed 1 September 2023).
94 P. Laing, D. Steven and M. Nissanka, *Emergency Housing: Exploratory Study, January–February 2017* (Ministry of Housing and Urban Development 2018).
95 Ministry of Social Development, *Homelessness in New Zealand and Emergency and Transitional Housing Responses* (Ministry of Social Development 2014).
96 Ibid.

housing places.⁹⁷ Transitional housing is housing provided by a community housing organization which is intended to last for 12 weeks – in practice, this is frequently lengthened, and some residents have lived in transitional housing for years.⁹⁸ By June 2018, funded places had increased to 2,341, rising to 2,789 in 2019.⁹⁹ Simultaneously, MSD established an Emergency Housing Special Needs Grant (EHSNG) to meet the demand for emergency housing. *Emergency housing* is defined as housing lasting for a few days and up to a fortnight. The EHSNG is prioritized for circumstances when people have no other suitable housing options available, including transitional housing places.¹⁰⁰ Emergency housing is often provided by commercial private accommodation, such as motels. One EHSNG allocation lasts seven days before people must apply for a new grant.¹⁰¹ MSD EHSNG allocations between 1 June to 30 September 2016 were estimated as 5,450 for 2,140 households, at a cost of $4.34 million NZD, compared with more recent figures for the quarter ending in September 2019 of 29,266 EHSNG for 6,064 individual households, at a cost of $41.6 million.¹⁰²

More recently, HUD and the Ministry of Business, Innovation, and Education (MBIE) have funded people to stay in emergency and transitional housing as part of the Covid-19 pandemic response. Over two years, transitional housing places jumped from 3,324 in June 2020 to 4,432 in June 2021, then 5,520 in June 2022.¹⁰³ As in many countries, the fragmentation of policy, funding, and communication between health, housing, and homelessness sectors in Aotearoa NZ became acutely apparent during the pandemic.¹⁰⁴ These systemic gaps still remain to a certain extent, despite additional government resources and the significant efforts of those working in government, health, community housing sectors, and Māori and Pacific organizations. At the time of writing (December 2022), HUD has prioritized the increase in the supply of transitional housing places, partly to reduce the cost and burden of administering the EHSNG. In September 2022, HUD funded 5,738 transitional housing places. In the same quarter, MSD made 31,164 EHSNG allocations for 7,204 individual households at a cost of $91.7 million.¹⁰⁵ This was a decrease from the March quarter, where MSD made 35,222 EHSNG allocations for 8,486 individual households.¹⁰⁶ Caution is required in interpreting this data, and it is too early to draw conclusions about whether this is a trend due to reduced demand for emergency housing or another explanation, such as a change in policy or tightening of MSD's housing assessment and public housing entry criteria.

---

97 Ministry of Housing and Urban Development (n 88).
98 Ministry of Housing and Urban Development (n 93); M. Cooke, 'Data Reveals Hundreds Living in Transitional Housing for Months on End' *Radio New Zealand* (Wellington, 3 August 2021) <www.rnz.co.nz/news/national/448323/data-reveals-hundreds-living-in-transitional-housing-for-months-on-end> (accessed 1 September 2023).
99 Ministry of Housing and Urban Development (n 88).
100 Work and Income, *Emergency Housing* (Ministry of Social Development 2022) <www.workandincome.govt.nz/housing/nowhere-to-stay/emergency-housing.html> (accessed 1 September 2023).
101 Ibid.
102 Ministry of Housing and Urban Development (n 88).
103 Ibid.
104 F. Gatzweiler and others, 'COVID-19 Reveals the Systemic Nature of Urban Health Globally' (2021) 5 *Cities & Health* s32.
105 Ministry of Housing and Urban Development (n 88).
106 Ibid.

The benefits of enabling people to maintain their housing and avoid homelessness were recognized in the government's Sustaining Tenancies programme, introduced in 2017 to provide wrap-around services to people at risk of losing their tenancy.[107] Funding for the scheme has subsequently been expanded.[108] This is managed by HUD, which provides funding to community agencies to provide practical and holistic support to public and private rental tenants, including facilitating access to welfare provisions, budgeting advice, access to physical and mental health services, and any other help needed to maintain the tenancy.[109] Tenants can self-refer or can be referred through a community or other agency, including their landlord. While there is provision to connect the Sustaining Tenancies programme with the operation of tenancy services, potentially reducing the rate of eviction, this is yet to be explored.[110] Kāinga Ora, the national state housing provider, also adopted a policy of sustaining tenancies at the same time, taking a problem-solving and supportive approach to tenancy issues.[111] As a housing provider of last resort, tenants evicted from Kāinga Oranga will have few subsequent housing options, making a policy of sustaining tenancies integral to avoiding homelessness.

The Healthy Housing Initiatives (HHIs) also play a role in supporting people to access housing. These were established in eight regions by the Ministry of Health in 2013 and have expanded to cover most of the country in the years since.[112] These initially targeted low-income families with children at risk of rheumatic fever who were living in crowded households, and have now expanded their focus to providing warm, dry, and healthy housing to pregnant people and low-income families with children who have been hospitalized for a housing-related condition or who are subject to certain risk factors.[113] HHI kaimahi/assessors visit homes to provide healthy housing education, provide household items such as heaters, curtains, and bedding where required, to advocate for housing improvements to landlords – or housing transfers, for Kāinga Ora/public housing tenants – and to refer to other services, such as benefit entitlement assessments, tenancy law advocacy, budgeting advice, and insulation provision. In many cases, they work with people who meet the definition of *homelessness*, as they are living in emergency accommodation, substandard housing – including garages – or overcrowded housing. Kaimahi/assessors will assist people to access emergency housing and check if they are on the public housing register (waiting list). In some cases, they are able to support people into a new home. This is not always possible, however; as one HHI assessor explained:

> [W]e end up managing expectations and saying 'look you're in an overcrowded home and you need another bedroom but the reality is that you can go on the social housing

---

107 Toy-Cronin and Bierre (n 75).
108 Ibid.
109 Ministry of Housing and Urban Development, *Sustaining Tenancies* (Ministry of Housing and Urban Development 2022) <www.hud.govt.nz/our-work/sustaining-tenancies/> (accessed 1 September 2023).
110 Toy-Cronin and Bierre (n 75).
111 C. Denisse Sanchez Lozano, C. Wilkins and M. Rychert, 'Outcomes from the New Zealand Tenancy Tribunal After a Review of Policy on Residential Housing Methamphetamine Contamination' [2022] *Journal of the Royal Society of New Zealand* 1.
112 E. Chisholm and others, 'Promoting Health Through Housing Improvements, Education and Advocacy' (2020) 31 *Health Promotion Journal of Australia* 7.
113 Ibid.

wait list but you're still not going to get anything anytime soon because the wait list is what it is.'¹¹⁴

A major success of the HHI project is that it brings together qualitative and administrative data using the Integrated Data Infrastructure (IDI). The IDI is a research database curated by Statistics New Zealand containing de-identified linked microdata from government agencies, Statistics New Zealand surveys, and non-government agencies. Information on over 9 million people who have ever been residents of Aotearoa NZ is contained within the IDI.¹¹⁵ The HHI dataset is one of 70 housing-related projects registered with the IDI and one of the largest community datasets linked to the database with information on over 21,000 children who have been a part of the programme.¹¹⁶ With the IDI, linked datasets were used to connect the referred children to their household and provide further information on their living conditions and outcomes post-intervention. In the IDI, the Aotearoa NZ Census is a significant source of information on housing. Amore, Viggers, and Howden-Chapman illustrated the use of the census data in the IDI in their work estimating severe housing deprivation in Aotearoa NZ, including that which is 'uninhabitable'.¹¹⁷ Using a similar methodology, the IDI has been used to capture 5,550 children and their families (7%) in the HHI data who are potentially experiencing housing instability or homelessness.¹¹⁸

Looking to the Future

Housing, particularly homelessness prevention and support, remains a dynamic and changing area of policy and legislation. In terms of upstream efforts that will serve to prevent homelessness, much work has been undertaken in recent years to address the wider housing crisis.¹¹⁹ Some of this includes work to increase the housing supply. Census data shows that, between 2013 and 2018, the population grew more quickly than did the number of dwellings. For example, Tāmaki Makaurau/Auckland's population increased by 150,000 during that time, while its housing stock increased by just under 27,000.¹²⁰ The number of consents for new builds issued has increased in the past decade, including due to the work of the new Crown agency Kāinga Ora – Homes and Communities to build public and private housing, but it is still at a much lower rate per capita than in the 1970s. The decline in housing supply since the 1970s is largely the result of councils implementing increasingly restrictive and complex rules; for example, central Tāmaki Makaurau/Auckland's capacity for housing was halved.¹²¹ In recent years, a number of initiatives have attempted to promote housing supply through easing zoning restrictions, in order to increase

---

114 Ibid at 33.
115 S. Gibb, C. Bycroft and N. Matheson-Dunning, *Identifying the New Zealand Resident Population in the Integrated Data Infrastructure* (Statistics New Zealand 2016).
116 Nevil Pierse and others, *Healthy Homes Initiative: Three Year Outcomes Evaluation* (Te Whatu Ora 2022).
117 Amore, Viggers and Howden-Chapman (n 9); Viggers, Amore and Howden-Chapman (n 12).
118 Pierse and others (n 116).
119 Fraser (n 55).
120 R. Goodyear and others, 'Understanding the State of Our Housing: Housing in Aotearoa 2020' (2021) 47 *New Zealand Population Review* 33.
121 New Zealand Infrastructure Commission, *The Decline of Housing Supply in New Zealand* (New Zealand Infrastructure Commission 2022).

A Snapshot of a Fragmented Landscape

intensification. In Tāmaki Makaurau/Auckland's case, under the 2015 Unitary Plan, consents for new builds are now at an all-time high, and new builds tend to be multiunit complexes in existing urban areas.[122] The government has now stepped in to force all councils to allow for intensification in their plans. Under the Medium Density Residential Standards, it is possible to build up to three storeys (or three units) on most sites in cities without any need for resource consent. Under the National Policy Statement on Urban Development, councils are required to allow at least six-storey building heights in areas within walking distance from urban commercial centres and major public transport routes. These changes are predicted to increase housing supply by tens of thousands over the coming decades.[123] They are supported by other initiatives, such as the Housing Acceleration Fund, a contestable fund to provide infrastructure and increase the pace and scale of housing development, and the ongoing reform of the Resource Management Act.[124] It is hoped that this increase in supply will relieve pressure on the stressed, competitive housing market – particularly for renters.

In terms of homelessness service provision, a particular area of focus – both now and into the future – is the ways in which emergency and transitional housing are run and funded. The 2020 amendments to the RTA (discussed earlier) also served to make emergency and transitional housing providers exempt from the RTA, meaning, providers do not have to meet the standards set out in the HHGA, and that residents are unable to take providers to the Tenancy Tribunal.[125] Prior to this, emergency and transitional housing had been covered by the RTA – though this was not widely known, and Official Information Act requests show providers were deliberately not made aware of this throughout 2019–2020.[126] This exemption was met with criticism from a range of individuals, social service providers, and other non-governmental organizations. Concerns have repeatedly been raised during recent months about the safety and suitability of emergency and transitional housing, particularly for children and young people. Subsequently, HUD is working to develop a 'code of practice' for transitional housing providers.[127] While this is a necessary first small step, it will not apply to emergency housing providers (primarily moteliers) and will not give residents the legal protections of the RTA. The Human Rights Commission has expressed apprehension about these amendments and has noted that once the code has been developed, it will not be enforceable until it is proactively included into contracts upon renewal – which could take several years.[128] Alongside this, residents will not be able to lodge complaints with Tenancy Services or the Tenancy Tribunal, as they will not have legal protections; grievances

---

122 Auckland Council 'Submission to the Environment Select Committee on the Resource Management (Enabling Housing Supply and Other Matters Amendment) Bill 2021'.
123 PricewaterhouseCoopers, *Cost-Benefit Analysis for a National Policy Statement on Urban Development* (Ministry for the Environment 2020); PricewaterhouseCoopers, *Cost-Benefit Analysis of Proposed Medium Density Residential Standards* (Ministry for the Environment 2021).
124 Ministry for the Environment, *Resource Management Reform* (Ministry for the Environment 2022).
125 Residential Tenancies Act 1986.
126 S. Olley, 'Emergency Housing: Government Warned of Human Rights Risks Years Ago, Documents Reveal' *Radio New Zealand* (Wellington, 5 October 2022) <www.rnz.co.nz/news/political/476085/emergency-housing-government-warned-of-human-rights-risks-years-ago-documents-reveal> (accessed 1 September 2023).
127 Ibid.
128 Ibid.

will instead need to be raised as contractual issues.[129] In 2021, the United Nations special rapporteur on housing expressed concerns that Aotearoa NZ had not yet fully enshrined the right to housing in legislation.[130] Many of these misgivings remain.

With a population of only five million, Aotearoa NZ has high rates of homelessness and fragmentation of policy and service provision. Despite a unitary central government, policy, contracting, funding, and support are the responsibility of several government agencies, often in complex and confusing ways. The evolution and changing nature of political rhetoric, government agencies, and the public service, combined with ideological shifts, have resulted in an intertwined web of support available to those experiencing, or at risk of experiencing, homelessness. While we have been able to tease out some of these complexities in this chapter, the reality remains that for those who are trying to find support, the process can be complicated and confusing – to the extent that MSD has funded roles for 'navigators' to assist people who are seeking housing support since 2019. Navigators provide a higher level of support than both case managers and intensive case managers, coordinating services and providing ongoing support for those who have a high level of housing need.[131] MSD contracts to community organizations for these roles, and navigators work with housing and social service providers, the health system, and relevant government agencies to help individuals and whānau navigate the housing support system and its many complexities. High-level, cross-agency strategies like the HAP and MAIHI Ka Ora indicate an ongoing commitment to address some of these complexities, as well as a desire to prevent homelessness from occurring in the first place.

129 Ibid.
130 L. Farha, *Special Rapporteur's Report on New Zealand Housing* (United Nations 2021).
131 C. Sepuloni and K. Faafoi, 'More Measures to Help Those Facing Homelessness' *The Beehive* (2019) <www.beehive.govt.nz/release/more-measures-help-those-facing-homelessness> (accessed 1 September 2023).

INDEX

Note: Page numbers in *italics* indicate a figure and page numbers in **bold** indicate a table on the corresponding page. Page numbers followed by "n" with numbers refer to notes.

Aboriginal people 469–470
All Party Group on Homelessness 35
Aotearoa, New Zealand, homelessness in 500; definitions of 501–503; factors contributing to 503–504; initiatives to support people 510–513; key drivers of 506; rates of 503
Aotearoa, New Zealand, homelessness policy of 506–509, 515–516; emergency and transitional housing 506–507, 511–512; Emergency Housing Special Needs Grant (EHSNG) 513; financial supports 511; Government Policy Statement on Housing and Urban Development 508; Healthy Homes Guarantee Act 2017 (HHGA) 508–509; Healthy Housing Initiatives (HHIs) 514–515; homelessness action plan (HAP) 507; Housing First (HF) services 510; MAIHI Ka Ora 508; mediation process 509; Sustaining Tenancies programme 511; Tenancy Tribunal 509; Waitangi Tribunal 506
Aotearoa, New Zealand, housing policy 504
assistance system 62–70; classification of homeless people 65–66; financing methods 63; hierarchical and segmented nature of 63–64; history of 63; non-take-up 67–68; overnight shelters for women 70; recurrent displacement 67; repressive approach 65; waiting periods 67
Athens Olympic Games 127
Australia: law and order policing in 468–469; social housing law of 493–497

Australia, homelessness in 465, 481; banning notices 470–471; crimes of survival 474–477; criminalization of 469–470, 472–474; definitions of 466–467, 481–482; factors contributing to 483, *483*; move-on powers 470; offensive behaviour offences for 472–473; police powers to tackle 470–472; policing of public space 468–469; 'public nuisance' offences for 473–474; search-and-seizure powers 471–472; specialist courts for people experiencing 477–480; ticketing use for 474; trends in 467–468, 483–484
Australia, homelessness services in: cost of 481; Homelessness Bill 2013 482; social housing law 493–497
Australian residential tenancies law, homelessness prevention in: Covid-19 eviction moratoriums 491–492; marginal rental 492–493, tenancy termination 484–491

Baccaro, L. 365
Bandauko, E. 374
Bankruptcy Law 139
Beggary regulation 439–442
Beloved Community Village 289–293
Belshaw, Cyril 243–244
Benjaminsen, L. 316
Biden, Joe 35
Bodnar, Adam 189
Bombay Prevention of Begging Act of 1959 440–442, 446–447

bottom-up housing strategies 413–415
Brazil: homeless social participation in 313–315; housing problem in 306–308
Brazil, homelessness in 318–319; assessment of 315–318; definition of 301–303; historical perspective of 303–306; homeless protagonism 313–315; as housing problem 306–308
Brazil, homelessness policies in: Federal Constitution and 309; Homeless Population Specialized Reference Centres (Centros POP) 311–312; housing social movements 308–309; intersectoral 314; Intersectoral Committee for Monitoring and Evaluating (PNSR) 314; Municipal Policy for the Homeless Population 311; National Council of Justice (CNJ) resolution 313; National Homeless Population Movement 311; National Human Rights Council (CNDH) resolution 312–313; National Policy for the Homeless Population Law 310–311; National Social Assistance Policy Regulation 310; National Social Assistance Services Regulation 311; Organic Social Assistance Act 310; Social Assistance Specialized Reference Centres (CREAS) 311–312; Street Clinics (CnR) 312
Brazilian Federal Constitution of 1988 309
Burt, Martha 261

Callahan v Carey case 261–262
Calle Program 322
Canada: as federal political system 226; housing providers in 229–230; multiculturalism 227; third sector organizations 229–230
Canada Emergency Response Benefit 235
Canada, homelessness in: in Alberta 226, 235; annual cost of 226; in Calgary 225–226; causes of 227–228, 234–235; Covid-19 impact on 235; criminalization of 236; crisis management model for 235–236; with cuts to social housing 229–230; definitions of 228; encampments 236; estimations of 225–226; history of 225–226; housing programmes for 225; income security programmes for 225; of Indigenous peoples 230–233; inflation and recession impact on 235–236; as 'national crisis' 230; National Housing Strategy for 235; OAG report on 235; preventative practices for 233–234; problems of 234–235; public policy issues 237; social policies for 225
Canada, Indigenous homelessness *see* Indigenous homelessness, Canada; Indigenous homelessness policy, Canada
Canada Mortgage and Housing Corporation 235
Canadian Constitution 226
Cape Town, homelessness policy of 362
CARES Act 269
Catalan Civil Law 118
Catalan Economic and Social Emergencies Assessment Board 122
Catalan service 120
Center for Housing and Homelessness Research 284
Chan, K. C. 407–408
Chilean Solidarity Social Protection System 322
Chile, homelessness in 320–321; definition of 324–327, **325–327**; dimensions of 325; factors tackling 329–330; frameworks for understanding 324; prevalence of 322; social service to address 322
Chile, homelessness policies of 327–332; Chile Solidario Social Protection System 327; Dignified Night Program 328–329, 334; effectiveness assessment of 332–334; fragility of design of 333–334; Housing First model 330; Housing with Support programme 321; limitations on scope of 333; public–private working model 333; Street Program 328, 333, 334; Supported Housing Program 330–332
Chretien, Jean 234
'Chronic Homeless Action Plan 2019-22' 34
chronic homelessness 34, 276
CIAMP-RUA 313–315
Citizenship Income 102, 103
Colorado Safe Parking Initiative 285–288
ComCare hotline 456
Common Housing Register 29
Community-Oriented Substance Use Programme 356–357
Comprehensive National Homelessness Strategy 2015-2020 110–111, 116
Comprehensive Social Security Assistance 408
Condominium Act 149
Condominium legislation 119
Constitutional Tribunal 191–193
Constitution of Republic of Poland of 1997 191–193
COOPAMARE 304
'Coverage' programme 140–141
Covid-19 pandemic 1; Canadian homelessness 235; 'Cure Italy Decree' and 106; English and Wales homelessness services 18–19; eviction moratoriums 491–492; homelessness in Greece 132–134; Italian homelessness 98–99; Scottish homelessness policy 25; Scotland homelessness services 25; Spain homelessness services 114, 121
Crisis (homeless charity) 13, 37
Cross Departmental Team on Homelessness 42

Culhane, D. P. 276, 278
'Cure Italy Decree' 106

DALO Act 68
Damon, Julien 63
Dapur Jalanan 425
debt relief and debt cancellation 122
demand-side subsidies 51
Denner Initiative 211
Denver Basic Income Project (DBIP) 294–296
Destitute Persons Act 1977 422
Dignified Night Program 328–329, 334
Domestic Abuse Act 2021 17, 18
Donovan, Mark 294
dualist housing system 160
Dublin Housing First Demonstration Project 52–53
Dublin Regional Homeless Executive (DRHE) 41
Dutch homelessness law and policy: Approach to Social Relief 178; exclusion from services 179–181; future of 186–187; Housing First programmes 179, 185, 186; initiatives 184–185; problems of coordination 181–184
2023–2030 Dutch national action plan on homelessness 176

Early On (Vroeg Eropaf) 185
economic crisis of 2009: homelessness in Greece before 126–128; impact on homelessness in Greece 128–132
economic structural adjustment programme 372–373
EEA Agreement 146
Ekpo, A. 338
elderly homeless people 62
Ending Homelessness Act 268–269
Ending Homelessness Together Action Plan 33–34, 36–37
'Ending Homelessness Together – Homelessness strategy 2022-27' 34
England and Wales, homelessness in: estimation of 13–14; legal definition of 14
England and Wales, homelessness policy in 13–20, 36; Covid-19 pandemic impact on 18–19; history of 15–18; optimism for reform to 19–20
episodic homelessness 276
Erundina, Luiza 309
ETHOS typology 110, 110n6, 111, 117, 162, 324
European Typology on Homelessness and Housing Exclusion (ETHOS) 75, 176, 324
'Everyone In' programme 18
Everyone Needs a Safe Home (2021–2024) 156
eviction procedures 120–121

'Fachstelle Wohnungssicherung,' concept of 88–89
Family Hubs 51–52
Farha, L. 219
Federal Social Assistance Act of 1961 77–78
Fernandes, E. 373
Food Not Bombs Kuala Lumpur 425–426
France, homelessness in 56; assistance system for 65–70; population affected by 56, 58–59; repressive measures for 65
France, housing exclusion in 57–62, 71; age and 61–62; definitions of 57–58; housing inequality 59; INSEE survey on 58; living spaces 58–59, 62; in lower social classes 59; migration 60; proportion of women 60–61; rising cost of housing 59–60; social housing requests 60
France, public policies on homelessness in: assistance system 62–68; 'DALO' Act 68; enforceable right to housing 69; 'Housing First' policy 70–71; overnight shelters for women 70
Freire, Paulo 304
'Frostschutzengel' ('frost protection angels') 91
Fund for European Aid to the Most Deprived (FEAD) programmes 135

Gauteng Province 363
GBI see Guaranteed Basic Income
Germany, homeless care and policy in: Caritas associations 76; community-oriented approaches 78; Criminal Code and 77; development of 76, 77; reforming welfare law 77–78; systematic orientation 76
Germany, homeless in: 'case in urgent need of housing' 75; continuities of exclusion of 76–78; definitions of 73–74; roofless 74–75; 'settled' and 'non-settled' 76; terms for 73
Germany, homelessness good practice in 88, 87–92; accommodation of acutely homeless persons 90–91; Housing First 87, 93–94; housing provision and aftercare 92; Mobile Mieterhilfe ('Mobile Tenant Assistance') 89; municipal instrument 92–94; prevention of housing losses 87–89; support system 87
Germany, homelessness in 72; complementary reporting 84–85; definitions 72; first official statistics 83–84, 84; historical background of 76–78; involuntary 74–75, 80–81; national and local strategies to overcome 85–86; need for nationwide statistics 82–83; outlook 94–95; supplementary reporting 84–85; target group 83–84

Germany, legal basis of homelessness in 78–82; help for people with particular social difficulties 79–80; homelessness prevention 81–82; legal entitlement 80–81; social assistance 78–79; Social Code Books II and XII 82; state's obligation 80–81; unemployment benefit II 78–79
Glasser, M. 373
Global Financial Crisis of 2008 1
GMI *see* Guaranteed Minimum Income
'Good Banking Practices Code' 120
Good Friday Agreement *see* Northern Ireland Act 1998
Greece, homelessness in: causes of 138–139; Covid-19 pandemic impact on 132–134; before economic crisis of 2009 126–128; impact of economic crisis of 2009 on 128–132; measures to deal with 126–127
Greece, homelessness law and policy in: Bankruptcy Law 139; 'Coverage' programme 140–141; before economic crisis of 2009 126–128; effectiveness of 135; FEAD programme 135; financial support social programmes 135; fragmented actions 141; future of 138–141; GMI programme 135–136; Housing Allowance 136; 'Housing and Work for the Homeless' programme 137–138; Housing First approach 135; Humanitarian Crisis Response Programme 136; ideological transformation in 132–134; Katseli Law 139; Law 5006/2022 139–140; legal and policy framework 135–138; 'My Home' programme 139–140; 'National Network of Direct Social Intervention' 136–137; need for 128–132; 'Renovate-Rent' programme 140; Stathakis Law 139; transitional hospitality hostels 137
Greek austerity policies 128; fiscal adjustment programmes 129; impact on employment sector 128–129; impact on social policy 129
Guaranteed Basic Income 293–294
Guaranteed Minimum Income 135–136
Gysin, Remo 212

Harare, homelessness in 370, 383; built-environment legislation 378–379; commodification of city 380–381; eviction crisis 380–381; methodology to study 376; policy pathways 381–383; qualifying and quantifying 377–378; results from case study of 376–381; 'right to the city' approach to 373–374; 'urban modernism' approach to 375–376; 'world-class city visioning' processes 380
Hargey, Deirdre 36

Hartman, L. 166–167
Harvey, D., 374
Hawthorn, Harry 243–244
HDB Joint Singles Scheme (JSS) 451
Health and Care Services Act 150
Health and Personal Social Services (NI) Order 1972 28
Health and Social Services Boards 28
Hearne, R. 52
hidden homelessness 111–112, 163
Holston, J. 375
Homeless Action Coalition 362
Homeless Bills of Rights 265
Homelessness Act (2003) 31
Homelessness Act 2002 17
Homelessness Action Group 20, 36
homelessness action plan 41–42
homelessness consultative forum 41–42
Homelessness Etc. (Scotland) Act 2003 22
Homelessness in Northern Ireland (report) 32
Homelessness Monitor 32, 33
homelessness prevention initiatives 1
Homelessness Reduction Act 2017 17, 19, 36
Homelessness Rough Sleeping Action Group (HRSAG) 22–24
Homelessness Strategy of 2015 116
Homeless Strategy 2017–2022 33
Homes for All Act 269
Hong Kong: approach to welfare service 407–408; as 'economic city 408; economic prosperity 408; negative approach to welfarism 409; positive non-interventionism approach 408–409; public and voluntary sectors 409; social security programme 408; socio-economic composition of 408
Hong Kong Special Administrative Region (HKSAR), homelessness in: definition of 406, 407, 426–427; street sleepers **406**, 406–407
Hong Kong Special Administrative Region (HKSAR), homeless services in 405–407, 428–429; areas for propelling change 426–428; bottom-up housing strategies 413–415; IMF crisis and consolidation of 409–413; positive non-policy to 409; transitional social housing 415–421; understanding causes contributing to 427
Housing (Scotland) 2001 Act 22
Housing (Homeless Persons) Act 1977 15, 36
Housing (Scotland) Act 1987 22, 36
Housing Act 1988 39, 46–47
Housing Act 1992 39
Housing Act 1996 15–16
3/2015 Housing Act 119

Index

Housing (Traveller Accommodation) Act 1998 40, 47
Housing (Wales) Act 2004 20
Housing (Miscellaneous Provisions) Act 2009 46, 47
Housing Act (Miscellaneous Provisions) 2009 51
Housing (Amendment) Act (Northern Ireland) 2010 31
Housing (Scotland) Act 2010 23
Housing (Wales) Act 2014 16, 17
Housing (Homeless Persons) Act of 1977 20–21
Housing Allowance Act 150–151
Housing and Urban Development Corporation 443
'Housing and Work for the Homeless' programme 137–138
Housing Assistance Payment scheme 50–51
housing authorities 46–47
Housing Bank 148–149, 151, 156
Housing Benefits (Northern Ireland) Order 1983 27
Housing Bill for 2023 24
Housing Cooperatives Act 149
Housing First (HF) services 19–20, 26, 36, 52–53, 70–71, 87, 93–94, 102–105, 107–108, 122, 135, 170–172, 179, 185, 186, 270–271, 280–282, 281, 330, 510
Housing for All – A New Housing Plan for Ireland 42–43
Housing for Welfare (2014–2020) 156
housing inequality 59
Housing Is a Human Right Act 268
Housing Is Infrastructure Act 269
Housing (Northern Ireland) Order 1983 27
Housing (NI) Order 1988 27–29
Housing (Northern Ireland) Order 1988 29
Housing (NI) Order 2003 30
Housing Promotion Act of 2003 210–213
Housing Selection Scheme Review Committee 28
Housing Supply Strategy 2022–2037 35
'Housing Support Duty' 23
'Housing the Homeless' 30
Humanitarian Crisis Response Programme 136
human rights law and social housing 496–497
Hunt, Paul 166

Independent Expert Review Traveller Accommodation 47–48
India, anti-begging legislation in 439–442
India, challenges faced by homeless in: access to healthcare 436; denial of human rights 437; mental health conditions 437–438; women and children 436–437
India, homelessness in: begging and destitution 439–441; civil society organizations initiatives 444–445; definition of 431; drivers of 434–436; Indian government programs to eradicate 442–443; prevalence of 430; statistics on 432–433; types of 433–434; way forward for 445–447
India, legal provisions for housing in: Indian Constitution 438–439; signatory to human rights laws 439
Indigenous homelessness, Canada 230–233, 255–256; definition of 240; dimensions of 240–241; estimation data 238; historic reality of 243–245; history of 239–240; institutional overview of 241–243; policy 245–254; prevalence of 239; urban 231, 238–239
Indigenous homelessness policy, Canada 245–256; Dominion Housing Act 245; federal funding programmes 246; housing schemes 247–250; lack of Indigenous participation at 247; National Housing Act 245; opportunities and challenges 250–254; post–World War II 245–246; Rowell-Sirois Commission 245
Inkathalo Conversations 362
Institutional mediation services 120
'An Inter-Departmental Action Plan 2017–18' 33
Interim Rental Housing Scheme 457–458
Interim Tenancy Sustainment Protocol 53
Ireland, homelessness in 38; action plans to address 41–42; challenges of 48–50; constitutional issues and 55; drivers of 44; history of 39; housing authorities 46–48; legal framework addressing 45–50; precarious housing and 43–44; traveller accommodation 47–50; traveller housing 44–45; travellers and 39–40
Ireland, homelessness law and policy in 38; defining homelessness 53–54; future of 53–55; governance/oversight bodies to develop 41; history of 39; homelessness strategies 40–41; *Housing for All – A New Housing Plan for Ireland* 42–43; 'strategy'-based approach to 38
Ireland, homelessness preventative practices in 50–53; Family Hubs 51–52; Housing Assistance Payment scheme 50–51; Housing First initiatives 52–53; Tenancy Support Schemes 53
IRHS *see* Interim Rental Housing Scheme
Italian National Institute of Statistics (ISTAT) 97
Italy, homelessness in: Caritas report 98; during Covid-19 pandemic 98–99; definitions of 96–99; economic crisis of 2008 and 99; ISTAT surveys 96–98; poverty and social exclusion 99

Italy, homelessness preventative practice in 103–106; city of Turin 105; 'Cure Italy Decree' 106; housing-led and Housing First services 104–105, 107–108; minimum income scheme 103; rapid rehousing services 106; RRNP 104–106, 107; secondary forms of prevention 104; 'Solidarity Fund' 106; territorial differentiation of 104

Italy, policy framework on homelessness in 99–103; bottom-up approach 101; financing innovative services 102–103; Fio.PSD 101–102, 107; FNPS and constitutional reform 100; future of 106–108; Housing First initiatives 102–104, 107–108; Italian welfare regime 99–100; Law 328 100

Jamieson, Stuart 243–244
Japan: economic growth of 387; economic stagnation of 387; residential deprivation in 387–388
Japanese housing policy 388, 404; Basic Act on Housing and Living Conditions 401; challenges for 401–404; Housing Safety Net Law 400–401
Japan, homelessness in 387; causes of 388, 393–394; definition of 388–389; demographic changes with 392–399; duration of 396–398; employment status and 397; future prospects and expectation with 397–399; occupations before 394–396; structural changes with prevention of 398–401; survey on 390–391
Japan, homelessness policy in: Basic Policy on Supporting the Independence of Homeless People 391; challenges for 401–404; Homeless Independence Support Act 2002 387, 389–391; Housing Safety Net Law 2007 399; Law for Supporting the Independence of the Needy 398–400; Nagoya City 391–392, 392; self-reliance counselling 400
Jawaharlal Nehru National Urban Renewal Mission 443
João Pinheiro Foundation 306
Johannesburg, homelessness policy of 363

Kamete, A. Y. 372, 376, 382
Karlsruhe, city of 88–89
Kaseh4U 425
Katseli Law 139
Kechara Soup Kitchen 424–425
Kennedy, John F. 257
Kjellevold, A. 152
Koshish 444
Kothari, Miloon 218–219
Kuhn, R. 276, 278

Latin America, homelessness in 320–321, 323–324
Lau, H. M. M. 418
Law and Justice Political Party 188
Lee, A. 372
Lefebvre, Henri 373, 374, 382, 383
Lei Orgânica da Assistência Social 310
'local connection' test 21
Local Government Act 153–155
Löfstrand, C. 160, 164–165
Lonsdale, Joe 271
low-cost housing 350; collaboration and capacity building for 348–349; encumbrances affecting 341–342; housing finance reform for 348; private sector engagement in 349; revamping Nigeria's government role in 347–348; sustainable city planning for 349
Lowenheim, O. 134
low-income earners (LIEs), in Nigerian cities 338, 341, 347
Lula da Silva, Luiz Inácio 309, 311

Malaysia, homelessness in 428–429; definitions of 421–423, 426–427; homeless numbers and geography 423–424; understanding causes contributing to 427
Malaysia, homeless services in 405; areas for propelling change 426–428; Food Not Bombs Kuala Lumpur (FNBKL) 425–426; Kaseh4U 425; Kechara Soup Kitchen (KSK) 424–425; Nasi Lemak Projek 425; Need to Feed the Need (NFN) 425; non-governmental support 424–426; PERTIWI Soup Kitchen 424; public sector service landscape 421–423
Mandisvika, G. 374
Marais, Hein 364
marginal rental 492–493
Marra, Michael 212–213
Maslow, Abraham 338
Mbiba, M. 376, 382
McKinney–Vento Homeless Assistance Act of 1987 260, 262–263, 278–279
Mekhoe, Tich 356
migration and housing exclusion 60
minimum income protection 122
MNPR see National Homeless Population Movement
Mobile Mieterhilfe ('Mobile Tenant Assistance') 89
Moore, E. A. 337, 340, 341
Municipal Health Services Act 152
Murphy, M. 52
'My Home' programme 139–140

Nagoya City, homelessness self-reliance support scheme structure of 391–392, *392*
Nakagawa, C. Teixeira 316
Nasi Lemak Projek 425
12/2023 National Act on the Right to Housing 111, 116
National Anti-Drug Agency 422
National Board of Health and Welfare 162, 169
National Coalition 262
National Homelessness Consultative Committee 42
National Homeless Population Movement 305, 317–318
National Housing First Implementation Plan 2018–2020 53
National Housing Plan 2009–2012 117
National Housing Plan 2018–2022 117
National Housing Plan 2022–2025 117
National Housing Trust Fund 270
'National Network of Direct Social Intervention' 129, 136–137
National Plan for Interventions and Social Services 2021–2023 102, 104
National Poverty Plan 2021–2023 102
National Secretariat of Income and Citizenship (SENARC) 311
National Secretariat of Social Assistance 311
National Social Assistance Council 311
National Strategy to Combat Homelessness in Spain 2023–2030 110
National Strategy to Prevent and Tackle Poverty and Social Exclusion 2019–2023 116
NBHW *see* National Board of Health and Welfare
Need to Feed the Need 425
Neglected and Criminal Children's Act 1864 469
New Zealand *see* Aotearoa, New Zealand, homelessness in
Netherlands, homelessness in: definition of 175–177; ETHOS Light classification 176, 177; historical background of 177–179; institutionalization 178; new framing of 179; official statistics of 175–176, 178; preventing 184–185; *see also* Dutch homelessness law and policy
'Network Housing First Italia' 102
Networks for Homeless People 123
NHTF *see* National Housing Trust Fund
Nigeria, homelessness in 338–339, 350; definition of 340; housing deficit and 339–340; root cause of 340–342; way forward to tackle 347–349
Nigeria, housing in 337–338
Nigerian government housing policies and programmes 343-37
Night Shelter programmes 443

NIHE *see* Northern Ireland Housing Executive
NIHE Homeless Strategy 2022–2027 36
'non-settled personality' 76
Nordfeldt, M. 168
Northern Ireland Act 1998 30
Northern Ireland Assembly 13, 30; collapse 33, 34; report of enquiry into homelessness 30
Northern Ireland, homelessness in 34–35
Northern Ireland, homelessness policy in 26–27, 37; history of 27–30; NIHE homelessness strategies 30–36
Northern Ireland Housing Executive 26–27, 37; attempts to revitalize 36; homelessness strategies 30–36; Housing Selection Scheme Review Committee 28; Working Group 29
Norway, homelessness in: definitions of 145; numbers and profile of 146–148, *147*; registration of population 145; surveys of 142
Norway, housing-led homeless policy in 158; allocation agreements 156–157; assignment agreements 156–157; change in 142–143; Condominium Act 149; Everyone Needs a Safe Home (2021–2024) 156; Health and Care Services Act 150; Housing Allowance Act 150–151; Housing Bank 148–149, 151, 156; Housing Cooperatives Act 149; Housing for Welfare (2014–2020) 156; Local Government Act 153–155; in market-driven housing system 148; Municipal Health Services Act 152; Pathway to a Permanent Home (2005–2007) 155–156; Planning and Building Act 149; Project Homeless 155; Regulations of Loans from the Housing Bank of 2022 151; Regulations on Competence Grants for Social Housing Work from Norwegian State Housing Bank 151; Social Housing Act 152–153; Social Housing Competence Fund 156; Social Services Act 150, 152; soft measures and funding 155–157; strengthen individual right to housing 152–155; Vagrancy, Beggary, and Drunkenness Act of 1900 143–144
Norwegian Building Research Institute 145
Norwegian national homeless surveys 144–145

Obama, Barack Hussein 281
Oberholzer, Leutenegger 212
O'Connell, C. 49
Ofideute 120
Olsson, L.-E. 169
Omar, Ilhan 269
Operation Murambatsvina of 2005 369
'Organização de Auxílio Fraterno' 304
O'Sullivan, Eoin 40, 44
Oyediran, O. S. 338

Papadakis, K. 365
Partners Engaging and Empowering Rough Sleepers Network 458–459
Pathway Accommodation and Support System 41
Pathways Operational Centre 357
Pathway to a Permanent Home (2005–2007) 155–156
PEERS Network *see* Partners Engaging and Empowering Rough Sleepers Network
People's Response Act 268
Personal and Family Counselling Service 166–167
Pertubuhan Tindakan Wanita Islam (PERTIWI) Soup Kitchen 424
Petit, Louis-Julien 61
Planning and Building Act 149
Poland, homelessness in 188; criminalization of 200–201; definition of 194; emerging role of cities in 202–204; history of 190; lack of access to medical care 198–200; prevention of 189
Poland, legal framework on homelessness in: Constitution of Republic of Poland of 1997 191–193; future of 202–204; lack of coordination 196–197; local connection rules 197–198; Ombudsman 195–197; positive aspects in 201–202; Social Welfare Act 193–195, 197–198
Policy Appraisal and Fair Treatment (PAFT) analysis 29
Política Nacional da Assistência Social 310
Política Nacional da População em Situação de Rua 311
Poor Law 39
'priority need' criterion 15–20, 21, 26, 29
Project Homeless 155

Ramaphosa, Cyril 360
Ramokgopa, Kgosientso 355
rapid rehousing mechanisms 122
rapid rehousing services 106
Rapid Rehousing Transition Plans 24, 37
Rauws, W. 373
RdC *see* Citizenship Income
REACT EU 103
Reading, C. 239
Reagan, Ronald 257–259
Recovery and Resilience National Plan 102–105, 107
Reddito di Inserimento 102
Regulations of Loans from the Housing Bank of 2022 151
Regulations on Competence Grants for Social Housing Work from Norwegian State Housing Bank 151

rehousing approach 23–24, 26
'Renovate–Rent' programme 140
Rental Accommodation Scheme 51
Rent Supplement 51
Resource Group Assertive Community Treatment 185–186
right to adequate housing 324
right to housing 46–47
rising cost of housing 59–60
'Roof Over Your Head' guarantees 165
Rooms with Attention (Kamers met Aandacht) 185
Roosevelt, Franklin D. 257
rough sleeping 13, 18–19, 23, 74–75, 90
Rough Sleeping Initiative (RSI) programmes 19–20
Rudd, Kevin 482

Safe and Sound Sleeping Places (S3Ps) 459
safe parking lots 285–288
Sahlin, Ingrid 171
Scotland, homelessness policy in 36–37; Covid-19 pandemic impact on 24–25; devolution and 20–22; 'Housing Options' approach 23; impact of UK welfare reforms on 25–26; limitations of 26; post-devolution 22; preventative strategies 23–24; progressive approach to 25; right to housing 23–24
Sé Square massacre 305
SGB XII 79–80, 82
shared ownership 118
Singapore, homelessness in 448, 450, 459–460; agency-vs-structure cause of 449; classification of 449; definition of 449, 451–452; homeless families 453–454; homeless singles 452; manifestations of 448
Singapore's approach to tackle homelessness 454–461; ComCare hotline 456; comprehensive and coordinated social assistance 456; homeownership culture 455; housing loans/mortgage payments 455–456; Interim Rental Housing Scheme (IRHS) 457–458; PEERS Network 458–459; policy principles and policy leads 454–455; Safe and Sound Sleeping Places (S3Ps) 459; transitional shelters 456–457; welfare homes for destitute 458
Singapore's housing policy: impact on homeownership rate 450; Public Home Ownership Program 450; public rental schemes 451
Single Homelessness Accommodation Programme 19

Social Assistance Unified Registry (CadÚnico) 312
Social Code Book II 82
Social Code Book XII 79, 82
Social Housing Act 152–153
Social Housing Competence Fund 156
social housing, statutory frames for: Condominium Act 149; Health and Care Services Act 150; Housing Allowance Act 150–151; Housing Bank 148–149, 151; Housing Cooperatives Act 149; Planning and Building Act 149; Regulations of Loans from the Housing Bank of 2022 151; Regulations on Competence Grants for Social Housing Work from Norwegian State Housing Bank 151; Social Services Act 150
social innovations: Beloved Community Village (BCV) 289–293; Colorado Safe Parking Initiative (CSPI) 285–288; Denver Basic Income Project (DBIP) 294–296; Guaranteed Basic Income (GBI) 293–294; safe parking lots 285–288; tiny home communities 288–293; Universal Basic Income (UBI) 293–294; vehicle homelessness 284–285
social rental housing stock 119
Social Security and Housing Benefits Act 1982 27
Social Service Offices 456
Social Services Act 150, 152
'Social Structures for Direct Response to Poverty' 129
Social Territorial Ambits 103, 104
Society for Promotion of Youth and Masses 444
South African cities, homelessness in 351, 368; considerations from national policy perspective 363–364; definitions of 353–354; disparate government approaches to 358–360; lack of national policy on tackling 360–363; street homelessness 353; structural causes of 352; suburbanization of 352
South African homelessness policymaking: collaborative action in 366–367; Community-Oriented Substance Use Programme (COSUP) 356–357; disparate government approaches 358–360; Homeless Action Coalition and 362; lack of national policy 360–363; macro-challenges in relation to 363–364; Pathways Operational Centre (POC) 357; promises, pitfalls, and processes 364–366; Tshwane Homelessness Forum 355–356
South African Social Security Agency 359
Southern European countries, housing insecurity problem in 127–128
Soziale Wohnraumhilfe (SWH) 92–93

Spain, homelessness in: causes of 112–114, **113**; challenges for tackling 123–125; Covid-19 measures to tackle 120–121; definition of 109, 111, 117; ETHOS typology 110, 110n6, 111; legal and policy framework on 114–118; official data on 109–111; reactive measures to tackle 121–123; recommendations for tackling 123–125; structural measures to tackle 118–119; treatment measures to tackle 120–121; urbanization and hidden 111–112
Spanish legal system 121
Spanish National Institute of Statistics 109
Stathakis Law 139
Stellenbosch, homelessness policy of 362–363
Street Program 328, 333, 334
structural homelessness 163
Stuurman, Sipho 360
Supported Housing Program 330–332
Supporting Mental Assistance Responder Teams (SMART) Community Policing Act 268
Swärd, H 167
Sweden, homelessness in 159; BHW's official statistics on 162; definition of 162–164; estimates of 163; modes of 163; municipal responsibility 161; preventative practice for 169–172; Swedish Social Service Act 161, 164–165
Sweden, homelessness policy and practice in 159; future of 172–174; Housing First programmes 170–172; local housing services 166–169; Municipal Act 161, 166; Personal and Family Counselling Service (PFS) 166–167; prevention of evictions 169–170; right to housing assistance 164–165; staircase model 170
Sweden, social services in 159–160, 163; privatization 167; right to housing assistance within 164–166
Swedish housing policy 160
Swedish municipality 159; homelessness in 163; right to housing assistance 165
Swedish unitary housing system 160
Swiss Federal Constitution (FC) 206–208
Switzerland, cantons as responsible bodies 206, 208–209; social assistance 208–209; as welfare state 207–208
Switzerland, homelessness in 205; cantons and municipalities preventing 214–215; drug consumption and 211; guiding frameworks in assessing 215–217; lack of definition of 206–207; legal and policy framework pertaining to 213–221; preventative practice for 217–218; social rights connected with 213–214; Swiss parliamentary debates on 210–213

Take Medicine Hat 235
Tata Institute of Social Sciences 444
temporal ownership 118
Tenancy Support Schemes 53
tenancy termination 484; by landlords 485–487; tribunals' considerations and discretion in 487–491
Thistle, Jesse 240
tiny home communities 288–293
Torres Strait Islander peoples 469–470
transitional homelessness 276
transitional shelters 456–457
transitional social housing 415–421
travellers and homelessness 39–40
Trudeau, Justin 251–252
Trump, Donald 271
Tsemberis, Sam 170
Tshwane Homelessness Forum 355–356
Tshwane, homelessness in 351; Community-Oriented Substance Use Programme (COSUP) for 356–357; definition of 353; disparate government approaches to 358–359; estimation of 357–359; Pathways Operational Centre (POC) for 357; social housing delivery for 359–360; street homelessness 353–354; Tshwane Homelessness Forum for 355–356; *see also* South African cities, homelessness in
Tshwane Leadership Foundation 359
Tshwane Street Homeless Policy 351
Turin, homelessness preventative practice in 105

UBI *see* Universal Basic Income
Under the Rooftiles (Onder de Pannen) 185
UN Habitat 337, 446
United Kingdom, homelessness law and policy in 13, 36–37; Covid-19 pandemic impact on 18–19; history of 15–18; optimism for reform to 19–20
United States and housing as human right 266–267
United States, homelessness in 296–297; background and causes of 257–259; categorization of 276; challenges of 270–273; communications challenges 273; criminalization of 264–266, 271–273; definitions of 260–261; emergency assistance systems 263; forced institutionalization 272–273; grassroots movements 273–274; Housing First programmes and 270–271; legal and policy framework for 261–264; opportunity of 273–274; prevalence of 261, 264, 275–276; short-term measures for 271–272
United States, homelessness policy landscape in 267; for affordable housing 269; CARES Act 269; coordinated entry process 282–283; ending criminalization 268; Ending Homelessness Act 268, 269; for funding 268; HEARTH Act 281; Homes for All Act 269; housing affordability challenge 283; Housing First model 280–282; Housing Is a Human Right Act 268; Housing Is Infrastructure Act 269; increased funding 268; McKinney Act of 1987 279–280; National Housing Trust Fund (NHTF) 270; People's Response Act 268; A Place to Prosper Act 269; preventing evictions 269; social innovations 283–296; staircase model of care 279–280; Supporting Mental Assistance Responder Teams (SMART) Community Policing Act 268; tax credits 270
Universal Basic Income 293–294
Universal Declaration of Human Rights 266, 337, 431, 432, 437, 439
urbanization and hidden homelessness 111–112
Urban modernism 375
Urban planning legislation 373
URJA Trusts 444
Uruguay, homelessness in 320–321
US Department of Housing and Urban Development (HUD): Continuum of Care system 282; definition of homelessness 260–261; estimation of homelessness 264; guidelines for Housing First programming 281; Point-in-Time Count (PIT) 276–278; programmes administered by 263–264

Vagrants, Gaming, and Other Offences Act 1931 469
vehicle homelessness 284–285
visible homelessness 163
von Bodelschwingh, Friedrich 76

Wales, housing policy in 36; as devolved matter 16; Housing (Wales) Act 2014 16–17; intentionality test 16; person-centred ideology 16
Waters, Maxine 269
Watson, V. 382
Welfare Reform Act 2012 25
Westminster and Holyrood, tensions between 25–26
Wien, F. 239

Index

'Wohnungsnotfall' ('case in urgent need of housing') 75
'Wohnungsnotfallhilfe' ('help for cases in urgent need of housing') 75
women, growing proportion of: in homeless population 60–61; overnight shelters for 70

Yeast City Housing 359
young people, in homeless population 61–62

Zami, M. S. 372
Zimbabwean cities: housing deficit 370; as orderly spatialities 370; urban informality in 369; urban planning legislation 370–371
Zimbabwe, homelessness in 369, 384; affordability gap 372; in Harare 370; Harare case study 376–383; literature review of 371–373; theoretical underpinnings 373–376; *see also* Harare, homelessness in
Zulkifli, Masagos 461

Milton Keynes UK
Ingram Content Group UK Ltd.
UKHW010351101224
451979UK00007BA/110